T1
SHAPED AMERICA

"I have greatly enjoyed reading *The Laws That Shaped America*, a fast-moving narrative, with colorfully drawn settings and nuanced descriptions of major players. Dennis Johnson addresses major themes fundamental to lawmaking and representative democracy while effectively illustrating the inherent frustration, sluggishness, complexity, and unpredictability of the legislative process. He has brilliantly mastered a vast amount of source material with proper tone, balance, and emphasis. I learned a great deal from this book."
—**Richard Baker**, author of *The Senate of the United States: A Bicentennial History*

"Dennis Johnson's *The Laws That Shaped America* is an invaluable scholarly resource. Most scholars and serious students will know the basic story of how fundamental laws, like the Northwest Ordinance, the Land Grant College Act, the Social Security Act, and the Voting Rights Act were passed, but few will know the full back stories in all their fascinating detail. This is policy history at its best. Dennis Johnson's fine book goes on the shelf right next to David Mayhew's classic *Divided We Govern*."
—**Cal Jillson**, Southern Methodist University

"Dennis Johnson has produced a masterly account of America's landmark acts of Congress, which will be of interest to anyone interested in history and politics for years to come. It is both highly readable and exhaustive in its research. I highly recommend this book."
—**Robert B. Dove**, Parliamentarian Emeritus of the United States Senate

For better and sometimes for worse, Congress is a reflection of the aspirations, wants, and priorities of the American people. During each two-year session of Congress, thousands of pieces of legislation are proposed, many hundreds are given serious consideration, but far fewer are eventually enacted into law. Most enactments have limited impact, affect few, and are quietly forgotten in the flow of legislative activity. However, a small number of laws have risen to the level of historical consequence. These are the laws that have shaped America, and they are the subject of this book.

Dennis W. Johnson tells the story of fifteen major laws enacted over the course of two centuries of American democracy, for each looking at the forces and circumstances that led to its enactment—the often tempestuous political struggles, the political players who were key in proposing or enacting the legislation, and the impact of the legislation and its place in American history.

Dennis W. Johnson is professor and former associate dean of the George Washington University Graduate School of Political Management, Washington, D.C.

THE LAWS THAT SHAPED AMERICA

Fifteen Acts of Congress and their Lasting Impact

Dennis W. Johnson

Routledge
Taylor & Francis Group

NEW YORK AND LONDON

First published 2009
by Routledge
711 Third Avenue, New York, NY 10017, USA

Simultaneously published in the UK
by Routledge
2 Park Square, Milton Park, Abingdon, Oxon OX14 4RN

Routledge is an imprint of the Taylor & Francis Group, an informa business

© 2009 Taylor & Francis

Typeset in Baskerville by
Keystroke, 28 High Street, Tettenhall, Wolverhampton

Library of Congress Cataloging in Publication Data
Johnson, Dennis W.
The laws that shaped America: fifteen acts of congress and their lasting
impact/by Dennis W. Johnson.
p. cm.
Includes bibliographical references and index.
1. Law–United States–History. I. Title.
KF352.J64 2009
349.73–dc22
2009005998

ISBN10: 0–415–99972–3 (hbk)
ISBN 10: 0–415–99973–1 (pbk)
ISBN10: 0–203–87758–6 (ebk)

ISBN13: 978–0–415–99972–4 (hbk)
ISBN 13: 978–0–415–99973–1 (pbk)
ISBN13: 978–0–203–87758–6 (ebk)

TO THE MEMORY OF MY DEAR WIFE
LINDA BUCHANAN JOHNSON
(1948–2009)

CONTENTS

PREFACE

All legislative Powers herein granted shall be vested in a
Congress of the United States, which shall consist of a
Senate and House of Representatives.

> Article I, section 1, U.S. Constitution

We have in this country the greatest law factory
the world has ever known.

> Charles Evans Hughes (1924)

On the morning of June 10, 1964, the lawmakers were exhausted but flush with anticipation. First-term senator Robert C. Byrd (Democrat–West Virginia) had kept his colleagues up throughout the night with a fourteen-hour, thirteen-minute speech, a last-ditch effort to stop consideration of the pending civil rights legislation. Byrd, forty-six years old and young by Senate standards, was the final speaker in a coordinated filibuster that had begun in late March and stretched over seventy-five calendar days, consuming nearly six million words in the *Congressional Record*, protesting the legislation, arguing for states rights, pontificating far and wide, trying to stall passage of the Civil Rights Act of 1964. Southern Democrats, led by Richard B. Russell of Georgia, formed a platoon system, coordinated by three old bulls, Allen J. Ellender of Louisiana, John C. Stennis of Mississippi, and J. Lister Hill of Alabama. Each of these wily veterans stage-managed a team of six senators, which would take its turn speaking non-stop on the Senate floor.[1] But then on June 1, it was time for the Senate leadership to act. Majority Leader Mike Mansfield (Democrat–Montana) and Minority Leader Everett M. Dirksen (Republican—Illinois) announced that they would file a long-anticipated cloture petition to cut off debate. This was a high-stakes move, never before successful in civil rights measures and rarely successful in others, which required the vote of two-thirds of the senators, or sixty-seven if all 100 were present. Then, on June 10, Majority Whip Hubert H. Humphrey (Democrat–Minnesota) determined that he had the votes needed to close off this longest of Senate debates and move on to final passage. Byrd, who wrapped up his withering all-night speech at 9:51 in the morning, warned his Senate colleagues that a vote to cut off debate and pass this legislation would be a disaster. It would "impair the civil rights of all Americans. It cannot be justified on any basis—legal, economic, moral or religious."[2]

For many Washington tourists, the ornate Senate gallery was just another stop along the way through the gleaming U.S. Capitol. A group of Roman Catholic nuns, school children, and tourists dressed in shorts and T-shirts were in the gallery. But crowded together in the back of the Senate chamber and up in the gallery were some 150 House members, former senators, and congressional staffers; hundreds of others waited outside in a long line. Scattered throughout the visitors' gallery were a few African-Americans, including Clarence Mitchell, director of the Washington chapter of the NAACP, who listened intently. History was about to be made.

Promptly at 11:00 a.m., the clerk began calling the roll. "Mr. Aiken." "Aye," announced George D. Aiken (Republican–Vermont). "Mr. Allott." "Aye," replied Gordon Allott (Republican–Colorado). When the clerk got down to "E", the Senate reached a moment of high drama, rarely seen in its history.

Senator Clair Engle (Democrat–California), fifty-two, once a handsome and rugged liberal who had earned the sobriquet "Congressman Fireball," was now a mere shadow of his once robust self. His fragile, wracked body slumped in a wheelchair, gently guided onto the Senate floor by an aide. Ten months earlier, Engle had undergone an operation to remove a malignant brain tumor, with more surgery in April; since then his condition had deteriorated to the point where he could not walk, could barely move his arms, and was unable to utter a word. Clair Engle was the hundredth senator present, and he was determined to have his vote count. Gallery spectators watched in respectful silence as several times Engle weakly lifted his crippled arm, pointed to his eye, and tried to mouth the word "Aye." There were tears in the eyes of many of his distinguished colleagues. Senate procedure did not require that a vote be uttered out loud, and Engle's vote was recorded in the "Aye" column, along with what turned out to be seventy-one votes, four more than needed, to cut off the filibuster.

In the end, forty-four Democrats and twenty-seven Republicans voted to close off debate; predictably all eighteen southern senators—seventeen Democratics and one Republican—voted against cloture and were joined by Byrd of West Virginia, Albert A. Gore, Sr. (Democrat–Tennessee), and Barry Goldwater (Republican–Arizona), among others. Goldwater, in the thick of his bid for the Republican presidential nomination, later told reporters that he wasn't against civil rights reform, but that, as a matter of principle, he always voted against closure attempts in order to protect the interests of small states, like Arizona.[3] As the clerk proceeded alphabetically down the roll of senators, John J. Williams (Republican–Delaware) provided the crucial sixty-seventh vote to close off debate, and as he did, a relieved Majority Leader Mike Mansfield exclaimed, "That's it!"[4]

Clair Engle had one more vote left in him. He mustered the strength and courage to vote one last time, for final passage of what would become the Civil

Rights Act of 1964. Soon thereafter, on July 30, Engle died. In clinging to life and to his convictions, Engle and his vote became a small, but memorable, episode in the grand sweep of legislative history.

The Civil Rights Act of 1964 was one of the most important and far-reaching pieces of legislation enacted by the federal government. The fight for its enactment was contentious, filled with bitter threats, impatient outbursts of moral indignation, calculated foot-dragging and legislative subterfuge. But, in the end, it was a landmark achievement for a determined president and a Congress stiffened by public opinion and effective grassroots protest. The Civil Rights Act and its companion, the Voting Rights Act of 1965, removed some of the most oppressive stains of racial discrimination and fundamentally transformed life in the United States. Like the other pieces of legislation in this book, they were laws that shaped America.

For better and sometimes for worse, Congress is a reflection of the aspirations, wants, and priorities of the American people. It reflects the kaleidoscope of special interests and service to others, of favors sought and sacrifices made. During each two-year session of Congress, thousands of pieces of legislation are proposed, many hundreds are given serious consideration, but far fewer are eventually enacted into law. It may not be the law factory that Chief Justice Hughes wryly observed, but, throughout its history, Congress has churned out nearly forty thousand pieces of legislation.[5] Most enactments have limited impact, affect few, and are quietly forgotten in the flow of legislative activity. However, a small number of laws have risen to the level of historical consequence. These are the laws that have shaped America and they are the subject of this book.

Which of those pieces of legislation were the most significant for the development of the Nation, which have had an immediate or lasting impact on our society, which laws so affected us that we could not imagine how our lives would be without them? Several historians and social scientists have looked at the great legislative initiatives throughout America's history and have identified the most important ones. Recently, the National Archives and Records Administration enumerated the one hundred most important American documents: legislation, treaties, Constitutional amendments, speeches, and other writings. The Indiana University Center on Congress identified fifty-six notable federal legislators and the laws they sponsored from 1862 to the present. Political scientist David R. Mayhew surveyed historians, political scientists, and newspaper accounts in selecting 300 laws considered important from 1945 through 1990. Political scientist Paul C. Light surveyed 450 historians and political scientists when he identified fifty categories of greatest legislative achievements since World War II that grew out of a list of 540 pieces of legislation. The *Congressional Quarterly Almanac* and the yearly wrap-up edition of the *Congressional Quarterly Weekly* list the most significant legislative accomplishments of each year. To commemorate its fifty years of covering Capitol Hill, the newspaper *Roll Call* gathered together a panel of legislative scholars to consider the ten most important pieces of legislation passed since 1955. A comprehensive list of landmark legislation comes from congressional scholar Stephen W. Stathis, who analyzed each of the 107 Congresses from 1789 through 2002 plus the sessions of the Continental and Confederation Congresses from 1774 to 1788, and compiled a list of 1,200 laws and treaties considered landmark pieces of legislation. Finally, an encyclopedia of major Congressional legislation, edited by Brian K. Landsberg, features compact essays on 262 enactments.[6]

My approach is more modest and focused. It is a study of fifteen major laws enacted over the course of two centuries of American democracy. Each of these laws was examined, looking at the forces and circumstances that led to its enactment; the sometimes fierce political struggle involved in crafting its language; the members of Congress, presidents, and others who were key in proposing or enacting the legislation; and, finally, the impact of the legislation and its place in American history.

With a focus on just fifteen, many other worthy candidates, of course, had to be left aside. There is no magic number in fifteen; but those selected span the entire range of American history and cover events, circumstances, and policies that were compelling and instrumental in the development of the United States. You might be able to compile a separate and equally valid list of major legislation, or would want to add a sixteenth or seventeenth to this roster. What guided me in selecting these fifteen laws, was the answer to this simple question: "Where would we be without this law?" What would America be like today if tough federal civil rights laws were not enacted forty years ago? How would America's elderly fare without the security of health care and social insurance? How congested and dangerous would our surface transportation system be without the backbone of an interstate highway system? What if Congress in the early years of the republic had rejected the land deal of the century and decided not to purchase the vast stretches beyond the Mississippi River? Each of these fifteen laws had a lasting impact on American society and history, and has had consequences far beyond its enactment.

Technically, this book considers "legislative actions," and not simply "laws" in our usual meaning of the term. In addition to laws, there is a treaty ratification, a proposal for a constitutional amendment, and one ordinance enacted before the creation of the U.S. Constitution. I chose not to quibble about the strict meaning of the word "law," but include them in this list because of their importance to American democracy and history. The laws chosen for this study are given no further ranking but are presented here chronologically: The Northwest Ordinance (1787); the Louisiana Purchase Ratification (1803); the Kansas–Nebraska Act (1854); the Homestead Act (1862); the Morrill Land-Grant College Act (1862); the Nineteenth Amendment (1919); the National Labor-Relations Act (1935); the Social Security Act (1935); the GI Bill (1944); the Marshall Plan (1948); the Interstate Highway Act (1956); the Civil Rights Act (1964); the Voting Rights Act (1965); Medicare/Medicaid (1965); and the National Environmental Policy Act (1969).

Many other laws were considered for this book and many have a legitimate claim as a substitute for or supplement to the laws chosen here. In the Appendix, there is a roll-call of more than 200 laws, featured chronologically, that deserve further attention. What about laws passed in more recent times? It is perhaps too soon to make a reasoned judgment on laws that have been enacted during the past two decades. One or two, such as the USA Patriot Act (2001) or the Emergency Economic Stabilization Act (2008), might be considered of such importance that they could become one of the fifteen laws. But for now, they will have to undergo an historical marinade, waiting for time, perspective, and judgment to place them in a larger context. Chapter 13, the concluding chapter, discusses lawmaking during the last three decades, and probes the question: have we reached the point where large pieces of legislation (at least expensive ones) are a thing of the past? Has a deadlocked Congress lost its will to enact such legislation? Is the Congress bereft of leadership that could accomplish such policymaking? Is the lawmaking function so ensnared by special interests that legislators are incapable of crafting landmark legislation? Finally, we will speculate on what possible landmark legislation might still lie ahead.

ACKNOWLEDGMENTS

This book covers an enormous expanse of American history, politics, and public policymaking. I am indebted to the hundreds of historians, political scientists, congressional and public policy scholars, and others who have explored the themes and issues before me. As the more than 1,500 endnotes attest, they have laid the foundation for this study.

To assist me with this wide range of history and interpretation, I have called upon many colleagues and associates, both in academic circles and beyond. I am especially grateful to Peter Albert, Richard Baker, Todd Berkoff, Edward Berkowitz, Allida Black, Kate Bouve, John Buchanan, Robert Chartrand, Charles B. Cushman, Robert Dove, Eva DuGoff, Michael Edwards, Julius Hobson, Jr., Matthew Jeanrette, James T. Patterson, Heather Rothman, Richard Weingroff, and Tom Wolfson.

From our university staff, I thank Melissa Donner and David Marshall, and, from the Gelman Library of George Washington University, I give special thanks to Patricia Southard and Glenn Canner and their crack staff for tracking down my many hundreds of requests for books and manuscripts.

I am grateful for the advice and assistance of several anonymous reviewers and particularly to Michael Kerns, my editor, Felisa Salvago-Keyes of Routledge, and the fine production team, especially John Banks, Maggie Lindsey-Jones, Emma Wood, Jo Aston, and Rictor Norton.

Dennis W. Johnson
Washington, D.C.

1

WESTWARD EXPANSION

The Northwest Ordinance of 1787 and the Louisiana Purchase Ratification of 1803

Excepting only the Constitution, for at least seventy years,
the Ordinance of 1787 was the most famous of American state papers.
Francis S. Philbrick (1965)

No event in all American history, not the Civil War,
nor the Declaration of Independence nor even the signing
of the Constitution, was more important.
Bernard DeVoto (1953) on the Louisiana Purchase

During the early decades of the seventeenth century, French traders and missionaries explored the St. Lawrence River valley and established settlements and trading posts at Quebec, Montreal, and other sites. These expeditions led them westward to the river's source, the "Sweet Seas," as the Great Lakes were designated on contemporary French maps. The Europeans were told by several tribes of Native Americans that beyond the Great Lakes was a magnificent river that flowed to the sea. This vast but unfamiliar and unexplored land soon would be claimed in its entirety by France. At a colorful pageant staged before the chiefs of fourteen tribes, French colonial authorities in 1671 declared that not only were the Great Lakes annexed to the kingdom of Louis XIV, but also "all other countries, rivers, lakes . . . those discovered and to be discovered, bounded on one side by the Northern and Western seas, and on the other by the South Sea, this land in all its length and breadth."[1]

Two years later, the colonial government began its voyages of discovery, sending Louis Joliet and Jesuit priest Jacques Marquette to find and explore this great river, which the Indians called the "Father of Waters," the Mississippi. They did not reach the mouth of the Mississippi, but knew that it would empty into the Gulf of Mexico. At the end of their voyage, the twenty-nine-year-old Joliet wrote Governor Comte de Frontenac, "the great river . . . having been discovered in these last years of 1673 and 1674 . . . passes between Florida and Mexico to empty into the sea, crossing the most beautiful country that has ever been seen. I have never, even in France, seen anything more beautiful than the

1

prairies I have admired here, nothing could be more pleasing than the variety of groves and forests . . ."[2]

Five years later Robert Cavelier de La Salle followed up on Joliet's explorations and reached the mouth of the great Mississippi. There on April 9, 1682, in a ceremony of possession, La Salle annexed this territory and gave it the name *La Louisianne*, in honor of his king.[3]

The next year, at the end of his four-year voyage of discovery to the upper Mississippi Valley, Father Louis Hennepin wrote to the King: "It seems, Sire, that God had destined you to rule this territory, because of the happy coincidence between your glorious name and the name *Louis* by which the Indians designate the sun . . . [T]he name of Your Majesty is ever on their lips, for they undertake nothing without first paying homage to the sun under your name of Louis."[4]

It was a land so immense, so wild and bountiful, beyond the seemingly impenetrable Appalachian mountains, reaching from the northern headwaters of the Mississippi to the Gulf of Mexico. These vast reaches of forest and plains were populated mostly by Native Americans, as they had been for centuries. *Voyageurs*, missionaries, and fur traders were the first European settlers, followed later by squatters, land speculators, and adventurers. By the early 1700s, the French had established forts and trading posts throughout the territory: at Detroit, three villages on the Mississippi, a settlement on the Wabash River at Vincennes, and, most importantly, the village of New Orleans. The French occupation at the mouth of the Mississippi was particularly important. Henri de Tonty, La Salle's successor, saw the land's commercial and military importance: from a port at New Orleans, the French could bring furs and iron ore from the interior, dispatch troops to Mexico, and, most crucially, prevent the British from gaining mastery over the West.

Throughout the earlier part of the eighteenth century, French and British forces had fought for control of Canada, New France and the interior of the American wilderness. Young George Washington and his troops skirmished with French forces in western Pennsylvania, sparking the Seven Years' War, the largest conflict of the eighteenth century; in America it was befittingly called the French and Indian War. The British finally conquered the French in the fateful battle of Quebec on the Plains of Abraham in 1759 and Montreal fell the following year. When the Paris Peace Treaty was signed in 1763, ending the Seven Years' War, the French had lost to the British New France (Canada) and the immense wilderness beyond the Appalachians to the Mississippi River. France's reluctant ally, Spain, claimed the mostly unexplored territory west of the Mississippi and was given New Orleans. Both Britain and Spain claimed portions of West Florida, while Spain ceded the rest of Florida to the British.

Of immediate importance to American colonists was the Proclamation of 1763, a royal decree which prohibited them from settling in the new British-controlled areas beyond the crest of the Appalachian mountains. The area west of the mountains was to be a preserve for Native Americans. The proclamation was based not on benevolent accommodation but on a pragmatic assessment of the Indian threat to British America. Ottawa chief Pontiac, a former ally of the French, led a rebellion in August 1763, exacting a terrible toll on western settlers and the outpost of Detroit; other tribes attacked the key British fort at Michilimackinac and the smaller fort at Green Bay. The undermanned British authorities above all wanted to avoid a costly war with the Indians.[5] But many colonial land speculators and settlers were furious, seeing this proclamation as yet another example of British high-handedness and restrictions of their freedom to emigrate to this new territory. The proclamation did not stop colonists from moving into the restricted areas; it only fueled the distrust that had been building up between them and the mother country.

Another key event affecting western lands occurred during the Revolution when Major George Rogers Clark captured the former French outposts of Kaskaskia and Cahokia (in current southern Illinois on the Mississippi River) and then in 1779 captured the British Fort Sackville near Vincennes (Indiana). These military victories set the stage for the acknowledgment of American possession of the western lands at the Paris peace conference of 1783, which officially ended the Revolutionary War.

Following the war, the new nation was faced with one of its most vexing problems, the settlement of western lands. Land charters had been granted to the individual colonies and then to the states, but not to the Confederation itself. About half of the thirteen states had no western claims, while the others were rich in chartered land-grants. There was continued acrimony between the haves and the have-nots, with the sniping becoming so acute that it held up ratification of the Articles of Confederation for three years. Finally, Virginia, by far the biggest land claimant, ceded its western holdings to the national government; other land-rich states followed suit.

Nearing its last year of operation, the Confederation Congress enacted its most significant piece of legislation, the Northwest Ordinance. The Ordinance dealt with the Northwest Territory, the lands west of the Appalachians and above the Ohio River, in what would later become the states of Ohio, Indiana, Michigan, Illinois, Wisconsin, and a small portion of Minnesota. The Northwest Ordinance determined that new lands would eventually become full and equal states, not colonies of the original thirteen states. This principle, which was not at all inevitable at the time, applied not only to the five states carved out of the Northwest Territory but to nearly every new state thereafter. The Northwest Ordinance also proclaimed the first national version of a bill of rights, borrowing its language from the English Bill of Rights and the Massachusetts Constitution. Most remarkably, the Northwest Ordinance established the principle that slavery would not be allowed in the states carved out of the Northwest Territory. It was an imperfect gesture, and one that was scoffed at in the emerging southern territories, but it was the first, and only, national articulation of anti-slavery policy before the Civil War. The Ordinance also confirmed the consequential principle that land would be set aside in each six-mile-square township for public education. Although written in sometimes impenetrable language, lacking the grace and force of the others, the Northwest Ordinance stands with the United States Constitution and the Declaration of Independence as one of the most important early American state documents.

In the last years of the eighteenth century, the United States was facing deteriorating relations with France, its ally during the Revolutionary War. The two countries were engaged in what became known as the Quasi War, with the real threat of open hostilities. The new president, Thomas Jefferson, who for much of his public career had been sympathetic to French culture, policies, and alliances, was shocked to learn that Spain had secretly given back to France the lands west of the Mississippi it had gained in 1763. France now posed a bigger threat than Spain or England, and, with Napoleon's expanding imperial ambitions, the American government feared a strong European power on its western borders. For the moment, however, American western lands were no longer of great strategic importance to Napoleon, who was looking elsewhere to satiate his imperial ambitions. With the unexpected and catastrophic defeat of French troops sent to quell an on-going slave insurrection in Saint Domingue (Haiti) and the prospects of renewed warfare with Britain, Napoleon in 1803 decided to unload New Orleans and the western lands.

American envoys in Paris, James Monroe and Robert R. Livingston, were instructed to purchase the port of New Orleans and West Florida from the French, or to encourage the French to persuade Spain to sell West Florida if the French did not own it (such was the murkiness of the land claims). Instead, the Americans were handed the land deal of all times, the entire Louisiana territory west of the Mississippi. The boundaries were not clear, nor were the long-range consequences of the purchase. If the United States agreed to the purchase, it would double its territory in one fell swoop and remove a powerful European threat from its frontier. Most Americans and policymakers were elated; but the devil was in the details.

The treaty had to be ratified within six month of its signing in Paris in April 1803, and there was a strong possibility that the quixotic Napoleon would renege on the deal. Word of the treaty did not reach President Jefferson until early July; then the president promptly called a special session of Congress to convene in October. While there were some major concerns, the treaty was ratified in short order; but larger questions emerged soon thereafter. What would become of this vast new territory? What were its exact boundaries? Would it belong to the federal government and follow the steps toward statehood outlined by the Northwest Ordinance? Would slavery be allowed? What would become of the fairly even balance of power between southern agrarian and northern mercantile states with this newly acquired land? Some of the answers had to await the conclusion of the War of 1812, the admission of Louisiana into the Union, and the bitterly fought battles around the statehood admission of Missouri, Kansas, and Nebraska. Some answers only came through blood and force in the Civil War.

The purchase of the Louisiana territory was of enormous consequence for the new nation on its way to becoming the dominant country in the Western hemisphere, in determining how the west would be settled, in wrestling with the complex issue of slavery, and in coming to grips with the concept of Union and the meaning of the Constitution.

The Northwest Ordinance

In America, the Seven Years War was touched off by a skirmish in the western wilderness of Pennsylvania. While the French troops occupied forts in the Ohio Valley, the Virginia colony claimed the land as its own; the British colonial and French governments were determined to use force to back up their competing claims. Virginia governor Robert Dinwiddie dispatched a young officer, George Washington, to the western wilderness. On May 28, 1754, Washington together with Indian allies under Chief Tanaghrisson came upon an encampment of French soldiers under the command of Joseph de Jumonville. No one knows who fired the first volley, but the French were surrounded, quickly defeated, and butchered by Tanaghrisson's warriors. This bloody, senseless skirmish marked not only the start of the Seven Years War, but also the beginning of the end of the French empire in North America.[6]

On February 10, 1763, Spanish, French, and British envoys gathered in Paris to sign the peace treaty that formally ended hostilities. Under the terms of the Treaty of Paris, France ceded to Britain its North American territories in French Canada and all the territory east of the Mississippi River. Earlier, in November 1762, through the Treaty of Fontainebleau, Louis XIV ceded to his ally and cousin Carlos III of Spain the territory of West Louisiana and the enormous area west of the Mississippi River. This was to compensate Spain for ceding Florida to Britain and to keep the Louisiana territory out of the hands of the British. With Canada ceded, Louisiana lost much of its importance to France, particularly with the French treasury losing money on this faraway outpost. But there was trouble almost immediately. To the French-speaking majority in the port of New Orleans, Spanish rule was unacceptable. Local rebels were determined to set up their own independent republic, and the Louisiana Revolt of 1768 caused serious problems for Spain until it was quelled the following year. Spain was a somewhat reluctant landlord, slow to establish authority in the Orleans Territory, unwilling to spend from its treasury, but recognized that the land was a valuable buffer between Britain and other Spanish claims in western America.[7]

Despite the Proclamation of 1763, which forbade colonists from entering the newly acquired western frontier, many ignored the Royal order and moved over the mountains. Most were newly arrived immigrants who would make a significant impact on the American frontier. From 1760 through 1775, at least 125,000 Protestant Irish, Scots, and English came to North America; so too did 12,000 German-speaking immigrants.[8] Many of these immigrants headed directly to the frontier and to the West. In addition, some 84,000 African or West Indian slaves entered North America during this time, allowing southern planters to increase their land holdings and prompting poor whites to seek cheaper farm land on the frontier.[9]

During the Revolution, the western lands were in the balance. In 1778, on the instructions of Virginia governor Patrick Henry, Colonel George Rogers Clark was dispatched to protect Virginia's far-flung lands west of the Appalachians in Kentucky and the area north of the Ohio River. Clark was successful in his mission, capturing Kaskaskia and Cahokia in July and during the dead of winter 1779, defeating British forces at Fort Sackville at Vincennes in a daring raid. The British were unable to regain control of this territory and with the Paris Peace Treaty of 1783, formally ending the War of Independence, the western lands, including the Northwest Territory, became part of the new nation.

One of the vexing issues facing the Continental Congress was the organization and control of the western lands. There were sectional and economic rivalries between those states with western claims and those without. Four southern states, Georgia, South Carolina, North Carolina, and especially Virginia, claimed lands to the South Sea, or, with the peace negotiations of 1763, at least to the Mississippi River. Massachusetts, New York, and Connecticut also claimed western lands. The "landless" states, Rhode Island, New Jersey, New Hampshire, Pennsylvania, Delaware, and particularly Maryland, resented the vast claims made by Virginia and others. Historian Francis S. Philbrick considered the tangled web of state jealousies and rivalry "greater in potential consequences for good or evil than anything in the field of international relations."[10] Congress had to contend with several divisive issues: should it favor settlers or speculators, should it force the states to cede their land to the Confederation, should settlement in the West be controlled or unrestricted, and, most importantly for a government strapped for funds, how should the lands be sold and who should get the proceeds?

When the Articles of Confederation were drafted in 1776, all attempts to give Congress powers over the western lands were blunted. John Dickinson from the landless commonwealth of Pennsylvania, drafted an article that would limit the boundaries of states with extended western charter claims. This proposal drew swift reaction from the Virginia delegates: not only did they oppose the draft article, but the Old Dominion reasserted its land claims in its new state constitution.[11] Historian Jack N. Rakove argued that this dispute over western lands posed "the single greatest obstacle not only to the completion of the Articles of Confederation, but arguably to the survival of the nation."[12]

Congress tried once more in 1778 to set state limits on western lands, but again failed, with only five states supporting the idea. By July, eight states agreed to the Articles of Confederation; however, all thirteen states were needed for ratification. Five months later Maryland declared that it would never join the Confederation until the issue of the western lands was resolved; in May, 1779,

Connecticut agreed with Maryland, and the ratification was held hostage for three more years.[13]

Virginia's extensive claims made it the focus of the opposition. The Old Dominion claimed lands between the Appalachian Mountains and the Ohio River, and the territory north of the Ohio which became known as the Northwest Territory. Landless Maryland insisted that, since all the states were fighting and shedding blood in the Revolution, then the western lands should be considered the property of all. But despite these patriotic sentiments and national vision, the real issue boiled down to money. As historian Don E. Fehrenbacher observed, the political disposition of the West was fairly undisputed: there was not much sentiment for extending the boundaries of eastern states out to the Mississippi River. However, "the real bone of contention . . . was the substantial income expected from the sale of western lands over the years."[14]

Many politicians, planters, and merchants speculated in western lands; it was just about the fastest way to make a financial killing.[15] Politicians and speculators sought land grants from the states, or failing that, from the Indian tribes. Speculators from Maryland, Pennsylvania, and New Jersey formed the Indiana Company, seeking title to an area that was roughly the current state of West Virginia. But Virginia had already made a grant in 1749 to a group called the Ohio Company for approximately the same territory, and Virginia would not listen to the other claims. This prompted the Indiana Company to reach an agreement with Indian tribes at the Treaty of Fort Stanwix (1768), and receive lands from the Six Nations of the Iroquois Confederacy.[16]

Philip Schuyler, representative from New York, urged Congress to take up the question of the peace with the Six Nations; he was led to believe that New York would lose its western lands under a treaty with the Indian tribes. Schuyler then hurried home and, with the New York legislature in session, convinced the state to cede to Congress its western land claims.[17] With the New York cession in early 1780, Virginia found itself in the awkward position of being opposed by the northern states and with neighboring Maryland noisily refusing to ratify the Articles of Confederation.

On January 2, 1781, the Virginia General Assembly passed an act that ceded all lands northwest of the Ohio River, but kept its claims on what would later become Kentucky. Virginia hedged its actions by putting a number of restrictions on the cession, prompting Congress to delay the ratification vote for three years, and only by a narrow margin was it eventually accepted. Finally, two months after Virginia's offer to cede, in March 1781, Maryland signed the Articles of Confederation. Thus, five years after the Articles were first drafted, the states were united, more or less, under the Confederation.

In six months, the War for Independence was all but over, with the victory over Lord Cornwallis's troops at Yorktown in October 1781. Through the Paris Peace Treaty of 1783, negotiated by John Adams, Benjamin Franklin, and John Jay, the United States was recognized as an independent sovereign nation and the western lands were ceded from British to American control. At the same time, Florida, which had been in British hands for twenty years, was now restored to Spain.

Between 1781 and 1787, the cession of western lands was completed, putting vast stretches under the jurisdiction of the Confederation Congress. A major portion of the ceded territory was the land above the Ohio River, the Northwest Territory. Now came the hard part: what to do with the land, how to handle competing claims, and how to establish a rational policy for lands so distant.

Following the acceptance of the Virginia western territory, a congressional committee headed by Thomas Jefferson began preparing a plan for the lands beyond the Appalachians. At the end of April 1784, Jefferson and Hugh Williamson of North Carolina presented a report that would divide the entire trans-Appalachian region, using a grid plan, between the Thirty-First and Forty-Seventh Parallels into at least fourteen states, each rough rectangles of approximately the same size.[18]

In devising this plan, Jefferson did not want to repeat the mistakes of the heavy-handed British colonial officials.[19] Once the western territories had reached a minimum population of 20,000 free inhabitants, they could start drafting their own state constitutions along republican forms. Jefferson added several provisions in the report to Congress, which became the Ordinance of 1784. One provision mandated that the new states would "for ever remain a part of the United States." Another was an anti-slavery clause: "after the year 1800 of the Christian era, there shall be neither slavery nor involuntary servitude in any of the said states, otherwise than in punishment of crimes, whereof the party shall have been duly convicted to have been personally guilty." Here, for the first time, the issue of slavery was considered in an act or ordinance by the national legislature;[20] certainly it would not be the last time.

The anti-slavery provision needed seven states for passage; it was supported by six, with three southern states, including Jefferson's Virginia, voting against it. Despite its defeat, some historians have credited Jefferson with inspiring the anti-slavery section found in the Northwest Ordinance three years later. Historian Garry Wills, however, has been less charitable, noting that Jefferson's plan would have permitted slavery to exist in the territories for sixteen more years, becoming "irrevocably entrenched in the life of the settlers."[21] Wills noted further that Timothy Pickering, then the Quartermaster General, should be given some credit for anti-slavery language. Pickering in 1783 pursued the idea of creating a new state from the Northwest Territory as payment to veterans of the Revolutionary War. In that new state, Pickering proposed the "total exclusion of slavery," a provision that would be "essential and irrevocable" in its new constitution. After the defeat of the 1784 Ordinance's anti-slavery provision, Pickering worked with Elbridge Gerry of Massachusetts and Rufus King of New York to resurrect it, but without the 1800 grace period.[22]

The Ordinance of 1784 was not officially communicated to the states for their approval until May 28, 1785.[23] By that time, events had overtaken it.

Congress badly needed revenue, and settlers, as well as squatters and speculators, were moving into the fertile Ohio Valley. Legislators worried that,
without a rational plan for surveying and selling the western lands, Congress
would not be able to recoup badly needed funds or defend the widely dispersed
westerners from Indian or white predators. To resolve these issues, Congress on
May 20, enacted a new measure, the Land Ordinance of 1785.

The Land Ordinance declared that as soon as seven ranges of townships,
each six miles square, had been properly surveyed and recorded, the land would
go up for competitive bidding, selling for no less than one dollar per acre. This
meant that squatters, who would not or could not pay for land, were not
welcome; nor were speculators who were seen as direct competition with the
government. To be successful, the government had to offer clear titles to the
new land.[24]

One of the unique features of the Land Ordinance was the dedication of
parcels of land in the new territory for education. This was a departure from
Jefferson's Ordinance of 1784, which contained no reference to education or to
public schools.[25] In the new Ordinance, each township was divided into thirty-
six lots, each one mile square (or 640 acres), and the sixteenth such lot was
reserved for public schools. The Ordinance helped establish the idea of the
public common school from grades one through eight, and in doing so
"promoted the equality of all citizens and the revolutionary notion that true
democratic government demands an educated citizenry."[26] This also set a
precedent for national land grants in education, as seen in Chapter 3.

But the Land Ordinance of 1785 still needed to be perfected, and, in the next
two years, it was transformed into the Northwest Ordinance of 1787.

Making the Law

When Thomas Jefferson left Congress to become American Minister in Paris,
his successor James Monroe took the lead in preparing a more workable version
of the land ordinance, completing in May 1786 what might be considered a
rough draft of the Northwest Ordinance.[27] When Monroe left Congress,
Nathan Dane of Massachusetts became the most prominent member of the
drafting committee. In September 1786, a new congressional committee consisting of Dane and five others presented a draft report outlining a temporary
government for the western territories. While the report received a favorable
hearing in April 1787, it failed to pass because of the lack of a quorum. Then
another committee, with Dane, Melancton Smith of New York, Virginians
Richard Henry Lee and Edward Carrington, and John Kean of South
Carolina, crafted a new version, using some of the language from earlier
ordinances.[28]

The legislators had some help: years before the term was coined, this congressional committee was assisted by a "lobbyist" for a major land speculation
company. During the winter of 1785–1786, a group of Revolutionary War

veterans from New England formed the Ohio Company of Associates, an organization seeking to purchase western lands. Its chief agent was the Reverend Dr. Manasseh Cutler of Massachusetts, to whom many historians have given some credit in shaping the legislation that eventually became the Northwest Ordinance.

During the late spring and summer of 1787, attention was focused on Philadelphia, as delegates gathered to debate and eventually craft the United States Constitution. Many members of the Confederation Congress left New York to join the other delegates in Philadelphia. Left behind to carry on the legislative work of the Congress were just eighteen representatives. They quietly carried on their business in New York during the summer of 1787, and produced the most important document in the history of the Confederation Congress.

On July 11, 1787, Congress received what looked like the completed draft of the Northwest Ordinance. Then at the last minute, Nathan Dane inserted a final provision from the floor:

> Article VI: There shall be neither Slavery nor involuntary Servitude in the said territory otherwise than in the punishment of crimes . . . provided always that any Person escaping into the same, from whom labor or service is lawfully claimed in any one of the original States, such fugitive may be lawfully reclaimed . . . .

The amendment passed quickly, and then the eight state delegations present voted unanimously for the Northwest Ordinance on July 13, 1787.

In the new lands north of the Ohio River, there would be no slavery and there would be no waiting period until 1800, as in Jefferson's earlier plan. At the time, only Massachusetts prohibited slavery altogether. How was it that the measure passed, and particularly, how did the southern delegations agree to this no-slavery clause? Historians have offered several explanations. One is that the South got something in return because the anti-slavery article was also a fugitive slave article, requiring the return of slaves who sought freedom in the Northwest. A second explanation was that, by agreeing to no slavery in the Northwest, there was a tacit agreement that slavery could exist in the Southwest. A third rationale was that the anti-slavery provision was part of a much larger compromise of 1787: the Northwest Territory would be free of slaves, while the South would gain the three-fifths clause, the continuation of the international slave trade for twenty years, the fugitive slave clause, and the prohibition on export taxes, which favored the products of slave labor. But the evidence of a collaboration between the Confederation Congress in New York and the constitutional convention in Philadelphia is fairly thin.

Altogether, southerner lawmakers believed that the Northwest would be mostly settled by southerners, and become pro-South in attitudes and politics.[29] Indeed, the southern congressional majority in the waning days of the

Confederation Congress may have thought that they had engineered a victory for their region with the Northwest Ordinance.[30]

Historian Paul Finkelman has argued that the anti-slave provision, hastily drawn up, slipped in at the last minute, and subject to no debate, was a bad example of how to draft an important piece of legislation. If there had been a full debate, there might have been a better understanding of how to enforce the article and how to resolve its internal contradictions. Pennsylvania, Rhode Island, and Connecticut either had enacted or were considering gradual emancipation laws, but none of their delegates was present when the Ordinance was passed.[31]

In a letter written three days after the Northwest Ordinance was enacted, Nathan Dane explained to his colleague Rufus King some of the pressures facing Congress: the Ohio Company was about to purchase a large tract of federal land, he speculated six or seven million acres (the company soon purchased 1.5 million acres), and Congress wanted to abolish the old system and get a better one in its place. Dane said that they "found it necessary to adopt the best system we could." Dane continued, telling King that he had "no idea that the states would agree to the sixth art[icle] prohibiting slavery" since Massachusetts was the only one of the eastern states present, and the article had been omitted in the final draft "but finding the House favorably disposed on this subject, after we had completed other parts I moved the art[icle], which was agreed to without opposition."[32]

While Dane was surprised that his anti-slavery article was agreed to, legal historian David Currie was impressed by the audacity of Congress to enact the Ordinance at all. He noted that there "really is no evidence in the Articles of Confederation giving Congress the power to adopt such a measure."[33]

Through Article V, the Northwest Ordinance established the important principle of equal footing: once a territory had acquired 60,000 free inhabitants, it could be added to the Union, on equal footing with the original thirteen states. There would be intermediary steps as the territories established their governments, chose governors and appointed judges, selected representatives for territorial legislatures, and adopted civil and criminal codes from those of existing states.[34] The Ordinance contemplated between three and five states to be carved out of the Northwest Territory, and rejected the concept of territorial statehood that had been a central tenet of the 1784 Ordinance.[35]

There was also an extended section on rights and privileges, taken mostly from the English Bill of Rights of 1689 and the Massachusetts Constitution.[36] Among those rights were the freedom of worship (no one "demeaning himself in a peaceable and orderly manner" was to be "molested on account of his mode of worship or religious sentiments"); guarantees of habeas corpus; jury trial by one's peers; judicial proceedings according to the common law; bail allowed in most cases; moderate fines; and no cruel or unusual punishment. These provisions, with some modification, later found their way into the Bill of Rights of the U.S. Constitution.[37]

Highlights of the Northwest Ordinance

The Ordinance in its fourteen sections outlawed primogeniture, and set the governmental structure for the Northwest Territory, mechanisms for the formation of a permanent government, the enforcement of civil and criminal laws, and a means by which the territories could apply for statehood.

It contained six articles of compact between the original states and the people and states of the Northwest Territory.

- The first article provided freedom of religion.
- The second article provided basic rights, many lifted from the English Bill of Rights in 1689: benefit from the writ of habeas corpus, trial by jury, proportionate representation in the legislature; no excessive fines; no cruel and unusual punishment; and the protection of private contracts.
- The third article encouraged schools and education ("Morality and knowledge being necessary to good government and the happiness of mankind, Schools and the means of education shall forever be encouraged"), and "utmost good faith shall always be observed towards the Indians, their lands and property shall never be taken from them without their consent . . ."
- The fourth article proclaimed that the new states would be forever a part of the Union, and when admitted to the Union would be on equal footing with the original states in all respects.
- The fifth article determined that no fewer than three and no more than five states would be created out of the Northwest Territory.
- The sixth article prohibited slavery and required the return of fugitive slaves.

Aftermath

It took nearly four months after approval of the Northwest Ordinance before the territorial officers were selected. Agents from the Ohio Company negotiated with Congress, trying to get favorable terms for land sales. They also tried to influence Congress in the selection of new territorial leaders. The Rev. Dr. Cutler recommended Arthur St. Clair, the current president of the Confederation Congress, to become the new governor of the Northwest Territory. St. Clair, a major general in the Revolutionary War, was an able choice: unlike other territorial officers, he was honest and never got involved in land speculation.[38] Not so his second in command. Winthrop Sargent, the second-ranking territorial officer, described as arrogant and selfish, however, saw money to be made. He had been a former major general in the Revolutionary Army and a land surveyor. When the Ohio Company on October 26, 1787, bought 1.5 million acres for a million dollars, Cutler and Sargent each purchased 750,000 acres for half a million dollars, payable over a three-year period.[39]

Others were involved in outright land speculation. Probably the most notorious was John Cleves Symmes who had purchased millions of acres between the Great Miami and Little Miami rivers. He was unable to pay for the lands, then carelessly or fraudulently sold to others land he did not own; then Symmes sat as a judge in suits concerning his own property. Ultimately,

Symmes was ruined, but not before he became "one of the most hated men in the Northwest Territory."[40]

The first permanent settlement in the Ohio Valley, the village of Marietta, was founded in 1788, at the confluence of the Ohio and Muskingum Rivers; later that year, the village of Losantiville (Cincinnati) was settled. In his first speech as governor, Arthur St. Clair addressed the citizens of Marietta, praising them for their industriousness in bringing civilization to the wilderness; he then admonished them to treat the Indians with Christian kindness. The town's spokesman replied that they always treated Indians "like friends, like brothers."[41]

The Ohio Company of Associates placed advertisements in the *Pennsylvania Packet* in early 1786 soliciting stockholders. The ads touted "incontestable evidence" that the western lands were of much better quality than any known in New England, and that the climate, seasons, and produce were "equal to the most flattering accounts which had ever been published of them." Later advertisements forewarned readers about lurid stories of the "horrors of an Indian war," suggesting that such tales probably did not originate in the western country, but likely were "fabricated in some of our cities of refinement (perhaps New York)" so that unnamed speculators could make a killing on this land with the "most luxuriant soil in the universe."[42]

Key Individuals in the Making of the Northwest Ordinance

Historians have puzzled over the authorship of the Northwest Ordinance and there is no definitive claim. Some have argued that Thomas Jefferson, the author of the Ordinance of 1784 and its anti-slavery provision, should be considered a forerunner; others promote James Monroe who took over the committee after Jefferson, or Rufus King who also penned an earlier anti-slavery provision.[44] Probably the strongest argument for authorship would go to Nathan Dane of Massachusetts and, from outside the Congress, the lobbying of land speculator Manasseh Cutler.

Nathan Dane (1752–1835) served as a member of the Confederation Congress, 1785–1788, from Massachusetts. A lawyer from Beverly, Dane was elected to the Massachusetts state senate in 1790–1791 and 1794–1797. In 1795, he was appointed a commissioner to revise the laws of Massachusetts, working on the project until 1812. In 1814, he was a delegate to the Hartford Convention, which many believed was an attempt by New England Federalist forces to secede from the Union. Earlier, Dane had been involved in the so-called Essex Junto, another abortive plot by New Englanders to leave the Union.[45]

Mannaseh Cutler (1742–1823) was descended from a long line of New England clergy. He broke tradition by becoming a lawyer then later a clergyman. During the Revolution, Cutler studied medicine, then became an amateur botanist, astronomer, and anthropologist. In 1786, Cutler joined several other veterans in forming the Ohio Company of Associates. He lobbied Congress on behalf of this organization, serving as its chief agent. George Washington appointed him judge of the U.S. Court of Ohio, but Cutler declined the position. He later served in the Seventh and Eighth Congresses (1801–1804) as a Federalist from Massachusetts.

But it was a hard sell and the flow of settlers was disappointing. Many would-be settlers had read of Indian atrocities and were afraid. The Indians in the West presented the new republic with some of its most vexing issues.[43] The Northwest Ordinance briefly mentioned native Americans: "laws founded in justice and humanity shall from time to time be made, for preventing wrongs being done, and for preserving peace and friendship with them [Indians]." This benevolent language, however, belied the harsh and brutal reality on the western frontier. There were outbursts of violence and dangerous clashes between Indians and settlers north of the Ohio River, discouraging many would-be settlers from moving into the fertile lands.

In 1790, President George Washington was determined to quash the Indian attacks in the West. A major confederation of Indians from the Shawnee, Delaware, Mingo, Wyandot, Ottawa, Miami, Potawatomi and Chippewa tribes had united under Chief Little Turtle. Both Brevet Brigadier General Josiah Harmar and Governor St. Clair had been badly defeated earlier by the Indian fighters. In 1794, General Anthony Wayne regrouped forces at the site of St. Clair's defeat in 1791 and built Fort Recovery, near the current border between central Ohio and Indiana. Little Turtle's forces attacked the fort, but were repulsed.

The Treaty of Paris of 1783, ending the Revolutionary War, contained a clause that allowed the British to remain in the Northwest Territory until the United States had resolved the land issue with Indians who were British allies. In 1794, the issue was about to be resolved. The British had just built Fort Miamis, and about 100 British volunteers joined 1,100 Indians against Wayne's forces. The decisive battle was at Fallen Timbers on August 20, 1794, in present-day Toledo, Ohio, with Wayne and his soldiers decimating the Indian forces.[46] The British then made peace with the Americans and abandoned their Native American allies.

In 1794, Chief Justice John Jay was dispatched to England to resolve several outstanding issues. Americans were disturbed over the seizure of their ships with cargoes unrelated to war, the impressment of American seamen, and continuing British occupation of western posts within U.S. borders. The Treaty, controversial in America, succeeded in withdrawing British soldiers from frontier posts and from supplying Indians with firearms; it established a commission to settle outstanding border issues between the United States and Canada and another commission to resolve American losses in British ship seizures and Loyalist losses during the Revolution. Missing, however, was a provision for the British to refrain from stopping American ships and impressing American seamen. This omission caused an uproar in Congress: Washington and Jay were sharply attacked, but it was probably the best that could have been accomplished for a young nation lacking a strong military and international political clout.

Key Events involving the Northwest Ordinance	
1763	Treaty of Paris, ending the Seven Years' War, made the Mississippi River the boundary between British and Spanish possessions in North America.
1780	Congress recommended that states cede portion of their territorial claims; adopted resolution to divide ceded western territory into new states, with equal privileges as original states.
1782	The United States signed a preliminary treaty with Britain, providing for the British to move their fortifications from the Northwest and established the Mississippi River as western boundary of the United States.
1783	Treaty of Paris was signed in France by the United States and Britain, officially ceding its empire north of Florida and west of the Appalachian mountains to the United States.
1784	Congress accepted Virginia's cession of western land claims; Ordinance of 1784 enacted.
1785	Land Ordinance of 1785 passed in Congress; New York ceded its land claims in the west.
1787	Northwest Ordinance passed; Constitutional Convention in Philadelphia.
1796	Land Act of 1796, provided for survey of all public lands within Northwest Territory, and public auction of lands. Minimum sale was 640 acres, at $2.00 per acre; benefited large land speculators.
1803	Ohio became the first state created from Northwest Territory and seventeenth state of the Union. France ceded all of Louisiana to the United States, doubling its land mass.

This led to peace discussions in January 1795 between the United States and the Ohio Indian tribes. On August 3, 1795, the chiefs of twelve Indian tribes met General Wayne at Fort Greene Ville in eastern Ohio to sign a treaty, relinquishing all Native American claims to the Ohio Valley and gave the Americans control over key trading areas, including the site of the future Chicago, Illinois.[47] Under the terms of the Treaty of Greenville, Native Americans were permitted to hunt on the lands they had ceded, but there still were tensions. White settlers quickly encroached on Indian lands and many Indians refused to honor the treaty.[48]

Although the Ordinance prohibited it, slavery persisted in the territories, especially in Indiana and Illinois.[49] Slaveholders did not explicitly break the law, but rather they evaded it by enacting long-term indenture clauses and rental contracts, or legally recognizing the slave status of those brought into the territories before 1787. They also repeatedly petitioned Congress to permit the importation of slaves for a limited time. The Territory of Indiana adopted a law, borrowed from Virginia, entitled "An Act concerning Slaves and Servants," which historian Paul Finkelman described as "nothing less than a full slave code for Indiana."[50] President Thomas Jefferson, who had penned the 1784 anti-slavery provision, made no protest to William Henry Harrison, the Virginia-born governor of the Indiana territory.[51] By the time Indiana became a state in 1816, the opponents of slavery had the upper hand in its legislature.

The new Indiana constitution declared that "no alteration of this constitution shall ever take place so as to introduce slavery or involuntary servitude in this State, otherwise than for the punishment of crimes, whereof the party shall have been duly convicted."[52]

The Territory of Illinois in 1813 placed an absolute prohibition on the immigration of free blacks into the territory; nevertheless, by the time it became a state in 1818, Illinois had more than a thousand slaves or indentured servants living within its borders. The state's constitution of 1818 specifically allowed the use of slaves in Illinois salt mines, and, in one of the first acts of the new free state of Illinois in 1819, all slaves were required to register, their movement was restricted, and they were subject to whippings for violating the law. Sixty years after the Northwest Ordinance was passed, Illinois, in 1848, enacted its second state constitution, which finally included the abolition of all slavery within the state.[53]

Transforming Legislation

During the first years of the Republic, three new states were added: Vermont in 1791, Tennessee in 1792, and Kentucky in 1796. Next to be settled was the area of the Northwest Territory. The Northwest Ordinance built upon the rational system of township grids established by the 1785 Land Ordinance. Today, anyone flying over Ohio, Indiana, or the other states of the old Northwest Territory will be struck by the straight roads, the six-mile by six-mile township grids established by legislation well over two hundred years ago. While the land sale business was fraught with greed, fraud, and speculation, the Ordinance brought order and rationality to the system of land purchases. So too did the rules established for the orderly transition from territory to statehood. What was developed in the Northwest Ordinance became a pattern used in twenty-six other states as they moved from territory to states of equal footing with those in the Union.[54]

The Northwest Ordinance stated that "religion, morality and knowledge, being necessary to good government and the happiness of mankind, schools and the means of education shall forever be encouraged." Building upon the Land Ordinance of 1785, the Northwest Ordinance made local education a national priority. Education historian Jurgen Herbst considered the Northwest Ordinance and the Morrill Act of 1862 the "two most important documents in the history of the national government's influence over American higher education."[55] Chapter 3 features the Morrill Act and its impact on education policy.

The push for educational institutions in the new Northwest came largely from the efforts of Manasseh Cutler on behalf of the Ohio Company. In order to attract industrious settlers, particularly from New England, there had to be more than fertile, abundant land; there had to be marks of civilization, particularly schools and religious instruction. The final contract between the federal government and the Ohio Company included the setting aside of lot number sixteen in each township for education, as was earlier articulated in the Land Ordinance of 1785; lot number twenty-nine was reserved for religion; and two complete townships were to be dedicated for a university.[56]

The anti-slavery provisions became a rallying cry for abolitionists during the 1830s and 1840s. However, when southern territories were admitted to the Union, the anti-slavery precedent was tossed aside. In 1830, Daniel Webster praised the anti-slavery clause, laying the philosophical groundwork for nineteenth-century historians and commentators who saw moral righteousness and the creation of a strong republic as the main motives behind the Ordinance. Indeed, for much of this time, the Ordinance was known primarily as the measure which prohibited the expansion of slavery.[57]

School children do not recite from memory passages from the Northwest Ordinance; its language does not soar or inspire. Nor do we today hold it with the same reverence as the Declaration of Independence and the Constitution. It was not a perfect document; those who crafted it were not all wise patriots, and greed and self-interest were not far from the surface. Yet, for much of early American history it was an exceptionally important document. As Americans opened up the new, fertile lands of the Midwest, the Ordinance provided sense of freedom and order, the promise of education, and the courage to prohibit slavery.[58]

The Louisiana Purchase Ratification

One of the chief concerns of the new American government was that the Mississippi River should be open and free for navigation for the western settlers who were pouring across the Appalachians. The river was the lifeblood of commerce for the settlers in the Ohio and Mississippi Valleys. With Spain in control of the Orleans territory, it was vital for the United States to have assurances that the port of New Orleans would be open to American shipping. American officials were concerned that, if they could not guarantee an open trade route, remote western settlers might decide to set up their own independent country, or align themselves with a European power.[59] George Washington, who had extensive experience in the western lands, warned in 1784 that settlers there had different views and interests than found in the East, and that they could become a "formidable & dangerous neighbour."[60]

New Orleans, and lower Louisiana, were experiencing an upsurge in commerce, population, and economic activity. The Spanish tried to keep a grip on the Louisiana economy, by trying (but failing) to monopolize trade with Native American tribes, blocking foreign traders, and, in 1784, closing the lower Mississippi to foreigners, especially Americans. Spain declared that it owned both banks of the river up to the Thirty-First Parallel (north of Baton Rouge, where the Red River connects with the Mississippi) and could thus assert its monopoly. Western farmers were outraged; for twenty years now, the

Mississippi had been open and free to them. They were joined by southern politicians who demanded that Spain reopen the port of New Orleans.[61]

Spain's first envoy to the United States, Don Diego de Gardoqui, a polished diplomat who spoke excellent English, thought that the Spanish position was sound: there would be no concession on the issue of American navigation of the lower Mississippi, although His Catholic Majesty's government was willing to make some trade concessions and discuss boundary claims in West Florida. Congress appointed John Jay, the Secretary of Foreign Affairs, to negotiate with Gardoqui. The Spanish envoy also knew that the Americans were not solidly lined up behind the demands of western settlers and southern politicians. The longer he negotiated, the more Gardoqui sensed that New England was more interested in local commerce, fishing rights, and commercial concessions that Spain might offer than in protecting free access to the port of New Orleans. Gardoqui also had been involved in earlier negotiations in Madrid when Jay was American minister there, he knew how New England and other eastern politicians felt, and, with that knowledge, he, in the words of historian Jon Kukla, "played them like a violin" throughout the spring and summer of 1786.[62]

Westerners and southern legislators were enraged when they grasped the terms of Jay's proposed treaty with Spain. Acceding to New England and eastern interests, the treaty would have the United States forgo use of the Mississippi for twenty-five or thirty years so long as it could have trading privileges with other parts of the Spanish empire. The southern states, through the leadership of James Monroe of Virginia, were able to prevent the ratification of any such treaty; but the result was a bitter sectional fight, with some equally outraged New England delegates discussing the formation of a northern confederation.[63]

Spanish officials resorted to "honeyed guile" rather than open resistance to American frontier advances: they subsidized Indians who wanted to block settler expansion and they encouraged separatist activity, particularly from American land speculators James Wilkinson and John Sevier. At the same time, between 1784 and 1787, Carlos III authorized a series of land concessions, extending American land claims further south into what later became the Mississippi Territory.

In December 1788, Madrid issued a royal decree allowing American ships to pass and sell goods in New Orleans, subject to a stiff 15 percent tariff.[64] Then came a policy of encouraging immigration and offering land-grants, on the condition that the new immigrants (mostly Americans) would swear allegiance to Spain. Four years later, the policy was reversed and Spanish officials tried to block Americans from coming to Louisiana. In the next year, 1793, Spain was at war with France, leading the Spanish government to open up economic activity in Louisiana, hoping that American goods would become available to New Orleans and other Spanish ports. Throughout all these twists and turns, one ineluctable truth stood out: despite repeated Indian raids, tariffs, threats, and intrigue, American settlers kept coming.

During all this, French officials never gave up on the dream of reacquiring Louisiana. There were rumors that France had its eye on Louisiana when it signed the Franco-American Alliance of 1778, and even more so after the British were defeated at Yorktown in 1781. The rumors were so persistent that in 1786 the French envoy in New York had to disavow any French designs on the territory. John Jay sharply questioned the envoy, Louis Guillaume Otto, who, of course, denied any possibility that France would retake possession of Louisiana.[65]

A major concern of American officials was that the United States would be sucked into the maelstrom of European wars and the shuffling of colonial territories, particularly against a strong, unstable, but ambitious France. The Revolution in France, beginning in 1789, remained essentially an internal struggle for two years; then in 1791, it escalated into an international war. By 1793, Spain and Britain joined the war between France, Austria, and Prussia, and alliances would be broken and re-formed until Napoleon's defeat in 1815. During this twenty-five-year period, there were just two years of relative peace between the French and the British, crafted from the Treaty of Amiens of 1802.[66]

Jay's Treaty of 1795 between the United States and Britain caused great alarm in France, especially America's abandonment of neutral rights which had been proclaimed in the Franco-American alliance of 1778.[67] The treaty caused trouble for Spain as well. When Spain signed a peace treaty with France in July 1795, it knew that war with Britain was imminent (and in fact hostilities would later break out in the autumn of 1796). But with the war over, for the moment, France wanted Spain to retrocede Louisiana; Spain refused, but later in the same year of 1795 changed its mind, and offered France the territory of Louisiana in exchange for the eastern part of the Caribbean island of Santo Domingo. But France refused to go along, arguing that the price was too high, but wanted to continue negotiations.[68]

Then, against the objections of France, the King of Spain and the United States signed the Treaty of San Lorenzo ("Thomas Pinckney's Treaty") in 1795, which guaranteed Americans free navigation of the Mississippi and the right of transshipment of goods in New Orleans and ceded to the United States virtually all of the current states of Mississippi and Alabama, except for the strip bordering the Gulf Coast, known as West Florida.[69] The territory of New Orleans, north to Baton Rouge, remained in Spanish hands.

War between Britain and France broke out in the autumn of 1796. The French insisted that the United States uphold its end of the Franco-American Treaty of 1778 and actively join France against Britain. The United States replied that the treaty was signed between the U.S. and Louis XVI, and, since the Revolution in France and the king's untimely death, that treaty was null and void. The United States, which had barely avoided war with Britain and had patched things together with Jay's Treaty, now faced a hostile France. By the summer of 1796, French privateers began seizing American ships on the high seas and using Spanish ports to waylay American commerce. Over the next twelve months, over 300 American merchant ships had been captured. President Washington during his last few months in office sent Charles C. Pinckney to Paris in an attempt to negotiate a settlement. But the revolutionary government threatened to arrest Pinckney and he was forced to flee to the Netherlands.

The new president, John Adams, tried again, sending Pinckney, John Marshall, and Elbridge Gerry to France in August 1797 to negotiate a commercial agreement to protect U.S. shipping, but the Directory officially refused to accept the American envoys. Behind the scenes, however, the wily French foreign minister Charles Maurice de Talleyrand-Perigord demanded a loan for his country and bribe money for himself. Three of Talleyrand's agents (later called XYZ) approached the U.S. ministers, suggested a bribe of $250,000 for Talleyrand, and a loan of $10 million to France before negotiations could begin. While the American envoys wanted quick resolution of the commercial agreement, Talleyrand just bided his time.

When Marshall and Pinckney returned home in mid April 1798, their dispatches recounting the demand for a bribe and loan were shared with an outraged Congress and public. Congress unilaterally cancelled the 1778 alliance with France, expanded the navy, prepared for war, and President Adams sent ships against the French in the West Indies. John Adams, who had generally been dismissed by the public, became a national hero; pro-British Federalists were gleeful; pro-French Republicans were demoralized. The public flooded Congress with petitions of support for Adams and denouncement of French perfidy.[70] Many Americans could not trust France to be an ally and further demanded that the United States have nothing to do with European affairs.[71] Over the next two years, the small U.S. Navy captured more than eighty French ships. During this period, called the Quasi-War, both countries wanted to avoid open warfare and tensions were eased with a new commercial agreement, the Convention of 1800 (Treaty of Mortefontaine); they also terminated the earlier Treaty of Alliance of 1778.

Before the Treaty of Mortefontaine was signed, Talleyrand, sensing the way the political winds were blowing, resigned from office in July 1799. Five months later, Napoleon Bonaparte overthrew the Directory and established a new government, headed by three consuls. As First Consul, Bonaparte wielded the authority of the government, and quickly revived the idea of a western empire. Talleyrand was back in power, and, in July 1800, Bonaparte ordered him to restart negotiations with Spain. Bonaparte had his eye on not only the Louisiana territory but the Floridas as well.[72]

While French officials were working with Americans in Paris to end the Quasi-War another group of French negotiators was secretly meeting in Madrid, working to return the Louisiana territory to France. On September 30, 1800, American and French officials concluded the Treaty of Mortefontaine restoring normal relations between the two countries; the next day, Spain and France signed a secret deal, the Treaty of San Ildefonso, giving Louisiana back to the

French in exchange for some duchies in Italy. Not wanting to provoke the British or the Americans, the French and Spanish governments agreed not to make the treaty public before Napoleon's troops could be sent to defend Louisiana.[73]

Saint-Domingue

The western portion of the island of Hispaniola, called Haiti by its natives and Saint-Domingue by the French, was of immense importance to Napoleon as a military installation for the Western hemisphere. Its fate was closely tied to that of Louisiana. Once Britain and France had signed their peace agreement in 1802 through the Treaty of Amiens, Saint-Domingue could become the staging area for a return of French military power to the Americas. With the still secret retrocession of Louisiana signed in 1800, Napoleon might be able to build a base in New Orleans and then absorb other Spanish colonies and provinces, like the Floridas, Cuba, and Mexico.[74] But events turned out much differently than Napoleon had expected.

Saint-Domingue was also enormously important for its agricultural products: it was the world's largest producer of sugar and coffee. These crops required cheap, back-breaking labor, which was supplied by over half a million slaves. This was the largest single concentration of slaves in the Western Hemisphere, nearly half the size of the entire slave population in the United States, but packed into an area no bigger than the state of Maryland.[75] They were treated brutally, often literally worked to death, whipped, mutilated, and discarded when no longer able to work in the scorching sun. The French Revolution of 1789 had an important impact on Saint-Domingue, raising rebellious spirits and animosities against the rich and powerful. There was intense hatred of French landowners and officials, and agitation against them first started with poor whites, then the mixed-race population, and finally, in 1791, an open rebellion of the half-million black slaves led by the brilliant former slave Toussaint L'Ouverture.

White plantation owners were killed or driven out as slaves and free blacks gained power. The white owners sent out pleas for help to the British and Americans, not wanting to rely on the revolutionary forces in France. Their pleas fell on receptive ears: the British were worried that a successful slave rebellion in Saint-Domingue would spark a similar rebellion in British-controlled Jamaica; rumors spread throughout the slave-holding American South that Saint-Domingue was just the start of a much wider revolution. The British, at war with France, sent provisions and a contingent of its army. President Washington's two principal advisors, the pro-abolitionist, but pro-British Alexander Hamilton and slave-holding, freedom-loving Thomas Jefferson, agreed to assist the slave holders.[76]

Toussaint's forces were successful in repulsing local French forces, then sided with the Spanish, then changed allegiance back to France once the French Assembly had outlawed slavery. Toussaint then became the governor of the independent nation of Saint-Domingue; his soldiers defeated British troops who had come to the island by 1798, then defeated Spanish forces on the other two-thirds of the island, Santo Domingo. Napoleon, however, wanted to regain his military bases in Saint-Domingue. In 1802, he sent his brother-in-law, General Charles Leclerc with over 20,000 of the best French troops, to defeat the former slaves. Despite some defeats in early encounters with Toussaint's general Jean-Jacques Dessalines, Leclerc's forces appeared to be winning. Toussaint surrendered and later Leclerc invited him to dinner, one gentleman to another, and, fearing that the defeated slave leader would reignite warfare, Leclerc had Toussaint arrested. Napoleon then sent him to Fortress Joux in the Swiss Alps, where he quickly died from the damp and cold weather.

In 1802 Napoleon reinstated slavery; the reaction on Saint-Domingue was catastrophic for the French forces on the island. There was an uprising of blacks; the French were destroyed by the local forces and by yellow fever. Leclerc himself succumbed to the fever in November 1802.[77] This enormous setback for Napoleon, coupled with impending restart of war against Britain the following year, set into motion his decision to abandon grand schemes for the Americas.

Rumors of Louisiana Retrocession

The rumors had been swirling around for some time, even in American newspapers in the summer of 1801: Spain had returned Louisiana to France. Secretary of State James Madison warned the French representative Louis Pichon that the secrecy about a proposed retrocession was causing great alarm in the United States, and that any move by France in the American West would make the western territories bind together and would cause the United States to work more closely with France's nemesis, Britain.[78]

In mid-October 1801, Jefferson dispatched Robert R. Livingston to be U.S. minister to France to find out what he could about that country's intentions. By the time Livingston and his party reached Paris in early December, the president had received conclusive word about the retrocession from Rufus King, the American minister in London. Jefferson had to find out the details of the San Ildefonso agreement, to find out what Napoleon was up to, and to beef up American military power. News was still sketchy about the details of the transfer, and one major question was still unanswered: were the Floridas included in this deal?[79]

One of the problems that Jefferson had to consider was that France, Spain, and Britain had signed the Treaty of Amiens in March 1802, a peace agreement which meant that France now could free up to 40,000 troops for a possible Louisiana expedition.[80] The French expedition did take place, but it went to Saint-Domingue with General Leclerc and was destroyed.

Adding to the tensions, the Spanish Intendant of New Orleans, Juan de Dios Morales, abruptly and without notice closed the port to foreign shipping in October 1802. This startling news, when it reached Washington five weeks later, prompted government officials and ordinary citizens to look past Spanish authority and blame the French. The French, as was conclusively learned over 100 years later, were just as surprised as the Americans; this was a Spanish reprisal against American smuggling of gold and silver through the Port of New Orleans, nothing more. Frontiersmen in Kentucky and Tennessee were furious, threatening to march to New Orleans to settle the matter right then and there. Rumors swirled around that Napoleon was mounting a massive army to be sent to Louisiana.

Jefferson, however, tried hard to keep the port closure incident separate from the question of Louisiana cession. He decided to appoint former U.S. minister to France James Monroe, who was just completing a term as governor of Virginia, to join Livingston in Paris to see if they could negotiate with Napoleon.[81]

On December 15, 1802, Jefferson presented to Congress his Second Annual Message, noting the cession of Louisiana and warning that this would cause a change in American foreign relations. In early January 1803, the House debated Spain's cession, and passed a resolution on January 7 affirming its "unalterable determination" to maintain American navigation of the Mississippi. Federalists in Congress were calling for armed intervention. Senator James Ross (Federalist—Pennsylvania) moved that the president be given authority to raise 50,000 troops to seize New Orleans. Finally, after weeks of spirited, even intemperate, debate, a softer resolution was substituted. On January 12, the Senate approved the nominations of Livingston and Monroe to enter into a treaty or convention with Napoleon. All along, the goal was to purchase New Orleans and West Florida, and the House of Representatives appropriated $2 million for that purpose on the same day. While the Senate discussed the American rights to free navigation of the Mississippi navigation, Jefferson sent a secret letter to the House, asking for $2,500 appropriations for what would be the Lewis and Clark expedition of the American West.[82]

Louisiana Purchase Negotiations

Secretary of State James Madison wrote to Livingston to see what he knew, and, if France had reclaimed Louisiana and Florida was part of that deal, to see if Livingston could persuade Napoleon to transfer the Floridas, or at least West Florida, to the United States. If the Floridas were not part of the retrocession, then Madison wanted Livingston to work with U.S. minister Charles Pinckney in Madrid. Spanish officials said that the Floridas were not included in the cession; but the French said they were. When asked directly by Joseph Bonaparte whether the United States was interested in Louisiana or Florida, Livingston said that his government had no interest of extending westward of the Mississippi, and that the prime American goal was security, rather than extension of territory.[83]

What was Napoleon thinking? François Barbe-Marbois, the French Minister of the Public Treasury, was given the task of negotiating a deal with the American envoys. In private conversations in the Tuileries, Napoleon expressed his greatest concern: that the British, if left unchecked, would reinstate their rule in America. Napoleon thought it necessary to balance Britain's influence with another power "that may one day become her rival; that power is the United States."[84]

On April 10, 1803, Napoleon called on Marbois and Denis Decres, Minister of the Navy and Colonies, for further discussion; Marbois urged the sale, Decres argued for retaining Louisiana. Early the next morning, Napoleon summoned Marbois, commanding him to action.

"I renounce Louisiana," said Napoleon. "It is not only New Orleans that I will cede, it is the whole colony without any reservation. I know the price of what I abandon . . . I renounce it with the greatest regret. To attempt obstinately to retain it would be folly."[85]

Livingston's biographer, George Dangerfield, argued that the cessation of the whole of Louisiana came about probably because of several complex and nearly simultaneous pressures as well as the British threat: the fierce fighting of blacks in Saint-Domingue, the loss of Napoleon's brother-in-law Leclerc and his entire army; the failure of another military operation in Holland; American fury over the closing of the port of New Orleans and Spanish obstinacy; the diplomatic bluffs of Jefferson and Madison, the uncertainty of the impending Monroe instructions; and, finally, the prodding of Livingston in Paris.[86]

For several months, Livingston had been negotiating with Talleyrand, hoping to complete talks before Monroe arrived in Paris. The talks ranged from the sale of West Florida, New Orleans, and Louisiana above the Arkansas River; through it all, Talleyrand kept a skeptical silence. Then, on April 11, Talleyrand invited Livingston to his headquarters and casually asked if the United States wanted to purchase the entire Louisiana territory. For the moment, Livingston did not know what to say; he had no knowledge of Napoleon's decision the day before.[87]

Napoleon was now directing Marbois, not Talleyrand, to meet with Livingston as soon as possible. James Monroe arrived in Paris on April 13, and Livingston held a dinner party in his honor. Waiting outside was Marbois, who, after Monroe and the other guests had left, informed Livingston of Napoleon's decision. Without waiting to inform Monroe, with whom there were growing personal tensions, Livingston stayed up until three o'clock in the morning to draft a diplomatic dispatch. Monroe felt snubbed, but the two American envoys were able to patch up their differences, and later bargain down the asking price to $15 million ($11.25 million for the purchase and $3.75 million for payment of claims), made available through the issuance of stock at 6 percent interest, which the French could sell on the open market.[88]

All that was left was the question of the precise boundaries of the Louisiana territory, which, as it turned out, would not be settled for several more decades.

Making the Treaty

Word of the purchase of Louisiana reached American shores in late June. The headlines in the *Boston Independent* on June 30 exclaimed, "Louisiana Ceded to the United States!" President Jefferson heard indirectly three days later. Livingston and Monroe handed over a dispatch to Rufus King, who was returning immediately to the United States from London; King transmitted the letter from New York to Secretary of State Madison.

Most citizens in Washington just saw a simple announcement in the *National Intelligencer*, the official organ of the government, on July 4 stating that

> the Executive have received official information that a treaty was signed on the 30th of April between the Ministers Plenipotentiary and Extraordinary of the United States and the Minister Plenipotentiary of the French government; by which the United States obtained full right to and sovereignty over New Orleans and the whole of Louisiana, as Spain possessed the same.[89]

Though there was jubilation and congratulations throughout the land, there was occasional sniping and grousing, especially from Federalists and New Englanders. George Cabot, in a letter to Rufus King, thought that France got the better end of the deal: "It is like selling us a ship after she is surrounded by the British fleet."[90] King hinted that an even better deal could have been reached had not Livingston and Monroe been so anxious to sign the deal.[91]

Soon after learning about the purchase, Jefferson developed a plan to turn most of the new territory into a long-term homeland for eastern Indians. This meant that the land west of the Mississippi and north of the Thirty-First Parallel would be reserved for Indians. However, this scheme was put aside in the late summer and early fall. So, too, was Jefferson's idea of first seeking a constitutional amendment that would legitimize the purchase.[92]

There was nothing in the Constitution that explicitly permitted the United States to acquire territory, and Jefferson thought that a constitutional amendment would be needed in order to clarify this point. In a letter, written in January 1803, Attorney General Levi Lincoln, anticipating the problems of territorial acquisition, came up with a solution: let the existing states extend their boundaries to newly acquired areas, then there would be no need to worry about the Constitution. But Treasury Secretary Albert Gallatin would have none of it: if the federal government could not acquire new land, how does it become more legal to let the states do the same? Under Lincoln's scheme, Gallatin asked, what would prevent "the President and Senate, by treaty, annexing Cuba to Massachusetts, or Bengal to Rhode Island . . . ?"[93] Gallatin laid out a broad construction of the Constitution: there should be no difference "between a power to acquire territory for the United States and the power to extend by treaty the territory of the United States."[94] Jefferson was finally won over to the argument that Congress had the broad authority to acquire territory and that an amendment to the Constitution was not necessary.

Then there was the practical problem: the ratification clock was ticking. A constitutional amendment would take time, far more time than allowed by the treaty's six-month deadline. Further, Jefferson feared that Napoleon might change his mind and did not want to risk losing this opportunity. The president had received a letter from Livingston warning that Napoleon might be looking for an excuse "to weasel out of the bargain."[95] The niceties of a constitutional amendment would have to go by the wayside. Historian George Dangerfield put it this way: "To so magnificent an event as the Louisiana Purchase, a magnificent disregard for the Constitution was, perhaps, appropriate: and Jefferson's un-Jeffersonian behavior has justly been greeted with more applause than alarm or condemnation."[96]

The Treaty called for ratification within six months of the date of signing, which was April 30, 1803. The French had already signed and delivered their copy by June 7. While Jefferson received unofficial word on July 3, the official documents did not arrive in Washington until July 14; time was running short. Jefferson called Congress back into special session, convening on October 17, leaving only fourteen days to complete the ratification before the deadline.[97]

The debate in Congress over the Louisiana Purchase was rather limited. Yet, many who endorsed the plan had serious doubts: they praised the purchase, but questioned what the effect might be on the federal system of government.

Boundaries

Just what had the United States purchased? No one really knew the exact boundaries of the Louisiana territory. The original instructions to Livingston and Monroe were to purchase New Orleans and the east bank of the Mississippi River and the territory of West Florida, from whoever owned it. Instead, the United States purchased a vast territory, from the headwaters of the Mississippi River in Minnesota to the Gulf of Mexico. But it was not that simple. As George Dangerfield observed, "no American was able to define just what it was that had been purchased; no Frenchman was willing to do so; no Spaniard would admit that the purchase was valid."[98]

Eighth Congress, 1st Session
(October 17, 1803–March 27, 1804)

Senate: 18 Democrat-Republicans;
13 Federalists

House: 64 Federalists;
42 Democrat-Republicans

President: Thomas Jefferson

It was not until years later, with the purchase of all of Florida in 1821 and the Adams-Onis (Transcontinental) Treaty, that the western borders of the Louisiana Territory were established.

The Purchase Price

Money was not going to be an issue. In 1802, the national government had a good year financially. The U.S. Treasury had brought in nearly $12.3 million in revenue in 1802, and federal expenditures, including interest on the national debt that year, were just $3.7 million. Further, in early 1803, Congress had already appropriated $2 million as the first installment on the probable purchase of New Orleans and Florida. The Louisiana territory would cost the United States $15 million in stock, payable over six years' time. As General Horatio Gates wrote to Jefferson just three weeks after news reached America of the purchase: "Let the land rejoice, for you have bought Louisiana for a song."[99] How could anyone object to this deal?

Highlights of the Louisiana Purchase

There are three separate documents in what is known as the Louisiana Purchase. The first is the Treaty of Cession, in which France ceded its holdings in North America. There was no description of the land, except that it was "the Colony or Province of Louisiana with the Same extent that it now has in the hand of Spain, & that it had when France possessed it" (Art. I). This document also provided for the inhabitants of Louisiana to be incorporated into the Union as soon as possible, and to enjoy the rights, advantages and immunities of U.S. citizens (including, but not mentioned, the right to own slaves) (Art. III).

In the second and third documents, Conventions between the U.S. and France, the purchase price is set and diplomatic relations are spelled out.

Treasury Secretary Albert Gallatin did complain about the method of payment: the French could dispose of the stock for cash, which in fact they did, but the United States could not begin to pay down the debt for fifteen years.[100] But, apart from Gallatin, few argued about the price to be paid.

New England Federalists

But New England Federalists, their power and influence on the wane, launched biting, but ultimately futile, criticism of the Purchase. Manasseh Cutler, the old Ohio Company agent and now a member of Congress (Federalist–Massachusetts), termed the treaty a "flagrant violation of the principles of the Constitution," and expressed what many New England politicians had said before him. Cutler wasn't so much worried about the purity of the Constitution, however. He, and many of his colleagues, worried that the admission of

Louisiana "would throw the balance of political power to the South, and in all probability will lay the foundation for a separation of the States."[101]

William Plumer (Federalist–New Hampshire) worried about this new political reality: "admit this western world into the union, & you destroy with a single operation the whole weight & importance of the eastern states in the *scale* of politics."[102] The fear, very simply, was that, with this new territory, the commercial and manufacturing centers of the northeast would be overwhelmed by the political power of the plantation, slaveholding southern states.[103] That southern political power further was enhanced because of the three-fifths clause, boosting its representation in Congress and the Electoral College.

Key Individuals

Who should take credit for the Louisiana Purchase and its subsequent ratification? Both Livingston and Monroe made their claims, and Secretary of State James Madison acknowledged that both diplomats should receive some credit, but that the "state of things" which led Napoleon to his offer to sell Louisiana was probably the main reason.[104] Both Madison and President Jefferson had impressed upon the French and other European powers that the United States had special interest in the Mississippi. However, the most American important figure throughout was Thomas Jefferson.

Thomas Jefferson (1743–1826) was a member of the Continental Congress (1775 and 1776) and principal author and signer of the Declaration of Independence; he was governor of Virginia (1779–1781); then he returned to the Continental Congress (1783–1784). In 1784, he was appointed minister plenipotentiary to France and minister to the king of France in 1785. He served as the first secretary of state (1789–1793) under George Washington; was elected vice-president (1797–1801) under John Adams; and became president in 1801 on the thirty-sixth ballot in the House of Representatives. He was re-elected president in 1804, serving until March 1809. In his eight years of office, the Louisiana Purchase was the most important legislative and diplomatic act.

Easterners, particularly from New England, also raised the old fear, seen in the debates of the Northwest Ordinance and in the Constitutional convention, that, by opening up the West, streams of settlers would cross the Mississippi, the American population would be further scattered, and land values in the East would be depressed.[105] Jefferson was reviled by most Massachusetts Federalists, but he received support from two important leaders, John Adams and his son John Quincy Adams. Jefferson had defeated the senior Adams in the bitter presidential election of 1800, but Adams was pleased with the purchase and, years later in a letter to Josiah Quincy, concluded that, without the Purchase, "we could never have secured and commanded the navigation of the Mississippi. The western country would infallibly have revolted from the Union. Those States would have united with England, or Spain, or France, or set up an independence, or done anything else to obtain the free use of that river."[106] John Quincy Adams, the newly chosen senator from Massachusetts, was just presenting his credentials to Congress as the ratification debates began in October 1803. Young Adams broke with his party and supported Jefferson, both on Louisiana and later against Britain during the Napoleonic Wars. As a result of his disloyalty, the Federalist-dominated Massachusetts legislature took the extraordinary step of electing a successor to Adams in 1808 nine months before his term was completed. John Quincy Adams resigned in protest.[107]

The New England Federalists, however, turned out to be a minority within a minority party: most Federalists were expansionists, and like most other Americans, wanted to see the Purchase Treaty ratified.[108]

Statehood

One of the core principles of early republicanism came directly out of the political philosopher Montesquieu: "It is natural for a republic to have only a small territory, otherwise it cannot long subsist."[109] But by 1787, with the expansion into the West, that element of political theory was losing some of its appeal. In 1803, Senator John Breckinridge (Democratic Republican–Kentucky), a strong supporter of Thomas Jefferson, attacked the "old and hackneyed doctrine: that a republic ought not to be too extensive," arguing that the "Goddess of Liberty" was not restrained by geographical limits. For Breckinridge, "the more extensive its dominion the more safe and durable [the union] will be."[110]

Breckinridge stated the administration's case: "To acquire an empire . . . from the most powerful and warlike nation on earth, without the oppressing of a single individual, without in the least embarrassing the ordinary operations of your finances, and all this through the peaceful forms of negotiation," this, Breckinridge concluded, "was an unparalleled achievement."[111]

Key Events involving the Louisiana Purchase	
1795	Treaty of San Lorenzo between the United States and Spain, guaranteeing American right to deposit good free of charge in New Orleans.
1797–1798	XYZ Affair; Quasi-War, military confrontations between U.S. and France.
1799	Napoleon's ascendancy to power in France.
1801	Thomas Jefferson becomes president; James Madison becomes secretary of state. U.S. learned that Spain had secretly returned Louisiana to France.
1802	Spanish officials in New Orleans abruptly announced new restrictions on American merchants. French army was repelled by a revolt in Saint Domingue.
1803	Napoleon surprised American envoys by offering entire Louisiana Territory for sale; Senate quickly approved treaty on October 20. Legislation to create the Territory of Orleans.
1812	Louisiana became a state; beginning of War of 1812.
1815	Battle of New Orleans.
1820	Missouri Compromise.

In the Senate, the Federalists were definitely in the minority, with only nine members, and the final vote for the treaty, on October 20, coming after just two days of debate, was 24 to 7.[112]

Then there was a set of implementing laws, requiring the participation of both the House and the Senate. The president was authorized to take control of Louisiana; funds were appropriated to pay for the land and the federal statutes, and tariff provisions were incorporated into it. The land was originally divided into two sections: the Territory of Orleans, below the Thirty-Third Parallel, and the District and later the Territory of Louisiana.[113]

On November 10, 1803, Jefferson signed into law an authorization for the creation of $11.25 million in stock for purchase of Louisiana. The official transfer came in December 20, 1803, when William C. C. Claiborne, who had been governor of the Mississippi Territory, and James Wilkinson, the senior officer in the U.S. Army, signed documents at the Cabildo in New Orleans to transfer Lower Louisiana from France to the United States.

Impact

The debates over both the Louisiana Purchase Treaty in the Senate and the enabling legislation in the House and Senate were relatively short, somewhat heated, but in the end accomplished the task at hand. But underlying the debates were struggles over the balance of power between the North and the South. The hard part was still to come as the issues of slavery, the loyalty of the citizenry in Orleans Territory, and sectional division would have to be confronted.

Exploration and Boundaries

First, however, was the question of staking an authoritative claim to the new territory and resolving the disputes over boundaries. In May 1804, with forty enlisted soldiers, Meriwether Lewis and William Clark began their celebrated scientific exploration crossing the new Louisiana Territory, reaching the Columbia River and the Pacific Ocean, before returning to St. Louis in September 1806. Another exploration, more military than scientific, was launched under the command of Lieutenant Zebulon M. Pike. Together with twenty men, Pike traveled in a keel boat to the headwaters of the Mississippi River in northern Minnesota on a nine-month voyage (1805–1806), to inform both Canadian traders and Sioux Indians that the United States now had sovereignty over this land. A second Pike expedition, launched in the summer of 1806, took another military party to the source of the Arkansas River and to the mountains of present-day Colorado. Pike also escorted home a contingent of Osage and Pawnee chiefs and their tribesmen who had been visiting Washington.[114]

While there were more expeditions, it took years before the final boundaries of Louisiana were established. The main sticking problem was the western border between Louisiana and Texas, which was then held by Mexico. Spanish officials maintained that the western boundary was near Natchitoches; the United States argued that the boundary was further west, at the Sabine River or perhaps the Rio Grande River. Diplomatic relations between the United States and Spain broke down in 1805 and war was feared on the disputed border. Eventually a neutral strip was negotiated between the two countries, a no-man's land which lasted for another decade. Finally, a treaty signed in 1819 by Secretary of State John Quincy Adams and Spanish Minister to Washington Luis de Onis settled the boundary of the Louisiana Purchase; it was not ratified by the new Republic of Mexico, however, until 1821.

In exchange for renouncing claims on Texas, the United States received favorable terms by getting the western border of Louisiana set at the Sabine River, together with the rest of the Louisiana Purchase boundary set at the Red and Arkansas Rivers to the Continental Divide; then it followed the Forty-Second Parallel to the Pacific Ocean. Spain retained control of Texas, present-day California, New Mexico, Arizona, Nevada, Utah and parts of Wyoming and Colorado, but relinquished its claim to Oregon above 42° north latitude, the current California–Oregon border. This Adams–Onis (Transcontinental) Treaty also called for Spain to cede all of East Florida (east of the Apalachicola River), to give up all claims to West Florida (west of Apalachicola River and much of present-day Alabama and Mississippi); in exchange, the United States assumed $5 million in claims of American citizens against Spain.

Slavery

While the tensions between North and South greatly increased, northern legislators refrained from attacking slavery as an institution or slave representation for fear that they might lose southern support.[115] While slaves were still held in some parts of the Northwest Territory and in northern states, by the day of Jefferson's inauguration as president, March 4, 1801, eight out of sixteen states sanctioned slavery. Kentucky had entered the Union in 1792 without ever having been a territory; Tennessee entered as a slave state in 1796. At this time, the United States was the largest slave-holding country in the world: 900,000 slaves out of a total population of 5.3 million.[116] The slave population was about to increase substantially. Later, the Alabama and Mississippi Territories, which were ceded from North Carolina and Georgia, stipulated that Congress could not interfere with the existing slave status in those areas. By 1810, the white population of the Territory of Orleans was 34,311; its slave population was 34,660; there were 7,585 free people of color. By 1860, the proportion of whites and slaves in the state of Louisiana stayed equal, but had grown roughly tenfold.[117]

The life of slaves, harsh and cruel that it was, became worse in the Louisiana Territory under American rule. Before 1803, slaves were guaranteed certain rights under the *Code Noir*: they were to be instructed in religion, able to cultivate their own plot of ground for their own use; testify in court when white witnesses were not available (but not against their masters); they had the right to observe Sundays as holidays and be buried in consecrated ground. Husbands and wives could not be sold separately; slave children under fourteen could not be sold away from their mothers; and, if mistreated, slaves could appeal to colonial authorities. After coming under United States jurisdiction, the Black Codes adopted by the new Territory of Orleans wiped out all of these protections.[118]

In 1804, Representative James Hillhouse (Federalist–Connecticut) offered an amendment to the bill organizing the territory of Louisiana that prohibited slavery in the entire area ceded by the French. The amendment predictably failed, but Hillhouse successfully led an effort to ban the importation of foreign slaves into Louisiana. But Jefferson, author of the anti-slavery provision for the Land Ordinance of 1784, reasoned that a ban on slave labor would cripple the production of sugar, a crop vital to the agricultural independence of the country. He also understood that the terms of the Louisiana Purchase had precluded a federal abolition of slavery, because the French had written into the treaty that the citizens of Louisiana should enjoy rights and privileges of American citizens, and among those rights and privileges was the ownership of slaves.[119]

Jefferson refused to allow Louisiana citizens the right to buy slaves imported from other countries. It was still four years away from the constitutional requirement that the importation of slaves be prohibited, and Louisiana slave owners objected strongly. But a curious coalition of northern and southern legislators banded together: many of the northerners objected to the importation of slaves on moral and constitutional grounds, while a major objective of the southerners was to be able to sell their own surplus slaves to planters in Louisiana.[120]

The free people of color and slaves in the Territory of Orleans constituted a majority of persons; the slaves had the most to lose with the new, harsher Black Codes. In January 1811, in probably the largest such insurrection in American history, hundreds of slaves joined together in revolt outside of New Orleans. They were dispersed by federal troops and local militia, but tensions lingered, and local officials were constantly worried about a slave rebellion.[121]

Admission into the Union and Battle of New Orleans

The laws in place in Louisiana at the time of transfer to the United States were those of Spain. Later, in 1808, the Louisiana territorial government adopted a civil code, not based on Spanish law, nor on Anglo-American concepts, but to a large extent on the new French code, the Code Napoleon.[122] Now with a population of some 76,000, well above the minimum of 60,000 required for statehood, the U.S. Congress in 1811 authorized the calling of a state convention. The new Louisiana constitution of 1812, modeled after that of Kentucky, strictly limited voting and office holding to white men of property, disqualifying nearly two-thirds of the adult white males, and, of course, all nonwhites and all women.[123] On April 30, 1812, Louisiana was admitted as a slave state, the eighteenth state of the Union.

Ever since the transfer of power in 1803, many Americans questioned the allegiance of Louisianans, wondering, if there were another war with a European power, whether they and other westerner settlers would leave the United States to form alliances with other countries.[124]

The Battle of New Orleans proved beyond a doubt that Louisianans were loyal to the United States and fiercely opposed to British intrusion. On December 24, 1814, American and British commissioners met at Ghent, Belgium, to sign a peace treaty to end the War of 1812. In the meantime, however, the first battle for New Orleans had begun, followed by two bloodier fights in early January, 1815. The British outnumbered the American soldiers and militia men by at least two to one. But on January 8, in the most famous battle, Major General Sir Edward Packenham, commander of the British forces, was killed, over 2,000 British soldiers became casualties (compared to 71 Americans), and the remnants of the British forces retreated to their ships, never to return. Among General Andrew Jackson's defenders were members of the Louisiana and New Orleans militias, the First and Second Battalions of Free Men of Color, home guards, slaves and citizens who helped widen canals and build fortresses.[125] They had proved their mettle and their loyalty to the Union.

Jefferson had proclaimed an "Empire for liberty," built on a commitment of continental expansion. But, as historian John H. Murrin observed, it was a remarkable achievement, but one for whites only. The harsh legacies of Jefferson's dream meant the forcible removal of Indians from the East and South, continued slavery, and thoughts of African colonization.[126] Free now of hostilities with foreign powers, the West continued its inevitable growth, with the life pulse provided by the Mississippi River. New territory would be added and new states admitted into the Union, with the growing tension between free soil and slave. After Louisiana had been established as a state, the remainder of the Louisiana Territory became known as the Missouri Territory. There was no anti-slavery provision for this immense expanse, as there was for the Northwest Territory. For a time, there was a balance in the admission of new states: one free state admitted and then a slave state shortly thereafter. By 1818, the territory of Missouri had enough settlers to petition for statehood; if admitted, Missouri would become a slave state.

Then a one-term congressman from New York proposed that slavery be gradually removed from the Missouri territory; his proposal did not pass, but in its place came the Missouri Compromise of 1820. Missouri could enter the Union as a slave state, but, from that point on, there would be no slavery in the remainder of the Louisiana Purchase lands above the southern border of Missouri, at the latitude line of 36°30′ north. For the next twenty-five years, the delicate question of slavery in new states and territories seemed resolved. Then came the annexation and statehood of Texas and an anti-slavery proviso, proffered by a young congressman from Pennsylvania. Later came the Compromise of 1850 which dealt with the admission of California and the status of the New Mexico and Utah territories, runaway slaves, and other issues. Shortly thereafter came the Kansas–Nebraska Act of 1854 which repealed the Missouri Compromise, inflamed tensions between the North and South, fractured political party alignments, ushered in Bleeding Kansas, and was one of the fateful steps leading to the breakup of the Union.

2

SLAVERY AND THE TERRITORIES

The Kansas–Nebraska Act of 1854

*I passed the Kansas–Nebraska Act myself. I had
the authority and power of a dictator throughout the
whole controversy in both houses.*

Stephen A. Douglas (1854)

*This law may have been the most important single
event pushing the nation toward civil war.*

James McPherson (1988)

*The Kansas–Nebraska Act was a gross miscalculation.
And the nation paid a heavy price for it.*

Robert V. Remini (2006)

The legislation was introduced with the best of intentions. The ambitious, confident Stephen A. Douglas, Democratic senator from Illinois, was determined to lay the groundwork for a transcontinental railroad from his hometown of Chicago to the Pacific coast. To do so required that the lands west of Missouri be organized into territorial governments and eventually become states. This would permit the settlement of land and the orderly growth of communities in the West.

But quickly the debate over the Kansas–Nebraska Act shifted from railroads to the bitter fight over the extension of slavery into the remaining unorganized territory of the Louisiana Purchase. Douglas needed southern Senate support and he bowed to pressure from powerful southern leaders, who insisted that this new territory permit slavery. Douglas and his allies accomplished this by insisting on implementing popular sovereignty: let the people who settle this new land determine for themselves whether it will be slave or free.

However, popular sovereignty ran directly counter to an older, seemingly settled national policy concerning slavery in the territories. In 1820, the Missouri Compromise determined that the Missouri would became a slave state but that the remaining land of the Louisiana Purchase above the current Arkansas–Missouri border would be "forever free" of slavery.

Douglas knew that his Kansas–Nebraska Act would raise indignant cries from northern free soilers and abolitionists. But, in one of the more tone-deaf decisions in American history, he forged on, publicly declaring the Missouri Compromise to be inoperative; along the way, he recruited a reluctant President Franklin Pierce to join him. All thoughts about rail transportation were put aside during the four months of acrimonious debate. Old wounds and long-standing personal insults festered, sectional animosity resurfaced, and threats of secession again were cried out.

The political fallout was immense. The Democratic Party suffered heavily in the North, the Whig Party disintegrated, the nativist Know Nothing movement surged before quickly fading, and the new Republican Party emerged. A former one-term Illinois congressman, utterly dismayed by the Kansas–Nebraska legislation, left the lifeless Whigs. Abraham Lincoln re-entered politics, leading the new Republican Party in Illinois, sparring with the powerful Douglas in a series of historic debates.

Less than two years later after it was enacted, civil insurrection raged in Kansas, and the principle of popular sovereignty, so dear to Douglas, had been made a mockery. In a decisive break with both the southern wing of the Democratic Party and President James Buchanan, Douglas excoriated the fraudulent LeCompton constitution and fought to deny slave-state Kansas admission into the Union. The divide between northern and southern Democrats was now irreparable; soon to follow were Harpers Ferry, Fort Sumter, secession, and brother fighting brother.

Unlike all other laws in this book, the Kansas–Nebraska Act is most known for its unintended consequences and the fateful steps taken in its aftermath. It was a law that shaped America, but in a way unimaginable to its author and those who grappled with it.

Background

The forty years preceding the Civil War saw the creation of the dominant Democratic Party, the rise and fall of the Whig Party, and the birth of the Republican Party. Those years were marked by increased sectional rivalries between North and South, grandiloquent spokesmen, and tumultuous relations in Congress. It also was an era of both weak and strong presidents: a dominant two-term president (Andrew Jackson), a strong one-term president (James K. Polk), two who died in office (William Henry Harrison, Zachary Taylor), two who were defeated for re-election (John Quincy Adams, Martin Van Buren), and three who were passed over by their own parties for re-election (John Tyler, Millard Fillmore, Franklin Pierce). What follows is a thumbnail sketch of the politics of that era.

Through the early years of the nineteenth century, the Jeffersonians and Virginia dominated national politics. The Federalist Party had all but withered away by 1815, and the followers of Jefferson called themselves the

Democratic-Republican Party. During the eight-year presidency of James Monroe (1817–1825), the Democratic-Republicans were so dominant that there was no opposition political party; in fact, Monroe received all electoral votes but one in his 1820 re-election. This period, called the Era of Good Feelings, however, was punctuated by the Missouri Compromise of 1820, a foretaste of the heated sectional battles yet to come.

In 1824, bitter personal rivalries surfaced during the presidential election. It was a four-way race: war hero Senator Andrew Jackson of Tennessee, Secretary of State John Quincy Adams of Massachusetts, Secretary of the Treasury William H. Crawford of Georgia, and Speaker of the House of Representatives Henry Clay of Kentucky. Jackson garnered the most popular and electoral votes, but not enough for a clear majority. For the second time in American history, the presidential contest was decided in the House of Representatives, following the procedures laid out in the Constitution. Before the voting began, Clay, who had the lowest total of both popular and electoral votes, swung his support to Adams, who then won on the first ballot. Later, Adams awarded Clay the position of secretary of state. Jackson's supporters were outraged, vowed retaliation, and pointed to examples of political chicanery as a campaign theme against Adams four years later. John C. Calhoun of South Carolina was elected vice-president.

In 1828, the Democratic-Republican Party split in two: those supporting Andrew Jackson and the legacy of Thomas Jefferson now called themselves Democrats, and those who opposed Jackson were the National Republicans. This year marked the acrimonious rematch between Adams and Jackson, with Jackson unseating Adams; for the second time in America's early history a president named Adams was defeated for re-election. Again, Calhoun was chosen vice-president. By the mid-1830s, two national political parties had begun to emerge. The first was the Democratic Party, under the leadership of Jackson and under the management of his second term vice-president, Martin Van Buren.[1] The Democratic Party became the dominant political organization from 1828 through 1860, winning six out of nine presidential elections, and controlling the House of Representatives for twenty-four out of thirty-two years and the Senate for twenty-eight of those years.[2]

However, the Democrats soon encountered strong competition and the second American party system was born, lasting from the early 1830s until the mid-1850s. Opposing the Democrats and Jackson was a new party called the Whigs, so named because its supporters considered themselves the political legatees of the British Whigs who opposed King George III. The American Whigs' opponent was "King Andrew" Jackson and his bold assertion of political power.

Daniel Webster's Senate speech denouncing the Jackson veto of the national bank bill in 1832 marked the beginning of Whig opposition. It took several years before the Whigs organized, but they were able to cobble together a viable political organization under the leadership of three strong, but very different, personalities: Henry Clay of Kentucky, Daniel Webster of Massachusetts, and

John C. Calhoun of South Carolina. It was not an ideological connection but more a distaste for Jackson that kept the Whigs together during this time.[3]

The Whigs ran three candidates for the presidency in 1836, gambling on a divided electorate and a chance to win in the House of Representatives. However, Jackson's vice- president Martin Van Buren, the key strategist behind the creation of the Democratic Party, prevailed. Van Buren ran for re-election in 1840, but, thanks in large part to the Panic of 1837 and its economic consequences, he lost to Whig candidate William Henry Harrison. The Whig Party, born just five or six years earlier, now had succeeded in electing a president, had taken over 62 percent of the seats in Congress, and won nearly all the gubernatorial contests as well.[4] But Harrison died one month into his presidency, and was succeeded by his vice-president, John Tyler of Virginia, a former Democrat. This was the first time that a president had died in office, and Tyler had to set the precedent—not accepted by everyone—that he was not simply a caretaker or acting president, but the president in fact. However, Tyler bumped heads with his party's legislators and political leaders, especially Henry Clay, over a presidential veto of a second national bank bill, and Tyler was denied the Whig Party nomination for re-election in 1844.

That year, the Whig Party chose Clay as its presidential nominee, while the Democrats nominated James K. Polk. Polk was a protege of Andrew Jackson, a former speaker of the House, and former governor of Tennessee who had just lost two successive gubernatorial contests to Whig candidates. In choosing Polk, the Democrats passed over former president Martin Van Buren, who publicly opposed annexation of Texas. In a campaign dominated by the issue of Texas annexation, which Polk advocated and Clay opposed, the Polk Democrats prevailed in a narrow victory over the Clay Whigs.

In 1844, the Liberty Party, a small single-issue party created in 1839, played a role. The party opposed slavery and called for its abolition in Washington, D.C., and other federal territories. In the extremely tight contest for the presidency in New York state, the Liberty Party gathered enough votes to make the difference between Polk and Clay, and thus the election.

During Polk's four-year term, the United States went to war against Mexico and expanded its territory by one-half, with the annexation of Texas, the Oregon territory, and the vast territory of New Mexico, California, and Deseret. Polk, whom many historians now rate as one of the strongest presidents of the nineteenth century, pledged to serve only one term in office. In 1848, the Whigs nominated Zachary Taylor, the Mexican war general, and the Democrats chose Senator Lewis Cass of Michigan as their standard bearer. Taylor, who beat out Clay and Major General Winfield Scott for the Whig nomination, barely defeated Cass, whose chances were hurt in part because former president Martin Van Buren withdrew his support from the Democratic Party to run as a third party candidate, representing the new Free Soil Party. The Free Soilers opposed extension of slavery into the newly annexed territories, an issue that loomed large as the antagonism between North and South increased.

Presidents and Vice-Presidents, 1825–1861	
President	*Vice-President*
John Quincy Adams (1825–1829)	John C. Calhoun (1825–1829)
Andrew Jackson (1829–1837)	John C. Calhoun (1829–1832)
	None (1832–1833)
	Martin Van Buren (1833–1837)
Martin Van Buren (1837–1841) (Dem.)	Richard M. Johnson (1837–1841)
Wm. Henry Harrison (1841) (Whig)	John Tyler (1841)
John Tyler (1841–1845) (Whig)	None (1841–1845)
James K. Polk (1844–1849) (Dem.)	George M. Dallas (1845–1849)
Zachary Taylor (1849–1850) (Whig)	Millard Fillmore (1849–1850)
Millard Fillmore (1850–1853) (Whig)	None (1850–1853)
Franklin Pierce (1853–1857) (Dem.)	William King (1853)
	None (1853–1857)
James Buchanan (1857–1861) (Dem.)	John C. Breckinridge (1857–1861)

Taylor was the second Whig president to die in office; with his death in 1850, he was succeeded by Vice-President Millard Fillmore. Fillmore became president in the midst of the fight over the Compromise of 1850, the five pieces of legislation that for a time dampened the slavery and territory fervor. However, many northern Whigs were irreconcilably opposed to Fillmore once he had signed the Fugitive Slave Act, which was part of the Compromise. This resistance cost Fillmore the 1852 presidential nomination. Later, Fillmore became the candidate of the American, or Know Nothing, Party in 1856.

In 1852, Democrat Franklin Pierce, who won his party's nomination on the forty-ninth ballot, bested Whig candidate General Winfield Scott, the last presidential candidate the Whig Party would mount. By the congressional elections in late 1854, the Whigs were on their last legs, if not already politically moribund. Ironically, many legislators who had been Whigs won re-election, but, with the full implications of the Kansas–Nebraska Act now being felt, the Whigs split apart, with Southern Whigs joining Southern Democrats, and Northern Whigs joining a wide assortment of coalitions. By the 1855 session in Congress, the Democrats were in the decided minority, with former Whigs combining with Know Nothings, Know Nothing-Democrats, Know Nothing-Free Soilers, Free Soilers, anti-Nebraska factions, and non-partisan alliances constituting a shaky majority.

In 1854, a new secretive organization, the Know Nothings, experienced a surge in growth. Emerging as the American Party, the Know Nothings were stridently anti-immigrant, anti-Catholic, anti-liquor, and anti-slavery. The party had particular strength in New England and parts of the old Northwest, but, once the national American Party decided to support the Kansas–Nebraska Act at its 1855 convention, northern sympathizers left to join a new organization, the Republican Party.[5]

In 1856, the new Republican Party fielded its first presidential nominee, explorer John C. Fremont, who lost to Democrat James Buchanan, who had swept the South and won a number of northern states as well. But neither Buchanan nor congressional Democrats could hold North and South together. By 1858, the Democratic Party was torn apart over the LeCompton affair in Kansas when Stephen A. Douglas led northern Democrats in revolt against their president and southern Democrats. That split was fully evident in the presidential election of 1860, with Douglas running as the candidate for Northern Democrats and Buchanan's vice-president John C. Breckinridge of Kentucky the candidate for the Southern Democrats. Added to the mix was John Bell of Tennessee, for the Constitutional Union Party, an organization made up of former Whigs, Know Nothings, and others. The Democratic Party, fractured and contentious, presented the Republican Party with its historic opportunity. Meeting in Chicago, the Republicans by-passed their putative leader Senator William H. Seward of New York for the far less known Abraham Lincoln, a former one-term Whig Party congressman and twice-defeated candidate for the Senate from Illinois.

The Sectional Crises

From the first days of the Republic, there had been sectional tensions. Historian David M. Potter characterized the problem of sectional bickering and tension as "chronic in American history."[6] As seen in the previous chapter, much of the tension initially was between East and West, between the settled original states and the new states and territories beyond the Appalachians. Certainly slavery was a contentious question, only partially mollified by the three-fifths compromise and future ban on imported slaves. But more immediate were commercial and financial tensions between the agrarian South and the increasingly commercial, manufacturing North. Tariffs, the Hamiltonian financial system, and Jay's Treaty were flash points between the North and South.[7]

In reaction to the Alien and Sedition Acts passed during the John Adams administration, Kentucky and Virginia enacted their famous resolutions, which articulated the doctrines of strict construction, state sovereignty, and nullification. However, much of the fight about southern separation and sectionalism was temporarily mitigated when Jefferson was elected president in 1800. After that, New England increasingly became the embattled minority section of the country.[8] Some of the first plots to secede from the Union were contrived by New Englanders, with the most serious coming in late December 1814 and early January 1815. New England delegates met in Hartford, Connecticut, to air their grievances and plot secession from the United States. They were bitter about the War of 1812 and its effects on commercial and trading interests in New England. However, by the time they had completed their deliberations and delivered their grievances to Washington, the war was over.[9]

But ineluctably, the issue of slavery, and, more particularly, the extension of slavery into new territories and states, formed the core of tensions between the North and South. With the great territorial expansion from the Louisiana Purchase, Jefferson made no effort to stop the spread of slavery into this new territory. In the acquired Louisiana territories, slavery already was legal, under Spanish and French territorial law. All Jefferson and his allies had to do was pass an organic law for the territory, containing no provisions excluding slavery.[10]

The three-fifths clause was a bone stuck in the craw of many northerners. Over the years they had realized, as Gouverneur Morris had predicted in 1787, that the three-fifths clause had nothing to do with direct taxes and everything to do with political power.[11] Through it, slave-holding states artificially increased their power by over one-third in the House of Representatives and the Electoral College. In 1793, for example, the slave states had forty-seven seats instead of thirty-three that would have been allotted solely on white population; in 1833, they had ninety-eight seats instead of seventy-three.

However, the South never attained a majority in the House of Representatives; the great influx of immigrants and population growth came mostly in the North and the new states created from the Northwest Territory. From 1789 through 1792, the North had thirty-five representatives, and the South had thirty; from 1811 to 1822, the North had 107 representatives and the South had seventy-nine.[12] No matter what happened in the House, however, the South would always have the Senate to protect its interests. With equal representation in the Senate, southern states could always count on blocking any measures passed by the northern-dominated House, provided, of course, that there was a parity and balance in the admission of free and slave states.

But from a northern point of view, the three-fifths clause violated the principles of fairness and one-man, one-vote. The slave-holding South was getting too much power, not only in the House of Representatives but also in the Electoral College. With fourteen extra electoral votes, southerners were able in 1800 to elect Thomas Jefferson and oust the sitting president, John Adams.[13] Jefferson's victory continued what would be a thirty-two-year Virginia Dynasty: eight years of Washington, eight years of Jefferson, followed by eight years each for Madison and Monroe. Only John Adams in 1796 and his son John Quincy Adams in 1824 put a dent in that dynasty.

The balance between slave and free states became critical. Of the original states, eight generally could be considered free: Pennsylvania, New Jersey, Connecticut, Massachusetts, New Hampshire, New York, Rhode Island (admitted in 1790), Vermont (1791);[14] slavery was legally permitted in Delaware, Georgia, Maryland, South Carolina, Virginia, and North Carolina (1789).

By 1820, four new free states were admitted: Ohio (1803), Indiana (1816), Illinois (1818), and Maine (1820); five new slave states were admitted: Kentucky (1792), Tennessee (1796), Louisiana (1812), Mississippi (1817), and Alabama (1819). This brought the total to twelve free and eleven slave states.

By 1845, just one free state, Michigan (1837), was added, while four slave states were admitted: Missouri (1821), Arkansas (1836), Florida (1845), and Texas (1845). The balance now was thirteen free and fifteen slave states. In the fifteen years preceding the Civil War, five new free states were admitted to the Union: Iowa (1846), Wisconsin (1848), California (1850), Minnesota (1858), Oregon (1859); there were no additional slave states. This brought the balance to eighteen free and fifteen slave states, but slavery was waning in Maryland and Delaware and was negligible in the mountainous regions of Kentucky, Tennessee, and western Virginia. South Carolina then seceded from the Union on December 16, 1860, and Kansas became a free state in January 1861. Soon, ten other states joined South Carolina in secession; however, Maryland, Kentucky, Delaware, and Missouri, all slave-holding states, remained in the Union.

In the three decades before the Kansas–Nebraska Act, Congress was involved in three serious sectional crises, relating to the Missouri Compromise (1820), the Texas Annexation and the Wilmot Proviso (1845), and the Compromise of 1850. All were rooted in the issue of slavery in new states and territories. In addition, Congress was embroiled in the Tariff of Abominations (1832) which set off a secessionist threat in South Carolina and the anti-slavery gag rule (1835–1844), which further stoked regional tension.

The Missouri Compromise. By 1818, the territory of Missouri had gained enough settlers to qualify for statehood; and it intended to apply as a slave state. Most settlers came from the South, and with them came their slaves. By 1820, there were 10,222 slaves in Missouri comprising 15.8 percent of the total territorial population.[15] Louisiana was the first state to be carved out of the Louisiana Purchase lands; now came the application for a second state and some thorny questions. Would this set a precedent, permitting slavery in all of the Purchase lands? Would this upset the delicate balance between slave and free states? Would the North, simmering over the strength of the southern states, balk at further slave expansion? To a friend, the aged Thomas Jefferson wrote that the Missouri issue was as "a fire bell in the night" which "awakened and filled me with terror."[16]

It fell to a one-term northern congressman to frame the issue of slavery in the new territories. On February 13, 1819, in the last weeks of the Fifteenth Congress, James Tallmadge, Jr. (Republican New York), "tossed a bombshell into the Era of Good Feelings." He introduced two amendments: the first would bar future slaves from entering Missouri, the second would free slaves who were born in Missouri once they had reached twenty-five years of age. This was not the first time that Tallmadge had introduced anti-slavery legislation. He had helped New York state emancipate its slaves in 1817; his home state that year had roughly the same number of blacks as the Missouri Territory had in 1820.[17] Tallmadge inveighed against slavery on both moral and political grounds: bondage in the new states would mean additional slave votes inevitably lined up against the North. In the Senate, the venerable Rufus King (Federalist–New

York) argued even more forcefully than Tallmadge about the "unjust and odious" nature of slave extension. The House of Representatives passed the Tallmadge amendments a week later, but the measures were blocked in the Senate.[18] In both chambers, on both amendments, the votes turned overwhelmingly North versus South.

Certainly, northern politicians resented the dominant power of the Virginia Dynasty and what was being called "Slave Power."[19] Now in the second decade of the nineteenth century, America was becoming more democratized: it was going through a transition from Jeffersonian elitism, where property (and slaves) mattered above all, to a new, yet-to-be articulated Jacksonian democracy, where individual white men mattered, not their property, either real or in slaves. Slave Power, however, was blocking that seemingly natural transition, and was redefining and shaping the new egalitarian impulses.[20]

Just what was Slave Power? According to abolitionist Senator Salmon P. Chase (Free Soil–Ohio), speaking decades later, Slave Power consisted of about 350,000 or so slave owners in the South. Chase may have been wildly erroneous in his estimates of the number of slaveholding families in the South, or he was focusing on just those who held economic and political power. By 1860, in the lower South (South Carolina, Georgia, Florida, Alabama, Mississippi, Louisiana, and Texas), the proportion of slave-holding families ranged from 28 percent in Texas to 49 percent in Mississippi; in the upper South (Delaware, Maryland, Virginia, North Carolina, Kentucky, Tennessee, Missouri, and Arkansas), the proportion ranged from 2 percent in Arkansas to 29 percent in North Carolina. Five states (Virginia, South Carolina, Georgia, Alabama, and Mississippi) had between 400,000 and 500,000 slaves each in 1860; Delaware had 1,798 slaves. In Mississippi, the slave population of 436,631 constituted the highest proportion of slaves in the total population, 55.1 percent.[21]

Some defended slavery and Slave Power stoutly and aggressively. Few southern politicians were as vocal and undisguised as William Smith (Democratic Republican–South Carolina), who enthusiastically defended slavery: it was universal throughout history, found in the Bible, justified by Aristotle and Plato, and now, in America, was needed to help the helpless servant. "No class of laboring people in any country upon the globe are better clothed, better fed, or more cheerful, or labor less," Smith opined, than "our indulged serviles."[22] Some southerners wished that they could roll the clock back and never have gone down the path of slavery. Others felt that slavery would eventually die off, under its own economy-deadening weight. Some, like past president Thomas Jefferson and future president John Tyler (Democratic Republican–Virginia), advocated the diffusion of slaves into the territories. If slavery were spread out among the territories, there would be a far better chance for eventual emancipation. Confining blacks to an ever tighter black belt, this reasoning went, would only lead to slave insurrection and the resultant clamping down by white slave owners. But Tallmadge's amendments to the

Missouri statehood bill smacked against any frangible wishful thinking about the diffusion of slavery.

However, southerners in general during the summer of 1819 were "blissfully unaware" that there was a sectional fight going on in Congress. Far more important than the extension of slavery was the impact of the Panic of 1819, America's first economic crisis and depression. It was not until there were anti-slavery meetings and pamphleteers in northern cities that most southerners became aware of this looming fight.[23]

The Fifteenth Congress adjourned on March 3, 1819, without settling the issue, and the next Congress did not meet until December 6 of that year. It was customary in the nineteenth century for Congress to begin its first session in December then go through to the early part of the summer of the following year; the second session was often shorter, convening in December and adjourning in March of the next year.

Tallmadge declined to run for re-election to the Sixteenth Congress (1819–1820). Into his place stepped Senator Jesse B. Thomas (Democratic Republican–Illinois) with a compromise plan. Thomas, the owner of five black apprentices (slaves), had voted against the Tallmadge amendments in the previous session. Nevertheless, his idea was to link the admission to statehood of slave Missouri with non-slave Maine. The Thomas bill would grant statehood to both Missouri and Maine and outlaw slavery in the Louisiana Purchase territory (except for Missouri) above 36°30' north latitude. This meant that future states carved out of the Arkansas Territory could become slave states; the rest of the old Louisiana Territory above 36°30' (the border between Missouri and Arkansas), which later would include Kansas and eight other states, would be free of slaves. Despite some squabbling from southern colleagues, the Thomas bill passed 22–16 in the Senate, but it had a far more difficult time in the House. Northerners did not want to abandon the Tallmadge amendments of the previous session, and southerners did not want to sell out on slavery so quickly. In the end, Henry Clay, using all of his power as Speaker, worked a compromise through the House.

Finally a conference committee came up with a solution to break the stalemate: there would be separate votes on 36°30' and on admitting Missouri as a slave state. Both passed; the 36°30' vote passed readily, thanks to a solid North and an evenly split South; and the slave-state Missouri squeaked by with all southerners and fourteen northerners joining together for a 90–87 victory. Thanks to the extra seventeen three-fifths clause votes in the House, the South was able to bring Missouri into the Union without the offensive Tallmadge amendments. A northern congressman had started this fight, but Slave Power had won the day. In these fateful deliberations and votes, the South rejected Tallmadge's gradual emancipation approach; southern legislators, in their virtual unanimity and persistent voice, committed themselves to slavery as a permanent condition.[24] President James Monroe signed the Missouri

Compromise measures in early March 1820, and, from that day, slavery was "forever prohibited" from what would be known as the Nebraska territory.

The Missouri constitution, ratified in 1820, banned freed slaves and mulattoes from entering the state. This was unacceptable to many in Congress, and a second Missouri Compromise was engineered in 1821 by Clay, which allowed Missouri to come in as a state, on the condition that it not pass legislation to enforce its own constitutional ban of freed slaves.

Historian Glover Moore argued that the Missouri Compromise "marked the end of the liberal phase" of antebellum southern history. The fifteen years from 1820 through 1835 were a transition period, followed by twenty-five years (1836–1861) of hardening of pro-slavery positions. Tallmadge's amendments to stop slavery gradually in Missouri, the increased northern criticisms of southern institutions and slavery, the threat of slave insurrection as seen in Denmark Vesey's 1822 plot in South Carolina, the expansion of cotton as an important cash crop, and acquisition of slave-potential territory—all of these added to the hardening attitudes, fears, and prejudices.[25] Nonetheless, the Missouri Compromise held.

The Tariff of Abominations. In 1816, Congress passed the nation's first protective tariff, taxing imported goods at 25 percent; a second tariff was enacted in 1824, raising the rate to 33 percent. The purpose of these tariffs was to protect manufacturing and industry in New England and other areas of the North. The South, which was overwhelmingly agricultural and produced raw materials for export, was hurt by such tariffs. Then, in 1828, Congress enacted a third tariff which boosted the tax on imported goods to 50 percent. Southerners quickly castigated it as the Tariff of Abominations. The tariff was engineered by Senator Martin Van Buren (Jacksonian–New York), in hopes of hurting President John Quincy Adams and promoting former Senator Andrew Jackson in the upcoming presidential rematch in 1828. Historian Robert V. Remini characterized the tariff legislation as a "ghastly, lopsided, unequal bill, every section of which showed marks of political preference and favoritism."[26] Nonetheless, Adams signed the tariff and in the presidential election of 1828 was soundly defeated by Jackson.

South Carolina particularly was hurt by the tariff: it had to buy imported manufactured goods at a much higher price and saw a further reduction in the sales of its raw materials. The new tariff immeasurably compounded the state's economic rough times: South Carolina had suffered through poor crop management and depleted soil, over-leveraged absentee owners, and devastating coastal hurricanes. Probably the most important economic factor was the competition from cotton cultivation in the lower South, from Georgia west to Texas. In the 1820s, some 56,000 whites left South Carolina and 30,000 slaves were sold or taken away; the exodus was even larger in the 1830s.[27]

The South Carolina legislature in 1828 turned to its most powerful advocate, Vice-President John C. Calhoun, to determine how the state could thwart this federal law. Calhoun secretly wrote for the state legislature the *South Carolina Exposition and Protest*, articulating his theory of nullification. The *Exposition* asserted that a sovereign state had the right to declare an act of Congress unconstitutional, to interpose state authority in its place, and declare the federal act null and void within the limits of the state.[28]

The doctrine of nullification became known nationally when it was introduced in the U.S. Senate by Robert Y. Hayne (Jacksonian–South Carolina) in January 1830, and produced the famous Hayne–Webster debates on the nature of the Union and the doctrine of nullification. In those debates, Daniel Webster (Anti-Jacksonian–Massachusetts) articulated what historians regard as one of the most important congressional speeches of the nineteenth century, and the most critical in defense of nationalism and union.[29] Calhoun, once an ardent nationalist, then the secret author of the *Exposition*, was now publicly espousing nullification: the idea that ultimate sovereignty rested with the separate states not the federal government, and that states could declare a federal law null and void if it harmed state interests. Calhoun could see what was coming: the North was growing stronger and more powerful with each passing year. Soon there could be concerted northern attacks on the South, through tariffs, economic pressure, control of money, and ultimately, the control over slavery.[30]

Congress passed another tariff bill in 1832, moderating some of the provisions of the 1828 legislation, but this was still too much for the South Carolina legislature. A popular convention was called, and in November 1832 the lawmakers declared null and void the two tariff bills, proclaiming that they had no force in South Carolina, and established legal penalties against any government official, state or federal, who dared uphold the federal laws. Further, the nullifiers threatened to secede from the Union and organize an independent country if forced by the federal government.

Fellow southerner Andrew Jackson would have none of it: nullification was unconstitutional and illegal, secession was revolution, and leaving the Union was tantamount to treason. On January 16, 1833, he asked Congress to "solemnly proclaim that the Constitution and the laws are supreme and the Union indissoluble." Congress then passed the Force Bill, authorizing the President to use his authority to support federal law against any obstruction by the states. Jackson backed up his assertions by sending a U.S. Navy man-of-war and seven smaller vessels to Charleston. No other southern state would openly side with South Carolina, which now had to make do with a face-saving compromise tariff bill enacted the same day as the Force Bill.[31] Calhoun in late December 1832 had resigned the vice presidency, took the Senate seat of Robert Hayne who had resigned, and for much of the next two decades became the leading states' rights, pro-slavery voice in Congress.

The Gag Rule. The first slavery controversy in the Jackson administration concerned the so-called Gag Rule Crisis, which began in late 1835. Historian William W. Freehling characterized it as "the Pearl Harbor of the slavery controversy."[32] Abolitionist sentiment continued to grow in the North. The American Colonization Society, founded in 1816, advocated the gradual resettlement of emancipated blacks to Africa. Much more incendiary was the work of William Lloyd Garrison, who in 1831 began publication of his abolitionist newspaper *Liberator* in Boston, and the American Anti-Slavery Society (AASS) formed the following year. Both called for immediate and universal emancipation of slaves. The AASS used the postal service as its weapon for disseminating thousands of pamphlets and publications throughout the country. Southerners objected to the abolitionist literature and blocked its dissemination. Jackson's postmaster general Amos Kendall, from the slave state of Kentucky, admitted that there was no legal authority to exclude abolitionist materials from the southern mails, but he also adopted the southern view that these radical tracts "were calculated to fill every family with black assassins and to repeat the horrors of Santo Domingo."[33] The memories of Denmark Vesey and the Nat Turner uprising of 1831, the largest slave revolt ever in American history, also were fresh in the minds of many. Fifty-five whites in Southampton County, Virginia, had been murdered by Turner and his followers; eventually fifty-five blacks were executed by official sources, and over 200 were murdered by white vigilantes.[34]

On December 7, 1835, Jackson recommended that Congress pass a law prohibiting the circulation in the South of "incendiary publications intended to instigate the slaves to insurrection." Anti-slavery efforts, Calhoun warned, were "unconstitutional and wicked."[35] Jackson, the man of the people, was making it clear that the right of petition, guaranteed in the Constitution, would not apply when the subject of protecting slavery was concerned. But Calhoun objected on principle: it should not be a federal law, but states, particularly northern states, should stop these subversive activities and the fanatical presses. There were also personal political considerations involved. Jackson had short-circuited Calhoun's presidential ambitions and his firm stance against nullification angered Calhoun. Jackson's own choice to succeed him as president was Vice-President Martin Van Buren, and Calhoun hoped to discredit Van Buren as an ally of the abolitionists.[36] Six months later, Congress enacted a law reorganizing the Post Office Department, protecting abolitionist literature and making it a misdemeanor for postmasters to delay or not deliver these items; however, the law was simply ignored throughout the South.[37]

Abolitionists had another weapon. Since 1831, they had been petitioning Congress. One of their immediate targets was ending slavery or the slave trade in the District of Columbia. Pro-abolitionists kept pushing petitions and amendments, keeping the issue alive, and frustrating many southerners. At the beginning of the Twenty-Fourth Congress, in December 1835, James Henry Hammond (Nullifier–South Carolina) had had enough. Two petitions had already been introduced in the new Congress, and now a third. Hammond, a first-term congressman who married his way into South Carolina aristocracy and fancied himself as his generation's John C. Calhoun, argued that anti-slavery petitions were insults to the honor of the South and that henceforth all such inflammatory materials must be stopped before they ever reached congressional hands.[38]

But the petitions kept coming. In the first three months of the Thirty-Fourth Congress (December 1835 to February 1836), there were more than 300 petitions, with 40,000 signatures or names, calling for the abolition of slavery in the District of Columbia. The movement was growing dramatically: in May 1834, there were sixty anti-slavery societies in the United States; by Christmastime 1835, there were 350 such organizations.

The so-called gag rule battle disturbed many in Congress. Southern moderates thought Hammond was too much the fanatic. Vice-President Van Buren, hoping to win southern support for his presidential bid in 1836, had a big problem on his hands: as a Democrat from New York, how could he walk the fine line between increasing anti-slavery sentiment in the North and moderate pro-slavery Democrats in the South? Van Buren had to fend off the demands of the anti-slavery movement, but also put some distance between himself and the firebrand Hammond.[39] He also needed to give other legislators, both northerners and southerners, some political breathing room.

In the House, Van Buren, living up to his sobriquet "The Little Magician," finessed the gag rule problem by getting another South Carolinian, the son of one of the pillars of South Carolina society, to do his work. In early February 1836, Henry Laurens Pinckney (Nullifier–South Carolina) proposed the creation of a select committee to receive all such slavery proposals. Called a traitor by Hammond and other fire-eaters, Pinckney's language nevertheless gave many congressmen just enough wiggle room so that northern and southern moderates could agree. By doing this, the debate on slavery slowed, and calm seemed to return to the House. In May, Pinckney's committee published its report and proposed a resolution, completely unanticipated by friend or foe, that all petitions and other actions related to the subject of slavery (not just in the District of Columbia), be tabled and no further action be taken. John Quincy Adams complained bitterly, but the House adopted Pinckney's resolution, 117–68. This proposal only emboldened abolitionists, and they resolved to inundate Congress with petitions. In the next eighteen months, over 300,000 petitions flooded Congress. Pinckney's gag rule not only galvanized abolitionists,[40] it also led to a censure motion against Adams.

Adams, defeated and humiliated by Jackson in the 1828 presidential contest, spent two miserable years in retirement; then the old puritan was asked by his neighbors to return to the fray of politics. The former senator, ambassador, secretary of state, and former president became a lowly freshman member of the House of Representatives. From 1831 through 1848, Adams had found his new stage: he was Old Man Eloquent, fighting for Yankee principles and agitating against slavery and the gag rule.

For months, Adams exasperated southerners with his presentation of petitions and his insults of slavocracy. "Expel him! Expel him!" came the cries from southerners in the House. One cried out to the Speaker of the House, "We demand that you shut the mouth of that old harlequin."[41] In his most famous defiance, in February 1837, Adams presented what he called a petition from twenty-two persons, declaring themselves to be slaves. Speaker of the House, James K. Polk (Democrat–Tennessee), asked to see the slave petition, but, before he could make a ruling, Waddy Thompson, Jr. (Whig–South Carolina) called for Adams's imprisonment. Then Dixon H. Lewis (Democrat–Alabama) called for Adams's censure on the grounds that he attempted to introduce a petition from slaves for the abolition of slavery in the District of Columbia. No, remarked Adams, the petition came from slaves who asked that slavery *not* be abolished. There were giggles and titters in the House galleries, but Waddy Thompson was not amused. Adams had silenced his flummoxed indicter and had turned the debate into an issue of civil liberties and denial of white liberties of petition. Should a member of Congress be indicted for presenting a petition, Adams implored. "If that, sir, is the law of South Carolina," charged Adams as he turned the rhetorical knife blade, "I thank God I am not a citizen of South Carolina."[42] Waddy Thompson's censure motion failed, 105–21.

In 1842, there was another gag rule censure motion, this time against Joshua R. Giddings (Whig–Ohio). Unlike the more adept Adams, Giddings was censured. He immediately resigned his seat, and won re-election by an overwhelming eighteen-to-one margin. This was the first clear referendum dedicated to the issue of slavery, and it sent a definite message.[43]

The gag rule was renewed each year by strong majorities and in 1840 it became one of the permanent standing rules of the House. Finally, in late 1844, John Quincy Adams moved its repeal. Public sentiment in the North and West had become much more sympathetic to abolition over the nine years since the first gag rule was imposed, and Adams's measure passed by a comfortable margin, 108–80.[44] The gag rule had became an irritant, a constant reminder in the eyes of many northerners of the unfair power held by southerners in Congress and by the growing doubts about democratic values and bondage. For southerners, the petitions and northern haranguing were equally irritating reminders that their honor was being impeached and their way of life was under assault.

Texas Annexation and the Wilmot Proviso. By 1846, Texas had been an independent republic for a decade, having defeated Mexican forces at the decisive battle of San Jacinto in 1836. Earlier, the United States had tried to purchase Texas from Mexico. In 1827 Adams offered $1 million and in 1829 Jackson upped the offer to $5 million; both were rejected by the Mexican government. By the late 1830s, however, Adams and other northerners saw a darker side of annexation: they were convinced that the revolution in Texas and proposals to make Texas a state were part of a larger southern conspiracy to extend slavery to the southwest.[45] So convinced was Adams that he filibustered for twenty-two days to try to prevent Texas annexation.

In the South, cotton was now king. It was flourishing in the southwest, especially in Mississippi, Alabama, Louisiana, and in the Republic of Texas, and the economic power and wealth in the South had shifted from tobacco (Virginia) and rice (South Carolina) to this dynamic labor-intensive agricultural staple. To meet the labor demands, some 835,000 slaves had been relocated to the southwest, especially to cotton plantations, from 1790 to the 1860s.[46]

In the 1840s, there was serious talk that the Republic of Texas would be split into four or possibly five new slave states once it became a part of the United States. President John Tyler, a slave-holding Virginian and proponent of annexation, launched a campaign for Texas annexation in the summer of 1843. He was encouraged by the success of the Webster–Ashburton Treaty, the agreement that resolved a long-festering boundary dispute between New Brunswick and Maine. His secretary of state, Daniel Webster, was able to claim more than half of the disputed territory for the United States. Tyler now hoped to add far more territory.

Tyler was also looking for a popular issue that would help propel him into a full term in office. "His Accidency," as his critics called him, had assumed the presidency on the death of William Henry Harrison, and soon bitterly disappointed his Whig colleagues. Tyler vetoed the second national bank bill, a key provision advocated by fellow Whig Henry Clay. The Whigs disowned him and threw their 1844 presidential support to Clay. However, Tyler was not going away quietly, and planned to run as an independent in the next election. All he needed was an issue that would distinguish him from Clay and the Democrat's Martin Van Buren. Tyler chose Texas annexation as his issue. Historian William J. Cooper, Jr., argued that Tyler's decision to advocate the annexation of Texas as a slave state had a profound political impact: it was the death knell for Van Buren, it destroyed the new Clay Whig Party in the South, and guaranteed the supremacy of the politics of slavery in the South.[47]

In April 1844, Tyler presented to the Senate a treaty to annex Texas as a slave state.[48] Tyler said that he was worried about reports that Britain had designs on Texas. Sam Houston, president of the Republic of Texas, did nothing to stop those rumors, cunningly suggesting to Washington that, if the United States did not care about Texas, then perhaps Britain would. John C. Calhoun had resigned from the Senate and became Tyler's secretary of state in 1844, replacing Webster. Calhoun had sent a letter to the British ambassador, Richard Pakenham, stating that American annexation of Texas was necessary in order to protect and preserve the institution of slavery, and that slavery was in fact beneficial to blacks.[49] Calhoun's frank and controversial letter was part of the supporting documents submitted to the Senate to accompany the proposed treaty ratification. But both Van Buren of the northern Democrats and Clay, leader of the Whigs, came out against annexation, fearing that it would provoke sectional hostilities. The Senate defeated the treaty proposal by over two to one.

Van Buren, who for many years had been labeled by the Whig Party as the "northern man with southern principles," now had lost the support of southern

Democrats because of the annexation issue, and, when the Democratic presidential nominating convention met in Baltimore, Van Buren received just a few southern votes.[50] In 1844, the Democrats rebuked Van Buren, the father of their party, former vice-president, and former president, and turned to James K. Polk as their nominee. Van Buren was done in by the party's two-thirds rule, which was contrived by Senator Robert S. Walker of Mississippi and supported by his southern colleagues. Van Buren was the biggest vote getter at the convention, but could not surmount the two-thirds needed for the nomination. Van Burenites, while dismayed, supported Polk unstintingly during the campaign, but they were soon to be disappointed by the new president. Polk failed to reach out to any Van Buren supporters for cabinet positions.[51]

Tyler was not done with Texas. In the lame duck period between Polk's election in late 1844 and early March 1845 when the new president was sworn in to office, Tyler pushed ahead once more for the annexation of Texas, this time by joint resolution rather than through the treaty process. Supporters were now talking about "manifest destiny" and brandishing the pro-annexation pamphlet written by Senator Walker. His *Letter of Mr. Walker, of Mississippi, Relative to the Annexation of Texas*, written in early 1844, was circulated in millions of copies. In it Walker extolled the virtues of an annexed Texas. He used the old diffusion theory: rather than perpetuating slavery, a slave-sanctioned Texas would help diffuse blacks away from the oldest part of the South and eventually from an emancipated North America. Failure to annex Texas would mean slaves would be bottled up in the old South, the British would try to emancipate Texas, the Yankees would emancipate the old South, and freed blacks would engulf their liberators in the North.[52] It was fear-mongering and race-baiting at its worse.

Van Burenites did not want to press the matter, but felt forced when southerners refused to compromise. Southern Democrats looked at the Texas annexation resolution as a test of northern friendship of the South and a continued endorsement of slavery. The northerners were also worried that the annexation of Texas would tip the balance of sectional power to the South, especially if the rumored four or five states, presumably all slave, were carved out of the territory. Tyler pushed ahead, and, in the last week of his administration, convinced incoming president Polk to accept a version crafted in the House of Representatives. After annexation formally was approved by the Republic's legislature and its voters, then by both houses of Congress, Texas became the twenty-eighth state on December 29, 1845.

With annexation, however, came war with Mexican and American troops clashing on the southern Texas border on April 25, 1846. By August of that year, more northern Democrats and others were coming around to Van Buren's thinking, and were willing to oppose the further extension of slavery. There was added resentment from western Democrats when Polk hesitated to push for northward expansion of the Oregon territory but seemed ever so eager to gain Texas. In his campaign for the presidency, Polk pledged to support an expanded Oregon, promising "Fifty-four Forty or Fight!" But once in power, his administration settled on the current American–Canadian western border, at the Forty-Ninth latitude. Disgruntled westerners now joined Van Buren New Yorkers who felt betrayed by the Texas annexation.[53]

In August 1846, Polk requested $2 million from Congress to conduct negotiations with Mexico. This was the opportunity for anti-slavery forces, Whigs, abolitionists, and disgruntled Van Buren Democrats to strike. First-term congressman David Wilmot (Democrat–Pennsylvania) offered a fateful amendment: the Polk appropriations bill could go forward, provided that slavery be barred from any land acquired from Mexico. Wilmot and about ten congressional allies belonging to the Van Buren wing of the party, were irritated at Polk but also apprehensive over the influence of Slave Power. As Wilmot wrote later to a colleague, "I am jealous of the *power* of the South ... [S]o dangerous do I believe the spirit and demands of *Slave Power*, so insufferable its arrogance, if I saw the way open to strike an effectual and decisive blow against its domination at this time, I would do so, even at the temporary loss of other principles."[54]

Quickly, the Wilmot Proviso was agreed to, 87 to 64, and then the appropriation as amended was adopted, 85 to 79. But the vote did not come along party lines; partisanship was thrown completely out the window. Sectionalism ruled the day: it was South versus North, not Democrats versus Whigs.[55]

The Wilmot Proviso never was adopted by the Senate because it reached the floor only one hour before the end of the session. In a bungled parliamentary move, Senator John Davis (Whig–Massachusetts), who supported the Proviso, kept talking and talking, hoping to finish debate, and then send the bill to the House at the very last minute. Unfortunately for Davis, there was an eight-minute difference between the House and the Senate clock. Once Davis got done talking, the House had adjourned for the session, and never had the chance to vote on the Senate version.[56]

The initial reaction to the Proviso showed a country "strangely indifferent" to the issues of slavery in the territories, with little attention given to it in the South.[57] When Congress reconvened in December 1846 it was apparent that many northern legislators were determined to press ahead with Wilmot's demand. Alexander H. Stephens (Whig–Georgia) ventured that the North was going to stick the Wilmot Proviso into every appropriation and the South would do everything to block it. "I tell you," said Stephens, "the prospect ahead is dark, cloudy, thick and gloomy."[58] Indeed, Stephens was prescient: the Wilmot Proviso was reintroduced in session after session by northern congressmen. Northern state legislatures also got into the policy debate. During the first three months of 1847, nine state legislatures had officially sanctioned non-slavery extension and had instructed their congressmen and senators to vote for their positions; eventually fourteen of the fifteen northern states would adopt versions of the Proviso.[59] With similar provisos being introduced in the House and a growing solidarity among northern legislators, southerners increasingly became worried.

Many, including Calhoun, had not seen the danger in the Proviso when it was first introduced, but soon Calhoun realized that a united North had to be met by an equally united South. In February 1847, he introduced the first in a series of resolutions that argued the basic southern principles that the territories belonged to the states and Congress had no power to deprive any state of its full and equal rights and that the federal government could not interfere with the rights of citizens along with their property (slaves) in these new territories.[60]

Wilmot was essentially adopting the language of the Northwest Ordinance and restating what free soilers believed as a fundamental principle: new territory should be free territory. It would become central to national politics during the next two decades, and particularly decisive in the Kansas–Nebraska fight. Like James Tallmadge in 1820, David Wilmot was in his first term in Congress. Wilmot left the Democratic Party in 1850, joining up with Martin Van Buren and other former Democratic leaders to form the new Free Soil Party, and later became a Republican senator in 1860.

The Compromise of 1850. In just six decades the population of the United States had jumped from 4 million in 1790 to 23 million by 1850 and the U.S. territory had grown from 890,000 to 2,997,000 square miles. The original thirteen states were now twenty-nine, with the majority of those states owing their existence to federal action through the Northwest Ordinance, the Louisiana Purchase, the purchase of Florida, and the annexation of Texas and the Mexican Cession.[61]

In May 1848, at their presidential nominating convention in Baltimore, the Democrats chose Senator Lewis Cass of Michigan, passing over senators James Buchanan of Pennsylvania and Levi Woodbury of New Hampshire. The Whig Party turned to "Old Rough and Ready" Zachary Taylor, the Mexican War general, now sixty-four years old. Taylor had never voted in an election before and was ill-prepared for public office. Yet, it was thought, his coattails would help many southern Whigs who were running for Congress that year.[62] His running mate, Millard Fillmore, was a four-term congressman and the current state comptroller of New York. In Buffalo, northern Whigs, Democrats, and others put aside their political differences and formed a new party, the Free Soilers, and nominated former president Martin Van Buren as their candidate. The Free Soilers pledged to fight against any extension of slavery into new territories, and adopted the motto: "Free Soil, Free Speech, Free Labor, and Free Men." Taylor and Fillmore prevailed in the presidential election, but the Free Soilers made a significant showing and picked up thirteen seats in the House of Representatives. The Ohio legislature sent to the Senate the first Free Soiler, Salmon P. Chase, an ardent abolitionist, who earned the sobriquet of the "attorney general of fugitive slaves."[63]

The biggest news of 1848 did not concern presidential politics but the discovery of gold at John Sutter's mill near Sacramento. Gold mania had reached San Francisco by June and the frenzy had made its way to the East by August. The Gold Rush was on and thousands headed west to claim their fortunes. To meet this onslaught, the military government in California pleaded with Washington to set up a territorial government as soon as possible.[64] In his final message to Congress in December 1848, Polk announced the gold discoveries and urged Congress to create territorial governments for California and New Mexico. Further, he proposed that the demarcation between free and slave state, the Missouri Compromise 36°30' line, be extended to the Pacific. But Congress was too divided and contentious to reach any agreement. Northerners in the House seized the moment, reintroduced the Wilmot Proviso, called for the abolition of the slave trade in the District of Columbia, and urged California be admitted as a free state. Southerners were insulted, fist fights broke out, and repeated threats of secession were shouted out. A bill by Stephen Douglas was offered to admit the entire area of ceded Mexican territory as a state, but it went nowhere.[65]

Congress tried again, in the very last days of its session, on March 3–4, 1849, pulling an all-nighter; it turned ugly with several drunk senators making threats, insulting one another, throwing punches, and again threatening secession. Finally, at seven o'clock the next morning, without solving any of the territorial questions, Congress mercifully adjourned.[66] Zachary Taylor was sworn in as president on March 4, and it was now his turn to deal with a bitterly divided Congress. But Taylor in his opening address to Congress talked only in bland generalities, saying nothing about the territories then, nor during the next three months. Yet Taylor, ever the old army general, had a plan: he would not wait for Congress to make the decision, rather he would get the western territories to call their own constitutional conventions and request statehood. He dispatched Congressman Thomas Butler King (Whig–Georgia) to California, on a mission to encourage Californians to apply for statehood themselves. The day before he arrived, General Bennet Riley, the military governor of California, announced that a constitutional convention would be called. The Californians drew up a free-state constitution, based on the constitutions of Iowa and New York. Taylor tried the same maneuver with New Mexico, but the citizens there were not able to craft a constitution until May 1850.[67]

Another territory, which was not under the control of government forces in Santa Fe, had its center in Salt Lake City, under the authority of the Mormon Church. In March 1849, on their own initiative, the Mormons drafted a constitution for a provisional State of Deseret, covering present-day western Colorado, western New Mexico, Utah, Nevada, Arizona down to the Gila River, and California east of the Sierra Nevada mountains.[68]

Congress, which had recessed in March 1849, now returned for the first session of the Thirty-First Congress on December 4, 1849. "Never before in six decades under the federal Constitution," wrote historian Holman Hamilton, "had the House been more chaotic."[69] In the Senate, Democrats were dominant, if only the northern and southern wings of the party could stay together: there were thirty-four Democrats, twenty-four Whigs, and two Free Soilers. In the House, it was a virtual deadlock, no matter the sectional politics:

111 Democrats, 105 Whigs, and thirteen Free Soilers. This was the first Congress in American history when the president's party controlled neither the House nor the Senate.[70]

Before it could consider the territorial issue, Congress was embroiled in a fight for the election of the Speaker of the House; three weeks and sixty-three ballots later, Congress finally chose Howell Cobb (Democrat–Georgia), an ardent backer of slavery in the new territories but also a pro-Unionist. While a Georgian was now their leader in the House, many southerners nonetheless were worried. If California and New Mexico were admitted as free states along with the inevitable free states of Oregon and Minnesota, the tenuous balance between free and slave states would be upset in the North's favor. There would be greater agitation to remove slavery from the District of Columbia, and northerners would continue to resist attempts to return runaway slaves. Insults and accusations were hurled: Vermonters called slavery a moral evil, a crime against humanity; southerners likened free soilers to criminals and assassins.[71] The talk among southerners grew: it was time to think seriously about dissolving the Union.

Zachary Taylor, son of Louisiana, owner of more than one hundred slaves, was nevertheless an ardent nationalist. He was soon scorned by fellow southerners as a southern man with northern principles: he pushed for California and New Mexico to go directly for statehood, knowing full well that they would do so as free states. He further appalled some of his southern brethren by his counsel and friendship from Senator William Seward (Whig–New York), not only a Yankee but an abolitionist to boot.

By January 21, 1850, various bills had been introduced in Congress to settle a border dispute between Texas and New Mexico and to compensate Texas; to bypass the territorial phase and admit California and New Mexico into the Union; to enact a forceful fugitive slave law; and to outlaw slave trade and slavery itself in the District of Columbia.[72] How could an increasingly ill-tempered Congress, seething with sectional and personal rivalries, sort out these contentious issues? What was necessary was for someone with the legislative skill, temperament, and stature to step forward.

That role fell to Henry Clay. The old Whig leader was back in his seat as senator from Kentucky. Clay's long national career began in the Ninth Congress in 1805 when he was chosen senator, despite not yet having reached the constitutional minimum age of thirty. He served in the Senate (1805–1810, 1831–1842, 1849–1852), in the House (where he was Speaker for four years) from 1811 to 1826, and ran for the presidency in 1824, 1836, and 1844. Now seventy-three, wracked with pain, weakened by a terrible winter cough, Clay made an unannounced visit to the home of another old lion, Senator Daniel Webster (Whig–Massachusetts), who gave his blessing to Clay's compromise plan.

On February 5, 1850, Clay had to be helped up the stairs of the Capitol. The Senate chamber was jammed, and, in the overheated, suffocating room, Clay spoke for three hours, pleading that lawmakers compromise for the good of the country; then he spoke again the next day. He had two weeks earlier introduced eight resolutions before the Senate, each carefully offering concessions to northern or southern interests. Clay summed up and defended his compromise legislation. California, Clay declared, had the right to join the Union as a free state; there was no violation of anyone's principles there. Northerners, stop insisting on the Wilmot Proviso; you have made your point, and besides, nature is on your side: the new territories are unsuitable geographically for slavery anyway. The Texas–New Mexico boundary compromise was good for both parties, gave Texas a vast territory, and took care of its public debt. Prohibiting the slave trade, but not slavery itself, in the District of Columbia was a reasonable compromise between northern and southern demands. (It was shocking to our sensibilities, Clay confessed, to see "a long train of slaves" trudging down the avenue connecting the Congress and the chief magistrate of "one of the most glorious Republics that ever existed.") It was the duty of the federal and state governments, even private citizens, to return runaway slaves, Clay argued; beefing up the fugitive slave law would go far to placate southern demands. Finally, Clay urged that Congress had no right or business interfering with the slave trade between slave states; the North should back off.[73]

Clay summed up by saying that no state or group of states had the right to secede from the Union. He begged his countrymen to pause "at the edge of the precipice, before the fearful and disastrous leap is taken into the yawning abyss below, which will inevitably lead to certain and irretrievable destruction."[74]

The reactions to Clay's speech were predictable: abolitionists condemned it, southern extremists picked it apart. Then, President Zachary Taylor threw a wrench into any talk of compromise. Privately, he told Georgia Whig representatives Alexander H. Stephens and Robert Toombs that he would hang all "traitors," which meant any one who tried to secede from the Union.[75] All talk of compromise seemed thrown out the window.

Following Clay in the weeks ahead there was a series of speeches in both chambers, denouncing and praising the Whig patriarch. But those orations were mere prologue, because those aging giants, John C. Calhoun and Daniel Webster, were soon to have their say. The Great Triumvirate—Clay, Calhoun, and Webster—in their last days of office, would deliver some of the most famous speeches in the history of Congress.[76]

Calhoun, the conscience and intellect of the slave-South, former vice-president under both John Quincy Adams and Jackson, secretary of war under Monroe, secretary of state under Tyler, and long-time senator from South Carolina, now sixty-eight years old, rose in opposition to Clay's plan. Gaunt, suffering from tuberculosis, his white mane of hair contrasting with the black flannels that enwrapped him, Calhoun was too fragile to speak and asked Senator James Mason (Democrat–Virginia) to read his address. It was one of his most eloquent and, from Clay's position, most dangerous of speeches. Calhoun took the high ground: the South was morally right and it derived its authority from the Constitution; the North was to blame for this crisis; and there would be no compromise. His speech finished with these ominous words: "Having faithfully done my duty to the best of my ability, both to the Union and my section, throughout this agitation, I shall have the consolation, let what will come, that I am free of all responsibilities."[77] *Let what will come*. Everyone knew: that meant secession and war.

In three weeks, Calhoun was dead. But before succumbing, he mustered enough strength to attend the Senate one more time, to hear Daniel Webster deliver his speech of March 7. Daniel Webster, also sixty-eight, began his career in Congress in 1813, had served in the House and the Senate, was secretary of state under Harrison and Tyler, and ran unsuccessfully for the presidency in 1836. He was a famed lawyer and orator, renowned for his brilliant defense of Dartmouth College before the Supreme Court in 1819 and his advocacy of the Union in the Webster–Hayne debates of 1830. In the debates with Hayne, Webster gave us those memorable words: "liberty and Union, now and forever, one and inseparable."[78]

Now twenty years later, for three and a half hours, Webster spoke, laying out in one of the opening sentences his purpose and cause: "I speak today for the preservation of the Union." He pleaded with the northerners to calm their passions, not to press the Wilmot Proviso, and not to taunt the South. Webster said that the issue of slavery and territories had long been settled, first by the Northwest Ordinance and then by the Missouri Compromise. The new territory, because of its geography, was not suited to slavery. He argued that slavery was a settled fact in the South, and that northerners should assist by returning fugitive slaves. Abolitionists blasted Webster for his remarks about fugitive slaves, but the reaction throughout the country, even in parts of the South, was of universal praise. Webster hit a responsive chord with those in the North who wanted compromise and wanted to preserve the Union; the speech also calmed some of the southern fires of secession. The Seventh of March speech became one of the most famous in American history; it was widely reprinted in newspapers and over 120,000 copies of the address were distributed throughout the North.[79]

Webster spoke of compromise, of holding the Union together. He had gravely disappointed abolitionists, but now one of their own took the floor. Newly elected senator and confidant of the president, William Seward, would concede nothing. His famous "Higher Law" speech of March 11 minced no words: he rejected the whole notion of compromise. In response to Calhoun's justification for slavery in the Constitution, Seward proclaimed, "there is a higher law than the Constitution." This was a moral question: God opposed slavery; it was unjust, immoral, and must give way; emancipation was not only inevitable, but near. Seward created a firestorm of protest: to many of his southern colleagues and the southern press, Seward was evil, diabolical, an unscrupulous demagogue. He was denounced by southerners of all stripes, by Clay, and even by his friend Zachary Taylor.[80]

Various proposals were brought up in Congress, with Senator Douglas offering one of the compromise versions. A special Senate committee of thirteen senators headed by Henry S. Foote (Democrat–Mississippi) tried to take control of Clay's legislation by combining it into a single omnibus bill. Douglas and Clay both opposed this approach and saw it as cutting the legs from underneath Clay's legislation. Zachary Taylor, too, was suspicious of the legislation. By spring and early summer, however, the attempts at compromise were ripping apart. The upper-South Whigs and lower-North Democrats tried to patch the compromise together, but they were outnumbered in both chambers by Northern Whigs and Southern Democrats who fought against compromise. Too many legislators hated some parts of the patchwork legislation; and too many despised the whole package. Clay denounced Taylor for concentrating just on California and leaving four other problems unresolved; Taylor became increasingly hostile to Clay and Webster.[81]

Then, on July 4, there was a sudden turn of events. In the suffocating heat and withering humidity that only Washingtonians can appreciate, Zachary Taylor dutifully listened to the patriotic exhortations staged at the yet unfinished Washington monument. To cool off, Taylor later quaffed large amounts of water, then cherries soaked in bourbon and cream. He contracted a severe intestinal ailment and died five days later.[82] Now came the more conservative Millard Fillmore, the second vice-president in nine years to succeed a deceased president. With Taylor's death, opposition to the compromise was swept away; Fillmore was a friend and political ally of Daniel Webster, and an ardent supporter of compromise legislation.

Once again, Daniel Webster used his oratorical skills in mid-July to convince his Senate colleagues of the need for settlement. He and Douglas worked together to move legislation through the Senate. First, they had to kill the omnibus bill, which in effect destroyed Clay's earlier work. Douglas broke up the Clay legislation into five separate bills, and with that came the key to ultimate legislative success. Even Clay, who had left Washington dejected and exhausted, agreed to this approach by the first of August.[83] There had been nine months of argument, threats, and give-and-take, and Douglas was leading the legislative drive now that Webster had resigned to become Fillmore's secretary of state.

Over the span of six weeks in August and September, the five separate parts of the Compromise of 1850 were enacted. First, California was admitted into the Union as a free state. Second, the territorial governments and boundaries were established for Utah and New Mexico, and their status as free or slave states would be determined by the territories themselves through their constitutions. Third, the slave trade would be abolished in the District of Columbia by 1851. Fourth, the 1793 Fugitive Slave Act was amended by removing cases from the states and appointing federal commissioners to conduct hearings and issue arrest warrants; it also prohibited slaves from having the right of trial by jury or testifying on their own behalf. Finally, the

Texas–New Mexico boundary was established, and Texas was paid $10 million in compensation for its loss of New Mexico lands.

A fatigued Stephen Douglas summed up the compromise: "The measures are right in themselves, and collectively constitute one grand scheme of conciliation and adjustment . . . . Neither section has triumphed over the other. The North has not surrendered to the South, nor has the South made any humiliating concessions to the North."[84] Millard Fillmore, in his first annual message to Congress in December 1850, praised the Compromise, assuring the country that it was the "final and irrevocable" settlement of the sectional tensions.[85]

The Compromise bought a measure of peace and bought some time. However, it did not fully accomplish what it set out to do: in California, a free state, the senators during the 1850s were pro-southern; slavery continued to exist in Utah and New Mexico; the slave trade was not fully shut down in the District of Columbia; and Texas creditors were not paid immediately.[86]

One of the sorest points of contention was the Fugitive Slave Act. For southerners, the principle of states' rights was a basic article of faith: the federal government could not and should not tell the states what to do. For southerners, states' rights meant the federal government should not interfere with slavery, pure and simple. But for some northern states, states' rights meant that they had the right to protect runaway slaves. That's not what southerners had in mind at all. They demanded the federal government use its power against recalcitrant northern states to help capture and return runaway slaves.[87] Eight years before the 1850 Fugitive Slave Act was created, the U.S. Supreme Court decided in *Prigg* v. *Pennsylvania* that enforcement of the fugitive slave clause in the U.S. Constitution was a federal, rather than a state, responsibility. Free soil states saw this as an opening to protect runaway slaves. Vermont in 1850 enacted a law which guaranteed a jury trial for runaway slaves. After 1854, nine northern states enacted so-called personal liberty laws, which forbade state and local law enforcement officers to enforce the fugitive slave provisions or to use local jails for such cases.

The mood in the North was shifting toward sympathy for runaway slaves and, in many circles, for complete abolition. There had been some widely publicized cases of slaves being rescued in the North or Canada, but the greatest impact on public opinion came from the publication of Harriet Beecher Stowe's sensational and heart-tugging *Uncle Tom's Cabin or Life Among the Lowly* in March 1852. The book, a best-seller in the North and throughout the world, profoundly shaped public opinion in the North about slavery and hardened opinions in the South.[88]

Despite all this, during the first years of the 1850s, the nation was experiencing relative prosperity, and some of the talk of secession had cooled. Reflecting the prevailing mood, the *Arkansas State Gazette and Democrat* wrote that the Compromise of 1850 had brought about a welcome relief from the agitation of the issue of slavery and territorial expansion.[89] The Nashville Convention, urgently called for in 1849 to stir up secessionist action, had met in June 1850, but only nine southern states sent delegates, and they could not agree on a course of action. Politicians who wanted to keep the Union together were elected in Georgia, Mississippi, and South Carolina. Both Whigs and Democrats wanted to cool the rhetoric on slavery, and both of the party platforms in 1852 treated it as a settled issue.[90] But right below the surface, slavery–anti-slavery tensions were sharpening, and into the mixture were increasingly vocal anti-Catholic and anti-immigrant nativist sentiments.

The Compromise of 1850 had bruised both parties and their presidential aspirants. The Whig Party, however, probably was hurt the most. President Fillmore was running for a full term; war hero Major General Winfield Scott, "Old Fuss and Feathers," was the candidate of the northern Whigs who were against the Compromise; and, for his last shot at the presidency, there was Daniel Webster. Whigs turned away from Fillmore, bitterly disappointed Webster, and turned to the sixty-six-year-old Scott. Democrats, fairly united, but torn between old Lewis Cass, the available James Buchanan, and the overly eager Stephen Douglas, took forty-nine ballots to nominate a reluctant Franklin Pierce, a forty-seven-year-old former senator from Vermont. Pierce, and his running mate William R. King, senator from Alabama, defeated Scott and third party candidate John P. Hale of New Hampshire, running as a Free Democrat.[91]

In choosing Franklin Pierce, voters were looking for someone to calm the waters. They were weary of sectional disputes and fights over slavery; they wanted peace and harmony.[92] In his inaugural address, on March 4, 1853, Pierce pledged his full support of the Compromise, a vigorous enforcement of the fugitive slave law, and support of territorial expansion.

The Pierce administration had the support of two-thirds of the congressmen of the new Thirty-Third Congress, which would meet for the first time in early December 1853, nine months after Pierce had been inaugurated.[93] But that congressional support was soft: there were many new members without fixed party loyalties and without allegiance to the president. Furthermore, many Democrats were irritated at Pierce over his patronage activity. He tried to please every faction of the party in his appointments to cabinet positions and lesser jobs, but in the end no one was happy. The Democrats were divided into their own factions in virtually every state, especially in the critical state of New York.[94]

However, the issues of slavery and territorial expansion were never far from the surface. California, just admitted as a free state, was slow to force its few slave owners to relinquish their human chattel; southerners were indignant when a New York court freed slaves from the vessel of a Virginia man who came to the New York harbor before sailing to Texas; in Missouri, the state supreme court had just ruled that a black man, Dred Scott, brought back to Missouri by his owner had lost the freedom he thought he had in Illinois and the Wisconsin territory; and Harriet Beecher Stowe was becoming a best-selling author.[95]

Another issue facing policymakers in the early 1850s concerned communication between the Pacific settlements and the East. In 1844, a New York merchant named Asa Whitney proposed a transcontinental railroad from Milwaukee to the Columbia River in Oregon. The following year, the young Stephen Douglas, in his first year in Congress, proposed an alternative route, starting in Chicago instead of Milwaukee. To facilitate settlement along this proposed rail line, the bill Douglas introduced called for the area west of Iowa to be organized into a new territory, called Nebraska. The bill was not adopted, but it established Douglas as an advocate of a transcontinental rail scheme.[96] With the discovery of California gold in 1848, the pressure for a transcontinental route increased; so too did the pressure from those potential settlers who saw the value in the rich lands along the Kansas and Platte rivers. The two issues, railroads and new territory, would collide with a third issue, the question of extension of slavery, with disastrous results in 1854.

Making the Law

In March 1853, Douglas, who was now a senator, joined his Illinois colleague in the House, William A. Richardson, in introducing legislation to organize the Nebraska territory, covering most of the remaining part of the Louisiana Purchase above the 36°30′ line. Douglas and Richardson, both interested in railroad development and in territorial expansion, were the chairmen of the Committees on Territories in the Senate and House, respectively. The measure easily passed in the House, but was tabled in the Senate.

Other legislators had their eye on a southern route for a transcontinental railroad, starting in New Orleans running through Texas and ending up in Southern California. Just the year before, the United States had acquired from Mexico a strip of territory below the Gila River in present-day Arizona and New Mexico. Secretary of War Jefferson Davis urged Pierce to appoint his friend, railroad entrepreneur James Gadsden, as U.S. Minister to Mexico to negotiate the purchase of some 30,000 square miles for $10 million, thus giving the United States land for the most practical railroad route through the southwest.

But southerners wanted more. Southern senators, particularly the members of the "F Street Mess" (senators who ate together at a boarding house on F Street in Washington), told Douglas their price: if he wanted to organize the Nebraska territory Douglas would have to repeal the Missouri Compromise and permit slavery there. It was a powerful group of senators, all Democrats, all committee chairmen: James M. Mason and Robert M. T. Hunter of Virginia, Andrew P. Butler of South Carolina, and particularly David R. Atchison of Missouri.

Atchison could see what was in store for his Missouri slaveholders if Nebraska were free. Transcontinental trains would arrive in slave Missouri from free

Illinois carrying northern settlers; at the other end, the trains would leave Missouri to free Nebraska. "Every train whistle," commented historian Allan Nevins, "would be a salute to freedom."[97] Slave state Missouri would be hemmed in on three sides by free territory, and the railroads would just bring more farmers and settlers who had no business with slavery. Atchison had more on his mind: he was in a bitter election rematch with the venerable Thomas Hart Benton, the man he had unseated after thirty years of service in the Senate; Atchison was determined that the wily Old Roman was not going to outflank him and capture the support of Missouri slave holders.[98]

At the beginning of the new Thirty-Third Congress in December 1853, Senator Augustus Caesar Dodge (Democrat–Iowa) reintroduced the territories bill that had been passed the House in the previous session. There was no mention of slavery, and it was assumed that the Missouri Compromise would continue to be in force.[99] The bill went to Senator Douglas's committee and immediately was transformed into the chairman's bill.

The Key Individuals in the Kansas–Nebraska Act

Stephen A. Douglas (1813–1861), from Illinois, a Democratic two-term member of Congress (1843–1847) and three-term Senator (1847–1861). Three times he ran for the presidency: in 1852 and 1856, he was an unsuccessful candidate for the Democratic nomination, and in 1860 was the nominee of the Northern Democrats. His life intersected with that of Abraham Lincoln through the historic Lincoln–Douglas debates of 1858 and the presidential election of 1860. During the 1850s, Douglas was far better known and more powerful than Lincoln and served as chairman of the important Senate Committee on Territories. Early in his career, Douglas developed a reputation for brashness, brilliant oratory often laced with sarcasm and profanity, and aggressive political action. He was a stout defender of Manifest Destiny, a harsh critic of the abolitionists, but was a strong Union man who worked hard to keep the increasingly fractious Democratic Party together. At five feet four inches, dubbed the "Little Giant," Douglas was a tobacco-chewing, whiskey-drinking Midwest lawyer, who transformed himself, with assistance from his Southern wife, into a cigar-smoking, cognac-sipping socially and politically ambitious fixture in Washington.[100]

Douglas's chief rival was *Salmon P. Chase* (1808–1873) of Ohio, who was the first Free Soil Party candidate elected to the Senate (1849–1855); he then was elected governor of Ohio (1855–1859) and returned to the Senate as a Republican in 1860. Soon thereafter, he resigned to become Lincoln's secretary of the treasury (1861–1864), then chief justice of the United States (1864–1873). As chief justice, he presided over the impeachment trial of Andrew Johnson. Chase was an ardent abolitionist and defender of runaway slaves. As senator he was an outspoken critic of the Compromise of 1850 and particularly the Kansas–Nebraska Act. The "Appeal of the Independent Democrats," coauthored with fellow Ohio legislator Joshua Giddings (Whig), was a forerunner of the Republican Party platform. As treasury secretary, Chase devised the modern system of paper money (his portrait is on the reverse side of the $10,000 bill); and the Chase Manhattan Bank was named in his honor, though he had no connection with it.

Atchison was the president *pro tempore* of the Senate. He proposed that the legislation remove the Missouri Compromise restriction on slavery in Nebraska and let the settlers decide for themselves if they wanted slavery or wanted to prohibit it. The Missouri Compromise *forever* forbade slavery north of 36°30′, the southern boundary of the state of Missouri; now, if Atchison had his way, it would be up to the settlers to decide. It should be presented as a matter of popular sovereignty. In 1848, presidential candidate Lewis Cass had advocated popular sovereignty as a solution for the slave issue in the newly acquired Mexican Cession.[101] What could be more democratic and in agreement with American liberties and local government than to let the people decide?

Douglas agreed and then crafted his legislation for organization of the Nebraska territory. He used the same language that he had authored in the Utah–New Mexico Acts: "And when admitted as a State or States, the said Territory, or any portion of the same, shall be received into the Union, with or without slavery, as their constitution may prescribe at the time of their admission." It was a clever piece of legislative legerdemain. Douglas had essentially skirted the Missouri Compromise: it was not repealed, nor was it rescinded; it was simply ignored.[102]

> Thirty-Third Congress, 1st Session (December 5, 1853–August 7, 1854)
>
> House: 159 Democrats; 71 Whigs; 4 other
>
> Senate: 38 Democrats; 22 Whigs; 2 other
>
> President: Franklin Pierce

But Atchison was furious. Douglas failed to consult him on the precise wording and, by using the Utah–New Mexico language, which only applied to the statehood stage, he left too much to interpretation. It might be left to the courts to decide if the Missouri Compromise still was valid; furthermore, if the Missouri Compromise language prevailed during the territorial stage, then the territory might never have a chance for slavery.[103] Douglas was now under intense pressure from Atchison to clarify the language so that the South would find it acceptable. The territorial bill had been defeated in the last session because Douglas could not get enough southern senators to sign on; now, if he wanted any chance, he would have to placate them.

On January 7, 1854, the Nebraska bill was printed in the Washington *Sentinel*, the official printer for the Senate. By now, the territory covered in the first bill had been greatly expanded to cover all unorganized territory from the Louisiana Purchase, up to the Canadian border, not just the territory west of Iowa and Missouri. On the 10th, the bill was printed again, to clarify a "clerical error." A whole section had been left out of the original, Douglas said, and, by adding this twenty-first section, his bill now expressed what he had wanted to say all along. Added to the original bill was now further strong language that popular sovereignty would be the rule, that local courts would decide questions of slavery, and that the Fugitive Slave Act would apply to the new territories.[104]

Douglas knew that there would be opposition, but he was ill-prepared for the storm of protest that erupted. The first reaction came from senators who saw this as a political move, to test the resolve of Democrats, to back the party's platform, and to test the loyalty of those free soil Democrats who had received big patronage rewards from Pierce. Others saw a deeper, more insidious purpose: he had not said so, but Douglas was repealing the Missouri Compromise, his critics charged. Douglas had "out-southernized the South," charged Senator Chase of Ohio; many southerners did not want to go so far, but now they were forced to stand and fight.[105] Then Douglas supporters retorted that the Missouri Compromise had already been breached when California came in as a free state, and that vast area below 36°30′ was not open to slavery.

This was not the fight that Douglas wanted. He wanted to concentrate on opening up the territories and helping create a transcontinental railroad; he did not want all attention to center on the Missouri Compromise and all the explosive baggage of the slave extension fight. But Douglas did not control the Senate. The first to enter the fray was Senator Archibald Dixon (Whig–Kentucky), the senator who replaced Henry Clay after he resigned in 1852. On January 16, 1854, Dixon introduced an amendment stating affirmatively that the Missouri Compromise did not apply to the territory in this bill or in any other U.S. territory. Now it was out in the open: a clear-cut repeal of the Missouri Compromise. Douglas did not want to go that far, but many of his southern colleagues liked Dixon's explicit language and put pressure on Douglas. Then on a carriage ride where they could talk privately, Douglas listened to Dixon's logic about specific repeal, and impulsively said, "By God, Sir, you are right. I will incorporate it in my bill, though I know it will raise a hell of a storm."[106]

Douglas reworked the bill, added specific language that repealed the Missouri Compromise and split the territory in two, creating the Kansas territory which would be west of Missouri and the Nebraska territory which would be west of Iowa and Minnesota. It was assumed that, given the course of things, Nebraska would be a free territory and Kansas slave. The split of the territory into a slave and a non-slave state further infuriated anti-slavery northerners.[107]

It did not take long for that storm and fury to be released. Douglas, Atchison, and their colleagues knew they needed the president to weigh in on their side. Franklin Pierce had not thought much about Douglas's legislation and was none too happy about repealing the Missouri Compromise. But, just days before Douglas was to introduce his bill in late January, Pierce agreed publicly, and in writing, to support the direct repeal of the Missouri Compromise. His statement declared that the Missouri Compromise had been superseded by the Compromise of 1850, and thus was inoperative.[108] Historian Eugene H. Roseboom characterized Pierce's decision as "one of the costliest blunders in White House history."[109]

A small group of Free Soil legislators struck first. In January, Salmon Chase and Charles Sumner (Free Soil–Massachusetts) from the Senate and Joshua Giddings (Whig–Ohio) and several others from the House published an "Appeal of the Independent Democrats in Congress to the People of the United States," in *National Era*, an anti-slavery weekly published in Washington. Chase later boasted that the "Appeal" was "the *most valuable* of my works."[110] The "Appeal" let it fly: Douglas's bill was a "criminal betrayal of precious rights," it was part of an "atrocious plot" to deny new immigrants and free laborers access to this vast land and convert it into a "dreary region of despotism, inhabited by masters and slaves." The "blight of slavery," it warned, "will cover the land."[111] Then it got personal. The "Appeal" denounced Douglas, asserting that the senator from Illinois was fanning his own presidential ambitions while wrecking the tranquility of the nation, and flayed the "servile demagogues" who served the "slavery despotism." Historian David M. Potter characterized the "Appeal" as "the first cannonade in what is, perhaps to this day, America's fiercest congressional battle."[112]

Douglas was stunned and hurt by these accusations. He was not pro-slavery, he insisted privately to a friend; bondage was a curse on both blacks and whites. But he was unwilling to violate the Constitution to end slavery because that would mean an even bigger evil, the splitting up of the country. The "integrity of the Union was worth more to humanity than the whole black race."[113] When he formally replied to the "Appeal" on January 30, his remarks in the Senate drew a capacity crowd; so many congressmen came over from the House side that there were not enough left in the lower chamber to hold a quorum. Douglas lost his temper; he was coarse, crude, and bombastic. He called Chase and Sumner the "pure, unadulterated representatives of Abolitionism, Free Soilism, Niggerism in the Congress of the United States." Yet, as historian Allan Nevins summed up, "the speech was in fact an adroit combination of argument and arraignment, and a skillful appeal to various prejudices."[114]

Douglas's fundamental appeal was for self-determination: "Let all this quibbling about the Missouri Compromise, about the territory acquired from France, about the Act of 1820, be cast behind you; for the simple question is, will you allow the people to legislate for themselves upon the subject of slavery?"[115] Douglas argued that when settlers moved into Kansas or Nebraska, when labor became plentiful, "it is worse than folly to think of its being a slave-holding country."[116]

Like Seward in 1850, Douglas believed in his own higher-law doctrine. Douglas adhered to the Compromise of 1850, but also to "a higher and more solemn obligation," to "that great fundamental principle of Democracy and free institutions which lies at the basis of our creed, and gives every political community the right to govern itself in obedience to the Constitution of the country."[117]

Key Provisions of the Kansas–Nebraska Act

The Act had thirty-seven sections, many of which dealt with territorial governance. The land west of Missouri would be divided into two territories. The territory of Nebraska would extend from the Fortieth parallel (current dividing line between Nebraska and Kansas) up to the Forty-Ninth parallel (the American–Canadian border) and extend westward to the eastern boundary of the Territory of Utah. The second territory was that of Kansas, carved out of the land south of the Fortieth parallel.

The most contentious point was section 32: the Constitution and the laws of the United States would have the same force and effect in the Territory of Kansas, except for section 8 of the Missouri Compromise (the slavery "forever prohibited" section); that section was inconsistent with the principle of non-intervention, as recognized by the Compromise of 1850, and was "declared inoperative and void; it being the true intent and meaning of this act not to legislate slavery into any Territory or State, nor to exclude it therefrom, but to leave the people perfectly free to form and regulate their domestic institutions in their own way, subject only to the Constitution of the United States."[118]

While Sumner, Chase, and others had clearly staked out their opposition, and others were on Douglas's side, there were plenty of legislators caught in the middle. Despite the sometimes vitriolic oratory, the caucusing and drafting of amendments and clarifications, few minds were changed.[119] At first, many southerners were unwilling to enter into the fray. They did not see the fight as worth it: it would just open up old wounds and, besides, slavery was not really suited for the climate and geography of Kansas. But southerners were drawn to battle by the agitation, name calling, and the utter rage of northern lawmakers. Just like the Wilmot Proviso fight, this became a point of southern honor.[120] For Midwest farmers, the question was one of possible loss of economic opportunity. Since 1820, they had been promised that the fertile territory of the West would be open to them as free soil. Increasingly, they saw the Kansas–Nebraska Act as a conspiracy of Slave Power, and one of their own, the senator from Illinois, being the lead conspirator.[121]

Douglas did not take part in much of the debate; he made his opening speech and then a final summation; more important was his role as floor manager. Salmon P. Chase was his leading opponent on the floor. The debate went on for four months, riveting the attention of the nation. "We are on the eve of a great national transaction," said Seward, "a transaction that will close a cycle in the history of our country." Charles Sumner pleaded against repeal of the Missouri Compromise, arguing that the true danger to the Union was not abandonment of the "peculiar institution" of the South, but the abandonment of freedom. "Not that I love the Union less, but Freedom more, do I now, in pleading this great cause, insist that Freedom, at all hazards, shall be preserved."[122]

Key Events in the Kansas–Nebraska Act	
1820	Missouri Compromise.
1832	Tariff of Abominations and South Carolina secession crisis.
1846	Texas annexation and Wilmot Proviso.
1850	Compromise of 1850.
1854	Kansas–Nebraska Act.
1857	LeCompton Constitution accepted by Buchanan; rejected by Senate in 1858.
1860	Presidential election.

The Kansas–Nebraska bill, originally introduced by Douglas on January 4, 1854, passed the Senate on March 3. There had been a flurry of speeches and amendments, with a still angry Douglas, in a three-hour harangue, defending once again the principle of popular sovereignty and leveling a final salvo of invectives at his opponents. At five o'clock in the morning, after seventeen hours of debate, the final vote was taken: forty-one Senators voted for and seventeen against. The southern states were firmly for the law, but the northern states were bitterly divided. For the most part, Democrats were able to keep together, but discipline among Whigs had fallen apart along sectional lines. In late May, the legislation passed in the House, 115–104, thanks to considerable pressure by Douglas, Pierce, and his cabinet.[123] After working out differences in the bills, the Kansas–Nebraska Act was sent to Franklin Pierce for his signature on May 30.

Aftermath

Despite the bruises and scrapes, Stephen Douglas considered this legislation a triumph. "I know the Bill is right," he wrote a month before it was passed.[124] But what he did not anticipate, or fully appreciate, was the extraordinary centripetal forces that the legislation had unleashed. Historian William E. Gienapp surveyed the damage done by the Kansas–Nebraska Act: "It weakened the Democratic Party throughout the North, disrupted the sectional balance within the parties, gave additional momentum to the ongoing process of party disintegration, and fundamentally altered the nature of anti-Democratic opposition."[125] Alan Nevins wrote that Stephen Douglas had "torn open all the wounds of 1848–1850, and reawakened the pain, fear, and anger of the fearful struggle of those years; he had split the Democratic Party asunder; he had completed the destruction of the Whig Party."[126]

The Democrats, prodded by Douglas and other leaders, held together, but they soon faced electoral disaster. Initially, Whig leaders like Seward and Abraham Lincoln were optimistic. Not one northern Whig had voted for the Kansas–Nebraska Act, and the Democrats rightly were getting most of the blame. Northern Whig leaders thought that the Democrats might take a beating during the fall elections and the Whigs could pick up votes from disaffected Democrats. They were partly right: the Democrats lost sixty-six congressional seats in the North alone in 1854. But Northern Whigs were not the beneficiaries. In the Midwest, Whigs abandoned their party to form anti-Nebraska coalitions, forming the Peoples, Independent, or Republican parties. Even in New England, where there were no great threats to the Whig anti-Nebraska position, the Whigs were not able to pick up support. Many were now joining the new Republican Party.[127] In the South, enemies of the Whigs used guilt-by-association tactics, tarring the southern Whigs for the actions of their northern party brethren who had strongly opposed Kansas–Nebraska. Whigs turned on each other: southern Whigs were chastised by their northern party colleagues. Truman Smith (Whig–Connecticut), for example, resigned from the Senate in disgust on May 24, 1854, repudiating southern Whigs who had voted for the Kansas–Nebraska Act: "The Whig Party has been killed off effectually by that miserable Nebraska business . . . . We Whigs of the North are unalterably determined never to have any [even?] the slightest political correspondence or connexion" with them.[128] Abandoned both in the North and in the South, the Whig Party was soon moribund. As historian Michael F. Holt has written, the Whig Party in 1854 and 1855 essentially "bled to death."[129]

While the Democrats lost ground and Whigs imploded, another political movement was gaining extraordinary momentum, a nativist organization called the Know Nothings. The Order of the Star Spangled Banner, a secret fraternal society, was founded in New York City in 1850, growing rapidly especially in the northeast. Sometime between May 1853 and May 1854, the organization became known as the Know Nothings.[130] Meeting in wigwams, lodges, or councils, sworn to secrecy, greeting outsiders with the words "I know nothing," their numbers had swelled in the summer of 1854. Beginning in June 1854, there were about fifty thousand members; by the end of October, there were over a million. Conventional parties had failed, and now there was a surge of citizens fed up with the Democrats and the Whigs who were moving to the Know Nothing movement.[131] These citizens considered themselves patriots: they were native-born folk who were anti-slavery, against the Kansas–Nebraska Act, and opposed to liquor. They also had a "searing hatred of Catholics and immigrants and of politicians who pandered to them."[132] This was an age with a strong temperance movement and an era with a surge in immigration, mostly Catholics and mostly Irish. Know Nothings knew what they liked and knew whom they despised.

By local and state election time in 1855, the Know Nothings had made extraordinary gains in Pennsylvania, Massachusetts and other parts of New England, and California. But they also won elections in the South, controlling the Tennessee legislature and gaining at least 45 percent of the vote in five other southern states. They had effectively replaced the southern Whigs as the alternative to the Democrats; or, as historian James McPherson noted, the Know Nothing Party was essentially the Whig Party under a new name.[133]

However, the issue of slavery soon split the Know Nothings. By 1855, now calling themselves the American Party, the nativists had their first national meeting in Philadelphia. At that meeting the new American Party endorsed the Kansas–Nebraska Act, leading to a mass defection of nearly all of its northern delegates. They and their followers now found a new home in the Republican Party.

Indeed, the new Republican Party, fueled by its opposition to the Kansas–Nebraska Act and slavery extension, abetted by the disintegration of the northern Whigs, was dependent on nativist support. Some Republicans, like New Yorkers Thurlow Weed and Seward, repudiated nativist bigotry, but they were in the minority. Most Republicans found it necessary to form an alliance with the anti-slavery northern Know Nothings, embracing some of their nativist sentiments, especially anti-Catholicism.[134]

In the new Thirty-Fourth Congress, which convened December 3, 1855, Democrats still held control in the Senate, but an anti-Nebraska coalition had the majority in the House. Of that coalition of 117 anti-Nebraskans, only forty-six would later call themselves Republicans.[135] Seventeen anti-Nebraska candidates vied for the position of Speaker of the House; after five excruciating weeks and 133 ballots, Republican Nathaniel P. Banks of Massachusetts bested Democrat William Aiken of South Carolina. The election of the forty-year-old Banks, who first entered offices in 1853 as a Democrat, re-elected as an American, and now standing as a Republican, was the first national victory for the new party, still feeling its way.[136]

Bloody Kansas and LeCompton

Stephen Douglas argued that popular sovereignty, the driving principle of the Kansas–Nebraska Act, was a fulfillment of the Declaration of Independence and the U.S. Constitution. But in bloody Kansas itself, instead of any glowing expansion of liberty and freedom, there occurred the "greatest attack on political liberties" in the nineteenth century.[137] There was a rush of northern and southern settlers into Kansas. The New England Emigrant Aid Company, formed to promote free soil in Kansas, sent money to Midwest farmers who wanted to resettle in Kansas. But pro-slavery men were not far behind. Under the encouragement of Senator Atchison, Missouri "border ruffians," a description they proudly embraced, came pouring into Kansas to help vote in a pro-slavery candidate for territorial delegate to Congress. Later, Atchison personally led a gang of Missouri ruffians to stuff the ballots for the territorial legislature elections in March 1855. The pro-slavery forces elected thirty-six of their own, while free soilers garnered only three seats. "Come on, Southern men!," proclaimed the *Leavenworth Herald*. "Bring your slaves and fill up the Territory. Kansas is saved."[138]

But the territorial governor, Andrew Reeder, a Democrat from Pennsylvania, would not permit the rigged elections. In about one-third of the districts, Reeder ordered new elections, which were won by free soilers. But when the new territorial legislature met, it pushed the new representatives aside, and swore in the original pro-slavery men. Free soilers would not stand for this; they gathered in Topeka to create their own government and draft a free-state constitution. In January 1856, there were two competing territorial governments: the LeCompton pro-slavery official government, and the Topeka free-soil unofficial government.

By spring 1856, a gang of 800 Missouri ruffians attacked the town of Lawrence, the abolitionist stronghold. Its newspapers were destroyed, and the hotel and the home of the free-soil governor were burned.[139] News of blood and burning in Kansas alarmed Washington. During these contentious years of the 1850s, it was not uncommon for fist fights and shouting matches to erupt in the barrooms and hotels of Washington between pro- and anti-slavery forces; sharply partisan newspapers knifed away at opponents. It was not unusual for legislators to arm themselves with pistols. While the Speaker's fight was going on in early 1856, one estimate had it that there were 300 loaded pistols in the halls and galleries of Congress one day.[140]

On May 22, 1856, Congressman Preston Smith Brooks (Democrat–South Carolina) strode over to the Senate chamber, approached the desk of Senator Charles Sumner of Massachusetts who was catching up on some letter writing, viciously clubbed him more than thirty times with his gold-tipped cane.[141] Brooks's accomplice Laurence M. Keitt (Democrat–South Carolina) kept senators and other onlookers at bay. What brought on this assault, which took Sumner over three years to recuperate from, was Brooks's reaction to Sumner's famous "Crimes against Kansas" speech given three days earlier, in which he denounced slavery and slaveholders, particularly going after South Carolina and one of its senators, Andrew Pickens Butler, a relative of Brooks. Sumner, one of the country's most outspoken anti-slavery advocates, who had a penchant for needling southerners, had insulted Brooks's home soil and his larger family.

Sumner had argued that the crimes against Kansas originated with one idea, that Kansas had to be a slave state. He launched into the absent Senator Butler, whom he called the Don Quixote of slavery: he has "chosen a mistress to whom he has made his vows, and who, though ugly to others, is always lovely to him; though polluted in the sight of the world, is chaste in his sight . . . the harlot, Slavery." Sumner labeled Senator Douglas as "the squire of Slavery, its very Sancho Panza, ready to do all its humiliating offices."[142]

The honorable thing for Brooks to do would be to demand a duel, but duels are fought out by social equals; no, Sumner would have to be whipped, the way a southern gentleman would treat his social inferiors, a misbehaving dog, or his slaves.[143] News of the brutal caning shocked and horrified northerners, delighted and emboldened southerners. Brooks had violently thrashed, nearly killed, the chief symbol of abolitionism in the Congress. More than 5,000 filled the Tabernacle in New York City, listening to speaker after speaker denounce

Brooks.[144] Southern reaction was equally fierce: Sumner deserved, and got, a good whipping. The Richmond *Enquirer* editorialized: "Our approbation is entire and unreserved. We consider the act good in conception, better in execution, and best of all in consequence. These vulgar Abolitionists in the Senate are getting above themselves. They have been humored until they forgot their position. . . . They must be lashed into submission."[145]

In July 1856, the House of Representatives voted to expel Brooks, but fell short of the two-thirds necessary; his accomplice Keitt was censured. Both resigned from the House and immediately were re-elected to fill the ensuing vacancies. Brooks renounced his national Democratic allegiances and became a rabid, fire-eating spokesman for southern nationhood; however, he died early in 1857, at the age of thirty-seven. Sumner returned to the Senate in 1860, more determined in his abolitionist fervor; so did the threats against his life.[146]

In Kansas, an abolitionist who drew his strength from Old Testament zealotry was enraged. John Brown, hearing what had happened to Sumner and convinced that pro-slavery men had murdered five free soilers, took it upon himself to extract divine retribution. Brown and a band of abolitionists abducted five innocent pro-slavery settlers from their cabins in Pottawatomie and hacked them to death in front of their families. Whatever uneasy peace there was in Kansas was now shattered; Kansas was now the theater for guerilla war.[147]

In the thick of the civil war in Kansas came the 1856 presidential election. Once again, a sitting president was denied nomination by his party. The Democrats opened their convention on June 2, 1856, at Cincinnati; they rejected Franklin Pierce, turned back Stephen Douglas, and on the seventeenth ballot nominated James Buchanan, who had been sitting out the partisan fray as U.S. minister to Great Britain. Buchanan and running mate, former congressman John C. Breckinridge of Kentucky, won twenty states, all of the South, plus his home state of Pennsylvania, Indiana, Illinois, and California, for 174 electoral votes. The first Republican Party presidential candidate, John C. Fremont, the dashing forty-three-year-old California explorer and son-in-law of Senator Benton, won eleven states, including all six New England states, New York, Ohio, Michigan, Wisconsin, and Iowa, for 114 electoral votes. Former president Millard Fillmore, running as a Whig-American, won only Maryland. It was a fervent campaign, sparked by torchlight parades and supporters chanting "Free Soil, Free Speech, Free Men, Fremont!" With its solid showing in the North, the Republican Party now affirmed that it was the successor to the Whigs.

Two days after Buchanan had been sworn in as president in March 1857, the Supreme Court, through Chief Justice Roger B. Taney, announced its momentous decision in *Dred Scott* v. *Sandford*. The Supreme Court ruled that all blacks, whether free or enslaved, were not nor could they ever become citizens of the United States. The Court went further in declaring the Missouri Compromise unconstitutional and that Congress had no power to exclude slavery from the territories, nor could slave property be excluded. The reactions against the Court decision were fierce and predictable. "Atrocious," "wicked," "abominable," charged Horace Greeley's *New York Tribune*. William Seward was convinced that there was a collusion between the Court's majority of five southerners (all of whom once owned slaves) and Buchanan. Two days before the decision, Buchanan announced that slavery should be settled by the courts and that he, as president, would "cheerfully submit" to the final decision.[148]

Stephen Douglas was happy with the Court's opinion: "I am opposed to Negro equality. I repeat that this nation is a white people . . . and I am in favor of preserving not only the purity of the blood, but the purity of the government from any mixture or amalgamation with inferior races."[149] Abraham Lincoln, upon his nomination for the Senate in 1858, charged in his famous "House Divided" speech that there was a conspiracy to nationalize slavery, and that conspiracy had been hatched by Taney, Buchanan, and Douglas, his Senate opponent. Many Republicans saw this as the last in a series of blows in favor of Slave Power and vowed to break that power through the ballot box. Black abolitionist Frederick Douglass was remarkably optimistic: the "Court had gone too far and its decision would raise the National Conscience"; this would begin the great cataclysm that could destroy slavery.[150]

Before becoming president, James Buchanan had a long public record, with forty years as a congressman, senator, cabinet member, and foreign emissary. Buchanan, now sixty-five years old, "Old Public Functionary," as he was derisively called by his critics, was on paper one of the best prepared men to run for the presidency.[151] But he had to deal with strong southern voices in his Cabinet and the festering problems of Kansas, especially the attempt to ratify the LeCompton Constitution. Pro-slavery forces, through trickery and intimidation, had confounded a succession of territorial governors. Free soilers held a two-to-one majority in the territory, but pro-slavery forces constituted the lawful government. They drew up a severe slave code, in defiance of the governor, and fabricated a constitutional convention that was rigged in their favor. Governor John W. Geary, whose life was under constant threat, called it a "felon legislature" and resigned the day Buchanan became president.[152]

Popular will had been trampled, through threat, chicanery, and stuffed ballots, but also because free soil Kansans refused to vote. The constitutional convention finished its work in the seedy little town of LeCompton, including in its document the protection of slave property, no provision for amending the constitution for seven years, and no provision to alter the property rights of slave owners. Further, the LeCompton Constitution and the petition for statehood had not been subject to a popular referendum, as promised by Buchanan and his territorial governor, Robert J. Walker.

Governor Walker denounced the decision not to go directly to the voters, but Buchanan, who worried about criticism from southerners in his cabinet, went against Walker, reversed his own policy, and in November 1857, accepted the fraudulent LeCompton constitution. Buchanan, an experienced politician, perhaps was being fixated on legalisms, accepting the work of the LeCompton Convention because it was a legal body, or perhaps he was intimidated by the force of proslavery southerners in Congress and in his Cabinet. Whatever the reason, historian Kenneth A. Stampp called Buchanan's acceptance of the LeCompton constitution "one of the most tragic miscalculations any President has ever made."[153]

Stephen Douglas, proud defender of the concept of self-determination, denounced the LeCompton constitution even before Buchanan accepted it. Battered by the *Dred Scott* decision, confronted by a Senate re-election fight in 1858, and determined to defend popular sovereignty and majority rule, Douglas defied his Democratic president, called the LeCompton constitution a travesty, and vowed to defeat it in the Senate. On the Senate floor on December 9, 1857, before a packed chamber, Douglas delivered probably the most significant speech in his career. "If this constitution is to be forced down our throats, in violation of the fundamental principle of free government, under a mode of submission that is a mockery and insult, I will resist it to the last," he concluded.[154] Douglas made his point; nevertheless, the Senate accepted the LeCompton constitution, although it was later defeated in the House.

Douglas had defied the president, disappointed southern Democrats, and surprised several prominent Republicans who now were ready to view him a little less harshly. One Republican who still saw him as a bitter opponent was Abraham Lincoln. The Kansas–Nebraska Act marked a turning point in the public life of Abraham Lincoln. At the time, Lincoln was a leader of the politically lifeless Whig Party in Illinois; however, he was infuriated that the Missouri Compromise had been abrogated. He had served in the Thirtieth Congress (1847–1849), but declined to run for re-election. Lincoln was still a Whig in February 1855, when the Illinois legislature by-passed him and, then with Lincoln's support, chose Congressman Lyman Trumbull as senator.[155] Then in May 1856, Lincoln accepted an invitation to attend the Bloomington, Illinois, Anti-Nebraska convention, and to lead the new Republican Party in Illinois.

There was a vigorous grassroots effort on the part of Illinois Republicans to draft Lincoln for the Senate, and on June 16, 1858, at the party convention in Springfield, Lincoln announced that he would run against Douglas for the Senate. In his most famous speech to date, Lincoln intoned that "a house divided against itself cannot stand. I believe this government cannot endure permanently half slave and half free. I do not expect the Union to be dissolved—I do not expect the house to fall—but I do expect it will cease to be divided."[156] Lincoln then accused Douglas, the Supreme Court through *Dred Scott*, and Buchanan of being part of a conspiracy to spread slavery to the North. There was no such conspiracy, but Lincoln's remark became fodder for the celebrated debates between Lincoln and Douglas later that fall.

Lincoln bested Douglas in the popular referendum, but the Illinois legislature, dominated by Democrats, re-elected the Little Giant to the U.S.

Senate. In 1860, Stephen Douglas made his third try for the Democratic nomination for president. James Buchanan and southern Democrats were still seething over Douglas's LeCompton actions; fear of slave rebellion was gripping the South in the wake of John Brown's October 1859 raid on Harpers Ferry. No Yankee was safe anywhere in the South; some were lynched, others were tarred, feathered, and ridden out of town.[157] Of all the places to hold their nominating convention in April 1860, the Democrats chose Charleston, South Carolina. The Democratic Party could not hold together; the fights over a slave-code plank were fierce and irreconcilable. Exhausted, dispirited, and divided, they adjourned, then later met in Baltimore. But to no avail; the rupture was irreparable: northern Democrats nominated Douglas while the breakaway southern Democrats nominated Vice-President John C. Breckinridge.

The Republicans met in Chicago, hometown of Democrat Stephen Douglas. National Republican leaders William Seward, Salmon P. Chase, Simon Cameron of Pennsylvania, and Edward Bates of Missouri had support, but they were all found wanting, for one political reason or another. Least known among the contenders was the home state favorite, Abraham Lincoln; but so obscure was he that many in the national press covering the convention did not even have his name included in their list of the twenty or so potential candidates.[158] On the third ballot, Lincoln prevailed over front-runner Seward.

It was a four-way presidential contest, but in most respects it was two separate contests: Lincoln against Douglas in the North, and John Bell of the Constitutional Unionist Party against Breckinridge of the southern Democrats in the South.[159] Sectionalism triumphed; Lincoln was elected, and the Union was about to be ripped asunder.

The other major laws featured in these chapters each claim a positive good for American society, worthy policy that made America the country it is. The Kansas–Nebraska Act was the exception; it was the final legislative straw leading to the breakup of the Union. It was based on a plausible sounding, but deeply flawed, doctrine of popular sovereignty: let the people in the new territories decide if they want to live free or live with slavery. It is an example of a legislative gamble by an ambitious politician, who, trying to placate his own constituents and his southern colleagues profoundly misread public opinion. Stephen Douglas's biographers and other historians still ponder why a man so politically astute could so badly falter. What was gathering in the North was widespread popular disapproval of the extension of slavery. The Kansas–Nebraska Act stoked the fires of sectional conflict, profoundly altered partisan alliances, and led us into the dark days of secession and conflagration.

3

THE PROMISE OF LAND

The Homestead Act of 1862 and the
Morrill Land-Grant College Act of 1862

*The Homestead Act of 1862 may justly be considered
the most important legislative act since the formation
of the Government.*

George W. Julian (1885)

The Emancipation Proclamation of higher education.

James Morrill, President, University
of Minnesota (1945–1960), on the Morrill Act

In the late spring and early summer of 1862, within a space of six weeks, President Abraham Lincoln affixed his signature to two of the most consequential pieces of legislation of the nineteenth century. Both concerned the disposition of America's most bountiful resource, its vast holding of public lands. The Homestead Act gave millions of acres of federal land to individual settlers, and the Morrill Land-Grant College Act offered millions more to the states for the establishment of agricultural and mechanical colleges and universities. Federal land sales and grants were nothing new. Many millions of acres of federal lands had been given away or sold at bargain prices in earlier years; land was given to military veterans and to states so that they could create educational institutions; land was given to help build roads, canals, and railroads, and other purposes. In the 1850s, there was great popular pressure for Congress to do even more. Yet like so many national issues, the disposing of public lands was wrapped in sectional controversy, with the South generally opposing the sale of such lands and the North and West in favor. Beleaguered President James Buchanan, trying to placate the South, vetoed earlier versions of both the homestead and land-grant college bills. His 1860 veto of a homestead bill became a campaign issue in that momentous presidential election year, an issue seized by the Republicans and Abraham Lincoln.

Both the Homestead and Land-Grant College Acts became law during the remarkable Thirty-Seventh Congress (1861–1863). The country had been fragmented by civil war, and, with recent Confederate victories, many were beginning to realize this fight would be a long, brutal, and costly. The southern congressional delegation had departed *en masse* with secession in 1861; only ardent Unionist Senator Andrew Johnson of Tennessee refused to leave Washington. President Lincoln called the Thirty-Seventh Congress into emergency session, meeting for the first time on July 4, 1861. There was much to be done. The war had to be waged, emergency measures enacted, resources appropriated for the Army and Navy. All this was crammed into the short, month-long emergency session. Then Congress resumed its normal cycle, meeting for its regular session on December 2, 1861. Wartime concerns still dominated congressional debate, but during this session legislators enacted several far-sighted pieces of legislation, which, together, laid the foundation for the modern American nation. Like the New Deal's Seventy-Fourth Congress (1935–1936) and the Great Society's Eighty-Ninth Congress (1965–1966), the Civil War's Thirty-Seventh Congress generated two of the landmark pieces of legislation selected in this book.

Both the Homestead and Morrill Land-Grant College Acts passed with relative ease, but both were beset by underlying tensions. Westerners chafed because public lands located in their states were going to the benefit of more populated eastern states for the development of colleges and universities. Easterners feared the homestead provisions would lead to a mass migration, leaving their states with fewer workers and depressed land values. Nativists worried that the new lands would be overrun by immigrants, with foreign ways and ideas. Settlers complained that the available homesteading land was of poor quality and often inaccessible to markets and transportation. Some lawmakers wanted to give land to Union veterans, and no land, they insisted, should go to rebellious southerners until the war had been won and the South subdued. Many lawmakers worried about railroad barons, land speculators, and swindlers who cheated honest but gullible settlers and made fortunes for themselves and eastern monied interests.

Despite these tensions and the sometimes sloppy administration of the law, well over 1.7 million homestead farms outside the South had been created on public lands by 1880, and over 2.4 million by 1900.[1] By the mid-1930s, the homestead program had nearly run its course, and the last homesteader settled on land in Alaska in 1985.

The land-grant college legislation favored the populated, eastern states like New York and Pennsylvania. Many of the eastern states no longer had any public lands, but the state legislatures could receive federal allotment of land or scrip (land procurement certificates) from the vast regions of public lands available in the West. Land was apportioned according to the number of congressmen and senators in each state, allotting 30,000 acres for every member of Congress and for each of the two senators in every state.

While some states had already set up state-supported universities before the enactment of the Morrill Land-Grant College Act, others used the proceeds from the sale of land-grant acres to add courses and professors for courses in agricultural and mechanical arts. Some state legislatures were short-sighted and made poor return on their windfall of western lands, others invested more wisely. The land-grant college movement slowly, haltingly picked up steam in the two or three decades following its enactment. A second Morrill Act was passed in 1890 to include black institutions in the South, and other laws gave the land-grant movement greater support and backing.

The land-grant schools became important additions to American higher education, transforming its nature and purpose, opening it to a far broader constituency of students and those who would benefit from their research, and adding to the fundamental democratization of American society. America's greatest natural gifts, its billion-plus acres of public lands, were put to a variety of uses, but none more important than the far-sighted actions of Congress in 1862 in extending free land to eager settlers and land to foster and endow higher education.

Background

By the 1780s the states had relinquished their claims to western lands, giving the federal government 200 million acres of public lands beyond the Appalachians. The Louisiana Purchase of 1803 added 500 million acres; the Florida Purchase of 1819 brought in another 43 million acres. While the land did not become federal public lands, the annexation of Texas in 1845 involved another 200 million acres. The Mexican Cession of 1848 added 334 million acres of public lands, while the Gadsden Purchase in 1853 brought in 19 million acres, and the Oregon Territory added another 181 million acres.[2] Altogether, by 1850 the United States had claimed 1.2 billion acres of public domain land, about one-half of the present-day size of the country.

For much of its first century, the federal government was preoccupied with the business of managing, selling, and giving away much of this vast public domain. Historian Paul W. Gates commented that "it is difficult for people of later generations to realize the extent to which the government was engaged in the land business in the nineteenth century."[3]

The first federal approach to public lands was to treat the sales as a source of income that would help fill the federal treasury. The national government relied chiefly on tariffs and duties, and it could now supplement that income with the sale of land in the public domain. But there were inequities and controversies. Speculators could buy large chunks of fertile land, squatters would be ejected, and would-be settlers of modest means often found it difficult to purchase suitable acreage. There were many complaints from ordinary citizens who wanted to settle western lands. One example came from Representative Albert Gallatin of Pennsylvania, who in 1797 presented a petition to Congress from one hundred persons from the Ohio country who complained that they were unable to purchase land because of the "conspiracies" on the part of the land speculators.[4]

The Land Act of 1796 established the rectangular system of land surveys: the essential unit was the township, six miles square, which was divided into thirty-six sections, each containing 640 acres. This made for uniformity and rationality in the laying out the land, but ignored its natural contours, rivers and marshes, and acres of poor and fertile soil. The land sold for $2 per acre with credit extended for over a year after the purchase. Yet sales were relatively slow and delinquencies were high. Credit was extended for a longer period of time, and some of the tracts were reduced in size in the new territories of Ohio, Mississippi, and Alabama.[5]

By the early 1800s agricultural interests began to assert their political power, and Congress, still looking for land sales for revenue, began liberalizing the terms of land purchase. Rather than having 640 acres as the minimum purchase size, Congress lowered it to 320, then in 1820 reduced the minimum purchase to 80 acres with a minimum price per acre at $1.25 cash.

The credit system adopted in 1800 caused headaches in Congress for the next twenty years. One of the biggest problems came from the land speculation in the Southwest, where dreams of cotton plantations and cheap slave labor pushed up prices of fertile land. Speculators often bought on federal credit, and the amount owed the government went from just over $3 million in 1815 to $16 million in 1818. America was living in an inflationary bubble during these three years, and that bubble burst with the collapse of cotton prices at the Liverpool cotton market in Britain. American land prices plummeted by 50 to 75 percent.[6] Then came the Panic of 1819, which exacerbated credit problems for rich speculator and poor settler alike. By the end of December 1820, when Congress halted the land credit program, over $21 million (half of which was from Alabama and Mississippi) was owed to the federal government.[7]

In 1830, in a major change in federal land policy, squatters were given a limited preemptive right to land; then in 1841, through the Preemption Act, squatters were given the full right to have first crack at the purchase of surveyed public land at $1.25 per acre.[8] However, with the great amount of land available and unsettled economic times, some public lands by 1854 were selling for just 12.5 cents an acre.[9]

In his fourth annual address to Congress in 1833, President Andrew Jackson stated that it was no longer necessary to rely on public land sales as a source for federal revenue, that the lands should be sold to settlers at reduced prices, and that whatever was not sold should be given over to the states. The latter point, however, was counter to the prevailing federal land policy. While the states were rapidly being added to the Union, they did not automatically receive ownership of former territorial lands once controlled by the federal government. Federal statutes admitting new states explicitly said that the federal government would retain title of public domain lands and that those lands would be insulated from state taxation.[10]

From 1789 to 1837 more than 4.5 million people had settled in the areas west of the Appalachians, spurred on by the availability of cheap public lands. It was one of the greatest mass migrations the world had known. Altogether, during this fifty-year period, Congress had passed 375 laws dealing with the lands in the public domain. Now this era of land sales was coming to an end.[11]

Senator Henry Clay of Kentucky was the principle advocate of the "American System," a program of protective tariffs, a new Bank of the United States, federal support for internal improvements such as canals, railroads, and highways, and the selling off of public lands. The American System was in full force during the presidency of John Quincy Adams (1825–1829), but, when Jackson came in, he swept aside the national bank and vetoed proposed federal funds for a sixty-mile extension of the National Road near Maysville, Kentucky.[12] His actions also helped establish an anti-Jackson political force that eventually became the Whig party.

Land policy made for interesting political alliances. Southerners were confronted by northern policies of high tariffs and growing anti-slavery sentiments. While western states traditionally supported the Northeast and these policies, westerners also wanted cheap land, and they turned to the South for assistance. Southern politicians, particularly John C. Calhoun and Andrew Jackson, were happy to oblige, especially if it would prise the West away from its traditional support of the northeastern states. The western state leader on land reform was Senator Thomas Hart Benton (Democrat–Missouri).[13] Benton's "log cabin" bill, first brought up in 1824, favored those who actually settled on the land and gave them the right of first refusal for its purchase. Ultimately, Benton's policies were enacted in the Preemption Act of 1841.

Two problems were not solved, however, by this approach. First, settlers had seized the best land possible, leaving much of the public domain lands unwanted; second, it did nothing to stop speculators from acquiring massive chunks of land, often paying individuals to squat on the best land, then selling it off to other speculators or individuals. Benton also favored a graduation scheme, which would adjust the price of the available land according to its value. He also believed that the federal government should simply give away to poor settlers land that could not be sold.[14]

The Homestead Legislation

The fundamental idea of homesteading was for the national government to give away or sell at rock-bottom prices federal public lands to individuals, who, after working the land for a defined period of time, would be given title to it. Proponents saw this as an enormous benefit to the countless thousands of would-be settlers who could not afford to purchase land on their own, but with hard work, ambition, and drive would help populate the West. Earlier versions of the homestead idea were floating around Congress by the mid-1830s, but could not muster enough support for passage. By the 1840s, the interest in homestead legislation picked up considerably. In 1842 Congress passed the Florida Occupation Act, which gave settlers 160 acres of free land on the condition that they occupy it for four years, build cabins, and fence in five of those acres. The next year, the Senate approved a generous homesteading bill for settlers in Oregon.[15]

During the first session of the Twenty-Ninth Congress (1845–1846), separate national homestead bills were introduced in the House of Representatives by Felix Grundy McConnell (Democrat–Alabama), Andrew Johnson (Democrat–Tennessee), and two Democrats from Illinois, Robert Smith and Orlando B. Ficklin.[16] Then in 1848, two additional homestead bills were submitted, by Johnson and Horace Greeley (Whig–New York), who later became better known as editor of the *New York Tribune*. At the beginning of the congressional session in 1849, Stephen Douglas also introduced a homestead bill. However, none of these measures passed.

In December 1851, at the beginning of the new Thirty-Second Congress, Andrew Johnson reintroduced his homestead measure. There was growing homestead support from the new western states. In the South, there were plenty of poor farmers who would have jumped at the opportunity for free land. But the biggest opposition came from fellow southerners, the defenders of Slavocracy: They feared Congress would have to raise tariffs to offset the loss of land-purchase funds to the treasury and the increasingly strident abolitionist sentiment. At this time, northern views on homesteading legislation were all over the map, both in support and in opposition.[17]

In this same month, December 1851, Galusha Grow (Democrat–Pennsylvania) was sworn in for his first term in Congress. At twenty-eight, Grow was the youngest member of the House, an ardent free soiler who strongly favored homestead legislation. His own party was lukewarm to the idea of homesteading, but Grow wasted no time and in his first address before Congress in March 1852 lashed out against land speculators, land companies, and their agents. He introduced a homesteading amendment and argued that settlers who work the land should have the inherent right to occupy it, just as they had the right to breathe the air or drink the waters. However, young Grow and his legislation would have to wait their turn.

Instead, the House turned to the homestead legislation of Andrew Johnson and on May 12, 1852, approved it by 107 to 52. But about one-third of the House members did not vote at all, probably not wanting to go on record just before their parties' national conventions.[18] When the Senate received the bill, it dawdled for several months, and finally in February 1853, the last week of the lame duck session, voted 33–23 against taking up Johnson's legislation, thus killing it.

Galusha Grow tried again in December 1853, the beginning of the new Thirty-Third Congress; Andrew Johnson had left Congress, returning home to serve as governor of Tennessee. Prospects now seemed a little better for homestead legislation; several others brought forth bills too, including John L. Dawson (Democrat–Pennsylvania), Bernhart Henn (Democrat–Iowa), W. R. W. Cobb (Democrat–Alabama) in the House and Salmon P. Chase (Free Soil–Ohio) and William Gwin (Democrat–California) in the Senate.[19]

But soon Congress was embroiled with the Kansas–Nebraska fight and most of its attention was centered on that increasingly volatile situation. Nonetheless, another land-grant dispute was working its way through Congress. Since 1848, the redoubtable social reformer Dorothea Dix had pushed and cajoled Congress to support a land-grant endowment program to finance asylum facilities for the indigent insane. Earlier, President Millard Fillmore had endorsed her idea of providing endowment funds from the sale of 12.5 million acres of public lands, and both houses of Congress separately had voted in favor of her proposals in 1851, 1852, and 1853. In 1854 the Dix legislation came up again, this time calling for the national government to grant states 10 million acres of public land for the care of the insane. Many congressmen who were against the Dix bill suddenly disappeared and failed to vote, fearing that reformers would seek retribution against them. Consequently, with a sizable portion of the opposition cowering in absentia, Dix's land-grant bill passed in both houses of Congress. It was left to President Franklin Pierce to play the heavy and veto the legislation, declaring it unconstitutional: "I cannot find any authority in the Constitution for making the Federal Government the great almoner of public charity throughout the United States."[20] Right after the veto of the Dix legislation, Congress considered grants of four million acres of public lands in Michigan, Wisconsin, and Minnesota to subsidize a canal around Niagara Falls and to aid public schools in the District of Columbia. Both bills failed.[21]

In 1857 Andrew Johnson returned to Washington, now serving as senator from Tennessee. The Thirty-Fifth Congress had just convened for its first session in December 1857, and he immediately introduced his homestead bill. Johnson reminded his new Senate colleagues that his homestead legislation had been introduced in the House in 1846 and later passed in the House in 1852, and that he hoped that the Senate would act quickly on this legislation.[22] But this was a very difficult time: the *Dred Scott* decision, bloody Kansas and the LeCompton constitution had further soured relations in the Senate. Southerners were suspicious of homestead legislation, even if it came from a familiar ally from nearby Tennessee. Old Calhoun Democrats like Virginians James M. Mason and Robert M. T. Hunter, Thomas L. Clingman from North Carolina, and Clement C. Clay of Alabama led the fight against Johnson's homestead plan.

Andrew Johnson stood to make his most important speech in the Senate, on May 20, 1858. In pleading for his homestead bill, he shared his alarm over the growth of cities and the twin evils of urban pauperism and vice. "Our true policy is to build up the middle class; to sustain the villages; to populate the rural districts, and let the power of this Government remain with the middle class," he implored. "I want no miserable city rabble on the one hand. I want no pampered, bloated, corrupted aristocracy on the other." Johnson defended those virtuous middle Americans who had their own homes to defend, wives and children to protect. These, "the great mass of the people, the great middle class," Johnson reminded his colleagues, "are honest."[23]

But Johnson could not shake the accusation by fellow southerners that homestead legislation was nothing more than a "Black Republican" plot. Southerner newspapers branded him a traitor, but he gained considerable support and interest from the North and West, doing nothing to dampen Johnson's interest in a possible run for the presidency in 1860. But the Senate had its say and voted to postpone further discussion of Johnson's legislation until the following session.[24]

Finally, in 1860, during the second session of the Thirty-Sixth Congress, both the House and the Senate passed homestead legislation. Galusha Grow shepherded his bill through the House, and on March 22, 1860, gained a 115 to 66 victory, but with clear regional distinctions: only one vote for the bill came from a slave state (Missouri) and just two votes against the bill came from free states (Delaware and Pennsylvania). Every Republican had voted for the homestead bill; here, indeed, was a campaign issue they could rally behind in the upcoming presidential contest. Andrew Johnson, fighting off some southern objections and acceding to others, saw his watered-down homestead bill accepted by the Senate on May 10, by a vote of 44 to 8. It took three conference committees to iron out the considerable differences between the more far-reaching House and weaker Senate versions, but at last, and for the first time, both chambers agreed to compromise homestead legislation on June 19, 1860.[25] But it all came to naught.

On June 22, lame duck President James Buchanan vetoed the homestead bill, stating that he was worried about the financial stability of the United States. He had inherited a $4 million surplus from Franklin Pierce, but by 1859 there was a $27 million deficit. The Pierce administration had been able to bring in some $273 million in federal revenue, thanks to the sale of public lands and customs fees. But the Buchanan administration saw revenues drop substantially, mostly because of the Panic of 1857 and the interruption of land sales in bloody Kansas. In the end, Buchanan was able to run the country on about $39 million less than Pierce, but did not want to give more public land away for free because he saw the land as a form of collateral for public loans.[26]

Buchanan also saw the homestead bill as a blatant attempt by the Republican Party to lure voters: Here it was, free land for small farmers and settlers; who could resist that kind of offer? Buchanan feared that the West would be inundated with new settlers and the still tender wounds of the slavery/anti-slavery battles would be reopened. He was determined not to repeat the mistakes of the Kansas–Nebraska fight. Further, his own Democratic Party was on record as against homestead legislation. Buchanan knew that he risked the political wrath of northerners, and that he would be accused of buckling to the wishes of the slave-holding South and halting westward progress, but those were risks he was willing to take.

In his written veto message to Congress, Buchanan explained his actions: The bill was unconstitutional, unjust, and discriminatory. It was unconstitutional because the small sum asked, 25 cents per acre, was tantamount to giving the land away, and Congress did not have the power to give away land to either settlers or to the states. The bill was unjust because, by encouraging settlers to go west, it would render useless the lands in the older settled states and the bounty lands held by veterans would lose value. The bill was discriminatory because unmarried citizens could not take advantage of it, while immigrants were eligible for the lands. Worst of all, said Buchanan, the honest man does not want charity, either from the government or from his neighbors, and this bill just demoralizes that spirit of rugged independence.[27]

Historian Paul W. Gates characterized the Buchanan homestead veto statement as "perhaps the most irrational, ill-conceived and amazingly inaccurate veto message that has ever emanated from an American President."[28] Andrew Johnson and Galusha Grow were furious; northern and western politicians condemned Buchanan and so did the northern press. Horace Greeley of the *New York Tribune*, however, was delighted. Homestead legislation was one of his top priorities, and now, at last, here was a clear-cut campaign issue.[29] Buchanan, exasperated, tired, and beaten back, had refused even this modest crumb to farmers and the working class of America. Despite the overwhelming majorities in both the House and Senate, the homestead bill did not survive the presidential veto. In the Senate, the veto override won 27–18 but fell three votes short of the two-thirds needed. All of the opposition came from the South.[30]

Republicans, meeting in Chicago to select their presidential nominee, were firm on their land policies and their politics. Section thirteen of the Republican Party platform demanded "the passage by Congress of the complete and satisfactory homestead measure"[31] With the Republican presidential victory in 1860, the secession of the southern states, and the hostilities at Fort Sumter, there would be no more solid southern bloc to obstruct northern domestic policies.

Land-Grant Colleges

The federal legislator most responsible for the land-grant college act was Representative Justin Smith Morrill of Vermont. Morrill, a Whig turned Republican, in his second term in Congress, introduced his first land-grant bill on December 14, 1857, at the beginning of the first session of the Thirty-Fifth Congress. Morrill's legislation was hardly the first time that land had been granted to the colonies or states for education. In 1619, the Crown had chartered Henrico College in Virginia by giving it a substantial land-grant. But with few English settlers in Virginia, failed crops, and not enough money from land sales to sustain the fledgling school, it soon folded and the charter was revoked by the Crown.[32] The first colleges established during colonial times were founded by religious institutions, particularly the Congregationalists in the North and the Anglicans in the South. Between 1636 and 1769, nine such schools were founded: Harvard, William and Mary, Yale, Princeton, Columbia, Pennsylvania, Brown, Rutgers, and Dartmouth.[33] The colleges all had some form of state-supported assistance. Harvard, Yale, and William and Mary supplemented their incomes from lotteries, license fees, ferry tolls, and certain taxes, while later Princeton, Columbia, Brown, and Dartmouth were assisted by land-grants.[34] From the 1770s through 1787, there was a growing interest in higher education. Three colleges were chartered in South Carolina, two each in Maryland, Virginia, and Pennsylvania, and one chartered in Georgia and what later would become Kentucky.[35]

During the summer of 1787 at the Constitutional Convention in Philadelphia, Charles Pinckney of South Carolina proposed that the new federal congress establish a national university at the seat of government of the United States. James Madison of Virginia also argued for a national university, and, in the last days of the convention, Madison and Pinckney tried again, only to have their proposal fail six to four. However, the Constitution as adopted was silent not only about a national university but about education itself.[36] Some delegates feared that a national university would be influenced by religious organizations; others felt that education was a state and local, not a national, concern.

President George Washington recommended that Congress consider a national university in his first message to Congress, January 8, 1790. Later Washington used his executive authority to set aside land in the capital city for a national university, with the hope that Congress would charter such an institution or private donors would come forward. Congress balked at the idea, but Washington, himself, left in his will a gift (which eventually became worthless) to be used as an endowment for a national university when eventually established. Washington had better luck when advocating for a military academy, and in 1802 Congress created the Academy at West Point.[37]

Each of the first six presidents urged Congress to create a national university. Finally, in 1821, Congress granted a corporate charter to the Columbian College, and then donated land in the District of Columbia valued at $25,000. The donation of land, rather than a donation of money, followed an acceptable federal government principle. Columbian College, as a private liberal arts college, limped along, "isolated, perennially down on at the heels, and regional"; it became Columbian University in 1873, then the George Washington University in 1904.[38] But this institution fell far short of becoming a national university.

In 1836 James L. Smithson left a $500,000 bequest for the "increase and diffusion of knowledge" and the endowment of a national agricultural university in Washington, D.C., but nothing came of this national university idea.[39] After the Civil War, there were several attempts in Congress to create a national university in the 1870s and again in the 1890s. In the next several decades, there had been twenty-six bills introduced in the House to create a national university; none survived.[40]

The first educational land grant for higher education came under the Northwest Ordinance: the territorial legislature of Ohio chartered American Western University on January 2, 1802; in 1804, it became Ohio University, and in 1808 it opened its doors to three students.[41] Its principal source of income was the educational land grant established through the 1787 Ordinance.

The Northwest Ordinance set the precedent for national land grants for education. From the founding of the United States until the Civil War, seventeen states had received federal land grants for higher education. Tennessee (admitted into the Union in 1796) received 100,000 acres through a special congressional act in 1806; Wisconsin (1848) and Florida (1845) each received 92,160 acres from three federal land-grants; Minnesota (1858) received 82,640 acres from three such grants; and Ohio (1803) received 69,120 acres from two grants. Twelve other states each received 46,080 acres from a variety of federal land-grants.[42]

The development of state universities was delayed, in part, by the landmark Supreme Court decision concerning Dartmouth College.[43] The central issue before the Supreme Court in 1819 was whether Dartmouth was a public institution or a private corporation. Founded in 1769 by Eleazar Wheelock and supported by the Congregational Church, Dartmouth had received a royal charter calling for a self-perpetuating board of trustees and a president who could name his own successor. Eventually John Wheelock, son of the founder, became president; but he soon ran afoul of church teachings and was fired. Young Wheelock exacted revenge, however; he was elected governor and encouraged the state legislature to pass a law changing private Dartmouth College into a state-supported Dartmouth University.

In a much-quoted, impassioned plea before the Supreme Court, Dartmouth's lawyer Daniel Webster framed the question: "Shall our state legislature be allowed to take that which is not their own, to turn it from its original use, and apply it to such ends or purposes as they, in their discretion, shall see fit!"[44] Through Chief Justice John Marshall, the Supreme Court ruled that Dartmouth was not a public institution and that the New Hampshire statute creating a state university out of the private college was an unconstitutional impairment of the obligation of contract. Education historian Paul Westmeyer observed that the Supreme Court's decision delayed the founding of state universities and immediately resulted in a spurt of founding of small colleges from the 1820s through the 1870s.[45]

Nevertheless, there were twenty-one state-supported colleges and universities founded before the Civil War. Beginning with the University of Georgia in 1785, twenty of the thirty-four states of the Union had created state universities. Six original states (Georgia, North Carolina, South Carolina, Maryland, Virginia, and Delaware) created state universities, as had fourteen new states (Vermont, Kentucky, Tennessee, Ohio, Louisiana, Indiana, Mississippi, Alabama, Missouri, Michigan, Iowa, Wisconsin, California, and Minnesota); Ohio had established two.[46] In addition, there were also six colleges or universities that were semi-state or municipal. Of the original states, seven (New Hampshire, Massachusetts, Rhode Island, Connecticut, New York, New Jersey, and Pennsylvania) had not founded state universities before the Civil War.

Seven new states (Illinois, Maine, Arkansas, Florida, Texas, Oregon, and Kansas) likewise had not created state universities.[47] From 1800 to 1860, liberal arts colleges had increased their enrollments from 1,156 students to 16,500. Altogether, 241 liberal arts institutions had been created during this time span, with just forty failing to survive.[48]

Fifteen years before the introduction of the Morrill legislation, professor Jonathan B. Turner of Illinois College persistently and forcefully argued for the establishment of college courses in agriculture and mechanical arts. His ideas were formulated in a speech before a convention of farmers in Granville, Illinois, November 18, 1851. It was published, widely distributed, and became known as the "Turner Plan." The professional classes, Turner declared, had enough literature to "sink a whole navy of ships," but where was the training and instructional materials for the industrial or agricultural arts? It just wasn't there. He argued that the Smithsonian Institution should be a center for disseminating practical learning, and that there should be a university in each state devoted to industrial and mechanical arts.[49]

On February 8, 1853, the Illinois state legislature adopted a resolution, written by Turner and some of his colleagues, directing the Illinois delegation in Congress to work with other legislators for a law that would donate public lands, worth at least $500,000, to each state for the endowment of industrial universities and to cooperate with the Smithsonian Institution. Representative Richard Yates (Whig–Illinois) was prepared to introduce a bill in 1854 but for some reason did not do so. When it looked more politically favorable in 1857, Senator Lyman Trumbull (Democrat–Illinois) said he would be glad to introduce it, but thought, given that so much land had already been turned over to western states, that perhaps the legislation should come from someone representing the East. Then, on December 17, 1857, Justin Morrill, a Vermonter, introduced his own piece of legislation.

Slowly, the movement for agricultural and mechanical colleges had gained strength. Editors of farm journals and journalists like Horace Greeley and Solon Robinson, educators like Jonathan Turner, and agricultural leaders like Marshall O. Wilder, president of the National Agricultural Society, turned to Washington for help. Their plea was simple and persuasive: if Congress can support industry and commerce through tariffs, patent law, subsidies for ships and harbors, and land grants for canals, why not help out agriculture? So little had been done for this vital segment of the American economy.[50]

Morrill's 1857 legislation called for a total grant of a little over 6 million acres of federal land, with an estimated value of $7.5 million, or $1.25 per acre. This sum was modest and the portion of public lands was relatively small. But the plan was also revolutionary, based on a much different land distribution scheme than the homestead proposals. Morrill's legislation would benefit the older, more populated eastern states at the expense of the newer western states. Eastern states had little or no public lands left, and, under Morrill's legislation, these states would now be able to pick lands in the West. The bigger the population of the state, the more land it would receive. The public land would be apportioned to each state based on the size of its congressional delegation, just like the Electoral College.[51] Using the 1850 census, New York, the most populous state, would receive 20,000 acres for each of its thirty-three representatives, and 20,000 acres for each of its two senators; Ohio would receive the same 20,000 acres for each of its twenty-one representatives and two senators. Tiny Rhode Island, with two representatives, would receive the same amount of acreage as Iowa or the vast, but sparsely populated, California.[52]

Each state would establish at least one college or university with a major focus on agriculture and mechanical arts. The secretary of the interior would issue western land scrip to eastern states that did not have public lands of their own. The states could sell these certificates and finance the institutions through the proceeds of the sales.

Morrill wanted his bill to go to the committee he sat on, the Agriculture Committee, but instead it was assigned to the Public Lands Committee, under the hostile glare of its chairman, Williamson R. W. Cobb (Democrat–Alabama). Morrill described the bulky and heavy-voiced Cobb as a man of weak intellect, with the "humor of a buffoon at times and the manner of a tin-peddler."[53] Cobb and the Public Lands Committee sat on the bill for months, and then on April 15, 1858, recommended that it not be passed. However, Morrill was good at counting heads, and knew that if the full House could consider his legislation, he would have a good chance of winning. He enlisted the help of two of his House colleagues to pull some parliamentary legerdemain, and Morrill soon found his bill before the full House of Representatives.[54]

Standing before his colleagues on April 20, Justin Morrill, now in his second term in Congress, argued that land grants for education were well within the authority of the Constitution: the federal government had invested millions in lighthouses, harbors, coastal surveys, and the military academies; authors and inventors had received federal copyright and patent protection; and railroads had received generous land-grant benefits. Why shouldn't agriculture be encouraged as well?

Morrill also warned about the falling productivity of American farmlands. Wheat production in New England, potato harvests, and tobacco in Virginia had all declined by the 1850s, principally because of depleted soil. What the United States should do was emulate the scientific agricultural programs in Europe. Belgium, England, and especially France had invested in agricultural programs and schools, in veterinary science and horticulture, with impressive results. "We have schools to teach the art of manslaying and make masters of 'deep-throated engines' of war," Morrill argued, "and shall we not have schools to teach men the way to feed, clothe, and enlighten the great brotherhood of man?"[55]

Morrill estimated that his land-grant bill would give over 5.8 million acres to the states for building agricultural colleges. This was far less than the 61 million acres parceled out to veterans, the 25 million acres given to states to build railroads, and the nearly 68 million that had already gone to the states for schools and universities. That would still leave over a billion acres of federal public land left for other uses.[56]

The House debated further and finally voted 105–100 in favor of Morrill's bill. It took longer in the Senate. First, Charles E. Stuart (Democrat–Michigan) tried to steer it through, but the vote was delayed until the next session. Then Benjamin F. Wade (Republican–Ohio) took over the task of getting it through the Senate. He argued that support for land-grant legislation was widespread: many state legislatures and nearly every agriculture society had endorsed the idea. But there were some vociferous opponents in the Senate, with westerners and southerners the biggest critics. Henry M. Rice (Republican–Minnesota) derided higher education for farmers: "We want no fancy farmers; we want no fancy mechanics." Southerners were particularly worried about federal disposal of public lands. They argued that it was against both the spirit and the letter of the Constitution to give away land to settlers, to railroads, or to colleges and universities. To James M. Mason (Democrat–Virginia) this was nothing more than an "unconstitutional robbing of the Treasury for the purpose of bribing the states." From the floor of the Senate in February 1859, Clement Claiborne Clay, Jr. (Democrat–Alabama), railed against Morrill's bill, calling it "one of the most monstrous, iniquitous and dangerous measures which have ever been submitted to Congress."[57]

Others, particularly western state legislators, worried about land speculators. They remembered the bitter experience of the grants given to veterans of the Mexican War. More than 61 million acres had been awarded to the veterans; but quickly the land value depreciated, sometimes down to 50 cents an acre. The land was then scooped up by speculators who purchased it in tracts of 5,000 to 100,000 acres. These were more often than not absentee land owners from the East, who found it convenient not to pay property taxes on their newly acquired lands. Land speculation meant that settlements were widely dispersed, and improvements like roads and rail lines had to be made by local governments. Speculators were getting the rewards, and locals were getting the bills. Many veterans fell victim to land speculators and schemers, and that could easily happen with the scrip awarded to colleges and universities, they feared.[58]

But in the end, Wade and his Senate supporters voted 25–20 in favor of Morrill's legislation. Thirty years earlier, Senator James Buchanan had voted for a land-grant bill, and there were hopes that he would be committed on principle to the college bill. But at the urging of John Slidell (Democrat–Louisiana) and other southern legislators, President Buchanan vetoed the Morrill bill, calling it unconstitutional and unnecessary. Given the closeness of the votes in both houses, Morrill and Wade knew that they could not gain a two-thirds vote to override the veto. The public was behind the legislation, thirteen states had instructed their federal legislators to support it, and national and state agricultural societies also gave their assistance. Charles B. Calvert, a leading agriculture proponent, even tried to deny Buchanan honorary membership in the United States Agricultural Society.[59] As Morrill later remarked, "Nothing more could be done except to wait for a possible change of the administration and certain change of the President."[60]

Making the Laws

On the eighty-fifth anniversary of America's independence, President Abraham Lincoln called Congress into special session. When Congress met on July 4, 1861, it was for the serious purpose of waging war and the survival of the nation. As one account described it, "excited multitudes" packed the visitor galleries in both the House and the Senate, and many pushed vainly to try to be admitted.[61] The Capitol had just been cleaned up, scrubbed of the lingering odors and detritus left by the Union soldiers temporarily billeted there. What legislators and visitors now smelled was the freshly baked bread, 58,000 loaves a day, coming from the army's gas-fed bakeries in the Capitol's basement.[62] On the floor of the House and Senate, visitors and legislators saw stark evidence of a nation torn apart: the empty seats of the fifty-six southern congressmen and twenty-one senators who had gone home, to defend their property, their honor, and the Confederacy. Only Andrew Johnson of Tennessee would remain and soon he would resign his senate seat to become the military governor of Tennessee.

Republicans dominated both the House and Senate, and in the House they chose thirty-seven-year-old Galusha Grow as their speaker. Rather than selecting either Schuyler Colfax of Indiana or Francis Blair of Missouri, the two moderate contenders, the Republicans chose the fiery, brilliant Grow, who in his maiden speech as speaker lashed out at the South and its rebellion against the Union. The Democrats were dispirited and leaderless; secession had robbed the party of its strength, and their most able northern leader and opponent of Lincoln, Stephen A. Douglas, had died just one month before the new Congress convened.[63]

Lincoln asked Congress for an additional 400,000 troops, the staggering sum of $400 million to execute the war, and approval of the emergency wartime powers that the president had already begun exercising. Congress obliged, going even further by authorizing 500,000 volunteers, increasing the regular army by eleven regiments, closing southern ports, and strengthening the army and the navy. To pay for the war, Congress authorized $250 million, to be paid for the first time by a direct tax upon incomes.[64]

Thirty-Seventh Congress, 2nd Session (December 2, 1861– July 17, 1862)

Senate: 31 Republicans; 10 Democrats; 8 other

House: 105 Republicans; 43 Democrats; 30 other

President: Abraham Lincoln

A shocked Congress was spurred on by the first major engagement of the war. In July, some 35,000 Union troops had gathered in Washington, under the command of Brigadier

General Irvin McDowell. The Confederate Congress was to meet in Richmond on July 20, and there were war cries of "Forward to Richmond" from Horace Greeley's *New York Tribune* and other northern papers. The first step would be for McDowell's troops to defeat the rebels at Bull Run in nearby Manassas, Virginia. Brigadier General Pierre G. T. Beauregard's 22,000 Confederate troops were reinforced by another 10,000 Confederates brought in by General Joseph E. Johnston. In the final attack on July 21, with Union forces seemingly poised for victory, a Virginia brigade under Thomas J. Jackson formed a defensive line, held back the enemy, giving Confederate forces time to mount a successful counterattack. Jackson would forever be known as "Stonewall," and Union forces, green, overconfident, and unprepared, would stampede back to the safety of Washington, pushing and shoving aside incredulous Union politicians and horrified spectators who had come out to watch their boys teach the rag-tag rebels a lesson.

This Union humiliation and defeat, however, left Lincoln and Congress more determined than ever. Immediately, Lincoln signed a bill for the enlistment of 500,000 troops, and a second bill for an additional 500,000 three days later. The total congressional appropriation reached $350 million, more than five times the national budget in the session immediately before hostilities commenced.[65]

The Homestead Bill

Just four days after the session began, on July 8, 1861, second-term congressman Cyrus Aldrich (Republican–Minnesota) introduced a homestead bill. But given the shortness of the session, which lasted only until August 6, and pressing war-related business, Aldrich's proposal was not heard from again in that special session. The second session of the Thirty-Seventh Congress began at the usual time for legislative business, on December 2, 1861, and went through July 17, 1862. Homesteading was an important plank of their party platform, and, now fully in power, Republicans wasted little time in introducing legislation. The Aldrich bill reappeared and was referred to the Committee on Public Lands, chaired by John Fox Potter (Republican–Wisconsin). On December 10, 1861, Potter reported a homestead measure to the full House. It called for the transfer of public lands to citizens, or those who declared that they wanted to be citizens, who were twenty-one years old and heads of their household; these settlers would pay a $10 entry fee and occupy the land for five years. The homesteaders would receive either 160 acres, valued at $1.25 per acre, or 80 acres, valued at $2.50. The Potter bill also would pay out cash bounties of $30 to men who had served in the Union army for three months or longer.[66]

Some legislators, like William S. Holman (Democrat–Indiana) argued that Union soldiers should receive land grants, not just cash bounties. Others wanted Congress to act immediately: the sooner settlers got their land, the better. A few legislators thought the homestead program should wait until after the war was over. One of those who wanted to wait was Justin Morrill, who was trying to get his own land-grant college bill through Congress and did not want homestead bills blocking his legislative efforts.[67]

Key Provisions of the Homestead Act

The Homestead Act provided for the transfer of 160 acres of non-occupied and surveyed public land to individual homesteaders who paid a nominal fee and resided on that land for five years.

- Eligible was any person who was the head of a family, or was twenty-one years old and a citizen of the United States, or who had declared the intention to become a citizen, and had never borne arms against the United States government or given aid and comfort to its enemies.
- Claimants also could receive title to their land early by paying $1.25 per acre for the 160 acres, or $2.50 per acre for 80 acres or less.
- The Act took effect on January 1, 1863.

For the next two months, the homestead legislation was put on hold while Congress considered other matters. Then on February 21, 1862, the House once again took it up. The legislation that came from Potter's committee was almost identical to the bill that Galusha Grow had introduced in 1859. By now, Speaker Grow had reached the end of his patience. He took the dramatic and unprecedented step of summoning Elihu Washburne (Republican–Illinois) to the Speaker's chair to serve as Grow's temporary substitute. Grow stepped down, took his place on the floor of the House, and spoke forcefully for immediate passage of the bill. The homestead bill had been passed in the House five times in the past ten years, he implored; discussion had gone on far too long, and it was time to vote approval. A week later, the House overwhelmingly approved the legislation, 107–16.[68]

The Senate wrestled with the question of whether to include land-grants for veterans, but in the end Grow's friend and senate ally Ben Wade from Ohio cleared the path by eliminating the bounty for veterans. On May 6, 1862, by a vote of 33–7, the Senate passed the homestead bill, and nine days later both the House and Senate approved the final version, with no discussion and no recorded vote.[69] Lincoln signed the legislation on May 20.

The Land-Grant College Bill

Representative Justin Morrill wasted little time in getting his land-grant college bill introduced in Congress. Four days into the second session, on December 6, 1861, Morrill announced that he would submit his legislation, and did so ten days later. Like Galusha Grow's homestead bill, Morrill's land-grant college bill had won congressional approval but had been vetoed by Buchanan. This time, Morrill sweetened the pot, proposing that 30,000 acres (rather than 20,000) be awarded to states for each representative and senator. Morrill also included a provision to require each land-grant institution to add military science and tactics to its curriculum.[70]

But Morrill's legislation faced a tougher time in the House Committee on Public Lands than did the homestead legislation. Chairman John Potter was adamantly opposed to the bill and there was only lukewarm support, at best, from other committee members.[71] After a delay of nearly six months, Potter recommended on May 29, 1862, that the full House not pass the legislation. The biggest hurdle was that westerners did not want the eastern, more populous states, to benefit from the sale of western state public lands.

While Morrill was awaiting a decision from the Committee on Public Lands, he worked with Ben Wade from Ohio to get the land-grant bill introduced in the Senate. Westerners again voiced their objections. Senator Henry M. Rice (Democrat–Minnesota) complained that the land agents would cull out the choicest land, "blighting, like the locusts every region which may attract them . . ." James H. Lane (Republican–Kansas) worried that all the good land in Kansas would be snatched up by out-of-staters. Like many others, Senator Morton S. Wilkinson (Republican–Minnesota) worried that land speculators, "a remorseless class of vampires," would wipe out the good done by the homestead grants. They "care little for common prosperity," Wilkinson pleaded, "and still less for the cause of education."[72]

Key Provisions of the Morrill Act

The act called for support in each state (originally the non-rebelling states, then in 1866, all states) of at least one college devoted to agriculture and the mechanical arts.

- For each senator and representative under the 1860 apportionment, the states would receive public lands or the equivalent in land scrip of 30,000 acres. Altogether, there would be 17,430,000 acres of public land dedicated to this land-grant provision.
- The proceeds of the sale of land were for the endowment, support, and maintenance of at least one college "where the leading object shall be . . . to teach such branches of learning as are related to agriculture and the mechanical arts . . . in order to promote the liberal and practical education of the industrial classes in the several pursuits and professions of life."
- The funds would be used to set up an endowment at no less than 5 percent interest.
- Any unused funds would be returned to the federal government in five years.

Former executive director of the National Association of State Universities and Land-Grant Colleges Russell I. Thackrey observed that the Land-Grant College Act was one of the most "beautifully vague pieces of legislation in the history of education, and therein lies much of its greatness."[73]

Throughout the debate on Morrill's legislation, there was much discussion about how lands would be taken from western states for the benefit of easterners, but there was remarkably little discussion of education itself. Historian Carl L. Becker was struck by the "singular indifference" that the members of Congress paid to the educational provisions of the act. Most of the discussion was focused on how the use of public lands would increase the nation's prosperity, not reform its educational system.[74]

On May 12, 1862, Senator Wade called up the bill, but then the Senate held it up in deference to the objections of Lane of Kansas. It came up again ten days later, only to meet with "violent speeches," in Morrill's words,[75] by Lane and Wilkinson; but, on June 10, the Senate finally, and easily, supported the land-grant college bill by a vote of 32 to 7. In the House, Public Lands Committee chairman John Potter tried a number of dilatory tricks to prevent Morrill's bill from coming to a vote, but finally, on June 17, the full House passed the land-grant college bill by a resounding 90 to 25.

Two months earlier, on May 15, Lincoln had signed the law creating the Department of Agriculture. This had fulfilled his plea, as seen in his annual message to Congress in December 1861, to take special care of agriculture. "Agriculture, confessedly the largest interest of the nation, has not a department, nor a bureau, but a clerkship only, assigned to it in the government." Lincoln, however, had no recorded comment on the land-grant legislation. He had not fought for either the homestead or the land-grant college legislation, although he did endorse both.[76] Now, on July 2, 1862, Lincoln signed into law the Land-Grant College Act, which was destined to play a vital role in the development of agriculture and science.

Key Individuals in the Homestead and Land-Grant College Acts

Several legislators had proposed versions of homestead legislation, but two stand out as the most important.

Galusha Aaron Grow (1823–1907) served in Congress from 1851 through 1862. Grow, a Pennsylvania Democrat, then a Republican, was the youngest member of Congress when he entered at twenty-eight, and was only thirty-seven years old when he was chosen as Speaker of the House in 1861. At the height of his power in 1862, his legislative district was reconfigured, and he lost re-election to Congress. He later served as president of the Houston & Great Northern Railroad Company in Texas and then returned to Pennsylvania to pursue interests in coal, oil, and lumber. After thirty years away from Washington, Grow returned to Congress in 1893 and served until 1903.

Andrew Johnson (1808–1875) had a long political career that culminated in the presidency in 1865–1869. Johnson, a Democrat from Tennessee, served in the House of Representatives from 1843 to 1852; he then returned to Tennessee as its governor (1853–1857). He was elected by the Tennessee legislature to the U.S. Senate in 1857 and served until 1862. At that time, he returned to Tennessee as the military governor. In 1864 he was selected as the vice-presidential candidate to run with Abraham Lincoln; he became president upon Lincoln's assassination in March 1865. Johnson's presidency was marked as the first time a president had been impeached, and he came within one vote in the Senate of being found guilty of an impeachable offense. He became the second president (after John Quincy Adams) to return to the Congress. He was an unsuccessful candidate to the House in 1869 and also unsuccessful for the Senate in 1872 but was chosen by the Tennessee legislature once again as U.S. Senator, serving in the Forty-Fourth Congress from March 1874 until his death in July 1875.

A number of historians have argued that the key inspiration for the land-grant college movement was professor Jonathan B. Turner, who advocated for agricultural and mechanical colleges in the 1840s and 1850s. However, in Congress, the most important voice was that of the legislator whose name is intimately associated with the land-grant movement.

Justin Smith Morrill (1810–1898) served as a Whig, then Republican, representative from Vermont from 1855 through 1866. Morrill, whose formal schooling did not reach past the age of fifteen, was a tireless advocate of agricultural education throughout his long, and very productive, legislative career. He served as senator from Vermont from 1867 until his death thirty-one years later and was a key figure in the Republican Party. The Land-Grant College Act of 1862 was supplemented by the so-called second Morrill Act of 1890, which provided additional permanent funds to the land-grant schools and led to the creation of separate black land-grant institutions in seventeen states. Morrill was also known as the author of the Tariff Act of 1861.

Aftermath

In its wrap-up of legislative activity for the Thirty-Seventh Congress, the *New York Times* ran a two-line announcement simply noting that "The President has approved the Homestead bill and it is therefore a law." It said nothing about the Morrill Land-Grant Act.[77] However, these two enactments, approved during the dark years of civil war, were essential to the development of America. Implementation did not always go smoothly and results were not always evident, but in the end, these two enactments, based on the bounty of public lands, helped shape America.

Homesteading

A total of 285 million acres, or 10 percent of the land mass of the United States, was claimed and settled under the Homestead Act.[78] The law went into effect on January 1, 1863, the very day that another historic pronouncement, the Emancipation Proclamation, became law. Ten minutes after midnight on the first day, Daniel Freeman filed his claim in the Land Office in Brownville, Nebraska. He paid a $10 dollar filing fee and a $2 dollar commission, built a home, and, after five years of farming the land, Freeman most likely asked two neighbors or friends to sign a document attesting that he had "proved up," that is, that he had fulfilled the requirements for ownership. Freeman then paid a final $6 fee and received patent for the land in the form of a fancy certificate signed by the president of the United States. In 1865 the bachelor Daniel Freeman proposed marriage through the mail to Agnes Suitor, a young woman from LeClaire, Iowa, who had been engaged to Freeman's brother James, who had died during the Civil War. Daniel Freeman brought his new bride to his homestead claim and over the years they had eight children.[79]

Soon after passage of the Homestead Act, a popular song was heard throughout the country, with this refrain:

> Come along, come along, make no delay,
> Come from every nation, come from every way,
> Our lands they are broad enough, have no alarm
> For Uncle Sam is rich enough to give us all a farm.[80]

During the next several decades, some two million individuals would follow the same dream as Daniel Freeman and apply for homestead patents. However, homesteading was not for everyone, and perhaps only 40 percent were successful in overcoming the harsh and lonely climate and soil, periodic skirmishes with Native Americans, cyclones, and locusts. Many European immigrants were attracted by the possibility of free land, but even that enticement was not an overwhelming motive.[81]

The Homestead Act, however, treated the South differently. Southern farmers and would-be settlers were frozen out of the free lands until after the end of the war, and there were strong sentiments in Congress to continue to treat the South differently. Before 1861, there were nearly 48 million acres of federal public land, almost one-third of the entire territory of Alabama, Arkansas, Florida, Louisiana, and Mississippi. Much of that land was swamp-filled, or of poor timber quality, and had been for sale before the war at prices ranging from 12.5 cents to one dollar an acre.[82]

The South became the laboratory for land policy experimentation. From 1866 to 1876, southern public lands were reserved for homesteaders only, and it was illegal to make large land purchases. Congressman George W. Julian (Republican–Indiana), a long-time abolitionist and the chairman of the House Public Lands Committee, wanted to restrict southern homesteading only to loyal citizens and to break up the old southern aristocracy. In 1866, pushed on by the Radical Republicans, Congress enacted the Southern Homestead Act, which restricted the southern public lands to parcels of 80 acres each to be given only to individual homesteaders. With the southern states being readmitted over the next years, one of the first things that southerners wanted to do was repeal the 1866 law. To many, the Southern Homestead Act was another insult, of northerners trying to rub the war into their noses and retard growth and economic prosperity. Finally, in 1876, after a long, heated fight, with southern lawmakers unified in their determination, the 1866 law was repealed. Now, the South was open once again to land and timber speculation. But ironically, it was monied interests from the North that swooped down and bought control of the best land, the best cypress and yellow pine acres, and reaped the profits from the southern timber industry.[83]

Altogether, over 1.03 billion acres of public land were disposed of, with 285 million going to homesteaders, and the rest to railroads, the states, and other claims.[84] In the eight years following passage of the Homestead Act, a total of 127 million acres were granted to railroads and another 2 million to the building of canals and wagon roads. Another 140 million acres of public lands were given to state governments to produce endowments for state institutions. After 1862, between 100 and 125 million acres of Indian reservation land was also sold off to white settlers.[85]

Timeline of Homesteading and Land Policy

1796	Land Act of 1796 established rectangular system of surveys in townships consisting six miles square. Public land sold for $2.00 per acre, with credit extended. Relatively low sales, and high delinquencies.[86]
1820	Credit for purchases of public lands was discontinued; land had to be surveyed first, and sold at public auction at a minimum of $1.25 per acre.
1830	Squatters given limited preemptive rights; a major change in federal land policy.
1841	Pre-emption Act fully established the right of the squatter on surveyed public lands to have first crack at purchase, at $1.25 per acre.
1857	Nearly 44 million acres auctioned off, with over 25 percent of the land in California.
1862	Homestead Act.
1867	Purchase of Alaska for $7 million; 365 million acres.
1873	Timber Culture Act, which transferred title to settlers at no charge, provided forty acres (then reduced to ten) of a quarter section were cultivated in trees. Over 290,000 entries, for 43 million acres, almost all in Kansas, Nebraska, and the Dakota Territory.
1902	National Reclamation Act using federal money from sale of public lands to irrigate 10 million acres of the West.
1934	Taylor Grazing Act substantially decreased the amount of land available for homesteading.
1976	Federal Land Policy and Management Act repealed the Homestead Act in the contiguous forty-eight states.

As popular as it was, the Homestead Act did have its critics, the famed explorer and naturalist John Wesley Powell foremost among them. Powell, who became a national hero after his three-month, 1,000 mile expedition down the Colorado River and through the Grand Canyon in 1869 and 1871, was later appointed to the U.S. Public Lands Commission and in 1881 became director of the U.S. Geological Survey. Powell sought to learn more about the environment and ecology of the West and to apply scientific methods to its study. His most important insight was that the West was different from the rest of the United States because of one key factor, its aridity. Using the rain charts compiled by Charles A. Shortt of the Smithsonian Institution and his own observations, Powell concluded that apart from the rain-abundant strip of land along the Pacific coast from San Francisco to Seattle, the rest of the West received less than twenty inches of rainfall annually. He divided the West into a "subhumid" region (most of Texas, Oklahoma, Kansas, and Nebraska) which covered 10 percent of the continental United States, and an "arid" region, which covered another 40 percent of the country.[87]

Powell argued that, except for a few oases of sustainable land, the West simply did not have the moisture for farming and ranching. He criticized the long-held system of rigid grids and 160 acre quarters, arguing that Congress should go back to the more realistic system of metes-and-bounds that was used by the original colonial settlers, which allowed property lines to follow natural lines, rather than a rigid grid system. Further, Powell wanted to scrap the whole homestead program. He would allow just two types of land ventures in the West: small irrigated farms of no greater than 80 acres, with all the farms clustered together in irrigation districts, and livestock ranches that were no larger than 2,650 acres.[88]

Powell frequently testified before the House Select Committee on Irrigation of Arid Lands in the United States, serving as the professor he once was to explain the harsh facts of the arid West. One in nine acres, at most, in the West could be irrigated, Powell observed. Powell went further in 1890, calling for a radical new system of dividing of the lands. His plan called for 140 new governmental units in the West, based on watersheds; the federal government would retain title to the lands, but settlers would make the rules and create self-reliant, self-governing commonwealths.[89] However, Congress did not appreciate this somewhat utopian vision. Many members of Congress, particularly from the West, wanted the federal government to give the lands to the states, letting them dispose of the lands however they pleased.

The U.S. Census Bureau in 1890 announced the end of the frontier. By that time, the seventeen western states and territories had reached a total population of 6,451,000. There were so many westerners, spread out over the vast landscape, that there was no longer a way to define a frontier line. By 1890 new urban centers had developed in the West: San Francisco had 298,000 residents; Los Angeles, 50,000; Denver, 107,000; and Salt Lake City, 45,000.[90] Three years later, historian Frederick Jackson Turner presented a paper before the American Historical Association entitled "The Significance of the Frontier in American History." The central theme of this seminal paper was that "the existence of an area of free land, its continuous recession, and the advance of American settlement westward, explain American development."[91] A special American character had been formed, Turner argued, based on democracy, individualism, pragmatism, and egalitarianism. By 1890 that frontier was gone, and a new foundation for American life must be created.[92]

While the frontier might be gone, land was still available. Powell and the U.S. Geological Survey had estimated that some 30 million acres of western land could be irrigated, but, by 1890, just 3.6 million of those acres were being farmed. At the urging of George Maxwell, a spokesman for the national irrigation movement, and Frederick Newell, chief hydrographer of the U.S. Geological Survey and a protege of John Wesley Powell, Senator Francis E. Warren (Republican–Wyoming), and Congressman Francis G. Newlands (Democrat–Nevada) worked on legislation for a system of federally-funded irrigation projects.[93] Out of this came the National Reclamation Act of 1902, signed by President Theodore Roosevelt, which used federally money from the sale of public lands to irrigate areas in the West. Eventually 9 to 10 million western acres became productive because of this legislation. Historian Donald Worster has argued that the National Reclamation Act was the "most important single piece of legislation in the history of the West, overshadowing even the Homestead Act in the consequences it has had for the region's life."[94]

The Taylor Grazing Act of 1934 substantially decreased the amount of land available to homesteaders. The West was threatened with overgrazing and dust bowl conditions, prompting Congress to regulate public lands for the first time, requiring permits for grazing. In summing up the lengthy history of homesteading and public land sales, Paul W. Gates observed in 1971, "yet with all the poorly drafted legislation, the mediocre and sometimes corrupt land officials, the constant effort of settlers, moneyed speculators, and great land companies to engross land for the unearned increment they might extract from it, the federal land system seems to have worked surprisingly well."[95]

Then the Federal Land Policy and Management Act of 1976 repealed the Homestead Act in the contiguous forty-eight states, but left a ten-year extension for Alaskan claims. In 1974, Kenneth Deardorff, a native of California, staked out an 80-acre claim to land on the Stony River in southwestern Alaska. He had proved up his claim in five years' time, and finally received his patent in May 1988, making him the last of a breed of settlers and pioneers who worked the land and enjoyed the fruits of federal land policy.[96]

A new generation of homesteading is making modest headway in parts of the Great Plains. The small Kansas towns of Ellsworth, Kanopolis, Holyrood, Wilson, and Minneapolis have offered free lots (not 80 acres), sometimes free water and sewer hookups, free cable television, and even cash payments to entice settlers. The Great Plains region, from North Dakota to north Texas, has been losing population steadily since the Great Depression and dust bowl days. In 2003 Senator Byron L. Dorgan (Democrat–North Dakota) introduced a new Homestead Act that would offer business tax credits, establish a $3 billion investment fund, and pay half of college loans for people who relocate to such areas.[97]

Land-Grant Colleges

In 1862, there were just three collegiate institutions that described themselves as agricultural colleges; they would later become known as Michigan State University, the Pennsylvania State University, and the University of Maryland. Soon, individual states would begin taking advantage of the federal land-grant opportunities. Two months after it became law, Iowa was the first state to accept the conditions laid down by the Morrill Act, then Vermont and Connecticut soon followed. Fourteen more states agreed in 1863, and, by the end of the Civil War, a total of twenty-one states had signed up.[98] Some legislatures, like those in Minnesota, Wisconsin, and Missouri, assigned funds to existing universities; funds were also given to the existing agricultural colleges in Iowa, Pennsylvania, Maryland, and Michigan. Several private universities were given funds: Massachusetts Institute of Technology and Amherst (later dropped) in Massachusetts, Brown University in Rhode Island, and Cornell University in New York. In Delaware, Illinois, Kentucky, and California, new schools were created.[99]

The Morrill Act gave away 17.4 million acres of federal public land, with a return of $7.5 million for the creation and use of agricultural and mechanical colleges. The return was hardly the $1.25 per acre that Congress had sought, but more on the order of 58 cents per acre. State legislatures could choose federal acreage anywhere they wanted from the land allotted by the Department of the Interior. Only three states east of the Mississippi River—Illinois, Wisconsin, and Michigan—had any public lands remaining in them; all other eastern states would be given land procurement certificates (scrip) for their allotments of western public lands.[100] The smart decision was to choose fertile soil or good timberlands. But a number of states let the opportunity slip through their fingers, through either incompetence or collusion with speculators.[101]

Brown University was assigned the scrip for 120,000 acres by the Rhode Island legislature to create a department of agricultural and mechanical arts. After spending the summer of 1863 out west looking at land, a committee headed by Brown's president decided the task was just too complicated, they threw their hands into the air, and accepted the convenient offer of one of their members, the Rev. Horace T. Love, a professional money-raiser, who offered $50,000 for the whole of the 120,000 acres. He paid over a period of years, at no interest, and gained the land for 42 cents an acre; soon after, Love sold the acres to land speculators Stebbins & Porter of Kansas for an average of 93 cents an acre.[102]

New Jersey, New Hampshire, Connecticut, and Pennsylvania had similar tales of impatience, incompetence, the rush to get the money quickly, or the pull from greedy speculators. Too often, land was sold when the markets were saturated and prices were low. New Jersey obtained just a little more than 50 cents an acre; New Hampshire, 43 cents. Connecticut sold its land and received just $7,000, enough to add three professors at the Sheffield Scientific School at Yale. Pennsylvania, which, next to New York, received the largest of all the land grants, succumbed to the twin pressures of speculators wanting to get the land quickly and state college officials wanting the money as soon as possible. The 780,000 acres of land was sold for just $439,000, or just 56 cents per acre.[103]

In Wisconsin, Henry Barron, the speaker of the state legislature, introduced a resolution to make sure that none of the state's 240,000 acres would be sold for less than $1.25. Much of the land was valuable white pine timberland, and the price should be fair so that Wisconsin farmers could have a chance to buy it at a reasonable rate. But most of the land ended up in the hands of big timber companies, speculators, and wealthy investors, like politician Caleb Cushing of Massachusetts, who purchased 33,000 acres of the land through the good offices of speaker Barron.[104]

The first truly successful program coming out of the land-grant legislation was Cornell University. New York received the largest land-grant of all, 980,000 acres, with those acres located in the pine lands of Wisconsin. One-time professor of history at the University of Michigan and now New York state senator, Andrew Dickson White convinced his fellow lawmaker, the phil-anthropist Ezra Cornell, to assist. Cornell had intended to use his considerable wealth to help two competing, though struggling, schools become land-grant institutions. White convinced Cornell otherwise: Why not create a real university, from the ground up? Cornell finally came around to seeing it White's way, and in January 1865 quietly confided to him: "I have about half a million dollars more than my family will need: what is the best thing I can do with it for the State?"[105]

Seventy-six thousand acres of the New York land-grant had already been sold for about 85 cents per acre. Ezra Cornell agreed to purchase the remaining 813,920 acres of scrip for $300,000. Cornell was no charlatan or dishonest land speculator, ready to make a quick investment. He ultimately doubled the $300,000 endowment and, more significantly, held on to the remaining land until 1905, when the university bearing his name received $5.8 million, or $5.82 per acre. Chartered as a private land-grant institution in 1865, Cornell University opened its doors with Andrew D. White as its founding president.[106]

Land-grant institutions were required to maintain military training for their students, although it was up to each school to determine if such training was compulsory. A number of non-land-grant schools also set up their own military science programs. On the eve of World War I, the land-grant schools had furnished three times the number of officers to the U.S. Army as did West Point, including fifty general officers, 2,000 field officers, and 25,000 captains and lieutenants. After the first World War, Congress established the National Defense Act of 1920, which created the Reserve Officers Training Corps (ROTC), a military training program at schools, colleges, and universities, whether or not they were part of the land-grant college program.[107]

By 1870 all thirty-seven states had created or were planning to create land-grant colleges and universities. But all was not well. Many of the schools were underfunded, with faculty paid miserably, and students ill-prepared. In a number of instances, new colleges had opened, but there were few high schools that could supply students. Indeed, the push for agricultural and mechanical education did not come from the bottom up, with students clamoring to get into college. Rather, it came from federal reformers and lawmakers pushing a new experiment in higher education.[108] By 1876 some of the schools were barely getting off the ground. Delaware College, for example, had just seven faculty and forty students; Illinois Agricultural College had four faculty and forty-one students. Louisiana State University had more faculty (five) than students (three). In 1877 there were literally no students applying to the land-grant school in New Hampshire; the farmers' college in College Park, Maryland (University of Maryland) went through five presidents and graduated only eight students during the first eight years after the war; and the "Farmers' High School" (Pennsylvania State University) had to reach down into the common-school level to meet its student shortfall. Only strong programs like Cornell University (forty faculty and 304 students) and the University of Wisconsin (nineteen faculty and 225 students) had reached impressive numbers.[109]

Historians of the land-grant college program basically agree that the first twenty-five years of the land-grant program was a "dismal period," with college and university programs still not able to begin fulfilling the promise of Morrill's legislation.[110] Farmers' organizations, like the Grange and the National Farmers' Alliance, were openly hostile or suspicious of the schools, and in many there were internal fights on what emphasis to place on a traditional curriculum, new courses in agriculture and engineering, and the role of mechanical arts.

The new University of California at Berkeley saw its share of difficulties. Unlike some states, California decided not to divide the land-grant funds among existing colleges, but to create a new institution in Berkeley, the University of California.[111] The state was growing dramatically, from roughly 50,000 persons in 1850 to nearly 870,000 in the 1870s. By 1872 there were two buildings on the Berkeley campus, with a university enrollment of 151 students, including 28 women. Soon, however, the new university was under attack: it was commendable that the university charged no tuition and admitted women, but, its critics charged, it had low enrollment, relied too much on classical curriculum, and was elitist in nature. The Workingmen's Party and the farmer-based California Grange, which was now asserting its political power, led the attack on the university's regents and its president, Daniel Coit Gilman. Professor Ezra Carr, head of the university's agriculture college, charged that land-grant funds were being diverted for the purpose of "gentlemanly training." Gilman, one-time Yale University professor, "frustrated over the meddling of the state legislature and popular clamor," resigned his presidency after three years and headed back east to become the founding president of The Johns Hopkins University in 1875.[112]

While the land-grant program languished during its first twenty-five years, it received an important boost in 1887 with the enactment of the Hatch Act, a program where the federal government would furnish an annual appropriation of $15,000 to each state for the establishment of agricultural experiment stations at land-grant universities. The prime movers behind the Hatch Act were George W. Atherton, the president of the Pennsylvania State College, and, in Congress, William H. Hatch (Democrat–Missouri), chairman of the House

Agriculture Committee. The Hatch Act helped to legitimate agricultural research, in essence developing a federally subsidized program for the academic study of agriculture.[113]

Timeline on Land-Grant Colleges and Universities

1787	Northwest Ordinance.
1862	Morrill Land-Grant College Act.
1887	Hatch Act, establishing agricultural experimental stations.
1890	Second Morrill Land-Grant Act, creating separate black institutions in seventeen southern and border states.
1914	Smith–Lever Act, authorizing land-grant schools to offer extension programs away from their universities.
1935	Bankhead–Jones Act, added funding for agricultural research and extension programs.
1994	Inclusion of twenty-nine Native American institutions, bringing the total of land-grant institutions to 105.

Session after session, Congress turned its back on legislation that would increase funding to land-grant colleges. Finally, twenty-eight years after the first enactment, Justin Morrill was successful in getting a second Morrill Act (Morrill II) passed in 1890. Led by Henry E. Alvord, president of the Maryland Agricultural College, land-grant college presidents mounted a successful campaign to boost federal funding of agricultural schools. This legislation provided additional funds for land-grant colleges or universities, starting at $15,000 per year and increasing by $1,000 per year until there was a permanent annual payment of $25,000. The Morrill II, unlike the first act, specified that funds were to go to specified fields of study, especially agriculture, mechanical arts, English, mathematics, physical and natural sciences, and economics. States would have to provide annual reports on the finances, enrollment, and educational research conducted at schools that received Morrill II funds. This sudden infusion of federal cash to the states was like "manna from heaven," and became a particular boon to engineering and mechanical arts programs. Further, the act established a closer, more formal relationship between the universities and the federal government.[114]

No state that made a distinction based on race in its admission policies was to receive Morrill II funds; however, the states could create separate institutions and be in compliance.[115] If a state were to give funds to a white school and to a black school, the land-grant funds had to be equitably divided. Thus, six years before the Supreme Court endorsed the "separate-but-equal" doctrine in *Plessy* v. *Ferguson*, the U.S. Congress and President Benjamin Harrison had given their approval to that principle in higher education.[116]

Seventeen states in the South and border areas would create separate colleges for blacks and maintain a whites-only policy for their principal land-grant institutions.[117] There was much ground to be covered for black education in the

South. These 1890 institutions began with elementary and secondary school enrollment as their largest portion. By 1915 there were just sixty-four public high schools for blacks in the South, and only forty-five of them offered four-year curricula.[118] A landmark survey by the Phelps–Stokes Fund, published by the U.S. Bureau of Education, found that in 1914, in all of the seventeen state-supported land-grant colleges for blacks, just twelve students were enrolled at the collegiate level.[119]

By 1928 there were just 3,527 students enrolled in the black land-grant colleges. In these early years, concentration was on teacher training and thus devoted to traditional curriculum: classics, letters, humanities, other aspects of liberal arts. Formal curriculum in agriculture and mechanical arts did not begin until after 1900. Black colleges, unlike white, spent most of their resources on sub-collegiate-level instruction. Not until 1931 were there more college students than secondary students enrolled in black land-grant schools.[120]

Despite this, and despite the fact that black faculty salaries at state schools were roughly half those of whites, most of the 1890 schools were able to develop bona fide four-year, standard college degree programs and receive accreditation by the 1930s.[121] However, the individual states that maintained both black and white land-grant schools did not treat them equally, and, inevitably, the black institution suffered. Until 1950, for example, the University of Maryland-College Park took most of the land-grant funds set aside for Princess Anne Academy, the black institution set up through the 1890 law. The academy then became the University of Maryland-Eastern Shore, and College Park could no longer monopolize land grant funds.[122] In Tennessee, the historically black school, Tennessee State University, had been subordinated to the flagship school, the University of Tennessee in Knoxville. A 1977 federal court order merged Tennessee State University with the new "budgetarily overfavored" Nashville campus of the University of Tennessee. In Texas, since 1923 about $2 billion in oil royalties had gone into the Permanent Improvement Fund at the University of Texas. Not until the 1980s could the land-grant schools of Texas A&M and the predominantly black Prairie View A&M share in the oil revenue.[123]

Beyond Morrill II, other legislation has assisted the land-grant university system. The Smith–Lever Act of 1914 authorized land-grant schools to offer extension programs away from their campuses and to set up agricultural and home economics extension services. The Bankhead–Jones Act of 1935 added more funds to allow agricultural research and cooperative agricultural extension programs.[124]

The University of Alaska, Fairbanks (with branches in Anchorage and Juneau), is the youngest of the state land-grant universities, although it has its roots as a land-grant institution in the Alaska Agricultural College and School of Mines, which was established in 1922. The most recent land-grant college was designated in 1968—Federal City College, now the University of the District of Columbia.[125] In 1994, twenty-nine Native American tribal colleges also gained land-grant status.

There are now 105 land-grant institutions, enrolling approximately 3 million students, producing half a million graduates each year. Each state has at least one such institution, providing an important component of the state's commitment to higher education. The schools vary in size, scope, and reputation, and, with addition of the Native American tribal colleges, in mission and purpose. Many came into their own during the early part of the twentieth century. They were among the first schools to offer advanced training to women and minorities. Several of the land-grant institutions are world-class universities.[126]

Agriculture, today, at land-grant colleges and universities constitutes but a fraction of the curriculum, faculty, and research budgets. Many institutions are questioning both their relevance and their future. Agriculture professor Neil E. Harl, among others, worries that the land-grant schools are giving attention to research, but have de-emphasized their duties of teaching and extension service. Further, the institutions are concerned over the decreasing portion of state funds spent on higher education.[127] Harl argues that the land-grant university "is on a trajectory that will narrow, dramatically, the traditional constituency of the land-grant university to the point of invisibility."[128]

Martin C. Jischke, president of Purdue University, addressed the National Association of State Universities and Land-Grant Colleges annual meeting in 2004 and pointed out the challenges these institutions face in the new century. At the time of Morrill's 1862 legislation, roughly 60 percent of all jobs were directly tied to agriculture; now the figure is less than 2 percent. Today, agriculture constitutes less than 10 percent of the enrollment at land-grant institutions, and, to serve modern agriculture, Jischke argued, the land-grant schools must give greater emphasis to engineering, technology, pharmacy, nursing and health science, management programs, and the liberal arts.[129] He argued further that the Department of Agriculture is "too slender a reed upon which to build our future" and that the land-grant university system has to reach out for research and engagement to other departments of the federal government, such as the Environmental Protection Agency, the National Institutes of Health, and the Department of Commerce.

Among the more than 4,000 accredited colleges and universities in the United States, the land-grant institutions have played an important role in the development of agricultural science, technology, engineering, and military science. In searching for their role in the twenty-first century, the land-grant colleges and universities will need to reach beyond agriculture, with more interdisciplinary programs, embracing a larger agenda. As Martin Jischke observed, the "land-grant universities cannot be synonymous with agriculture if they are to serve contemporary American and contemporary American agriculture, and if American agriculture is to grow and prosper."[130]

4

WOMEN'S RIGHT TO VOTE

The Nineteenth Amendment to the
U.S. Constitution (1919)

*Resolved, That it is the duty of the women of this
country to secure to themselves their sacred right to
the elective franchise.*

Declaration of Sentiments and
Resolutions, Seneca Falls (1848)

*Kaiser Wilson: Have You Forgotten Your Sympathy
With the Poor Germans Because They Were Not Self-Governed?
20,000,000 American Women Are Not Self-Governed.
Take the Beam Out of Your Eye.*

Suffragist banner outside
the White House (1918)

On March 3, 1913, Washington, D.C., was decked out for a celebration, eagerly awaiting the next day's inauguration of Woodrow Wilson as the twenty-eighth president of the United States. Buildings were festooned with streamers and bunting; thousands of dazzling electric lights were strung along the main thoroughfares. The nation's capital, as one reporter wrote, was a "gay, thronged city of fairyland."[1] Wilson and his entourage had slipped into the city, arriving at a strangely quiet Union Station at 3:45 in the afternoon. A few onlookers waved and clapped as the party headed to the Shoreham Hotel. "Where are the people?" Wilson asked, expecting a throng of well-wishers to greet him. "On the avenue, watching the suffragist parade," came the reply.[2] Woodrow Wilson had been upstaged. Just blocks away, lining Pennsylvania Avenue, were half a million people, the largest crowd ever assembled in Washington, watching 5,000 women march for the right to vote.

The march on Washington was planned by the feisty, young militant Alice Paul, designed to grab the headlines during the presidential inaugural festivities. Special trains had brought the suffragists from all over the country. In midwestern town squares and western state capitals there were send-off ceremonies and official well-wishes. The largest contingent came from New York; other New Yorkers, under the leadership of "General" Rosalie Jones, had forsaken the train and tramped on foot for fourteen days covering 250 miles from New York City to Washington.

The parade started at the Peace Monument on the west grounds of the Capitol and proceeded westward up Pennsylvania Avenue toward the White House. Awaiting the marchers, on the steps of the Treasury Department building, with its marble Greek columns, was a suffrage tableau. Six actresses portrayed allegorical figures, with eighty-seven young girls as their attendants. As the parade brochure noted, when the lead figure, Columbia, heard the approach of the parade, she would summon to her side Justice, Charity, Liberty, Peace, and Hope, and they would review the procession.

Grand Marshal Mrs. Richard Coke Burleson, mounted on her horse, gave the order to march. Newspaper accounts all noted the strikingly beautiful social reformer and lawyer Inez Milholland, wearing a flowing white robe, sitting astride a white horse, leading the parade.[3] A women's cavalry unit, dressed in white corduroy riding habits and plumed hats, rode alongside a wagon bearing an enormous sign: "We Demand an Amendment to the United States Constitution Enfranchising the Women of the Country." Next came a contingent from the National American Woman's Suffrage Association, led by its president Dr. Anna Howard Shaw. It was a brilliant, brisk day, with just enough crisp in the air to make marching enjoyable. Many women were riding, but most were on foot. Floats had been assembled to illustrate the seventy-five years of progress that the suffrage cause had achieved.

But soon there was trouble. By the time the marchers had reached Seventh Street, all order had broken down, and the suffragists were hemmed in by rowdy, drunken spectators who had broken through the cordoned lines. Some of the marchers were forced to walk single file through a wall of hostile onlookers. Worried about just such a scene, the U.S. Senate days earlier had passed a resolution to keep Pennsylvania Avenue clear, but that gesture had no effect on this surly crowd. Marchers were jeered, insulted, jostled and spat upon; many were injured, a dozen people had their arms broken, and many others fainted. In all, Washington Emergency Hospital had 175 ambulance calls and over 200 people had to be treated for wounds.

The suffragists and their supporters were furious, especially at the District of Columbia police. "Here, politically, we have long been treated as criminals and imbeciles," said one woman, "but what shall we say of the treatment we received yesterday? They would have taken better care of a drove of pigs being driven through the streets by some farmer than they did of us." Genevieve Stone, wife of Representative Claudius U. Stone (Democrat–Illinois), said a policeman insulted her by shouting, "If my wife were where you are, I'd break her head." Alice Paul complained that the Boy Scouts "were the only ones who did any effective police work." Ultimately, a detachment of Marines had to be brought in to dampen the riotous behavior and protect the marchers.

The next day, inauguration day, the Senate adopted two resolutions seeking to determine why the local police had failed to protect the marchers. Harriot

Stanton Blatch of the Woman's Political Union, returning to New York, sent a biting telegram to president-elect Wilson: "As you ride to-day in comfort and safety to the capital to be inaugurated as the President of the people of the United States, we beg that you will not be unmindful that yesterday the Government, which is supposed to exist for the good of all, left women, while passing in peaceful procession in their demand for political freedom, at the mercy of a howling mob on the very streets which are being at this moment so efficiently officered for the protection of men."

There was no comment from Wilson, nor any mention of woman suffrage or women's struggles in his inaugural address. In his short speech, Wilson concluded: "This is not a day of triumph; it is a day of dedication. Here muster, not the forces of party, but the forces of humanity. Men's hearts wait upon us; men's lives hang in the balance; men's hopes call upon us to say what we will do. Who shall live up to the great trust? Who dares fail to try? I summon all honest men, all patriotic, all forward-looking men, to my side. God helping me, I will not fail them, if they will but counsel and sustain me!"[4]

Wilson eventually came around to support the women's cause, but it would take another five years before the House of Representatives would approve the Nineteenth Amendment, another full year before the Senate endorsed it, and finally in August 1920 the thirty-sixth state, Tennessee, by the narrowest of margins ratified the amendment and made woman's suffrage the law of the land.

The journey was long, often exasperating, filled with both triumphs and setbacks. Those arguing for woman suffrage drew upon the solid democratic principles of equality and citizenship, but at times played on the fears of class distinction and racial superiority. The suffrage movement was led by a small cadre of remarkable, determined women, working together but at times at odds with one another, and by a grassroots movement that waxed and waned over the decades. It also attracted opponents, less well-known, but equally bent on preventing women from voting. The movement was at its beginning radical, then turned conservative, and, in the end, it embraced elements of militancy and political sophistication. National and local societies were formed, leaders endured the rigors of cross-country travel and went on national speaking tours, petition drives were launched, supporters marched on Washington, New York, state capitals and cities throughout the country. Supporters targeted congressmen who voted against suffrage and fought to have them defeated, they picketed the White House, engaged in hunger strikes, were arrested and thrown into jail.

In early 1918, Woodrow Wilson, now halfway through his second term as president, surprisingly announced his support for the Nineteenth Amendment, urged on wavering members of Congress, and, once it passed in Washington, cajoled governors and state legislative leaders to support its ratification. At last, 20 million women were eligible to vote in the national presidential elections of 1920. By this time, the early leaders of the drive for woman suffrage—Lucretia

Mott, Elizabeth Cady Stanton, Susan B. Anthony, Lucy Stone, and others—had been dead for decades. Carrie Chapman Catt, the leader of the principal suffrage organization at the time of ratification, bitterly recalled the long battle: over fifty-two years of political wrangling, woman's suffrage forces conducted 56 referendum campaigns, 480 campaigns to urge state legislatures to submit suffrage amendments to voters, 47 campaigns to include woman's suffrage in state constitutions, 277 fights to have political parties include woman suffrage in their platforms and 30 platform fights during presidential elections, and 19 campaigns in 19 successive Congresses spanning thirty-eighty years.[5] Theirs had been the longest sustained grassroots effort in American history, and the moment that started it all, the 1848 meeting at Seneca Falls, was for many a distant but proud memory.

Background

Eighteenth-century state constitutions made it clear who could vote and who could not. Pennsylvania, Maryland, Delaware, and North Carolina defined voters as "freemen"; Vermont used the designation "man"; Georgia chose "white male inhabitants," and South Carolina enfranchised "free white men." Only one state, New Jersey, had a gender-free designation. In its 1776 constitution, a New Jersey voter was defined as an adult inhabitant with a "worth of fifty pounds" who had lived in the state for one year. This meant that unmarried or widowed women were eligible to vote; married women, however, were excluded because the property of the family was in the husbands' names, not theirs. This suffrage provision was not a technical oversight nor did it merely slip through the cracks; the constitutional convention in New Jersey debated the issue and determined that unmarried women indeed should have the right to vote.[6] In 1790, that right was reaffirmed by statute. Both the Federalists and the Republican candidates actively courted women voters, particularly in the elections of 1800. Seven years later, however, New Jersey women lost their right to vote. Opponents of woman's suffrage claimed that women were susceptible to being manipulated and subject to fraud, and in 1807 the state legislature decided, for the "safety, quiet, good order and dignity of the state," to disenfranchise women.[7]

It took thirty-one more years before another state would permit even a limited version of woman suffrage. In 1838, the legislature of Kentucky permitted "widows with children of school age" the right to vote in school elections. The education and care of children was seen as a woman's role, and, for a majority of lawmakers, school suffrage seemed to be a proper, limited reform.[8]

While they did not have the vote, many women nonetheless were involved in political activities during these early years. The work that they did, however, was perceived not as political but as benevolent and charitable: providing social services for widows and orphans, health care for the indigent, assistance for the aged, launching fund raisers and organizing boycotts. While the women of benevolent societies in eighteenth-century America operated under a deferential mode of politics, their daughters, the reformists of the early nineteenth century, were not so quiescent and participated in a variety of civic activities. They organized pressure groups, transformed political parties, debated national and local politics, assisted candidates for office, edited partisan newspapers, and engaged in civil disobedience and fomented agitation.[9]

Women played a prominent role in the emerging abolitionist movement.[10] In 1833, several small anti-slavery societies scattered throughout New England and the Middle Atlantic states met in Philadelphia to form the American Anti-Slavery Society (AASS), with William Lloyd Garrison, and the Tappan brothers, Lewis and Arthur, as the founders. Many women had been members of the smaller regional societies, but at the Philadelphia meeting they were barred from membership in AASS and from signing the organization's "Declaration of Sentiments and Purposes." After AASS adjourned its meeting, about twenty women gathered, under the leadership of Lucretia Mott, to form the Philadelphia Female Anti-Slavery Society. Mott, then forty, had been a Quaker minister for twelve years, and was becoming increasingly involved in the abolitionist movement.

What followed was a rapid rise in women's involvement in anti-slavery agitation with a network of female anti-slavery societies developed by 1836. Women circulated and signed anti-slavery petitions by the tens of thousands and sent them to Washington protesting the gag rule imposed on any discussion of slavery within the halls of Congress. Special clerks had to be hired to handle the avalanche of petitions.[11]

Once women were accepted into AASS, Lucretia Mott became active in its Pennsylvania executive committee. Along with others, she organized the Anti-Slavery Convention of American Women, which held its 1838 convention in Pennsylvania Hall in Philadelphia. The meeting was interrupted by a pro-slavery mob and two days later Pennsylvania Hall was burned to the ground and Mott's own home was threatened. In March 1840, she was elected as a delegate from the militant wing of AASS to the British and Foreign (World) Anti-Slavery Convention held in London. A whole day of the convention was consumed in a debate on what to do with the women delegates. They were not given credentials and were forced to sit in an alcove, curtained off from the convention; the American women were joined by prominent British woman anti-abolitionists.

At the London convention, Lucretia Mott by chance met the young bride of delegate Henry B. Stanton. Elizabeth Cady Stanton, fifteen years younger than Mott, was not a delegate, but, as historian Louise M. Young observed, she was "exactly the right fuse for the older woman's practiced hand, ready with the spark."[12] Stanton later wrote that "woman's suffrage in England and America may be dated" from the sting and indignation of not being recognized at the London convention and the coming together of Stanton and Mott.[13] Stanton and Mott would not meet again until Seneca Falls eight full years later.

The organized abolitionist movement in the United States had ended with the split between the moderates and Garrisonian militants. While the movement was active, many women were involved and learned valuable lessons. Much later, Elizabeth Cady Stanton and Susan B. Anthony wrote that, in the early anti-slavery conventions, "the broad principles of human rights were so exhaustively discussed, justice, liberty, and equality, so clearly taught, that the women who crowded to listen, readily learned the lesson of freedom for themselves, and early began to take part in the debates and business affairs of all associations." The abolitionist movement also taught women how to turn the cause of women's rights into a political movement.[14]

During the summer of 1848, most Americans were concerned about the upcoming presidential elections and the war with Mexico. But in a small upstate town of Waterloo, New York, there was a different concern. Five women gathered around a tea table in mid-July. Elizabeth Cady Stanton, who lived in nearby Seneca Falls, spoke earnestly of her disappointment in the constricted roles that women of her age were forced into. Listening to Stanton were Lucretia Mott, her sister Martha Jane Wright, Jane Hunt, and Mary Ann McClintock.[15]

On July 14, the five women issued a Call to a Woman's Rights Convention "to discuss the social, civil and religious condition of women." Five days later, three hundred women and men attended the two-day meeting and produced a call to action, the Declaration of Sentiments and Resolutions. They deliberately copied Thomas Jefferson's preamble to the Declaration of Independence, adding just one word: "women." "We hold these truths to be self-evident," the Declaration of Sentiments read, in those familiar words, "that all men and women are created equal." Among the several resolutions, number nine stood out: "That it is the duty of women of this country to secure to themselves their sacred right to the elective franchise." It passed by a small margin, while other resolutions were approved unanimously.[16]

The convention, held in the Wesleyan Methodist chapel, was, in Stanton's words, "in every way a grand success."[17] But she and others were dumbfounded, just days afterwards, when their meeting and resolutions which they considered as "so timely, so rational, and so sacred," would be the subject of biting sarcasm and fierce ridicule by the press. Only abolitionist newspapers and Frederick Douglass stood by the signatories. One by one, many of the men and women who attended and signed the declaration withdrew their support. "Our friends," Stanton wrote, "gave us the cold shoulder and felt themselves disgraced by the whole proceeding."[18]

The Seneca Falls meeting drew the most attention and the most controversy, but soon there were women's conventions held in Rochester, New York, then in Salem, Ohio, and later in Indiana, Massachusetts, Pennsylvania, and New York City. Reform was in the air: not only were women talking about the right to vote, but also about reform of laws that placed onerous burdens upon them in the area of divorce, property rights, wages paid, and working conditions. They drew parallels between the condition of slaves and women, argued for increased access to education, wrote feminist tracts, and, with the introduction of "bloomers," loose-fitting "Turkish" pants under a knee-length skirt, women rebelled against current clothing fashion of heavy dresses, petticoats and whalebone stays.

These early meetings culminated with the first national women's convention in Worcester, Massachusetts, in October, 1850. The convention brought together the most famous feminists in America, including Lucretia Mott, Angelina Grimke, Paulina Wright Davis, Ernestine Rose, and Abby Kelley Foster. New voices came as well, particularly Sojourner Truth and Antoinette Brown. Several of the leading abolitionist men, Wendell Phillips, William Lloyd Garrison, Gerrit Smith and Frederick Douglass, spoke at the convention in support of women's rights. There was widespread press coverage, much of it unflattering. The *New York Herald* called the Worcester meeting "that motley gathering of fanatical radicals, old grannies, male and female, of fugitive slaves and fugitive lunatics, called the Woman's Rights Convention."[19]

Despite criticism and ridicule, the fledgling women's movement continued to hold annual conventions until 1860, missing only one year. In the early 1850s, the three most important voices in woman's suffrage for the second half of the eighteenth century would meet, work together, and later part ways.

Lucy Stone, the first woman from Massachusetts to earn a college degree, began her public speaking career in 1847. She was a spellbinding orator, who enthralled thousands at a time with her speeches on abolition and women's rights. She outdrew the leading star of the day, opera singer Jenny Lind, and became so famous that P. T. Barnum tried to hire her for a series of lectures in 1854.[20] Stone was one of the organizers of the first national convention in Worcester, and her speech in defense of women's rights at the closing of the convention electrified the audience. The country's most influential newspaper, Horace Greeley's *New York Tribune*, devoted extensive coverage to the entire two-day convention, including Stone's concluding speech. Those newspaper articles reached a wide audience. In England Harriet Taylor (who was soon to marry John Stuart Mill) read about the Worcester meeting, and wrote that the women of Sheffield, England, had presented a petition to the House of Lords demanding the right to vote. Another reader who was influenced by Stone's speech and the proceedings was a young school teacher and temperance advocate, Susan B. Anthony.[21]

By 1846, Susan B. Anthony, now twenty-six years old, became headmistress at Canajoharie Academy, a well-known boarding school in upstate New York. She pursued a long-standing family interest in the temperance movement and increasingly became interested in the abolitionist cause. Anthony had founded the Woman's State Temperance Society, and, once she became acquainted with Stone, Stanton, and Antoinette Brown, she became increasingly active in women's labor issues, women's rights, suffrage, as well. Anthony's confidence, determination, and speaking skills flourished by her association with these women and their activities.[22]

The third woman was the oldest and best known, Elizabeth Cady Stanton.[23] A cofounder of the Seneca Falls conference and a delegate at the 1840 London anti-slavery conference, Stanton advocated changes in New York's property laws and later created a sensation when she called for divorce reform at one of the 1860 national women's rights convention.

Through much of the mid-1850s, however, Anthony carried the burden of the women's movement. Much of her work concentrated on New York legislators to amend the Married Women's Property Law, which thanks in large part to her determined efforts was enacted in 1860. Through this law, women gained the right to own property separately from their husbands, engage in business transactions, handle their own money, sue and be sued, and be joint guardians of their children.[24] Stanton, now in her forties, had given birth to her sixth child, Harriot, and Stone was now married to abolitionist Henry Blackwell and gave birth to her first child, Alice. Both children would later become important feminist advocates and writers. With the approach of the Civil War, a decision had to be made: should women pour their energies into the war effort, demonstrating their loyalty to the Union, or should they press on for women's rights and suffrage? Stanton advocated the former, while Anthony argued that women must press for their rights no matter the wartime circumstances. The Stanton view prevailed and it was not until after the war that the federal government was prepared to open up the franchise. But many of the leaders of the woman's movement would be bitterly disappointed. The franchise would be expanded, but not for them.

At the end of the Civil War, the pressing matter of assimilating former slaves overshadowed woman's rights and suffrage issues. Feminists wholeheartedly supported the Thirteenth Amendment (1865), which declared slaves to be free and overruled the *Dred Scott* decision.[25] However, some woman's rights leaders—particularly Stanton and Anthony—were alarmed at the language of the proposed Fourteenth Amendment (1868). The amendment defined citizenship and nationalized privileges and immunities of citizens through the protections of due process and equal protection of law. But in section 2, dealing with representation, Congress deliberately added the word "male," leaving women, black and white, in constitutional limbo.[26] Anthony urged her abolitionist colleagues Senator Charles Sumner (Republican–Massachusetts) and Representative Thaddeus Stevens (Republican–Pennsylvania) to remove the word "male" from the amendment, but to no avail. Anthony and Stanton then drafted a petition for woman suffrage, collected 10,000 signatures, and presented it to Congress. But they ran into a wall of resistance from Radical Republicans and many of their abolitionist colleagues: woman's suffrage would have to wait. This was the "Negro's hour," not theirs.[27]

In May 1866 at the eleventh National Woman's Rights Convention in New York, a new organization was formed, the American Equal Rights Association (AERA), which pledged to fight for universal suffrage, the vote for both African-American men and all women. The AERA was the inspiration of Theodore

Tilton,[28] the young editor of the *Independent*. It was his idea to merge the American Anti-Slavery Society (AASS) with the woman's rights movement, and Stanton agreed. At her insistence, Lucretia Mott became AERA president, Stanton first vice-president, and Anthony the recording secretary. But Wendell Phillips, the leader of AASS, balked at the idea of a merger. He was determined that African-Americans should be given their voting and citizenship rights first. It was not simply a matter of enlightened interest in the welfare of black voters. Phillips and other Radical Republicans hoped that, by giving the vote to black men, who would vote overwhelmingly Republican, their party could retain its political power.[29]

While the states were still ratifying the Fourteenth Amendment, an important test of public opinion took place in Kansas, where voters in 1867 were considering referenda on Negro suffrage and woman suffrage. Kansas Republicans fought hard for Negro suffrage and against woman suffrage; Democrats opposed both. In the end, both measures lost by wide margins. The Kansas fight greatly strained the relationship between Anthony and Stanton, on the one hand, and AERA abolitionists, particularly Lucy Stone, on the other. The source of contention was Anthony and Stanton's unholy alliance with George Francis Train, a wealthy, flamboyant, publicity-seeking advocate of woman's suffrage, who also was an unrepentant racist demagogue who was bitterly opposed to giving black men the vote. In their last-ditch effort to sway the suffrage vote, Train accompanied Anthony throughout Kansas, funneled money into the cause, and helped for a time to finance Stanton's radical newspaper *The Revolution* in 1868.[30] It showed the lengths to which Stanton and Anthony were willing to go to support woman's suffrage and the depth of their alienation with former abolitionist and Republican allies.

The reform movement became further split over the Fifteenth Amendment. One group, under Charles Sumner and other long-time abolitionists argued that the Fifteenth Amendment should be limited to blacks. Another group, which included Lucy Stone and Henry Blackwell, argued they should try as hard as possible to incorporate woman suffrage into the amendment, but, if they failed to do so, go ahead and support the amendment and then try later for a woman's suffrage amendment. The third group were the hard-liners under Stanton and Anthony: if women were not included in the Fifteenth, then the amendment should be scuttled altogether.[31]

The Fifteenth Amendment was approved by both houses of Congress in February 1869, and sent to the states for ratification. Black males, and not women, were to be given constitutional protection: "The right of citizens of the United States to vote shall not be denied or abridged by the United States or by any State on account of race, color, or previous condition of servitude."

In May 1869, after Congress had approved the amendment but before its ratification by the states, resentment boiled over at the anniversary meeting of the American Equal Rights Association. On May 13, in Steinway Hall in New York City, Anthony appealed to her fellow delegates for universal suffrage, but, if that could not happen, then women, through a new Sixteenth Amendment, should have preference over former slaves and ignorant foreign men flooding to America's shores. "Think of Patrick and Sambo and Hans and Yung Tung, who do not know the difference between a monarchy and a republic, who cannot read the Declaration of Independence or Webster's spelling-book, making laws for Lucretia Mott" and other women leaders, Anthony said in scorn.[32]

Then spoke Frederick Douglass, a long-time friend of woman's suffrage. Politely Douglass said that he had come to the meeting more to listen than to speak, and he congratulated Stanton on her earlier speech calling for universal suffrage. He argued that the AERA delegates should indeed support the Fifteenth Amendment, because there was a much greater urgency for black votes than for women's votes. "With us," said Douglass, "the matter is a question of life and death, at least, in fifteen States of the Union. When women, because they are women, are hunted down through the cities of New Orleans; when they are dragged from their houses and hung upon lamp posts; when their children are torn from their arms and their brains dashed out upon the pavement; when they are objects of insult and outrage at every turn . . . then they have an urgency to obtain the ballot equal to our own."[33] Great applause followed, noted a *New York Times* reporter. Douglass added that he objected to the words "Sambo," "Paddy," and "Hans," but acknowledged that this was only "good-natured criticism." "Let us all come in; let us all have equal rights and equal political privileges," Douglass concluded.[34]

Others then had their say, but Anthony would not back down. The old antislavery school argued that "women must stand back and wait until the Negroes shall be recognized. But we say, if you will not give the whole loaf of suffrage to the entire people, give it to the most intelligent first. If intelligence, justice, and morality are to have precedence in the Government, let the question of woman be brought up first and that of Negro last."[35]

Two months earlier, on March 16, Representative George W. Julian (Republican–Indiana) submitted a joint resolution to Congress proposing that woman suffrage become the Sixteenth Amendment: His resolution declared that "the right of suffrage in the United States shall be based on citizenship" and that "all citizens . . . shall enjoy this right equally without any distinction or discrimination whatever founded on sex."[36] Anthony and other leaders had pinned their hopes on Julian's legislation, but Congress was in no mood to listen. The focus and success had been with black male votes. In March 1870, Secretary of State Hamilton Fish certified that twenty-nine states had ratified the Fifteenth Amendment, which now extended the franchise to all male citizens.[37]

Immediately after the May meeting of AERA, Stanton and Anthony created the National Woman Suffrage Association (NWSA), which would focus solely on the battle to enfranchise women. Lucy Stone would not go along, and the women's movement formally split. There were personal disagreements, hostility over George Francis Train, and the large rift concerning the Fifteenth Amendment and black suffrage. Stone and her associates founded their own rival organization, the American Woman Suffrage Association (AWSA) in October. Stanton and Anthony would not reunite with Stone for another twenty years.

Working together, Stanton and Anthony would spend the long, arduous years of the 1870s through the end of the century, fighting for women's causes. It was a remarkable team. As historian Judith E. Harper observed, "Anthony was the incomparable administrator, the doer, the propulsive force . . . Stanton was the thinker, the writer, and the rhetorician."[38]

Suffragists also tried a new tactic. During the early 1870s, Anthony and a number of other women decided to take direct action and challenge the ambiguous meaning of the Fourteenth Amendment. They were encouraged by Francis Minor, a lawyer from St. Louis, who suggested that the newly ratified Fourteenth Amendment gave women a means to assert their right to vote. The Fourteenth Amendment stated that "All persons born or naturalized in the United States . . . are citizens of the United States . . . No State shall make or enforce any law which shall abridge the privileges or immunities of citizens of the United States." Minor claimed that women were equal in citizenship to men and thus entitled to vote. In 1872 Minor's wife, Virginia, a leader of the Missouri suffrage movement, brought suit against the voting registrar for failing to allow her to vote. The case ultimately reached the U.S. Supreme Court in 1875, and, for the woman suffrage cause, its ruling was disastrous. In *Minor* v. *Happersett*,[39] a unanimous Supreme Court ruled that voting had nothing to do with the rights of national citizenship as protected under the new Fourteenth Amendment. The Court took a narrow and, at the time, accurate view of voting and citizenship, but failed to grapple with the larger issue: can a country which excludes over 50 percent of its citizens truly be considered a democracy?[40]

This decision, so resounding in its unanimity, helped focus the attention of suffragists on drafting a constitutional amendment protecting their rights. For the woman's suffrage movement, however, the tide was turning away from them. The mid-century pro-democratic sentiment had crested, and was now falling away.[41]

The following decades were bleak for the woman enfranchisement movement. Yet, there was some local progress in partial enfranchisement. Kansas entered the Union in 1861 and gave all adult women the right to vote on school elections, but denied them full suffrage in that bitter 1867 referendum. In the 1870s, Michigan, Minnesota, New Hampshire, Oregon, and Massachusetts offered limited local suffrage, while nine other states introduced similar legislation. Montana allowed women to vote on local budget issues and Kansas, beginning in 1887, also offered local municipal suffrage.[42]

In 1874, a temperance movement began to emerge in the Midwest, through the creation of the Women's Christian Temperance Union (WCTU). With strong religious overtones, the temperance movement grew dramatically, winning converts, shutting down thousands of saloons. The temperance movement drew far more activists than did the suffrage movement. There was some cross-over. Frances Willard, the dynamic second president of the WCTU, openly called for women to be able to vote on issues concerning local alcohol restrictions. Some suffragists welcomed the additional forces of the temperance movement, but others were worried that mixing temperance with suffrage could only give the enemies of women's vote another reason to oppose them.[43]

First Efforts in Congress

In December 1866, Congress took its first vote on woman suffrage on a bill to extend the voting right to African-American men in the District of Columbia. Senator Edgar Cowan (Republican–Pennsylvania) moved to strike the word "male" from the provision, thus prompting the first debate in Congress on woman suffrage. His motion, however, failed, with just nine senators voting in favor and thirty-seven voting against.[44] Then, in March 1869, George Julian submitted his proposed Sixteenth Amendment. In an increasing conservative political climate, Julian's constitutional amendment would go nowhere.

Nine years later, in 1878, Senator Aaron A. Sargent (Republican–California) introduced a new Sixteenth Amendment to the Constitution, called the Susan B. Anthony Amendment. Penned by Anthony herself, the text read: "The right of citizens to vote shall not be abridged by the United States or any State on account of sex." Nothing came of his proposal, but it was destined to be introduced in Congress every year for the next forty-one years until it was finally passed in 1919.

In 1882, both Houses of Congress appointed select committees on woman's suffrage and both reported favorably, but it took nearly five years before there was a recorded vote. On January 25, 1887, the Senate took that first vote, and woman's suffrage was defeated, 34 to 16; twenty-five senators were absent from the vote. In an editorial, the *Washington Post* noted that, for nineteen years, the National Women's Rights Association had held its sessions in Washington. "These persistent, remarkable women, had pressed the matter before Congress, repeatedly, only to be disappointed. There is something at once sublime and pathetic in their persistence. They are undismayed. Opposition is nothing. Defeat and overthrow is nothing." But, the *Post* declaimed, voting is not a right, it is a concession. These women have wasted their energies on Congressmen, mere "men of straw." They should be out there in the states, large and populous states like Massachusetts, Georgia, or Ohio. Make their case in the states, because Congress would not run the risk of creating a constitutional amendment protecting them.[45] The *New York Times* likewise chastised the suffragists: "It is, with all due respect to the advocates of woman suffrage, absurd to ask Congress to propose an amendment on this point requiring the assent of three-fourths of the States, when not a single State has adopted unqualified woman suffrage."[46]

Granted, the territories of Wyoming (1869), Utah (1870), and Washington (1883) had permitted full woman suffrage, but it would be another six years before a state, Colorado in 1893, would do so. The sentiments of the *Washington Post* and *New York Times* reflected the mood in Congress: if women want the vote, then they had better go out to the states and get it for themselves, and not bother trying to convince Congress.

But Congress had already made several decisions about national voting policy. First was the Fifteenth Amendment; then, in the 1880s, Congress passed legislation dealing with the voting rights of Indians and Mormons. In February 1887, the Dawes Severalty or General Allotment Act set the conditions for Indian citizenship and guaranteed those living on allotted lands and who were willing to adopt the habits of "civilized life" the same rights and privileges of other American citizens. Utah presented a different picture. Critics charged that here was a territory that embraced a most liberal view of women's rights, the right to vote, but at the same time permitted polygamy, the most enslaving of a circumstances for married women.[47] The next month, Congress passed the Edmunds–Tucker Act, which disenfranchised women in Utah; this was one of several measures aimed at punishing Utah for the continued practice of polygamy. While the National Woman Suffrage Association, Susan B. Anthony, and Belva Lockwood lobbied in defense of women's right to vote in Utah, the Women's Christian Temperance Union and anti-polygamy associations campaigned for the disenfranchisement of Utah women.[48] These two laws in 1887—one granting voting rights to Indians and the other stripping it from Utah women—convinced some suffragists that Congress did indeed have the power to create a national solution to voting, and the federal government could be the vehicle for adopting a nationwide policy for woman suffrage.[49]

But progress towards woman's suffrage in Congress was maddeningly slow. It was not until January 1887 that the Senate took its first vote on woman suffrage, with the amendment losing 16 to 34. Over the years, the Senate committee reported out the amendment to the full body twelve times, usually with a favorable report, and finally in 1917 with a unanimous favorable vote. In the House, the committee reported out in ten different sessions, but with some adverse or no recommendations. There were no further recorded votes in either chamber until 1914, when the Senate voted 35 to 34 in favor. But a simple majority would not do. This was legislation proposing a constitutional amendment and required a two-thirds vote. The next year, the House had its very first recorded vote on the subject, with the amendment easily defeated 174 to 204.[50]

The Passing of the Suffragist Pioneers

By the first years of the twentieth century, the first and second generation of suffragist and woman's rights leaders had passed from the scene. The women were remarkable in many ways, but particularly for their determination, stamina, and longevity. The oldest, Lucretia Mott, born in 1793, was active until the end of her life, dying at the age of eighty-seven in 1880. Lucy Stone, born in 1818, was the chairman of the reunited National Woman's Suffrage Association when she was seventy-two, and gave her last public address at the World's Columbian Exposition in Chicago shortly before her death in 1893. Sojourner Truth, born in 1797, petitioned President Ulysses Grant to give freed slaves western lands; she was seventy-three at the time, and lived another thirteen years until 1883.

Elizabeth Cady Stanton, born in 1815, was still active in the late 1890s. In early 1892, at the age of seventy-six, she spoke before the House Committee on the Judiciary, delivering her masterful statement on feminist ideology, a powerful speech entitled "The Solitude of Self." Congress reprinted ten thousand copies of her address.[51] When she was eighty years old, Stanton published part I of *The Woman's Bible*, a work that reflected her firm belief that organized religion repressed women. Published in 1895, it became an immediate, and controversial, best-seller. Stanton wanted to correct biblical passages that were demeaning to women, and point out errors and prejudices of male biblical writers and clergymen. The publication sparked immediate public debate and outcry: conservatives labeled it blasphemous and worse, and Stanton was branded as a heretic. But *The Woman's Bible* also upset tradition-minded suffragists, and, at the next year's NAWSA board meeting, the suffrage leaders voted to censure Stanton.[52] Twenty years later, Stanton's controversial book would be used by anti-suffragists to show how radical this woman and her movement were.

Susan B. Anthony, born in 1820, retired from the National American Woman Suffrage Association at the age of eighty, and lived six years into the new century. She never lost her fire or determination. On November 15, 1904, shortly after Theodore Roosevelt had been elected to a full term as president, Anthony, Ida Husted Harper, and Harriet Taylor Upton met with him at the White House. Anthony, now eighty-four and in frail health, pleaded: "Mr. Roosevelt, this is my principal request—it is almost the last request I shall ever make of anybody. Before you leave the presidential chair, recommend Congress to submit to the legislatures a constitutional amendment which will enfranchise women, and thus take your place in history with Lincoln, the great emancipator. I beg of you not to close your term of office without doing this."[53] Despite the flattery and comparison with Lincoln, Roosevelt gave no assurances and sent no suffrage measure to Congress.

Less than two years later, in 1906, in the last days of her life, Anthony received a seemingly endless outpouring of congratulatory letters and telegrams marking her eighty-sixth birthday. She said only, "When will the men do something besides extend congratulations? I would rather have President Roosevelt say one word to Congress in favor of amending the Constitution to give women the suffrage than to praise me endlessly!"[54]

New Century

In the late 1880s, Lucy Stone softened her criticism of Susan Anthony, and extended an olive branch to her. Stone proposed a merger of the more conservative American Woman Suffrage Association with the Anthony–Stanton National Woman's Suffrage Association. There were lingering suspicions and hard feelings, but Anthony was determined to accept the peace offering. A new organization emerged in 1890, the National American Woman Suffrage Association (NAWSA), with Stanton elected president, Anthony vice-president at large, and Stone as chair of the executive committee. NAWSA concentrated on state suffrage campaigns during this era, and two new leaders emerged, Anna Howard Shaw and Carrie Chapman Catt.

It became clear by the late 1890s that Carrie Chapman Catt had the leadership and political skills to run NAWSA. She had served as chair of its organizing committee, had participated in twenty hearings before Congress, and was an excellent speaker. However, Catt irritated some of the old guard whom she saw as weak or ineffective. In 1900 she succeeded Anthony to the presidency of NAWSA. Anthony admired Catt, and wrote to a friend in 1901 about her protege: "I know of no other woman with leisure, with no children, with a husband who backs her morally and financially, with the brains and disposition to do for the sake of the cause, and seemingly no personal ambition, but Mrs. Catt."[55]

Catt was shocked to find that the organization had so atrophied during the last years of Anthony's leadership. She served as president of NAWSA for four difficult years; tirelessly she spoke throughout the country and raised money, but, at the end of her term in 1904, was exhausted. Her health had suffered; her mother was ill, and her husband did not have long to live. The leadership of NAWSA was turned over to Dr. Anna Howard Shaw, a long-time lieutenant to Anthony. All along, Shaw had assumed that she would succeed Anthony in 1900 but was bitterly disappointed when Anthony chose Catt as her replacement.[56] Catt later effused praise on Howard, calling her the "greatest orator among women the world has ever known."[57]

During the presidency of Anna Shaw, from 1905 to 1914, NAWSA increased its membership and money poured in, but there was a growing sense of frustration from young suffragists, in particular, that the movement had lost momentum, that legislatures and voters in too many states were defeating suffrage referendums. The frustration mounted, and there were increasing calls to bring back Catt to lead the organization. During the intervening twelve years, Catt had concentrated her efforts on the presidency of the International Women's Suffrage Alliance, and from 1909 through 1911 embarked on a world tour helping women fight for the right to vote. Catt became an international celebrity and one of the most recognized voices in the woman's suffrage movement.[58] In 1914, the criticism of Howard and her organization became particularly evident when the young militant Alice Paul and her supporters broke off from NAWSA to form a more radical organization, the National Woman's Party.

At the state level, woman suffrage was most successful in the West. By 1915, ten western states[59] had granted women the full right to vote; however, none of the southern, midwestern, or eastern states permitted full participation. A number of states, including those outside the West, granted women the right to vote in school board elections or other local contests. Why the West? Sociologists Holly J. McCammon and Karen E. Campbell argue that woman suffrage came first to the West because of the political mobilizing for woman suffrage but also because of greater political and gender opportunities available to women in that part of the country. Western women were moving into education and the professions, blurring the lines between men and women and making the move toward woman suffrage an easier transition. There was also in the West a stronger sense of populism, less complicated rules for voter reform, and the lack of a politically entrenched opposition to woman suffrage than found in the South or in eastern big-city political machines.[60] Woman suffrage grass-roots campaigns were strong in the East, but they met with strong resistance from anti-suffragist women and other interests opposed to extending the right to vote.

The Antis

Momentum stalled in part because of the activities of the anti-suffragist forces. Organized opposition to woman suffrage first appeared in 1869 when Congress considered the first attempt at a constitutional amendment. Madeleine V. Dahlgren, Eleanor E. Sherman, and Almira L. Phelps presented a petition to Congress in 1873, allegedly with 15,000 signatures, protesting the extension of suffrage to women.[61] In the same year, opponents were fighting a woman's suffrage proposal in the Massachusetts legislature. Two hundred women signed a petition objecting to the Massachusetts proposal, arguing that woman suffrage would divide the household, and diminish the dignity and moral purity of womankind. The legislature decided not to take action.

Fourteen years later, another woman's suffrage proposal came up in Massachusetts and met considerable resistance. After this battle, the anti-suffragists were determined to stay together, and formed an organization called the Boston Committee of Remonstrants and by 1890 published an annual, then quarterly, publication called *Remonstrance*. The Antis, or Remonstrants, organized as the Massachusetts Association Opposed to Further Extension of the Suffrage to Women and spread their conservative viewpoint to other states.[62] In a non-binding suffrage referendum in 1895, the Antis collaborated with the Man Suffrage Association, and outmaneuvered the suffragists forces. To better assess public opinion the legislature permitted woman and well as men to vote in this referendum. The Antis encouraged women not to vote, and, when the referendum was defeated, they gleefully pointed to the lack of women's interest to vote, even when they had the chance.[63]

In 1911, under the leadership of Josephine Dodge and Minnie Bronson, the National Association Opposed to Woman Suffrage (NAOWS) was formed, with its headquarters in New York City. Both Dodge and Bronson were powerful speakers, well-known for their lectures and rallies throughout the nation. The Antis were strongest in the urban and industrialized states of the East and New England.[64] As historian Jane Jerome Camhi describes them, the anti-suffragists for the most part were "urban, wealthy, native born, Republican and Protestant—members of established families either by birth or marriage, or both."[65]

The Antis printed thousands of pamphlets, fliers, and tracts, aimed at the general public, and specific groups such as farmers' or women's clubs; they even took out ads in the freshman Red Book at Harvard College and bought advertising in the game-day programs of the Boston Red Sox and Boston Braves. They adopted the red (or pink) rose as their symbol, and their pamphlets were printed in pink. The Antis petitioned and spoke before the legislatures, infiltrated and sometimes disrupted pro-suffrage meetings, and were especially active during statewide suffrage referendums. Anti-suffragists portrayed themselves as the defender of home, domesticity, and women's honor; and they made sure others knew how fortunate women were to be under the legal protection of men.[66]

The anti-suffrage movement reached its peak of influence from the mid-1890s through about 1910. One indication of their strength was the fate of their opponents' efforts. From 1898 through 1909, woman suffragists absorbed 164 defeats, with proposals bottled up in state legislatures throughout the country.[67]

Up until 1917, the anti-suffragist argument focused on a "sentimental vision" of Home, Mother, God, and the Constitution.[68] Women were linked to the home and their profession, by their sex, as full-time homemakers and mothers. They argued that God had created men and women with different roles and different places in society. Woman was a complement to man; she was man's helper. This was not a position of social inferiority, the Antis argued, but insured woman's superiority provided she remained in her assigned sphere and role. Further, women had distinctive biological traits different from men. Femininity strongly suggested emotionalism, illogic, and idealism; masculine traits represented judgment, practicality, and hard-headedness. Women were also too delicate to withstand the rigors of public life; if a woman were active in political life, she might neglect her children and her duties at home. Within the home itself, the woman, as homemaker and mother, was the leader; but, to the outside world, there was, and could be, just one spokesman, and that was the husband and father.[69]

There was a major shift in the rhetoric of the anti-suffragist movement when NAOWS moved to Washington, D.C., in 1917, to take up the suffrage fight in Congress. Its new leader was Alice Wadsworth, the wife of Senator James Wadsworth, Jr. (Republican–New York). More men were appointed to the executive committee and the official paper changed its name from *Woman's*

Protest to *Woman Patriot*. Historian Kristy Maddux noted that the organization broadened its focus from simply stopping the passage of the Nineteenth Amendment to a broader defense of the conservative status quo and to fight against what it considered radicalism.[70] Part of their strategy was to focus on Stanton's *Woman's Bible*. The *Woman's Bible*, the Antis claimed, was a revolutionary writing: it attacked the sacred original Bible and its authors, and called for a new religion, based on feminism. It did not take too many steps to link the radical writings of Stanton and the suffrage movement with feminism, socialism, and even Bolshevism.[71] All, the Antis argued, were evil, all demanded radical change, and all had to be defeated.

There were other forces that worked to defeat woman suffrage, but not necessarily allies of the anti-suffragist women. Historian Thomas J. Jablonsky notes that the women found themselves in the company of people "whom they not only did not admire but at times openly scorned."[72] Suffragist organizations were convinced that the anti-suffragist forces were being supported and perhaps manipulated by the liquor industry. Liquor producers and distributors were fighting against the forces of the Women's Christian Temperance Union and the Anti-Saloon League, and saw the suffrage movement as a natural ally of the prohibitionists. They were not allies, but charges and accusations were hurled from all directions. Suffragists condemned the liquor lobby for abetting the anti-suffragists; the liquor lobby accused the suffragists and prohibitionist of working together.[73]

The women anti-suffragists found allies in the Roman Catholic church hierarchy, which, while never coming out with an official doctrine against woman suffrage, let it be known that it did not sympathize with the suffrage efforts. Immigrant groups, particularly German-Americans, Bohemians, Russians, Italians, and some Scandinavians also opposed suffrage. For many, this violated the long-standing cultural norms of *Kinder, Kuche, und Kirche*—that women were to raise the children, cook the meals, and be the moral force of the family. Immigrant groups were reminded that much of the early suffragist rhetoric pointed to the dangers of giving the vote to the great masses of unwashed and illiterate immigrant men.[74] Much of the opposition came from settled immigrant Catholic communities in the industrial northeast.

Opposition also came from the South, where many associated woman suffrage with the abolitionist movement of the late antebellum period, and the fears and suspicions of the "Negro problem." If the Nineteenth Amendment became a reality, the balance of power in many southern communities could turn on black women voting. Of even greater concern was the possibility that this Nineteenth Amendment would do what the Fifteenth Amendment failed to do: give black males protection and possibly encouragement to vote. The Yankees would once again exact revenge. The *Clarion-Ledger* in Jackson, Mississippi, claimed in 1919 that white women in Mississippi were so wild and crazy about the ballot that they forgot that the amendment "would make their cooks and washerwomen voters."[75] In the U.S. Senate, Ellison D. Smith

(Democrat–South Carolina) argued that the South considered the Fifteenth Amendment to be a crime against civilization and that adding another amendment would permit "an alien and ignorant race to be turned loose on us." His colleague, Park Trammell (Democrat–Florida) acknowledged that, in his state, the black vote was negligible, and announced his opposition to "any proposal which would possibly invite greater and more extensive participation in our election on the part of the Negro population."[76]

Some political leaders did not object to having white women vote, and emphasized that the best solution would be a states rights decision: let each state decide for itself. The threat of universal suffrage boiled down to a threat to the dominant white male power structure. It was a threat to the Democratic Party because it was feared that enfranchised blacks would flock to the Republican Party, possibly breaking up the solid Democratic South. Democratic leaders only had to count heads to see the potential of black voting. In Mississippi and South Carolina, the black population exceeded the white population and there were 219 southern counties where blacks outnumbered whites in the 1920 census.[77]

The suffragist leaders knew that they had to be very cautious with the South. If the South remained solid and voted as a bloc against a federal amendment, they would have enough strength to block ratification, particularly if the border states joined in. National leaders saw clearly how difficult their problem would be when two prominent suffragist leaders from the South, Laura Clay of Kentucky and Kate Gordon of Louisiana, withdrew from NAWSA and opposed a federal constitutional amendment, fearing federal takeover of voting and the enfranchisement of black women. In 1913, Gordon founded the Southern States Woman Suffrage Conference which fought for woman's suffrage on a state-by-state basis.[78]

Turning to Washington

Suffrage was not the only concern of activist women. They were becoming increasingly vocal as they chafed under dreadful working conditions, long hours, and low wages. By 1909, thousands of women were on strike in the garment industry. In Chicago, Philadelphia, New York, and Lowell, Massachusetts, there had never been strikes of this size or duration. Women and men were beaten and arrested; thousands joined them in sympathy strikes and protests.[79]

Some of the tactics used by striking workers found their way into the suffrage movement. Elizabeth Cady Stanton's daughter, Harriot Stanton Blatch, created in 1907 the Women's Political Union, an organization more radical than NAWSA. Blatch, a graduate of Vassar College, moved to Europe, married an Englishman, William Henry Blatch, and became involved in socialist politics. When her mother died in 1902, she returned to the U.S., hoping to use her growing political skills and knowledge of the more militant English version of suffrage mass politics. Her biographer called Blatch "modern suffragism's first great politician."[80]

In 1910, the Women's Political Union held the first suffrage parade in New York City, and, the following year, its parade grew to three thousand marchers and seventy thousand onlookers. Then came the tragedy of the Triangle Shirtwaist Company fire: 146 women, mostly young immigrants, trapped on the ninth floor of the Asch building in Washington Square, had died from asphyxiation, from burns, or from leaping to their death. When asked why the women did not have fire protection, a Tammany leader bluntly said, "They ain't got no votes."[81] On a rainy, cold day in April, 1911, nearly a half million persons marched through Washington Square Arch, silently mourning their deaths. This tragedy was one of the sparks that led female labor leaders, like Leonora O'Reilly, to insist that women be given the power to vote. The following year, the New York City suffragist parade swelled to twenty thousand marchers and nearly a half million onlookers.[82]

NAWSA president Anna Howard Shaw had seen a suffragist parade in England in 1907, and in the following year derided such spectacles as a "kindergarten method of demonstrating to the manhood of the world that woman should be free." But she soon changed her mind, and suffrage parades became commonplace: with yellow banners and ribbons for NAWSA supporters, purple, white and green for Harriot Blatch's Women's Political Union, and purple and white for Alice Paul's Woman's Party. The suffragists also displayed elaborate pageants and *tableux vivantes*, with costumed figures dramatizing the plight or the aspirations of women.[83]

In both 1914 and 1915, both houses of the Massachusetts legislature had passed a suffrage amendment by the needed two-thirds margin. Suffragists were optimistic that the measures would also be accepted by the voters, and the anti-suffragists, who had a long history of strong opposition in Massachusetts redoubled their efforts. The Antis held large rallies, raised $61,300 to fund their campaign. The tide seemed to be turning toward the suffragist side: there was growing support for women's vote from the pulpit and the press, and suffragists were able to raise $106,967 for their efforts. But, in the end, the suffragists were crushed, receiving only 35.5 percent of the vote in Massachusetts in 1915. On the same day, suffragists lost in Pennsylvania and New York, and one month later, lost again in New Jersey.[84] The loss in crucial New York was especially bitter. Carrie Catt had taken charge of the New York suffrage effort in 1912 through 1914, and Harriot Stanton Blatch had battled there for the 1915 referendum. It was time, everyone agreed, to change tactics.

Catt resumed the presidency of the NAWSA in 1915. At an emergency meeting held in Atlantic City, New Jersey, in 1916, Catt outlined a new tactic to push forward the suffrage movement. Catt, frustrated like many others with the slow, piecemeal progress at the state level, was determined to concentrate forces and focus on getting a constitutional amendment passed through Congress. It was time to end the state-by-state battles and go for a national amendment, by convincing members of Congress of the rightness of woman's suffrage. She presented to NAWSA a political outline called "The Winning Plan." NAWSA headquarters would be moved to Washington, efforts would focus on a federal amendment, and senators and congressmen who were foes of suffrage would be targeted for defeat. The delegates to the NAWSA convention enthusiastically endorsed Catt's vision and her initiative, and she won the endorsement of outgoing president Anna Shaw as well.[85]

There were risks involved. Several of the outspoken southern suffragists leaders, especially Kate Gordon and Laura Clay, worried that people from the South would object to having another constitutional amendment rammed down their throats like the Fifteenth and the Fourteenth Amendments. There still were too many raw feelings from the post-Civil War era to remind southerners of Yankee edicts.[86]

Blatch and her Women's Political Union pressed for a broad range of reforms, not content to narrowly focus on suffrage. Blatch believed firmly that the way to woman's suffrage victory was through the vast numbers of working women, the wage-earning women who were becoming so much more numerous.[87]

Into this mix of woman's political leadership came a third woman, who made Blatch's tactics and actions appear tame. Alice Paul, who, like Blatch, had experience in the British struggle for suffrage and had spent time in jail for hunger strikes and civil disobedience, came to Washington in 1913, at the age of twenty-eight. She had just completed her doctorate at the University of Pennsylvania, and came to work for the NAWSA's Congressional Committee. She was charismatic, brash, and eager for change. She found the committee too slow, too conservative, and set up her own, semi-autonomous Congressional Union to focus on the amendment ratification. Anna Shaw, in her last year as president of NAWSA, was upset by what she saw as the divisiveness, disloyalty, and militancy of Alice Paul and her colleague, Lucy Burns. After some bitter encounters, the NAWSA board asked Paul to resign in 1914. She did, and took loyalists from the Congressional Union with her. By 1916, Harriot Blatch's Women's Political Union had merged with the Congressional Union, and their cause was aided by the wealthy patron Alva Belmont. The following year, Alice Paul established the National Woman's Party.[88]

Carrie Catt and Nellie Shuler wrote that the suffragist lobbying forces constituted the largest lobbying force ever maintained in the nation's capital. Toward the end of their fight, NAWSA women came in waves, groups of dozens, fifties, and hundreds from all parts of the country. Under the leadership of chief lobbyist Maud Wood Park, they got to know Congress. They learned "its way of work, its machinery; its tricks; the men in it, their pet foibles, their fundamental weaknesses, their finer abilities, their human quality." The women also learned of the "cheap bi-partisanship that dominates the Congress; its insensate capacity to block justice for party advantage."[89]

In terms of policy advocacy, the suffragists did not have a uniform point of advocacy. As historian Gayle Veronica Fischer has written, the suffragists "ranged from conservative to radical in what they hope to achieve through the vote, and they ranged from conservative to militant in the methods they employed to get the vote."[90]

What brought widespread attention were the tactics employed by Alice Paul and her associates. They picked the White House, flying banners that chided and cajoled Wilson, they burned Wilson in effigy, were arrested, and engaged in hunger strikes. Suffragists had used street rallies, marches, were pioneers in using films, plays, and slide shows. NAWSA and the Women's Political Union contracted with movie companies to produce three melodramas and a comedy about suffrage. In 1919 the National Woman's Party sent off a Prison Special train, with women who had been imprisoned, wearing copies of their prison garb.[91]

Wilson on Suffrage

Woodrow Wilson held conventional Victorian views of women, believing that the ideal woman was a "homemaker, helpmate, and genial hostess." He was contemptuous of career women, and his views were shared and reinforced by his first wife Ellen Louise Axson Wilson, who was born in Rome, Georgia. In 1911, when cornered by reporters while campaigning for the presidency in California, Woodrow Wilson stated that suffrage was "not a national issue, so far. It is a local issue for each State to settle for itself."[92] Wilson was quiet and noncommittal about suffrage during his first years in office. He said nothing publicly after that large suffrage parade upstaged his March 1913 inauguration. But with that parade, its spectacle, and the violence, came front-page headlines across the country. Suffrage was now back in the news. Four days after his inauguration, a delegation of women led by Alice Paul came to the White House to make its case for a constitutional amendment. Wilson said that he had no opinion on the matter of woman suffrage, but that he would give it his utmost consideration.

On April 7, the opening day of Congress, another mass demonstration was held at the Capitol. Women delegates, representing each of the 435 congressional districts, carried petitions from suffrage supporters back home. The woman's suffrage amendment was in both houses, and, for the first time in over a quarter century, there was debate on the floor of the Senate on the subject.[93]

In December of that year, Wilson met with a group of fifty-five women from NAWSA. He implied that he personally endorsed woman suffrage but would not make a public statement because the Democratic Party had not taken a stand on the issue.[94] Then October 1915 Wilson publicly declared that he intended to vote for woman's suffrage in a special referendum in New Jersey. While this certainly was welcome news, overall 1915 was a particularly difficult year for pro-suffrage forces: they had lost ballot issues in Massachusetts, New York, Pennsylvania, and Wilson's New Jersey by comfortable margins.[95]

126

The 1916 platform of the Democratic Party, written primarily by Wilson, recommended the extension of the franchise to women, but through the states; it did not mention or endorse a constitutional amendment.[96] During this presidential election year, Wilson and his opponent, Charles Evans Hughes, were personally asked about their suffrage policy. On June 17, a deputation from NAWSA met Hughes in New York. Hughes, a former governor of New York and associate justice of the U.S. Supreme Court, stated quite frankly that he approved of a constitutional amendment but wanted to hold it in confidence until he was formally nominated by the Republican Party; on August 1, Hughes then issued a public declaration of support. Wilson, visited by a NAWSA delegation that same day, reiterated his belief: the answer must come from the states. Hughes declined an invitation to the NAWSA annual convention in Atlantic City, but Wilson agreed to come. Catt and Shuler believe that Wilson's conversion to the woman's suffrage cause came at that momentous gathering. Wilson said to the assembled members, "I have come to fight not for you but with you, and in the end I think we shall not quarrel over the method." Dr. Anna Shaw ended the evening by saying, "We have waited so long, Mr. President. We have dared to hope that our release might come in your administration and that yours would be the voice to pronounce the words to bring our freedom." According to Catt and Shuler, the great audience rose to its feet, without a word, every eye on the president: "silent, unmoving, the audience stood, a spellbound living petition to the most influential man in the nation—the President of the United States." From that moment, Wilson never declined an invitation nor turned away a delegation from NAWSA.[97]

Making the Law

On April 2, 1917, Congress convened for a special war session. The infamous Zimmerman telegram[98] had been made public in February, German submarines were sinking American vessels, and, on April 6, the United States declared war on Germany. Congress was determined to limit its deliberations to wartime emergency efforts, and the suffragists were equally determined to make the amendment a part of the war effort. Prior to the session, the NAWSA executive council met in Washington, pledged its loyalty in the event of war, and offered its services to the country. With idealism and talk of democracy so much in the air, NAWSA decided to make a concerted effort to appeal to Congress for the immediate adoption of the suffrage amendment. Hundreds of thousands of letters and telegrams poured into Congress. NAWSA leaders also vowed that, if the Sixty-Fifth Congress failed to submit a suffrage amendment before the next congressional elections, they would adopt Carrie Catt's Winning Plan and work for the defeat of reluctant legislators. This was also the historic occasion when Jeannette Pickering Rankin (Republican–Montana) was sworn into office on April 2, the first woman elected to Congress.

Suffrage amendments were introduced in both the House and the Senate. For the first time, the Senate Suffrage Committee voted unanimously for passage of the amendment. Until this point, there was no suffrage committee in the House of Representatives. The Rules Committee had routinely blocked any move to create such a body, but on September 14, 1917, the House, after years of ceaseless agitation, voted to create its own Woman Suffrage Committee. It was chaired by John E. Raker (Democrat–California) and ten of its thirteen members were committed to a federal amendment.[99]

Congress could look to the states to gauge the growing pro-suffrage sentiment. While it was a mixed year for state suffrage action, for the most part there was forward movement. Earlier in the year, the state legislatures of Indiana, Michigan, Nebraska, Rhode Island, and Ohio each granted women suffrage. Limited suffrage was approved in Arkansas, but a referendum was defeated in Maine, and the earlier action by the Ohio legislature was defeated in a statewide referendum. Then came the most important state suffrage vote, the decisive passage of a suffrage bill in New York state in November 1917. Under the leadership of Mary Garrett Hay, the New York suffragists convinced Democratic Tamany Hall to adopt a "hands-off" policy and not oppose the bill. With the New York City political machine neutralized, suffrage passed, despite continued upstate opposition. Carrie Catt marked the New York victory as the "Gettysburg of the woman suffrage movement."[100] The momentum seemed to be with the suffragists. As Catt and Shuler wrote, after the New York victory of woman suffrage, "up and down and across the nation resistance began to crumple."

In early 1918, the House of Representatives decided to take up the constitutional amendment. Two days before the decisive House vote, four cabinet members announced their support. The evangelist Billy Sunday, who would open the House session with a prayer on the day of the vote, endorsed the amendment. The suffragists counted the solid support of sixteen state delegations, particularly from the Midwest and West, and the large New York and Pennsylvania delegations were strongly behind the amendment.

The biggest surprise came on the day before the vote, on January 9, when President Wilson offered his support. Up until this time, Wilson had been quietly sticking with his position that woman suffrage was a question to be determined by each of the states, not through a constitutional amendment. That day, a delegation of Democratic lawmakers headed by Representative Raker met with Wilson at the White House. They talked about the support woman suffrage had received in Belgium, England and France. The day before, Wilson had lunched with the governor general of Canada, who

> Sixty-Sixth Congress, 1st Session
> (May 19–November 19, 1919)
>
> Senate: 49 Republicans;
> 47 Democrats
>
> House: 240 Republicans;
> 190 Democrats; 3 other
>
> President: Woodrow Wilson

declared that his country would also support women. Following the meeting, a short message was prepared and read to the public by Raker: "The committee found that the President had not felt at liberty to volunteer his advice to members of Congress in this important matter, but when we sought his advice he very frankly and earnestly advised us to vote for the amendment as an act of right and justice to the women of the country and of the world." At last, Wilson was on board.

The suffrage leaders were ecstatic: "Onward with our President, the great leader of democracy," exclaimed Anna Howard Shaw. Lucy Anthony, the niece of Susan B. Anthony, cried, "Washington, Lincoln, Wilson!"[101]

In the House, suffragists would need 274 votes in order to produce a two-thirds margin necessary for a constitutional amendment. For five hours the debate went back and forth. Jeannette Rankin led the pro-suffrage supporters on the Republican side. The vote would be extremely close. As the tally came closer, Democrat after Democrat backed away from Wilson and dug in against the amendment. The hundreds of men and women who packed the galleries were electrified when Representative Joseph J. Russell (Democrat–Missouri) bounded up to the Speaker's desk. He had missed the first roll call vote and on the second demanded that his vote be counted in favor of the amendment. James R. Mann (Republican–Illinois), the leader of his party, left his hospital bed in Baltimore to support the amendment; three other representatives, weak and feeble, came to support the amendment. Speaker of the House James Beauchamp (Champ) Clark favored the amendment, but would not vote unless necessary. Speeches droned on for hours. Catt and Shuler described the scene:

> Men rose to make interminable speeches on man's God-given right to tell woman what she must and must not do, sentimental speeches, speeches that put all womanhood to blush by the reflection of womanhood in some man's mind. . . . They rose to score a party advantage. They rose to points of order. They rose merely to get into the picture, the *Congressional Record*.[102]

Several limiting amendments were defeated, and on the final vote, suffrage won by the exact two-thirds margin needed, 274 to 136. The margin of victory came from the thirty-five members of the New York delegation, all of whom voted for the amendment. Outside, thousands of women who could not get into the packed House gallery lustily cheered.[103]

Now it was on to the Senate and to a much more difficult reception. But suffragists' spirits were buoyed two days after the House vote when four senators, heretofore opposed or noncommittal, now publicly backed the proposed amendment.[104] But time was running out on the legislative calendar: if the Senate did not act quickly, then the whole exercise would have to be repeated in the new Sixty-Sixth Congress.

The Nineteenth Amendment

The right of citizens of the United States to vote shall not be denied or abridged by the United States or by any State on account of sex.

The Congress shall have power by appropriate legislation to enforce the provisions of this article.

From early June through September, Wilson wrote to eight southern senators and, as the vote approached, telegraphed six of them. To Christie Benet (Democrat–South Carolina), Wilson wrote: "I need not assure you that I would not venture to make this direct appeal to you, were I not convinced that affirmative action on the amendment is of capital importance not only to the party, but to the country, and to the maintenance of the war spirit . . ."[105] Benet had just entered the Senate on July 6, following the death of the legendary anti-suffrage Benjamin R. (Pitchfork Ben) Tillman, and Wilson thought he had a chance of persuading him to vote for the suffrage amendment.

In late September 1918, the Senate resumed deliberation on the amendment. Pro-suffrage senators counted noses and did not have the two-thirds needed. A number of pro-suffrage senators had not arrived in Washington yet, and, on September 25, the pro-suffrage forces filibustered, waiting for their return. Meanwhile the anti-suffrage leaders were confident that they could hold thirty-five votes, and stop the amendment.

Key Individuals in the Nineteenth Amendment

Unlike the other laws in this study, no legislators stand out as decisive champions of woman's suffrage. President Woodrow Wilson deserves some credit for his belated, but important, support of the proposed amendment, and certainly a long list of women activists and suffragist leaders, from Lucy Stone, Anna Howard Shaw, Harriot Stanton Blatch, to Alice Paul deserve mention.[106] However, we concentrate on three influential suffragists.

Elizabeth Cady Stanton (1815–1902) was active in women's legal rights reform, pushing for New York legislation to grant married women the right to hold real estate, to expand women's property rights, and the right to wages and custody of children; later she pushed for divorce reform. She was one of the organizers of the 1848 Seneca Falls convention and during the Civil War formed the National Woman's Loyal League, which pushed for immediate abolition of slavery through constitutional amendment. In 1868, Stanton proposed a Sixteenth Amendment that would grant suffrage regardless of color, race, or sex. She also served as an early president of the National American Woman Suffrage Association, and at the age of eighty published the first volume of her controversial *Women's Bible* and later wrote her autobiography, *Eighty Years and More*.

Susan Brownell Anthony (1820–1906) left her teaching career to become the principal leader of the woman's suffrage movement, leading its organizations and agitation for

---

reform. Much of her activity was done in tandem with Elizabeth Cady Stanton. Early in her career, Anthony was interested particularly in abolition reform and women's labor issues, and the temperance movement. Her work in 1860 led to the passage in New York of the Married Women's Property Act, which became a model for women's property laws in other states. After the Civil War she returned to the issue of woman's suffrage and formed the Women's Suffrage Association in 1869. Along with twelve others, she was arrest for voting in the presidential election in 1872; Anthony was also the first woman to run for a seat in the U.S. Congress. She also penned the words that ultimately would be called the Susan B. Anthony Amendment, the Nineteenth Amendment. At age eighty, she retired from the National American Woman Suffrage Association.

Carrie Chapman Catt (1859–1947) succeeded Susan B. Anthony as the president of NAWSA. Catt graduated from Iowa State University, became a school teacher then a school superintendent, and became a political activist when she joined the Iowan Woman Suffrage Association. She served as a delegate to the national convention. Anthony soon recognized Catt's talents for organization and speaking, and chose her as the next president. Catt served in that capacity for just four years, curtailing her activities so that she could attend to her dying husband, wealthy engineer George Catt. Soon, she was involved in the suffrage movement worldwide, organizing the International Woman's Suffrage Association. She resumed leadership of NAWSA and through her determined, progressive leadership persuaded Woodrow Wilson to support the amendment. After ratification, Catt helped create the League of Women Voters, then worked on issues related to working women, pacifism, and Jewish relief efforts.

The next day, debate resumed, this time for five hours. The galleries were jammed; yellow ribbons and red badges were everywhere. Senator John Sharp Williams (Democrat–Mississippi) added a new twist: the proposed amendment read, "The right of citizens of the United States to vote shall not be denied or abridged by the United States or by any State on account of sex." Williams inserted the word "white" before the word "citizens." His colleague James K. Vardaman (Democrat–Mississippi) followed, saying that he knew "only too well" the danger that would come to the South if Negro women obtained suffrage, but he would vote for the amendment regardless of the issue of colored women. On a Saturday session, one of the stormiest of the year, pro-suffragists still were one short of the sixty-four votes needed for passage. Tempers were raw: Key Pittman (Democrat–Nevada) charged that Reed Smoot (Republican–Utah) had deliberately misled pro-suffrage Democratic senators into thinking there were enough votes for passage. Smoot angrily shouted back that Democrats had better come up with their own votes. There were charges that Republicans were working with the militant wing of the suffrage movement to defeat Democrats in the upcoming mid-term elections.

Early in the day of September 30, Senator Benet, who had been courted by Wilson and had been presumed to be in favor of the amendment, defected to the Anti side. That made it thirty-four votes against, one more than needed. Smoot cried out that this was a trick and that Pittman who had put Benet down in the pro-suffrage column was deliberately trying to fool unsuspecting Democrats. Pro-suffragist senators began a desperate filibuster, and after an hour, Benet had a chance to speak. "I do not think woman suffrage is necessary at this time," he said. "I cannot regard it as a war measure. I fail to see how politics can have anything to do with it. I put principle above party interests and I put war measures above anything else. That is why I want to announce to the Senate that I intend to vote against the woman suffrage amendment." With that, Benet sat down.[107] Pro-suffrage forces were aghast and dazed.

At one o'clock on the same day, President Wilson, giving the lawmakers just a half hour's notice of his intentions, arrived at the Senate chamber and pleaded for the amendment. He slowly read his fifteen-minute speech, as senators and the gallery visitors listened intently. "Gentlemen of the Senate," he began, Senate concurrence in the suffrage amendment was "vitally essential" for the war effort. If America is to show the world and lead the way in democracy, then it must "give justice to women." Wilson ended his speech, with his voice ringing through the Senate chamber: "I tell you plainly that this measure which I urge upon you is vital to the winning of the war and to the energies alike of preparation and of battle." But in the end, after the drama of an unanticipated visit from the chief executive, no votes were changed. Barely minutes after he left the Senate chamber, Oscar W. Underwood (Democrat–Alabama) rose to speak against the amendment.[108]

On October 1, with just eighty-four senators present, fifty-six votes would be needed. All the amendments, including the "whites only" provision of Senator Williams, were defeated. On final passage of the constitutional amendment, reality set in: the pro-suffrage forces could muster only fifty-three votes, three short of victory. Twenty-one senators from Wilson's own party, mostly from the South, had voted against, as had ten Republicans. Now it was time to face the voters.

"This defeat is only temporary," said Alice Paul, who vowed that the amendment would be brought up again after the elections and before the end of the Sixty-Fifth Congress.[109] Wilson, in his December 1918 State of the Union address, once again recommended passage of the suffrage amendment. Women were important in the war effort and "the least tribute we can pay them is to make them the equals of men in political rights. . . ."[110]

The suffrage amendment came up again in the Senate during the third, lame-duck session of the Sixty-Fifth Congress on February 10, 1919; but, once again, it fell short by one vote, 55 to 29. The day before, angry suffragists burned Wilson in effigy in front of the White House, blaming him for not swaying recalcitrant senators to his position. Wilson had sent telegrams to fence-sitting senators urging them to support the measure, but that was not enough. The effigy, which looked like an oversized stuffed doll, was thrown into the flames by Sue Shelton White of Nashville, Tennessee. "We burn not the effigy of the President of a free people, but the leader of an auto-cratic party organization whose tyrannical power holds millions of women in political slavery," cried out Miss White before she was pushed into a police patrol wagon.[111]

Key Events in the Making of the Nineteenth Amendment

1848	Seneca Falls Conference.
1850	First national women's rights conference.
1869	Creation of rival suffrage organizations: NWSA and AWSA.
1878	The Susan B. Anthony Amendment introduced in the Senate.
1893	Colorado became the first state to permit full woman suffrage.
1913	Suffrage parade in Washington before Wilson inauguration.
1916	NAWSA adopted the "Winning Plan."
1919	Congress adopted the Nineteenth Amendment.
1920	In August, Tennessee was thirty-sixth state to ratify the Nineteenth Amendment.

Senator Andrieus A. Jones (Democrat–New Mexico), the chair of the Committee on Woman Suffrage, who led the fight for the amendment, now had tasted bitter defeat twice within five months. He knew there was no further chance to get the measure passed in the Sixty-Fifth Congress, but, when the new Congress convened in May 1919, it would be a different story.

Before the new session, suffrage supporters redoubled their efforts. There were over 500 resolutions sent to Congress from religious, civic, labor, and education organizations and societies. A further six more state legislatures had given women the vote in presidential contests.[112] During January and early February, 1919, twenty-four state legislatures had sent messages to Congress, proclaiming their support of the suffrage amendment and urging Congress to send it to them for ratification.[113]

The congressional elections in November 1918 had taken their toll on Democrats, and suffragists rejoiced, claiming victory for their cause. Woman suffrage had emerged as a partisan issue, with the continued resistance from southern Democrats dragging down the party nationwide.[114] For the first time in eight years in the House and six years in the Senate, the Republican Party was now in control, gaining twenty-five seats in the House and four seats in the Senate. There were 117 new members of the House, most of whom committed to woman's suffrage. This was a special session of the new Congress, convened by President Wilson, who was still in Paris with peace negotiations, and who had cabled his 4,500-word message to Congress. Many postwar issues were on the agenda: the Paris peace treaty, the demobilization of troops, the return of railroads to private ownership, and the restoration of telephone, telegraph, and cable systems. Still Wilson put in a strong word for the suffrage amendment: "every consideration of justice and of public advantage calls for the immediate adoption of that amendment and its submission forthwith to the Legislatures of the several States."[115]

Congress responded. On May 21, 1919, two days after this momentous session began, the House adopted the suffrage amendment by 304 to 89, with 42 votes to spare. Most of the support came from the Republicans, 200 of whom backed the measure while 102 Democrats joined in. Significantly, just 58 southern Democrats voted against the measure, as opposed to 90 who had opposed it a year earlier.[116] By receiving 77 percent of the members voting, it was in stark contrast to the 47 percent gathered in the 1915 House vote. In the intervening four years, there was a dramatic increase in support for woman suffrage in the Midwest and the East, near unanimous support from the western states, with southerners firmly opposed. At the state level, there was significant progress. In 1915, there were only thirteen states with woman suffrage; by 1919, there were thirty.[117]

In the Senate, the vote was also expected to favor the suffrage amendment, and, after some last-minute maneuvering, and after four hours of debate and an attempted filibuster, the Senate on June 4, 1919, adopted the constitutional amendment, 56 to 25, with two votes to spare. The same language as originally penned by Susan B. Anthony in 1875 was endorsed by both the House and the Senate in 1919: "The right of citizens of the United States to vote shall not be denied or abridged by the United States or by any State on account of sex."

It had been a long time coming in Congress. The Senate had rejected the amendment in 1878, 1914, 1918, and 1919; the House had rejected it in 1915, but passed it in 1918 with no votes to spare. The United States was now joining democracies around the world which had given the vote to women. Woman suffrage became law in New Zealand (1893), Australia (1902), Finland (1906), Norway (1907), Iceland (1913), Denmark (1915), Russia (1917). In 1918, those countries were joined by Canada, Austria, England, Germany, Hungary, Ireland, Poland, Scotland, and Wales; in 1919, Holland and Sweden added woman's suffrage.[118]

Ratification

Now it was up to the states. In order for the measure to become the Nineteenth Amendment to the Constitution, three-quarters of the state legislatures, thirty-six, had to ratify. Ratification was by no means a forgone conclusion nor in many states was it easy to enact. The spotlight moved from Congress to the forty-eight state legislatures, each with its own power structures and personalities, public and private agendas, and governors and legislative leaders cooperative with or hostile to the suffrage movement. In some states, suffragists were very well organized, in others they were not; suffragists in the South were reluctant to support a federal amendment. Further, anti-suffragist forces, knowing that this was their last chance, dug in and fought ferociously.[119]

Quickly on June 10, the Illinois and Wisconsin legislatures, already in regular session, passed the amendment; a special session was called in Michigan, and it became the third state to ratify. By the end of June, Kansas, Ohio, New York, Pennsylvania, Massachusetts, and Texas also ratified. Five more states were added in July, three more in September. In some legislative sessions, the amendment passed enthusiastically and with acclamation; in others, like Texas, Arkansas, and Oklahoma, there was bitter opposition before passage. By the end of 1919, twenty-three of the needed thirty-six states had approved the amendment.[120] Many supporters now were hopeful that women would be able to vote in the 1920 presidential election.

Ironically, the states in which women had longest enjoyed the right to vote were some of the slowest to ratify. NAWSA worked furiously to rouse the governors and legislatures of the West. Wyoming dawdled until January 26, 1920, when it became the twenty-seventh state to ratify; Washington, where women had enjoyed suffrage for a decade, came in as the thirty-fifth state on March 22. One more state was needed to meet the three-quarters requirement of the Constitution.

The problem lay in the South: While Texas and Arkansas had ratified during the summer of 1919, the prospects were grim for suffrage in Louisiana, Mississippi, Alabama, Georgia, Florida, South Carolina, Virginia, and even Maryland and Delaware did not look promising. Georgia, Alabama, and Florida had rejected outright the amendment. In the Georgia debate, Representative J. B. Jackson echoed a common theme in southern resistance: that abolitionist Frederick Douglass was the father and Susan B. Anthony was the mother of the amendment and "if you ratify this Nineteenth Amendment you ratify the Fifteenth and any Southerner . . . [so doing] is a traitor to his section."[121]

By the time Washington became the penultimate state, only two other northern states, Connecticut and Vermont, had not ratified, and their anti-suffrage governors were not eager to call special sessions of their legislatures. In June, Delaware's lower house refused to consider the amendment. Now, in August all suffrage hopes were pinned on North Carolina and Tennessee.

What followed in Tennessee and North Carolina was a series of great surprises, mixed with disappointments, for the suffrage supporters. Carrie Catt arrived in Nashville on July 17, 1920, expecting a short stay, but found herself in the thick of things for nearly a month.[122] Both President Wilson and Sue White, the woman who burned Wilson in effigy in Washington, pressed Governor Albert H. Roberts to call a special session of the legislature. He did so, but waited until after the state primary had been held. Catt recalled the rough reception she received: "I have been called more names, been more maligned, more lied about than in the thirty previous years I worked for suffrage."[123] On a steamy August 13, the Tennessee Senate, to the surprise of everyone, voted overwhelmingly for the amendment, by 25 to 4; on the same day, a North Carolina Senate committee issued a favorable report, by the vote of 7 to 1. Suffragists were elated, assured of victory perhaps easily in both states.

Then things turned quickly. It was a complete shock when the full North Carolina Senate voted, 25 to 23, to postpone the ratification vote until the following year. Now all eyes were on the Tennessee House. President Wilson sent a telegram to the speaker of the Tennessee House urging the passage of the amendment, but it was going to be a tough fight. Hundreds of women and men set up their unofficial headquarters at Nashville's Hermitage Hotel. It became the site of the "war of the roses"—the suffragist forces decked out in yellow roses and the Antis wearing red. One historian remarked that the scene "smacked of Mardi Gras and Barnum and Bailey."[124]

The Tennessee House engaged in four hours of bitter personal debate, where just about every conceivable issue was thrown into the mix: home rule, *The Woman's Bible*, black voting, railroad interests, national interests, the vote in North Carolina and the possibility of postponing the Tennessee decision until 1921. Every legislator was stopped before going to the floor by women, hundreds of them, who pinned on the lawmakers either red or yellow roses. The women were on the floor of the House making their pleas, until the legislators finally voted to bar everyone from the floor except House members. One legislator left his hospital bed to vote for the amendment. At the last minute, Speaker Seth Walker, who had supported suffrage for years, switched sides. When the opposition called to table the bill one more time, the vote came up a tie. Parliamentary rules required that, in case of a tie, the amendment would be voted on.

Twenty-four-year-old Harry Burn, the youngest member of the legislature, up until this point had been publicly quiet about his vote. The political leaders in his rural east Tennessee district were against ratification, but he privately promised he would vote for, if his vote were absolutely necessary. His mother, a strong suffragist, wrote her son: "Vote for suffrage and don't keep them in doubt . . . Don't forget to be a good boy and help Mrs. Catt put 'Rat' in Ratification."[125] Harry Burn quietly voted "yes," and the amendment carried 49 to 47. After the vote, Burn said to the Tennessee House, "I believe we had a moral and legal right to ratify . . . . I appreciated the fact that an opportunity such as seldom comes to a mortal man to free seventeen million women from political slavery was mine."[126]

There were vigorous attempts to invoke the legislature's three-day rule, which permitted bills to be reconsidered. In a last-ditch effort, Speaker Seth Walker and thirty-eight Antis crossed the state line into Alabama, hoping to prevent a quorum and hoping to wait out the majority. But it did not succeed, nor did an attempted last-minute judicial restraining order. Governor Roberts signed the ratification certificate and sent it on to Washington.

On August 26, 1920, at 8:00 in the morning, at his home in Washington, Secretary of State Bainbridge Colby quietly signed a proclamation announcing the Nineteenth Amendment to the United States Constitution. Colby did so without ceremony and with none of the woman's suffragist leaders present. With that signature, seventy years of political struggle had ended, and

22 million women would now be able to cast their votes in the upcoming presidential election.[127]

Aftermath

Had Tennessee not been the thirty-sixth state to ratify, Connecticut would have been when it approved the amendment three weeks later on September 14. By then, of course, its vote was merely symbolic, since the Nineteenth Amendment was now in full force. The last northern state, Vermont, voted in favor in February 1921; Delaware followed two years later. The southern states eventually acknowledged the vote for women: Maryland's 1941 assent was eventually certified in 1958, Virginia and Alabama approved in the 1950s; South Carolina and Florida in 1969; Louisiana, Georgia and North Carolina in the early 1970s. Finally, on March 22, 1984, on a voice vote, with no objections, Mississippi became the last state to acknowledge what had been decided sixty-four years earlier.

On election day, November 2, 1920, some 22 million women were eligible to cast their vote. In a number of western states, women had enjoyed that right during several previous presidential contests; others were getting the vote for the first time. Women in Alabama and Georgia, however, could not vote in the presidential election: Alabama required citizens to register four months before the general election and Georgia required six months. It had only been three months since the amendment had been certified. Other southern women encountered more pernicious obstacles. In order to vote, African-American women in Columbia, South Carolina were required to read and correctly interpret long passages from the civil and criminal code; white women were exempt from such impediments.[128]

In early 1919, Carrie Catt founded the first chapters of the League of Women Voters, and following ratification, the National American Woman Suffrage Association resolved itself into the national League of Women Voters. Catt was determined that women should work to change policies and remove legal barriers through the existing Democratic and Republican parties. Alice Paul took another direction: Women should work through the National Woman's Party and should blot out discrimination and unequal treatment by enacting an equal rights amendment. In 1923, an equal rights amendment was adopted by the Woman's Party, and was introduced in the House and the Senate. Catt disagreed with the equal rights amendment, arguing that working women needed the hard-won protective legislation that had been passed by progressive states and that such an amendment might negate those protections. Many others, including Eleanor Roosevelt, Frances Perkins, and other leaders of the League of Women Voters, also objected to an equal rights amendment because of the probable impact on working women.[129] The amendment languished in Congress until 1972, when both Houses approved it. The amendment came close, but was never ratified by two-thirds of the states, and in 1982 the National Organization of Women, its principal lobbying advocate conceded defeat.

In the suffrage amendment struggle, Catt and her allies had chosen a successful, single-issue strategy: concentrate on women's right to vote and leave aside other social reforms and goals. During the ratification battles, anti-suffragists had predicted disastrous radical social reforms if the suffragists had their way; but their shrill predictions fell flat. Once the fight for suffrage was over, women were no longer seen or treated as a separate class of citizens; nor did they act as a cohesive political force. Candidates and political party bosses had nothing to fear from women: they were not a bloc vote, they could not carry out the threat of using their unified muscle and clout.[130]

What then did the long, frustrating, fight for woman suffrage accomplish? Many historians of the women's movement point out that woman suffrage had little impact on public policy or on the lives of women. Yet, historian Paula Baker argues that the battle was an important turning point, marking the "endpoint of nineteenth-century womanhood and woman's political culture."[131] Women activists became effective political forces. Above all, the suffragist gave the country a social model of how a class of citizens could fight for its rights. Suffragists developed effective grassroots lobbying techniques at both the state and national levels that were later used by others. They made political and strategic mistakes, fought against harsh criticism and internal dissension, but in the end became an effective political machine, a lobbying force that knew how to exert its muscle and its persuasive powers.[132]

Women did not immediately take advantage of their right to vote or participate in political activities. Voter turnout during the early years of the 1920s was lower than in previous decades, owing partly to the drop off of voting by men but mostly because women were still not fully participating.[133] By the end of the 1920s, the difference in voter participation between men and women voting had shrunk dramatically, from a 25 percent differential at the beginning of the 1920s to 20 or even 10 percent in some jurisdictions in 1930. A League of Women Voters study in 1930 found that, while it was still unusual to find women in elected office in America, there had been important gains. From the 1920s to 1930s, voters chose two female governors (Nellie Tayloe Ross of Wyoming and Miriam "Ma" Ferguson of Texas), 149 state legislators, thousands of minor officials, a dozen statewide elected officials, and a dozen mayors, including the mayor of Seattle.[134]

Yet, for most of the twentieth century, women's political participation continued to lag behind that of men. By the 1960s, with the beginning of significant social activism in the United States, women were less likely to vote and less likely to become involved in political activities. A 1990 national survey confirmed that women were less politically active than men.[135] Today, women are more politically active than before; their rate of voting in presidential elections is higher than that of men, while their overall participation in campaign activities still lags. Women have the one critical ingredient, education, which fosters greater political participation, but they are less likely to have the personal income, a profession that makes it easier to engage in politics, or the sense that they can make a difference.[136]

By the beginning of 2006, a total of 202 women had followed Jeannette Rankin into the House of Representatives. In the Senate thirty-three women have served, beginning with the one-day ceremonial appointment of Rebecca Latimer Felton (Democrat–Georgia) in 1922. However, twelve of those women, like Felton herself, were widows of senators or political caretakers who served for short periods of time, until a successor could be chosen.[137] In the 111th Congress (2009–2010), there were seventeen women senators (17 percent of the total)[138] and seventy-four in the House of Representatives (17 percent), more women serving in Congress than in any time in U. S. history. At the state level, there were eight women governors in 2006 and fifteen lieutenant governors; 1,680 women hold state legislative seats (22.8 percent).[139] Hillary Rodham Clinton was not the first, but certainly the most prominent, woman to run for the presidency. Governor Sarah H. Palin became the first vice-presidential candidate for the Republican Party.

Suffrage did not emancipate women, it did not immediately solve long-standing social ills or remove discriminatory treatment. The women's movement would later enjoy numerous policy successes but also endure the bitter defeat of the Equal Rights Amendment. But with the ratification of the Nineteenth Amendment a fundamental element of democratic life was now open for the first time to one half of the population. The barrier had been broken. Women could now vote, use their own political judgment, voice their own concerns, and participate in the messy, vital process of democracy.

5

PROTECTING THE WORKING FAMILY

The National Labor Relations Act
of 1935

*I am confident that it will prove itself the
Magna Carta of Labor of the United States.*

William Green, president,
American Federation of Labor (1935)

*It is simply absurd to say that an individual,
one of 10,000 workers, is on an equality
with his employer in bargaining for his wages.*

Senator Robert F. Wagner (1935)

*Perhaps the most radical piece of legislation
ever enacted by the United States Congress.*

Karl E. Klare (1978)

By March 4, 1933, the day Franklin D. Roosevelt was sworn in as the thirty-second president of the United States, over thirteen million Americans had lost their jobs and many millions more had seen their wages cut or feared that they too would become unemployed. The stock market had crashed three and one-half years earlier and the country was faced with an unprecedented economic and financial crisis. Throughout the country banks had collapsed, wiping out the savings of hundreds of thousands of families; farmers, who had experienced Depression-like conditions for nearly a decade, saw the value of their produce plummet; makeshift shanty towns, Hoovervilles, became the last shelter for the desperate and unemployed. More than half the country lived on less than subsistence wages. Workers, small business owners, industrialists, financiers, and politicians feared the worst: an unending stagnant economy, failed businesses, lost jobs, and shattered dreams.

On that cold, damp inauguration day, Roosevelt spoke to the fears, anxieties, and hopes of the American people. He had vowed to get the country back to work and he assured the millions who heard him on the radio or saw him on the newsreel that the only thing the country need fear was fear itself. Roosevelt called Congress into emergency session and thus began the first One Hundred Days of the New Deal.

While economic recovery was foremost on everyone's minds, Roosevelt and his advisers had developed no comprehensive plan to tackle the most intransigent problems. Only when confronted by aggressive alternative plans in Congress did the president support recovery legislation, called the National Industrial Recovery Act. Initially, there were high hopes for the NIRA, the agency it created, the National Recovery Agency, and the Blue Eagle campaign devised to support economic cooperation and recovery. Through voluntary action, industries and workers pledged to do their part to lift the country out of the Depression. Big business firms were no longer bound by antitrust regulations and collectively could set production and prices; labor had the assurance that it could organize and bargain collectively. But small businesses were most wary, fearful that they would be squeezed between the demands of labor and the competitive advantage of large corporations. A National Labor Board was created to monitor the progress of the voluntary codes, but it had no enforcement power. The Blue Eagle campaign began with great fanfare and enthusiasm, but soon cooperation broke down. Manufacturers ignored workers' right to organize or circumvented the law by forming company-controlled unions. The National Recovery Administration rapidly lost its authority and legitimacy and, within a year, many considered the NIRA and its recovery mechanisms to be failures.

During 1934, there was a series of high-profile, violent labor strikes. Organized labor, which in the 1920s had lost membership and suffered from weak leadership, now asserted itself, encouraged by new federal protections. But corporations became increasingly aggressive, digging in against labor demands. The federal government could offer little help. The NIRA was scheduled to lapse in mid-1935 and many critics thought that expiration would come none too soon. Nonetheless, Roosevelt half-heartedly endorsed an extension of the NIRA and reluctantly Congress obliged. But it was the U.S. Supreme Court that sealed the fate of the NIRA, ruling unanimously that it was unconstitutional. An intricate web of hundreds of ineffective, often contradictory, industry-wide codes collapsed.

Senator Robert F. Wagner, a Democrat from New York, had been one of the authors of the NIRA in 1933, sat on the original National Labor Board, and was convinced that new legislation was needed to protect workers' rights to organize and collectively bargain. While the NIRA was still on the books and months before the Supreme Court decision, Wagner introduced the National Labor Relations Act, or, as it was commonly called, the Wagner Act. It was an extraordinary piece of legislation: for the first time, the full authority of the federal government backed workers, protecting their right to join unions of their own choosing and to bargain collectively. The National Labor Relations Board was resuscitated, with clear powers of enforcement. Unfair labor–management practices were proscribed, including wholesale bans on corporate intimidation and interference with labor organizing, and most importantly, company unions were banned. Under the Wagner Act, government was clearly on the side of the workers: there were no corresponding protections for management nor proscriptions against illegal labor activities.

Roosevelt was uninterested in Wagner's ground-breaking legislative proposal and remained so until the Senate passed it and the Supreme Court overturned the NIRA. Only then did Roosevelt fully embrace the Wagner Act, putting it on his "must pass" list of critical legislation. On July 5, 1935, Roosevelt, with Senator Wagner and the president of the American Federation of Labor at his side, signed the historic legislation. It was part of a burst of legislative activity during that hot, steamy summer in Washington. The summer of 1935 became known as the Second Hundred Days, as Congress passed milestone pieces of legislation, including, just six weeks after the Wagner Act, the Social Security Act, the subject of the next chapter.

The Wagner Act passed with relative ease, though it was harshly criticized by the National Association of Manufacturers and other industrial interests. Many were convinced, however, that the law would be ruled unconstitutional, just as had the NIRA and other New Deal legislation. Many industries dragged their feet, would not accept union recognition, and fiercely avoided compliance with the new legislation. Then, in the spring of 1937, the Supreme Court, by the narrowest of margins, affirmed its constitutionality. Union organizing activity increased, particularly through the new, assertive Congress of Industrial Organizations (CIO), membership in unions surged, and critical industries like steel and automobile manufacturing reluctantly accepted unionization.

Along with an upsurge in union successes came harsh critics, with conservative Democrats and Republicans, together with their allies in business and industry, mounting attacks against the Wagner Act. When Republicans finally regained control of Congress in 1946, and public confidence in President Harry Truman was at a low point, lawmakers enacted sweeping changes in labor–management relations through the Taft–Hartley Act. Truman vetoed the legislation, but Congress passed it over his objections; labor called it a "slave labor" law while proponents called it a much-needed corrective. Its most important provision was to trim the federal government's supposedly one-sided protection of labor unions.

Despite Taft–Hartley, unions continued to grow, and, in 1955, the American Federation of Labor and the Congress of Industrial Organizations merged into an organization representing 15.5 million workers. Ironically, this was the high point of union activity and political clout. Highly publicized labor corruption hearings led to widespread public disapproval and federal legislation designed to clean up and democratize unions. The decades since have seen a steady, perhaps ineluctable slide in union strength, failure of organized labor to tap into new markets, globalization of the workplace, and loss of manufacturing jobs.

Today organized labor is undergoing an agonizing period of retrenchment, re-evaluation, and division.

Background

Throughout American history, workers faced major hurdles from employers, the government, and, particularly, from the courts as they fought for higher wages, shorter hours, and safer working conditions. One of the early impediments was the legal principle that equated the act of forming a union with a criminal conspiracy. First articulated in 1805, this legal precedent was followed until 1842; during that time, there were nineteen such conspiracy trials and convictions in the United States, effectively thwarting union activity. At the same time, there were no findings by the courts that businesses had engaged in illegal combinations with others to prevent workers from gaining higher wages and better working conditions.[1]

Labor had lost momentum, too, during the Panic of 1819; even skilled workers found it difficult to secure jobs. With the return of better economic times, the union movement started making a come back. By the mid-1830s, union activity, despite the threat of conspiracy charges, became more widespread. Then in 1842, the Massachusetts Supreme Judicial Court, under Chief Justice Lemuel Shaw, ruled for the first time that workers had the right to organize and seek collective bargaining. In this historic decision, *Commonwealth v. Hunt*, the Massachusetts court laid down the important principle that forming a labor union, in and of itself, was not a crime.[2]

After *Hunt*, labor unions began to take root. Some of the biggest problems that workers encountered were long hours and low wages. In 1830, the average working day was twelve and a half hours; thirty years later, the average working day was reduced slightly to eleven hours, with reductions hard won through increased agitation, militant campaigns, and strikes.[3] The federal government was more sympathetic to worker demands. Through an executive order in 1840, President Martin Van Buren authorized a ten-hour work day for federal employees on public works projects, with no reduction in wages.

This federal policy was an exception, however. Increased competition, a surge in cheap immigrant labor, and the use of power looms, steam engines, and other technological improvements led to harsh conditions for New England textile and other industrial workers. From the mid-1830s through the mid-1840s, workers found themselves laboring longer hours (sometimes thirteen and a half hours a day), for less money, and often in overcrowded, dangerous, poorly lit, and badly ventilated rooms or factory floors. Such conditions led to several reform movements.[4]

In 1847, New Hampshire became the first state to adopt a ten-hour work day, followed the next year by Pennsylvania, which set maximums of ten hours or sixty hours a week in cotton, silk, paper, woolen, and other factories. Soon, Maine, Connecticut, Rhode Island, Ohio, California, and Georgia established ten-hour work day statutes. But, in nearly every case, there was an escape clause which allowed the ten-hour requirement to be circumvented through "special contracts," which workers would sign waiving the hours worked requirement.[5]

Apart from the depression year of 1857, the decade before the Civil War was fairly robust economically. Working conditions improved, and workers tended to form unions around crafts and skills, focusing on hours, wages, and working conditions, maintenance of apprenticeship rules, and the closed shop. There was an increasing division between skilled and unskilled workers. Skilled craftsmen generally were American-born, Protestant workers, while unskilled factory workers tended to be recent immigrants, Catholics, women and children. On the eve of the Civil War came the largest strike up to that point in American history, when the shoemakers of Natick and Lynn, Massachusetts, refused to work. They were joined by 20,000 shoemakers in other New England towns. As the strike wore on and violence inevitably erupted, local police and state militias were brought in to maintain order; in the end, the strike was only partially successful.[6]

During the Civil War, labor unions grew and strengthened, and, by 1864, there were 270 unions, mostly local, with approximately 200,000 members.[7] By 1870, there were about thirty national labor unions, with the first such organization being the National Labor Union (NLU), a labor federation established in 1866, composed of both laborers and professionals. Under the presidency of William H. Sylvis, the NLU veered toward a middle-class reform movement and by the early 1870s had lost its focus and momentum as a working-class labor organization. While the NLU was short-lived, it did press for several important issues, particularly the eight-hour working day, an issue that was gaining ground throughout the country. The federal government made the eight-hour day the standard for all its employees in 1868, and six states had established it as the normal working day.[8]

In 1873, the United States experienced another economic panic; this time millions of workers lost their jobs. Labor unions suffered particularly. Before the panic, the thirty national unions had a total labor strength of roughly 300,000; in 1877, there were just nine national unions and 50,000 members.[9] In this period came one of the most violent and important strikes in the nineteenth century, the railway strike of 1877. Most of the major urban centers in the East were affected, and, in Pittsburgh, mobs rampaged, the militia was called out in force; twenty-six people were killed.[10]

The Knights of Labor, originally a secret society founded in Philadelphia in 1869, became the first effective labor organization in the nineteenth century. Its goal, under Grand Master Workman Terence V. Powderly, was to unite all wage earners (except Chinese immigrant laborers). The Knights of Labor hoped to use political action and education to improve the workers' lot, rather than resort to strikes. By 1886, the Knights of Labor had a membership of nearly 700,000, but, following a series of bitter and unsuccessful actions against railroads and the Chicago stockyards, the organization rapidly declined. Of greatest harm to the labor movement was the Haymarket Square riot in 1886. Stoked by labor anarchists, a strike at the McCormick Harvester plant in Chicago led to a bomb explosion, police firing on hundreds of protestors, seven policemen and five workers killed, and more than a hundred persons wounded. Anarchists were blamed, but the entire labor movement suffered from this bloody incident.[11]

The chief rival of the Knights of Labor was the American Federation of Labor (AFL). Samuel Gompers, who began his organizing activities with the International Cigar Makers' Union, became the first president of the AFL in 1886 and held that job, with the exception of one year, until his death in 1924.[12] The AFL was craft-based, with autonomy given to each trade, and, though the AFL was almost entirely the force and personality of Gompers, the real strength was in the individual member unions. By 1886, there were forty national unions, with the strongest affiliated with the AFL. As historians Foster Rhea Dulles and Melvin Dubofsky observe, the unions "could exist without the AFL, but the AFL had no meaning without them."[13]

Unions, of whatever affiliation, went through difficult times during the early 1890s. The year 1892 witnessed the most bitter labor strife up to this point in American history: a general strike in New Orleans, a railroad switchmen's strike in Buffalo, a coal miners' strike in East Tennessee, a copper miners' strike in Coeur d'Alene, Idaho, and a steelworkers' strike in Homestead, Pennsylvania.[14]

The private warfare between workers and the Carnegie Steel Company at its Homestead plant was intense. Skilled workers from the Amalgamated Association of Iron, Steel, and Tin Workers refused to accept wage cuts, went on strike and were joined by other workers. Henry Clay Frick, the tough anti-union head of the steel company, shut down the entire plant, and brought in three hundred armed Pinkerton detectives on barges up the Monongahela River. Workers opened up fire, the Pinkerton forces were driven back, and seven persons were killed. Six days later, 8,000 members of the state militia, called up by the governor of Pennsylvania, marched into the Homestead works. Now operating under martial law, 2,000 strikebreakers were brought in and nearly 3,200 of the original 4,000 workers were barred from the plant.[15]

Another major labor dispute occurred in Chicago, at the Pullman Palace Car Company. George M. Pullman provided a unique setting for his workers: he established a model town, a planned community where all workers were required to live. Pullman's paternalistic benevolence, however, came at a substantial price. Workers paid rent, utilities, garbage fees, library subscriptions to Pullman, and bought their goods at the company store. The rent was 25 percent higher than surrounding communities, but workers had no choice: they had to live on Pullman grounds. Following the Depression of 1893, the Pullman Company laid off 3,000 of its 5,800 employees, and cut the wages of those remaining by 25 to 40 percent, but made no reductions in the cost of its mandatory housing. Many workers were now surviving on one dollar a day after their rents and other charges were deducted. A committee of workers appealed in May 1894 to Pullman to either raise wages or cut rent, only to be rebuffed and have three of their number fired.

The men fired by Pullman belonged to the American Railway Union, the union organized by Eugene V. Debs, which had 150,000 members in 465 local chapters. When Pullman refused to negotiate, the union directed its membership not to handle any Pullman cars or equipment. The railroad companies that contracted with Pullman had their own organization, the General Managers' Association, composed of twenty-four railroads. A local labor dispute had now involved thousands of workers in more than twenty-seven states, making it America's first nationwide strike. The General Managers' Association brought in strikebreakers from Canada, and attached U.S. mail cars to its trains, so that, if the strikers refused to run the trains, they would be charged with interfering with the U.S. Postal Service. Violence and looting erupted and President Grover Cleveland ultimately was compelled to bring out federal troops, putting Chicago under martial law. The railroads had the ultimate weapon, however. They persuaded Attorney General Richard Olney to intervene; the attorney general then received a blanket injunction from a federal judge forbidding any interference with the U.S. mail. Seeing the handwriting on the wall, Debs offered to halt the strike, but it was too late. Pullman refused, the injunction went into effect, and Debs and three aides were arrested, with Debs spending six months in jail. The strike collapsed; 515 persons were arrested and charged with murder, arson, burglary, assault, and rioting, and seventy-one were indicted on federal charges of obstructing the mail and conspiracy to restrain trade.[16]

While the AFL had grown from 250,000 members in 1897 to 1.6 million in 1904, some labor leaders were dissatisfied with Gomper's job-oriented, conservative approach. In 1889, Daniel de Leon became the leader of the Socialist Labor Party. De Leon argued that the AFL approach of job-oriented bargaining should give way to Marxist socialism and that class-oriented ownership should be labor's goal. He had utter disdain for both the AFL and Gompers, whom he characterized as a "greasy tool of Wall Street."[17] Another faction of the socialist workers coalesced around Eugene Debs, who, after prison, became more radicalized, and eventually was five times a presidential candidate under the Socialist Party of America.

The Western Federation of Miners had left the AFL in 1897 and with the help of the Socialist Labor Party created in 1904 the Industrial Workers of the World (IWW), the "Wobblies."[18] Under the colorful but erratic leadership of William D. (Big Bill) Haywood, the IWW managed to win a number of important strikes, but, within a few years, its actions were so chaotic that both the Western Federation of Miners and the Socialists disavowed them. As economists E. Edward Herman and Alfred Kuhn observed, the IWW's most durable legacy was to instill a "strong public fear and distrust of unions."[19] Union militancy, tinged with socialist and Marxist ideology, was often met with brutal repression from local police, state militia, and private protection forces hired by employers. The only viable union movement left standing was the more conservative, yet tough-minded AFL.[20]

Employers struck back at unions in a variety of ways. One of the most effective was through the yellow-dog contract, an agreement between the worker and employer, written by the employer, stating that the worker did not at that time belong to, nor would attempt to join, a union. Workers who refused to sign the contract were dismissed or never hired. There were various legislative attempts, both at the federal and state levels, to protect workers' right to organize and to outlaw the yellow-dog contract. But every such initiative ran up against judicial challenges and were defeated. In 1898, Congress passed the Erdman Act which outlawed yellow-dog contracts in the railroad industry; however, the law was ruled unconstitutional by the U.S. Supreme Court in 1908, as a violation of contract between workers and employers, as protected by the Fifth Amendment. In 1913, the Kansas legislature prohibited the yellow-dog contract, but it too was struck down. Four years later, the Supreme Court, in *Hitchman Coal and Coke Company* v. *Mitchell*, explicitly backed the constitutionality of yellow-dog contracts.[21]

Before *Hitchman*, the yellow-dog contract was a "little-used annoyance" to unions. Now, it had the full sanction of the Supreme Court, and was used vigorously to prevent workers from joining unions. By the end of the 1920s, some 1.25 million workers had signed yellow-dog contracts, promising not to join unions.[22]

Another major weapon used against labor was the court-ordered injunction. First used to restrain workers in the railway strike of 1877, it was often employed during the bitter labor fights for glass workers, coal miners, and railroad workers in the 1880s. The injunction was given constitutional sanction when the U.S. Supreme Court approved a lower court finding of contempt against Eugene Debs during the Pullman strike.[23] So notorious was the labor injunction, that it became an issue during the 1896 presidential campaign. The Democratic Party platform that year decried "government by injunction" as it castigated judicial intervention in labor disputes. Republicans struck back. Workers got notices in their pay envelopes, warning them that a Democratic victory for candidate William Jennings Bryant would mean that more factories would be closed and more jobs lost.[24]

Injunctions were used most frequently in the 1920s; over a fifty-year period of the court-ordered labor injunction, nearly one-half, or 921, occurred during that decade. One of the most infamous was issued by federal circuit judge John J. Parker in 1927, the Red Jacket injunction, which effectively barred the United Mine Workers from organizing anywhere in West Virginia. The mine workers were enjoined from "trespassing upon the properties" or "inciting, inducing, or persuading the employees of the plaintiffs to break their contract of employment." This injunction covered 316 coal companies and 40,000 workers who had signed yellow-dog contracts, and was considered the most hated labor injunction of this era.[25]

The Sherman Antitrust Act of 1890 was enacted to curb the growing monopolistic practices of big corporations, such as the Standard Oil Company. No state, acting alone, could effectively control multi-state corporations and curb their abuses, such as restraining trade and monopolizing markets, and thus, the federal government claimed jurisdiction. Did Sherman also apply to the activities of trade unions? Could unions be held culpable under antitrust provisions? There was no specific mention of labor disputes or labor combinations in the law, but, in 1908, the U.S. Supreme Court decided, in *Loewe* v. *Lawlor*, that the Sherman Antitrust Act did apply to, and thus did not protect, labor unions.[26]

Another blow to the union movement came in 1911 when the Supreme Court found Samuel Gompers and other AFL leaders guilty of contempt of court for violating a lower court injunction based on the Sherman Act. That injunction was imposed by a District of Columbia court against the AFL for publishing a "do not patronize" list in its magazine. One of the businesses on that AFL blacklist, the Buck Stove Company, had sued Gompers for restraint of trade.[27]

During the 1912 presidential campaign, President William Howard Taft and his two challengers, former president Theodore Roosevelt and governor Woodrow Wilson, agreed on at least one thing: that the Supreme Court had been too lenient on big business and that the antitrust laws had to be strengthened. Congress responded in 1914 with the Clayton Antitrust Act, which appeared to give labor needed protection. Section 6 of the act stated that "Nothing contained in the antitrust laws shall be construed to forbid the existence and operation of labor, agricultural, or horticultural organizations . . . nor shall such organizations, or the members thereof, be held or construed to be illegal combinations or conspiracies in restraint of trade, under the antitrust laws."

This seemed to clear up the antitrust issue, and a pleased Samuel Gompers proclaimed the Clayton Antitrust Act the "Magna Carta of labor." However, the Supreme Court in 1921 ruled against labor, stating that despite the language of section 6, there was nothing that exempted unions from antitrust in the Clayton Act. The Court reasoned that the Clayton legislation covered only peaceful activities by unions and that the federal courts had never prohibited such activities. Thus, Clayton did not change anything.[28]

The antitrust provisions of the Sherman Antitrust Act thus remained and became important legal tools for quelling union activity. By 1928, unions had been prosecuted eighty-three times under the antitrust provisions, constituting 18 percent of the overall caseload brought under Sherman.[29]

During the latter stages of World War I, the federal government created the National War Labor Board to develop guidelines for postwar labor relations. For the first time in American history, the federal government established the right of workers to organize: "this right shall not be denied, abridged, or interfered with by the employers in any manner whatsoever." However, despite this clear, unambiguous language, corporations refused to comply, and the Board was given no authority to enforce this fundamental principle.[30]

The year 1920 was a high point in union membership, with 5 million workers belonging to unions; but it was also a period of intense labor strife, with nearly 20 percent of the workforce engaged in labor disputes. One of the most bitter strikes involved the largest corporation in America, the United States Steel Corporation, which in the fall of 1919 crushed a strike of some 365,000 steelworkers. Twenty-six workers were killed, the strikers won no concessions, lost over $100 million in wages, and were painted by the implacable Elbert H. Gary, chairman of U.S. Steel, as agents of Bolshevism.[31]

With the inevitable slowdown in the postwar economy, union membership fell sharply from 5 million in 1920 to 3.6 million in 1923.[32] It wasn't simply the economic downturn that caused union membership to decline, it was also the persistent anti-labor tactics used by employers, big and small, backed by compliant court systems and sympathetic governments at all levels.

Corporations used the many tools at their disposal. Injunctions during the 1920s were at an all-time high and the yellow-dog contract was widely used as a weapon against unionization. Companies used blacklists, threats, intimidation, their own private armed security forces, and found assistance in the state and federal courts, state militias, and local law enforcement. The success of U.S. Steel in smashing the 1919 strike helped the anti-union movement go to the next level. There was also an aggressive open-shop drive, dubbed "the American Plan," spearheaded by the National Association of Manufacturers and others. It established a network of open shop organizations throughout the country to push for legislation to guarantee that workers could not be compelled to join labor unions. The anti-union drive delivered its own political spin, attempting to tie labor unions with Bolshevism and communism, trying to expose the riches and spoils taken by union bosses at the expense of workers.[33]

The administration of Warren G. Harding also gave open support to the anti-union movement. In 1922, President Harding replaced Wilson appointees to the Railroad Labor Board, and those conservative replacements promptly slashed wages, leading to a walkout of 400,000 railroad shop men. The board then instructed the railroads to set up company unions, a move that cost striking workers their seniority. Then Attorney General Harry M. Daugherty obtained a sweeping injunction against the railroad workers. Daugherty declared, that as long as he spoke for the federal government, "I will use the power of the government to prevent the labor unions of the country from destroying the open shop."[34]

Perhaps the most important Supreme Court decision involving labor during the 1920s was *Adkins* v. *Children's Hospital* (1923) which decided that a District of Columbia minimum wage law for women was unconstitutional as a violation of the so-called freedom of contract. For progressives, this was a shocking ruling, going against the strong tide of recent legislation and legal rulings. Since 1912, seventeen states and the District of Columbia had enacted minimum wage statutes; and when cases were heard in federal court over the constitutionality of such laws, thirty-two judges voted in favor and only nine against. But now, the Supreme Court had spoken. Soon thereafter, state supreme courts using *Adkins* as the controlling doctrine nullified state minimum wage laws.[35]

However, the 1920s did produce some progressive federal labor legislation. The Railway Labor Act of 1926 was a breakthrough in creating a new national labor policy. The law was aimed at minimizing strikes and lockouts on railways and gave railroad workers the right to select their own bargaining representatives "without interference, influence, or coercion." This was the first time that the federal government had declared an unqualified right of workers to join (or not join) a union. It was also the only piece of federal labor legislation of any significance during the 1920s; however, with no established federal grievance board, thousands of complaints were left unresolved.[36]

For years, Fiorello La Guardia (Republican–New York) in the House and George W. Norris (Republican–Nebraska) in the Senate had been advocating federal anti-injunction legislation.[37] During extensive Senate hearings in 1929, Norris called in leading academic and legal experts, including Harvard law professor Felix Frankfurter, who, together with his colleague Nathan Greene, was just completing the seminal work on the subject of the labor injunction and its impact on the labor movement.[38] While Norris's legislation did not pass in 1929, it was reintroduced in early 1932, during the Seventy-Second Congress.

The time was ripe for reform, and anti-injunction sentiment was running high in the wake of the Red Jacket decision and Hoover's ill-fated attempt to nominate Judge James H. Wilkerson, the notorious "injunction judge," to the Seventh Court of Appeals. Norris worked the legislation through the Senate, winning with an extraordinary 75 to 5 margin. In the House, La Guardia shepherded it through some contentious debate, but ultimately with the same lopsided support, 362 to 14. The landmark Norris–La Guardia Act of 1932 cut away two of the most pernicious obstacles to workers and organized labor: the court-ordered injunction and the yellow-dog contract. The legislation severely limited the use of labor injunctions and judge-made labor law, and made yellow-dog contracts unenforceable. Federal courts could not forbid strikes, peaceful picketing, or other activities, such as publicizing a strike or giving out strike funds.

Historian Howard Zinn observed that the Norris–La Guardia Act could rightfully be considered "as launching the legislative 'new deal' for labor."[39] This was the pinnacle of La Guardia's career in Congress; ironically, later that year, he was defeated for re-election in the Democratic tidal wave that swept in Franklin Roosevelt and the New Deal.[40] Hoover signed the legislation, then without comment made public a letter from Attorney General James D. Mitchell which questioned the constitutionality of the legislation. George Norris was outraged. In the closing hours of the 1932 presidential campaign, the Republican Party, trying desperately to claim some credit, listed among Hoover's victories for labor the "approval in the face of forceful opposition of the bill outlawing the yellow-dog contract and providing relief from the use of injunction in labor disputes."[41]

Employers had yet another weapon to blunt, or at least co-opt, the drive toward unionization and collective bargaining. Businesses began creating their own company unions, or so-called employee representation plans. Such plans, however, were, as historian David M. Kennedy characterized them, "docile and housebroken creatures of management."[42] They were established, maintained, and controlled by management.

The track record of organized labor was not at all encouraging. Since 1875, labor had won few major fights, and organized labor's grip on working men and women was tenuous. By the beginning of the Depression and the Hoover administration, organized labor had lost its muscle and its drive. It was losing battles on minimum wage and hours, sweatshops were returning, and child labor was increasing.[43] Furthermore, organized labor lacked dynamic, vigorous leadership. Samuel Gompers, long past his prime as AFL president, had died in 1924, and his successor was the docile William Green. Labor historian Irving Bernstein characterized Green as an "uncomplicated intellectual mediocrity" without the power to lead. United Mine Workers president John L. Lewis was less charitable: "I have done a lot of exploring in Bill's mind and I give you my word there is nothing there."[44] Rather than fight for workers' demands, Green chose respectability and acceptance of business' dominance in the American economy. In the great political and legislative fights to come, organized labor was only a minor player.

On the day that Roosevelt defeated Hoover, November 8, 1932, there were 13.2 million Americans who had lost their jobs. By the time Roosevelt was sworn into office on March 4, 1933, that number had swelled to 15 million. "Grim poverty stalks throughout our land," Roosevelt told increasingly desperate voters while on the campaign trail. "It embitters the present and darkens the future."[45] European nations were defaulting on their debt installments and, beginning in January, the number and frequency of American bank closings sent anxious chills through the financial community.

During those last days bleak days of the Hoover administration, labor leader John L. Lewis spoke before the Senate Finance Committee, and gave a foretaste of both Franklin Roosevelt's inaugural address and early New Deal policy, most of which was crafted by Congress.[46] On February 17, 1933, Lewis warned the senators that the time for half-hearted measures and a fixation on a balanced budget had passed, and that it was now time for action. He argued that there needed to be created a national emergency board, composed of representatives from labor, industry, agriculture, and finance, that would have the power to reduce hours worked, guarantee the right of labor unions to form, stabilize prices, and have the authority to implement national economic planning.[47]

Also during the 1932 lame-duck session, Senator Hugo L. Black (Democrat–Alabama) introduced legislation requiring a maximum thirty-hour week in all industries. AFL president William Green testified on behalf of the bill and bluntly predicted that if the legislation were not passed, there would be a "universal strike."[48] With the New Deal Congress now convening in emergency session, Black, on March 10, 1933, urged Roosevelt to include a thirty-hour work week provision in his relief package. Roosevelt ignored him, prompting the senator to bring his bill to the floor, where it passed by 53 to 30 on April 16. For Roosevelt, the Black bill was too revolutionary, too much of a threat to the nation's economy. Roosevelt's new secretary of labor, Frances Perkins, who considered the bill unconstitutional, rushed to the House hearings to sidetrack the Black legislation.[49]

In the Senate, the most persistent champion of national industrial planning was Robert F. Wagner (Democrat–New York).[50] He headed one of three groups of policymakers who would craft the National Industrial Recovery Act (NIRA); a second group came from the Department of Commerce, while the third was headed by presidential advisor Raymond Moley.[51] After considerable wrangling, Roosevelt told the competing groups to go into a conference room, lock the door, and not come back until they had agreed. On May 15, the administration's bill was sent to Congress.[52]

The National Industrial Recovery Act suspended antitrust laws to permit employers within a single industry to form trade associations or industrial groups that set production quotas or fixed prices under "codes of fair competition." Employers would establish minimum wages, maximum hours, and other conditions of employment. Once approved and promulgated by the president, these codes would have the force of law. To encourage unions to participate, section 7(a) guaranteed employees "the right to organize and bargain collectively through representatives of their own choosing" without employer interference or coercion, language taken directly from the Norris–LaGuardia Act.

The National Association of Manufacturers pushed to soften the collective bargaining provisions, but Wagner insisted, issuing an ultimatum to the House-Senate conferees: "No 7(a), no bill." The disputed section stayed. Curiously, the administration and labor were at best lukewarm about this key provision. Industry did not support 7(a); organized labor was more interested in pushing the thirty-hour bill; both administration officials who would be put in charge, General Hugh Johnson and his successor, Donald Richberg, opposed it; and the president didn't understand the provisions or the long-term ramifications of protecting workers' rights.[53]

In the House, the NIRA easily passed, with minor changes but then ran up against stiff opposition in the Senate from progressives, particularly William E. Borah (Republican–Idaho), who warned that, with the suspension of antitrust provisions, big business would dominate the code-making process. But the administration prevailed, the Senate beat back Borah's objections, and the NIRA became law on June 16, 1933.[54] At the signing ceremony, Roosevelt promised that the NIRA would put millions back to work that summer, permitting them to buy goods and services, and get the economy going again.

Despite the fact that he was not really fully engaged in the legislation, Roosevelt remarked to the newsmen at the signing ceremony that "history will probably record the NIRA as the most important and far-reaching legislation ever enacted by the American Congress."[55] Senator Wagner, who certainly was engaged, was equally confident, saying that he felt that the "greatest victory in my war against human misery had been achieved."[56] But there were many policymakers and critics who had their doubts; not the least of those doubters was Justice Louis D. Brandeis.

The NIRA called for the creation of the National Recovery Administration (NRA) to oversee the creation of industry codes and a National Labor Board (NLB) to settle disputes. The NRA devised the Blue Eagle public relations campaign: businesses large and small pledged to comply with the NRA program, display the Blue Eagle sign or flag on their premises, and proclaim, "We Do Our Part." Codes would be developed for each industry, which would promise to produce higher wages, lower working hours, and better labor conditions. In exchange, industries would be exempted from antitrust regulations. Over two million employers enlisted.[57]

The country was ecstatic: finally, everyone seemed to be pulling together, all doing their part. A *Washington Post* report captured the flavor of a Blue Eagle rally in New York:

> Two million of New York's seven million citizens watched another quarter million that September [1933], banging and blaring and drumming away along the canyon that is New York's Fifth Avenue, marching in the Blue Eagle drive. Rickety prideful floats creaked by. Men and women shouted and cheered to their leaders in the red-white-and-blue reviewing stands opposite the library. They joked, broke step, gloried in the end of depression.[58]

Roosevelt beamed, "There is a unity in this country which I have not seen and you have not seen since April, 1917 . . ." Happy days were here again![59]

While the NRA began its work one week after the law was enacted, the National Labor Board (NLB) was not created until August 1933. It wasn't until late October that the board members received notification of their duties, and not until mid-December did the NLB become official through a retroactive executive order.[60] While its role and jurisdiction were vague, the NLB did have the responsibility of trying to settle strikes and disputes over recognition of a union, and to interpret and uphold section 7(a). Nearly three-quarters of all the disputes centered on employer interference with collective bargaining, especially since many employers construed section 7(a) to permit company unions or employee representation plans. At first, the NLB was having some success, but then, in November 1933, the National Association of Manufacturers publicly attacked the NLB, saying it interfered with sound employment relations. Weirton Steel and the Budd Manufacturing Company soon refused to cooperate with elections to see if employees wanted to form independent unions. After this, employers persistently refused to cooperate with the NLB.[61]

The trouble was, the NLB had no enforcement authority. It could try to mediate or obtain an agreement. If there was non-compliance, the only thing that the NLB could do was turn the matter over to the NRA administrator, the compliance division, or the attorney general for "appropriate action." All that could be done was to remove the Blue Eagle symbol from stores or business letterhead stationery. The attorney general could institute injunction proceedings or prosecute, but there were only four instances when Blue Eagles were removed during the life of the program.[62]

In February 1934, Roosevelt issued two executive orders empowering the NLB, if requested by employees, to conduct elections under the principle of majority rule. But then NRA's Hugh Johnson and general counsel Donald Richberg effectively repudiated the majority rule principle, favoring instead the right of minorities and individuals to bargain separately.[63]

In early 1934, Roosevelt decided to personally intervene in automobile labor negotiations. The automobile companies had a deserved reputation of bitterly fighting against outside unions, but, with the growing militancy of the automotive unions and the importance of the industry to the country's economy, Roosevelt offered a compromise. If the unions would call off the strike, the president would personally intervene. He did so, and, on March 25, announced his decision: the automobile manufacturers would be removed from the jurisdiction of the NLB, and placed in a special Automobile Board. The president went further, as labor historian Melvin Dubofsky summed it up: "Roosevelt had apparently condemned majority representation, endorsed company unionism, neglected collective bargaining, and demanded that unions as well as firms be regulated by law."[64] In effect, by his hands-on meddling, Roosevelt killed off the NLB. Labor secretary Frances Perkins warned Roosevelt not to become involved in detailed negotiations; later, the president averred, "I must never again do a thing like that."[65]

By early December 1933, Senator Wagner, who served as chairman of the NLB, was telling the reporters that section 7(a) needed strengthening and clear enforcement powers. On March 1, 1934, Wagner introduced a new labor disputes bill that would reconstitute the National Labor Board and give it enforcement powers through the federal courts. His proposal was met by vehement opposition from the U.S. Chamber of Commerce and the National Association of Manufacturers, and universal scorn from individual companies and their company union representatives.[66]

Wagner's labor disputes bill was bogged down in Congress and, with mounting labor strife throughout the country, Roosevelt stepped in and offered Public Resolution No. 44, which authorized the president to establish a board to investigate section 7(a) controversies which obstructed interstate commerce. Congress accepted the president's offer, and under the authority of Resolution 44, Roosevelt created the National Labor Relations Board (NLRB) in late

June 1934. However, the new NLRB had a basic, but familiar, flaw: it lacked enforcement power against employers who would not agree to section 7(a) proscriptions. All the NLRB could do was recommend, and, with public opinion increasingly hostile to labor demands and a reluctant Justice Department, this new three-member board became powerless and moribund.[67]

There was growing tension between workers and management, boiling over in 1933 and particularly in 1934. In the first six months after signing the NIRA, there were 1,695 work stoppages involving 1.1 million workers. The main reason for the stoppages were employee protests against violation of NIRA codes: 35,000 garment workers, 60,000 dressmakers, 50,000 silk workers, and 70,000 miners all walked off their jobs in August and September 1933.[68] In 1934, there was an explosion of labor–management strife: 1,856 work stoppages involving 1.47 million workers. It was a year, as Irving Bernstein observed, which "ripped the cloak of civilized decorum from society, leaving exposed naked class conflict."[69]

Four clashes stood out for their violence and for the involvement of labor militants, abetted, sometimes led, by radicals and sympathizers of the Communist Party. In May 1934, a violent clash between labor militants of the American Workers Party led by A. J. Muste and the Electric Auto-Lite Company in Toledo, Ohio, resulted in two men dead of gunshot wounds. Later that summer came a truckers' strike in Minneapolis, led by brothers Bill and Ray Dunne, a violent, protracted skirmish that witnessed police shooting sixty-seven Teamsters and killing two, and self-described radical governor Floyd B. Olson declaring martial law. In San Francisco, Harry Bridges, the militant leader of the International Longshoremen's Association, called for a general strike. Over 130,000 workers from throughout the city honored the strike and San Francisco was brought to a standstill for four days in July; two workers were killed in the violence. In each of these three strikes—Toledo, Minneapolis, and San Francisco—the workers won their grievances, but left in their trail bitterness and public resentment. Moreover, these strikes took place independently of the AFL and sometimes against its wishes. Then came the largest strike of all, the east-coast textile workers' strike in August, involving some 376,000 workers in twenty states. This strike, generated by the United Textile Workers and led by a conservative faction of the AFL, however, was completely unsuccessful.[70]

While citizens stood and cheered for the NRA in the fall of 1933, by the spring of 1934 there was growing popular disillusionment. The NRA, for many workers, minorities, and consumers, had become the "National Run-Around."[71] Former business friends, such as Gerard Swope of General Electric, and New Deal intellectuals turned against it. Midwest progressive senators Gerald P. Nye (Republican–North Dakota) and William Borah launched a relentless attack against the NRA, deploring monopolies and their devastating impact on farmers and small business owners.[72] To investigate charges of monopolistic practices, Roosevelt created a National Recovery Review Board, headed by the redoubtable, seventy-seven-year-old Clarence Darrow. The review board held twelve lengthy hearings, logged in 2,753 pages of complaints, and another 304 complainants waiting to testify about the NRA and the industrial codes. Darrow's final report, erratic and biased though it was, charged that big businesses dominated the code process, and squeezed small businesses, workers, and the public. Not the least of the NRA's problems was its administrator, the bombastic and at times unstable General Hugh S. Johnson, who finally resigned in September 1934.[73]

Making the Law

The 1934 midterm elections were an historic affirmation of Roosevelt and the New Deal. The *Washington Post* called the election results "one of the most spectacular expressions of confidence every tendered a president midterm."[74] Irving Bernstein concluded that "for all practical purposes the election eliminated the right wing of the Republican Party" and while, during the Seventy-Third Congress, the House had been considered the more progressive body, now, in the new Seventy-Fourth, the Senate was the more progressive chamber.[75] Democrats added nine pro-New Deal Senators, including Missouri's Harry S. Truman, who pledged 100 percent cooperation with President Roosevelt and his policies.[76] The victories were so sweet for the Roosevelts that the First Lady announced that wine would be served at the December cabinet dinner, the first time that alcohol had been served in the White House since the pre-Prohibition days of the Wilson administration.[77]

Roosevelt and Congress had their work cut out for them. The president was being squeezed hard by the U.S. Chamber of Commerce and other business interests for interfering with private enterprise, and he was attacked by progressive forces for not being aggressive enough in political and social reform.[78] One of the biggest problems for Roosevelt was the NIRA, which was scheduled to expire in the summer of 1935. On February 20, 1935, Roosevelt asked Congress to renew the legislation for another two years, despite its problems and shortcomings. There was stubborn opposition in both houses, but eventually Congress extended the NIRA in a greatly modified form for another ten months, to April 1, 1936.[79]

> Seventy-Fourth Congress, 1st Session (January 3–August 26, 1935)
>
> Senate: 69 Democrats; 25 Republicans; 2 other
>
> House: 322 Democrats; 103 Republicans; 10 other
>
> President: Franklin D. Roosevelt

In the fall of 1934, Senator Wagner directed his aide, Leon H. Keyserling, to revive the unsuccessful 1934 labor disputes legislation and draft what would become the Wagner Act. Keyserling, along with the general counsel and legal staff of the NLRB, had several sources from which to draft the legislation: the

Norris–La Guardia act, the NIRA, 1934 labor disputes bill, Resolution 44, and Wagner's experience on the NLRB and the old NLB.[80] The AFL assisted to some extent, sending over some policy suggestions, but was essentially content to let Wagner's staff work out the legislation.[81]

The day after Roosevelt half heartedly endorsed a two-year extension of the NIRA, Wagner introduced his own legislation. Roosevelt had done nothing to encourage Wagner and neither he nor any administration official was involved in its creation or in pushing it through Congress. Secretary Perkins was not consulted either during the drafting process, and, when she later testified in favor of the legislation, she showed little enthusiasm, and the focus of her testimony was to make sure that the new National Labor Relations Board would not be independent, but be housed within her cabinet department.[82] Congressman William P. Connery, Jr. (Democrat–Massachusetts), chairman of the labor committee, introduced the legislation in the House the following week.

Hearings began on March 11, with Wagner as the first witness before the Senate Committee on Education and Labor. He warned that there had been a "rising tide of industrial discontent" with employers ignoring NLRB orders and failing to uphold the labor-protection provisions of section 7(a) of the NIRA. Wagner told the committee that, of sixty-eight rulings by the NLRB, forty-eight had not been obeyed. The NLRB had ordered eight union elections, but just two had been held. Several hundred boards in the affected industries handled section 7(a) cases. This led to confusion, uncertainty, Wagner argued, and to the NIRA provisions being ignored and, consequently, section 7(a) was being "emasculated." It was time to clarify and toughen this fundamental protection for workers and unions. His legislation would re-enact the labor section of the NIRA and give it wide-scale application rather than limiting it to codified industries.[83]

Not unexpectedly, the National Association of Manufacturers was the chief opponent to Wagner's far-ranging bill. James A. Emery, the general counsel for the NAM, attacked the bill, claiming that it would "employ the government as the recruiting sergeant of an army in which workers refuse to enlist." During the course of the hearings, the NAM representative had several sharp clashes with Wagner; Emery hammered away that the bill violated the due process and commerce and judicial clause of the Constitution. Wagner said tartly: "Some day I am going to hear you approve some legislation in favor of social progress and that will be a great day." On the radio, Clinton L. Bardo, president of the NAM, attacked the legislation saying that it "attempts to overthrow that fundamental right of a man to sell his labor without being forced to affiliate with any group." Then Bardo took the gloves off and said, "the refusal to bargain collectively with an irresponsible, a communistic or racketeering union is by definition as illegal as the refusal of relations with a labor organization of reputation and integrity."[84]

Highlights of the Wagner Act of 1935

As stated in the preamble, it was "declared to be the policy of the United States to . . . [encourage] the practice and procedure of collective bargaining."

The heart of the legislation was found in section 7: "Employees shall have the right to self-organization, to form, join, or assist labor organizations, to bargain collectively through representatives of their own choosing, and to engage in concerted activities, for the purpose of collective bargaining or other mutual aid or protection." There was no parallel set of rights established for companies.

The next section listed five unfair labor practices that employers could not engage in: they could not (1) "interfere with, restrain, or coerce" employees who wanted to exercise their section 7 rights; (2) "dominate or interfere with" the formation or administration of any labor organization or contribute financially to it (thus, banning company unions); (3) discriminate between union and nonunion employees in any way that would encourage or discourage them from joining unions; (4) discriminate against any worker who filed charges or gave testimony; or (5) refuse to bargain in good faith. There was no mention of union unfair practices.

The Act also provided mechanisms for selecting union bargaining representatives, through government-supervised secret-ballot elections. It also established a reconstituted National Labor Relations Board, which, through its regional boards, could conduct hearings and decided charges of unfair labor practices. Such findings could then go to the national NLRB and then to the federal courts for enforcement.

The Wagner bill would outlaw company unions. At the time, roughly three million workers were organized in company unions, while four-and-one-half million members were in independent unions; company unions were also growing at a faster rate.[85] This brought an outcry from representatives of such unions, who argued that it would be the death knell of the employee representation plan and would "create strife and retard recovery." Senator Wagner heard their cry, but questioned their impartiality. Under his cross-examination, the witnesses admitted that they had been paid by their companies to come to Washington and testify, and that they might not be sufficiently impartial from the company.[86]

The AFL's William Green charged that, under the NIRA, section 7(a) had been "sabotaged" by industry and turned into an "instrument of persecution of the workers." He argued that it would be "better 10,000 times that Congress had never given us section 7(a) than that it should be used as an instrument of persecution of those who believed in it." The AFL leader, turning a charge often pinned on organized labor, linked the manufacturers with the communists.[87]

At the heart of Wagner's new legislation was section 7(a), which was taken verbatim from the NIRA:

> Employees shall have the right to self-organization, to form, join, or assist labor organizations, to bargain collectively through representatives of their own choosing, and to engage in concerted activities, for the purpose of collective bargaining or other mutual aid or protection.

Under Wagner's legislation, the federal government would throw its weight directly in support of workers and protect their right to organize. Accompanying language spelled out clearly the prohibited unfair labor practices that employers could not engage in: trying to influence elections, using force and intimidation, use of blacklists, and other tactics. The legislation was silent on any unfair labor practices or tactics that might be used by labor unions themselves.

The Wagner Act passed in the Senate on May 16, by the overwhelming vote of 63 to 12, then was reported out of the House committee four days later. Finally, on May 24, Roosevelt called Senator Wagner, Frances Perkins, Donald Richberg and others into his office. Despite the pressure from business interests, Roosevelt, after fifteen months of deliberation, agreed to endorse Wagner's bill. Not only did he endorse the bill, but Roosevelt then announced that this was a part of the "must pass" legislation for continuation of the New Deal.[88]

Then came Black Monday: May 27, 1935.

While Senator Wagner was shepherding his National Labor Relations Act through Congress, the Supreme Court was hearing a case challenging the constitutionality of the NIRA.

Author of the Wagner Act

Robert Ferdinand Wagner (1877–1953) served in the Senate from 1927 to 1949. Wagner was born in Germany, and with his family immigrated to the United States when he was a child. Wagner served in the New York State Assembly (1905–1908), then the State Senate (1909–1918), and chaired the State Factory Investigating Commission, which delved into the Triangle Shirtwaist Factory fire of 1911. Wagner also served as a justice on the New York Supreme Court (1924–1926). He put his progressive philosophy to work in the U.S. Senate. Two years before the start of the New Deal, Wagner had called for a public works program, a federal employment stabilization board, and a national system of unemployment insurance. He fought for anti-lynching legislation and for permitting Jewish wartime refugees to settle in the United States.

In her memoirs, Frances Perkins gave Wagner full credit for this landmark legislation: "It ought to be on the record that the president did not take part in developing the National Labor Relations Act and, in fact, was hardly consulted about it. It was not a part of the president's program. It did not particularly appeal to him when it was described to him. All the credit for it belongs to Wagner."[89]

Wagner was also responsible for shepherding the Social Security Act through the Senate in 1935. He later was a delegate to the United Nations Monetary and Financial Conference at Bretton Woods, in 1944.

The National Labor Board had convicted the Schechter brothers, New York City slaughterhouse operators who worked on a commission and sold to kosher retailers, of violating maximum hours and minimum wage provisions, selling sick, tubercular chickens, and failing to observe the "straight-killing" provisions of the Live Poultry Code, established under the authority of the NIRA. The case exposed the extreme lengths to which federal government regulation would go under this legislation. It also brought a few light-hearted moments in the courtroom. On May 3, 1935, Joseph Heller, counsel for the Schechters, argued that his clients were convicted by the federal government for matters that were purely local, involving only intrastate commerce, and wholly outside the jurisdiction of the NRA. When, in oral argument, a justice asked about the straight-killing method, Heller went into a long, detailed, and excited explanation of how someone reached into the chicken coop, took out whichever chicken he could grab, and handed it over to the rabbi for slaughter. A reporter for the *New York Times* observed that the normally staid justices were sent into "gales of laughter" by Heller's account.[90]

But the verdict was no laughing matter for the Roosevelt administration. On Monday, May 27, the Supreme Court, in a unanimous ruling penned by Chief Justice Charles Evans Hughes, ruled that the NRA had delegated too much power to the president and private organizations: "Such delegation of legislative power is unknown to our law and is utterly inconsistent with the constitutional prerogatives and duties of Congress." Indeed, the vast sweep of delegation by Congress, was, in the words of Benjamin Cardozo in his concurring opinion, "delegation run riot."[91] Roosevelt was stunned, and distressed by the unanimity of the decision. He had hoped at least to win over Louis D. Brandeis, "Old Isaiah" as Roosevelt called him, but Brandeis, who had disapproved the NIRA from the very beginning, publicly declared that "May 27 was the most important day in the history of the Supreme Court and the most beneficent."[92] Reporters dubbed that day "Black Monday."

In a free-wheeling press conference four days after the decision, over one hundred reporters jammed into Roosevelt's office wanting to know about the Supreme Court decision and the president's reaction. Roosevelt said that the ruling was probably more important than any since the 1857 *Dred Scott* decision, saying it raised the profoundly important question of whether the U.S. government has control over the national economy or would it be controlled by the forty-eight states. For ninety minutes, Roosevelt impressed the reporters with his grasp of the issues concerning interstate commerce, and stating further that, thanks to this decision, "we have been relegated to a horse and buggy definition of interstate commerce." The entire press conference was to be on background, without any quotes or attributions. But the press could not resist: the reporters asked for permission to use the horse and buggy quote, and the next day, newspapers nationwide proclaimed: "FDR: Horse and Buggy Decision" and editorials severely blasted the president.[93]

The NIRA was dead and, the next day, 411 NRA pending suits were dropped. Within days of the decision, the AFL reported that it was receiving reports from all around the country of wage cuts and forced increases in the work week.[94] Roosevelt would now turn his energies to the pending Wagner legislation, but first, he promptly set off on a weekend fishing cruise on the Chesapeake Bay.

The national press and administration opponents were convinced that *Schechter* had not only invalidated the NIRA but would do the same for the pending Wagner legislation as well. Undeterred, Wagner and Roosevelt pressed ahead. Some changes were made in the bill, particularly making clear in its preamble the connection between industrial disputes and commerce. Differences between the House and Senate versions were ironed out in conference, and approved by their respective chambers on June 27. On July 5, 1935, Roosevelt signed the National Labor Relations Act, giving ceremonial signing pens to Senator Wagner and AFL's Green. Echoing Gompers's pronouncement in 1914, Green declared the Wagner Act was the Magna Carta of the labor movement. Yet many industrial opponents were convinced that the legislation was just as unconstitutional as its predecessor.

Wagner's National Labor Relations Act was the first piece of legislation passed in what became known as the Second Hundred Days of the New Deal. Since early June, just after the *Schechter* decision, lawmakers were itching to adjourn. It had been a difficult, bumpy first six months in Congress and official Washington always closed down during the stifling heat and muggy summer months. Air-conditioning was still a new luxury in Washington; it was installed in the White House in 1929 and in the Capitol building the next year, but hardly anyone had the comforts of air-conditioning in their homes or automobiles.

Roosevelt was determined to reassert his leadership and resuscitate the New Deal. Spurred on by the *Schechter* defeat, by partisan bickering and economic stalemate, and the sense that the New Deal would be stalled unless Congress acted boldly, Roosevelt insisted that lawmakers stay in session through the summer months of 1935 until the job was done.[95] Wending their way through Congress were the social security bill, legislation on banking, a "soak the rich" tax increase, and a public utility holding company bill. Roosevelt would capture every one of these major pieces of legislation.

The Wagner Act created a new, independent National Labor Relations Board to protect workers against unfair labor practices and to investigate any impediments to unions and workers. Progressives hailed the enforcement protections of Wagner Act as a "momentous libertarian victory," with First Amendment guarantees of freedom of speech and assembly for workers, backed up by the force of law.[96]

But soon, industry struck back. Historian Dexter Perkins concluded that "no legislation of the New Deal period met with more determined opposition than the Wagner Act."[97] The National Association of Manufacturers led the charge, issuing a bulletin to its members declaring that the Wagner Act did not apply to manufacturing and that the unfair labor practices proscribed in Wagner did not affect intrastate commerce. "Commerce does not begin until manufacturing has ended," the NAM bulletin declared, bolstering its argument with recent federal court decisions.[98] NAM already had begun its propaganda war. Beginning in 1934, and for the next thirteen years, the NAM's Information Committee spent more than $15 million on leaflets, radio speeches, movie shorts, films for schools, reprints of favorable articles by economists, had a daily column in 260 newspapers, for the "dissemination of sound American doctrines."[99] At the core of NAM's sound American doctrines was the emasculation of the Wagner Act.

Then in September 1935, the Lawyers Committee of the American Liberty League declared the Wagner Act to be unconstitutional. Fifty-eight lawyers from the American Liberty League, an organization composed primarily of business and manufacturing interests, declared that the Wagner Act was "a complete departure from our constitutional and traditional theories of government." Jouett Shouse, the League's president, said that this would be the first in a series of legal appraisals of New Deal legislation, with other reports to follow on the Social Security Act, the Public Utility Holding Act, the Bituminous Coal Conservation (Guffey) Act, the Tennessee Valley Act and other major pieces of progressive legislation.[100] Secretary of the Interior Harold L. Ickes sarcastically shot back at the "gross impertinence and flagrant impropriety" of "Chief Justice Shouse and his fifty-seven varieties of associate justices."[101]

The NLRB began conducting field hearings in the fall of 1935, and discovered that companies were intent on subverting the new law. Its first case involved the Greyhound Bus Company in Pennsylvania, where the NLRB uncovered industrial espionage and surveillance of union meetings. The NLRB then went to Detroit in November to hear evidence that the Fruehauf Trailer Company had fired several men who wanted to join the United Auto Workers union. The hearings uncovered a Pinkerton detective agency employee who was working as a spy for Fruehauf, had infiltrated the union and gave the company a list of union members. Later that month, the NLRB held hearings in St. Louis, where it heard charges against the Brown Shoe Company of Salem, Illinois, for employing industrial spies, forming citizens' groups to break up union activities, and using various forms of intimidation against workers.[102] All of these activities violated the provisions of the Wagner act.

The NLRB wanted to know more and was determined to investigate industrial espionage, strikebreaking tactics, the use of private detective agencies, and other forms of union intimidation. It turned to long-time investigator Heber Blankenhorn for assistance. At the same time, Gardner (Pat) Jackson, former newspaper reporter and official at the Agricultural Adjustment Administration, convinced four senators and three representatives to sponsor a dinner at the Cosmos Club in Washington to discuss the problems of employer abuse and determine whether congressional action were needed. Nearly fifty members of Congress, labor, church, and civic leaders attended, and out of it came action. Shortly after the dinner, Jackson contacted Blankenhorn and with several others they helped draft what became Senate Resolution 266, introduced by Senator Robert M. La Follette, Jr. (Progressive–Wisconsin),[103] to conduct investigations on alleged violations of civil liberties in the field of labor relations.

The primary target of La Follette's investigations was the National Association of Manufacturers and its "organized disregard for the National Labor Relations

Act." La Follette's committee also charged that NAM engaged in a "massive, covert propaganda campaign, against labor agitators" and government measures to protect workers using "newspapers, radio, motion pictures, slide films, stockholders' letters, payroll stuffers, billboard advertisements, civic progress meetings and local advertising."[104]

"Young Bob" La Follette, who had been appointed in 1925 to succeed his father in the Senate, was a strong backer of progressive labor legislation and champion of civil liberties. He was a leader in the fight for passage of the 1932 Norris–La Guardia anti-injunction legislation and an enthusiastic backer of the Wagner Act. When anti-union resistance continued to build, and companies refused to obey the section 7(a) and fair practices provisions of the Wagner Act, La Follette urged that the Senate conduct an investigation of the infringement of workers rights to organize and bargain collectively.[105] From 1936 through 1940, La Follette served as chairman of the Senate Civil Liberties Committee, which biographer Patrick J. Maney characterized as "one of the most extensive, productive, and controversial congressional probes in history, exposed the heavy-handed, often brutal manner in which many employers tried to prevent workers from organizing."[106] From September 1936 through the spring of 1937, the committee focused on industrial espionage, strikebreaking, the use of private police forces, and the stockpiling of guns, billy clubs, grenades and other weapons to be used against strikers.[107] The revelations of employer chicanery were both sensational and shocking.

Though La Follette wanted to conclude the investigations in the spring of 1937, they were continued following the Memorial Day 1937 tragedy at Republic Steel's South Chicago plant where ten striking steelworkers had been killed and more than one hundred had been wounded.[108] Court challenges soon followed enactment of the Wagner Act. On December 21, 1935, federal judge Merrill E. Otis declared the Wagner Act unconstitutional, ruling that manufacturing was not a part of interstate commerce, and thus could not be regulated by Congress. Despite this lower court ruling, the NLRB continued to operate, considering 2,072 cases that affected 750,000 workers during its next eighteen months of operation. Clearly, the Supreme Court would have to decide the fate of the Wagner Act, and it would fall to the steel industry to provide the circumstances.

On the Court's docket for the 1935–1936 term were cases challenging the Wagner Act, the new Social Security Act, and a number of other federal and state regulatory schemes. The Supreme Court had just moved to its new home, the beautiful marble edifice across the street from its old chambers in the Capitol building. On January 6, 1936, the Court, by a six-to-three vote, struck down the Agricultural Adjustment Act, stating that its tax provisions encroached on state power in contravention of the Tenth Amendment. In potentially the most serious blow to the Wagner Act, the Court, in *Carter* v. *Carter Coal Company*, struck down the Bituminous Coal Conservation Act, which had set minimum wages and maximum hours, and guaranteed the right of workers to organize. Finally, the Court ruled that the New York state minimum wage law was unconstitutional because it violated the freedom of contract.[109] As historian William E. Leuchtenberg summed up: "In 1935 and 1936, over an unwontedly destructive sixteen-month period, the Court demolished a number of acts of Congress, as well as important state legislation."[110] While the Court was unanimous in its opinion in *Schechter*, in most of these opinions there emerged a dissenting faction of Harlan Fiske Stone, Louis D. Brandeis, and Benjamin N. Cardozo, with Chief Justice Hughes occasionally joining in. Roosevelt could count on three, perhaps four, justices to support the New Deal, but could not reach that fifth to make a majority.

In the presidential election of 1936, Roosevelt and the New Deal trounced Alfred M. Landon and the Republicans. Alf Landon, the governor of Kansas, carried just two states, Maine and Vermont. Republicans insisted on attacking Roosevelt and the New Deal on constitutional grounds, arguing Roosevelt was running roughshod over Congress, usurping judicial powers, shoving through legislation that was clearly unconstitutional, and encroaching on the powers and sovereignty of the states. Landon, the party's standard bearer, was in the wholly uncomfortable position of chastising the New Deal programs while at the same time admitting that many of the reforms had merit, but arguing that the Republicans could do better. Voters, however, were in no mood to derail the New Deal or to trust the Republican Party. Democrats now held 333 of the 435 House seats and added six more seats in the Senate, now controlling 75 out of 96 seats.

With an overwhelming mandate from voters and a heavy majority of New Deal backers in Congress, Roosevelt and his supporters turned to reforming the Supreme Court. The aging, conservative Court—the "Nine Old Men"—had ruled unconstitutional key elements of the New Deal, and Roosevelt supporters were bitter and ready for revenge. In particular, the administration scorned the four conservatives: James C. McReynolds, seventy-four years old in 1937, Willis Van Devanter, seventy-seven, George Sutherland, seventy-four, and Pierce Butler, seventy-one. Born in the Civil War era, each of these "Four Horsemen" had served since the Wilson or Taft administrations. Three justices were thought to be sympathetic to New Deal programs: Brandeis, eighty-one (despite his *Schechter* comments), Cardozo, sixty-seven, and Stone, sixty-five. The two justices who could go either way were Chief Justice Hughes, seventy-four, and Owen J. Roberts, the youngest justice at sixty-two. Ironically, Sutherland and Van Devanter probably would not have been on the Court in 1937 had not Congress passed the Economy Act in 1933. That law reduced the salaries and pensions of all federal employees and the justices felt compelled to stay on the bench rather than suffer reduced pensions.[111]

Roosevelt had been calculating a move against the Supreme Court for some time. During 1935 and 1936, Justice Department lawyers, at Roosevelt's urging, tried to draft a constitutional amendment to curb the Supreme Court's powers, but, by early 1937, they had not been able to come up with an acceptable version.[112] Congressional allies also were intent on clipping the judiciary's wings. One extreme proposal was to enact a constitutional amendment to forbid the Supreme Court from ruling acts of Congress unconstitutional; another would allow Congress to re-validate laws declared unconstitutional by the Supreme Court if Congress could repass them by a two-thirds vote of both houses.[113]

Roosevelt kept quiet throughout 1936 and there was not even a hint of his intentions in his January 1937 second inaugural address. On February 5, 1937, Roosevelt presented to Congress his plan to reorganize the federal judiciary. His message to Congress and the accompanying legislation caught nearly everyone by surprise. Roosevelt turned his attention to aged or infirm judges, a subject, he conceded, "of delicacy and yet one which requires frank discussion." A problem was that "a lower mental or physical vigor leads men to avoid an examination of complicated and changed conditions. Little by little, new facts become blurred through old glasses fitted, as it were, for the needs of another generation; older men, assuming that the scene is the same as it was in the past, cease to explore or inquire into the present or the future."[114] The accompanying legislation stated that for every federal judge who had served ten years or more and did not retire within six months of reaching his seventieth birthday, the president could then appoint an additional judge. Under this bill, the president could appoint up to fifty additional federal judges and the maximum size of the U.S. Supreme Court would become fifteen, giving the president authority to appoint up to six justices.

A clerk in the House began reading Roosevelt's message, which was being carried live throughout the nation by radio. When the Senate reading clerk did the same in the upper chamber, Vice-President John Nance Garner stepped down from the dais, then walked out of the chamber, "holding his nose with one hand and vigorously shaking his thumb down with the other."[115] Garner wasn't the only disappointed politician. Conservatives, Republicans, and Democrats alike, cried foul, clearly seeing this court-packing scheme for what it was. The Democratic majority in the Senate was hopelessly divided, with majority leader Joseph T. Robinson (Democrat–Arkansas) gamely trying to rally Democrats to the president's defense.[116]

Then came an historic day, March 29, 1937, when the Court made a doctrinal shift of immense proportion. In *West Coast Hotel* v. *Parrish*, a case involving enforcement of a 1913 Washington state minimum wage law, the Supreme Court, by a five-to-four majority, ruled that the law was a reasonable regulation. The Court overturned a 1923 ruling that had held that minimum wage laws were unconstitutional because they violated the freedom of contract between an employer and an employee. But what was this freedom of contract, the Court asked in *Parrish*? "The Constitution does not speak of freedom of contract. It speaks of liberty and prohibits the deprivation of liberty without due process of law."[117]

It had been assumed by many then and later that the Court caved to pressure from the White House and the President's court-packing scheme: the "switch in time that saved nine" as it became labeled. But Chief Justice Hughes later wrote that Roosevelt's proposal had "not had the slightest effect" on the Court's decisions, and the fifth and deciding justice, Owen Roberts, had made up his mind months before the Roosevelt scheme was made public.[118]

Despite *Parrish*, many believed that the Wagner Act would suffer the same fate as the NIRA in *Schechter*, and be ruled unconstitutional; board members of the NLRB were in fact "haunted" by that prospect. That decision would come just two weeks after *Parrish* in *NLRB* v. *Jones & Laughlin Steel Corporation* and related cases.[119] From September 1936 through May 1937, labor flexed its muscle. The newly formed labor union, the Congress of Industrial Organizations (CIO), aggressively pushed for collective bargaining and worker benefits in mass production, industrial plants. Workers began using the weapon of the sit-down strike, and during this period some 484,000 workers were engaged in sit-downs that closed plants and crippled production. The best remembered sit-down strike occurred in March 1937, right in the middle of the Supreme Court deliberations on the Wagner Act, when the CIO targeted the Flint, Michigan plant of General Motors and 192,642 workers went on strike.[120]

One of the most contentious battlegrounds for unionization was the steel industry. In defiance of the Wagner Act and the NLRB, the Jones & Laughlin Steel Corporation fired ten workers who were engaging in union organizing activities. The steel company dispute was consolidated with four others and brought before the Supreme Court. Over three days in early February 1937, the court heard from over a dozen attorneys who argued for more than twelve hours. Spectators filled the courtroom, with hundreds waiting outside in long lines, hoping to hear the historic oral arguments.[121] During the hearings, the Court was presented with a 1,000-page federal government brief describing the far-flung operations of the steel company and the far-ranging effects on interstate commerce. Manufacturing, the government contended, was not simply a local event, isolated from the reach of federal control and regulation.

On April 18, Chief Justice Hughes, in a strong voice, spoke for the majority of five justices in affirming the authority of the Wagner Act. The chief justice went to the heart of the matter: "Although activities may be intrastate in character when separately considered, if they have such close and substantial relations to interstate commerce that their control is essential or appropriate to protect that commerce from burdens and obstructions, Congress cannot be denied the power to exercise that control."[122] With that, the Court for the first time acknowledged that local manufacturing could come under the regulatory authority of Congress, and, in consequence, workers would come under the full protection of the Wagner Act provisions. "Employees," wrote Hughes, "have as clear a right to organize and select their representatives for lawful purposes as the respondent has to organize its business and select its own offices and agents."[123]

Arthur Krock, writing the next day in the *New York Times*, found these decisions to be "electric," particularly since they were so unexpected. Labor leaders were ecstatic. Labor secretary Frances Perkins noted that more than half the 1,015 strikes in the past six months were for union recognition, and now employers would have to recognize the established rights of workers and their unions. NLRB chairman J. Warren Madden agreed, saying that "[t]his means industrial peace."[121]

The decision, however, brought neither industrial peace nor a slackening of business for the NLRB. Before *Jones & Laughlin*, there were few cases brought before the NLRB and its twenty-one regional offices. In the eighteen months before *Jones & Laughlin*, the NLRB averaged about 150 cases per month; one month after the Supreme Court decision, in May 1937, 1,064 cases were filed; two months later, there were 10,000 cases, completely swamping the regional offices.[125]

Immediately following the ruling, auto magnate Henry Ford, bitter opponent of labor unions, allowed that his auto workers were "free to join anything they want to," but then added, "Of course, I think they are foolish if they join a union."[126] So did other industrialists, who vowed to strike back. The National Association of Manufacturers, the U.S. Chamber of Commerce, and their conservative allies in Congress proposed amendments to curb the powers of the NLRB and to "equalize" the effect of the Wagner Act.[127]

Aftermath

Labor had been growing increasingly restless under the conservative, deferential leadership of the AFL. By 1934, there had been few victories for organized labor. Only 3 million workers, or about 12 percent of the nonagricultural work force, belonged to trade unions; this was a smaller percentage than twelve years earlier.[128] Labor historian Nelson Lichtenstein noted that much of the early New Deal labor activism was a false start: 600 AFL local unions were discontinued or suspended, while hundreds of thousands of workers abandoned their new unions.[129]

Dissident labor leaders, particularly John L. Lewis, were upset with the lackluster performance of the AFL and the fact that it was missing out on a golden opportunity to recruit new workers in major industries. During the last days of the 1935 AFL convention, Lewis and other discontented leaders met informally to decide what to do next. Lewis was joined by union presidents David Dubinsky (Amalgamated Clothing Workers), Sidney Hillman (International Ladies Garment Workers), and Charles Howard (International Typographical Union). Later, on November 9, 1935, the group, now joined by four other union presidents, met again to announce the creation of the Committee of Industrial Organization (CIO), with the purpose of organizing unskilled workers in mass production industries. Lewis formally resigned as vice-president of the AFL in late November and the CIO, later renamed the Congress of Industrial Organizations, eventually made a clean break from the AFL.

One of the first targets of the new CIO was the formidable steel industry. The history of union activity in the steel industry was not promising: the bloody Homestead strike of 1892, a crushing defeat in 1901, and the back-breaking U.S. Steel strike of 1919 were bitter reminders of labor's inability to make inroads, and the ethnic and racial tensions fomented by the steel companies, pitting one group against another. In June 1936, the CIO created the Steel Workers Organizing Committee (SWOC), placing Lewis ally Philip Murray of the United Mine Workers as its head. SWOC's target was "Big Steel," the dominant U.S. Steel with 222,000 employees, Bethlehem Steel with 80,000, Republic with 49,000, and Jones & Laughlin with 29,000. The other steel manufacturers, Youngstown Sheet & Tube, National (Weirton), Inland, and American Rolling Mill, dubbed "Little Steel," would also become targets of union organizing.[130]

The historic turning point in labor relations came, however, in the automobile industry, not steel. On February 11, 1937, John L. Lewis stepped into the GM building in Detroit and signed an agreement with General Motors making the new United Auto Workers (UAW) the sole bargaining representative for striking auto workers. General Motors, the largest manufacturing company in the world, operated 110 plants in fourteen states and eighteen countries, employed 250,000 people, was highly profitable even during the Depression, and was considered the best managed big corporation in America. Two months earlier, it had been hit by an historic sit-down strike.

On December 30, 1936, UAW workers at the Fisher Body Plant No. 1 in Flint, Michigan, began a sit-down strike. The strike target was chosen carefully: for the entire line of 1937 GM automobile models only two sets of body dies had been made, and they were found in Fisher No. 1 in Flint and the Fisher plant in Cleveland. For forty-four days, the assembly lines were shut down and UAW workers refused to leave the Flint plant. In a rare and refreshing action, newly elected governor of Michigan Frank Murphy vowed not to take sides or intervene with the state militia. Other GM plants were struck in Ohio, Indiana, Michigan, and Wisconsin. Within two weeks, General Motors' sprawling manufacturing system had been "brought to its knees."[131] While not getting everything it wanted, the UAW did gain recognition from GM. Quickly Hudson, Packard, and Chrysler corporations, as well as a large number of automotive parts manufacturers, agreed to unionization.

The prominent holdout was the Ford Motor Company. On May 26, 1937, when Walter P. Reuther, president of UAW Local 174, and three other union officials climbed the stairs to the overpass leading to Gate 4 of Ford's massive River Rouge assembly plant, they were brutally attacked by some forty men from Harry Bennett's infamous "Service Department" at Ford.[132] Members of the press accompanied the UAW contingent and captured the violence for the world to see. The "Battle of the Overpass," like the pictures of police dogs unleashed on civil rights protestors some thirty years later, became iconic images of labor strife and the thuggery of industrial resistance. Yet it would be four more years before the 1941 crippling strike at River Rouge and Ford's capitulation to the clear mandates of the Wagner Act.

Soon after the General Motors signed the February 1937 contract, U.S. Steel agreed to unionization. U.S. Steel chairman Myron C. Taylor had been secretly meeting with Lewis, and ironed out an historic, peaceful agreement: recognition of SWOC (later the United Steel Workers) for its members, an eight-hour work day, forty hours a week with time-and-a-half for overtime, and a ten cent raise, bringing wages up to 62.5 cents an hour, or $5 a day. Soon, fifty-one companies signed with SWOC, with basically the same terms as U.S. Steel. Jones & Laughlin, which had just been ordered by the Supreme Court to reinstate discharged workers, signed a union contract in May. But Little Steel, led by the pugnacious Thomas M. Girdler, dug in its heels and would not negotiate for union recognition. This led to a bloody confrontation on Memorial Day 1937 at the Republic Steel Company's plant in South Chicago: police rioted, ten union protestors were killed, another 120, including thirty-five police, were injured. This was soon followed by deaths of workers in Youngstown and Massillon, Ohio. Little Steel would not give in, the unions would not back down, and the federal government, despite the Wagner Act protections, the NLRB, and the bully pulpit of the White House, did nothing. Not until 1941 did Little Steel capitulate and recognize SWOC.[133]

Timeline of the Wagner Act and Labor Rights

1896	Creation of the American Federation of Labor.
1919	Breaking of the steelworkers strike against U.S. Steel.
1920s	"American Plan" push for open shop legislation.
1932	Norris–La Guardia Act outlawing yellow-dog contracts and court-imposed injunctions against strikers.
1933	Creation of the National Industrial Recovery Act (NIRA), and through it the National Recovery Administration, the National Labor Board, and the Blue Eagle campaign.
1934	Divisive strikes in Toledo, Minneapolis, San Francisco, and in textile industry.
1935	The *Schechter* decision holding the NIRA unconstitutional (June); enactment of the Wagner Act (July); creation of the CIO.
1937	UAW sit-down strike against General Motors, union acceptance (February); *Jones & Laughlin* decision upholding the Wagner Act (April); bloody Republic Steel strike (May).
1947	Enactment, over Truman's veto, of the Taft–Hartley Act.
1949	CIO expelled eleven unions with ties to communists.
1955	Merger of the AFL-CIO.
1957	McClellan hearings into labor racketeering; Teamsters kicked out of the AFL-CIO.
1959	Landrum–Griffin legislation designed to bring union democracy and rid out corruption in unions.

The CIO had formed unions in the auto, glass, radio, rubber, and steel industries, and by the end of 1937 had 3.7 million members, while the AFL had 3.4 million members. Unity negotiations between the CIO and AFL collapsed, however, in December 1937, and the AFL severed its ties and revoked the remaining CIO chapters. The fault lines formed around conflicting egos and personalities, craft versus mass industrial unions, tactics, and, increasingly, ideology. John P. Frey, president of the metal trades department of the AFL, accused the CIO of having 145 Communist Party members on the CIO payroll, and accused John L. Lewis of being a frequent guest at the Soviet embassy. Later Frey was the lead-off witness against the CIO before the House Committee for the Investigation of Un-American Activities in 1938, pouring out a "goulash of half-truths and inaccuracies." The AFL and CIO battled each other to become the bargaining agents, with the AFL gaining an upper hand.[134]

Labor grew dramatically in strength in the late 1930s and into the war years. Total union membership increased from 3.7 million (6.7 percent of the total workforce) in 1935 to 8.9 million (15.5 percent) in 1940 and 14.8 million (21.9 percent) in 1945. During this time, the NLRB was involved in some 36,000 cases involving unfair labor practices and 38,000 concerning employee representation. Of all these cases, 15.9 percent required official NLRB hearings. Ultimately, some 2,000 company unions were disestablished, 300,000 workers were reinstated with back pay amounting to $9 million when employers were found to be guilty of unfair labor practices.[135]

Despite the growth in membership, increases in average wages and greater job security for workers, unions faced continuing hurdles, both internally and externally. Throughout this period, the AFL and CIO bitterly competed against each other, and, despite Roosevelt's attempts at peace and unity, the labor movement was divided against itself.

Just two years after *Jones & Laughlin*, the Supreme Court dealt a crippling blow to the right of unions to strike by ruling that it was not an unfair labor practice for an employer to replace striking workers. Employers have the right to protect their businesses, the Court reasoned. In another case, the Court ruled that sit-down strikes were against the law.[136]

Opposition in Congress was also beginning to mount, with conservatives striking out against the Wagner Act, particularly after the 1938 mid-term elections. Senator Carter Glass (Democrat–Virginia) decried the Wagner legislation: "I think the National Labor Relations Act the worst law ever put on the federal statute books, and would gladly vote for its repeal or its modification in any respect." Most conservatives publicly would not go this far, but they had hoped to insert crippling amendments or trim back the power of the NLRB through congressional investigations. Since 1939, Republican leaders, particularly Charles A. Halleck of Indiana, had been determined to amend the Wagner Act.[137] However, a full-scale conservative assault would have to wait until after the war and the chance for Republicans to regain control of the Congress.

With the beginning of American involvement in World War II, the key labor issue dramatically shifted from unemployment and union recognition to labor shortage. It was vital for the country to meet the spiraling military demands as well as domestic needs, to keep labor strife to a minimum, and to prevent rapid inflation. Throughout, organized labor was "solidly and unswervingly" behind the war effort. Both labor and industry accepted the decisions of the War Labor Board; labor agreed not to strike, to accept wage controls, and businesses further agreed to abandon the use of the lockout.[138]

After World War II, organized labor flexed its muscle. There were some 14.8 million union workers, representing 35.5 percent of the nonagricultural work force. The wartime economy, with its restrictions on wages, rationing of goods, and common sacrifice had given way to the new peacetime economic realities: loss of overtime pay, inflation, and a decline in the value of take-home wages. Labor–management problems reached a boiling point: there were 4,985 work stoppages in 1946, involving 4.6 million workers.[139]

Two labor actions in particular drew the ire and fury of President Harry S. Truman: a coal miners' strike engineered by the implacable John L. Lewis and a threatened nationwide rail strike. Twice Truman ordered the secretary of the interior to seize the coal mines, but the 164,000 workers refused to work. Yet, after the miners settled in May, Lewis called them out again in late November, just before the winter season. Truman stood firm and took the labor leader to court. Lewis and the UMW were fined by a federal court an unprecedented $10,000 and $3.5 million, respectively, for criminal and civil contempt for violating a government contract. Lewis finally capitulated and the strike was broken. With the threat of a devastating national rail strike, a furious Truman ordered the railroads seized and vowed to draft striking railroad workers into the military. As Truman prepared to address a joint session of Congress to draft striking workers, the railroad unions backed off. Union leaders denounced Truman as the "No. 1 strikebreaker" and vowed vengeance in the next presidential elections.[140]

Following the war, the South seemed to be ripe for union activity and organizing. During the war, one-quarter of the farm population left for employment in southern cities or moved north to manufacturing jobs.[141] The war had opened up federal contracts to manufacturing plans in the South and, for union activists, liberal Democrats, and civil rights leaders, had opened to promise of organizing this region of the country notorious for anti-union activity. In early 1946, the CIO launched Operation Dixie, a million-dollar campaign to organize the South. At first, there was some success, with about 280,000 new union members in the South by late 1947. But the South had always been a region where union repression, racism, and red-baiting were familiar tools. The drive to unionize met fierce resistance and it ultimately collapsed.

The CIO was going through extraordinary internal difficulties, with battles between Communist and anti-Communist leadership in 1946 beginning to tear apart the federation. In 1949, the CIO purged itself of eleven of its own unions and nearly a million workers for their radical political leanings, and alleged communist domination.

The public was becoming increasingly fed up with big labor and relentless postwar strikes. And many were fed up with the New Deal, Democratic control, and, particularly, Harry Truman. During the 1946 strikes, Francis H. Case (Republican–South Dakota) introduced in the House and the Congress ultimately passed a bill creating a Federal Mediation Board, requiring a sixty-day cooling off period before any strike could be called, and mandated that workers who quit their jobs during the cooling off period would lose all Wagner Act rights. Truman promptly vetoed this, and Congress could not override the veto.[142] But that was just a foretaste.

Republicans gained control of both the House and Senate in 1946, for the first time since 1930. The National Association of Manufacturers seized the opportunity. NAM published its "Declaration of Principles," appealing to anti-labor Republicans and conservative southern Democrats, finding increasing support from a public fearful of unbridled union power. On that first day of the new Eightieth Congress in 1947, Republicans introduced seventeen anti-labor bills. Truman had earlier warned AFL's William Green: there was "little doubt" in Truman's mind that there was "a definite plot . . . to smash, or at least to cripple, our trade union movement. . . ."[143]

Republicans preferred to consider it a long-overdue reform. The drive would culminate in legislation introduced by Robert A. Taft (Republican–Ohio) and Fred A. Hartley, Jr. (Republican–New Jersey). The Taft–Hartley bill, while it would not overturn the Wagner Act, profoundly changed the relationship of the federal government to organized labor. The government would no longer be the advocate of labor, but now would be a neutral umpire. Under Taft–Hartley, the closed shop was prohibited; management could sue unions for breaking contracts, states were allowed to draft legislation prohibiting union shops, and union officers had to swear that they were not Communists. Borrowing from the Case legislation, Taft–Hartley created a Federal Mediation and Conciliation Service and allowed the federal government to obtain an eighty-day cooling off period under special circumstances.[144]

Historian R. Alton Lee observed that Taft–Hartley "aroused as much controversy and political contention as any domestic policy formulated by Congress in the decade after World War II."[145] The law was extraordinarily complicated, but that did not stop vociferous public opinion about it. NAM and the U.S. Chamber of Commerce poured millions of dollars into the Taft–Hartley drive; the AFL spent nearly $1 million on newspaper and radio advertising to defeat the legislation, charging it would bring about "slave labor." The volume of mail that the White House received was the greatest on any issue or controversy, not equaled until the controversy surrounding General Douglas MacArthur's dismissal in 1951.[146]

On May 12, 1947, the day before the final vote on Taft–Hartley, Senator Robert Wagner rose to speak. This was his only contribution to the debate and it turned out to be his last speech in the Senate. In a fifteen-minute speech before a packed Senate chamber, Wagner, nearly seventy and in failing health, branded Taft–Hartley as "untimely, trouble-making, reactionary, unfair, and unduly political."[147]

For Truman, the veto of Taft–Hartley was particularly important. Vilified by labor leaders because of his firm stands against the United Mine Workers and railroad unions, through his veto, though overridden, Truman brought back nearly all of organized labor to the Democratic Party fold.[148] Truman, labor, and their liberal allies stood together, bruised and bloodied and ultimately losing the fight as Congress swiftly overrode Truman's veto. Suffering from a heart ailment, and convalescing in New York City, Wagner later said to Truman, after the override of Truman's veto, that this was "one of the bitterest disappointments I have ever experienced. For I was forced to see the work of a lifetime destroyed, while I lay on my back in bed."[149]

For decades on, the repeal of the Taft–Hartley law became a fervent, but fruitless, goal of organized labor and a litmus test for Democratic candidates for high office.

Within weeks of each other, in 1952, the long-time presidents of the CIO, Philip Murray, and the AFL, William Green, died. Replacing them were UAW's Walter Reuther as head of the CIO, and George Meany, Green's second in command, at the AFL. Both were convinced that the labor movement could survive and become stronger only through a merger. Still it took two exhaustive years of negotiations before the AFL and the CIO worked out the agreement to create the AFL-CIO in 1955. George Meany was elected, unanimously, as the first president of the combined labor federation. Meany vowed further improvement in the status of workers and pledged to become a force in the political movement. In a revealing article in *Fortune*, he outlined labor's goals and ambitions: "We do not seek to recast American society in any particular doctrinaire or ideological image. We seek an ever rising standard of living. Sam Gompers once put the matter succinctly. When asked what the labor movement wanted, he answered, 'More.' If by a better standard of living we mean not only more money but more leisure and richer culture, the answer remains, 'More.'"[150]

Soon, however, big labor, representing some 15.5 million workers, faced another round of extraordinary challenges. The McClellan Committee on Improper Activities in Labor-Management Affairs, better known as the Senate Labor Rackets Committee, spent two-and-a-half years investigating charges of union corruption and misuse of funds. At the beginning of its investigations in 1957, the committee, under the chairmanship of Senator John L. McClellan (Democrat–Arkansas) and his chief investigator, Robert F. Kennedy, tried to maintain its impartiality but gradually the focus turned toward the personal gain, corruption, and ties to organized crime of the Teamsters Union and its leader, James R. Hoffa.[151] The sensational McClellan hearings, coupled with the earlier Kefauver committee hearings on organized crime, gave the public a sense of the seriousness of union corruption. It also led to the expulsion of the Teamsters Union and two other unions from the AFL-CIO in 1957. Hoffa's predecessor, David Beck, was convicted of embezzling union funds that year and Hoffa later was convicted of jury tampering, fraud and conspiracy in 1964.

There was a false sense of security for labor leaders when Democrats won heavily in the 1958 congressional elections and throughout the country attempts to enact right-to-work laws were defeated in state referendums. Congress had heard from the public, and the public wanted reform.[152] Twelve years after passage of the Taft–Hartley Act, President Dwight D. Eisenhower signed the Labor-Management Reporting and Disclosure Act of 1959, the Landrum–Griffin Act. With this legislation, the federal government took further steps to control and regulate union activities.[153] Named after the co-sponsors, Phillip M. Landrum (Democrat–Georgia) and Robert P. Griffin (Republican–Michigan), the legislation sought to prevent union corruption and to guarantee that unions would be run democratically. The first title of this law, inserted by Senator John F. Kennedy (Democrat–Massachusetts), has been dubbed the union bill of rights. It protected freedom of speech and assembly for union workers at their own meetings and secret ballots in periodic union elections. Landrum–Griffin required unions to report to the secretary of labor, provided procedures and regulations for union elections, union accountability of their fiduciary responsibilities. Yet, if the legislation was meant to be a "get Jimmy Hoffa," it failed in doing so.

Throughout the latter part of the twentieth century, labor's voice, power, and presence have steadily diminished. By 2004, there were 15.4 million members of labor unions, representing 12.5 percent of the work force. "Union density," that is, the percentage of labor union workers in the total work force, has been declining since 1960, when it reached its high of 23.6 percent.[154] In some states, unionization is much higher than the average, such as Michigan (21.6 percent), Hawaii (23.7 percent), and New York (25.3 percent). However, in many states union density is below 10 percent, and in five southern states it is less than 5 percent.[155]

A number of students of labor economics and history have tried to explain the current low state of union strength and power. Business professor Hoyt N. Wheeler surveyed the probable causes, including the inability of labor unions to use effective recruitment tactics; increased opposition to unionization from employers; an American legal system that has permitted employers to vigorously, and successfully, oppose organizing efforts; union strength in only selected states resulting in a weakness as a nationwide force; loss of union solidarity through an increased racial and ethnic diversity of the workforce; increased competitiveness both domestically and worldwide; the outsourcing of manufacturing and other labor-intensive jobs; and the shift of jobs from heavily union states to nonunion southern and western states.[156]

Whatever the current shape of organized labor, workers owe a debt of gratitude to the far-reaching legislation crafted by Senator Wagner. It survives to this day as the foundation of modern labor–management relations, despite the best efforts of its opponents and the flawed performance of its beneficiaries.

6

THE GRAND CONTRACT
The Social Security Act of 1935

If the Senate and the House of Representatives
in this long and arduous session had done nothing
more than pass this bill, the session would be regarded
as historic for all time.

Franklin D. Roosevelt, on signing
the Social Security Act (1935)

In many ways, the law was an astonishingly inept and conservative piece
of legislation . . . Yet for all its faults the Social Security Act of 1935
was a new landmark in American history.

William E. Leuchtenburg (1963)

Practically every American is either a beneficiary,
a contributor building protection for the future, or the
dependent of a contributor.

Gaylord A. Nelson (1978)

By the summer of 1935, as the United States was deep into its fifth year of economic crisis, fifteen million workers were searching for employment. The jobless, up to 25 percent of the labor force, were forced to fend for themselves, rely on extended families, or seek out private charity, hoping to make ends meet while confidence in the economy eroded and prospects for recovery grew dimmer. Government, at all levels, was of little assistance. Many state legislatures had considered relief programs for the unemployed, but not until 1932 did the first state, Wisconsin, enact legislation to help workers get back on their feet. By 1935, there had been a growing clamor for states to do something to protect the jobless, with fifty-six unemployment bills under consideration in state capitals. The federal government, however, did little to assist. One measure of the federal government's indifference was the fact that it did not maintain reliable employment statistics until the 1930 census. In the latter days of the Hoover administration, Congress held hearings on unemployment relief, but nothing came of this legislative hand-wringing until 1934, when measures were finally considered.

Likewise, there was little relief for the most vulnerable of citizens, the elderly, many of whom were forced out of economic necessity to work well past their sixty-fifth year. Jobs were increasingly scarce and infirmity robbed many elderly of the prospects of earning a living wage. Nevertheless, state governments were more willing to assist the elderly than the jobless. By the first years of the New Deal, thirty-eight states had created a patchwork of programs to assist the elderly, but only 10 percent of older Americans were receiving benefits, and these benefits averaged just $15 a month, paltry even by early 1930s standards. Furthermore, funds were unevenly distributed. In some states, county governments were permitted to opt out of old-age assistance programs, leaving their residents without recourse to state funds; in the South, where the needs were particularly acute, the legislatures in every state shunned old-age assistance programs. The federal government had no program of relief for the elderly, and Congress finally considered, but ultimately failed to pass, old-age assistance legislation in 1934.

While the states and the federal government dawdled on social relief, other voices called for quick and radical action. Muckraking journalist Upton Sinclair came up with a plan to end poverty in California, calling for the replacement of capitalism with a cooperative socialist society. Retired medical doctor Francis E. Townsend offered a tantalizingly simple proposal that called for the national government to give all retired persons aged sixty and above the princely sum of $200 per month, provided that they spent all the money received during that month. The idea spread like wildfire, and soon one out of every five American adults had signed petitions in support of Townsend's plan. Father Charles E. Coughlin, the enormously popular radio priest, first praised Roosevelt, then excoriated him, blaming America's social ills on the bankers, the wealthy, New Dealers, and the communists. Louisiana senator Huey P. Long, along with demagogue preacher Gerald L. K. Smith, created the "Share Our Wealth" scheme, which called for the liquidation of the personal fortunes of the wealthy and distribution of those funds to everyone else, so that every family, no matter its circumstances, could purchase a radio, purchase an automobile, and even buy its own home. "Every Man a King," proclaimed Long in a February 1934 nationwide radio address, and, by mid-1935, some 27,000 Share Our Wealth clubs, with over 7 million members, were set up throughout the country.

For Roosevelt, mid-1934 was the time to call for a comprehensive program to address the problems of income security. He issued an executive order, creating a cabinet-level committee to study the issues of economic security so that legislation could be introduced during the new 1935 legislative session. Roosevelt had no exact notion of what the legislative package should look like, but he wanted it to be as comprehensive as possible and have the federal government work with the states to administer it. After the administration's package was submitted in January 1935, it almost immediately had to be reconfigured: categories of wage earners, like farmers and domestic workers, were excluded, and the method of financing was changed so that funds would come out of employer and employee payroll taxes, rather than through general revenues.

Congress was able to beat back alternative plans and fervent opposition from business groups, and in August 1935, just six weeks after signing the National Labor Relations Act, the Social Security Act became law. Once the states enacted their own legislation for unemployment relief and assistance to the elderly, the federal law began providing limited, but immediate relief. The remarkable feature was that the cornerstone of Social Security, old-age insurance, did not begin sending out regular pension benefit checks for nearly five years. Another feature was the efficient way a wholly new bureaucracy was created to administer these wide-ranging programs. Millions of employment records had to be collected, and, decades before computers and software, the task became known as the world's biggest bookkeeping enterprise.

The Social Security Act was soon challenged in court and emerged, like the Wagner Act, with the constitutional blessing of the Supreme Court. This Grand Contract, which today affects such an extraordinary number of citizens and absorbs such a large portion of our treasure, had a far more humble beginning. At the onset, just 1 percent of the elderly were covered and received modest benefits; today coverage is nearly universal with expanded benefits tied to the cost of living. Social Security became the law we know today only through a series of congressional actions over the decades. Just four years after its enactment, the Social Security Act was amended so that widows and orphans of deceased elderly could receive benefits. In 1950, after a decade of little action on the subject, Congress vastly increased the benefits and included more individuals in the system. In 1956, Congress incorporated disability insurance and later created SSI, the Supplementary Security Income program for the indigent aged not eligible for regular Social Security benefits. During nearly every election cycle, Congress would amend Social Security and increase its benefits, but in 1972 lawmakers created a method to index benefits with an automatic cost-of-living adjustment. The most significant and far-reaching amendment to the Social Security Act came in 1965, with the creation of Medicare and Medicaid, a law of such importance that it is the subject of Chapter 11.

In recent decades, there have been several attempts, some successful and others less so, to place Social Security on sound long-term financing. There have been countless seminars, policy papers, and learned treatises on how to secure this most important program with a strong financial foundation. During this time, there also has been a steady drumbeat of critics calling for fundamental reform of the system. President George W. Bush joined the critics, all the while praising Social Security but calling for its partial privatization. His proposals have met with solid opposition from Democrats and nervous, tentative support from many Republican lawmakers.

Whatever the shape and direction of future social insurance reform, Social Security continues to touch nearly all our lives. It has been the foundation of America's social insurance policy and the nation's most important anti-poverty program. For the twenty-first century, Social Security and Medicare present a formidable policy challenge to Congress and the American people: how to continue protecting the health and financial well-being of the growing elderly population while assuring younger workers that their needs will be met, without bankrupting the country or neglecting other public needs.

Background

At the beginning of the twentieth century, American workers and their families, particularly those living on the economic margins, were at the mercy of raw capitalism and cold market forces. When economic hard times hit, as during the Panic of 1893, workers were on their own: unions were still in their nascent stages, offering limited reserves, and beyond the almshouses and private charity, little was done to help the unemployed. In 1893, one of America's largest railroads, the Philadelphia and Reading Railroad, went out of business, followed quickly by the bankruptcy of the National Cordage Company. This started a near chain-reaction of collapses on the stock market: steel mills, railroads, and banks, especially, had over-extended themselves, and, in short order, some 15,000 businesses were forced to close. During the Panic of 1893, unemployment soared, reaching 25 percent in some sectors.

One frustrated and desperate businessman took matters into his own hands. The owner of a sand quarry in Massillon, Ohio, Jacob S. Coxey banded together jobless workers and formed a protest movement called "Coxey's Army." He was determined to march to Washington, to demand that the federal government provide public works jobs for those who were unemployed. Coxey claimed that 100,000 workers joined him in April 1894 to begin their march, but five weeks later only some 500 straggled into Washington. President Grover Cleveland and the Congress refused to help and Coxey and the other leaders were arrested on the humiliating charge of unlawfully walking on the grass of the Capitol grounds. The ragtag contingent of followers dispersed and nothing came of their protest. The economy improved and the Panic of 1893 was over by the end of 1897.[1] During this most severe economic downturn before the Great Depression, neither the federal nor state governments had either the power or the inclination to assist the jobless.

Nonetheless, federal assistance to individuals and their families was not a foreign concept, and, by the time of the Panic of 1893, much of the federal budget was devoted to providing veterans' pensions. As will be seen in the next chapter on the GI Bill, the federal government has had a long history of assisting war veterans and their families. Following the Civil War, Congress enacted pension legislation that aided hundreds of thousands of Union soldiers, their widows and orphans, and disabled veterans. In fact by 1894, some 37 percent of the entire federal budget was devoted to veterans' benefits and by 1900, Congress had laid out $5 billion in such pensions. By 1910, approximately 90 percent of the remaining Civil War veterans and their survivors were receiving disability, survivors', and old-age benefits. This extraordinary outlay of funds, consuming such a large part of the federal budget, however, reached only a fraction of the U.S. population, less than 1 percent in 1910.[2]

Apart from veterans' benefits, the federal government simply was not in the business of providing pensions, social insurance, or other forms of assistance. Such relief, when it did come, was from the private sector or from state or local government. The federal government would not follow the lead of Germany, which in 1884 created the first national workmen's compensation program, and was soon followed by national plans in Austria, Hungary, Norway, and other European countries. Nor would the federal government follow the example of Britian, which in 1911 created the first compulsory unemployment compensation law, covering some 2.2 million wage-earners in four industries; sixteen other countries followed through in the 1920s, with compulsory or voluntary forms of unemployment compensation.[3]

The first large-scale involvement of state governments came through the enactment of workmen's compensation laws. Between 1911 and 1920, legislatures in forty-five states passed such laws. The old system, where individual workers were forced to sue their employers, worked to the advantage of neither the workers nor their employers. The legal system was often ponderous, with families waiting for years before final decisions on their claims. Employers were worried because, as more workers turned to the courts, the awards were getting larger and the premiums they had to pay on liability insurance soared. State-sponsored workmen's compensation became the answer, shifting the burden from employer to the state, and became the most universally adopted form of social legislation before the New Deal.[4]

While there was widespread adoption of workmen's compensation laws, before the Depression the states paid scant attention to protecting the unemployed. Only one state, Wisconsin, had enacted an unemployment compensation program and did so only in 1932. The Wisconsin program came in large part because of the pioneering work of professor John R. Commons of the University of Wisconsin who in 1921 designed a model state unemployment compensation plan. A decade later, his plan was refined by professors Harold R. Groves and Paul A. Rauschenbush, then pushed through the state legislature by governor Philip F. La Follette. This 1932 unemployment insurance law was called, appropriately enough, the "Wisconsin plan" or the "American plan," to distinguish it from the compulsory unemployment legislation created earlier in Britain.[5] The Wisconsin legislation required employers to build reserves in order to take care of their own workers. This involved a "merit rating" system: the employer's contribution was determined by the success of keeping workers on the job. Companies with the highest unemployment had to pay the highest rates. Through this merit rating system, employers would be encouraged to stabilize their employment.[6]

There was a competing state plan, created by the Ohio Commission on Unemployment, which called for a pooled fund, rather than one having each employer maintain its own funds, and called for contributions from both workers and employers. No funds would be coming from the state government. But critics of this Ohio plan, such as Abraham Epstein of the American Association for Old Age Security and Paul H. Douglas of the University of Chicago, asserted that it was inadequate and that government had to be involved in its funding. While unemployment insurance programs were introduced in twenty-eight other states, none but Wisconsin's became law. One of the motivations for not passing legislation was the fear in many state capitals that, if the state passed a law requiring employers to fund unemployment compensation, then businesses and manufacturers would be at a competitive disadvantage to companies in other states without compensation laws.

Congress showed some interest in unemployment insurance during the latter days of the Hoover administration. The Senate Select Committee on Unemployment Insurance held hearings in 1931 and issued a report the following year urging employers to be allowed to deduct a 30 percent portion of their contribution to a bona fide unemployment reserve. Senator Robert F. Wagner (Democrat–New York) had introduced this concept two years earlier, but neither he nor the Select Committee got any further during the last days of the Hoover administration or the early frenetic days of the New Deal.[7]

Paul Rauschenbush and his wife Elizabeth Brandeis, both professors at the University of Wisconsin, met in Washington with New Dealers, offering them a proposal that had a new twist on the Wisconsin plan. The idea came from professor Brandeis's father, Supreme Court Justice Louis D. Brandeis: the enactment of a payroll tax that could be deducted from federal taxes. The Wisconsin Plan and this new wrinkle were taken up in Congress in 1934 by Senator Wagner and Representative David L. Lewis (Democrat–Maryland).[8]

Beyond protecting the jobless, the other major concern was coming up with some kind of protection for the growing number of elderly Americans. By 1890, there were just over 3 million individuals aged sixty-five or older, constituting 4.1 percent of the total population of 76 million. Of all men sixty-five and older, nearly two-thirds were still in the workforce. The private sector had no widespread system of retirement and little compulsory retirement: older workers stayed on the job out of sheer economic necessity. By 1930, the number of elderly would more than double to 6.6 million, representing 5.4 percent of the total population of 122.7 million.[9] Many of the elderly were living on the edge of survival, fearful that injury, infirmity, or economic downturn would ruin their lives.

Beginning in 1921, a men's organization, the Fraternal Order of Eagles, took up the cause of old-age pensions, and, in state capitals throughout the country, law makers who belonged to the Eagles introduced such legislation. In 1923, Montana became the first state to enact an old-age pension law, and its governor, Joseph M. Dixon, in thanking the Eagles for their assistance, exclaimed, "you could no more stop progress of old-age pensions in the United States than you could stem the tide of the Pacific Ocean."[10] Hyperbole aside, the governor was fairly prescient: by the time that Roosevelt affixed his signature to the Social Security Act, thirty-four states and two territories had enacted old-age pension programs.

Yet the old-age pension laws were less than they seemed. They were a patchwork of inconsistent, poorly funded, and incomplete programs. In many of the states, county governments had the choice of opting out of participation. During 1929, in six states that had enacted old-age pensions, just 53 out of the 264 counties actually participated in the program. Where the programs were needed the most, in the destitute South, none of the state legislatures had enacted bills; and 87 percent of the pension money went to elderly citizens in just three states: California, New York, and Massachusetts.[11] By 1934, a total of $32 million was being spent by states for old-age assistance, with the average grant just $14.69 per month, and only about 10 percent of the eligible persons actually receiving assistance.[12]

There were other voices for reform, coming from self-proclaimed champions of the poor, the elderly, and the unemployed.

In September 1933, Francis E. Townsend, a retired medical doctor, wrote a letter to the editor of a Long Beach, California, newspaper, under the title "Cure for Depressions." Townsend made this tantalizingly simple proposal: all Americans over sixty-five years of age would be given $200 at the beginning of each month by the government. Persons accepting this money had to be retired, could not have criminal records, and had to spend the money by the end of each month. The Townsend plan would be paid for by a 2 percent transaction tax, a form of a sales tax. This simple, easily understood idea caused a sensation; the response to it was both overwhelmingly positive and completely unexpected. The promised $200 a month payment was a far cry from the old-age pensions that the states had enacted, which ranged from just $8 to $30 a month. While Townsend had no plan for carrying out this idea, he soon joined with his brother and a friend to create a not-for-profit organization, Old Age Revolving Pensions, Ltd.[13] The Townsend plan movement spread rapidly throughout the nation, with millions joining Townsend Clubs and, in just three months, 20 million Americans (one out of every five adults) signed petitions in support of the doctor's income support scheme. In addition, sixteen out of the twenty-four California members of Congress supported a federal Townsend bill.[14]

But Townsend had plenty of critics. The transaction tax was highly regressive and the proceeds would become a windfall for the elderly. In 1935, more than 87 percent of Americans lived on less than $2,500 a year; Townsend's plan would allow a married couple, both over sixty, to reap a retirement income of $4,800 a year.[15] Economists and policy experts didn't like the system, nor did the strange ideological bedfellows of the conservative American Liberty League, the Socialist Party, the Communist Party, the National Association of Manufacturers, and the American Federation of Labor.

There were other plans as well. Upton Sinclair, best known as the author of the muckraking book *The Jungle*, ran for governor of California in 1934, and part of his platform was an appealing program to End Poverty in California

(EPIC), which called for replacing capitalism with a cooperative socialist society. In a vicious gubernatorial race, dubbed the "campaign of the century," Sinclair was vilified by his Republican opponents, was demonized by the press, and lost to conservative Republican incumbent Frank F. Merriam. Yet twenty-seven out of eighty members of the newly elected California state legislature had run on the EPIC platform, and Sinclair, despite his eccentricities as a candidate and his quirky ideas, managed to gain 37 percent of the gubernatorial vote in a three-way race. Sinclair decided to defer his EPIC program while Roosevelt's aides were crafting social security legislation, and Sinclair attacked the Townsend plan because of its regressive tax provisions.[16]

Both Townsend's simplistic plan and Sinclair's idealistic and naive ideas attracted a broad spectrum of support from cautious, yet anxious citizens, such was their anxiety and desperation. But there were more radical plans, particularly Senator Huey P. Long's soak-the-rich Share Our Wealth program and radio priest Charles E. Coughlin's National Union for Social Justice. During the 1930s, both Long and Coughlin had immense national followings. Huey (Kingfish) Long, Democratic senator from Louisiana, shrewd and ambitious country-bumpkin, once an ally of Roosevelt, now was a real threat to become a spoiler third-party candidate for president in 1936. Roosevelt privately considered Long "one of the two most dangerous men in the country" (the other was General Douglas MacArthur). Along with demagogue preacher Gerald L. K. Smith, Long created the Share Our Wealth program in January 1934, a scheme devised to liquidate personal fortunes and distribute the funds so that every family could own its own radio, purchase an automobile, even buy a home. "Every Man a King" was the rallying cry and, by early 1935, Long claimed 27,000 clubs with mailing lists of some 7.5 million persons.[17]

Based in Royal Oak, Michigan, Catholic priest Charles Coughlin captured an enormous radio audience, some 30–40 million listeners a week, the largest audience in the world.[18] No twenty-first-century talk show personality comes near the reach and popularity of this Canadian-born radio priest. Father Coughlin at first praised Roosevelt, declaring the country had a choice between "Roosevelt or ruin." But in short order, Coughlin was denouncing the New Deal and the administration; he saw bankers and concentrated wealth as the biggest problems in America, and charged that the New Deal was run by communists and bankers.

As historian Anthony J. Badger summed up, Townsend, Long, and Coughlin "brilliantly exploited the old political techniques of the stump, the new techniques of the radio and the mass mailing list, and new political constituencies of the unorganized and the old."[19] But these radical plans and movements faltered for lack of organization and direction; about all the followers could do was listen to the radio, do what their leaders asked of them, and write letters of protest to the president.[20] Huey Long was the exception: he held power and made good on his threat to run for president against Roosevelt, only to be cut down by an assassin a year before the election.

According to Labor Secretary Frances Perkins, Roosevelt had agreed to explore a program of unemployment relief and old-age insurance even before his March 1933 inauguration.[21] Once in office, Roosevelt encouraged Wagner and Lewis to move forward with their unemployment insurance bill, which they introduced in February 1934. In the meantime, Senator Clarence D. Dill (Democrat–Washington) and Representative William P. Connery, Jr. (Democrat–Massachusetts), introduced legislation to help states provide old-age assistance to needy persons, offering to pay one-third the cost of old-age assistance to aged dependents. The White House took no position on the Dill–Connery bill, which nearly passed in the Senate and was reported favorably in the House Committee on Labor.[22]

Making the Law

While Congress was considering social insurance legislation, Roosevelt decided that the administration should create its own comprehensive program for both old-age and unemployment relief. In a message to Congress, delivered on July 8, 1934, the president outlined three great objectives of security of the home, security of livelihood, and security of social insurance, all three of which, he argued, constituted "a right which belongs to every individual and every family willing to work." Roosevelt said that it was the government's "plain duty" to provide for the security of citizens and their families through social insurance, and that the next Congress, which would convene in January 1935, should consider a program of national scope. He assured Congress that his administration would commence, with the greatest care, the actuarial and other studies needed to formulate a social insurance program.[23]

Three weeks later, Roosevelt signed an executive order establishing the Committee on Economic Security (CES), an inter-agency, cabinet-level task force designed to coordinate and develop the administration's legislation. Labor Secretary Perkins chaired the group, which consisted of Secretary of the Treasury Henry Morgenthau, Jr., Secretary of Agriculture Henry A. Wallace, Attorney General Homer Cummings, and Federal Emergency Relief Administrator Harry Hopkins.[24] The CES would have a cluster of eight advisory committees composed of specialists in public health, social and child welfare, and actuarial science, along with a general advisory board of distinguished citizens.[25]

Roosevelt made it clear from the beginning of CES deliberations that he favored cooperative federal–state action and that he wanted a program of social insurance, not one that would be perceived as welfare and handouts. "You want to make it simple—very simple," Frances Perkins remembered Roosevelt saying in a cabinet meeting. "So simple that everybody will understand it. And what's more, there's no reason why everybody in the United States should not be covered. I see no reason why every child, from the day he is born, shouldn't be a member of the social security system. . . . Everybody ought to be in on it—the farmer and his wife and family. . . . Cradle to the grave."[26]

Beyond the general and vague instructions, Roosevelt did not have a fixed notion of what social insurance should look like; it would be up to the Committee, its staff, and advisory boards to craft the recommendations.[27] Serving as executive director of the CES was the very capable Edwin E. Witte, professor of economics at the University of Wisconsin. He was recruited by his friend and protege Arthur J. Altmeyer, who, as assistant secretary of labor, had authored both the CES executive order and Roosevelt's message to Congress on June 8.[28]

In tackling unemployment insurance, most experts favored a national plan, with the understanding that industry was a national, not a local, challenge. Those favoring a state approach worried about constitutional problems, arguing that it was not within the power of the federal government to set up a nationwide program.[29]

The president reminded the general advisory council of the CES in November 1934 that, while he was governor of New York, he recommended passage of an old-age pension act, describing it as the "most liberal in the country." But Roosevelt was worried that the time might not be ripe for creating a federal old-age security program. He noted that there were individuals and organizations out in the country promoting "fantastic schemes" that had aroused people's hopes but which could not possibly be fulfilled. Maybe this wasn't the right time for a federal plan, but, whatever the CES decided, it should be based on the principle of social insurance, and not be perceived as a form of welfare. Welfare, then and now, carried negative connotations; insurance did not. Under an insurance program, work and savings are encouraged, and individuals would not be on the dreaded "dole."[30]

Frances Perkins was also concerned, particularly about whether a far-reaching social insurance law would pose constitutional problems. In her view, the constitutional obstacles "seemed almost insuperable." But in one of those only-in-Washington moments, Perkins received some timely, unofficial advice from Justice Harlan Fiske Stone. Stone and his wife routinely held tea parties at their home on Wednesday afternoons. Perkins, not particularly fond of such events, nonetheless did her duty and responded to the kind invitation to sip tea. Seated next to the Supreme Court justice, they inevitably talked shop. Stone asked how things were going, and Perkins said that the administration had great hope in developing the social insurance program but was deeply concerned about the constitutional ramifications. "Your Court tells us what the Constitution permits," she laughed. Then Stone leaned over and whispered, "The taxing power of the federal government, my dear; the taxing power is sufficient for everything you want and need."[31]

Under Witte's direction, the Committee on Economic Security concluded its work and published its recommendations, and on January 17, 1935, Roosevelt sent a message to Congress requesting that it pass his economic security legislation. On the same day, the administration's bill was introduced in the Senate by Wagner and in the House by Lewis and Robert L. Doughton

(Democrat–North Carolina) of the Ways and Means Committee. Most lawmakers and certainly most of the public had never heard of the term "social security" before. It was not a term used by other countries when they developed similar social legislation. Abraham Epstein and the *Washington Post* were probably most responsible for coining that term. Epstein in 1933 had changed the name of his organization from the American Association for Old Age Security to the American Association for Social Security, and the *Washington Post* began calling Roosevelt's legislation by that name. It didn't gain currency until the Ways and Means Committee, in trying to find a title to distinguish its substitute bill for the administration's "Economic Security Bill," came up with the name the "Social Security Act."[32]

Before the introduction of the administration's bill, nearly all of the attention in Congress had been focused on unemployment issues; now, both in Congress and in the public, there was a shift to old-age security. Despite Roosevelt's concerns, the centerpiece of the administration's bill was a federal old-age pension program. The hearing began immediately in both Houses. But it was soon discovered that the bill, written by the Labor Department, had been poorly drafted, with little or no logic in the topics covered, with some of the language ambiguous, and, as remembered economics professor, and later U.S. Senator from Illinois, Paul H. Douglas, "indeed, in places unintelligible."[33]

Secretary Perkins, Senator Wagner, and Dr. Witte each testified on behalf of the administration's bill, but on February 7, James A. Emery of the National Association of Manufacturers launched a vigorous attack against it before the House Ways and Means Committee. Abraham Epstein of the American Association for Social Security defended the bill but told the Senate Finance Committee that it was just too complicated: "It would take nine Philadelphia lawyers to figure out what some of the sections in this bill mean," Epstein complained. Most business interests were dead-set against the legislation, but the U.S. Chamber of Commerce and the National Retail Dry Goods Association supported it.[34]

One of the principal questions was how to finance social security. The administration waffled on its financing plan, but Senator Huey Long said he knew what to do. Just two days after the administration's bill was introduced, Long in a radio address said that the only practical solution to finance an old-age program was to take the money from the rich and give it to the poor. Don't tax the common people, Long implored, they don't have the money and it just puts them further into poverty: "The common people haven't anything worth having and when you put a tax on them for the purpose of unemployment relief or for old-age pensions, or for anything else, you are giving nobody any relief, because you are taxing the same people who have nothing on the pretense that you are going to give it back to them."[35]

The administration worried about financing, too. The original plan by the CES called for an eventual federal subsidy or federal tax contribution once the payment of benefits exceeded the funds available. The CES estimated that this would occur sometime around 1965. Roosevelt did not fully comprehend these calculations, but, once he understood, he insisted that the formula be revised and social security become entirely self-sustaining. But it was too late to change the administration's bill before it was submitted to Congress. Three weeks after its submission, Secretary of the Treasury Morgenthau went before the House Ways and Means Committee and argued for a revised financial formula that would be self-sustaining: a plan to boost the tax paid by workers and employees and not require annual funds from general taxes.[36] Eventually, the maximum combined contribution would be 6 percent in 1949, and after that the reserve fund would meet the costs of the program in perpetuity. Funding the program through payroll contributions also made sound political sense. Workers would enthusiastically buy into the idea that it was their money that went in and their money that would be available at retirement time. As Roosevelt himself put it: "We put those payroll contributions there so as to give the contributors a legal, moral, and political right to collect their pensions. . . . With those taxes in there, no damn politician can ever scrap my social security program."[37]

It did not take long, however, before lawmakers were speculating on the extraordinary reserves, more than four times the original proposal, that would be built up under the new Morgenthau plan. It could reach beyond $50 billion by 1980, an extraordinary amount of money, considering that the federal budget outlays in 1935 were $6.3 billion and the accumulated national debt that year was $28 billion. Marion B. Folsom of the Eastman Kodak Company and member of the CES advisory council was one of those who strongly objected to Morgenthau's plan to build this extraordinary reserve: it would be too strong a temptation for politicians to increase social security benefits with such a large reserve building up.[38]

Highlights of the Social Security Act

There were four major elements in the Social Security Act. First, a federal–state unemployment insurance program, based on the Wagner–Lewis bill and administered by the states. A uniform nationwide tax on employers, against which there would be credit for contributions made to approved state unemployment compensation plans.

Second, federal grants to states for welfare payments (needy children, blind, and elderly).

Third, federal grants to states for vocational rehabilitation, infant and maternal health, aid to crippled children, and public health programs.

Fourth, and the "most revolutionary" provision: old-age insurance paid directly by the federal government to individuals. It was a national program, administered solely by the federal government, covering all workers except those who were exempted.[39] The Committee on Economic Security estimated that, of the 49 million persons gainfully employed, 26 million would be included in the old-age benefits program. Excluded were 12 million self-employed, owners and operators; 9 million employed in excluded industries, 1 million in included industries but over sixty-five years of age, and a half-million casual workers.[40]

The first retirement checks were to be issued in 1942 (later revised to 1940) to persons sixty-five years and older, who had worked at least five days in each of the years 1937 through 1941 in employment covered by the statute and who had earned a total of $2,000 during that time.[41]

Morgenthau also argued that certain categories of individuals should be excluded from old-age insurance coverage, including farm and domestic workers—marginal workers who probably needed more protection than most. Some historians and social critics have pointed to these exceptions as an example of racial politics: Roosevelt trying to placate southern politicians by excluding potential beneficiary groups with heavy concentrations of black workers. There was plenty of anecdotal evidence that white southerners and southern politicians had little sympathy for the welfare of black citizens. The Jackson, Mississippi, *Daily News* spoke for many in the South: "The average Mississippian can't imagine himself chipping in to pay pensions for able bodied Negroes to sit around in idleness on front galleries while supporting their kinfolks on pensions, while cotton and corn crops are crying for workers to get them out of the grass."[42] Critics have argued that African-Americans were consistently discriminated against by New Deal legislation and the agencies charged with carrying out its policies. Political scientist Robert C. Lieberman, for example, argued that, while the Roosevelt administration originally favored a comprehensive racially inclusive system, it "capitulated to southern racists."[43]

Others cautioned that fiscal conservatism and administrative problems were more determinant factors than racism. Edwin Witte told the Senate Finance Committee that, while the administration recommended including agricultural and domestic workers, "frankly, the administrative difficulties cannot be disregarded and you may wish to exempt these groups at the outset." Morgenthau argued for the exclusion of agricultural and domestic workers on fiscal and actuarial grounds, and other groups—self-employed, seamen, church, college, hospital, and charitable employees, and all government workers—were excluded as well.[44]

Few members of the House Ways and Means Committee favored an old-age insurance proposal and many senators were skeptical as well. Senator Harry Flood Byrd, Sr. (Democrat–Virginia), and other southern lawmakers worried that the bill would vest federal authority over the states, and would be an opening wedge for government interference in the "Negro question." Legislators were further concerned about old-age insurance when the Supreme Court in May 1935 held unconstitutional the 1934 Railroad Retirement Act in language that looked as though it might apply to the provisions they were then deliberating. But Roosevelt insisted on old-age insurance, and, with his endorsement, Congress responded.[45]

So, too, did Senator Wagner. Facing a skeptical crowd of 1,000 business leaders at the Hotel Astor in New York, Wagner spoke bluntly about the plight of the elderly:

> it is shocking to realize that about 50 percent, or 3.5 million, of our elderly folk have been reduced already to complete dependency upon others. With or without laws, every civilized community must and does take care of those who in their old age are not self-sustaining, unless we propose to kill the old as the Spartans slaughtered the weaklings among their young. The Americans of today do not want to be Spartans. But allowing for the passage of over 2,000 years since the decline of that famous nation, our own treatment of the weak is not deserving of applause.[46]

Competing for the legislators' attention were more radical ideas, and members of Congress were besieged with letters from the nation's elderly who pleaded for the Townsend plan or other schemes. The Townsend plan was also introduced in January 1935, then revised in April. It was easily rejected in the House, 206–56, but many members from the West took the easy way out: they conveniently were absent or did not vote, fearing the backlash from their constituents if they were on record against this extremely popular idea.

The House took the Townsend plan more seriously than did the Senate. On February 16, for two hours Dr. Townsend was grilled by the Senate Finance Committee. Some lawmakers' questions were thoughtful, others were filled with ridicule. Through it all, Townsend was grim and unsmiling; most of the questions revolved around the plan's financing. Townsend argued that increased spending, which would in turn increase the transaction tax, would revive American business. "Would shooting craps with half a dozen other fellows be services?" sarcastically inquired Senator Byron P. (Pat) Harrison (Democrat–Mississippi). "Oh, no," responded Townsend. "But buying the dice would be a commodity," retorted an equally skeptical Alben W. Barkley (Democrat–Kentucky). At the end of the hearing, chairman Harrison announced that the committee would try to craft a bill fair to all, but that the Townsend proposal would not be a part of it.[47]

> Seventy-Fourth Congress, 1st Session (January 3–August 26, 1935)
>
> Senate: 69 Democrats; 25 Republicans; 2 other
>
> House: 322 Democrats; 103 Republicans; 10 other
>
> President: Franklin D. Roosevelt

Frances Perkins, writing a decade later, observed that "one hardly realizes nowadays how strong was the sentiment in favor of the Townsend plan and other exotic schemes for giving the aged a weekly income. . . . The pressure from its advocates was intense."[48]

Other ideas were floated, particularly a plan presented by Congressman Ernest Lundeen (Farmer/Labor–Minnesota) which provided federal unemployment benefits equal to full wages, to be paid to any unemployed person as long as he or she remained without work. All relief funds would come out of the federal treasury. But Lundeen's plan was crushed in the House by a 158 to 40 vote.

On April 18, matters came to a head on the floor of the House of Representatives. From opponents of the administration there were cries of "stop the steamroller!" But the pleas were ignored, and all radical plans and approximately fifty amendments to the administration's bill were swept aside.[49] There was a "most scalding debate," observed the *Washington Post* when Harold Knutson (Republican–Minnesota) tried to get the federal government to pay $60 a month to the aged. Allen T. Treadway (Republican–Massachusetts) offered a bill to increase a federal old-age pension from $15 to $20; he was soundly defeated. Charles V. Truax (Democrat–Ohio) raced up and down the well of the House demanding passage of an amendment that would seize incomes above $1 million a year as a way to finance social security. Truax had in mind capitalists like the Mellons, Rockefellers, and Morgans: "if [J. P.] Morgan can't live on $1 million a year, let him go to England, where he pays all his taxes anyhow."[50]

With radical and even sensible amendments swept aside, the House took up the administration's bill. Many conservatives, Republicans, and business leaders were dumbfounded. In a moment of anguish and hyperbole, congressman John Taber (Republican–New York) cried out, "Never in the history of the world has any measure been brought in here so insidiously designed as to prevent business recovery, to enslave workers, and to prevent any possibility of the employers providing work for the people."[51] But conservatives were brushed aside. The House gave its overwhelming approval, with just thirty-three lawmakers voting against the social security bill.

Key Individuals in the Making of Social Security

While many individuals were responsible for the crafting and shaping of the Social Security Act, four stand out for their policy leadership.[52]

Franklin D. Roosevelt (1882–1945), the thirty-seventh president of the United States, 1933–1945. Historian Arthur M. Schlesinger, Jr., identified Roosevelt as the "single national political leader" associated with the cause of social insurance.[53] When Roosevelt was governor of New York (1929–1933), he established the first state relief agency and urged the state legislature to pass unemployment insurance and old-age bills. Frances Perkins noted that Roosevelt "always regarded the Social Security Act as the cornerstone of his administration, and I think, took greater satisfaction from it than from anything else he achieved on the domestic front."[54]

Frances Perkins (1882–1965) was the Secretary of Labor throughout the entire Roosevelt administration. Earlier, she had been a social worker and advocate for improved working conditions for women and children, served in a variety of commissions in New York state, and chaired the New York State Industrial Commission under governor Roosevelt. She helped draft the Social Security legislation and became one of the administration's public voices in support of it. After Roosevelt's death in 1945, Perkins resigned from the cabinet, but remained in government service as commissioner of the Civil Service Commission until 1953.

Arthur J. Altmeyer (1889–1972) was recruited by Perkins to be the assistant secretary of labor. In that role he authored Roosevelt's important 1934 address to Congress on economic security and played a key role as chairman of the technical board of the CES.[55] From 1937 through 1953, Altmeyer was chairman of the Social Security Board, and credited with the efficient creation of the new and far-flung bureaucratic apparatus needed to run the complex social security program. He oversaw the changes brought about by the major Social Security Act amendments of 1939 and 1950. His career ended abruptly when the new Eisenhower administration unceremoniously dumped him before he was about to take early retirement.

Edwin E. Witte (1887–1960) had been a professor of industrial relations at the University of Wisconsin and the head of the Wisconsin Legislative Reference Library. Many called him the "father of the Social Security Act."[56] Witte spent roughly half of his professional life at the University of Wisconsin, strongly influenced by the La Follette progressive thinkers and legislators, and the "Wisconsin Idea" of dedication to public service. He was instrumental in developing the Wisconsin unemployment compensation program and was brought to Washington to be the executive director of the CES. In that role, Witte synthesized the committee's work, crafted the legislation, and advocated and defended it before Congress.

The University of Wisconsin played a key role in the intellectual foundation of the Social Security Act. John R. Commons, who originally shaped the model unemployment legislation, was the academic advisor to both Witte and Altmeyer. Later, Wilbur J. Cohen (1913–1987), a student of Witte's, became a central player in the crafting of Social Security and Medicare policy.

The Senate Finance Committee reported its bill out on May 13, with the addition of a new provision for federal assistance to the blind. Neither the Townsend plan nor the Lundeen unemployment bill made any headway, with most of the Senate's attention fixed on an amendment offered by Joel Bennett Clark (Democrat–Missouri). One of the more contentious issues concerning old-age insurance was whether or not private pension plans would be exempted from the legislation. Private insurance companies pushed hard for this exemption and found their supporter in Clark. Ultimately, however, an exemption for private pension plans was dropped from the legislation, with the promise, never fulfilled, that it would be considered during the following session of Congress.[57]

On August 14, 1935, in the Cabinet Room at the White House, Franklin Roosevelt, using several ceremonial signing pens, rapidly affixed his name to the law. A *Washington Post* reporter said that it was unknown how many pens were used, but there were many requests for souvenirs at the ceremony. Roughly thirty people crowded around the president, and among the dignitaries were Congressman Lewis, Senator Wagner, and Labor Secretary Perkins. Photographers pressed around the signing table, but, remarkably, newspaper reporters were barred from the ceremony. A reporter groused that Roosevelt had urged in his short speech that he was anxious for widespread publicity for this new program, but, with reporters barred from the event, the working press could only rely on the accounts given to them by the cameramen photographing the ceremony.[58]

Four days later, Frances Perkins wrote a lengthy article in the *New York Times* on Social Security: "Few legislative proposals have had as careful study, as thorough and conscientious deliberation, as that which went into the preparation of our social security program. This program is embodied in perhaps the most useful and fundamental single piece of federal legislation in the interest of wage-earners in the United States."[59]

While Roosevelt, Perkins, and others touted this remarkable new legislation, its flaws were evident to many critics. Thanks to Morgenthau and the Ways and Means Committee, it was not a universal program. Roosevelt, Perkins, and others wanted an expansive program, but just over half of all adults would be eligible. The payroll tax which would support social security was regressive, with lower-income individuals paying a much larger percentage of their wages than those who had reached the maximum contribution level. The unemployment insurance program became a hodge-podge of differing state programs, with widely varying benefits based on forty-eight separate sets of policy standards.[60]

Congress had to appropriate the money so a new social security agency could be established. Even before Roosevelt signed the Social Security Act, Arthur J. Altmeyer had prepared the next year's budget for the new agency. One million dollars, Altmeyer gave as his best ballpark guess, to operate this new agency. House Appropriations Committee chairman James P. (Buck) Buchanan (Democrat–Texas), in order to save time at the end of the legislative session, convened a one-man committee of himself, and heard out Altmeyer. Buchanan, after listening to the testimony, put his feet on his desk and said, "I don't understand a damned thing that you're saying and I don't believe you do, either." He paused for a moment, then said, "But I'll give you the money anyway."[61] The full House then passed the appropriations bill to administer the program.

The Senate leadership, assuming the appropriation would be a routine matter, waited until the last day of the session, and put the item on its agenda for 6:00 p.m., hoping to finish this one last piece of important business, then take care of any last-minute legislative house-keeping before a midnight adjournment. Instead, the Senate fell right into a trap laid by Senator Huey Long, who was determined to talk and talk until the session had ended and the administration's new program would be denied operating funds. He got his way; the Senate adjourned, and the newly created Social Security Board had no funds to operate. But with the liquidation of the National Recovery Administration, the nucleus of its personnel, especially its clerical staff, and much-needed funding would go over to the new Social Security Board. Frances Perkins even chipped in an executive chair for Altmeyer.[62]

Social security scholars Eric R. Kingson and Edward D. Berkowitz saw the Social Security Act as a "near thing," an historic piece of legislation that the president "slipped through a window of political opportunity" that was soon to close.[63] It became a major issue in the 1936 presidential campaign, with Republican presidential candidate Alf Landon charging Social Security as a "fraud on the working man. The savings it forces on our workers is a hoax."[64]

The Republican National Committee distributed millions of fliers to be put in pay envelopes a week before the election. The RNC warned workers that starting January 1, 1937, a payroll tax would be taken out of their paycheck, but the flier was conveniently silent on the benefits that the program would ultimately yield. One pamphlet gave this warning: with a picture of a "New Deal Judge" saying "*You're Sentenced* TO A WEEKLY PAY REDUCTION *for* ALL OF YOUR WORKING LIFE. YOU'LL HAVE *TO SERVE THE SENTENCE* UNLESS YOU HELP TO REVERSE IT. NOV. 3, ELECTION DAY." The Social Security Board, anticipating such an attack, had also prepared 50 million leaflets which it distributed, mostly through labor unions, along with films shown at movie theaters explaining the benefits of the program.[65]

Landon and the Republican Party were dealt a political spanking. Roosevelt defeated Landon, gathering 523 electoral votes to Landon's eight, sweeping every state but Maine and Vermont.[66]

By 1937, some 26 million workers and 2.7 million employers were making payroll tax contributions into the new Social Security system. The Social Security Board, now headed by Altmeyer, was gearing up with 150 field offices already in operation.[67] But, like the Wagner Act, the new social security law was bitterly opposed by powerful business interests, some of whom refused to comply with the tax requirements until the Supreme Court had ruled on the constitutionality of this new law. Opponents did not have long to wait. Just six weeks after its historic affirmation of the Wagner Act in May 1937, the Supreme Court upheld the Social Security Act in *Steward Machine Company* v. *Davis* and its companion decision, *Helvering* v. *Davis*.[68] In the first decision, the Court ruled that the federal–state unemployment compensation program was a legitimate exercise of the federal power to lay and collect taxes and, in the latter case, the Court agreed that a federal old-age program was within the scope of the taxing and spending authority of Congress. Justice Stone was true to his word when he whispered his advice to Frances Perkins over tea.

In less than two years after passage of Social Security, unemployment insurance laws were enacted in all forty-eight states, the territories of Alaska and Hawaii, and the District of Columbia. Wisconsin was the only state able to begin paying beneficiaries before January 1938, but then on the first of the year, twenty-one states began their programs, and by July 1939, all states, the two territories, and the District of Columbia had implemented their programs.[69]

States had to establish their own old-age assistance programs in order to qualify for matching federal funds. They did so with varying degrees of urgency. The Virginia General Assembly dawdled, studied the question for two years, then the new governor, James H. Price, pushed America's oldest deliberative body to enact a proposal. It did so finally in March 1938, the last state, but funded just one-third of the $30 a month that the federal government would match.[70]

Aftermath

The new Social Security Board had the enormous task of creating an agency from scratch, assigning employee account numbers and maintaining files on millions of individual employee accounts. Hiring of personnel began on November 9, 1936, and by the end of the year, 2,500 workers were on board. The workers, mostly women, came from all over the United States, because the civil service rules at the time required that each state be given a proportion of available federal jobs. This was dubbed the "largest bookkeeping job in the world,"[71] and accomplished during the pre-computer days. The first bulky computer with vacuum tubes was still a decade away and electronic data storage using magnetic tape was another twenty years into the future. In September 1937, the Bureau of Old-Age Insurance began receiving from the Bureau of Internal Revenue the 1.7 million employer reports for the first half of 1937, covering 36 million employee wage items. By April 1, 1938, over 38 million social security accounts had been opened. Steel filing cabinets filled with social security records occupied half an acre in the cavernous Candler building in Baltimore, the site of a former Coca-Cola bottling plant and one of the few buildings in the entire Washington–Baltimore region large enough to contain this enormous collection of employment records, file clerks, and office equipment.[72]

It was a far-flung and complex enterprise, touching so many lives, both beneficiaries and those workers paying into the system. Overhead was far less than found in private industry and the programs were administered efficiently and with little complaint. Arthur M. Schlesinger, Jr., attributes this success to its senior administrator: "For this prodigious achievement, found on millions of records, clerks, and business machines, major credit went to Altmeyer."[73] In addition to creating and running an efficient operation, Altmeyer strongly believed that the government had an obligation to assist citizens in obtaining their federal benefits. This philosophy of affirmative government service smacked up against an obscure 1835 federal law prohibiting any official from encouraging a claim against the United States. The General Accounting Office pressed the case for the 1835 law, but Altmeyer persisted and the ethic of government assistance became a core value of the Social Security Administration.[74]

By 1937, thanks to the accumulation of funds through the payroll tax, the social security program had collected $511 million, while spending just $5 million in administrative costs. Old-age pensions were not to go into effect until 1942, a full five years after workers and employers started making their tax contributions. But the long-range surpluses were almost too large to be fathomed: it was estimated that by 1980, the social security reserve would be over $46 billion. Historians Edward Berkowitz and Kim McQuaid noted that this was a sum eight times more than the amount of money in circulation in the United States in the late 1930s and almost five times the amount of savings in banks.[75] Business leaders and conservative politicians were getting nervous, calling on Congress and the administration to cut back on its reserves by lowering pension benefits or lowering payroll taxes.

Arthur H. Vandenberg (Republican–Michigan) of the Senate Finance Committee pressed Altmeyer to create a commission to look into the funding of benefits. Altmeyer set up the Social Security Advisory Council, chaired by J. Douglas Brown of Princeton University and composed of a distinguished group of business leaders, academicians, labor leaders, and government officials.[76] Roosevelt weighed in with a strong recommendation for liberalizing the old-age provisions of the law. With the assistance of the advisory group and the input of social security officials, the Advisory Committee unveiled Plan AC-12, a program that would greatly change the original scope and reach of Social Security.[77] The original law provided retirement benefits, in lump sum, only to the worker, not to a surviving spouse or children. The new plan, drawn up in 1939, added two new categories of benefits: payment to a spouse and minor children of a retired worker, and survivors benefits paid to a family in the event of an early death of a covered worker. Benefits would be paid not in lump sum, but in monthly installments, and would be calculated on last wages rather than on total wage history. Further, the amendments increased the size of the benefits and pushed up the starting time for payments to 1940.[78]

The 1939 amendments were a pivotal point in the long history of the Social Security Act, a "tremendous step forward," Roosevelt noted in signing the amendments into law, "in providing greater security for the people of this country."[79]

Throughout the legislative struggles for social security during the 1930s and early 1940s, organized labor had sat on the sidelines; after World War II, it became an active, major voice for increasing benefits and including more workers in the social insurance system. Historian Robert J. Rosenthal, writing in 1948, noted the irony of labor's late arrival: "In terms of organized labor's present enthusiasm for social security, it seems almost inconceivable that one of the contributing causes for this county's late development was organized labor's lack of interest and active opposition to such a program."[80] Labor became particularly interested in the legislation introduced by Senators Robert

Wagner and James E. Murray (Democrat–Montana), and Representative John D. Dingell, Sr. (Democrat–Michigan). The Wagner–Murray–Dingell bill, introduced in 1943, would provide more liberal unemployment and old-age benefits, offer universal coverage for all workers, create a federal unemployment insurance system, and add health and disability coverage.

Key Events in the Making of Social Security	
1935	Social Security Act signed into law, August 14.
1936	Constitutionality of old-age insurance and unemployment insurance upheld by the Supreme Court.
1939	Amendments add dependent and survivors benefits; Old-Age Insurance now becomes Old-Age and Survivors Insurance (OASI).
1940	Ida M. Fuller, 76, of Ludlow, Vermont, becomes first person to receive monthly Social Security benefits checks; she was joined by 222,487 other recipients in 1940.
1942	OASI payroll tax rates frozen at 1 percent, until 1950.
1950	OASI coverage extended to 10 million more persons, including most non-farm, self-employed; liberalized eligibility, and benefits increased by 77 percent.
1956	Amendments add disability insurance; program becomes Old-Age, Survivors, and Disability Insurance (OASDI).
1965	Amendments create Medicare and Medicaid; liberalize OASDI benefits.
1972	A 20 percent cost-of-living adjustment (COLA) was authorized, making way for an index annual increase in 1975, based on consumer prices. Supplemental Security Income (SSI) program established to oversee benefits for needy aged, blind and disabled; these programs to begin in 1974.
1981	Certain benefits reduced or eliminated, including student benefits, and lump-sum death payments.
1983	National Commission on Social Security Reform; Congress passed amendments to augment Social Security financing, including taxing Social Security benefits, covering federal employees, raising retirement age beginning in 2000, and increasing reserves in Social Security trust funds.
1986	Social Security coverage for federal workers hired after 1983.
2002	Total of 46.4 million people received monthly Social Security benefits.
2003	Bush administration appeal to privatize parts of Social Security.

The Wagner–Murray–Dingell legislation was never reported out of committee, and officially died during the Seventy-Ninth Congress (1945–1946), but it did provide an opening for the inclusion of medical assistance for the elderly. Not until 1965, with the enactment of Medicare and Medicaid, did Congress respond with this component of social insurance.

The Townsend plan, first devised in the early 1930s, ridiculed and rejected by Congress in 1935, kept resurfacing in the public imagination. There was revived interest in it after Social Security was created because of citizen complaints that the new federal law just didn't go far enough to assist the elderly. Even as late as November 1949, a total of 179 members of Congress signed a discharge petition to force a bill embodying a Townsend plan out of committee. The discharge petition failed, but, had it succeeded, Congress would then have had to decide whether to replace Social Security with the Townsend plan. Supporters of Townsend fell thirty-nine votes short, but their persistence showed that there still was life in this simplistic and attractive idea some sixteen years after Francis Townsend penned his letter to the editor.[81]

Throughout the early postwar years, Social Security remained static: the benefits did not increase nor did the percentage of recipients increase. During the late 1940s, the absolute value of Social Security retirement benefits was quite low. Ida M. Fuller, the first recipient of social security benefits, received $22.64 in her first benefit check in January 1940; she received the same amount ten years later. Further, only one-quarter of all old people were protected.[82] In 1950, Congress enacted the first major change in Social Security since the 1939 amendments, increasing benefits by 77 percent and dramatically increasing their value for future recipients. This major boost in benefits was followed by double-digit increases in 1952 and 1954. Original social security recipients had now seen their benefits package double in value.[83] Wilbur J. Cohen, who was becoming one of the leading social security experts of his generation, wrote that 1951 marked a milestone. It was the first year in the nation's history when the total expenditures on social insurance exceeded old-age welfare benefits.[84] Then in 1952, with the national economy brightening, and, for the first time, with bipartisan support for expanded benefits, Congress enacted the first of many amendments in the 1950s and 1960s that demonstrated both the staying power of Social Security and its political popularity.[85]

In 1956, a new dimension was added to the social security program when Congress added a disability insurance program, providing benefits for disabled workers aged fifty through sixty-four and their dependents. Four years later, President Dwight D. Eisenhower signed into law an expansion of the disability payments program to cover disabled workers of any age and their dependents. By 1960, there were 559,000 persons receiving disability benefits, averaging $80 a month.[86] In the 1956 amendments, women were given the option of retiring early, at the age of sixty-two, with reduced benefits; men received a similar early retirement option five years later.

Many of the amendments to the Social Security Act were incremental, adding classes of workers to the eligibility rolls, increasing benefits, or lowering the age for early retirees. Then, thirty years after its enactment, the Eighty-Ninth Congress (1965–1966) made the biggest leap in the scope and nature of social insurance by creating the Social Security Act Amendments of 1965. As Chapter 11 will show, these amendments, Medicare and Medicaid, changed the face of health care for the aged and the poor, offering much-needed assistance, but also substantially increasing the federal government's involvement in health care and dramatically increasing its fiscal obligations.

In 1972, the Social Security Administration became responsible for a new program, Supplementary Security Income (SSI). Up to this point, a variety of state agencies—1,350 in all—administered programs for needy adults, the blind, and the disabled. The rules for eligibility and the administration of these programs were complex and inconsistent, and the payment of benefits varied widely from one state to another. These 1970 amendments put all the adult categories under the responsibility of the Social Security Administration, and converted over 4 million recipients from state welfare programs to the federal SSI.[87]

Until the 1970s, benefits could be increased only by specific action of Congress. Lawmakers obliged, adding amendments every two or four years, more often than not coinciding with the election calendar. This practice changed with an amendment in 1972 that instituted an annual cost-of-living adjustment based on the yearly consumer price index. Starting in 1975, benefits would automatically be adjusted to match increases in inflation. In 1980, the benefits increase was a whopping 14.3 percent, reflecting the period of considerable inflationary growth, but, by the mid-1980s, the yearly adjustment settled into an increase pattern of 1.5 to 5.0 percent.

In the early 1970s, the key issue of social security policy concerned the growing deficit in its trust fund. Three factors had brought about instability: the rapidly increasing number of disability claims, the impact on cost-of-living adjustments because of higher inflation rates, and demographic changes in the workforce.[88]

The trustees of the Social Security Administration released an alarming report in 1975, concluding that the trust fund would be exhausted by 1979 if there were no changes in the benefits, payroll taxes, or coverage. Congress responded in 1977 with amendments that increased the payroll tax from 6.45 percent to 7.65 percent, increased the wage base, slightly reduced benefits, and decoupled wage adjustments from the cost-of-living formula. The corrections to the formula, however, caused considerable problems for a small group of retirees. In the 1972 amendments, an error in the benefit formula gave extra funds to those born between 1912 and 1916; the 1977 amendments created a transition formula, lowering benefits for those born between 1917 and 1921. These recipients, called the "notch babies," vociferously argued that they were cheated out of benefits rightly due them, but a special Commission on the Social Security Notch in 1994 found that they were getting an equitable share and that no legislation was needed to adjust the benefit scale.[89]

The percentage of individuals covered by Social Security increased dramatically by the 1970s. In 1977, some 93 percent of persons sixty-five and older were now eligible for benefits and 95 percent of young children and their mothers were protected by survivors' insurance features of Social Security. Further, 80 percent of individuals aged from twenty-one to sixty-four had protection against loss of income caused by severe disability. By 1977, thirty-seven years after the first quarter of a million recipients began receiving modest monthly benefits, there were over 33 million beneficiaries, one out of seven Americans, with benefit checks averaging $240 per month.[90]

The intent of the 1977 amendments was to keep Social Security solvent for the next fifty years. However, the economy worsened and policymakers feared a rapid depletion of trust fund monies. To resolve the problems of financial stability, President Ronald W. Reagan and congressional leaders formed a bipartisan Commission on Social Security Reform and in 1983, Congress passed many of the commission's recommendations. A major force in social security reform was Robert M. Ball, a long-time public servant who was commissioner of the Social Security Administration under three presidents.[91] The 1983 amendments were the last major additions to Social Security. Congress provided for a gradual increase in retirement age for full benefits, from sixty-five to sixty-seven, added federal civilians and employees of nonprofit organizations (including even members of Congress, the president, vice-president, and federal judges), increased payroll tax rates, a one-time six-month delay in the cost-of-living-adjustment, and other measures.[92]

By 2005, more than 47.5 million persons were receiving Social Security benefits, with nearly two-thirds of those recipients being retired workers; another 13 percent were disabled workers, and over 8 percent were children. The Bush administration budget for fiscal year 2008 contained nearly $608 billion for Old Age, Survivors, and Disability Insurance out of a total budget of $2.9 trillion; Medicare and Medicaid constituted another $590 billion.[93]

Social Security, since its inception, has had its critics, from Alf Landon and the Republican National Committee in the 1936 presidential race, the National Association of Manufacturers, and other big business organizations, to conservative opponents in Congress, like Representative Carl T. Curtis (Republican–Nebraska) during the early 1950s. In the 1960s, economist Milton Friedman labeled it an unjustifiable incursion into personal liberty, presidential candidate Barry Goldwater vowed to repeal Social Security, and, in the 1980s, the Reagan administration sought to restrict its coverage.

For decades, Social Security critics have argued that a better solution to income security is through full or partial social insurance privatization. In the late 1970s, a third-year law student, Peter J. Ferrar, came up with what he acknowledged must have been the "craziest idea in the world."[94] His idea was to convert Social Security into a private investment program. Edward H. Crane, who had just founded the libertarian Cato Institute, picked up on the idea. This concept fit in well with Crane's philosophy and his challenge to the central purposes of government-sponsored social insurance. Ferrara then was commissioned to write Cato's first policy hardcover book, *Social Security: The Inherent Contradiction*.[95] In 1983, Heritage Foundation scholars Stuart M. Butler and Peter Germanis published a paper entitled "Achieving a 'Leninist Strategy,'" which called for "guerilla warfare against both the current Social Security system and the coalition that supports it," comparing their cause with that of Vladimir Lenin's efforts to undermine capitalism. "Before Social Security can be reformed," they wrote, "we must begin to divide this coalition [that supports Social Security] and cast doubt on the picture of reality it presents to the general public." Then, Butler and Germanis argued, "we must press for modest changes in the laws and regulations designed to make private pension options more attractive, and expose the fundamental flaws and contractions of the existing system."[96]

Over the years, the concept of privatization of Social Security took root in conservative circles. In 1988, former governor of Delaware Pierre S. (Pete) DuPont IV because the first presidential candidate to call for private accounts. Interest in private social insurance accounts accelerated with the booming economic years of the 1990s. George W. Bush, running unsuccessfully for a seat in Congress in 1978, was an early backer of private accounts, and later, while governor of Texas, he embraced this conservative policy. The National Association of Manufacturers became engaged in this issue in 1998, forming a business coalition that advocated self-directed private retirement accounts.[97]

In recent years, Social Security privatization has come under the broader guise of an "ownership society." Stephen Moore, president of the conservative Club for Growth, for example, argued that one of the key domestic policies of the Bush II administration was to go from an "entitlement society to an ownership society."[98] Privatization of Social Security would be key to fulfilling that vision.

In his inaugural address in January 2001, George W. Bush announced his intentions to reform both Social Security and Medicare, and, in his first speech before a joint session of Congress the following month, he announced the creation of a presidential commission to address possible reforms. Bush outlined three basic principles: all current retirees and those near retirement would have their benefits preserved; the Social Security system had to return to sound financial footing; and younger workers must be offered personal savings accounts, should they want them in lieu of Social Security.

At the beginning of his second term in office, Bush promised to make Social Security reform a top priority. He barnstormed throughout the country speaking to carefully selected friendly audiences, making his case that "the system is broken and promises are being made that Social Security cannot keep." Bush claimed that the Social Security system would be "flat bust, bankrupt" in forty years "unless the United States Congress has got the willingness to act now." Over the objections of many within the agency, the Social Security Administration developed a "tactical plan" for communications and marketing to demonstrate that Social Security faced dire consequences unless there was immediate reform.[99]

In the summer of 2005, Congress found itself at an impasse: Democrats dug in against privatization and personal accounts, and moderate Republicans became increasingly skittish in their support for a presidential initiative that was losing steam and popular support, and were desperately looking for an exit strategy from an increasingly uncomfortable position. But the events on the Gulf Coast soon overwhelmed any consideration of social security reform. The bungled federal response to Hurricane Katrina knocked social security off center stage. The continued disintegration of the war effort in Iraq and the party change-over in Congress following the 2006 mid-term elections removed any chances for Bush administration social security reforms.

Throughout the world, more than a dozen countries have converted their traditional government-financed pension systems to programs that were at least partially privatized. Chile, for example, since 1981 has provided a system of mandatory private individual accounts, with its traditional social insurance system being phased out. Workers there contribute 10 percent of their earnings to personal savings accounts. Mexico, since 1991, requires employers to contribute 2 percent of each worker's earnings into a private savings account, and workers are given the option to make additional, tax-free contributions. Since 1978, Britain has permitted workers to stop paying into one of the state pension systems if they redirect part of their payroll tax to an approved private pension plan. A *Washington Post* analysis of the Chilean and British pension schemes, however, showed decidedly mixed results.[100]

Alarm bells ring from both critics and supporters of Social Security, noting that, while payroll taxes now generate more funds than are paid out in benefits, that equation will soon change, and, if nothing is done, by 2040 Social Security will exhaust its trust fund assets and payroll taxes will be able to cover only 75 percent of the promised benefits. Yet to think that nothing will be done by Congress amounts to folly. Congress has tinkered with Social Security for decades, adding benefits, increasing payroll taxes contributions, increasing the range of workers covered, and other adjustments. Some of the changes have been conservative and incremental; other changes have come only because Congress has been forced to adjust benefits and taxes to protect the long-range solvency of the program. The next major amendment to Social Security most likely will attempt to put the system once again on sound financial footing, and, the sooner it comes, the easier will be the pain in adjusting to the new realities of social insurance. The solution will be a political one as much as an actuarial one, with Congress, listening closely to the wishes of the American people, young and old, determining whether benefits need to be reduced, eligibility requirements adjusted, upper income wages taxed, partial privatization introduced, and a variety of other adjustments to keep Social Security both solvent and vibrant.[101]

In 2006, social security payments were made to 53 million persons each month, with 3.8 million new applications for retirement and 2.5 million applications for disability benefits.[102] As the baby-boomer generation begins retirement in the early 2010s, the number of persons eligible for social security benefits will increase substantially. For many beneficiaries, Social Security is the difference between impoverishment and a modest retirement income. Without Social Security, nearly half of the elderly would be living below the poverty line. The survivors and disability portions are vital to children as well, making Social Security the most important anti-poverty program for children.[103]

The fairly conservative and modest program enacted in August 1935 has grown into this nation's Grand Contract. It has embodied the values of work, social insurance, and retirement. And it has represented a continuity of generations, as the productive workers of one generation help support those who have ended their labors. Further, the Social Security system consistently has received "extraordinary broad support" from the American people.[104] As the debate on the future of Social Security focuses on sound financing and the commitment to future generations, lawmakers would do well to remember the evocation of former Vice-President Hubert H. Humphrey: "the moral test of government is how it treats those who are in the dawn of life, the children; those who are in the twilight of life, the aged; and those who are in the shadow of life, the sick, the needy, and the handicapped."[105]

7

THE PROMISE TO
AMERICA'S VETERANS

The GI Bill of 1944

Long live the GI Bill of Rights!

Clark Kerr, president emeritus
University of California (1994)

*The GI Bill of Rights—and the enthusiastic response
to it on the part of America's veterans—signaled the shift
to the knowledge society. Future historians may consider it
the most important event of the twentieth century.*

Peter F. Drucker (1993)

The GI Bill of 1944 has been hailed by educators, social scientists, and historians as one of the most important pieces of legislation in the twentieth century. Enacted three weeks after the D-Day invasion of Normandy, and over thirteen months before the end of hostilities in the Pacific Theater, the GI Bill was a multi-dimensional piece of legislation that provided returning veterans with unemployment compensation, low-cost loans to purchase homes or businesses, and educational benefits. The legislation was enacted out of a sense of obligation to the millions of men and women who served in the armed forces; but the chief concern of the Roosevelt Administration, Congress, and the veterans' organizations that lobbied hard for this legislation was to prevent a return of economic hard times and political instability. The education of returning veterans was only of secondary concern. In fact, few policymakers in Washington predicted that veterans would jump at the chance for free college tuition or on-the-job training programs. But jump they did, flooding colleges and universities in the five or six years after World War II, and, to an even greater extent, flooding non-college programs, like on-the-job training, correspondence schools, and even programs for the completion of high school. It was the education provision of the GI Bill that proved to have the most far-reaching impact on American society.

The GI Bill's promise of educational assistance was an unusual feature in the history of veterans' benefits. Some educational relief was given to World War I disabled veterans, but typically the federal government gave only mustering-out pay, cash bonuses, or surplus public land. Following each American war, Congress has provided some level of benefits for its veterans, their widows, and survivors. Congress responded out of a sense of gratitude, but it was also prodded by organized veterans' organizations: the Society of the Cincinnati following the Revolutionary war, the United Brethren of the War of 1812, the National Association of Mexican War Veterans, and especially the Grand Army of the Republic following the Civil War. At times, the grants had been quite generous, particularly for Civil War and Spanish-American war veterans; and, by the beginning of the twentieth century, veterans' benefits constituted approximately 40 percent of the entire federal budget.

Four million Americans had served during World War I, and upon their release from military service each was given $60 mustering-out pay plus a train ticket home, while some disabled veterans received rehabilitation and educational assistance. Following the war, many civilian workers lost their jobs as the country demobilized, and, with the influx of veterans coming home, many veterans found themselves out of work, in bread lines. Out of the war experience came the most important veterans' organization, the American Legion. In the early 1920s, Congress gave World War I veterans a measure of relief and promised them a bonus, payable in 1945.

With the Depression tightening its grip on American life, desperate veterans in the spring and summer of 1932 demanded that the federal government pay the bonus immediately. Their hopes were raised when the House of Representatives passed such a measure, but then were dashed when the Senate, and especially President Herbert C. Hoover, rejected the House legislation. The desperation of the Bonus Army's march on Washington, the skirmishes with local police that left two marchers dead, and the burning of their encampment by General Douglas MacArthur's forces left Hoover shaken and vulnerable in the last several months of his administration.

President Franklin D. Roosevelt, the Congress, and the veterans' organizations were determined that the uncertainty and bitterness that accompanied the previous veterans' benefits legislation would not be repeated. For the first time since the Homestead and Land Grant College Acts of 1862, the Congress planned ahead for the eventual return of war veterans.

The official name of the legislation was the Servicemen's Readjustment Act of 1944, but it forever became known as the GI Bill of Rights after an American Legion publicist coined the phrase, calling for a " bill of rights for GI Joe and GI Jane." The American Legion was key to writing the basic contours of the legislation and putting pressure on Congress. Franklin Roosevelt was key to its passage; in a 1943 radio address to the nation, he urged Congress to enact legislation to assist soldiers returning from war. Although the legislation experienced smooth sailing through the Senate, it came up against the formidable and crafty Democratic Congressman John E. Rankin of Mississippi, who, fighting bitterly against unions, liberals, Jews, and any measure smacking of racial equality, delayed, twisted, and shaped the legislation.

Some educators, notably the presidents of Harvard and the University of Chicago, feared that academic standards would be compromised if hordes of returning servicemen were entitled to free education; others worried that decisions would be taken out of the hands of the education bureaucracy and placed under the Veterans Administration. But, for many institutions of higher learning, the GI Bill was nothing less than a godsend. Despite the overcrowding and the adjustments that had to be made to accommodate the flood of returning veterans, colleges and universities experienced a period of growth and relative prosperity. The federal government paid up to $500 for annual tuition costs, enough to cover the most expensive private universities, and supported veterans with modest living allowances. New classes were added, professors hired, summer school sessions extended, and dormitory space erected, some of it in tents or Quonset huts. College and university life, once the preserve of the upper-middle class, now broadened its reach. Elite private universities now opened their doors to Jews, children of twentieth-century immigrants, and students who were the first in their families to go to college. Academic curricula were expanded, reaching beyond the core of liberal arts education to technical and professional education. Catholic colleges and universities and 1890 Land Grant black colleges saw their enrollments soar. Colleges and universities, once the province of eighteen- to twenty-two-year-old students, now discovered an older student body, much of it married and with small children, bringing a new sense of maturity and seriousness to the pursuit of higher education.

The trend toward increased higher education had begun before World War II, and the GI Bill took advantage of that surge. During the six years of the original GI Bill, over 2.2 million veterans attended college or university at a total cost of $5.5 billion. The GI Bill during this time had been tinkered with, and eligibility and benefits were increased. Yet the GI Bill could not simply be geared toward veterans who wanted a college degree. Roughly 60 percent of returning veterans had not completed high school, and there had to be suitable non-college training and education programs available to them. There were problems with the bill, especially in the rapid increase of for-profit correspondence and fly-by-night schools that provided little or no education and were created only to siphon off the guaranteed federal tuition subsidy.

College and university population almost doubled from 1940 to 1950, then nearly tripled from 1950 to 1970, providing educational opportunities to a far wider swath of students. The GI Bill also set in motion the federal government's relationship with students and higher education. The principle was established that federal money would go to the student, not to the educational institution. That principle became the cornerstone of federal educational policy.

The GI Bill officially terminated in 1951, but soon thereafter, in response to the Korean War, a second GI Bill was enacted, followed by the Vietnam Era GI Bill in 1966, the Montgomery GI Bill in 1985, and the Post-9/11 Veterans Educational Assistance Act in 2008. Many of the provisions from the earlier legislation had changed. Benefits were increased, but so, too, were the dollar amounts that service personnel were required to contribute. In all, the GI Bill proved to be an extraordinary investment. By June 2004, the sixtieth anniversary of the GI Bill, 21 million veterans, service personnel, and their families had received a total of $77 billion in GI Bill benefits for education and training; in addition, 17.5 million veterans had taken advantage of the home loan guaranty program, for loans totaling $830 billion. Through its education programs for college and non-college bound students and its home loan guaranty program, the GI Bill helped to create the modern American middle class.

Background

The Veterans of the Revolution and the Nineteenth-Century Wars

Using the established English laws as their guides, several colonial legislatures crafted measures to assist wounded citizen-soldiers who had fought against Indians. The Plymouth Colony in 1636 proclaimed that any man who set forth as a soldier in the war against the Pequod Indians and came back injured would be "maintained competently by the Colony during his life." The Virginia legislature in 1644 provided relief for "hurt or maymed" men who had fought against Indians, and required local counties to provide them relief. Later, the Massachusetts Bay Colony (1676), Maryland (1678), New York (1691), and Rhode Island (1718) created similar laws protecting the disabled soldier. During the Revolutionary War, the Virginia and Pennsylvania legislatures enacted liberal provisions for the disabled, and the widows and orphans of those slain. In May 1778, Virginia promised full pay for life for any of its soldiers in the Continental Army who were disabled; in same year, the legislature promised half pay for life to widows of those slain in service. The Continental Congress had granted half pay for seven years for commissioned officers who served until the end of the war; in March 1780, the Commonwealth of Pennsylvania extended the benefit to half pay for life.[1]

Recruits to the Continental Army, drawn heavily from the poorest third of society, had mutinied over lack of pay, and officers three times threatened Congress with mass resignations unless they were granted half-pay pensions for life. As the major hostilities effectively ended with the Battle of Yorktown in October 1781, many officers worried that they would not receive either their back pay, which for some amounted to six years owed, or their pensions. Some soldiers feared that once they had been dismissed from wartime service they might be jailed and thrown into debtors' prison.[2] Four months before the Treaty of Paris was signed to officially end the war, a group of officers in May 1783 formed the Society of the Cincinnati. This became the main vehicle in later years for Continental officers to press their claim for war-related compensation.

There were two basic pension issues that confronted the new United States Congress: first, it had to devise a pension plan for injured or disabled soldiers;

and, second, it had to contend with the persistent clamor of Revolutionary army officers who demanded half-pay pensions for life for all officers who had served to the end of the war.[3]

Veterans were successful in gaining land grants in the newly opened western lands. As seen in Chapter 1, the Confederation Congress in 1787 passed the Northwest Ordinance, opening up the western lands above the Ohio River. One of the provisions was to reserve one-seventh of that land, or approximately 2.6 million acres, for Revolutionary War veterans.

During its first session under the new Constitution, Congress in September 1789 continued disability and death benefit payments that had been granted and paid by the states during the Revolution. Then, in 1792, it passed the first of several veterans' pension laws, providing that "any person . . . called out into the service of the United States . . . wounded or disabled while in actual service . . . shall be taken care of and provided for at the public expense."[4] This first federal pension law, vague though it was in its language, was important for the precedent that it set. According to historian William H. Glasson, "in miniature, its history shows most of the conditions which surrounded the passage and administration of later pension laws."[5]

The claims of both Revolutionary officers and enlisted men, however, were not settled until 1817. Following the recommendations of President James Monroe, Representative Joseph Bloomfield (Republican–New Jersey) introduced a veterans' pension that expanded the earlier legislation, giving officers $20 a month and enlisted men $8. All veterans were entitled to such benefits, regardless of income or financial status. By the next year, the costs of the benefits program had grown to $3 million a year, six times the original estimate when Bloomfield introduced the legislation.[6] The Pension Bureau, established to administer veterans' benefits, estimated that the total pension payments to Revolutionary soldiers and their widows amounted to around $70 million, and that the last surviving dependent received benefits up until 1911.[7]

Veterans of the War of 1812, or their families, were given land-grants by the federal government, but the original legislation required that they must have served for five years or died during their service. As a result only 29,000 of the 400,000 who served during the war were eligible for a grant of federal lands. What mobilized 1812 veterans, however, was the more generous treatment that was given to veterans of the Mexican war (1846–48). Under the Ten Regiments Act of 1847, Mexican war veterans were eligible for 160-acre land warrants after serving just one year. Further, the Mexican war veterans could either choose a land warrant anywhere on public lands or accept a cash award of $1.25 per acre instead; War of 1812 veterans did not have a cash option, and the lands given to them were in remote western sites, far removed from the great majority who had come from the East.[8]

Under pressure from 1812 veterans, who had organized as the United Brethren of the War of 1812, Congress passed a land-granting measure in 1850 to any veteran who had served at least a month in a war after 1790. But this legislation fell short of veterans' expectations. Under the 1847 Ten Regiments Act, many veterans had been cheated out of their land-grant by thieves and land brokers. To remedy this, the 1850 law barred the sale of the granted land. The 1850 law also set up a sliding ratio of service to land: if a veteran had served from one to four months, he received 40 acres; four to nine months meant an 80-acre grant; and more than nine months would mean a full 160-acre grant. Veterans objected, and a number of state legislatures petitioned Congress to reverse the 1850 law. The prohibition against selling land was overturned by an 1852 law, and in March 1855 Congress passed land-grant legislation to benefit 260,000 veterans (170,000 from the War of 1812), as well as their widows and heirs. This was by far the largest, and last, land-grant for veterans, awarding 34 million acres to veterans and their heirs.[9]

Historian James W. Oberly characterized the United Brethren of the War of 1812 as an organization that resembled modern veterans' groups, emphasizing conservatism, nationalism, and nonpartisan political positions, unlike Civil War veterans' groups which "existed as creatures of rival political parties."[10]

Fifty-nine years after the beginning of the War of 1812, the remaining survivors in 1871 finally received their long-sought service pensions. This was the signal for Mexican war veterans, now united as the National Association of Mexican War Veterans, to resume the fight for their own pension demands. At their first national convention in 1874, the Mexican war veterans asked Congress for a grant of $8 a month for all soldiers who had served sixty days or more.[11] Mexican war veterans, however, had difficulty in getting what they considered their just rewards. For one, they were less than politically astute, attacking Republican politicians and casting their lot with Democrats. Many of the Mexican war veterans were from the South, and by the time of their first convention, with the Civil War still etched in lawmakers' memories, they were frankly fighting on the wrong side. They also had to contend with a new, potent veterans' organization, the Grand Army of the Republic.

The War Department had estimated that over 2.2 million men served in the Union army during the Civil War.[12] By far the most powerful and largest Union veterans' organization was the Grand Army of the Republic (GAR), which was formed in 1866 and by the 1880s had seen its membership and political power grow dramatically. The GAR continued to grow rapidly, from 60,678 members in 1880 to 427,981 members in 1890. Further, about one-third of the members of Congress during the Forty-Ninth Congress (1885–87) were veterans from northern and border states. The GAR created its own lobbying presence through its Committee on Pensions, and in Washington there was a concentration of law firms that put pressure on both the Congress and the Bureau of Pensions.[13] General Benjamin F. Butler exhorted veterans at the twenty-fourth annual encampment of the GAR that, if they acted together, they could "make politicians dance like peas on a hot shovel."[14]

Butler, the GAR, and its forces in Washington had much to brag about. By the end of 1883, the 1 million survivors out of the original 2.2 million Union soldiers were collecting $150 million annually in pensions, nearly 40 percent of the entire federal budget of $385.6 million, a percentage which held relatively constant through the end of the century.[15] Congress was swamped with requests for private pension bills. In 1884, some 40 percent of all bills introduced in the House and 55 percent introduced in the Senate were for private pensions. Robert M. LaFollette, Sr. (Republican–Wisconsin), who served in the House from 1885 to 1890, estimated that about from a quarter to a third of his time was spent looking up pension cases for old soldiers in his congressional district; Representative William P. Hepburn (Republican–Iowa) estimated that he received 50,000 letters relating to pensions during his twenty-seven-year congressional career.[16]

Probably the high point in the GAR's political influence came with the presidential election of 1888. President Grover Cleveland, a Democrat, had vetoed the generous Dependent Pension Bill in 1887, which would provide pensions to disabled and dependent soldiers, whether or not their disabilities were service-related. The legislation had overwhelming support in Congress, but after Cleveland's veto and the fierce reaction against the bill from the press and much of the public, enough border state and northern Democrats had changed their minds, helping to sustain the veto. Cleveland further irritated veterans when he gave oral approval, with little thought of the consequences, for the return to the Southern states of some of the Confederate battle flags that were collecting dust in the attic of the War Department and later by failing to honor an invitation to appear at the GAR's annual encampment in St. Louis.[17]

On November 6, 1888, Grover Cleveland won the popular vote, but lost in the Electoral College to Republican challenger, former Senator Benjamin Harrison of Indiana. With Republicans now in control of both the White House and Congress, the GAR and its attorneys actively pursued a new service pension law. The ensuing law, the 1890 pension act was characterized as "the most extravagant pension law ever enacted."[18] In addition, Harrison appointed as Commissioner of Pensions a member of the GAR pension committee, James Tanner, who vigorously and enthusiastically aided veterans, to the point where he had to be removed from office six months later. But the tide was turning. The pension and tariffs were critical issues that led to Republican defeats in 1890 and 1892, and, with the Panic of 1893, there was no surplus left in the Treasury to distribute to veterans or any other programs. Soon, these issues lost appeal with the emergence of the free silver question.[19]

Then, with the conclusion of the war with Spain and the insurrection on the Philippine Islands, Congress enacted another, even more generous pension for these veterans. While there had been defeats and disappointments, in all, the veterans' lobbies had enjoyed remarkable success. By the end of the nineteenth century, nearly $5 billion had been paid out to Civil War pensioners alone, a testament to the strength and political power of the veterans' lobbies.[20]

World War I and the Bonus Army

Some 4 million American servicemen were demobilized within a year of the November 1918 Armistice. Of the total, 50 percent were volunteers; approximately 2 million had served overseas, and 1.9 million never left the United States.[21] The demobilized servicemen received $60 in separation pay and a railroad ticket home. Only disabled veterans received more. Under the Rehabilitation Act of 1919, the disabled veteran was eligible to receive federal payment of tuition, fees, books, and a subsistence allowance of $90 to $145 a month for rehabilitative or professional training. A total of 329,969 World War I veterans registered for vocational training and of those 118,355 were deemed rehabilitated and ready to enter the workforce.[22] At the same time, thousands of workers in war-related industries were being laid off, with no unemployment compensation to cushion the shock.[23]

The median educational level of servicemen was the sixth grade (in World War II, the median educational level was second year of high school), and there were 121,000 illiterate servicemen in the American Expeditionary Force.[24] Just after the Armistice, programs were launched in reading and writing to help illiterate and undereducated veterans. Some states provided better benefits than did the federal government for returning veterans. California, Colorado, Minnesota, New York, North Dakota, and Oregon provided free tuition to state-supported institutions. Wisconsin offered two attractive educational programs for its returning veterans.[25]

Several months later, in February 1919, Colonel Theodore Roosevelt, Jr., invited a group of twenty officers to a dinner in Paris to consider forming an organization for war veterans. Roosevelt and Major Joel Bennett Clark were chosen as co-chairmen. In March, another meeting was held in Paris, with nearly two hundred officers and enlisted men as delegates, making it the first caucus of the American Legion. Two months later, a thousand delegates met in St. Louis for the first public convention of the new organization. The delegates insisted that Colonel Roosevelt become their first national commander; Roosevelt, to the protests of many, declined the offer.[26] Instead, Major Clark was chosen. Clark was well positioned in political circles: his father, James Beauchamp (Champ) Clark, was the Speaker of the House of Representatives and had vied for the presidential nomination in 1912. The young Clark would become involved in national politics, would be elected senator from Missouri and would ultimately play a key role in the creation of the GI Bill. The American Legion would take on the role played by earlier war veteran groups, like the Grand Army of the Republic or the Veterans of Foreign Wars (VFW), to push for federal benefits for those who had served in the armed forces.[27]

After the war, several bills were introduced in Congress for veterans' benefits and, while opposed by many as financially and morally unsound, they did provide some assistance. The Adjusted Compensation Act of 1924 caused the most controversy. It provided a deferred bonus, of $1.25 per day for overseas duty and $1.00 per day for home military service, payable in full in 1945. President Warren G. Harding had earlier vetoed similar legislation, and in 1924 President Calvin Coolidge vetoed it as well, citing the enormous long-term cost, which earlier had been estimated at $3 billion, one-sixth of the public debt, and arguing that it violated the principle of equity, that is, it singled out one class of citizens, the veterans, for preferential treatment. Nevertheless, Congress overrode his veto. In addition to the deferred outlay of the 1945 bonus payout, there were the day-to-day expenses of providing compensation and benefits to the 530,000 veterans and 100,000 widows, and the hospital treatment for 500,000. From 1921 to 1931, the newly formed Veterans Bureau disbursed $14 billion.[28]

In the early days of the 1930s, as economic hard times became a constant, gripping reality, millions of Americans lost their jobs and faced the humiliation of bread lines and soup kitchens. Among them were thousands of war veterans. Their promised bonus payment was still fifteen years away, but many demanded that they receive their benefits when they desperately needed them. In the spring and summer of 1932, some twenty thousand veterans, calling themselves the Bonus Expeditionary Force, descended upon Washington, hoping to pressure Congress into passing a veterans' bonus bill, legislation that had been sponsored by Representative Wright Patman (Democrat–Texas). The bill, which would have cost $2.4 billion, was opposed by the leadership in both the House and the Senate, and by President Hoover, who promised to veto it. As the Depression began to sink in for the long haul, with the federal Treasury depleted and the price tag so high, legislators found themselves in a difficult position.

Representative Fiorello La Guardia (Republican–New York), who himself had a distinguished war record, was one of many who argued against the bonus bill: "You are to give $2 billion to 4 percent of the population. It will not solve a single problem. There are 8 million unemployed. I refuse, for one, to sacrifice them to this distorted, selfish purpose. Eight weeks after they get the bonus the veterans will have no money and the situation will be the same as before."[29] LaGuardia and other legislators had reason to worry: in 1932, veteran benefits counted as 25 percent of the entire federal budget.[30]

Nevertheless, the House of Representatives passed the Patman bill, 211–176, with most Democrats voting for and most Republicans against. Bonus marchers, scattered throughout the House gallery when final passage came, broke into applause, although warned repeatedly against any grandstanding. Then some 6,000 bonus marchers joined in a solemn funeral procession for Representative Edward E. Eslick (Democrat–Tennessee), an ardent supporter of the bonus bill, who had died on the floor of the House days earlier. Senator J. W. Elmer Thomas (Democrat–Oklahoma), a chief sponsor of the bill, was hopeful that the Senate would accept it, but, on June 14, the upper body resoundingly rejected the bonus bill, 62–18.

In early June 1932, with the arrival of the bonus army, Congress and Hoover secretly sought to give the demonstrators army cots, blankets, tents, food, and medical supplies; the U.S. Army, however, protested, telling Congress that such gestures would violate the "basic principles" of the Army and the War Department toward this motley so-called Bonus Expeditionary Force.[31] In June 1932, General Douglas MacArthur, Army chief of staff, wired all corps area commanders that, if any bonus army marchers came through their areas, the commanders were to determine if any communists were present. MacArthur added that he wanted the names of those with "known communist leanings."[32]

In early July 1932 Congress appropriated funds to help veterans return to their homes; many of the estimated 12,000 veterans in Washington left for home. Congress adjourned for the year on July 16, without passing a bonus bill.[33] On July 21, with 5,000 veterans still in Washington, members of the Bonus Expeditionary Force were informed that they were to be evicted from a government-owned building on Pennsylvania Avenue. The warning was reiterated on July 27, and eviction began the next morning. One building was cleared, but then a fight broke out between 200 marchers and city police, and two marchers were killed. By that afternoon, the District Commissioners reported to President Hoover that the situation was out of control.

Hoover, waiting an hour for the request to come in writing, then ordered MacArthur to clear the area. Federal cavalry, six tanks, and a column of infantry were called in. MacArthur was supposed to secure the contested buildings and contain the marchers at their bivouac site on the Anacostia River flats, but instead he used tear gas to rout the marchers from their base and he allowed the city police to burn down their forlorn camp.

Hoover was furious, demanding that MacArthur and Secretary of War Patrick J. Hurley publicly acknowledge their responsibility. But both Hurley and MacArthur stood their ground, arguing that they had prevented further bloodshed. MacArthur said he had uncovered machine guns and felt certain that "communist agitators" were planning a major confrontation. In the end, Hoover stood by both men and assumed full responsibility himself.[34]

This was probably the low point in Hoover's battered, contentious admin- istration. The sight of the beleaguered, rag-tag veterans, run out of town by the Army with its tanks and cavalry, left an indelible impression on voters. A discouraged Republican party renominated Hoover for another term as president, but, in these bleak months before the 1932 election, his presidency was all but over.

One of the first orders of business for Franklin D. Roosevelt after he was sworn into office on March 4, 1933, was to confront the issue of veterans' benefits. On March 5, Roosevelt issued a proclamation calling Congress back into immediate session and declared a four-day national bank holiday. The Emergency Banking Act, cobbled together by Roosevelt advisors in furious overnight sessions, reached Congress one hour after it convened, was subjected to perfunctory debate, and was passed almost unanimously. The second piece of emergency legislation sent to Congress on March 10 was the Economy Act, which slashed some $500 million from the $3.6 billion federal budget, reduced the pay of government employees (including members of Congress), and made a 50 percent reduction in veterans' benefits, despite furious protests from veterans' organizations. On March 20, Roosevelt signed this second emergency measure into law. Two days later, in anticipation of the ratification of the Twenty-First Amendment, Congress passed the Beer-Wine Revenue Act. As historian David M. Kennedy has noted, during this flurry of law making, Roosevelt "had taken on and vanquished two of the most powerful political lobbies in Washington: the veterans and the prohibitionists."[35] But certainly the fight over veterans' benefits was not over. The next year Roosevelt responded to angry American Legionnaires, remarking "that no person, because he wore a uniform, must thereafter be placed in a special class of beneficiaries over and above all other citizens."[36]

Making the Law

With war raging in Europe and the Far East, Congress passed, with a one-vote margin in the House, the Selective Service Act of 1940, requiring all men between the ages of twenty-one and twenty-six to register for military service. This was America's first ever peacetime draft and over the next two years there would be a second, third, and fourth registration, adding new twenty-one-year-olds and older men. With the United States entering the war in December 1941 and manpower needs becoming acute, fifth and sixth registrations were added in 1942, reaching down to eighteen-year-olds.[37]

In November 1942, at the time that the Allied forces were beginning their offensive in North Africa, Roosevelt appointed the Armed Forces Committee on Post-War Educational Opportunities for Service Personnel to look into postwar plans for demobilized veterans. The panel was chaired by Brigadier General Frederick H. Osborn and quickly became known as the Osborn Committee.[38] Roosevelt had two important considerations in mind. He had just signed the amended Selective Service Act of 1942 which had lowered the draft age to eighteen; he knew this would be an unpopular move and wanted to assure the public that his administration had plans to help returning servicemen with educational benefits. Roosevelt also was interested in getting the Army and the Navy to work together to avoid the lack of planning he saw when he served as assistant secretary of the Navy during World War I.

It did not take long for Congress to react. As a reporter for the *Washington Post* observed, the president's six-point program brought a rush of congressional endorsements. "I'll bet 100 bonus bills are dropped into the hopper in the next term of Congress," responded one member of the House Ways and Means Committee.[39] Eventually 640 bills dealing with some aspect of veterans' benefits and demobilization clogged the hoppers of the House and Senate.[40]

With the Osborn Committee recommendations and report now complete, Roosevelt on October 27, 1943, announced his goal to have the federal government make it financially feasible "for every man and woman who has

Seventy-Eighth Congress,
2nd Session (January 10–December 19, 1944)

Senate: 58 Democrats; 37 Republicans; 1 other

House: 218 Democrats; 208 Republicans; 4 other

President: Franklin D. Roosevelt

served honorably for a minimum period in the armed forces since September 16, 1940, to spend a period up to one calendar year" in a college, technical institute, or on the job training program.[41] Roosevelt concluded that "we have taught our youth to wage war; we must also teach them how to lead useful and happy lives in freedom, justice, and decency."[42] Also in the fall of 1943, the American Council on Education had produced a veterans' postwar education plan that in many ways paralleled those of the Osborn Committee.[43]

The American Legion was the most important group to push for postwar veterans' benefits. The Legion became the champion of the GI Bill, helped craft the language, and applied its considerable organizational pressure to see it enacted. At its annual convention in Kansas City in September 1942, the American Legion invited new World War II veterans to join its forces and adopted a resolution urging Congress to include vocational education for returning veterans when it crafted the Selective Service Act of 1942.

On November 30, 1943, Legion national commander Warren H. Atherton appointed a special committee to draft a "master plan" for the readjustment of World War II veterans; included on that committee were John Stelle, former governor of Illinois (chairman), Henry (Harry) Colmery, past Legion national commander, and Robert W. Sisson, head of the Legion's National Rehabilitation Committee, and several others. Meeting at the Mayflower Hotel in Washington, D.C., between December 15 and 31, the committee, with Colmery as its draftsman writing in longhand on hotel stationery, crafted the American Legion's proposal.[44]

The basic principles developed by the drafting committee were that GI benefits should be centralized under one agency, the new Veterans Administration; that World War II veterans should receive no less than their World War I counterparts; and that legislation should ensure that "returning servicemen could resume their civilian status right at the point at which the war had disrupted their lives." The draft was made public on January 8, 1944, as "a bill of rights for GI Joe and GI Jane," a phrase credited to the Legion's acting publicity director, Jack Cejnar. It soon became forever known as the GI Bill of Rights or, simply, the GI Bill.[45]

There were two major veterans' bills being considered by Congress in January 1944. The administration plan, introduced by Senator Elbert D. Thomas (Democrat–Utah), incorporated the recommendations of the Osborn Committee and attempted to link education benefits with the larger issue of national employment policy. Further, the administration proposal offered aid to veterans, but only for the first year of study, limiting additional years of study to those with "exceptional ability or skill."[46]

The second bill was that of the American Legion. Called the Veterans' Omnibus Bill, it was introduced by Joel Bennett Clark of Missouri, with seventy-nine other senators eagerly signed on as co-sponsors; the other sixteen lawmakers disappointed because they hadn't signed on before it reached the Senate floor. This was the same Clark who in Paris in 1919 was the co-chairman of the founding committee of the American Legion. In the House, the American Legion's bill was introduced by Representatives Rankin and Edith Nourse Rogers (Republican–Massachusetts) of the Committee on World War Veterans Legislation.

While there were many similarities between the administration's and the American Legion's proposals, the biggest difference was that for Roosevelt veterans' benefits were linked to the broader goal of domestic reconversion. The American Legion, however, was clearly focused: to "serve the veteran directly, unequivocally, and with no shenanigans."[47] The Legion bill called for rather modest education benefits: veterans who had served for at least nine months would be entitled to one full year of educational benefits; the Veterans Administration would then be able to choose those to continue for another three years of education. Single and married veterans enrolling in the education programs would receive a subsistence allowance of $50 and $75, respectively, per month. The bill also provided for low-interest loans for purchase of homes and farms, set at a maximum of $7,500 appraised value for homes and $12,500 for farms, a feature not found in the administration's bill. The omnibus Legion bill also addressed unemployment, by giving veterans $25 a week for up to fifty-two weeks.

Historian David R. B. Ross noted that there was a logical consistency to the American Legion's proposal: it centralized the administration of the GI Bill into one agency, the Veterans Administration, and focused on the basic theme of helping veterans readjust to civilian life. Further, the American Legion demonstrated "shrewd tactical insight" by presenting a fully developed omnibus bill, rather than the piecemeal approach that was employed by the Roosevelt administration.[48]

Federal legislation, whether for the Civil War or World War II veteran, set in motion a long-term commitment to the recipients and their survivors. The bonus that was so controversial for World War I veterans was finally paid off in full in 1936. At the same time that the GI Bill was being considered, the national leaders of the United Spanish War Veterans and its auxiliaries met in its Washington, D.C., headquarters to plot their own strategy for increased benefits. Their efforts focused on the Senate as it considered a bill that had already been passed unanimously in the House that would increase the Spanish–American war veterans' allotments from $60 to $75 a month. The bill also extended the date of marriage of a Spanish–American War veteran's wife from 1922 to 1938.[49]

Everyone wanted to help America's men and women in uniform, but there were difficult times ahead, for both the American Legion and the administration as they prepared their 1944 legislative packages. The American Legion, perhaps in its rush to craft legislation, perhaps in not wanting to share the credit with others, caused friction with other veterans' organizations, the Veterans of Foreign Wars (VFW), the Disabled America Veterans (DAV), the Military Order of the Purple Heart, and the Regular Veterans Association. These organizations wanted a traditional veterans' bonus, not the plan crafted by the administration or the American Legion. Their bonus plan, however, came with an extraordinary price tag of $25–30 billion and stood no chance against the American Legion or administration bills.[50] The VFW eventually joined forces with the American Legion, but the other groups remained opposed.

Further, the Disabled American Veterans worried that the Veterans Administration would be overloaded with responsibilities for all service personnel under the proposed GI Bill and that disabled veterans might suffer. They had seen this happen a few years earlier under the Economy Act, when hospital and other benefits were curtailed significantly.[51] Millard Rice, the national service director for the Disabled American Veterans, was afraid that the GI Bill would become an "administrative monstrosity" and overwhelm the Veterans Administration.[52]

Meantime, the relationship between Roosevelt and Congress during the winter of 1943–44 grew testy. Roosevelt, with an eye on an unprecedented fourth term in office, proposed a uniform federal ballot that would make it easier for armed forces personnel to cast their vote in the 1944 presidential election. But states rights forces fiercely opposed this, arguing that elections had always been the prerogative of the states, not the federal government. In early December 1943, the Senate defeated this administration proposal. Then in February 1944 Roosevelt vetoed a tax bill, causing such an outburst that Senator Alben W. Barkley (Democrat–Kentucky) resigned from his position as majority leader. As a snub to Roosevelt, the Senate immediately re-elected Barkley to the majority leader post.[53]

Despite the friction between Congress and the White House, the veterans' benefits bills went fairly smoothly through the Senate with the focus on the American Legion's version. Senator Clark's Subcommittee on Veterans' Legislation held nine sessions of hearings, concluding on March 10, 1944, and crafted legislation that went to the full Finance Committee. The senators revised and expanded the education and unemployment sections of the American Legion's proposal. They made the education and training benefits available to all veterans who were honorably discharged and had six months' service, rather than the Legion's version which just gave those benefits to those whose education or training had been interrupted; they also allowed benefits for veterans who wanted to be part-time students. The senators increased fee repayments to $500 and added an advisory board to assist the Veterans Administrator on education and training matters. Senators also expanded unemployment benefits, determining that the Legion's disqualification provisions were too harsh. The full Senate approved the revised bill unanimously.[54]

In the House the legislation had a more bumpy ride, especially because of the determined views and shrewd maneuvering of Chairman Rankin. He held back the GI Bill because of his heated opposition to its unemployment insurance features. Rankin could not tolerate the idea of giving unemployment benefits to either blacks or union workers. Rankin privately told the American Legion's Atherton that he opposed all unemployment insurance. Atherton publicly responded, "if Mr. Rankin means that he wants to deny unemployment insurance to the men now carrying a bayonet for Uncle Sam, the veterans of the American Legion intend to fight him right down the line and take the issue to every voter in the country."[55]

Rankin was also suspicious of the education title, fearing it gave the federal government too much opportunity to interfere with state policies and practices; above all, it might even lead to federal interference with sacrosanct southern policy of racially separated schools. He also distrusted the supposed left-leaning theories and ideas of academicians, once asserting that he'd rather send his child "to a red schoolhouse than to a red school teacher."[56] Rankin knew he was fighting a tough battle, and his tactics now shifted to delaying the legislation as much as possible. But after sixteen public sessions and nineteen closed-door executive sessions, Rankin's War Veterans Committee favorably reported the GI Bill, but, at Rankin's insistence, and to Atherton's disappointment, reduced the unemployment compensation feature by 50 percent of what had been approved in the Senate bill.[57]

In the meantime, the American Legion mobilized its forces, some 1.5 million members, of whom 200,000 were current World War II veterans.[58] On the twenty-fourth anniversary of the American Legion, in mid-March 1944, Atherton announced a nation-wide "sign-up day" urging Congress to pass the GI Bill. Atherton's telegram to all Legion departments was a call to arms: "I herewith call upon the 12,000 posts of the American Legion to give real meaning to the observance of our twenty-fifth anniversary by staging in every community throughout the land an all-day house-to-house, office-to-office, store-to-store, and factory-to-factory canvass for millions of signatures urging Congress to enact our omnibus bill."[59] In May the American Legion presented a petition to Congress with a million signatures urging passage of the GI Bill.[60] The political power of veterans and their families was no idle threat. Historian Roy V. Peel estimated that all persons retired to civilian life from armed forces in 1945 constituted 12 million citizens, a full one-quarter of the American voting population.[61]

Also coming to the aid of the American Legion and veterans' benefits was the Hearst publishing empire. William Randolph Hearst, who had little love of Franklin Roosevelt and his New Deal programs, stepped into the fight for the GI Bill thanks in large part to an incident between two Hearst reporters and Andrew Jackson May (Democrat–Kentucky), the chairman of the House

Military Affairs Committee. In early December 1943, May had been charged by the House leadership to write a bonus bill in time for Christmas for what became called the "Forgotten Battalion," a name given by the American Legion to those servicemen whose "bodies and minds had been broken" in defending the nation [62] The Legion wanted a $500 bonus, but May drafted a bill for just $300, went home to Kentucky for Christmas, and refused to report the bill out of committee in time for any floor action before the holiday break. Hearst newspapers pounced on May's seeming insensitivity, with newspaper stories appearing around the country. Readers were in an uproar, and May was furious at the coverage. In January, 1944, he and the Democratic leadership won a crucial final vote for a $300 mustering out payment; meanwhile, the Senate unanimously approved a $500 measure. In a Senate–House conference to iron out the differences, May's $300 proposal prevailed, disappointing not only the American Legion but also the Hearst newspapers. This could have been seen as nothing more than an inside-Washington legislative battle, until Congressman May confronted two Hearst reporters, threatening one with this riposte: "Remember—before you mention me again, you consult the undertaker—because brother, you'll need him." That was enough for Hearst; from that moment on, he decided to throw the full resources of his media empire behind the American Legion and its push for the GI Bill.[63]

With the public solidly behind the GI Bill, the American Legion fully mobilized, and the Hearst newspaper chain touting the legislation, the House took up four days of debate on May 11. At first there was little controversy; however, members were soon sharply divided over the education sections, with each of two sides accusing the other of trying to impose bureaucratic control from Washington over state and private schools. Chairman Rankin was firm: "We are in favor of maintaining the rights of the States and keeping as many bureaucrats out as possible." To protect the rights of smaller schools, including some black schools, Rankin said his committee's legislation permitted the Veterans Administration to add to lists certified by state educational bodies. Rankin asserted that "we want to be dead sure" that a veteran can attend a school of his choice.[64] After another heated discussion about the role of labor unions, the House unanimously approved the GI Bill on May 18.[65]

When it came time to iron out the differences between the House and Senate versions, things almost fell apart. When the House–Senate conference met, there was a deadlock on the unemployment provisions. Rankin's House bill was pitted against Clark's more generous Senate version. Representative John S. Gibson (Democrat–Georgia), one of the conferees, went home to Georgia because of illness. Originally, Gibson gave Rankin his proxy vote, with full authority to vote as Rankin wished. Then Gibson changed his mind, instructing Rankin to have Gibson's vote cast in favor of the Senate unemployment provisions. Rankin didn't honor this request, and the conference remained deadlocked. The American Legion learned late in the afternoon of June 9, 1944, that there would be a final conference vote at ten o'clock the next morning. They contacted

Gibson, pleaded that he return to Washington, and arranged for a local Legionnaire to pick him up, drive him to the Waycross, Georgia, airbase, and through a pelting rainstorm escort him two hundred miles to Jacksonville, Florida, where a commercial flight had been waiting for him. Gibson arrived just in time to cast the decisive tie-breaking vote the next day.[66]

Highlights of the GI Bill of 1944

- Unemployment compensation. Authorized up to fifty-two weeks of unemployment compensation at $20 per week, with adjusted compensation for self-employed veterans restoring themselves in business rather than seeking jobs from others.
- Home or business purchase loans. Guaranteed 50 percent of the loans up to $2,000 to veterans, at interest not more than 4 percent, to purchase a home or a business.
- Construction of hospital facilities. Authorized $500 million for the construction of additional veterans' facilities, including hospitals, and strengthened provisions to assist veterans in finding employment through the United States Employment Service.
- Education benefits. Authorized allowances for four years of individual grants of $500 a year for training and education, plus monthly subsistence of $50 a month for single and $75 a month for married veterans.

After going through conference committee, final passage was a foregone conclusion, with unanimous votes in both the Senate and the House. Using ten commemorative ink pens to affix his signature, a beaming President Roosevelt signed the "GI Bill of Rights" on June 22, 1944. He was surrounded by Senate and House leaders, representatives of the American Legion, the Veterans of Foreign Wars, and others. Roosevelt noted that the GI Bill gave "emphatic notice to the men and women in our armed forces that the American people do not intend to let them down."[67] He also commented at the ceremony that he wanted comparable benefits given to 155,000 members of the merchant marine. This, however, never materialized, and the GI Bill remained associated only with armed forces veterans.[68]

The Key Individuals in the GI Bill

Franklin D. Roosevelt (1882–1945), the thirty-seventh president of the United States (1933–1945) knew that early demobilization planning was key and, through the 1942 Osborn Committee and earlier studies, he prodded lawmakers and policymakers to give serious thought about veterans benefits and programs. He did not play an important role during the six months that Congress worked on the legislation, but his overall approval and his public endorsement were key to passage.

John Elliott Rankin (1892–1960), a Democratic congressman (1921–1952) from Mississippi, co-authored, along with Senator George Norris (Republican–Nebraska),

---

legislation to create the Tennessee Valley Authority and the Rural Electrification Authority. Later, he played a prominent role on the House Un-American Activities Committee. Rankin was the chairman of the House Committee on World War Veterans Legislation and was primarily responsible for shepherding the GI Bill through the House of Representatives. Thin and wiry, with wild gray hair, Rankin was a master of parliamentary procedure and legislative tactics, known for his acerbic tongue, his fervent belief in white supremacy, his contempt for organized labor, and his anti-Semitic harangues. Walter Goodman noted that Rankin "took glee in baiting his Jewish colleagues. . . . One day he referred to [New York Representative Emanuel Celler] as 'the Jewish gentleman from New York.' When Celler protested, Rankin asked, 'Does the Member from New York object to being called a Jew or does he object to being called a gentleman? What is he kicking about?'"[69]

Joel Bennett Clark (1890–1954), a Democratic senator from Missouri (1933–1945), had earlier served as parliamentarian of the House of Representatives (1913–1917). His father, James Beauchamp (Champ) Clark, served in the House of Representatives (1893–1920), was Speaker of the House (1911–1914; 1915–1918), and ran unsuccessfully for the Democratic presidential nomination against Woodrow Wilson in 1912, losing on the fortieth ballot. The GI Bill was Clark's greatest legislative triumph; he skillfully steered the legislation through the Senate and never lost a single vote. In November 1944, however, Clark was defeated for a fourth Senate term by Republican Forrest C. Donnell. From 1945 until the end of his life in 1954, Clark served as associate justice of the U.S. Court of Appeals for the District of Columbia.

Warren H. Atherton (1891–1976), an attorney, judge, and politician from Stockton, California, served as national commander of the American Legion. In a nationwide radio address, May 2, 1944, he warned that "veterans will be a potent force for good or evil in the years to come. They can restore our country or break it. The can restore our democracy or scrap it. . . . We do not want our sons and daughters selling apples on street corners."[70] He served on the California Board of Prison Terms and Paroles (1935–1937), was a consultant to the secretary of war then coordinator of international affairs. He ran unsuccessfully for the U.S. Senate in 1957.[71] While other American Legion senior officials, like John Stelle, Robert W. Sisson, and Harry W. Colmery played important roles in crafting the legislation, Atherton's overall role as national commander was key.

Aftermath

Several things stood out with the making of the GI Bill. This was the first time since the Homestead and Morrill Acts of 1862 that the federal government had planned in advance, not waiting for demobilization.[72] Roosevelt was concerned about political and economic instability in a postwar America, and in November 1942 created the Osborn Committee to make recommendations that would ultimately be the backbone of the administration's legislative proposal. A month later, Army Chief of Staff George C. Marshall began considering plans for the demobilization of American troops. He wanted a plan created, in the event that there would be a sudden armistice.[73] Roosevelt's concerns about the political and economic instability of a postwar America also prompted early administration actions.

Certainly there were the fears associated with demobilization. The President's Commission on Veterans' Pensions in 1956 described the situation this way: "When World War II ended . . . we were confronted with a domestic crisis that was a graver threat to our national unity than any attack mounted by the enemy." The Commission found that "World War II was a monstrous time bomb that could have split the country into two divisive factions."[74] There were major problems: the welfare of the demobilized soldiers as they returned to peacetime activities; economic stability of the country and possible threat of moving back to a depression-like economy; the impact of disillusioned veterans on government institutions; the educational deficit that occurred when so many young people were removed from the educational stream; and the potential, extraordinary demand for larger pensions.[75]

On September 6, 1944, the Department of War released information on a proposed "Adjusted Service Card," a point system that would help determine the priority of demobilization of troops following the cessation of hostilities in Europe. Veterans would receive points for their length of service, awards and decorations earned, and the number of dependent children. After the war ended, President Harry S. Truman relaxed the standards, giving priority to older veterans; in late 1945, the demobilization standards were loosened once more.[76]

But the pressure to demobilize was constant and fierce, even though most Americans felt that the demobilization plans were fair and proceeding at the right pace. Members of Congress, hearing from their constituents, agitated for quicker demobilization. Some 200 "Bring Back Daddy" clubs were organized; wives of servicemen flooded Congress with pictures of their husbands and their children. Then, in December 1945, members of Congress were "deluged . . . with baby shoes with attached cards pleading 'Please bring back my daddy.'"[77]

One million men were discharged from the Army in December 1945. General Eisenhower, Fleet Admiral Ernest J. King, and Air Force General Carl A. Spaatz warned against such a rapid demobilization, fearing that there would not be enough replacement troops to meet the military's needs. To achieve the minimum goal of having 1.55 million American troops in July 1946, the armed services would have to halt the demobilization of the remaining 1.5 million troops overseas. What resulted, however, were troop riots in Manila, with over 20,000 agitating for quick demobilization in January 1946. In Batangas, Philippines, servicemen pooled together $3,700 to cable their protest to the President and the chairmen of the House and Senate committees on military affairs, and to publish full-page advertisements in fifteen leading American newspapers. In Guam, 18,000 soldiers collected $3,600 to send a cablegram of their complaints, signed by 6,000, to syndicated newspaper columnists Walter Winchell and Drew Pearson. Other servicemen protested in Honolulu, Paris, London, and Frankfurt-am-Main.[78]

Problems were complicated by the sheer size of the returning forces. The Civil War saw 2.2 million Union soldiers (and another 237,000 captured or imprisoned Confederate soldiers), World War I had 4 million personnel; by May 1945, there were 12.3 million returning veterans from World War II, of whom 7.6 million were stationed overseas.[79] Some of those veterans had been born as early as 1900, but the great majority were born between 1920 and the middle of 1926. Among white enlisted men born between those years—men who would have turned 18 between 1938 and 1944—the proportion serving from each quarter year was around 75 percent. These were the biggest beneficiaries of the GI Bill. About 50 percent of veterans born between 1923 and 1928 used the GI Bill benefits; but, for those born five years earlier, the rate was only between 27 and 40 percent.[80]

In the early 1940s, a high school diploma was still a rare achievement, earned by only 25 percent of the population. The 1940 Census showed ten million adult Americans with a formal education of fourth grade or less; one out of every eight adult males was illiterate. Only 14 percent of the enlisted men in the Army and only 6 percent in the Navy had attended college before entering the military.[81] The armed services needed personnel who could read and write, and they began an historic attack on illiteracy, producing probably the most successful adult literacy program in America's history, especially for African-Americans. From June 1943 through October 1944, approximately 180,000 illiterates attended special classes; about 85 percent or 150,000 attained a sufficient degree of literacy. Of those 150,000, a total of 86,670 were blacks.[82]

During World War II, servicemen were sent to colleges or civilian training programs to increase their skills. Accelerated courses were provided on many military installations. The United States Armed Forces Institute, created in 1942, offered correspondence programs for servicemen throughout the world.[83] In July 1945 and for the next six months, three European universities (in Florence, Italy, Shrivenham, England, and Biarritz, France) opened courses tailored to GIs. A technical school was also established in Warton, England. By February 1, 1946, some 35,000 soldiers had attended one of these four schools.[84]

Above all, the shift from giving a bonus to offering education benefits was a monumental change in policy, yet one unappreciated by policymakers at the time. Most lawmakers and experts in education policy predicted that between 8 and 12 percent of returning veterans would take advantage of the GI Bill's educational benefits. The remarkable thing is how wrong these experts were; by the end of the original GI Bill, 37 percent, or 7.8 million veterans, were being educated or trained.[85]

Also proven famously wrong were the predictions of two of the most influential university presidents of the day, James B. Conant of Harvard University and Robert M. Hutchins of the University of Chicago. Conant found the GI Bill "distressing." In his opinion, the legislation, which put no barriers on entry, did not "distinguish between those who can profit most by advanced education and those who cannot." He feared that "we may find the least capable among the war generation . . . flooding the facilities for advanced education."[86] Hutchins wrote an article for the December 1944 issue of *Collier's* magazine entitled "The Threat to American Education." He called the education provisions of the GI Bill "unworkable," predicting that colleges and universities, in order to increase their tuition revenues, would admit unqualified veterans and would refuse to expel even the veterans who were doing substandard academic work. He feared that "colleges and universities will find themselves converted into educational hobo jungles. And veterans . . . will find themselves educational hobos."[87]

Don Balfour, a twenty-two-year-old student at George Washington University, was the first veteran to sign up for the GI Bill. The day after President Roosevelt signed the bill into law, Balfour, an honorably discharged former corporal in the Quartermaster Corps, was interviewing John M. MacCammon, a Veterans Administration vocational officer, for an article in the student newspaper, *The Hatchet*. Balfour asked to have the GI benefits explained, then asked if he could sign up. The forms had not yet been printed, but in August 1944 he started receiving benefits from the GI Bill.[88] Balfour was followed by millions of other returning veterans, not a hobo among them. The student population of George Washington University swelled, with 7,000 veterans registered for the 1946–1947 academic year and another 7,000 registered in the fall semester of 1947, doubling the student enrollment. The University of Wisconsin admitted 11,000 veterans in 1946, and its total enrollment went from 9,000 to 18,000; Rutgers University jumped from 7,000 to 16,000 students during the same period; Stanford University went from 3,000 to 7,000. A surge of veterans—some 100,000—enrolled in Catholic colleges through the GI Bill in the Fall semester of 1947, with hardly a word of protest about breaching a wall between church and state.[89] In all, 1 million returning veterans in the 1947–1948 school year accepted Uncle Sam's offer of free tuition plus living allowance and headed off to college; altogether, 2,232,000 veterans attended college under the original GI Bill, at a cost of $5.5 billion.[90]

Veterans who had served between September 1940 and July 1947 were eligible for benefits; significantly, grants were awarded to individuals, not to educational institutions. In the early 1940s, the average annual tuition was $91 for a four-year public college and $273 for private colleges; even the most expensive private universities, such as the Ivy League schools, charged less than the $500 allotted for GI Bill tuition and fees.[91] The monthly cash allowance was $65 per month for single veterans and $90 per month for those who were married. Then in December 1945, after months of pressure from returning veterans and their families, Congress liberalized the education program, raising subsistence amounts, removing restrictions on veterans over twenty-five, and lengthening the time they could have to complete their education.[92]

The college campus was transformed. Classes were crowded, professors were in short supply, and married student housing was at a premium. Eighteen- to twenty-two-year-olds, the typical student population of an undergraduate program, now rubbed shoulders with students who were five, even ten years older, often married with their own children, far more mature and education-minded. The rah-rah atmosphere on many campuses was replaced with serious study and goal-oriented students. Many educators remarked at the maturity and drive of the returning veterans. A survey of educators conducted by the *New York Times* concluded that "contrary to fears expressed when the bill was adopted in July 1944, the educators held that the men who studied under Government subsidy were serious-minded, attended to their studies, and in all other respects were a credit to their institutions. In almost every respect, the average veteran was a superior student on the campus and in the classroom."[93] Historian Keith W. Olson has argued that the World War II veteran generation established "perhaps the most distinguished record in the history of higher education."[94]

An even larger number of returning veterans took advantage of educational benefits in non-college settings than took part in college studies. Roughly 60 percent of the veterans had not completed high school, and for them opportunities were available for on-the-job training programs, agricultural and industrial schools and institutes, and courses to complete their high school degrees. Some veterans enrolled in dance classes, beautician school, flight training, and correspondence courses.[95] In all, during the first seven years of the GI Bill, 3.4 million veterans received education below the college level; another 760,000 received on-the-job training, and an equal number received farm or agricultural training.[96]

But not all returning servicemen benefitted. The GI Bill perpetuated racial discrimination found in training programs, admission to higher education, application business loans, and mortgages. In areas of the country with whites-only schools, blacks were denied admission; traditional black colleges could not accommodate the 70,000 returning black veterans. Blacks were denied insured mortgages; when they sought employment assistance, they were channeled into low-paying unskilled jobs. As social scientist Ira Katznelson has observed, "written under Southern auspices, the [GI Bill] was deliberately designed to accommodate Jim Crow."[97]

There were some problems, most coming from the educational institutions that were reaping the benefit of the $2.5 billion in tuition payments by 1950. Tuition charges at many schools jumped dramatically, and new, mostly for-profit schools sprang to life. More than 5,600 of the 8,800 approved non-college schools were established after the enactment of the GI Bill. In 1950 an investigation by the Senate Committee on Labor and Public Welfare charged that millions of dollars were being wasted by questionable schools and programs. The Veterans Administration tightened up, requiring schools to register and account for their educational practices. Over 1,200 schools were alleged to have inadequate documentation or irregularities in their reports; of that total, 963 were for-profit institutions.[98]

The last year to sign up for the GI Bill was 1951, with the completion of studies in the academic year 1956. With the Korean war under way, there was widespread sentiment to extend the benefits of the original GI Bill. Just two weeks after American troops began fighting, in June 1950, Congressman John Rankin began working on a veterans' bill for the Korean war.[99] In his January 21, 1952, budget message, President Truman urged Congress to extend the veterans' benefits program but also asked lawmakers to learn from the mistakes and what he called "significant imperfections" of the original GI Bill. The president was concerned about diploma mills, educational fraud, and the millions that were alleged to have been stolen by fly-by-night for-profit schools. In response, the Senate Committee on Labor and Public Welfare conducted public hearings on extending the GI Bill while the House Committee on Veterans' Affairs held its own hearings. A key contribution was made by the House Select Committee to Investigate Education Programs under the GI Bill, an eighteen-month study, headed by Congressman Olin E. Teague (Democrat–Texas). In all these deliberations, there were a large number of participants, many of them from veterans' organizations, the military, and higher education interests.[100]

While 75 percent of men born between 1921 and 1926 served during World War II, just 45 percent of men of comparable age served during the Korean war. In 1951, the Selective Service System introduced the general deferment (II-S) for college study, the forerunner of the doctrine of "channeling," which in the 1950s and 1960s directed men away from the service into college.[101] The new deferment increased congressional concern about justice and fairness: with so many young men in college or beginning their careers, it was necessary to assist those who did answer the call to arms.

There were three contentious issues of debate surrounding the Korean war legislation. First, the new legislation was less generous in its education benefits than the original GI Bill, and, unlike the 1944 legislation, money for education went directly to the veteran and not to the college or other education institution. Korean war veterans could receive up to thirty-six months of education, and, if studying on a full-time basis, they would receive $110 a month if single, $135 a month with one dependent, and $160 a month for two or more dependents. Out of this money would have to come tuition, books, and other supplies. They, or the educational institutions, would not receive a $500 tuition award. State-supported institutions, with smaller tuitions, benefitted from this policy, while private colleges and universities vigorously fought for extra money to cover the more expensive tuitions and fees at their schools. Private schools lost this debate.

A second issue concerned the administration of the educational program. Most education groups and the American Council of Education favored the Office of Education, but, because of pressure from veterans organizations, the Veterans Administration continued its role as the lead agency. As a compromise, the Office of Education was thrown a bone in a section of the legislation that urged cooperation with other agencies and set up a special advisory committee, of which the commissioner of education was a member. A third issue concerned the eligibility of combat versus non-combat veterans; however, the principle set in the original GI Bill applied here: no matter where the service was performed, veterans of the Korean war would be eligible for educational benefits.[102]

Key Events in the Making of Veterans' Benefits	
1917	War Risk Insurance Act, provided basic package of benefits for World War I veterans.
1919	Creation of the American Legion.
1921	Consolidation of executive agency responsibilities under new agency, the Veterans' Bureau.
1924	World War Adjusted Compensation Act, provided a bonus payment to veterans, payable in 1945.
1932	Bonus army march on Washington.
1944	GI Bill of Rights.
1952	Korean GI Bill.
1966	Vietnam Era GI Bill.
1985	Montgomery GI Bill.
1988	Department of Veterans' Affairs established.
2008	Post-9/11 GI Bill.

The Veterans' Readjustment Assistance Act of 1952, or the Korean GI Bill,[103] provided more than just educational benefits. Like the original GI Bill, it also provided for loan guarantees, unemployment compensation, assistance for job placement, and a cash settlement for mustering out.[104] The Korean GI Bill ended on January 31, 1965. By that time, 2.4 million of the 5.5 million veterans of the Korean war had taken advantage of the educational benefits. More than half of these veterans, 1.21 million, used the GI Bill benefits to attend a college or university, while another 1.18 million took advantage of non-college programs, on the job training, and on-farm training. The total cost of the benefits amounted to $4.5 billion.[105]

In March 1966 Congress passed the Veterans' Readjustment Benefits Act of 1966, or the Vietnam Era GI Bill. For the first time, armed service personnel on active duty were eligible for benefits. Further, the bill was retroactive to those post-Korean war veterans who had served between February 1, 1955, and August 4, 1964, as well as Vietnam war veterans. Another major change permitted disadvantaged veterans to finish high school without losing entitlements for college or other training programs. The Veterans Administration paid veterans directly, with the first stipends in 1966 of $100 a month to cover tuition, fees, books, and other expenses; increasing by 1984 to a rate of $376 a month for single veterans. By the time of last eligibility for this program, in December 1989, a total of 8.2 million veterans and service members had received benefits; the majority of them, 5.1 million, used the benefits for college and university education. In all, the cost of education benefits under this third GI Bill was $42 billion.[106]

Congress terminated the Vietnam Era GI Bill at the end of the 1976 session. In its place, it instituted the less generous Veterans Educational Assistance Program (Basic VEAP). The Vietnam Era GI Bill required no matching financial contributions of servicemen; however, Basic VEAP did. Furthermore, its benefits were much lower. The Vietnam Era GI Bill provided $14,000 in aid to a single individual, and $16,500 for a married person. Under Basic VEAP, the Department of Defense provided a two-for-one assistance: the serviceman could contribute up to $2,700, and the Department of Defense would contribute a maximum of $5,400.[107]

The Army in particular was having trouble meeting its recruitment goals, and it added a "kicker" to the basic benefits, called "Ultra VEAP," and in 1982, this was instituted nationwide as the Army College Fund. The goal was to attract more college-oriented recruits. Then, in 1985, Basic VEAP and the Army College Fund were reformed with the passage of the "New GI Bill" (replacing Basic VEAP) and the "New Army College Fund." Under the new legislation, later called the Montgomery GI Bill, eligibility remained unchanged, but maximum benefits provided by the federal government rose to $9,600 and maximum soldier contributions were reduced to $1,200.[108] The total educational benefits paid by the government for individuals enrolled in the New Army College Fund—$24,000—were almost identical to the "old" Army College Fund.[109] The new GI Bill was originally introduced in 1981 by G. V. (Sonny) Montgomery (Democrat–Mississippi) but it took nearly five years to get through Congress. Montgomery acknowledged that it "came as a shock to me that some leaders in both the House and Senate were opposed to the enactment of a GI Bill for the All-Volunteer Force."[110] There were, in effect, two Montgomery GI Bills, one for active duty personnel entering the service after June 30, 1985, and the other, for the first time, giving benefits for National Guard and Reserve forces, called the Selected Reserve Educational Assistance program.[111]

However, the legislation, while generous and expensive, was not the same as the original. Writing in 1994, William Celis III noted that GI Bill legislation, through the years, had lost much of its economic impact and its appeal to veterans. Since the passage of the Montgomery GI Bill in 1985, only one-half of the eligible veterans participated, and, while $1.6 billion had been awarded in educational benefits, another $1.9 billion earmarked for veterans sat in the U.S. Treasury, unspent. Many veterans were upset because, in Celis's words, the GI Bill had "evolved to resemble life insurance." By 2004, despite expanded benefits, a third of the veterans had not taken advantage of the veterans' educational programs. Veterans with at least three years' service could receive more than $36,000 for tuition, books, and living expenses, provided the money was used within ten years.[112]

A number of other pieces of federal legislation have been enacted over the years to assist veterans, their survivors, and their dependents, including benefits for Persian Gulf war veterans (1991), and enhanced benefits under the Montgomery GI Bill in 2001 and 2004. Most recently, the Post 9/11 Veterans Educational Assistance Act was enacted in 2008 to give benefits to the men and women who had served for three years of duty after the September 11, 2001, terrorist attacks. The legislation, which survived a threatened veto from President Bush, was sponsored by Senator James H. Webb (Democrat–Virginia), the highly decorated Vietnam veteran and former Reagan administration secretary of the Navy, and Representative Robert S. Scott (Democrat–Virginia).

Transforming Legislation

At the commemoration of the sixtieth anniversary of the GI Bill, legislators and agency heads paused to reflect on its accomplishments. Representative Christopher H. Smith (Republican–New Jersey), chairman of the House Committee on Veterans' Affairs remarked in May 2004 that the original GI Bill "produced 450,000 engineers, 238,000 teachers, 91,000 scientists, 67,000 doctors, 22,000 dentists, and another one million college-educated men and women." He noted that "another five million men and women received other schooling or job training on the GI Bill, helping to create the modern middle class."[113]

Representative Henry E. Brown (Republican–South Carolina) noted that the home loan section of the GI Bill "was so successful that it is credited with creating the suburbs in America. Before the GI Bill, the great majority of Americans were renters. Now, most Americans live in their own homes."[114] Later, Anthony J. Principi, secretary of the Department of Veterans Affairs, noted in June 2004 that 21 million veterans, service members, and their families had received more than $77 billion in GI Bill benefits for education and training since 1944; the home loan guaranty program was used by 17.5 million, for loans totaling $830 billion.[115]

Reflecting on the GI Bill ten years earlier, Clark Kerr, president emeritus of the University of California, Berkeley, emphasized the "enormous push" that the GI Bill provided for the long-term movement away from mostly elite access to higher education before the Civil War, toward mass access through the land-grant college movement, and then to universal access to education following World War II. Half of the college students who used the GI Bill came from homes where neither of their parents had attended college. "In just ten years," Kerr wrote, " higher education enrollment underwent a quantum leap, and American higher education was irrevocably changed."[116]

To meet the peak demand for GI Bill students, in 1947–1950, colleges and universities had to stretch their resources. During that time, there were only ten universities with student enrollments of 20,000 or more. Two decades later, there had been such a spurt in growth of higher education that in 1967 there were fifty-five universities with enrollments of 20,000 or more. A greater boom in higher education came at the two-year community college level. Before the GI Bill, there were only forty-four such schools; by 1947, there were 328 community colleges and enrollment had doubled from 1944 to a total of one-half million students in 1947.[117]

Another important legacy of the GI Bill was the funding mechanism. The original GI Bill funded the veterans' education benefits through the students, not through the institutions. Veterans were given a monthly living stipend and up to $500 in tuition and fees, which the federal government would then reimburse to the educational institution. With the Korean GI Bill, there was no designated amount reserved for tuition, and veterans had to use their stipends for living expenses and tuition. Many veterans chose to use their benefits at the relatively less expensive state-supported schools, rather than at private colleges and universities. By 1960, with both of the GI Bills having expired, there was a push to have a "civilian" GI Bill. The question turned quickly to funding: should funding stay with students or should federal funding go through higher education institutions? The Carnegie Commission on Higher Education and the Rivlin Committee of the Department of Health, Education, and Welfare, among others, wanted money to go directly to colleges and universities. Those institutions, of course, wanted the money, and wanted it with a minimum of strings attached from the federal government. According to Clark Kerr, this was a "crucial controversy in the history of higher education," and, because lawmakers reinforced the aid-through-students principle in the 1966 Vietnam GI Bill, it "proved fundamental to making the GI Bill a permanent force in American society."[118]

Since passage of the GI Bill, the federal government has enacted several other major laws dealing with higher education, especially the Higher Education Act (1965), which established a variety of programs and guaranteed loans, and established the Teacher Corps, and Title IX of the Education Amendments (1972), making illegal discrimination in education on the basis of gender.[119] Further, Congress has enacted a series of laws to assist veterans with health care and housing. Nothing, however, compares to the scope, range, and long-lasting impact of the original legislation. Designed as an economic measure to cope with the enormous number of returning veterans, the GI Bill surprised its creators, astounded the colleges, universities, and other schools that braced themselves for the crunch of eager students, and fostered serious, mature learning, to the gratification of professors and school administrators. Above all, a grateful nation paid its lasting tribute to the men and women who took up arms in its defense, and the United States, its veterans, and its educational institutions were all the better for it.

8

THE RECOVERY OF WESTERN EUROPE

The Marshall Plan of 1948

Never before in history has one nation faced so vast
an undertaking as that confronting the United States
of repairing and salvaging the victors as well as the vanquished.

Harry S. Truman (1956)

The United States ought not forget that the emerging European
Union is one of its own greatest achievements: it would never
have happened without the Marshall Plan.

Helmut Schmidt (1997)

In the summer of 1945 much of Europe lay in ruins. In the hardest hit areas, cities were reduced to rubble, bridges destroyed and highways made impassable, crops could not be planted; factories were crippled or demolished, and production fell to dangerously low levels. Everywhere in areas hit hardest by war, there were refugees and displaced people, many having lost everything but the clothes on their backs. While touring Berlin in July 1945, on the eve of the Potsdam Conference, President Harry S. Truman saw first-hand the ruined, burned-out buildings, but even more depressing was the "long, never-ending procession of old men, women, and children wandering aimlessly along the autobahn and the country roads carrying, pushing, or pulling what was left of their belongings."[1] Forty years later, Helmut Schmidt, chancellor of the Federal Republic of Germany from 1974 to 1982, reminisced about his country's fate immediately after the war: "I had imagined that when we lost the war we Germans would have to live in caves and holes in the ground. . . . There were days during the winter of 1946–47 when we stayed in bed because there was nothing to eat and nothing to burn for warmth."[2]

European rebuilding and reconstruction began immediately, with some progress made in the months that followed the conclusion of hostilities. But the task was overwhelming. The United States helped with an infusion of $4 billion in aid to Western Europe through the United Nations Relief and Rehabilitation Administration (UNRRA) between 1945 and 1947. These grants and loans to individual countries, however, were given on an ad hoc basis, following no overall scheme or pattern, and no recipient country was able to plan ahead, since the desperately needed funds could not be counted on to continue.[3]

The burden overwhelmed the funds available. While factories and manufacturing centers had been utterly destroyed in many parts of Europe, a greater problem was the wholesale interruption of supply lines to make products. Plants could not produce iron and steel because of the lack of coal; transportation networks were widely interrupted, with bridges, roads, and rail lines destroyed, and waterways clogged. The agricultural sector was in even worse shape, with wholesale losses of livestock, lack of fertilizer, and lack of farm equipment.[4] Black markets flourished, with cigarettes and cognac as the coins of exchange. Above all, Europe faced a major shortage of dollars and unfavorable terms of trade. If it were to recover, Europe needed staple products—petroleum, metals, milk and cheeses, cotton, meat, and grains. Given the depression in production elsewhere, these could only be purchased from the United States.[5]

Then came the winter of 1946–1947, the worst in memory, hitting Britain and Western Europe particularly hard, blanketing much of the area with massive snow drifts, downed power lines, and disruption of transportation; an alarming number of people suffered from frostbite and many thousands were on the verge of starvation.

These hardships were accompanied by political and social upheavals throughout the world. China was on the brink of civil war; the Middle East was in turmoil with the agitation for a new state of Israel; the government of Greece was challenged by insurrectionists; Iran and Turkey were threatened by the Soviet Union; communist parties were growing in strength and number in France and Italy; and France, Britain, and the United States were at odds with the Soviet Union over the division and destiny of Germany. Eastern European countries fell under the political and military hegemony of the Soviet Union, and shortly the world was talking about an "iron curtain" drawn between East and West in Europe and a "cold war" between the Soviet Union and the West.

The United States, like it or not, had been thrust into the role of a world leader, and, for an important moment in American history, the Republican-controlled Congress and the Democratic administration, bitterly scrapping against each other on many domestic fronts, came together to create a bipartisan foreign policy. Britain, which had suffered tremendously during the war and was facing the painful reality of losing the last remnants of its empire, abruptly informed the United States that it could no longer protect Greece and Turkey. At the same time, the Soviet Union, which had suffered immeasurably more than Britain, was aggressively fighting for its own self-interest and threatening not only Eastern Europe but Western Europe as well. In 1947 Congress agreed to emergency relief for Greece and Turkey, and, thirteen months later, supported an ambitious European Recovery Program, popularly known as the Marshall Plan. The plan, which bore the name of Secretary of State George C. Marshall, had been germinating in State Department and foreign policy circles for some time, and was unique in two respects. First, the

American offer of aid, which itself was quite vague, compelled the European countries to work together to formulate a coordinated European-wide response and request for assistance. Second, the sheer magnitude of the final aid package—over $13.5 billion for a four-year period—was an extraordinary amount of foreign assistance money when the annual federal budget was between $35 and $40 billion per year.

Western Europe quickly recovered during the next decade, primarily through each country's own determination and initiative but to a certain degree because of the timely infusion of Marshall Plan assistance. Historians and social scientists gave near universal praise to the Marshall Plan during the first decade after its implementation. However, some revisionist scholars in the 1960s took a much dimmer view, seeing the aid program as primarily an instrument of American capitalist hegemony. More recently, some historians and economists have argued that the Marshall Plan funds were not all that vital in the overall economic recovery of Europe, while others have sharply disagreed with that conclusion.

European recovery was clearly in America's self-interest, for overlapping economic, military, and political reasons. However, U.S. officials and policy were only partially successful in convincing recipient countries to adopt manu-facturing efficiencies, rationalize production methods, and adopt bureaucratic reforms.

The Marshall Plan, however, was more than foreign aid money and administrative reform; it was an important political and psychological boost to America's European friends and allies. It helped stabilize democratic govern-ments, assisted European countries to begin the first steps toward economic and political integration, and demonstrated to both former ally and foe, that the United States was willing to provide much-needed assistance at the most critical time possible. Further, the Marshall Plan also changed America: it was the seminal postwar gesture that thrust the United States into the role of inter-national leader.

Background

Termination of Lend-Lease

On May 8, 1945, Acting Secretary of State Joseph C. Grew and Foreign Economic Administrator Leo Crowley came to the Oval Office and handed President Truman an important document that had been approved but not signed by Franklin Roosevelt shortly before his death. It was an order autho-rizing the State Department and the Foreign Economic Administration to cut back on Lend-Lease shipments and supplies once Germany had surrendered. Germany had formally surrendered to U.S. forces on May 7 and to Soviet forces the next day. Truman recalled his meeting with Grew and Crowley: "What they told me made good sense to me; with Germany out of the war,

Lend-Lease should be reduced. They asked me to sign it. I reached for my pen and, without reading the document, I signed it."[6]

Lend-Lease was the first major American commitment to its World War II allies, not only in ammunition and war materiel, but in food, clothing, and supplies. It was drafted in early January 1941, ten months before the United States entered the war, and was passed quickly by Congress. Yet, it took longer for the appropriations to be approved, and it was not until late March that the desperately needed money was made available. Late in 1941, a grateful British Prime Minister Winston Churchill called the Lend-Lease program "without question . . . the most unsordid act in the whole of recorded history."[7]

But Truman's 1945 order to terminate Lend-Lease monies hit America's allies like a thunderbolt. Britain, which had received a total of $31.4 billion in Lend-Lease assistance, was hit particularly hard by its sudden termination. The British government knew that eventually Lend-Lease assistance would end, but it had assumed there would be at least eighteen more months of fighting in the Pacific Theater, and for planning purposes Britain would continue receiving assistance, permitting its economy gradually to be restored.

With this termination, Truman acknowledged that he had also "stirred up a hornets nest" in the Soviet Union, which also had received significant wartime assistance from the United States. Truman admitted that he should have decreased Lend-Lease aid on a gradual basis, so that no country could complain that it had been "deliberately snubbed."[8] In July 1945, both Winston Churchill, now the leader of the opposition, and Clement Attlee, the just-elected Labour prime minister, were shocked by this abrupt decision. The new Labour government based its platform on domestic social reforms and nationalization of industries, but now, with the loss of Lend-Lease funds, found itself with staggering overseas indebtedness.[9]

Following the Potsdam Conference, Truman dispatched William L. Clayton, the under secretary of state for economic affairs, to London to determine the extent of British economic suffering. Clayton urged immediate assistance, a $4 billion low-interest loan. The influential economist John Maynard Keynes, acting as an advisor to the British Treasury, thought that the United States could be persuaded to make a $6 billion grant or interest-free loan. Keynes accompanied Lord Halifax, the British ambassador, to Washington in September 1945 to see what could be arranged. Now with the war over, however, Washington was not in the mood to be overly generous. Fred Vinson, the new secretary of the treasury, knew little about international monetary issues, did not like Keynes, and helped persuade Truman and the American negotiators to drive a hard bargain. Ultimately, Truman settled on a loan of $3.75 billion at 2 percent interest, much to the disappointment of the British. In addition, Britain was compelled to join the World Bank and the International Monetary Fund, to agree to remove trade restrictions, and, the most bitter pill, to remove all restrictions to the free exchange of sterling.[10] Labour official Roy Jenkins observed that this loan package created "more dissension than gratitude and was not supported in Parliament." But the British had no choice; they were "too desperate to refuse" the conditions.[11]

While the Truman administration agreed to assist the British, the appropriations for the $3.75 billion loan did not come quickly or easily in Congress. There did not seem to be any coherent executive leadership pushing for the legislation, some in Congress resented the fact that American money was going to support a government bent on nationalizing private industries, and there was some resentment against Britain because of its opposition to Jewish immigration to Palestine.

For the British, this was another of several unhappy episodes in Anglo-American relations under the new Atlee Labour government. First came the abrupt loss of Lend-Lease funds; then the severance of a full exchange of information about atomic weaponry, which British officials thought had been agreed to in the Quebec Agreement of 1943; and now this, the failure of the Keynes mission to Washington to obtain a generous grant.

Finally in June 1946, Congress passed the legislation, prodded to a great degree by growing suspicion of and anger toward the Soviets.[12] Truman also was increasingly agitated over Russian activities. In a January 1946 letter to Secretary of State James Byrnes, the president noted that the United States was anxious to get the Soviets into the Japanese war, then found we did not need them. The Russians, observed Truman, "have been a headache to us ever since." "There isn't a doubt in my mind," wrote Truman, "that Russia intends an invasion of Turkey and the seizure of the Black Sea Straits to the Mediterranean. Unless Russia is faced with an iron fist and strong language another war is in the making. Only one language do they understand—'How many divisions have you?'" Truman told Byrnes that the United States should insist that Russia return American ships and force settlement of its Lend-Lease debt, and then concluded: "I'm tired babying the Soviets."[13]

Indeed, Truman had taken several aggressive actions against the Soviet Union, including a strong stand against Soviet incursion into Iran, the dispatching of U.S. naval forces into the Mediterranean to discourage Soviet moves against the Dardanelles, and accepting Secretary of State James Byrnes's plan for an economic merger of American and British zones in Germany. Truman had also fired Commerce Secretary Henry A. Wallace for publicly straying from the tough administration policy toward the Soviet Union.[14]

In February 1946 George F. Kennan, the charge d'affaires at the U.S. embassy in Moscow, sent a telegram that helped solidify perceptions about the Soviet Union in official Washington. Kennan, in bed with a cold, sinus problems, toothache, and fever, received a communique from the Treasury Department wanting to know why the Russians were reluctant to adhere to the World Bank and the International Monetary Fund. Could Kennan explain their behavior to the bewildered Treasury officials? In his memoirs, Kennan wrote that most of official Washington simply did not understand Russian motives and now the Treasury was asking his opinion.[15]

Kennan's eight-thousand-word message, sent in five separate parts, became known as the Long Telegram. In it, this expert of Soviet affairs threw a cold dose of reality on any American hopes of dealing with the Russians. The Soviets were fundamentally insecure, Kennan wrote, they feared foreign contact, were implacably opposed to the United States, and were bent on violent destabilization of the world.[16]

The Long Telegram influenced thinking among senior foreign policy makers; its timing was fortuitous, and its warnings and predictions were taken seriously. Commerce Secretary W. Averell Harriman, who had been U.S. ambassador to the Soviet Union, thought the piece was "well worth reading," and sent a copy to Navy Secretary James V. Forrestal, who became Kennan's promoter, sending mimeographed copies to other members of the Truman cabinet and senior military officials.[17] Two weeks after the Long Telegram, Winston Churchill, speaking at Westminster College in Missouri, told the world that "From Stettin in the Baltic to Trieste in the Adriatic, an iron curtain has descended across the continent."

In the summer of 1946, Truman ordered his aides Clark M. Clifford and George M. Elsey to prepare a report on U.S.–Soviet relations. Their report was even more alarming than Kennan's analysis, and when they submitted it in September 1946, Truman considered it so "hot" he ordered that it not be circulated and that all copies be kept in the White House safe.[18] Truman's growing frustration, Kennan's memorandum, the Clifford–Elsey report, together with Winston Churchill's "Iron Curtain" speech moved the United States into a get tough attitude toward the Soviet Union.[19]

Domestic Politics and Loss of Congressional Control

Truman was barely able to get the British aid package passed through Congress in 1946, when Democrats controlled both the House and the Senate. Then came the November elections and a Republican sweep in Congress. Democrats lost fifty-four seats in the House and ten in the Senate; Republicans were now in the majority for the first time since 1932, with a 51 to 45 advantage in the Senate and a 245 to 188 advantage in the House.

For many Americans, the early postwar years were exasperating, and they took out their frustrations on the party in power. People wanted to return to normal times and stake their claim to the American dream. As seen in the previous chapter, there was considerable agitation for the rapid demobilization of American troops. Wartime price controls were lifted in June 1946, but, with persistent shortages of household staples, prices shot up. New cars finally were being produced after a wartime freeze, but auto makers could not meet demand. Housing was in critical shortage, with a reported 100,000 veterans without housing in Chicago alone.[20] There was enormous tension between labor and management, with record numbers of strikes, as unions pressed for higher wages and benefits. Truman lost critical organized labor support, and many in the labor movement simply sat on their hands during the 1946 elections.[21]

Liberals were particularly disappointed in Truman: he was not Franklin Roosevelt, not by a long shot; he had replaced Roosevelt loyalists with what they considered party hacks, and he could not lead Congress. As journalist I. F. Stone remarked, the New Dealers were replaced by "big-bellied, good-natured guys who knew a lot of dirty jokes, [and] spent as little time in their offices as possible."[22] What was worse, less than three months before the 1946 mid-term elections, Truman clumsily fired Wallace, a favorite son of the liberal wing of the party, for advocating a softer line against the Soviet Union.

With the Republicans now in control of Congress, the mood was decidedly anti-New Deal. Out of power all those years, Republicans were ready to cut back what they considered the bloat and waste brought on by New Deal programs. On the domestic front, one of the first items of business for the new Republican majority was a tax cut; Truman vetoed it, and, the next month, Congress passed another tax cut; Truman vetoed it as well. The lines were drawn between the embattled president and the resurgent Republican majority. On the international front, Senate Republican leader Robert A. Taft of Ohio, in a radio address on January 3, 1947, predicted congressional resistance to large-scale foreign assistance, but otherwise had little to say about foreign affairs.[23]

In the Senate, Democrat Tom Connally of Texas was replaced by Republican Arthur H. Vandenberg of Michigan as chairman of the Foreign Relations Committee. Long a champion of isolationism before the war, Vandenberg was now a committed internationalist, who later proved key in passing the administration's foreign assistance programs. In the House, the new chairman of the Foreign Affairs Committee was Charles A. Eaton of New Jersey, also a strong internationalist.

While Vandenberg was the major voice on foreign affairs, Taft was the key senator for Republican domestic policy. He had powerful, natural ideological allies on the other side of the aisle. Southern Democrats—Richard B. Russell, Jr., and Walter F. George of Georgia, Kenneth D. McKellar of Tennessee, Harry F. Byrd, Sr., of Virginia, and James O. Eastland of Mississippi—had been committee chairmen when Democrats were in the majority, were still in office and were determined as ever to defeat Truman. Republicans and like-minded southern Democrats were a constant threat to the increasingly beleaguered president.[24]

While priding himself in his conservative values, and carrying the mantle of "Mr. Republican," Taft appeared almost a moderate in comparison to some of the new Republican leadership, especially in the House. The new Speaker of the House, replacing Sam Rayburn of Texas, was Joseph W. Martin, Jr., of Massachusetts, a bitter foe of the New Deal and a committed isolationist, who had been in office since 1924. One thing, however, that united all Republicans and the great majority of Democrats, was a fierce opposition to communism, particularly the Soviet Union. When it came to foreign assistance, defense spending, and international relations in general, anti-communism and the threat of the Soviet Union became the trump card that Truman and his allies played—often adroitly and sometimes clumsily.

Secretary of State Marshall

At the beginning of 1947, James Byrnes announced his resignation as secretary of state; this was a long-planned and amicable departure. Relations between Truman and Byrnes, however, had never been easy, and it was past time for Byrnes to step down. Truman biographer David McCullough observed that Byrnes thought he was better equipped than Truman to be president and he "was not always successful in concealing" that sentiment.[25] Truman, while considering Byrnes to be intelligent, could never trust him. One particularly galling episode for the president occurred in late December 1945 when Byrnes, returning from a Moscow conference, had released a communique to the public before reporting to the president; he compounded the error by notifying Truman's press assistant Charles Ross to arrange air time on the radio networks, again before Truman had been notified. "Clearly," observed McCullough, "Byrnes had forgotten his manners."[26]

Byrnes had submitted his resignation letter to Truman in April 1946, but Truman waited to replace him until his successor had completed an important mission. George Catlett Marshall had retired from the Army in November 1945 after a distinguished career that culminated in his role as chief of staff, commander of all American forces during World War II, and five-star General of the Army. No sooner had he retired than Truman appointed him as the president's special representative and head of the U.S. Mission to China. There Marshall spent over a year in what proved to be fruitless negotiations between the Nationalist and Communist Chinese forces.

"He's the great one of the age," Truman wrote on his appointment calendar. "I am sure lucky to have his friendship and support." Harry Truman felt that a number of people who served him were in one way or another more talented than he, but George Marshall may have been the "only one whom he considered a better man."[27] Indeed, as secretary of state during this extraordinarily difficult time in American diplomatic history, Marshall was the right man at the right time. He was well respected and trusted by the vast majority in Congress, he was widely admired by the general public as a man of integrity, and foreign leaders applauded his choice. Above all, in this new reality of divided government, he was not a partisan politician but a calm presence above the fray.[28] On the day his name came before the Senate in late January 1947, he was enthusiastically confirmed; such was the respect for Marshall.

Dean Acheson, who had been under secretary of state and a close advisor to Truman, was persuaded to stay on for several months to help with the transition. In his memoirs, Acheson observed: "The moment General Marshall entered a room everyone in it felt his presence. It was a striking and communicated force. His figure conveyed intensity, which his voice, low, staccato, and incisive, reinforced. It compelled respect. It spread a sense of authority and of calm. There was no military glamour about him and nothing of the martinet."[29]

Marshall did for the State Department what neither Byrnes nor Roosevelt had done: he paid serious attention to it. Byrnes had largely ignored the department; Roosevelt had by-passed it. But Marshall brought the State Department back into the center of foreign policy decision-making. Long-time career foreign service officer Charles E. Bohlen noted that while there was some initial nervousness in the department over having a military man as secretary, Marshall was greatly appreciated: "Under Marshall," Bohlen wrote, "all the senior officers were consulted, and when policy was decided, there was no question what it was. There was a greater clarity in the operation of the State Department than I had seen before or have seen since."[30]

Marshall had been shocked by the "complete state of disorganization" he found in the State Department. At Acheson's urging, the new secretary rescinded the Byrnes policy of dispersing intelligence and research among geographic divisions of the department and brought them together in a centralized function.[31] Marshall established the executive secretariat, consolidating a number of units and placing them under his former senior Pentagon aide Carlisle H. Humelsine. Then he established a long-range planning group, the Policy Planning Staff, appointing as its director George F. Kennan, now lecturing at the National War College. Kennan was a rising star in the foreign service and his knowledge of Russian language, culture, and history became crucial in this new era of Soviet–American relations.[32]

Crisis in Greece and Turkey

The first major international problem facing the president, the new secretary of state, and the Republican-dominated Eightieth Congress involved the increasingly precarious situation of Greece. The country was on the point of economic and military collapse, there was widespread starvation, and the reactionary government of Premier Constantine Tsaldaris faced a left-wing guerilla insurgency.

In early February, the American ambassador in Greece, Lincoln MacVeagh, cabled to the State Department the rumors that Britain would withdraw its troops from Greece.[33] Then on a Friday afternoon, February 21, Loy Henderson, director of the Office of Near Eastern and African Affairs, received Herbert M. Sichel, first secretary of the British Embassy. Marshall had left earlier in the day to go first to Columbia University and then to Princeton University to receive an honorary degree and make his first speech as secretary. Sichel carried with him a message from Lord Archie Inverchapel, the British ambassador, and needed to discuss an urgent matter. Henderson telephoned his associate, John D. Hickerson, and discussed the message: the British informed the United States that they were formally withdrawing from Greece and could no longer give aid to either Greece or Turkey. The State Department officials knew immediately: "Great Britain had within the hour handed the job of world leadership, with all its burdens and all its glory, to the United States."[34]

Acheson was in charge of the department in Marshall's absence, and by telephone he informed both Truman and Marshall of the British message. Greece needed between $240 and $280 million in foreign exchange. Britain would be unable to offer any further aid after March 31, the last day of the British fiscal year.[35] On February 24, Britain publicly announced its withdrawal from Greece. On the same day, Marshall shared the British memorandum with other cabinet secretaries. Navy Secretary Forrestal wrote in his diary, "Marshall said that this dumped in our lap another most serious problem—that it was tantamount to British abdication from the Middle East with obvious implications as to their successor."[36]

Joseph M. Jones, then a junior officer in the State Department, later wrote that "this sudden spark set off a dazzling process which within fifteen weeks [February 21 to June 5, 1947] laid the basis for a complete conversion of American foreign policy and of the attitudes of the American people toward the world."[37]

The difficulty now was to convince the Republican-dominated Congress, in no mood to spend additional money, to come up with the funds for Greece and Turkey. There were no dollars set aside for emergency contingencies and the House had already made substantial cuts for the next fiscal year.[38]

On February 27, Truman brought the congressional leadership to the White House to hear Marshall explain the crises in Greece and Turkey.[39] Acheson later wrote that Marshall had "flubbed his opening statement" before the leaders of Congress. (Truman, however, observed that the lawmakers were "deeply impressed" by Marshall's blunt assessment.)[40] Acheson, who felt that this was his crisis, asked to speak, to convince the congressional leaders of the dangers that lay before them. He outlined the Soviet pressure on the Dardanelles straits, Iran, and northern Greece. "Like apples in a barrel infected by one rotten one, the corruption of Greece would infect Iran and all to the east. It would also carry infection to Africa through Asia Minor and Egypt, and to Europe through Italy and France, already threatened by the strongest domestic Communist parties in Western Europe."[41] The metaphor of rotten apples would later be replaced by dominoes, one toppling over causing the next to fall.

Acheson then wrote: "A long silence followed. Then Arthur Vandenberg said solemnly, 'Mr. President, if you will say that to the Congress and the country, I will support you and I believe that most of its members will do the same.'"[42]

Truman proposed an immediate aid package of $250 million for Greece and $150 million for Turkey. Despite this request, Senator Taft, chairman of the Republican Policy Committee, declared that it would have no effect on Republican plans to slash the federal budget. The president's budget for fiscal year 1948 was $37.5 billion; the House had already adopted a resolution to cut $6 billion, and the Senate was about to consider a $4.5 billion cut. "Plain idiocy," said the feisty Representative Clarence A. Cannon (Democrat–Missouri), to the suggestion that the military budget could be cut at this time.[43]

The timing of the request for aid was, in columnist Walter Lippmann's words, "very awkward indeed." In the next few weeks both the president and Secretary Marshall would be out of the country, away from their military and diplomatic command, separated from Congress, and deeply preoccupied with other matters. But there was a fixed deadline of March 31; after that, no more British aid.[44]

On March 12, before a joint session of Congress, Truman outlined the case for aid to Greece and Turkey. The United States had taken the lead in establishing the United Nations, Truman said, and it must be "willing to help free people to maintain their free institutions and their national integrity against aggressive movements that seek to impose upon them totalitarian regimes." It should be the policy of the United States, the president said, to "support free peoples who are resisting attempted subjugation by armed minorities or by outside pressure." Truman warned that, if Greece and Turkey were to fall to armed minorities, "confusion and disorder" might spread to the rest of the Middle East and could have a "profound effect" on those European countries whose people were struggling to maintain their freedom.

Truman called for "immediate and resolute action" by supplying the $400 million in emergency aid to Greece and Turkey. He reminded the legislators that the United States had contributed $341 billion towards winning World War II, and that the aid requested here "amounts to little more than one tenth of 1 percent of this investment."

Truman concluded his remarks by arguing that "the seeds of totalitarian regimes are nurtured by misery and want. They spread and grow in the evil soil of poverty and strife. They reach their full growth when the hope of a people for a better life has died." If the United States faltered in its leadership, "we may endanger the peace of the world—and we shall surely endanger the welfare of our own Nation."[45] Thus was born the Truman Doctrine, and with it one of the opening chapters of the Cold War and an extension of the still-forming policy of containment.

Congress that night was described as shocked into silence and awed by the momentous worldwide implications. "A much-shaken Congress," wrote C. P. Trussell of the *New York Times*, "saw their country's foreign policy undergo radical change in the space of twenty-one minutes."[46] Congress was indeed shaken, but nevertheless cautious. During the speech, the assembled legislators had applauded enthusiastically only when the president promised that the loans to Greece and Turkey would be paid back promptly.[47] Speaker Martin and Senator Taft were reserving judgment, calling Truman's speech a complete reversal of American foreign policy. Senate Majority Whip Kenneth S. Wherry (Republican–Nebraska) characterized the speech as a "virtual declaration of war" against the Soviet Union, and Senator Edwin C. Johnson (Democrat–Colorado) denounced this extension of the Monroe Doctrine to the

Mediterranean, and warned that a Russian invasion of Greece might be the next step.[48] Many other law makers were noncommittal, but the two foreign affairs chairmen, Vandenberg in the Senate and Eaton in the House, both directly and forthrightly supported the President. More than two months later, on May 22, Congress responded to Truman's urging and appropriated the first postwar foreign assistance statute, providing $400 million in economic and military assistance to Greece and Turkey.[49]

In his speech, Truman never mentioned the Soviet Union by name. Marshall was on his way to a four-power Council of Foreign Ministers meeting in Moscow, and, not to make Marshall's work any more difficult, Truman agreed to leave the Soviet Union out of the speech.[50] Nonetheless, was the president engaging in Soviet-bashing? Historian Melvyn P. Leffler argued that, based on U.S. intelligence analysis, Soviet behavior in the months before Truman's speech "hardly justified the inflammatory rhetoric" used to secure congressional support.[51]

Before Truman gave his speech, Marshall and his aide Charles Bohlen had already left for Moscow. They saw a copy of it while making an intermediate stop in Paris. Marshall and Bohlen agreed that the draft was "a little too much flamboyant anti-Communism." Marshall cabled their thoughts back to Washington, but they were brushed aside: the White House was convinced that the Senate would not approve this measure without an emphasis on the dangers imposed by Communism.[52]

Up until the Moscow Conference in March 1947, Marshall, as well as General Dwight D. Eisenhower, "tried his best to get along with Stalin," observed Harriman. The fact that the Russians immediately had reinvigorated their attack on the Germans after D-Day had made a deep impression on both Marshall and Eisenhower. They were convinced, Harriman argued, that, since Stalin had kept his word on vital military commitments, he would do the same on political matters.[53]

Marshall's views changed following the disappointing Moscow conference. The conference, attended by Marshall, British Foreign Secretary Ernest Bevin and French Foreign Minister Georges Bidault, and hosted by Soviet Foreign Minister Vyacheslav M. Molotov, addressed a variety of postwar difficulties, with German industrial reconstruction at the foremost in Marshall's agenda. Marshall and Bevin argued that an economically viable Germany was important for Europe's recovery.[54]

But over six weeks of "frustrating and fruitless discussions," nothing was decided.[55] In the final days of the conference, on April 18, Marshall and Bohlen paid a courtesy call to Joseph Stalin. "I had not seen Stalin since December 1945, and was struck by how much he had aged, how much grayer, careworn, and fatigued he appeared," Bohlen observed. Stalin received his visitors late at night, met with them for an hour and a half, but he was in no mood to move discussions along. "Doodling the inevitable wolf's head with a red pencil, [Stalin] asked what difference it made if there was no agreement [about the German question]."[56]

Stalin's cold indifference made a lasting impression on Marshall. "All the way back to Washington," Bohlen wrote, "Marshall talked of the importance of finding some initiative to prevent the complete breakdown of Western Europe."[57] Marshall later confirmed that the Marshall Plan "was an outgrowth of the disillusionment over the Moscow Conference which proved conclusively that the Soviet Union was not negotiating in good faith and could not be induced to cooperate in achieving European recovery."[58] Shortly after returning from Moscow, Marshall shared his frustrations over Soviet tactics, telling a nationwide radio audience that "the patient is sinking while the doctors deliberate."

While worried about Germany, Marshall and his aides were equally concerned about deteriorating conditions in France and Italy. Will Clayton, after meeting in Geneva with French agricultural officials and U.S. Ambassador James C. Dunn in Rome, pleaded for emergency food shipments. So unstable were these governments and that of Greece that U.S. officials doubted that they could survive.[59]

Crafting the Marshall Plan

A number of individuals have made paternity claims on the Marshall Plan. At the public level, Walter Lippmann, the influential columnist who was read widely at the highest levels of government decision-making, wrote a series of articles in March 1947 on the necessity of European recovery. In his "Today and Tomorrow" column, Lippmann warned of the imminent collapse of European economies: "The danger of a European economic collapse is the threat which hangs over us and all the world." He argued that "the truth is that political and economic measures on a scale, which no responsible statesman has yet ventured to hint at, will be needed in the next year or so." Lippmann warned that "our own officials shrink from the ordeal of explaining it to Senator Taft and those who see things as he does."[60] Ronald Steel, Lippmann's biographer, asserted that Lippmann first suggested that the United States invite the Europeans to create their own plan for recovery.[61]

In government circles, Forrestal, John J. McCloy, Henry L. Stimson, Harriman, John Foster Dulles, Paul Nitze, Bohlen, Kennan, Acheson, and others had been thinking and writing about aid to Europe since the end of the war. Walter Isaacson and Evan Thomas argue that Harriman may have been the first to reduce his thoughts to paper. In one of his last cables from Moscow to President Roosevelt, Harriman urged a massive reconstruction aid program. Acheson, too, in drafting the Truman Doctrine, argued for a larger reconstruction program.[62]

However, in the United States government itself, there was no inter-agency coordination, and no comprehensive plan that addressed the challenges of European recovery.[63] The planning that occurred came primarily from the State Department. On March 11, Acheson established the State-War-Navy

Coordinating Committee (SWNCC), which a month later produced a report calling for a comprehensive recovery plan, with economic integration of Europe and reintegration of German as essential features.[64] Another group set up by Acheson, the Committee on the Extension of U.S. Aid to Foreign Governments, was given the responsibility of looking at European economic problems.

Kennan's Policy Planning Staff relied to a considerable extent on the findings of the SWNCC and the influence of junior State Department officers who championed European economic integration.[65] In late May, Kennan presented Acheson with the first effort of the Policy Planning Staff (PPS/1), a memorandum entitled "Policy with Respect to American Aid to Western Europe." The central point of the memorandum was that American assistance for Europe should not be for fighting communism but for restoring the economic health of Europe. The memorandum urged that "the formal initiative must come from Europe; the program must be evolved in Europe; and the Europeans must bear the basic responsibility for it."[66] This language was borrowed later by Marshall in his speech at Harvard. Historian Wilson D. Miscamble noted that Kennan's report "was obviously not a plan for American assistance" but was a strategy for such a plan. Kennan and his colleagues began "the complex task of transforming disparate ideas and policy recommendations into practice."[67]

On May 8, Acheson, substituting for President Truman, spoke before the Delta Council in Cleveland, Mississippi, in a hot, crowded gymnasium at Delta State Teachers College. Truman was supposed to have been there for this big annual agricultural event, but he did not want to get involved in a local political fight over who should succeed Senator Theodore Bilbo.[68] Acheson had tipped off three British journalists about this speech; Lippmann was also given a heads-up.[69] Acheson outlined a five-point program for implementing U.S. international economic policies, including "emergency assistance in areas where it will be most effective in building world political and economic institutions, in fostering liberal trading policies, and in strengthening the authority of the United Nations."[70] Later asked if Acheson's words represented administration policy, Harry Truman said yes, they did.

Another important contribution came from Will Clayton, the under secretary of state for economic affairs. Clayton was in Geneva in April 1947, heading up the U.S. delegation to the International Trade Conference and the newly formed Economic Commission for Europe. In late May, he flew back to Washington and on the way prepared a memorandum outlining the "desperate state of affairs" in Italy and France and the "urgent necessity for financial assistance," especially to help them avoid being taken over by a Communist coup.[71] In his memorandum, Clayton warned that the United States had "grossly underestimated the destruction" of the European economy, particularly the effects of economic dislocation. He noted that "without further prompt and substantial aid from the United States, economic, social and political disintegration will overwhelm Europe." It was necessary, Clayton continued, for the president and the secretary of state to make "a strong spiritual appeal to the American people to sacrifice a little of themselves, to draw in their own belts just a little in order to save Europe from starvation and chaos (not from the Russians) and, at the same time, to preserve for ourselves and our children the glorious heritage of a free America." He recommended a three-year grant program of six or seven billion dollars, and urged that the United States avoid getting bogged down in another UNRRA effort. *"The United States must run this show,"* Clayton concluded.[72]

The next day, Marshall, Clayton, and Acheson focused on Clayton's memorandum and Kennan's policy paper. Clayton forcefully described in more graphic detail the plight of Europe and the need for U.S. quick involvement.[73] Something had to be done quickly to inform the American people and Congress. Acheson met with a dozen senators on the same day and advised Marshall that a public announcement should be direct and forth-coming, but not "scare the hell out of the people," like the tactics used to sell the Truman Plan.[74] In the meantime, Truman was also lining up congressional support, quietly inviting key legislators to confidential meetings and especially gaining the support of Vandenberg and Eaton.[75]

The Speech

Originally, Marshall had planned to present his policy on European recovery at the University of Michigan, but he had to cancel because the details of the speech had not been worked out. Marshall also worried about the isolationist reaction he would find in the Midwest, particularly from "Bert McCormick and the *Chicago Tribune*," he later recalled. The next chance to speak would have been at Amherst College on June 16. But time was of the essence, and Marshall decided to accept a long-delayed invitation from Harvard University to speak at its commencement on June 5.[76]

Following the May 28 staff meeting, Marshall wrote to James B. Conant, president of Harvard, accepting the invitation to speak at its graduation: "As I wrote you on May 9th, I will not be able to make a formal address, but would be pleased to make a few remarks in appreciation of the honor and perhaps a little more."[77] The "little more" would have profound worldwide impact.

In this day of pageantry and ceremony, Marshall was one of twelve to receive an honorary degree. He did not speak at the formal morning graduation ceremony, but at the afternoon alumni gathering; Marshall was the eighth speaker of the day and his eight-minute speech was a bit underwhelming. Standing there at the podium in his business suit, rather than academic regalia, Marshall spoke in a "dull, off-hand way." Historian Robert H. Ferrell observed that Marshall spoke in a "soft and almost inaudible voice, with his marked Southern accent, gazing doggedly at the notes before him, playing with his spectacles, never looking at the audience."[78]

One of the other speakers that day was poet T. S. Eliot. Arthur Hartman, later U.S. ambassador to both France and the Soviet Union, then a student at Harvard College in 1947, remarked: "If you polled my class, you would likely have found that we were more impressed by what T. S. Eliot had to say than by the remarks of Marshall."[79]

In the end, what mattered was the substance, the written word, and not the delivery. "I need not tell you that the world situation is very serious," Marshall began.[80] He did not lay out a master plan but quietly focused on the urgent problem: "Our policy is directed not against any country or doctrine but against hunger, poverty, desperation, and chaos. Its purpose shall be the revival of a working economy in the world so as to permit the emergence of political and social conditions in which free institutions can exist."

Later came the point that Kennan had insisted upon earlier, that this must not be a unilateral adventure by the United States:

> It would be neither fitting nor efficacious for the government to undertake to draw up unilaterally a program designed to place Europe on its feet economically. This is the business of the Europeans. The initiative, I think, must come from Europe. The role of this country should consist of friendly aid in the drafting of a European program and of later support of such a program so far as it may be practical for us to do so. The program should be a joint one, agreed to by a number of, if not all, European nations.

U.S. aid, Marshall said, would be available to any European country that was willing to fully cooperate. Did this mean extending aid to the Soviets? Marshall had left the door open; at the May 28 staff meeting, he said that he had "decided to 'play it straight' and invite the Soviets to collaborate."[81] Then in a news conference a week after the Harvard speech, Marshall made it clear that the Soviet Union would be welcome to participate.

Thus was made public the Marshall Plan. But as Kennan made clear in a memorandum seven weeks after the Harvard speech, "We have no plan."[82] That was the point. The Europeans would be responsible for coming up with their own plan. They would be responsible for carrying out Marshall's dictum that the initiative must come from Europe.

The Reaction from Europe

Foreign Secretary Ernest Bevin first heard about the Marshall speech when he turned on the small wireless set at his bedside that evening to listen to the BBC's American commentary. Leonard Miall, Washington correspondent for the BBC, had been given advance notice of the speech by Acheson, but there was no word from official British channels. The British Embassy in Washington decided, given what they considered relatively little interest found in the

American press, that it would not spend the cable charges to send an advance copy of the speech to London.[83]

Allan Bullock, Bevin's biographer, wrote that "it is arguable that Bevin's action in the next few days was his most decisive personal contribution as Foreign Secretary to the history of his times."[84] He seized upon Marshall's line: "the initiative, I think, must come from Europe." Without waiting for advice from the British Embassy in Washington, Bevin came to the Foreign Office the next morning, and jumped at the chance to begin the process. Bevin fully knew the stakes for Britain and Europe. As he reflected nearly two years later at the National Press Club in Washington, "I assure you, gentlemen, it was like a life-line to sinking men. It seemed to bring hope where there was none. The generosity of it was beyond our belief."[85]

Bevin sent a message to Duff Cooper, the British ambassador in Paris, asking to see French Foreign Minister Georges Bidault. Cooper was to explain that Britain was "anxious to cooperate . . . in studying the new American approach to Europe."[86] On June 27, just over three weeks after Marshall's speech, Bevin and Bidault convened a meeting in Paris; also invited, to the consternation of many, was the Russian foreign secretary. Molotov showed up with a staff of eighty; perhaps this was a sign that Moscow was willing to cooperate with the West. U.S. and British officials had assumed that Molotov would do his best to undermine the talks. But then Molotov dug in his heels and insisted that the Soviets would welcome all the money Americans might want to give them, but there would be no economic cooperation, the money would be spent the way the Soviets wanted, and there would be no on-site inspection on how the money was spent.[87]

The United States refused Molotov's blatantly unacceptable conditions, and the Soviet Union on Stalin's orders withdrew its mission on the fifth day of talks, taking seven European satellite countries with it. U.S. Secretary of State Madeleine K. Albright, on the fiftieth anniversary of the Marshall Plan, commented that Jan Masaryk, foreign minister of Czechoslovakia, was told by Stalin in Moscow in 1947 that his country would not be permitted to participate in the Marshall Plan. Upon returning to Prague, Masaryk told his colleague Josef Korbel, Albright's father, that he then understood he was employed by a government no longer sovereign in its own land.[88] Under instructions from Moscow, Poland, Hungary, Romania, Bulgaria, Albania, and Yugoslavia all refused to join as well. Charles L. Mee, Jr., observed that "the startling casualness with which the United States and the Western European nations abandoned Eastern Europe . . . illuminates, as perhaps nothing else so clearly does, how completely the leaders of the West had by this time acknowledged that Eastern Europe belonged to Russia."[89]

In July, an invitation for a full European conference was accepted by sixteen European countries—Austria, Belgium, Denmark, France, Greece, Iceland, Ireland, Italy, Luxembourg, the Netherlands, Norway, Portugal, Sweden, Switzerland, Turkey, and the United Kingdom. Spain, under the fascist regime of Generalissimo Francisco Franco, was not invited, nor was West Germany, although it later was included. From July 12 through September 22, the sixteen countries, meeting as the Committee of European Economic Cooperation (CEEC), hammered out a program for increasing production, eliminating inflation, promoting economic cooperation, and solving the dollar payments problem. At times, the meetings were rancorous and France felt particularly vulnerable to suggested plans to revive Germany. The CEEC suggested a European-payments deficit of $22 billion and asked the United States to finance $19 billion of it. Will Clayton tried to gently tell the Europeans that their expectations of U.S. support were too unrealistic.

Truman set up three executive committees to study the ramifications of European aid. The first, chaired by Harriman, was the best known, with its nineteen members mostly from business, financial, agricultural sectors charged with advising the president on how best to spend European recovery money, now projected at between $12 and $17 billion.[90] A second committee, headed by Julius A. Krug, secretary of the interior, looked at the impact of the aid program on American natural resources, while the third committee, under Edwin G. Nourse, chairman of the new Council of Economic Advisers, studied the impact of aid on the national economy.[91]

During the late summer of 1947, Truman persuaded the leadership in the House of Representatives to send a fact-finding mission to Europe to see for itself the problems and challenges. The House was going to be particularly difficult to convince, and Truman believed that the best way to persuade reluctant Republicans and conservative Southern Democrats was to let them see the problem firsthand. An eighteen-member committee, headed by Representative Christian A. Herter (Republican–Massachusetts), chairman of the House Select Committee on Foreign Aid, spent over a month touring Europe and discovering the true nature of the challenges ahead.[92]

Making the Law

A $17 billion foreign assistance request was indeed an astounding amount. Even if stretched over several years, it constituted an enormous part of the federal budget. For fiscal year 1948, the estimated federal budget was $37.5 billion, which included $11.2 billion for national defense. Truman had been hoping that the federal budget would level off after the war at around $25 billion annually, with $6 billion or perhaps $7 billion devoted to defense.[93] Republicans continued to push for tax cuts and reductions in the federal budget. And now, this enormous price tag for the Marshall Plan. This was in addition to the $6 billion the United States had already given through UNRRA and direct grants and loans.

To have any chance of success in Congress, Truman and the administration would have to court Republicans, and the most important legislator was Arthur H. Vandenberg of Michigan, the new chairman of the Senate Foreign Relations Committee. For years, the jovial, cigar-smoking, bow-tie wearing

Vandenberg had been the symbol of Midwest isolationism, or, as he preferred to put it, "insulationism." That all changed for Vandenberg with the attack on Pearl Harbor. But his most important contribution came a little over three years later. As one historian put it, "Vandenberg became a senator on March 31, 1928, and a statesman on January 10, 1945."[94] It was the beginning of the Seventy-Ninth Congress, Franklin Roosevelt had just been elected to his fourth term as president, and he was having considerable difficulty with Congress. Legislative support for the United Nations was faltering, Roosevelt was having trouble getting State Department officials confirmed, and, with the Yalta Conference coming soon, the mood was suspicious and bitter between the executive and legislative branches. Vandenberg rose to the occasion, delivering a memorable, ringing endorsement for internationalism. Isolationism was dead, Vandenberg declared, and the United States must cooperate with other countries to prevent future warfare.[95]

Eightieth Congress, 2nd Session
(January 6–December 31, 1948)

Senate: 51 Republicans;
45 Democrats

House: 245 Republicans;
188 Democrats; 1 other

President: Harry S. Truman

With Republicans now in control of Congress, and with Vandenberg the foreign affairs chairman, Truman and the State Department were definitely paying attention. At the State Department, the Michigan senator was treated "as if he were a foreign dignitary."[96] While Marshall did not consult Vandenberg before his Harvard speech, he later became the secretary's "full partner." Starting in the summer of 1947, they consulted twice weekly at secret meetings at Blair House, across the street from the White House.

There was an immediate problem, however: the clock was ticking on European economic and political problems. The problem was soon called the "Marshall gap," that period between Marshall's speech in June and the time when, hopefully, Congress would pass legislation to support European recovery. The State Department, particularly through a steering committee headed by Acheson's successor, Under Secretary Robert A. Lovett, warned that European countries desperately needed interim financial assistance.[97] Responding to these needs, Truman, on October 23, called Congress back into special session and on December 23, by wide margins, Congress approved emergency interim aid of $522 million for Italy, France, and Austria, and $18 million for China.[98]

Gathering Support

Journalist I. F. Stone saw the worst obstacle to getting the Marshall Plan enacted as lying "in a kind of cantankerous impatience with Europe among the American people and in the absence of leadership gifted enough and courageous enough to make ordinary Americans understand their stake in European revival."[99]

It probably was not so much the impatience of the American people, but rather their apathy toward and ignorance of foreign affairs. In the months before the congressional action on the Marshall Plan, polls showed that only about 25 percent of American citizens could demonstrate some knowledge of foreign events; a full 30 percent were unaware of any international events. By February 1948, after nearly nine months of steady information about the upcoming Marshall Plan, just 14 percent could give a reasonably correct statement of the Plan's purpose.[100]

While the general public perhaps did not grasp the central points of the Marshall Plan, there was a steady increase in its support, particularly among specialized audiences. Newspaper editors and educators overwhelmingly supported the Plan; so too did business executives, foreign relations committees, farmers, and students. Three of the four radio networks invited a total of 145 speakers to discuss the Plan; of these, 120 urged adoption, and just twenty were opposed.[101] This support from leaders and opinion makers was critical, because many Americans in the two years after the war, while aware of and sympathetic to the economic problems in Western Europe, felt that the United States had done enough, and it was time for Europe to get back on its own feet.

In 1940–1941, when the Roosevelt administration was trying to drum up public support for Lend-Lease, journalist William Allen White created, at Roosevelt's request, the Committee to Defend America by Aiding the Allies. Dean Acheson was one of the participants in this public information program. Even before the Marshall Plan was formally launched, Acheson was thinking about a similar public information organization. However, Marshall was skittish about such an effort, worried that Congress would be sensitive to a public relations drive mounted by the State Department. But by the fall of 1947, such concern was put aside, and the Citizens' Committee for the Marshall Plan was formed, with two former secretaries of war, Henry L. Stimson and Robert P. Patterson, leading the effort.[102]

One objective of this committee and its local affiliates was to stir up grassroots support in congressmen's home districts; a second goal was to secure support from membership organizations. By March 1948, fifty-two such national organizations gave full support to the Marshall Plan and over one hundred local committees were formed to discuss the Plan.[103]

Political scientist Herbert Agar later observed that the fate of the Marshall Plan was not decided on the floor of the Senate, but by the American people. "There has never been a better example of how public opinion, in a sprawling federal nation, can inform itself and bring pressure to bear, once it has been aroused to make the effort."[104]

The Debate Begins

President Truman sent his lengthy message to Congress on December 19, 1947, outlining the proposal for European aid, asking Congress to authorize a four-year European Recovery Program to halt the march of "selfish totalitarian aggression" and to maintain civilization in which the American way of life is rooted. Most congressman had left for holiday vacation, and only twenty-two were on the floor of the House as the reading clerk began intoning Truman's important but unexciting message. It called for the expenditure of $17 billion from April 1, 1948, through June 30, 1952; an immediate appropriation of $6.8 billion for the first fifteen months; and the creation of an Economic Cooperation Administration to administer the program. This was thus far the largest program of expenditure in the nation's peacetime history.[105]

The president could have referred to this massive aid program as the "Truman Plan," as a complement to the Truman Doctrine. Indeed, White House aide George Elsey described the Marshall Plan as the "Truman Doctrine in action," and Truman later called the Truman Doctrine and the Marshall Plan 'two halves of the same walnut.'[106] Yet Truman not only wanted to honor Marshall but had practical politics in mind as well. As he told his aide Clark Clifford, it would be far easier for a Republican Congress in a presidential election year to support a program named for General Marshall than the same one named for Truman.[107]

After the holiday recess, Senator Vandenberg was the lead-off witness followed by nine government witnesses, eighty-six other witnesses, and seventy-six written communications. In all, the Senate hearings filled 1,449 pages of testimony; with the House hearings, 2,269 pages.[108] The pattern of testimony followed vintage Vandenberg methods: there would be exhaustive hearings, with the goal to separate the various components of the legislation, isolate the objections, and beat them back one at a time. Then there would be first-hand accounts from senators who had traveled to Europe and seen the devastation. Methodically, the process went on, until the committee had reached rough consensus.[109]

On January 8, 1948, Secretary Marshall took the witness stand before the Senate Foreign Relations Committee, during both the morning and afternoon sessions. Reporter James Reston noted: "He was clear. He was calm. He was patient and courteous. And yet he acted like a man who was determined to get substantially the Marshall Plan he wanted or, as is already rumored in the capital, retire at last to Leesburg."[110]

It was not at all clear that the president and Marshall would have their way. Republicans, in particular, were highly skeptical of the $17 billion that Truman had requested. Former President Herbert C. Hoover wanted to scrap the Marshall Plan in favor of a $3 billion relief fund and a $1 billion loan to revive European industries. To placate Republicans, Vandenberg was able to convince the administration to delete specific mention of the $17 billion price tag and to arrange for a twelve-month, rather than fifteen-month, first appropriation.[111]

Vandenberg and his colleagues in the Foreign Relations Committee also relied on the findings of the Krug, Nourse, and Harriman committees. Harriman later wrote that Vandenberg had acknowledged that the November

1947 report of the Harriman Committee "was really more help than anything else in getting legislation on the Marshall Plan through Congress."[112] Through its witnesses, reports, and testimony, the Truman administration played on the sympathies and fears of legislators: they would emphasize the economic benefits of the Marshall Plan, or its charitable dimensions, or note that such aid was a pivotal point in Western civilization; above all, they would address the underlying fear that the Marshall Plan would be a pivotal weapon in the fight against communism.[113]

Vandenberg's efforts were central; he was patient and took his time in the Foreign Relations Committee hearings. He also was able to win over his influential colleague, Walter F. George (Democrat–Georgia), as well as other members, by reducing the initial appropriation from fifteen to twelve months.[114] The Marshall Plan legislation, called the Economic Cooperation Act, passed unanimously in the Senate Foreign Relations Committee.

But before it could move to the full Senate floor, where there would likely be some heated opposition, events intruded in Czechoslovakia. On February 27, 1948, there was a *coup d'etat* in Czechoslovakia, as President Eduard Benes caved to Soviet pressure and named Stalin-backed Klement Gottwald as prime minister. Within hours, there were arrests, purges, and executions. Jan Masaryk fell to his death, probably assassinated. This coup, in the only Eastern European country with the semblance of a democratic government, in Truman's words, "sent a shock through the civilized world."[115] Furthermore, there was great concern that the communist party would win the national elections scheduled in Italy in late April.

Then, on March 1, Arthur Vandenberg gave the second most important speech of his career. He prepared carefully, rewriting the speech seven times. The Senate galleries were packed; corridors jammed with people wanting to hear him. Nearly all senators were present, and many representatives walked over to the Senate side and lined the walls of the upper chamber. Vandenberg spoke emotionally for one hour and twenty minutes, and noted that the Senate Foreign Relations Committee had voted 13–0 to approve the Economic Cooperation Act of 1948. "In the name of peace, stability, and freedom it deserves prompt passage. In the name of intelligent American self-interest it envisions a mighty undertaking worthy of our faith."[116] He reminded senators that they would bear the blame for failure if they delayed or whittled down the European recovery legislation.

Reporter Ferdinand Kuhn, Jr., observed: "When he had finished, about fifty senators on the floor jumped to their feet applauding him in one of the rare standing ovations in recent Senate history." Most senators, led by Tom Connally filed past Vandenberg's desk and shook his hand.[117] The Economic Cooperation Act survived attacks from both left- and right-leaning senators, beat back an amendment from Senator Taft to slice the funds, and passed the Senate, 69–17. Taft, with his eye on the Republican presidential nomination, emerged from this fight "satisfied but bruised," reluctantly voting for final passage.[118]

In the House, passage was not so certain. Although Representative Charles Eaton was an important proponent for international assistance, he was not the forceful advocate that Vandenberg was. In the House Foreign Affairs Committee, Republicans insisted on including aid to the Nationalist government in China and criticized the absence of military assistance. Vandenberg's and Eaton's attempts to limit the question to European aid was overruled by Republican Party leaders Martin and Charles A. Halleck (Republican–Indiana).[119] There were nearly fifty amendments proposed, nineteen of which were approved. But the pressure was on from business leaders, civic organizations, and others to pass the legislation. Key to the House debate was the Herter Committee report, coming from the respected Republican internationalist, which gave legitimacy to the Truman policy ideas.[120] The House stayed in session well into the night of March 31, and by 329 to 74 voted for the Marshall Plan. The Senate quickly resolved its differences with the House, and on April 3 Truman signed the Economic Cooperation Act, which became part of the larger Foreign Assistance Act of 1948. After four intensive months of hearings, debate, political posturing, and ultimately bipartisan cooperation, Congress had made its decision. Truman characterized the act as "Perhaps the greatest venture in constructive statesmanship that any nation has undertaken."[121]

Despite some bitter remarks, the aid package passed with nearly 84 percent of the vote in the House and 90 percent in the Senate. This was in line with a remarkable string of bipartisan foreign policy votes, from Bretton Woods in 1945, UNESCO in 1946, to the Greek–Turkish loan in 1947, where both the House of Representatives and the Senate averaged over 83 percent in favor.[122]

Highlights of the Economic Cooperation Act of 1948

The Economic Cooperation Act (Marshall Plan) constituted Title I of the Foreign Assistance Act of 1948. In all, the Foreign Assistance Act provided a little over $6 billion in economic assistance: the sixteen countries of Western Europe plus West Germany received $5.3 billion, and $700 million was given in economic and military aid to China, Greece, and Turkey. The ECA had to go through annual reauthorizations to fulfill its full $13.5 billion in assistance funds. The act established the declaration of policy, established the Economic Cooperation Administration, and outlined the nature and methods of the assistance.

The Marshall Plan authorization still had another hurdle to surmount: the program had been authorized, but now the funds had to be appropriated. House Appropriations Committee chairman John Taber (Republican–New York) took his sweet time, waiting three weeks before beginning hearings on the aid package. Marshall had hoped that the European relief legislation would be completed by April 1. But Taber's hearings dragged on until June 3, and the Appropriations Committee reduced first-year funding by $2 billion. The funds were restored, in large part because of heavy pressure from the House Foreign

Affairs Committee, Vandenberg, and Governor Thomas E. Dewey of New York, who was emerging as the leading Republican presidential nominee. Finally, the Senate and House approved the Foreign Aid Appropriation Act of 1948, which became law on June 28.[123] The Marshall Program received $5.3 billion for the first year of operation and each subsequent year had to go through the scrutiny of the appropriations process. Ultimately, $13.5 billion, rather than the original $17 billion, was funded for the four years of operation, and $12.5 billion was disbursed. After June 30, 1951, the remaining aid was folded into the Mutual Defense Assistance Program.

Key Individuals in the Marshall Plan

George Catlett Marshall (1880–1959) devoted his life to the service of his country. He was commissioned as a second lieutenant in the U.S. Army in 1902, served in the Philippine Islands, and later served with distinction during World War I. By 1938 Marshall was a brigadier general and head of the War Plans Division. Throughout World War II, he served as chief of staff and was appointed to the five-star rank of General of the Army in 1944. He retired briefly from the Army, but was soon appointed head of the U.S. mission to China, serving as Truman's personal representative. From early 1947 through the beginning of 1949, he served as secretary of state. Afterwards, he spent one year as head of the American Red Cross and then returned to the Truman Administration in 1950 as secretary of defense. Marshall was awarded the Nobel Peace Prize in 1953 for his contribution to European relief and stability.

Arthur Hendrick Vandenberg (1884–1951), a Republican senator from Michigan (1928–1951), served as chairman of the Senate Foreign Relations Committee during the crucial Eightieth Congress (1947–1948). He began as a newspaper editor and publisher and was appointed to fill a Senate vacancy in 1928. Vandenberg was an outspoken and committed isolationist before World War II, but soon became a prominent internationalist. He was a delegate to the United Nations Conference in San Francisco in 1945, the U.N. General Assembly at London and New York in 1946, and the Pan American Conference at Rio de Janeiro in 1947. Marshall later said of Vandenberg: "I feel that Vandenberg has never received full credit for his monumental efforts on behalf of the European Recovery Program. . . . Vandenberg was my right-hand man and at times, I was his right-hand man."[124]

On April 16, just two weeks after the Economic Cooperation Administration (ECA) was created, but well before money was appropriated, representatives of the sixteen European countries and the western-occupied area of Germany met in Paris to sign a multilateral aid agreement, establishing the Organization for Economic Cooperation and Development (OEEC) as the vehicle for closer cooperation and implementation of the Marshall Plan program.[125] The Europeans filled the OEEC with talented, committed internationalists, particularly Belgian Prime Minister Paul-Henri Spaak, who chaired the OEEC Council, Robert Marjolin of France who headed the OEEC International Secretariat, and Sir Edmund Hall-Patch of Britain, who chaired the executive committee.

There were rumors that Under Secretary Clayton, then Acheson, would be given the job of administrator of the new ECA. But the position went to Paul G. Hoffman, president of the Studebaker Corporation and a good friend of Vandenberg's. While Hoffman, a nominal Republican, reluctantly accepted the position, he carried out his responsibilities with a sense of urgency.[126] There were inevitable tensions between Congress, the ECA, and business interests. Hoffman opposed using Marshall Plan funds for short-term American business gains, and he was at times accused of selling American interests short. Soon, business interests demanded special exemptions: the shipping lobbying insisted upon, and ultimately received, a requirement that 50 percent of all American commodities transported under the Marshall Plan had to be carried by U.S. ships. Some members of Congress criticized Hoffman for not pushing U.S. tobacco sales abroad; others said he was not doing enough to force the British to buy more American wheat; still others complained that steel, cotton, machine tools, fur, and other commodities were not getting the treatment they deserved. Altogether, Hoffman told the Senate Foreign Relations Committee, there were 109 requests for exemptions, and the list was "being added to almost hourly."[127] Despite the carping and the pressure from special interests, Congress and Hoffman fought back virtually all requests for special treatment.

Key Events in the Marshall Plan	
1945	Lend-Lease program terminated, May.
1947	Britain withdrew aid from Greece and Turkey. U.S. aid to those countries; Truman Doctrine, February and March.
	Big Four Foreign Ministers Conference in Moscow, March–April.
	Acheson speech before Delta Council in Mississippi, May 8.
	Marshall speech at Harvard outlining Marshall Plan, June 5.
	Soviets turn down Marshall Plan offer; 16 European countries accept, establish Committee for European Economic Cooperation (CEEC), July.
	Soviets set up Communist Information Bureau (Cominform), consisting of East European parties along with communist parties of France and Italy, September.
	CEEC report put European deficit at $22 billion for next four years, called for establishment of OEEC, September.
	"Marshall Gap" aid approved, December.
1948	Communist coup in Czechoslovakia, February.
	Brussels Pact signed, March.
	Marshall Plan aid approved through Economic Cooperation Act, April.
	Economic Cooperation Administration began operations, April.
	OEEC has first meeting in Paris, April.
	West German currency reform, July. Berlin blockade begins.
1949	Russians call off Berlin blockade, May.
	Federal Republic of Germany officially enters OEEC, June.
1950	Schuman plan, European Coal and Steel; European Payments Union.
1951	Marshall Plan ends six months early, because of escalation in Korean War, December.

A key decision by Congress was to insert a "counterpart" clause in the Economic Cooperation Act, a procedure that followed the practices in UNRRA programs. Paul Hoffman, ECA Administrator, observed that the counterpart device was the key difference—"the essential catalyst"– between success or failure in both economically weak and strong recipient countries.[128]

The counterpart arrangement required all recipient governments receiving Marshall Plan grants to match every dollar with its equivalent in local currency. Five percent of that local currency was turned over to the United States and used to administer the local ECA missions and to purchase strategic materials. The remaining 95 percent would provide further relief, debt retirement, or other programs approved by the ECA.

In July 1948, Hoffman and British Chancellor of the Exchequer Sir Stafford Cripps inaugurated another section of the Economic Cooperation Act, the technical assistance program. First British, then later all recipient countries would send agricultural and manufacturing teams to the United States to study production methods. In all, more than one hundred such teams visited American factories and farms during the three-year period. This sharing of information helped lead to a great increase in productivity.[129]

Another important feature added by Congress was language in the preamble, urging the sixteen participating countries to work together toward economic cooperation. The Truman administration had earlier discussed European integration, but the State Department held back such language, not wanting to inject another political dimension into what was supposed to be a program of economic recovery.[130]

Aftermath

Eleven days after the Marshall Plan became law, on April 14, 1948, a freighter left Galveston, Texas, with 9,000 tons of wheat, headed for Bordeaux, while five other vessels sailed that same week with emergency food for France. Soon, there would be some 150 ships on the high seas at any given moment laden with food, tractors, oil, cotton, tires, and other commodities. The funds had not yet been appropriated, but nevertheless, the Marshall Plan had begun.[131]

The plans for European recovery came none too soon. The second half of 1948 was particularly challenging. In the United States, very few political pros gave Truman a ghost of a chance to win re-election against a confident Governor Dewey; even the Gallup poll stopped asking citizens six weeks before the election, since the conclusion was obvious to everyone that Truman would lose. In Europe, tensions between East and West had escalated: the Berlin blockade was in full force, labor unrest and communist agitation was spreading, the economic revival had not yet kicked in, and production was still anemic.[132]

For most countries, the largest single imported item was oil, a full 10 percent of all purchases. While accounting for less than 10 percent of Europe's energy supply in 1947, oil was the only source for aviation fuel and gasoline. About 50 percent of Western Europe's oil came from U.S.-owned companies operating abroad, and payment in dollars was required. In addition, about one-third of the Marshall Plan imports were agricultural.[133]

Journalist Daniel Schorr observed the Marshall Plan in action at the village level. Writing for the *Christian Science Monitor* from the Netherlands, Schorr wrote about Nyverdal, a village of 9,000, which was dependent on its spinning mill. The factory was in danger of shutting down because of the lack of cotton, which would be bought from the United States, if there hadn't been a shortage of dollars. Through the ECA mission in the Hague, such dollars were allocated. Bales of cotton arrived at the village, some 2,000 workers kept their livelihood, and the taxes generated from the factory helped build schools and finance social welfare programs. The bakery store in town displayed a sign: "The grain in this bread comes from the American Marshall Plan." Further, guilder equivalents to the Marshall Plan dollars became the counterpart funds, and were used to finance Dutch students studying as Fulbright Scholars in the United States.[134] These kinds of transactions were repeated thousands of times over in the course of the Marshall Plan years. Britain received the largest portion of Marshall Plan funds, 23 percent, while France received 20 percent, before considering intra-European transfers.

The ECA established its European administrative base in Paris, with offices in each of the recipient countries. W. Averell Harriman headed the 600-person Paris office, called the Office of the Special Representative. The ECA had varying influence in the recipient countries. In Greece, its influence was dominant, described as something akin to a "colonial relationship," with an influence strong in Italy, minimal in Britain, and somewhere in between in France. In addition, there were inevitable tensions between the ECA and the State Department, particularly in the area of economic policy and relations, and Harriman had especially difficult relations with Hall-Patch and his British colleagues.[135]

Recipients of Marshall Fund Monies

From April 3, 1948 to June 30, 1952 (before intra-European transfers):[136]
    Britain, $3.189 billion
    France, $2.713 billion
    Italy, $1.508 billion
    Federal Republic of Germany, $1.390 billion
    Netherlands, $1.083 billion
    Greece, $706.7 million
    Austria, $677.8 million
    Belgium, Luxembourg, $559.3 million
    Denmark, $273.0 million
    Norway, $255.3 million
    Turkey, $225.1 million
    Ireland, $147.5 million
    Sweden, $107.3 million
    Portugal, $51.2 million
    Iceland, $29.3 million

At the heart of the recovery program was West Germany. The OEEC report in September 1947 stated bluntly that "other Western European nations cannot be prosperous as long as West Germany is paralyzed." The tasks ahead, however, were significant: restoration of civilian government; currency reform; rehabilitation of essential industries, particularly mining and manufacturing; increases in food rations; clothing and other human necessities; and a resumption of trade relations between Germany and the rest of the world.[137]

The German economy had been hit the hardest by the war. By 1946, industrial production in western Germany was just 29 percent of its 1938 prewar levels, by far the lowest percentage in the recipient countries; nearly every other country had reached and exceeded prewar levels by 1948, but the West German economy in 1948 reached only 51 percent.[138] West Germany's monetary system was in shambles, there was hyperinflation, black markets thrived, cigarettes and cognac became the common currencies, hundreds of thousands of homes had been destroyed, and over 10 million desperate refugees from Eastern territories had to be absorbed.[139]

The U.S. Congress had channeled over $1 billion through the U.S. Army from 1945 to 1948 to the U.S. military zone in West Germany, and, when the West German government became a participant in OEEC, the unused portions of these funds were transferred to Germany's ECA account.[140]

The rebuilding of the West German economy began quickly after the war's end, and recent European economists have noted that it started before Marshall funds were available and contended that such funds were never at the center of German recovery.[141] Former economics professor Ludwig Erhard, who was director of the economic council for the joint Anglo-American occupation zone, stated emphatically that Marshall Plan funds and foreign aid had not made "*the least* contribution to the revival. . . . The economic recovery was achieved exclusively *by our own efforts*."[142] Erhard, who later became the West German Minister of Economic Affairs (1949–1963), then Chancellor (1963–1966), had clashed with General Lucius D. Clay, the American Allied Commander in the occupied zone. Erhard had abolished price controls at the same time that the Allies were introducing currency reform and the new Deutschmark. Erhard's actions, strongly criticized by Clay and his advisors, marked the beginning of *Wirtschaftwunder*, German's economic miracle and rebirth.[143]

The Marshall Plan also helped accomplish the important task of reintegrating Germany into Western Europe. The United States did not want to repeat the mistakes of Versailles following World War I, isolating and punishing Germany. There were clashes between American and German policymakers, as the United States tried, only partially successfully, to remold postwar West German institutions and economic practices in the image of America.[144] Economist Werner Abelshauser has argued that the Marshall Plan brought a new form of international economic cooperation and stabilization and helped West Germany recover its own resources; "at its core . . . the Marshall Plan helped Germany to help itself."[145]

Despite problems and miscommunications, West Germany's first postwar political leader saw American aid and German initiative as essential. Konrad Adenauer, chancellor of the Federal Republic of Germany (1949–63), wrote in his memoirs that "[w]ithout American help the reconstruction of Germany was impossible, but it was equally impossible without our own cooperation, our confidence and our own will to rebuild. The German interest and the European interest were identical and I warmly welcomed the fact that in explaining his proposals Marshall had described the German question as the heart of the European question."[146]

When Marshall Plan funds and monies from other U.S. programs were added together, France received more than any other European country. Historian Irwin M. Wall noted, that with the Marshall Plan, military aid, direct budgetary assistance, and help financing the war in Indochina, American aid to France was approximately $1 billion per year from 1945 through 1954.[147] France had suffered greatly from the long occupation of its enemy, and through the ambitious Monnet Plan tried to inject government funds for economic modernization. However, the political situation in France was unstable, with the United States casting its hopes on centrist "Third Force" governments. Successive Socialist, Christian Democrat, and Radical party governments would come and go, all the time being criticized and pressured by Gaullist and Communist party forces. Maurice Schumann recalled that, while most of the National Assembly was appreciative of the assistance, one-fourth of the French were voting Communists, and the French Communist Party and its sympathizers mounted a strong campaign against the Marshall Plan. "This was the beginning of a wave of anti-Americanism," Schumann noted.[148]

ECA officials during the unstable 1948–1950 period withheld counterpart funds, hoping to force France to stabilize its finances and reduce debt. In this effort, the ECA was only partially successful. By 1950, the French economy had begun to recover with inflation in check, industries producing more, and standards of living improving.[149]

The End of the Marshall Plan

The Marshall Plan was to cease on June 30, 1952; in actuality, it had ended in late November 1951, when the Chinese army intervened in the Korean war. The invasion had an important impact on both the foreign and the domestic policies of the Truman administration.[150] Congress cobbled together a new foreign aid program that combined military and economic programs, and by October 1951 it had created the first Mutual Security Act and the Mutual Security Agency. Two years later, the Foreign Operations Administration was created as an independent agency outside of the State Department, and in 1954 its operations were merged into the International Cooperation Administration (ICA). One of the features of the Mutual Security Act of 1954 was the Food for Peace program.

In September 1961, Congress passed the Foreign Assistance Act, which reorganized the U.S. foreign assistance program, separating military and non-military aid, and establishing an agency to administer economic assistance programs. The U.S. Agency for International Development (USAID), established in November of the same year, was the first such federal agency responsible for long-range economic and social development assistance. In proposing the new U.S. foreign assistance program, President John F. Kennedy addressed the question of why the United States should continue foreign economic assistance:

> The answer is that there is no escaping our obligations: our moral obligations as a wise leader and good neighbor in the interdependent community of free nations–our economic obligations as the wealthiest people in a world of largely poor people, as a nation no longer dependent upon the loans from abroad that once helped us develop our own economy—and our political obligations as the single largest counter to the adversaries of freedom.[151]

Transforming Legislation

Harry Truman, writing in 1955, judged the Marshall Plan as "one of America's greatest contributions to the peace of the world. I think the world now realizes that without the Marshall Plan it would have been difficult for western Europe to remain free from the tyranny of Communism."[152] In December 1953, the Nobel Committee awarded George Marshall its Peace Prize for his work in European recovery.

There has been an extraordinary outpouring of writings and commentary about the Marshall Plan, its purposes, and its impact. At the time of its creation, the Marshall Plan was embraced by both conservative and liberal legislators and policymakers. As political scientist Hadley Arkes observed in the early 1970s, while everyone might have reservations about the current U.S. foreign aid program, "no one finds anything objectionable in the Marshall Plan."[153] Many historians and commentators writing during the first two decades after its enactment came to the same laudatory conclusion: that the Marshall Plan was an important legislative landmark that advanced American foreign policy and contributed to the economic and political health and well-being of Europe.

By the late 1960s, particularly during the height of the Vietnam war era, revisionist historians emphasized that the Marshall Plan was primarily a tool in a global strategy of capitalist stabilization.[154] In more recent years, particularly with the opening of rich sources of documents both in the United States and Europe, there have been reassessments of the Marshall Plan from American and European historians, political scientists, and economists. Some have looked at American motives, how the European recovery program fitted into long-range U.S. foreign policy and domestic policy interests, the impact of the recovery programs on European society, and assessments of the actual economic impact on European recovery.

Some critics, particularly Alan S. Milward and Charles S. Meier, have argued that Marshall aid accounted for just a small portion of European capital formation.[155] Milward asserted that the Marshall Plan did not save Western Europe from economic collapse, and that the "ultimate purposes" of the Marshall Plan "were almost entirely political albeit that its mechanisms were almost entirely economic."[156] Milward further argued that the economic crisis Western Europe found itself in was a crisis of payments, not one of production, and that the Marshall funds helped the recipient countries cover their deficits with dollars and continue the recovery that had already begun.[157]

The Marshall Plan aid accounted for only 2.5 percent of combined national incomes of the recipient countries during the four years, and even at its height Marshall aid accounted for just 20 percent of capital formation. Yet economists Barry Eichengreen and Marc Uzan argue that the Marshall Plan had a "significant impact" on European recovery. They argued that Europe was principally suffering from a market crisis: political and financial instability compelled people to hoard commodities, and workers and companies were not investing in the marketplace. The Marshall Plan helped restore the financial markets, restore order to prices, and liberalize production.[158]

Another major reanalysis of the Marshall Plan comes from historian Michael J. Hogan, who disagrees with Milward, and considers the plan to be "one of the most successful peacetime foreign policies launched by the United States" in the twentieth century.[159] The Marshall Plan helped to modernize European budgetary systems, encourage economic planning, rationalize production methods, and develop public–private power sharing efforts. Hogan argues that American interests and Western European interests coincided to a great degree: they both wanted economic rehabilitation and political stability, and wanted to discourage communist activities. Further, Hogan considers the consistent U.S. efforts to move Europe toward integration. The American Marshall Planners shared what Hogan called the New Deal Synthesis, hoping to remake Europe in America's image: an integrated European economy, free trade, the full operation of market forces, and trade unions, agriculture and professional leaders working together for national planning. The other aspect of the New Deal Synthesis was a shared commitment to economic growth: using modern production techniques, American business techniques, and sharing the benefits more equitably with workers. Because of the emphasis on European self-help, Hogan argues, what resulted is not exactly what American policymakers wanted or anticipated, but became a European version of the New Deal Synthesis.[160]

The reasons for the Marshall Plan were many and varied, and, as seen in the congressional debates, advocates would push various pressure points when it suited them best. The Marshall Plan was considered a humanitarian program or a strategic policy to fight back communism and preserve Western civic values;

the plan promoted peace, freedom, and prosperity; worked for European stability and political-economic integration; helped stimulate world trade; and benefitted American workers and the American economy.

On January 22, 1948, in a speech before the House of Commons, British Foreign Minister Ernest Bevin wanted to dispel the image of America as a brash country offering money for some ulterior motives. Certainly America must regard its own interests, Bevin said, but it is time to pay tribute to the "great heart" of the American people. "I was quite convinced, and I am now, that there was no political motive behind the Marshall offer other than the valuable human motive of helping Europe to help herself and so restore the economic and political health of the world."[161]

The Marshall Plan also has to be considered for its political and psychological impact. Konrad Adenauer, reflecting on the Marshall Plan, wrote that, first, the aid program was a deed of "extremely great political significance." By including Germany in the program, the United States placed its former enemy on equal footing with other suffering countries, giving Germans both hope and confidence. "[Y]ou must not forget," Adenauer wrote, "that at that time there existed strong intentions among the victorious powers simply to efface Germany from history as a great country. That is why President Truman's decision had such an extraordinary good psychological effect on Germany."[162]

On June 5, 1972, the twenty-fifth anniversary of Marshall's address, West German Chancellor Willy Brandt delivered a speech at Harvard to commemorate the program for European recovery. Brandt announced the creation of the $47 million German Marshall Fund, a program for scholarly exchange and research financed by the German government but operating independently in the United States, as an expression of "our special gratitude for the American decision in 1947 not to keep us out."[163]

The Marshall Plan, enacted in a rare period of bipartisan foreign policy, marked the beginning of American postwar leadership in world affairs. Through decades of political and economic analysis and historical reflection, and through the examination of newly opened primary documents in the recipient countries and in the United States, the Marshall Plan has stood firm as legislation and policy that has shaped America.

9

RIBBONS OF HIGHWAY
The Interstate Highway Act of 1956

*The obsolescence of the nation's highways presents an appalling
problem of waste, death and danger.*

Dwight D. Eisenhower (1952)

*The [interstate] highways represent the height of
American technological achievement; but no one, not the
engineers, the planners, not even the naysayers . . . understood
how the roads would ripple through the culture.*

Tom Lewis (1997)

The interstate highway system is the transportation backbone of America, a
46,000-mile ribbon of superhighways that traverses the continental United
States connecting every major city from the Atlantic to the Pacific, from Maine
to Florida, and Canada to Mexico.[1] It is the critical infrastructure supporting
America's dominant automobile culture and has helped transform how and
where Americans drive, live, shop, and conduct their business. The highway
system, with its 54,663 bridges and 104 tunnels, is the envy of the engineering
and transportation world. Indeed, in 1994 the American Society of Civil
Engineers proclaimed it one of the "Seven Wonders of the United States."[2]
Others, however, have been less enthusiastic. Interstate rest stops up and down
the East Coast do a brisk business selling "I Hate I-95" T-shirts; travelers are
almost guaranteed to hit aggravating traffic congestion as Interstate 95, the
world's busiest highway, snakes through the heavily populated areas of the East
Coast megalopolis, from Boston through Washington, D.C. During any given
morning or evening rush hour, interstate traffic in Los Angeles, Seattle,
Chicago, New York, or other major urban corridors slows to a crawl, forming
the world's longest parking lots.

At its inception, the interstate highway system was the most complex and
expensive public works project ever undertaken in the United States, meeting
the burgeoning demand for safe, dependable limited-access highway transportation for a growing, increasingly prosperous nation. The project took much
longer than expected, cost far more than planned, and, twenty years behind the

original schedule, final appropriations for the interstate system were released by Congress from 1991 through 1996. One of the last completed portions was a massive, complicated, and incredibly expensive engineering marvel known as the Big Dig, tunneling through the bowels of downtown Boston, sections of which cost $15,782 per inch. With a price tag expected to reach $15 billion, it cost more than the entire 1,919-mile Interstate-95 from Maine to Florida.[3]

While the federal government considered developing and financing road construction early in the history of the Republic, it was not until just before World War I that it began funding highway construction and maintenance. Until that time, road building was almost exclusively a county or state government enterprise. Since 1916, the federal government has provided financial assistance and technical support for state primary, secondary and urban highways, and in 1944, after many years of hesitation, Congress enacted legislation to develop an interstate highway system yet failed to appropriate funds for its construction.[4]

The Interstate Highway Act of 1956—or to use its formal name, the Federal-Aid Highway Act of 1956—was the decisive, historic piece of legislation.[5] President Dwight D. Eisenhower played an important leadership role, making highway transportation a key domestic priority for his administration. The federal Bureau of Public Roads (BPR), state transportation officials, and corporate and union voices from the transportation field were all eager to tackle this grand project. Once the politically thorny question of funding had been resolved, the Interstate Highway Act quickly was adopted by Congress, hailed by its supporters as a long-overdue, indispensable measure to meet the insatiable demands of the American traveler and motor transportation industries.

But the interstate program soon encountered resistance and criticism. The billions of dollars released for road construction led to fraud, bid-rigging, and other well-publicized abuses by private citizens, corporations, and state government officials. The ambitious construction program soon fell behind schedule, and early cost estimates were quickly revised upward, with the final construction cost at nearly five times the original plan.[6] The interstate system was planned and implemented by state and federal engineers and transportation experts, long before countervailing political forces could coalesce: voices from the environmental and historic preservation movements, those representing urban poor, and those calling for the revival of urban mass transit alternatives. There were early bitter fights in San Francisco, New Orleans, Memphis, Washington, D.C., and other urban areas between neighborhood activists and historic preservationists on one side and government officials, business, and road construction forces on the other. Many inner cities and long-settled neighborhoods soon bore the ugly scars of demolition, relocation, and highway construction. The interstate highway program had an enormous policy leverage over alternative transportation systems. It drew its financing from a user fee, embodied in the Highway Trust Fund, that was used exclusively for highway construction during the first seventeen years. Not until

1973 were urban mass transit programs able to tap into this steady stream of funding.

Despite its critics, the interstate highway system has proven to be a remarkably efficient means of transportation and a catalyst for economic growth and prosperity. It comprises less than 1 percent of all highway mileage in the United States, yet transports nearly a quarter of all road traffic. It has spurred lower freight transportation costs, has permitted productivity gains through just-in-time shipping methods, and has been a critical boost to businesses dependent on safe, reliable highway transportation. Suburban economic growth has been greatly assisted by the interstate system and urban nodes, created around interstate beltways and corridors, have blossomed miles away from downtown. Hundreds of thousands of lives have been spared major injury or death because motorists use the far safer interstate system. It is difficult to imagine what America's transportation network would look like, or how it would function, without the limited-access multi-lane highway system established by Congress in 1956.

Background

Early in the Republic's history, the federal government became involved in road building. In 1806, Congress enacted a law to develop the Cumberland Road, a national turnpike from Cumberland, Maryland, to the new state of Ohio and the Ohio River; the road was to be financed by land sales and later by tolls. Two years later, Secretary of the Treasury Albert Gallatin presented to the U.S. Senate a comprehensive plan to develop an integrated system of great canals and a continuous turnpike for a inland navigation route from Massachusetts to North Carolina, and a turnpike from Maine to Georgia, uniting all the major seaports.[7] The federal government would sponsor the plan, build the roads, then turn them over to the states or to private corporations.

Work began on the Cumberland Road in 1811, reaching Wheeling in 1818; by 1838, now called the National Road, it extended to Springfield, Ohio, and then to Vandalia, Illinois, in 1841, ultimately stretching 800 miles. But it was soon overcome by new technology: the National Road was abandoned with the rapid growth of railroads.

But Gallatin's turnpike plans soon ran into political, economic, and constitutional difficulties. There was a persistent problem of economic sectionalism: New York and the New England states had already spent large sums of money on roads and canals. They were reluctant to help pay for improvements in other areas, such as Baltimore or points south, which would inevitably cut into their commercial transportation advantage. Some southerners also worried that growing federal power could ultimately be a threat to slavery. Virginia congressman John Randolph warned his colleagues in 1824: a federal government that could build highways could also free the slaves. Presidents James Madison (1817), James Monroe (1822), and later Andrew Jackson (1830) each vetoed appropriation bills for a national system of transportation facilities; each president maintained that, in order for the federal government to be involved in such schemes of road and canal building, there would have to be a constitutional amendment. With those presidential vetoes, the federal government withdrew from national road building and did not re-enter in a substantial way until nearly a century later.[8]

Good Roads Movement

The push for better roads and federal involvement came from the invention of the modern bicycle, the mounting demand from farmers for decent, affordable transportation, the creation of the Rural Free Delivery program of the U.S. Post Office, and, of course, the inception of the automobile age.

In 1878 Colonel Albert Augustus Pope introduced a geared, low-wheeled "safety bicycle" with a comfortable seat and air-filled rubber tires.[9] It quickly made obsolete the bone-jarring, dangerous old style bicycles with their enormous 58-inch front wheels and small rear wheels. The affordable safety bicycle was an immediate success, and recreational cycling became a national craze: city streets became crowded with cyclists, and preachers on Sundays complained that church-goers were emptying the pews to go out on their two-wheelers. Cycling was also seen as a liberating force for women. Susan B. Anthony once commented that the bicycle "has done more to emancipate women than anything else in the world. I stand and rejoice every time I see a women ride by on a wheel."[10]

By the 1890s bicyclists were everywhere in the United States, and over 100,000 enthusiasts had joined an organization called the League of American Wheelmen. In 1892 the League published *Good Roads*, which billed itself as the "first publication in the world devoted strictly to road improvement." Through this and other organizations, the Good Roads movement was born, becoming a popular political issue in the 1890s.[11]

In addition, farmers were growing increasingly dissatisfied with the monopolistic grip of the railroads. For two decades the federal government had heavily subsidized railroads, but by the 1890s there was a growing agrarian push to have an alternative form of moving produce and livestock to market. For farmers, highway transportation was that reasonable alternative. The push for better roads probably depended more on farmers than on enthusiastic city people and their bicycles. Much was at stake: over two million miles of dirt roads, often poorly maintained, prone to flooding and frequently impassable, crooked, and full of ruts. Historian Wayne E. Fuller asserted that farmers had been the "heart and soul of the good-roads movement."[12] Responding to this growing agrarian pressure, Congress in 1893 voted a $10,000 appropriation for the secretary of agriculture to promote the investigation of highways.[13]

In 1896 the federal government inaugurated an important new mail service, Rural Free Delivery. No longer would farm families have to make the long trek into the nearest town to pick up their mail; the mail would come to them, at no extra charge. Three years later, the U.S. Post Office Department adopted a policy that rural delivery routes would not be laid out in areas where the roads were unfit for travel. Immediately there was a demand for better rural roads The Post Office went further than merely declaring its policy, it actively promoted and pushed for better roads, admonishing postmasters, local officials responsible for roads, and even postal patrons that mail delivery would be in jeopardy unless the roads were better maintained. The most important contact point was the rural mail carrier, who often aggressively advocated improvement of roads.[14]

Then came the automobile. Two bicycle mechanics from Springfield, Massachusetts, Charles and Frank Duryea created the first American gasoline-powered internal combustion engine and attached it to a broken-down horse carriage. Under the cover of darkness, so as to avoid embarrassment if it failed, they chugged up and down the streets of Springfield in 1893.[15] The tinkering and experiments of hundreds of manufacturers of horseless carriages rapidly evolved into the automobile industry. By the first decade of the twentieth century, the automobile was becoming an essential part of American life. Press coverage was overwhelmingly favorable and many predicted the automobile would soon replace the horse and buggy as a cheaper, more reliable, means of transportation. By 1910 America, with 468,500 motor vehicles registered, was the world's foremost automobile consumer.[16] Soon Henry Ford revolutionized automobile manufacturing by introducing assembly-line mass production; the rugged and affordable Model T, introduced in 1908, quickly became available to thousands, then millions of new customers.

Highway production was spurred on by early social clubs like the American Automobile Club of New York and the Automobile Club of Southern California, and especially the American Automobile Association, founded in 1902, and its local affiliates. It was also boosted by business and state government associations bent on improving highway construction. In 1901 Horatio S. Earle, a local lawmaker and official with the Michigan branch of the League of American Wheelmen, advocated the creation of a national organization to push for a "Capital Connecting Government Highway," joining every state capital with every other state capital, and those cities connecting with Washington, D.C. Two years later, that emerging organization, the American Road Builders Association, held its first national convention, with Earle as its president.[17] In 1914, at a meeting of an American road congress in Atlanta, the American Association of State Highway Officials (AASHO) was created. This organization, which played a significant role in state road planning and construction, began with a modest, realistic goal: to get traffic "out of the mud!"[18]

One impatient entrepreneur wasn't satisfied with waiting for the federal or state governments to act. Automobile industrialist Carl G. Fisher, founder of the Indianapolis Motor Speedway and later the developer of Miami Beach, Florida, wanted to build a hard-surfaced, all-weather highway from New York to San Francisco. Unable to convince Henry Ford to back this $12 million project, Fisher nonetheless received financial backing of Henry B. Joy, head of the Packard Motor Car Company, who gave the road the memorable name of the Lincoln Highway. Parts of the highway were opened, but mounting costs and difficulties with local and state highway authorities caused the Lincoln Highway Association to disband after passage of federal legislation in 1925–1926 creating a U.S. numbered highway marking plan.[19]

The Lincoln Highway was followed by plans to build a Meridian Highway from Nuevo Laredo, Texas, to Winnipeg, Saskatchewan; another highway, called the Jefferson Highway, was planned from New Orleans to Winnipeg. Senator John H. Bankhead (Democrat–Alabama) was to be honored by a highway named after him from Memphis, Tennessee, to El Paso, Texas; then there was to be a Victory Highway following the cessation of World War I and a Theodore Roosevelt memorial highway between Washington and Los Angeles. Carl Fisher's new resort of Miami Beach would be served by a new Dixie Highway, running from the Mackinaw Strait in Michigan to Miami Beach.[20] Most of these grandiose private schemes, however, never were developed or took decades and state financing and construction to complete.

Push to Legislation

In the meantime, a major constitutional objection of a century earlier had been swept aside. In 1907 the Supreme Court affirmed, through *Wilson* v. *Shaw*, that the U.S. Congress had the authority under the Interstate Commerce Clause to construct interstate roads.

There was growing pressure in Washington to assist states and local governments in road building. In 1912 a good roads bill passed in the House of Representatives by a comfortable margin, calling for the federal government to make "rental" payments to counties for the use of their roads by the U.S. Post Office Department; those federal rental payments would then be used to help maintain the roads. But the Senate failed to pass the bill, primarily because of opposition from the American Automobile Association and other motoring groups. It was a variation on an old theme: a clash between rural and urban, farmers and city people. As Federal Highway Administration historian Richard F. Weingroff explained, "Farmers wanted all-weather, farm-to-market roads. Motorists groups and the automobile industry wanted hard-surfaced, interstate roads."[21]

By 1913 the House of Representatives created a new Committee on Roads and Congressman Dorsey W. Shackleford (Democrat–Missouri), author of the 1912 legislation, left his position on the Ways and Means Committee to become its chairman. But there was opposition, especially from the East and big cities, whose citizens did not want to pay for country roads in poor areas of the South and West. For example, two years earlier, Congressman Michael E. Driscoll (Republican–New York) rose in opposition to such programs: "Twenty-nine road bills have been introduced by the Democrats and ten by Republicans, but not one from an Eastern State, not one from a Middle State, very few from the Mississippi Valley; but all from the great broad states in the South and West of large areas, long roads, small populations, and small taxing power."[22]

In 1916 Congress passed the first legislation, the Federal-Aid Highway Act, providing states with matching funds for road construction. Paying for highway construction was always a vexing issue. At the beginning of the twentieth century, highways were funded through property taxes, poll taxes, and labor levies; it became clear, however, that these placed enormous strains on the limited taxing sources of local governments.[23] One of the main problems was that wealthier counties and cities were able to respond with decent funding for roads, but poorer counties could provide very little. The 1916 federal highway legislation helped, but still there was growing need for revenue. States developed new sources of revenue, such as automobile registration fees, bonds, and highway user taxes. The user tax was a novel idea, and after 1921 all of the states placed an increasing share of the burden for highway funding on motor vehicle users.[24] But still, such fees and taxes were inadequate to meet public demand for highways. In 1919 Oregon, Colorado, and New Mexico each adopted a gasoline tax, and by 1929 the tax had spread throughout the country, adopted even in Mexico and Canada. The tax was typically three to four cents per gallon, and by 1929 the states had collected $431 million in gasoline taxes.[25] Starting in 1932, the federal government began to impose a tax on gasoline, first as an "emergency" one cent per gallon to go into the general revenue fund, not toward highway improvement, and then additional taxes during World War II.[26]

Lt. Colonel Eisenhower's Transcontinental Expedition

In 1919, in the aftermath of the Great War, the future of the U.S. Army's Tank Corps was uncertain. Tanks were prone to breakdowns, they were slow, and clumsy, and many experienced officers questioned the tactical benefit of these awkward, noisy machines. The Army realized that tanks, trucks, and other mechanized vehicles had to run on reliable, better maintained roads. This became painfully evident in December 1917 when the Army Motor Transport Corps found it almost impossible to drive trucks from Toledo, Ohio, to Baltimore during one of the most severe winters in memory.

As a demonstration of the need for better roads, the War Department in the summer of 1919 decided to send a caravan of seventy-five trucks, cars, ambulances, and repair cars, manned by 295 officers and enlisted men and a fifteen-piece band, across the United States. The convoy began on July 7, at the Zero Milestone just south of the White House in Washington, headed to Gettysburg, Pennsylvania, where it picked up the partially completed Lincoln Highway and ended in San Francisco on September 6. The expedition was commanded by Colonel Charles W. McClure, and one of the officers who volunteered to join the expedition was Lt. Colonel Dwight D. Eisenhower. The trip lasted sixty-two days, as the convoy experienced countless mechanical failures and breakdowns; roads were crushed under the weight of the heavy equipment, and bridges were too fragile to carry the loads. At times, the convoy averaged only six miles an hour; on some days when seventy or a hundred miles would be the estimated progress, the convoy made only three or four miles. Forty-five years later, Eisenhower summed up the arduous trip, noting that they had finally arrived in San Francisco "sixty days and 6,000 breakdowns later." All along the route, they were greeted by well wishers, politicians and generals, bands, street dancing, and speeches, always speeches.[27]

The long, bumpy expedition in 1919 made an important impression on Dwight Eisenhower. So too, did the *Autobahnen*, the advanced highway system of Hitler's Germany. Eisenhower recalled in his memoirs, "I recognized then [upon seeing the *Autobahnen*], that the United States was behind in highway construction. In the middle 1950s I did not want us to fall still further behind."[28]

Growing Federal Role

After World War I, Americans were buying an unprecedented number of automobiles, with vehicle registration jumping from 10.5 million in 1920 to 26.7 million in 1929; and, even during the Depression years of the 1930s, automobile purchases only twice fell below two million units per year.[29] States responded by drastically increasing the construction of new highways, but there was a wide disparity in the amount of funds that individual states would commit. State highway bureaucracies took control of road building away from individual counties, which often were unable to build good-quality roads and would construct only for local use, rather than fit into a uniform statewide network. During the 1920 and 1930s, the United States was experiencing what many in the highway business considered the first "golden age" of highway construction.

The federal government assisted state highway builders in two major ways, with funding and technical assistance. Federal funding began with the 1916 Federal-Aid Highway Act then continued with regular appropriations over the years. Most important was the 1921 Federal-Aid Highway Act which established the key principle that the federal government would provide funds to the states, while the states would spend a larger portion of funds on roads that were "interstate in character." Amidst the diversity in state highway funding and priorities, the federal-aid roads program became the core of each state's road system.[30] The second important assistance came through the federal Bureau of Public Roads, which provided states with technical assistance, guidance, and political cooperation. Guiding the Bureau of Public Roads through its formative years was Thomas H. MacDonald, who served as chief of the BPR for thirty-four years, from 1919 to 1953. "Chief" MacDonald, as he was almost always referred to, worked closely and cooperatively with the

American Association of State Highway Officials charting out the role of federal aid in the 1920s and 1930s, working out political compromises to satisfy both the rural-farm and urban road-building constituencies, and helping to establish the foundation for the interstate highway system. Richard F. Weingroff characterized MacDonald as "the towering figure of road transportation in the twentieth-century."[31]

MacDonald had his own vision of an interstate, transcontinental system of highways; however, it ran up against the plans of another highway enthusiast, President Franklin D. Roosevelt. Franklin Roosevelt had long had an interest in highway planning and development. In 1924 he was president of the Taconic State Park Commission in New York and oversaw the planning of the 125-mile parkway; later as governor he worked to improve farm roads and shift the burden of construction and highway maintenance from the counties to the state. As president, Roosevelt took, in the words of historian Tom Lewis, "immense delight in not merely supporting the financing of roads but tinkering with the details of their construction."[32]

Lee Mertz, Federal Highway Administration historian, observed that "legend has it that the interstate [highway system] began with President Roosevelt drawing three lines East and West and three lines North and South on a map of the United States and asking the Bureau of Public Roads to build it."[33] Indeed, Roosevelt had been talking with federal officials and congressional leaders in 1935 about forming a network of superhighways. As the *Washington Post* reported, tentative plans called for three master roads connecting the Atlantic and Pacific coasts, Canada with Florida, and Canada with Mexico, linking international boundaries with "smooth, arrow-straight four-lane thoroughfares."[34] During the late 1930s, the Roosevelt administration submitted two highway proposals, and no fewer than fourteen bills were introduced in Congress.

In 1938 Roosevelt asked MacDonald to conduct a study assessing the possibility of three east–west and three north–south super toll roads. Congress, too, was looking for guidance and in that same year directed MacDonald's Bureau of Public Roads to produce a comprehensive study on the feasibility of a system of national toll roads.[35] Chief MacDonald was no proponent of toll roads, but he went ahead with a full-fledged study, and in 1939 the Bureau of Public Roads produced *Toll Roads and Free Roads*. This report's central conclusion was that the highway scheme proposed by President Roosevelt was not economically possible and that the country would be better off with a comprehensive system of 26,700 miles of low-cost non-toll roads that would be connected to the downtown of each of the country's major cities. *Toll Roads and Free Roads* was a direct rebuff to Roosevelt's aspirations, but also marked a decided shift in federal bureaucratic thinking about highway priorities, a shift from a rural to an urban emphasis.[36]

MacDonald's allies in this effort were AASHO, the American Automobile Association, the American Trucking Association, the National Association of

Bus Operators, and other highway lobbying groups. State highway officials, in particular, were concerned that they would be cut out of the toll road business, which was usually carried out by private engineering companies.

Soon after the BPR report was published, the Pennsylvania Turnpike, a triumph of highway engineering, was dedicated on October 1, 1940. It ran from the western side of the state capital at Harrisburg to the eastern side of Pittsburgh, cutting through the Allegheny mountains and trimming five hours off the trip between the two cities.[37] Officials at the Bureau of Public Roads had opposed the toll road concept and had tried to discourage private financial backing, but Pennsylvania was able to get a $35 million loan from the federal Reconstruction Finance Corporation and a grant of $29 million in work-relief funds from the Public Works Administration in order to build the road.[38] It was an instant hit, bringing in much larger toll revenues than predicted by the Bureau of Public Roads. Within a year, five states—New York, Maryland, Maine, Florida, and Illinois—had created toll road commissions.[39]

Toll Roads and Free Roads set the groundwork for future interstate highway consensus even though the issue of toll roads versus non-toll roads was yet to be resolved. However, the federal government actually cut back on funds available for highways at the outset of World War II, and, with the decision to transport war materiel by rail rather than highways, defense priorities shifted away from road building.

World's Fair and Futurama

Imaginations were stirred when visitors experienced the huge General Motors "Futurama" exhibit at the 1939 World's Fair in New York. Here they could catch a glimpse of a shiny, glistening tomorrow: the United States in 1960. Fairgoers, a capacity of 30,000 per day, trudged up the long ramps to the exhibit, called "Highways and Horizons," designed by Norman Bel Geddes. Many waited for hours to get in, but, once inside, they were bathed in blue twilight in a sixty-foot-high vault. In stages, the room changed, subtly, from blue twilight to purple, to a reddening dusk. Walking on heavy carpet, the fairgoers then came to a 140-ton passenger conveyor system, a moving platform that had a row of soft, plush blue velour winged chairs, two side by side. From the comfort of those seats, visitors could gaze at the future.

The diorama was huge, some 35,738 square feet, containing 500,000 model buildings, more than a million trees, and 50,000 miniature automobiles, with 10,000 of them gliding on the superhighways of the future. The ride took seventeen minutes to make the full circle around the exhibits of metropolises, farmland, and mountains—a vast landscape, all connected by a network of superhighways and access ramps. Inside the chair wings were small speakers, and as the fairgoers watched the exhibit, a soft voice whispered to them: "These are the express highways of 1960. Notice there are five different lanes, for various speeds, up to 100 miles an hour. Notice the feeder roads, how they enter on the main highways by ramps that do away with intersections. Your cloverleaf intersection, so new in 1939, was abandoned many years ago."

Visitors got a close-up view of the City of Tomorrow. "This is the metropolis of 1960," said the whispering voice. "It is a city of one million people." The voice assured visitors that there were no slums and that the city of 1960 was divided into separate zones for residential, commercial, and industrial use. The light automobile traffic flowed easily through this great metropolis.

The American Institute of Public Opinion (the Gallup Poll) surveyed Fair visitors and found that Futurama was the most popular exhibit. This vast diorama depicted many of the features that eventually ended up in the 1956 Interstate Highway Act, and it undoubtedly helped popularize the idea of a superhighway system, connecting metropolises and rural areas alike.[40] When they left the exhibit, visitors were given a lapel button that said "I have seen the Future." Hundreds of thousands were convinced that they had.

Postwar Realities

However, the reality of highway building and planning was far different from the utopian landscapes of Futurama and General Motors. Federal and state politicians, highway administrators, and planners had failed to come up with a coherent, fundable highway strategy. As historian Mark H. Rose observed, at the onset of World War II there was at each level of government a series of "complex, ambivalent, and inconsistent road programs, all of which together fostered construction of limited and often substandard highway mileage."[41]

In 1942 a coalition of some 240 automobile manufacturers, oil companies, automobile clubs, unions, state highway administrators, and others met weekly in Washington to secretly lobby for better roads. This coalition, the so-called Road Gang, succeeded when Congress passed the 1944 Federal-Aid Highway Act, which rearranged federal aid roads into the ABC system of primary, secondary, and urban arterial roads and designated, but did not fund, a national system of interstate highways, not to exceed 40,000 miles, that would stretch from the Atlantic to the Pacific and from the Canadian border to Mexico. With an extraordinary backlog of work to be done on the ABC roads, there simply wasn't money left over for an interstate system. Or there was not enough political will to make the money available.[42] Whatever momentum there was for an interstate highway system in 1944, it basically ground to a halt over the next decade.

In 1949 over 37,000 miles of U.S. highways were audited and found to be in poor shape. Many of the highways were over twenty years old and had not been maintained, and there were different types of pavement, varying widths of the roadways, and variation in the load capacities of bridges. When Eisenhower became president in 1953, just 6,417 miles of highways had been improved by funds authorized in the 1944 legislation.[43]

During the war, all automobile production had stopped, but, once the war was over, auto manufacturers worked furiously to meet the pent-up demand. The new cars were greeted with extraordinary enthusiasm by a hungry public; millions of potential buyers and window shoppers waited anxiously in front of showrooms to see the new models. Not only did the public want new automobiles, it wanted multi-lane, limited access superhighways. Especially at mid-century, automobile manufacturers, truck operators, bus lines, state and federal highway departments, and labor unions all clamored for better highway transportation.[44]

Along the way, the interstate highway movement gained a powerful ally in newspaper magnate William Randolph Hearst, Jr., who became the unofficial, but highly effective, cheerleader for better roads. Just as he did during the battle for the GI Bill, Hearst went all out to generate popular support for the highway movement. Between October 1952 and the end of 1955, Hearst papers printed almost three million lines, or enough material to fill 1,229 newspaper pages, on the highway problem. His constant drumbeat was that America needed and deserved safe and reliable superhighways. No wonder that in 1956 the American Road Builders Association along with the president of the Chrysler Corporation presented him an award for so effectively communicating the case for interstate highways to the American people.[45]

Making the Law

Eisenhower's Role

President-elect Eisenhower forcefully stated his position on highway construction in a statement that ran throughout the Hearst newspapers: "The obsolescence of the nation's highways presents an appalling problem of waste, death and danger. Next to the manufacture of the most modern implements of war as a guarantee of peace through strength, a network of modern roads is as necessary to defense as it is to our national economy and personal safety."[46]

Congress held extensive hearings on highway construction as it prepared for the next authorization, the Federal-Aid Highway Act of 1954. It was basically a stop-gap piece of legislation, authorizing just $175 million for the interstate system, trying to satisfy competing urban and rural interests, but it was important for establishing the basic consensus for the interstate system. In May 1954 Eisenhower signed the highway legislation into law but also decided that it was time to exert his executive leadership.

The forum for Eisenhower was the 1954 annual meeting of the National Governors' Association, held in July at a resort on Lake George, New York. However, Eisenhower was unable to attend the conference because of the death of his sister-in-law; in his place, Vice-President Richard M. Nixon read the president's remarks. Eisenhower repeated his charge that the American highway system was obsolete: "It is obsolete because in large part it just happened. It was governed in the beginning by terrain, existing Indian trails, cattle trails, arbitrary section lines. It was designed largely for local movement at slow speeds of one or two horsepower. It has been adjusted, it is true, at intervals to meet metropolitan traffic gluts, transcontinental movement, and increased horsepower. But it has never been completely overhauled or planned to satisfy the needs ten years ahead."[47]

The president called for a $50 billion, ten-year highway program: "[It is] a goal toward which we can—and we should—look."[48] The speech came as a complete surprise to the assembled governors; they were given no advance statements nor notification of what Eisenhower would say. According to Richard F. Weingroff, a number of governors favored removing the federal government entirely from the highway planning and construction business, and the governors had been debating how to get the federal government out of the highway gasoline tax business so that the states could use that revenue. Indeed, the impact of the Eisenhower speech had an "electrifying effect" on the governors and their aides.[49] Eisenhower, in offering his dramatic $50 billion program, had taken the initiative for highway policy away from the federal Bureau of Public Roads and the Congress and placed it in the White House.[50]

Some of the governors were perplexed or annoyed at the Eisenhower speech, worried that the federal government would take over the lucrative and vital business of road building. All were stunned by its boldness. But the road builders, who were suffering through an economic drought in the early 1950s, were quick to see the benefit. Lt. General Eugene Reybold of the American Road Builders Association spoke for his industry: "President Eisenhower, in a bold stroke, has blown the lid off any milquetoast, piecemeal planning. . . . There is no longer room for timidity in road building plans."[51]

However, there were major obstacles ahead for the president. It would be difficult for Congress to swallow such an enormous funding request, no matter how popular it might be. There were serious questions as to how such a highway system should be financed: through a massive bond issue, through a self-financed toll system, or a combination of higher taxes and user fees? Should the funds come from a dedicated source, such as a system of gasoline taxes and user fees, or should it come from the general federal revenue stream? How much should states be required to contribute?

Eisenhower ordered his senior aides and members of the administration to craft his highway plans. However, Secretary of Commerce Sinclair Weeks, whose department would have overall jurisdiction, opposed such large-scale federal expenditures, while his chief of the Bureau of Public Roads, the politically astute Francis V. du Pont, emphasized the importance of the federal government stimulating economic growth through the roads program.[52]

Two other key aides offered fundamentally contrasting ideas for the federal government's role. Chief of Staff Sherman Adams, a former New Hampshire governor, thought that the system of federal–state cooperation put in place by Thomas MacDonald was the right way to go, especially if the federal government appropriated more funds. Adams proposed a Continental Highway Finance Corporation that would finance the highway system but leave planning and construction to the BPR and state governments. Another aide, Major General John Stewart Bragdon, who had known Eisenhower since they were West Point cadets in 1915, came up with an altogether different idea: abolish the Bureau of Public Roads and the state highway agencies, bring all road building under the financial and construction authority of a National Highway Authority, and build a system of toll roads similar to those conceived of by Franklin Roosevelt. Bragdon may have been an astute general, but he was a bumbling naif in the world of highway and pork barrel politics. His nationalization scheme would have wrecked the long-standing political balance that MacDonald and others had crafted. As Tom Lewis described it: "Gone would be the pride that individual senators and representatives took when a road construction project went through their district. Gone would be the cooperative alliance between the federal and state governments that had characterized road building since the Federal-Aid Road Act of 1916."[53] With Bragdon and Adams at odds and Weeks and du Pont with different policy visions, there was a decided policy impasse in the administration.

To move forward, Arthur F. Burns, chairman of the Council of Economic Advisers, suggested that Eisenhower create two committees to explore the issues of building and financing a national highway system. The first, headed by du Pont, was an Interagency Committee composed of representatives from the departments of Commerce, Defense, and Treasury, the Bureau of the Budget, and the Council of Economic Advisers. This committee was to look into the economic requirements for the interstate system and report to the second committee, the President's Advisory Committee on a National Highway Program, headed by Eisenhower's friend and former colleague General Lucius D. Clay.[54]

General Clay carefully selected his committee members: David Beck, president of the Teamsters Union; William Roberts, president of Allis-Chalmers; Stephen D. Bechtel of the large construction firm bearing his family's name, and Sloan Colt of Bankers Trust Company in New York. The executive secretary, who could draw upon the full resources of the Bureau of Public Roads, was the veteran highway administration official Francis C. Turner. "These men," historian Richard O. Davies concluded, "were no enemies of the highway and the automobile."[55]

Nor were the witnesses who asked to speak. The highway lobby was out in full force at the Clay Committee hearings of October 7–8, 1954. There were representatives from American Farm Bureau Federation, the U.S. Chamber of Commerce, the U.S. Conference of Mayors, the American Road Builders Association, National Association of County Officials, the Automobile Safety Foundation, the American Automobile Association, the Associated General Contractors, the American Petroleum Institute, the Highway Municipal

Association, the Truck-Trailer Manufacturers Association, the Independent Advisory Committee to the Truck Industry, the American Association of State Highway Officials, the Private Truck Council of America, the American Trucking Association, the National Grange, the Toll Road Association, and the National Association of Motor Bus Operators. Two fundamental interests were represented: those who would have to pay for the highways and those who would gain from their construction. The American Transit Association, the national organization that spoke for urban transit interests and was no foe of the interstate system, however, was not invited.[56] Nor was there any participation from citizen organizations or interests.

Various financing proposals were floating around the administration, but General Clay decided to ignore them and sought instead the advice of Wall Street financiers. Ultimately, Clay's committee recommended the selling of bonds, administered through a newly created federal corporation. No taxes would be levied; the money would become immediately available, and the interstate highway system could become a reality in short order.

A report entitled *Ten-Year National Highway Program* was released by the Clay Committee in January 11, 1955, and became the basis for most of the legislation that was considered in Congress during the next six months. The report recommended spending $101 billion over a ten-year period on a combination of primary, secondary, and urban highways and an interstate highway system, which the report called a "top national economic and defense priority." Tom Lewis assessed the committee's report: "Masterful in conception, Clay's proposal—like Bragdon's—was foolish in its basic comprehension of political realities. It was destined to fail."[57] Eisenhower, too, was lukewarm to the Clay Committee report. The president originally preferred a system of self-financing toll highways, and, though he endorsed General Clay's recommendation, Eisenhower "grew restless with the quibbling over methods of financing." He just "wanted the job done."[58]

Passing the Law

In a February 22, 1955, letter transmitted to Congress, President Eisenhower argued forcefully for "comprehensive and quick and forward-looking" action to construct interstate highways. He stressed four urgent problems: the issue of safety, with an annual cost of 36,000 deaths and more than a million injured on highways; deterioration of the current road network and the increased cost of operating vehicles resulting from poor roads; the need for evacuation routes in case of an atomic attack; and, finally, traffic congestion,

Eighty-Fourth Congress, Second Session (January 3–July 27, 1956)

Senate: 48 Democrats; 47 Republicans; 1 other

House: 232 Democrats; 203 Republicans

President: Dwight D. Eisenhower

which Eisenhower predicted that "existing traffic jams only faintly foreshadow those of ten years hence."[59]

The president laid out the attractiveness of a coordinated interstate system: it embraced only 1.2 percent of total road mileage but joined forty-two state capitals and 90 percent of all cities with populations over 50,000. The interstate system would carry one-seventh of the country's automobile and motor transport traffic. In addition to this 1955 State of the Union address, Eisenhower spoke publicly and forcefully for the interstate highway system on fourteen separate occasions.[60] Nearly everyone—Democrat or Republican—agreed that a national system of interstate highways was vital. There was no partisan, ideological, or sectional cleavage; this was public works funding on a grand scale, and there was something for everybody. The sticking point, however, would be in how to finance the enormous project. Long a supporter of highway development, Senator Harry Flood Byrd, Sr. (Democrat–Virginia), was also a politician who hated indebtedness. Since 1835 Virginia had been a pay-as-you-go road state, never issuing a single bond, Byrd proudly told the Senate Public Works Subcommittee on Public Roads in 1955. He implacably opposed the Clay Committee's recommendation to finance a $20 billion, 30-year bond issue, which would require interest payments of $11.5 billion. Sticking to his fiscal principles, Byrd became the administration's chief critic of its funding proposal.[61]

Another powerful senator who had difficulty with the Clay Committee recommendations was Albert A. Gore, Sr. (Democrat–Tennessee), chairman of the Subcommittee on Roads in the Committee on Public Works. He characterized the scheme to impose a federal gasoline tax and have the revenue go to bond holders rather than to road building as "a screwy plan which could lead the country into inflationary ruin."[62] During testimony before Senator Gore's subcommittee in the Spring of 1955, it became evident that the administration's bill was going to have a rough time of it. Senator Dennis Chavez (Democrat–New Mexico) summed up the growing concern over debt service in the administration's bill: "A lot of people are writing me from all over the country and saying why issue $20 billion worth of bonds and pay $11 billion worth of interest in thirty years; this $11 billion could build lots of roads. In other words, they feel that this is an investment bill and not a road bill."[63]

A Gore substitute bill, which authorized partial funding for an Interstate system, was passed by voice vote. But in the House, lawmakers not only defeated Eisenhower's bill but also soundly defeated a measure proposed by Subcommittee on Roads chairman George H. Fallon (Democrat–Maryland).

Arthur F. Burns urged Eisenhower to call a special session of Congress if necessary to reconsider the legislation. Eisenhower recalled in his memoirs: "'Well,' I said somewhat ruefully, 'the special session might be necessary—but calling it could be at the cost of the sanity of one man named Eisenhower.' There was no sense in spending money to call them back when I knew in advance that the result would be zero."[64]

Eisenhower's State of the Union message to Congress at the opening of the 1956 session was as forceful as his remarks the previous year, but he did not recommend any specific method of financing. Then House Republican leader Joseph W. Martin, Jr. (Massachusetts), announced in January that Eisenhower had agreed to a pay-as-you-go tax program, similar to what Senator Byrd had advocated, in order to break the stalemate surrounding the administration's bond financing proposal.[65] In the 1956 session of Congress, the Highway Act of 1956 was introduced by Democrats Fallon and T. Hale Boggs (Louisiana) in the House and Gore in the Senate; their legislation managed to break a four-month deadlock. Title I of the legislation encompassed the Federal-Aid Highway Act of 1956, and Title II, the Highway Revenue Act of 1956, crafted by Boggs, addressed its financing. The Highway Act authorized nearly $31 billion in federal–state funds over a thirteen-year period ($26 billion of which was the federal portion) and earmarked highway user fees and gasoline taxes for a newly created Highway Trust Fund, with the provision that the Trust Fund could never show a deficit. This was a decisive step because it broke a long-standing congressional precedent of not earmarking specific tax revenues for specific projects. As historian Mark H. Rose summed it up, Boggs and Fallon had found the key ingredients: plenty of new roads for everyone, a financially secure way of financing construction, and a modest increase in taxes from the trucking industry.[66]

Gasoline taxes were always viewed as suspect by the automobile, trucking, rubber, and petroleum industries. They feared that, if the taxes became too onerous, citizens would drive less, buy fewer cars, and use less in motor freight. But with the Highway Revenue Act of 1956, the automobile, trucking, and rubber industries withdrew their opposition to higher and sustained federal gasoline taxes to pay for the interstate system. Only the petroleum industry continued to voice its strong opposition to such taxes.[67] With the highway lobby onboard, everything seemed to brighten.

A further breakthrough was the new cost-sharing formula: instead of the old 50/50 division, or 60 percent federal to 40 percent state, the new highway system would have the federal government bear 90 percent of the cost with the states picking up the remaining 10 percent.

The legislation passed in the House of Representatives by an overwhelming 388–19; then the Senate passed by voice vote a modified version of Gore's earlier bill. In James A. Dunn's words, the legislation rolled through Congress "like a tractor trailer on a downgrade."[68] A conference committee reconciled the differences in the two bills, both chambers quickly agreed, and on June 29, 1956, President Eisenhower signed into law the Federal-Aid Highway Act of 1956. As the *Saturday Evening Post* summed up the power of the highway lobby and the ease with which the Highway Act passed, "That should answer any questions as to who runs this country."[69]

Highlights of the Highway Act of 1956

The Highway Act provided for $31 billion ($26 billion federal) for interstate highways, based on a 90 percent federal and 10 percent state funding formula. A Highway Trust Fund was created, which would raise an estimated $14.8 billion over a 16-year period, from increased gasoline, diesel, and special motor taxes. Between 1957 and 1959, half of the funds would be distributed on the traditional formula of mileage, area, and population, and the other half by population alone. After that, funds would be allocated according to the needs of the system. The system was expanded by 1,000 miles to encompass 41,000 miles (then 42,500 miles in 1968), and renamed the National System of Interstate and Defense Highways. The entire system was to be completed by 1969, with Highway Trust Fund taxes lapsing in 1972.[70]

The legislation was a triumph for the automobile driving public, state and federal highway officials, and the highway lobby. In a way, this was a much simpler time to develop a comprehensive interstate system. Social critics, environmentalists, policymakers, and certainly lawmakers were still years, even decades, away from coming to grips with issues of environmental impact of road construction, highway blight, the impact of highway development on inner city neighborhoods, historical preservation, the balance of automobile traffic versus mass transportation. One lone voice was Robert F. Wagner, Jr., mayor of New York City, who asked that tenants in urban areas receive federal assistance to defray the costs of moving when displaced by an interstate highway; few others had even thought of such matters.[71]

Key Individuals in the Interstate Highway Act

Dwight D. Eisenhower (1890–1969) provided the executive leadership, urging Congress to enact the interstate highway legislation. He sparked interest in highway construction through his Grand Plan, outlined before the National Governors' Conference in 1954 and his State of the Union and other speeches. As Eisenhower later recalled, the interstate highway legislation "was one of the things that I felt deeply about, and I made a personal and absolute decision to see that the nation would benefit by it."[72] However, Eisenhower, by his military experience and temperament, was a delegator, who left the details of important issues in the hands of his subordinates, including the plans for an interstate highway system.

George Hyde Fallon (1902–1980), a Democratic congressman (1945–1970) from Maryland, chaired the roads subcommittee of the House Public Works Committee. During the long and bitter fight for freeways in Washington, D.C., Fallon insisted that all freeways could be approved by Congress, despite fierce local opposition, and their construction had to be assured before work could begin on Metro, the underground mass transit system. In 1970 the organizers of Earth Day, the grassroots event that helped launch the modern environmental movement, campaigned against the "dirty dozen" congressmen, those whom they considered to have the worst environmental record. One of those targeted was Fallon, who then was defeated in a Democratic primary by Paul S. Sarbanes. While environmental groups may have considered him an enemy, the highway lobby heaped praise upon him. While giving Fallon an award in 1959, a presenter for the American Road Builders Association said: "If highway people ever had a friend in Congress, it is George H. Fallon, and I believe the 'H' stands for 'highways.'"[73]

Albert A. Gore, Sr. (1907–1998), had served in the House of Representatives for fourteen years before defeating incumbent Senator Kenneth McKellar in 1952. He became chairman of the Roads Subcommittee of the Senate Public Works Committee in 1955. There he opposed the Clay Committee's proposals and crafted the Senate version of the Interstate Highway Act.[74] In 1959, Gore moved to the Foreign Affairs Committee, but he still maintained a strong interest in highway transportation. He sought the Democratic vice-presidential nomination in 1956 but lost out to fellow Tennessee senator Estes Kefauver. Gore, a moderate voice in the South, voted for federal civil rights legislation and opposed the Vietnam War. He was defeated in 1970 by Republican William Brock in a bitter campaign.

Thomas Hale Boggs (1914–1972) was elected to the House of Representatives in 1941, then served in the U.S. Navy during World War II. He returned to Congress in 1946 and by 1956 was in a key position on the Ways and Means Committee. He worked with George Fallon on the interstate highway bill, and, at the suggestion of Treasury Secretary George Humphrey, incorporated the idea of a Highway Trust Fund for the financing of interstate and other federal-aid highway projects.[75] He later became majority leader in the House, but his career was cut short when he died in a plane crash in Alaska, while helping fellow Democrat Nick Begich (Alaska) campaign for re-election.

Francis C. Turner (1909–1999), a highway engineer and senior federal administrator, began his career with the Bureau of Public Roads immediately following his graduation from college in 1929. During the critical negotiations in 1955–1956, Turner served as executive secretary of the Clay Committee, then was the key liaison between the Bureau of Public Roads and the congressional committees that wrote the legislation. By 1969 Turner had moved up the ranks to become administrator of the Federal Highway Administration. In its own history of the federal-aid highway program, that agency dubbed Turner as the "Father" of the interstate highway system and in 1994 *American Heritage* magazine, in its fortieth anniversary issue, cited him as one of the ten people, though completely unknown to the public, who had been "agents of change" during the same period of time.[76]

Aftermath

In just a few years after its enactment, the interstate program came under heavy criticism, particularly for its failure to meet national defense design requirements and for charges of graft and corruption in the awarding of lucrative highway contracts. In the 1950s lawmakers had uncritically accepted the argument that interstate highways were needed for national defense. While supporting interstate highways for other reasons as well, President Eisenhower had urged their construction so that, in the event of atomic attack, cities could be evacuated and troops and supplies transported quickly.[77] However, a 1960 congressional investigation conducted by Representative John A. Blatnik (Democrat–Minnesota) found that the Army, Air Force, Corps of Engineers, and Navy all had weapons systems or other materiel that when placed on trucks or other vehicles exceeded the fourteen-foot minimum clearance for interstate bridges and overpasses. That year, the Department of Defense and the Bureau of Public Roads agreed to a standard sixteen-foot minimum for interstate structure—which made obsolete some 2,200 interstate bridges and over-passes.[78]

In 1957 Congress began hearing complaints of fraud and abuse in highway contracting. A Senate Public Works Committee probe headed by Senator Gore noted that $80,000 in illegal profits were realized by former officials of the Indiana highway department. Later a federal grand jury issued indictments against two men and called former Indiana governor George N. Craig (Republican, 1953–1957), "morally if not legally responsible" for highway irregularities.[79]

A far-reaching, four-year investigation was being conducted in the House of Representatives. In 1966 a subcommittee of the House Public Works Committee, headed by Representative Blatnik, uncovered a wide range of fraudulent or illegal activities, including price-fixing and bid-rigging, collusion, and graft involving land transactions in twenty states. In late 1965 eighteen petroleum products manufacturers and seventeen individuals were fined a total of $2 million for illegal price-fixing activities in Missouri, and thirteen petroleum companies pleaded no contest to price-fixing in Kansas.[80]

Highways Cutting Through Cities

One of the most contentious interstate issues was the running of highway corridors through central cities. Highway officials saw these urban connections as necessary cogs in the completion of a coordinated interstate system; chambers of commerce and urban business interests saw them as vital links to suburbia, which would help revitalize the decaying, core city center. For years this was the dominant decision-making structure, and highway officials, mayors, city councils, and business interests got their way. They became even more enthusiastic knowing that 20 percent of interstate mileage and half of federal funding would be dedicated to urban areas.

New Yorkers got an early taste of urban highways well before the interstate highway system was inaugurated, when in 1945 Robert Moses, the controversial and powerful New York City parks commissioner, planned to build more than 100 miles of superhighways in the heart of the metropolitan area. His biographer Robert A. Caro observed, "Lump together all the superhighways in existence in all the cities on earth in 1945, and their mileage would not add up to as many miles as Robert Moses was planning in 1945 to build in one city."[81]

The controversial Cross-Bronx Expressway, one of thirteen projects, was a seven-mile project that would cross 113 streets, avenues and boulevards, hundreds of sewer, water and utility lines, one subway and three railroads, five elevated rapid transit lines, and seven other expressways or parkways that Moses was building at the same time.[82] This and other New York City projects were immensely difficult, expensive, and, for the most part, popular, except for the neighborhoods and small businesses, usually the city's least powerful, who were displaced to make room for the projects. To the inevitable protests, Moses would reply, "you can't make an omelet without breaking eggs."

This was not what President Eisenhower had in mind when he advocated the interstate system. In fact, he was frustrated and perplexed when he heard of plans to run interstate highways through urban areas. In an April 1960 meeting in the Oval Office with his senior highway advisers, Eisenhower remarked that running the interstate routes through congested parts of the cities was "entirely against his original concept and wishes; he never anticipated that the program would turn out this way." Eisenhower had carefully read the Clay Committee Report, and he was not aware that the interstate program would be used to build up an extensive intra-city route network. He reiterated his disappointment over the way the interstate program had developed against his wishes but had reached the point where his hands were virtually tied. A frustrated Eisenhower called public works projects one of the biggest "grab bags" for federal funds.[83]

Soon more criticism started coming in as federal and state highway planners began surveying urban corridors. The *New York Times* lamented in a 1966 editorial: "As neighborhoods are sliced in two and cemeteries are relocated, neither the quick nor the dead are safe. Every major city from Boston to Los Angeles is festooned, draped—or is it strangled—with ribbons of concrete."[84] Urban studies experts Alan Altshuler and David Luberoff wrote that interstate highways had subjected cities, especially the high-density, older cities to "major surgery, on a scale without precedent in American history."[85]

Neighborhoods, civic organizations, and eventually some city governments fought back. One of the earliest citizen revolts involved Interstate 480, the Embarcadero Freeway, an elevated stretch of highway in San Francisco. The short section of freeway which would cut right through picturesque Fisherman's Wharf was first proposed in 1951 as a route to serve downtown commuters coming across the Golden Gate Bridge from Marin County. It opened in 1959 but was subject to immense opposition, with over 30,000 people signing petitions of protest during its construction the year earlier. That same year, the San Francisco Board of Supervisors voted to cancel seven out of ten proposed freeway routes through the city and halted construction on the uncompleted portions of the Embarcadero Freeway. In 1969 San Francisco Mayor Joseph Allioto declared that no new freeways would be built: "San Francisco, truly one of the majestic cities in the world, is not going to be turned into a wasteland of freeways and garages."[86] Four years later, there were plans for the Embarcadero's demolition. But Nature had the last word: In 1989 the Loma Prieta earthquake severely damaged the Embarcadero Freeway, and for safety reasons it was demolished.

Plans for a series of elevated express highways had been developed for New Orleans in 1946, when the Louisiana Highway Department hired Robert Moses, who was at the height of his power and influence in New York. Nothing came of those plans, but in the 1950s a group of powerful business and civic leaders in the city banded together to plan the Vieux Carre Riverfront

Expressway, an elevated highway, to be designated I-310, that would run along the Mississippi River, abutting Jackson Park and the French Quarter. The business leaders, wanting to revive downtown New Orleans and make it more competitive with Houston and Atlanta, were aided by their powerful ally in Washington, Representative Hale Boggs.

In what was called the "Second Battle of New Orleans," neighborhood and community activists, after a long, difficult, and bitter struggle, delayed the project, made it into a national issue of historic preservation, and gained support during a period of shifting federal priorities. In 1969 the Riverfront Expressway project was cancelled by the newly appointed secretary of transportation, John A. Volpe, because it had not been considered by the Advisory Council on Historic Preservation as required by the National Historic Preservation Act of 1966. Highway backers and critics alike were astounded: John Volpe, a Nixon appointee, former Massachusetts governor and Eisenhower's first federal highway administrator, the only official recommended to head the Department of Transportation by the American Association of State Highway Officials, had withdrawn federal support. However, a less powerful African-American neighborhood coalition was unable to stop the construction of an elevated section of Interstate 10, which destroyed not only an extraordinary stand of old oak trees, but also the long-settled Claiborne Avenue neighborhood.[87]

Memphis, Tennessee, went through a protracted, twenty-four-year-long battle over an extension of Interstate 40, which was to cut through historic Overton Park toward downtown. Nearly a thousand businesses, churches, and homes, mostly of African-American residents, were destroyed, and several miles of the interstate were built, but heated public opposition blocked plans to have the interstate cut through the park. Congress in 1966 enacted the Department of Transportation Act; one of its provisions required that an interstate highway could not go through public parklands unless there was no "feasible or prudent" alternative. Interstate opponents, dubbed by the Memphis press "little old ladies in tennis shoes," won an important victory and ultimately saved the parkland, when the U.S. Supreme Court ruled in *Citizens to Preserve Overton Park* v. *Volpe* (1971)[88] that there indeed was an alternative, a planned beltway around the city, which the secretary of transportation was required to consider.

In May 1966 a long-smoldering freeway battle erupted in Washington, D.C. This fight, in the backyard of Congress and federal highway officials, was particularly bitter. It began with a 1955 proposal to have an eighteen-mile Inner Loop freeway, configured like a figure-eight, six lanes wide sunken below street grade, constructed in nine stages: the design was viewed as the "boldest answer yet conceived for the traffic snarl of Washington," according to reporter Robert C. Albrook of the *Washington Post*.[89] During the mid-1960s there were heated, bitter arguments over proposals for interstate connections in the District of Columbia. In 1965 Congress had authorized a subway system for the greater Washington metropolitan area. Highway proponents in Congress threatened to cut off subway funding unless all of the proposed highway routes were approved. Representative William H. Natcher (Democrat–Kentucky), chairman of the House Appropriations Subcommittee for the District of Columbia, scolded anti-freeway forces. It is "time to stop this foolishness," declared Natcher "I want the members of the Committee to know that I am unable to continue recommending . . . that money appropriated for the rapid transit system if the highway program is to be brought to a complete halt."[90]

The U.S. Court of Appeals had halted highway development, principally on the grounds that the plans were approved without public hearings. But, temporarily, the highway lobby had the last word. Congress passed the 1968 Federal-Aid Highway Act, crafted by Representatives John C. Kluczynski (Democrat–Illinois), chairman, and William C. Cramer (Republican–Florida), ranking minority member, of the House Public Works Subcommittee on Highways. In a section directed squarely at the District of Columbia, the act required completion of all interstate freeways, notwithstanding any court or administrative ruling directing otherwise. It also weakened protection for park lands and wildlife preserves, forbade the president from shifting any funds out of the Highway Trust Fund for other purposes, and, as a further slap against President Johnson, emasculated the highway beautification program, a pet project of Lady Bird Johnson. Reporters Drew Pearson and Jack Anderson, calling the act the "most lobby-dominated bill of this session," listed the leading highway lobbyists: Firestone Rubber Company, the American Road Builders Association, the American Automobile Association, the Asphalt Institute, the National Association of Auto Dealers, and the Portland Cement Association, and the National Association of Motor Bus Owners.[91]

Lyndon Johnson, now in his last six months of office, signed the bill, but in the end it was a hollow victory for pro-highway forces. Much of the interstate system for metropolitan Washington was never built.

Urban Mass Transit Policy

There was no question that federal surface transportation policy was dominated by highway forces. Key to that domination was the Highway Trust Fund which pumped a steady stream of funds exclusively for the interstate system during its first seventeen years. The federal government assumed the lion's share of the expenses, with the states obligated to put up only 10 percent of the cost of highway projects. No such federal funds or generous funding formulas were available for mass transportation. The highway lobby was no match for the weak, ineffective, and just-emerging mass transportation lobby. Further, as professor George M. Smerk has argued, there was limited support for mass transportation in Congress because up until the early 1960s it was considered mainly a problem limited to large cities and not seen as a national issue.[92]

Federal urban mass transit policy began in a small way in 1961 with the federal Housing and Urban Development Act, which offered small, low-interest loans for mass transit systems. At nearly the same time, urban transportation planning received a major boost with the 1962 Federal-Aid Highway Act, which required that any highway project in an urbanized area of 50,000 or more had to have a continuing, comprehensive, and cooperative urban transportation plan as a condition for receiving federal funds. By mid 1965, all 224 urbanized areas that fell within the guidelines of the 1962 legislation had such urban transportation planning under way.[93]

The first legislative effort to concentrate on mass transit was the Urban Mass Transportation Act of 1964, which provided federal capital grants for up to two-thirds of the cost of construction of a mass transportation facility; however, only $150 million was authorized per year, and even less was actually appropriated. An important institutional change was the creation of the Department of Transportation in 1967, which brought the disparate transportation agencies under one roof. The Urban Mass Transportation Administration (later the Federal Transit Administration), originally in the Department of Housing and Urban Development, was transferred in 1968 to Transportation. Now it was on the same organizational chart, though still not as influential and powerful, as the Federal Highway Administration, the successor of the Bureau of Public Roads. Then in 1970 Congress passed the landmark Urban Mass Transportation Assistance Act, authorizing $10 billion over a twelve-year period. Finally there was an infusion of funds for mass transit, but still the amount paled in comparison to the guaranteed funds that came to highway programs.

The Highway Trust Fund was a pot of gold. The highway lobby jealously guarded it but increasingly urban transportation interests along with more and more city and state governments hoped to prise away some of the money for non-highway use. Both presidents Lyndon B. Johnson and Richard M. Nixon tried, unsuccessfully, to impound highway trust fund monies. In 1966 Johnson cut $1.1 billion that Congress had already appropriated but soon reversed himself in face of the squealing and complaining of state transportation officials and legislators. Nixon in 1971 announced in an address to the Detroit Economic Club, ground zero of the automobile industry, that "we cannot be rigid with regard to the Highway Trust Fund."[94] The next year, Nixon impounded $2.5 billion of highway funds. The reaction against him was swift: more than thirty lawsuits were filed against the administration, and most of the time states won their cases, including a U.S. Court of Appeals ruling which held that the administration had illegally withheld Highway Trust Fund money apportioned to the state of Missouri.[95]

Undeterred, Nixon and Transportation Secretary John Volpe worked closely with the Democratic congressional leaders to break the hammerlock that the highway lobby had on the trust fund. The 1973 Federal-Aid Highway Act for the first time authorized use of some highway trust fund money for urban mass transportation and gave the secretary of transportation the authority to withdraw some of the more controversial urban highway plans. Highway and mass transit forces had been at loggerheads during much of the 1960s, and the anti-highway forces were growing in numbers and political strength, so much so that they were a significant factor in blocking passage of a 1972 highway bill. The bargain struck in 1973 was simply smart policy making; let urban transit have a piece of the action and wipe out much of the opposition to continued funding of highways.

Up until this time lawmakers permitted urban transit funds for capital improvements, but they were not prepared to provide much-needed operating subsidies. But many urban systems were in desperate shape, and in response the 1974 National Mass Transportation Assistance Act for the first time allowed federal funds to be used for operating subsidies, nearly $12 billion over a six-year period.

In 1975 President Gerald R. Ford, a former congressman from auto-dependent Michigan who had strongly supported the Highway Trust Fund in the past, proposed legislation that would have severely crippled it. Ford recommended giving the trust fund just one cent of the four-cent federal gasoline tax; two cents would go to the federal treasury and the other cent would go to the states. The highway lobby, along with its new partner, the mass transit lobby, was able to beat back Ford's initiative.[96]

Three years later the Surface Transportation Assistance Act became the first federal law that combined highway, public transportation, and highway safety authorizations into one piece of legislation. Then in 1982, urban mass transit forces got their long-sought "cut" of the Highway Trust Fund monies. The Federal Public Transportation Act, which became Title III of the Surface Transportation Act of 1982, increased the gasoline tax by five cents and dedicated nearly 20 percent of the total revenues generated from the Highway Trust Fund for mass transit. That 20 percent earmark has remained a fixture in federal policy ever since.

ISTEA and the End of the Interstate Highway Program

It was widely assumed that the Surface Transportation and Uniform Relocation Assistance Act of 1987 would be the final chapter in the interstate highway system funding. The act provided $17 billion for completing the interstate highway system, and once its authorization expired in 1991 so too would new funding for the interstate program. But there was one further chapter in the interstate highway system's construction history. In 1991 Congress enacted the most far-reaching and expensive road repair and reconstruction bill to date, the Intermodal Surface Transportation Efficiency Act (ISTEA); upon signing the legislation, President George H. W. Bush called it "the most important transportation bill since President Eisenhower started the interstate system thirty-five years ago."[97] ISTEA was critical for redirecting federal transportation policy: it authorized the FHWA to propose designation of routes for the new National Highway System, consisting of 155,000 miles of interstate, urban and principal rural roads. ISTEA highway grants, which would now have an 80 percent federal matching share, would now go to repair and reconstruct these strategic road systems.

ISTEA, immediately given the moniker "Ice-Tea," authorized over a six-year period a total of $124 billion for highway grants, $36 billion for mass transit, and $2.4 billion for bicycle paths and historic and scenic preservation. Most significantly, it reserved $6 billion to help state governments comply with federal air quality standards. While the great majority of funds were focused on highway rebuilding, funds were spread around so that urban transit, environmental, and historic preservation groups were placated. As Alan Altschuler and David Luberoff noted, "the surface transportation coalition, broadened to include transit advocates during the 1970s and 1980s, now included virtually all of its former critics."[98]

ISTEA earmarked funds for several final projects of the interstate system, including the Central Artery/Tunnel Project, the Big Dig in Boston, surely one of the most difficult, complex, and expensive construction projects ever attempted. The Big Dig completed I-90 in Boston, the longest section of the interstate system, and reconstructed I-93, the old controversial elevated highway, known as the Green Monster, in downtown Boston by putting it under ground. It was extreme engineering, removing centuries of debris, unstable landfill, and old utility lines, supporting the current interstate highway while a new one was built 140 feet below it, and running within inches of existing underground subway systems.[99]

While the Big Dig received much of the media attention, other projects quietly added to the interstate system. Since 1991 another 3,882 miles of new highway had been added, bringing the system to 46,677 miles. More miles are planned for Pennsylvania's I-99 and Wisconsin's I-39; there are also plans for an extended Interstate, I-69, an 1,800-mile-long highway passing through eight states and ten cities, connecting Mexico (at Laredo, Texas) and Canada (at Port Huron, Michigan).[100]

Then in 1998 President Bill Clinton signed the Transportation Equity Act for the 21st Century (TEA-21), a $218 billion measure which greatly increased the funding of highways and protected them with budgetary "firewalls." In addition, TEA-21 boosted public transit and rural transit and provided funds for environmental mitigation projects. The 2005 reauthorization provided another $286.4 billion for highway and other transportation projects. Tucked into its 1,752 pages were 6,371 specific projects, known as "earmarks" or more pejoratively as "pork." In 1982, there were only ten such earmarked highway projects and 1,850 in the 1998 legislation. 'I stuffed it like a turkey," admitted Don Young (Republican–Alaska), the chairman of the House Infrastructure Committee, commenting on the inordinate number of projects going to Alaska.[101]

Key Events in the Making of Highway Systems	
1880s–90s	Good Roads movement.
1921	Federal Highway Act.
1938	Federal-Aid Highway Act, called for study of toll networks, with no more than three east–west and three north–south routes. *Toll Roads and Free Roads* recommended a network of 26,700 miles of free roads.
1944	Federal-Aid Highway Act designated 40,000-mile network, the National System of Interstate Highways. No funds authorized.
1956	Congress approved 41,000 National System of Interstate and Defense Highways, and new Highway Trust Fund.
1967	BPR becomes Federal Highway Administration, part of the new U.S. Department of Transportation.
1969	National Environmental Policy Act and 1966 Department of Transportation Act applied environmental and public park restrictions.
1973	Federal-Aid Highway Act authorized withdrawal of controversial interstate segments and substitution of urban mass transit.
1989	National Transportation Policy (NTP) proposed.
1991	Intermodal Surface Transportation Efficiency Act (ISTEA), a major restructuring of federal-aid highway program.
1992	Interstate highway system, 99.7 percent complete.
1998	Transportation Equity Act for the 21st Century (TEA-21).
2005	Safe, Accountable, Flexible, and Efficient Transportation Equity Act (SAFE-TEA).
2008	Infusion of $8 billion in emergency funds for the Highway Trust Fund.

Transforming Legislation

Traffic and Congestion

Professors John R. Meyer and Jose Gomez-Ibanez have observed that the greatest disappointment with the interstate highway program was that "it did not seem to achieve its major objective of reducing traffic congestion."[102] While much of the interstate system traverses rural landscape and carries relatively light traffic, urban areas increasingly are choked with traffic. The beltways around urban centers, first conceived as routes to circumvent city traffic, are now integral parts of the local commuting patterns and carry heavy loads of both interstate and local automobile, bus, and truck traffic. The Texas Transportation Institute, which annually studies transportation mobility, noted in its 2004 report that traffic congestion was growing across the nation "in cities of all sizes, consuming more hours of the day, and affecting more travelers and shipments of goods than ever before."[103]

The grand plans of highway engineers and architects of an earlier era portrayed urban skyscrapers and superhighways, with very few automobiles, leading into them. The glowing drawings of the late 1930s to 1950s inspired by the International Style of the Swiss-born architect Le Corbusier and the

Futurama display at the 1939 World's Fair show metropolises, with shimmering skyscrapers, interlaced with new highspeed, limited access elevated highways, all of which were nearly devoid of automobiles. None depicted the grimmer urban reality of the late twentieth century: longer and longer peak-hour traffic periods, with vehicles traveling ten, not sixty, miles per hour, bumper against bumper, choking in each other's exhaust fumes. The highway planners and public officials of fifty years ago simply did not anticipate the extraordinary growth of motor vehicle usage.

Economist Anthony Downs in a book appropriately titled *Stuck in Traffic* noted that between 1981 and 1989, total highway miles increased only 0.6 percent while the number of cars and trucks rose by 24.0 percent and total vehicle miles driven went up by 33.6 percent.[104] Downs posited twenty-three policies to help reduce traffic congestion, from supply-side solutions like building more car or van pool lanes (HOV—High Occupancy Vehicle—in federal bureaucratese), and coordinating traffic signals, to demand-side solutions like instituting peak-hour variable tolls, HOT (High Occupancy Toll) lanes, or increasing gasoline taxes.[105] But many of these recommendations face stiff opposition and policymakers have been reluctant to impose unpopular, expensive remedies. However, at the heart of the problem of traffic congestion is the fact that Americans prefer driving to work by themselves from their auto-dependent suburban homes.

Downs's rather cynical but realistic answer: ". . . My advice to American drivers stuck in peak-hour traffic is not merely to get politically involved, but also to learn to enjoy congestion. Get a comfortable, air-conditioned car with a stereo radio, a tape player, a telephone, perhaps a fax machine, and commute with someone who is really attractive. Then regard the moments spent stuck in traffic simply as an addition to leisure time."[106]

The Suburbs and Edge Cities

The brilliant, stubborn, and acerbic automobile manufacturer Henry Ford had his own peculiar solution to urban woes: "We shall solve the city problem by leaving the city."[107] Millions of Americans did just that, especially after World War II, assisted by veterans' loans, and attracted by new suburbs and planned communities like those developed by William and Alfred Levitt. They were lured by lower land and building costs, the attractions of single-family dwellings with grassy yards, and the promise of rapid highway transportation to take them from suburban homes to urban places of work. Soon journalists and social commentators talked of "white flight," "crabgrass frontiers," and "suburban sprawl."

One of the biggest beneficiaries of the interstate highway system, aided by generous tax accelerated depreciation rules, was the suburban shopping mall, with some 22,000 built between the mid-1950s and 1970, with a total of over 43,000 malls by the late 1990s.[108] Other beneficiaries have been businesses with a natural connection to mobility and the automobile such as American icons like McDonald's, Burger King, and the whole fast food restaurant industry, and Holiday Inn and other franchised motels.

Interstate highways also helped foster the next wave of American life and culture, the growth of what journalist Joel Garreau called "Edge Cities."[109] There are over two hundred such cities, like Mahwah, Paramus/Montvale, Amtrak/Metropark, and Woodbridge in New Jersey, or Marina del Rey/ Culver City or Westminster/Huntington Beach in the Los Angeles area. These Edge Cities have five things in common: all have more than five million square feet of office space (larger than downtown Memphis); 600,000 square feet or more of leasable retail space; more jobs than bedrooms; they are perceived by the population to be a regional destination; and finally, were nothing like a city as recently as the 1960s.[110]

A great majority of these Edge Cities straddle the interstate highway system, often the beltway around a major metropolitan city center. Like pearls on a string, the Edge Cities of Westport and Stamford/Greenwich in Connecticut straddle Interstate 95, while Hauppage, Melville, and Great Neck/North Shore straddle Interstate 495 on Long Island; Troy and Auburn Hills straddle Interstate 75 north of Detroit, and more than a hundred other Edge Cities straddle interstate highways throughout the nation.

Robert E. Lang updates and refines our understanding of commercial suburbanization and metropolitan growth by focusing on a new category, which he calls "edgeless cities"—the clusters of office space that have sprung up along interstate highways and other metropolitan thoroughfares. While much attention was given to Garreau's Edge City analysis and the hope of smart growth urban planners, Lang argues that we have to understand the long-standing existence of the more mundane edgeless cities and accept the reality that "sprawl is back—or, more accurately, that it never went away."[111] No metropolitan area is without such edgeless cities, which are characterized as neither mixed-use, pedestrian-friendly, nor easily accessible by public transportation.

Critics

There have been plenty of critics of the automobile, superhighway construction, and the automobile culture in America. Early critics like Lewis Mumford (*The Highway and the City*, 1963) and Jane Jacobs (*The Death and Life of Great American Cities*, 1961) emphasized the negative impact of the automobile on urban spaces. A. Q. Mowbray (*Road to Ruin*, 1969) and Helen Leavitt (*Superhighway—Superhoax*, 1970) focus on the deleterious effect of interstate highway building in metropolitan areas. Dolores Hayden (*Building Suburbia*, 2003) argued that through the Interstate Highway Act, the federal government subsidized affluent citizens, and those who owned cars, rather than helping poorer citizens who had to rely on public transportation. Emma Rothschild (*Paradise Lost: The Decline of the*

Auto-Industrial Age, 1973) argued that the automobile was successful because the political system, from the highway lobby to sympathetic members of Congress and compliant federal agencies, heavily favored highway construction.

Historian James J. Flink (*The Car Culture*, 1975), writing at the height of citizen antagonism over urban highway construction, the energy crisis, and environmental and safety awareness, wrote that the United States was living through the "ending age of automobility." Writing thirteen years later, Flink (*The Automobile Age*, 1988) admitted that, while much progress had been made on automobile safety, energy efficiency, and pollution control, he was still reluctant to reverse his early forecast about the demise of automotive dominance. Architectural critic Jane Holtz Kay (*Asphalt Nation: How the Automobile Took Over America and How We Can Take It Back*, 1997) argued that "we're not just stuck in traffic, we are stuck in spending money that promotes more of the same." She called for citizen activism, from local to national levels, to ease the auto age into a new era that favors walking, bicycling, and relying on public transportation.[112] Deborah Gordon of the Union of Concerned Scientists (*Steering a New Course: Transportation, Energy, and the Environment*, 1991) argued that the urban interstate highways prompted people to move from urban centers, further from their workplace, and failed to integrate other modes of transportation, making comprehensive urban transportation planning that much more difficult.

Despite the sometimes bitter criticism of automobiles, the highway culture, and the planning and execution of the interstate system, there are many who defend the highway program. Proponents of the interstate highway system forcefully state that an America without superhighways would be a far different country. Consultants Wendell Cox and Jean Love, writing for the American Highway Users Alliance, argue that America would be "more risky, less prosperous, and lacking in the efficiency and comfort that Americans now enjoy and take for granted." They note that vacation time would be more restricted, freight charges would be higher, and intercity travel would occur less often and be more cumbersome.[113]

Interstate advocates point out that the highway system is indispensable to America's transportation network: while comprising only 1 percent of its total highways, the interstate system carries 23 percent of the nation's motor vehicle traffic and carries more than sixty times as many person-miles as Amtrak and all other urban rail systems. Using the interstate system, travel times have been cut by at least 20 percent between many cities, and by 1996 it was estimated that 187,000 lives were saved over the forty years of the system's history because of the greater safety of the interstate's limited-access, multiple-lane configurations.

Proponents further argue that the interstate system has had an extraordinary impact on the American economy, with freight costs that have been substantially lowered and the costs of operating tractor-trailer vehicles that have been reduced by an estimated 17 percent on interstate highways in comparison to other highways. The highways have added to Americans' mobility and have boosted the nation's international business competitiveness.[114]

The Interstate Highway Act of 1956 came at the right time in American history.[115] Following World War II, veterans returned home, eager to get back to work or to use their newly won GI Bill or Veterans housing allowances. They wanted to resume a normal life, and they wanted to buy new cars. But road building and improvement simply had not kept pace with the postwar boom in automobile purchases and the new sense of American mobility. The 1939 World's Fair had shown what could be imagined, and states like Pennsylvania, New York, and New Jersey, pioneers in developing limited-access toll roads, demonstrated what could be possible. State and federal highway officials had the skill and technical know-how, and the highway lobby of automobile manufacturers and suppliers, trucking, and petroleum interests all pressed for a new national system of roads.

An interstate highway system was something the motoring public craved. A popular president urged its passage, and a willing Congress quickly perceived this as the mother of all public works bills. The Highway Trust Fund turned out to be the master stroke: highways would be self-financed by a user fee, obligated never to go into the red. Furthermore, in 1956, Congress did not have to concern itself with pesky other voices: environmentalists decrying the destruction of ecologically sensitive areas, historic preservationists alarmed when highways gouged through long-settled communities, or civil rights advocates crying out that the poor, minority homes, and businesses in big cities were the first to appear in the cross hairs of the highway surveyors' telescopes. Those voices would emerge later, and the battles between highway advocates and urban non-highway forces would be fierce and more bitter. Nor did Congress in 1956 have to worry about the advocates of urban mass transportation; their voices were too weak and scattered, not fully heard until a decade later.

The interstate highway program succeeded because political will and popular support favored its construction. At the very core, the interstate highway system succeeded because it served the dominant automobile-mobility culture. America's prosperity depends on the automobile; the automobile depends on cheap and abundant energy sources; and federal government policy reinforces both needs. Gasoline taxes in the United States are among the lowest in the world; so too are taxes on automobile purchases. Federal mass transit policy has been late in coming and has played second fiddle to the highway programs. In the energy crisis of the 1970s, American consumers clamored for smaller vehicles; in the early twenty-first century they favored sport-utility vehicles and pickup trucks. Despite years of inconsistent government prodding, special car pool lanes, rebates on mass transportation, and the like, Americans demand the comfort, convenience, privacy, and safety of driving alone to work and play. We may have to pay the piper in decades to come with increasingly traffic-choked metropolitan areas, continued reliance on expensive and unreliable foreign oil sources for gas-guzzling vehicles, and nagging problems of air pollution and global warming. There is some hope. Presidential candidates have preached about the need for energy independence, consumers have begun to spurn behemoth SUVs, and public transportation has seen some significant increases. But there is much that needs to be done.

Road congestion alone is estimated to cost the U.S. economy $78 billion a year, with 4.2 billion hours in wasted time, and 2.9 billion additional gallons of gasoline.[116] As the deadly I-35W bridge collapse in Minneapolis in 2007 reminds us, we face a continuing, expensive challenge of infrastructure repair and maintenance. But in recent years, gas-tax revenues have plunged and in 2008 funds available for transportation were rapidly drying up. In September 2008, President Bush signed legislation to give the federal Highway Trust Fund an $8 billion emergency infusion, a stopgap effort to tide over the surface transportation program until the law expires the following year. It is clearly evident that the Highway Trust Fund, at its current level of taxing, cannot meet the exploding demands for repair, maintenance, and new construction. The Obama and future administrations and law makers will have the extraordinary task of making painful and expensive decisions.

At the heart of these important policy decisions will be health and continued well-being of the interstate highway system, the crown jewel of America's surface transportation system.

10

JUSTICE, EQUALITY, AND DEMOCRACY'S PROMISE

The Civil Rights Act of 1964 and the Voting Rights Act of 1965

It can be said of the Civil Rights Act of 1964 that, short of a declaration of war, no other act of Congress had a more violent background—a background of confrontation, official violence, injury, and murder that has few parallels in American history.

Robert D. Loevy (1997)

I want you to write me the god-damndest, toughest voting rights act that you can devise.

Lyndon Johnson to Attorney
General Nicholas Katzenbach (1965)

In July 1948, despondent and gloomy delegates to the Democratic Party's presidential nominating convention gathered in Philadelphia. The party was about to break apart; few thought President Harry Truman stood a chance against the Republican candidate, the popular New York governor Thomas E. Dewey, and his even more popular running mate, California governor Earl Warren. Making matters worse, the delegates were stuck in an un-air-conditioned auditorium, in the stifling summer heat, baking under the hot television lights, wiping their brows, cranky, irritated, and dejected.

On the final evening of the convention, one of the party's rising stars, thirty-seven-year old mayor of Minneapolis, Hubert H. Humphrey, approached the podium. Now a candidate for the U.S. Senate, Humphrey was risking his entire political future by insisting that the Democratic Party stand firm for civil rights reform. Truman earlier had presented a strong ten-point civil rights policy, but, once it got to the party's platform committee, its key provisions were compromised. Humphrey and his fellow liberals would not back down: the platform committee had eviscerated Truman's plan and they would not stand for it.

Humphrey, with his nerves frayed and little sleep from the night before, spoke for just eight minutes, but in that time he ignited the delegates, praised Truman for his stand on civil rights, and made that rarest of gestures, a plea for no compromise and a stand on high moral principles.

> Friends, delegates, I do not believe that there can be any compromise of the guarantees of civil rights. . . . There will be no hedging, and there will be no watering down . . . of the instruments and the principles of the civil rights program.
>
> My friends, to those who say that we are rushing this issue of civil rights, I say to them, we are one hundred seventy-two years late!

Then in his most memorable moment, Humphrey soared,

> To those who say that this civil rights program is an infringement on states' rights, I say this, that the time has arrived in America for the Democratic Party to get out of the shadows of states' rights and walk forthrightly into the bright sunshine of human rights.[1]

For the approximately seventy million Americans who heard Humphrey's speech on the radio and the new medium of television, this was an extraordinary moment. U.S. Senate candidate Paul Douglas, sitting as a delegate from Illinois, called the speech "the greatest political oration in the history of the country, with the possible exception of William Jennings Bryan's 'Cross of Gold' speech."[2]

Humphrey's pro-civil rights substitute prevailed in a roll call of the states, a stunning victory for Humphrey personally, for the liberal wing of the Democratic Party, and a humiliating loss for southerners. But the southern delegations would have none of it. Amid the noise and celebration, Eugene (Bull) Connor shouted out that the Alabama delegation was going to walk out; half of them did. Mississippi's entire delegation joined them in protest, waving Confederate battle flags as they left.[3] They were met with a rolling wave of boos from other delegates, along with scattered cheers.

Truman, sitting in the White House, watching Humphrey on television, characterized him and his liberal allies as "crackpots," who were just spoiling to have the southerners bolt from the convention.[4] Now the president would have to make his way to Philadelphia, the convention hall, and a sea of discontent and turmoil. Truman, his family, and his entourage boarded the special presidential train at Union Station in Washington and arrived in Philadelphia around 9:15 p.m. He finally was nominated for president at 12:42 the next morning, receiving 948 votes, while Richard Russell, the senator from Georgia, received 263 votes from those southerners who remained at the convention. At two in the morning, the president finally mounted the podium and, to everyone's surprise, ignited the exhausted, dispirited delegates with a fiery indictment of the Republican-dominated Congress. Republicans professed to be for all kinds of reforms, including civil rights, Truman charged, but they haven't done anything. He called them the "Do-Nothing Congress," and then dropped the bombshell: he was ordering the Eightieth Congress back into session on July 26 to complete its work.[5] Of course, it was pure political hyperbole and theater, but the feisty candidate, with his back to the wall, energized the delegates and blamed the Republicans for all the nation's troubles.

Meantime, the break-away southern delegates were getting ready to strike back. Governor Fielding S. Wright of Mississippi encouraged delegates to meet in Birmingham on Saturday to make a stand for states' rights. Six thousand boisterous convention-goers met in Birmingham that weekend and lustily cheered; South Carolina governor J. Strom Thurmond was unanimously chosen as the presidential candidate of the States Rights Democrats, as they called themselves, and Wright balanced out the ticket as his running mate.[6]

States Rights Democrats was the official name, but a newspaper reporter gave them the name that stuck, the Dixiecrats. Thurmond charged that federal anti-lynching legislation was simply "bait for minority votes and to arouse prejudice and to influence public opinion." If Truman got his way with his desegregation ideas, Thurmond charged, "lawlessness will be rampant. Chaos will prevail. Our streets will be unsafe" and there would be a "virtual revolution" in the southern states. As for the integration of the races, Thurmond was adamant: "All the laws of Washington and all the bayonets of the Army cannot force the Negro into our homes, our schools, and our churches."[7]

In November, Truman surprised nearly every one, defeating Dewey, carrying twenty-eight states, receiving 308 electoral votes, and 49.6 percent of the vote. Thurmond carried only the Deep South of Mississippi, Louisiana, Alabama, and South Carolina. Yet while Arkansas, Texas, Georgia, Florida, Virginia, and Tennessee remained loyal to the national Democratic Party, deep fissures were growing between southern and national Democrats. At the core of it all were the vexing, contentious issues of race, civil rights, and the role of the federal government.

Humphrey would win the 1948 Senate seat, but found in his first years in Washington that his celebrated stand on civil rights was something of a "political albatross" around his neck. Because of the southern domination of Congress, Humphrey observed that "the odor of magnolia was much stronger in Washington than it was in Montgomery or Richmond."[8]

Background

From the vantage point of the early twenty-first century, it is perhaps difficult to comprehend the depth and pervasiveness of racial discrimination in America during most of its years. In the land of equal opportunity where all men are created equal, the discrimination was widespread, knowing no geographic bounds, sometimes blatant, at times subtle, legal and extra-legal, enforced by law, custom, and community will. Over the decades, ethnic and racial discrimination affected many, including Native Americans, the Irish, eastern European immigrants, Asians, Hispanics and others. This chapter, however, focuses on the most pernicious form of discrimination, the laws and actions meted out against African-Americans in the South. It was the legacy of slavery and subjugation, rigid social hierarchy, regional values and mores, reinforced by the law and the whip. This is also a study of how southern lawmakers, acting on behalf of the majority of white constituents, fought tooth and nail to prevent federal law from righting these wrongs and how non-southern lawmakers, Democrats and Republicans alike, finally banded together to enact federal protections and to eliminate, once and for all, some of the most grievous state segregation laws and practices.

After the Civil War, the federal government enacted comprehensive civil rights protections, only to have those laws negated by court rulings, the re-emergence of the southern white power structure, and the loss of national political will. In 1870, the Constitution enfranchised African-American men and their numbers swelled on voting lists. Yet, by the end of the nineteenth century, southern state legislatures had created barriers and hurdles specifically aimed at stripping African-Americans of their right to vote. Jim Crow laws[9] were widespread and, in 1896, the U.S. Supreme Court validated the legal fiction of "separate but equal," giving state and local governments permission to continue segregating public conveyances and public schools, providing, of course, that they were "equal" (which they hardly ever were).

The domination of whites over blacks was comprehensive and pervasive.[10] First was economic domination. African-Americans were consigned to non-skilled, low-paying, menial, and often dangerous or dirty jobs: cooks, maids, janitors, non-union machine operators, or common laborers. "Help wanted" ads in newspapers typically were in columns "Jobs for Whites" and "Jobs for Coloreds." In a typical southern city, 50 percent of all African-American women in the workforce were domestic workers, while less than 1 percent of white women were so employed. In the rural South, with many African-Americans relying on farming, sharecropping beame a pervasive form of economic exploitation that tied African-Americans to the land.

The second form of domination was political oppression, through intim-idation, barriers to voting and political participation, poll taxes, and the domination of a white power structure. The pillars of democratic life—the fundamental right to speak out, to vote freely for candidates of one's choice, to do so without fear of physical reprisal or losing one's livelihood—all these were denied to or severely limited African-Americans.

The third form of domination was the denial of personal freedoms and dignity. There was an intimacy between blacks and whites: blacks cooking meals for white employers, changing their diapers and bed pans, caring for their children, tending to their needs. But this was not an intimacy of equals. In the public sphere, African-Americans were denied access to white-only hotels, restaurants, drinking fountains, and swimming pools. They were separated by race on railroads and buses. Prohibitions were explicit by the posting of signs that said "colored only"; more commonly, however, no signage was needed for African-Americans to understand that they were not welcome and their presence would not be tolerated. Jim Crow laws popped up everywhere. Black and white babies were born in separate hospitals, black and white children were taught in separate schools, black and white adults were segregated in all manner of public places, and black and white old folks were buried in separate cemeteries. Sometimes the laws bordered on the absurd: Alabama forbade African Americans from playing checkers with whites; Mississippi insisted on separate taxicabs; New Orleans segregated its prostitutes; Florida and North Carolina made sure that no textbook touched by an African-American would later be used by a white child.[11]

Some gains were made by African-Americans in the 1930s and 1940s, but they mostly came from the federal court system, not the Congress or the executive branch. World War II, probably more than anything else, opened up economic prospects for African-Americans. Halting steps were taken during the Roosevelt administration to include blacks in federal employment and the armed services.[12] Perhaps more important was the growing understanding by many white citizens that overt, blatant racial discrimination did not square with the ideals of democracy. In a series of legal challenges beginning in 1933, some of which culminated in Supreme Court decisions, the National Association for the Advancement of Colored People (NAACP) attacked racial segregation on higher education. Then the focus shifted to public school education and five consolidated cases that culminated in the 1954 and 1955 Supreme Court decisions of *Brown* v. *Board of Education*.[13]

The federal government began to take civil rights concerns seriously during the Truman administration, lead by the president himself. Truman, a son of Missouri, held fairly conventional border-state views about race relations, but he also could count votes and knew that his political fortunes depended on northern black support. Truman was worried that African-American voters might be drifting back to the Republican Party and worried about growing racial tension, increased Ku Klux Klan activity, and heightened racial violence during and following World War II. In December 1946, he appointed a distinguished panel of citizens to look into the growing racial divide in the United States.

On June 29, 1947, Truman made an extraordinarily blunt speech at the annual meeting of the NAACP, speaking in front of the Lincoln Memorial to a crowd of ten thousand and before a worldwide radio audience: "We must make the federal government a friendly, vigilant defender of the rights and equalities of all Americans. And again I mean all Americans." Turning to NAACP president Walter White, Truman concluded "We cannot wait another decade or another generation to remedy these evils. We must work, as never before, to cure them now."[14]

The civil rights panel report, a book-length study entitled *To Secure These Rights*, was released in October 1947. The recommendations were blunt, comprehensive, and, to many, startling: end poll taxes, create federal legislation against local police brutality, legislation to make lynching a federal crime, protection against racial discrimination in federal elections, home rule for the District of Columbia, and the elimination of racial segregation. The recommendations probably went beyond what Truman had anticipated; nevertheless, he endorsed them.[15]

Truman's standing with southern whites was becoming increasingly uncertain. The president wanted, indeed needed, the political support of the South, but he refused to back away on civil rights reform. He even refused to appear before segregated audiences in the South.[16]

In his 1948 State of the Union address, Truman outlined five "great goals" for the United States, the first being the securing of essential human rights. One month later, he expanded on that theme. In a special message to Congress on civil rights, Truman forthrightly stated that the protection of civil rights was "the duty of every government," not just the national government, but state and local governments as well. He charged Congress to enact "modern, comprehensive civil rights laws," many of which were outlined in the recommendations of the civil rights panel.[17]

Southerners were not pleased. Pollster George Gallup found that white southerners were "overwhelmingly opposed" to Truman's civil rights program; southern politicians reacted with equal ire. Senator Harry F. Byrd (Democrat–Virginia) compared Truman's actions with those of Hitler and Stalin, charging that the president's civil rights proposals "could very conceivably lead to dictatorship." Democratic leaders throughout the South, including some of Truman's close friends, began seriously thinking about rejecting him as their presidential nominee.[18] The party split, but Truman, in the end prevailed.

Brown and Its Impact

One of the most vexing civil rights issues was the segregation of public schools. Throughout the South and the border states, together with Indiana, Illinois, and Kansas, legalized segregation of the races was required in public elementary and secondary schools. Eighteen states in all required segregations and another six permitted local school board discretion.[19] The legal and constitutional basis for this separation rested on the 1896 decision of *Plessy* v. *Ferguson*, and its sanctioning of "separate but equal" facilities. The NAACP's deliberate and careful legal assault on separate education bore fruit in its first significant victories when the U.S. Supreme Court overturned Oklahoma and Texas practices of denying legal and general graduate education to African-Americans at the states' "white" law and graduate schools.[20]

The bigger challenge, of course, was public school education segregation, and that is where the NAACP turned to, gathering together five cases, from Delaware, Virginia, South Carolina, Kansas, and the District of Columbia. In all, there were over 200 plaintiffs seeking relief from racial segregation in their public schools. The cases had come before the Supreme Court in 1952, but now the court wanted them retried, giving special attention to the question of whether the Fourteenth Amendment banned racial segregation in public schools. One of the most famous Supreme Court litigants, John W. Davis, together with a battery of lawyers, argued on behalf of the states; while

Thurgood Marshall of the NAACP Legal Defense and Education Fund and his team argued on behalf of the school children.

On May 17, 1954, the U.S. Supreme Court handed down one of the most important decisions in its history. In *Brown et al.* v. *Board of Education of Topeka et al.*,[21] the Court, under Chief Justice Earl Warren, unanimously ruled that the doctrine of separate but equal had no place in public education. "We cannot turn the clock back to 1868," when the Fourteenth Amendment was first ratified, said Warren, as he read from the eleven-page decision, nor could the Court go back to 1896 when it crafted the "separate but equal" doctrine. The Court looked beyond the questions of congressional intent and focused instead on the sociological impact of segregation. It was harmful to Negro students, and it "generates a feeling of inferiority as to their status in the community that may affect their hearts and minds in a way unlikely ever to be undone." The reliance on social science quickly became a sore point for critics of the decision. Constitutional historian Alpheus T. Mason, for example, curtly remarked, that "instead of relying on solid legal arguments, Chief Justice Warren had based his opinion on the quicksand of social psychology."[22]

Nevertheless, the Court had ruled and thus came to an end the legal basis for maintaining racially separated public schools throughout the country. In a short companion case, the Court decided that the federal government could not maintain separate schools in the District of Columbia.[23] Many black leaders were joyful, optimistic, and eager to begin the historic process of dismantling segregated public education. Others were cautious, skeptical of any progress in this thorny area of life, and well aware that many white southerners weren't going to concede without a fight.

The Court did not set a timetable for implementation of its ruling. Rather it set aside time in the fall term for the attorneys general from the southern states and others to present re-argument. The Court was taking the highly unusual move of delaying for a full year the implementation of the children's right to education in non-segregated schools. But it was also giving the country some breathing room. By waiting a year for the implementation decision, the Court surely was hoping to avoid social turmoil in the South. On the last day in May, 1955, the Supreme Court ruled on implementation in *Brown II*: the cases would be sent back to the federal courts, which would enter the appropriate decrees to desegregate, and do so "with all deliberate speed." No timetables, no specific direction, rather the "curiously contradictory" phrase asking for both speed and deliberation. Historian James T. Patterson observed, "there is probably no Supreme Court language so hotly disputed as 'all deliberate speed.'"[24]

The decade of the 1950s was a period of increased visibility, friction, and turmoil in race relations. In 1955, the nation was shocked by the murder of fourteen-year-old Emmet Till, a black teenager from Chicago, who went to Tallahatchie County, Mississippi, to visit relatives and was killed by white vigilantes. On December 1, 1955, a seamstress named Rosa Parks refused to give her seat up to a white person on a city bus, was arrested, and helped to spark a 382-day boycott in Montgomery, Alabama, led by Martin Luther King, Jr., that gathered world-wide attention.

And now came the battle over school desegregation. The *Brown* decisions led to southern backlash and defiance. Many southerners blamed Eisenhower for appointing Earl Warren as chief justice. State governors and other politicians in the South loudly brayed their defiance of *Brown*. Senator Byrd of Virginia called for "massive resistance" to the Supreme Court decisions. Southern legislators dusted off the doctrine of "interposition," first used in 1798 against the Alien and Sedition Acts, but dormant since then, declaring *Brown* "null and void" and "of no effect" in their states.[25] In the spring of 1956, a "Southern Manifesto" was signed by seventy-seven (out of 105) congressmen and nineteen (out of twenty-two) senators from the Old Confederacy. Among other things, this "Declaration of Constitutional Principles" charged that the Warren court had no "legal basis for its action," and that overturning the separate-but-equal doctrine was a "clear abuse of judicial power," by justices who had "substituted their personal and social ideas for the law of the land." They pledged to employ "all lawful means" to reverse this decision which was "contrary to the Constitution."[26]

A 1956 federal court order required the University of Alabama to admit graduate student Autherine Lucy; another order required the desegregation of a public high school in Mansfield, Texas. Those judicial orders were defied; and President Eisenhower did nothing.[27]

Then, in 1957, Arkansas governor Orval E. Faubus, looking to gain support for a third term in office and not shy about whipping up racial animosity, proclaimed that desegregation of Little Rock's all-white Central High School would certainly lead to violence. Against the wishes of city officials, Faubus called out the Arkansas National Guard to prevent violence, block the desegregation order and defy federal orders. When a federal judge intervened, Faubus withdrew the guardsmen, leaving the school children under the care of local police, who were no help to them.

"Keep away from our school, you burr head," one of the white protesters shouted at fifteen-year-old Terrence Roberts. The boy later admitted to a reporter that he was scared, but said, "I think the students would like me okay once I got in and they got to know me." But the growing crowds of whites were in no mood for tolerance and understanding. Some spit on the black students, pushed them around, swore racial epithets. A white woman, Grace Lorch, tried to comfort one of the black children. "Nigger lover!" came the cry. "Why don't you calm down," Mrs. Lorch said. "I'm not here to fight with you. Six months from now you'll be ashamed at what you're doing."

After nearly three weeks of tense standoff, President Eisenhower was forced to send in U.S. Army troops, bayonets at the ready, and federalized Arkansas guardsmen. In announcing his action to the Nation, Eisenhower declared that "under the leadership of demagogic extremists, disorderly mobs have deliberately prevented the carrying out of proper orders from a federal court." Eisenhower, ever the moderate on issues of race, had been forced to act, and became the first president since Reconstruction to use armed forces to protect African-Americans in pursuit of their constitutional rights. With a force of 1,000 soldiers as their protectors, the nine black school children were finally admitted to Central High. But administrative delays, the shutting down of all four Little Rock high schools, protests and foot-dragging meant that the desegregation in the autumn of 1957 was but a hollow victory.[28]

That same year, 1957, Eisenhower urged caution to those assembled at the black National Newspaper Publishers' Association: "No one is more anxious than I am to see Negroes receive first-class citizenship in this country . . . but you must be patient." The NAACP's Roy Wilkins, looking at the slow progress during the Eisenhower years, observed: "President Eisenhower was a fine general and a good, decent man, but if he had fought World War II the way he fought for civil rights, we would all be speaking German today."[29]

White Citizens Councils, the somewhat more respectable cousins of the Ku Klux Klan, began sprouting up in the Deep South, vowing to protect the white race against forced integration. Mississippi went even further. The state legislature in May 1956 created the Mississippi State Sovereignty Commission, an executive agency which became that state's segregation watchdog. In its heyday in the early 1960s, it sent over 100 volunteer speakers and distributed 200,000 pamphlets to other parts of the country touting the rosy race relations in Mississippi and warning other states of the dangers of federal encroachment. More ominously, the Sovereignty Commission, chaired by the governor, also acted as a mini-KGB, employing informants, enemies lists, and surveillance to root out the activities of the NAACP and other civil rights groups.[30]

The protests, the angry white mobs, the boycotts, and the simple justice asked of black citizens—all this was making an indelible impression on the national consciousness. The Supreme Court had boldly declared segregation unconstitutional; the federal courts tried to enforce the law. Eyes now turned to Washington, to the Congress, which had not passed a single piece of civil rights legislation since Reconstruction and its aftermath.

The Southern Domination of Congress

When the Democratic Party regained control during the Eighty-Fourth Congress (1955–1956), William S. White, the Washington bureau chief of the *New York Times*, observed that "the southern Democrat . . . has returned to a place of unsurpassed power in the life of the United States. He bestrides the new Democratic Congress as so often, minority man though he is in his party, he bestrode Democratic Congresses of the past." This southern Democrat could not win a presidential contest, White noted, nor could he win Congress, but "when the dust and the smoke have cleared away, who is sitting at the top of Congress? The southern Democrat."[31] In the mid-1950s, southern Democrats constituted the most important part of the national Democratic Party, with sixteen southern and border states providing more Democrats than all other regions of the country combined. In 1956, for example, there were 235 Democrats in the House, and 134 of them were southerners.[32]

Throughout the 1940s and 1950s, southerners were able to keep civil rights legislation bottled up. In the deliberations, strategy and tactics of civil rights policymaking, four southerners mattered the most. *Richard B. Russell*, Jr., the senior senator from Georgia, who had been first elected to the Senate in 1932, led the southern forces in the Senate against civil rights legislation during the 1950s and 1960s. He was co-author of the Southern Manifesto, the "declaration of constitutional principles" signed by nearly all of the southern law makers protesting *Brown* and the threat of federal civil rights legislation. Russell became the principal strategist in the months-long filibuster against the 1964 Civil Rights Act. Clarence Mitchell, the director of the Washington office of the NAACP, unhesitatingly called Russell the ablest and most effective opponent of civil rights legislation.[33]

James O. Eastland, senior senator from Mississippi, began his senate career in 1943 and served until 1978. In 1955, when Democrats regained the majority in the Senate, the new majority leader, Lyndon B. Johnson, was instrumental in getting Eastland appointed chairman of the powerful Judiciary Committee, the committee of jurisdiction over civil rights legislation. Another signer of the Southern Manifesto, Eastland did not hide his contempt for African-Americans. Speaking in reaction to the Supreme Court decision in *Brown (I)*, Eastland delivered on the floor of the Senate this apologia for the southern way of life:

> Segregation is not discrimination. Segregation is not a badge of racial inferiority, and that it is not is recognized by both races in the southern states. In fact, segregation is desired and supported by the vast majority of the members of both races in the South, who dwell side by side under harmonious conditions.[34]

In the House of Representatives, one southerner stood out because of his crucial position as chairman of the Rules Committee. *Howard W. Smith* of Virginia, first elected to Congress in 1931, assumed the chairmanship of the Rules Committee in 1955. He played a vital role in blocking and delaying civil rights legislation by bottling it up in his all-important committee. From the floor of the House of Representatives, he castigated the 1964 civil rights legislation: "Already the second invasion of carpetbaggers and the Southland has begun. Hordes of beatniks, misfits, and agitators from the North with the admitted aid of the Communists, are streaming into the Southland on mischief bent, backed and defended by other hordes of federal marshals, federal agents, and federal power."[35]

Lyndon B. Johnson was first elected to the Senate in 1948 and in 1955 became the youngest majority leader in history. Ambitious and cunning, Johnson forged alliances both with his natural southern brethren and with liberal leaders like Humphrey and Paul Douglas. With his presidential ambitions, Johnson knew that no southerner could win the White House by adamantly sticking to civil rights resistance. He used all his persuasive skills to broker the watered-down 1957 and 1960 civil rights acts. As president, as we shall see, he was the driving force behind the two landmark pieces of legislation.[36]

In the legislative fights in Congress during the late 1940s, 1950s, and up through the early 1960s, the southern wing of the Democratic Party could count on several institutional and political weapons at its disposal: seniority, deference to committees, the conservative southern Democratic-conservative Midwest Republican coalition, and above all, the filibuster in the Senate. Following its long-standing tradition, Congress honored the seniority system, giving the most senior member of a committee the chairmanship; those chairs were disproportionately filled by southerners.[37] In the one-party South, Democrats were elected to Congress young and stayed in office for decades, inevitably rising to leadership positions.

In the Senate there was the filibuster, "the most effective parliamentary delaying tactic a legislative minority ever had," wrote Richard W. Bolling (Democrat–Missouri), a long-time liberal and advocate for congressional reform.[38] Southern Democrats would threaten to talk a bill to death with around-the-clock filibustering if necessary. The majority could attempt to invoke cloture and halt the filibuster, but it took an extraordinary two-thirds vote to do so.[39] It was a tough hurdle to overcome. J. Strom Thurmond, elected by an unprecedented write-in vote to the Senate in 1954, held the record for the longest individual filibuster on civil rights issues. During the deliberation of the 1957 civil rights bill, Thurmond spoke for twenty-four hours and eighteen minutes.[40] If the entire southern delegation worked together, coordinating the filibuster, it would be nearly impossible to stop.

In May 1956, Eisenhower's attorney general Herbert Brownell, Jr., and the Justice Department crafted a four-part civil rights bill for Congress to consider.[41] If passed, it would have become the first federal civil rights legislation since the late nineteenth century. It created a U.S. Commission on Civil Rights, gave more authority to a Civil Rights Division of the Justice Department, and increased the Justice Department's power to seek injunctions to protect the right to vote. The most controversial section permitted certain violations of the law to be tried in a court without the benefit of a jury trial. Liberals were in favor of this provision, arguing that southern white juries would be very reluctant to convict a white person accused of violating a federal civil rights law. But in the end, jury trials were included in the Act. In the end, southerners rightly concluded that the proposed legislation had little teeth and presented little threat to them.[42] Thus, the 1957 Civil Rights Act, with little other than symbolic meaning, was signed into law.

In 1959, Congress considered civil rights legislation in both houses, only to have the bills stopped cold. The chairman of the House Judiciary Committee, stalwart New Deal liberal Emmanuel Celler (Democrat–New York), reported a bill out of his committee, but then it was blocked in Howard Smith's Rules

Committee. The Senate version of the civil rights bill went nowhere once it got into the jurisdiction of the Judiciary Committee, headed by Eastland.

In 1960, Senate Majority Leader Lyndon Johnson had southerners crying "foul" when he tacked civil rights legislation onto a bill dealing with the leasing of Army land to a school in Missouri. Johnson did this so that he could avoid sending civil rights legislation to Eastland's committee, where it was sure to die. The Senate had no rule requiring that an amendment be germane; and certainly this civil rights amendment was not. Southern senators struck back by filibustering the bill on the floor, and proponents could not muster up enough support to invoke cloture.[43]

On the House side, civil rights legislation was frozen in the Rules Committee, and northern Democratic leaders were determined to wrest it away from Smith. They could do so by having a majority of House members, 218, sign a discharge petition. In January 1960, 145 Democrats and just 30 Republicans had signed the petition. Soon the list of petitioners was published in the *New York Times*, and some Republicans, embarrassed that so few in their party had affixed their names, clamored to sign on. The Republican leader in the House, Charles A. Halleck (Indiana), did not want northern Democrats to get all the credit for advancing civil rights, and encouraged his colleagues to sign the petition. Howard Smith, seeing this momentum and not wanting to lose control of the legislation, finally decided to hold hearings.[44]

Eventually, civil rights legislation was passed in both the House and the Senate, and President Eisenhower signed the Civil Rights Act of 1960 into law. But it was legislation watered down with significant compromises. At the signing ceremony, Eisenhower hailed the legislation as "an historic step forward in the field of civil rights"; however, NAACP lawyer Thurgood Marshall, like many others, complained that the law was "not worth the paper it's written on."[45]

The Kennedy Years

In November 1960, Senator John F. Kennedy defeated Vice-President Richard M. Nixon in the closest of presidential contests. Martin Luther King, Jr., was not particularly impressed with Kennedy's Senate record on civil rights and had little enthusiasm for his presidential bid. King's opinion changed somewhat after the two had a private breakfast, and Kennedy assured King that he, as president, would be a civil rights leader.[46] But King, James Forman of the Student Nonviolent Coordinating Committee (SNCC), Bayard Rustin of the Congress of Racial Equality (CORE), and other black leaders remained skeptical. During Kennedy's first six months in office, he had sent no civil rights legislation to Congress nor had he signed an executive order desegregating federally financed housing as he had promised during the campaign.[47]

With the election of 1960, Democrats not only won the presidency but also enjoyed an eighty-nine seat margin (262–173) in the House of Representatives. But this number was deceiving. Of those Democrats, 101 were from the South.

What had not changed was the southern hold on key committees, particularly the Rules Committee, chaired by Howard Smith. Often characterized as the "traffic cop" of the House, the Rules Committee could block, delay, and even kill legislation that had come from a committee of jurisdiction before it went to the House floor. For civil rights legislation, the committee of jurisdiction was the Judiciary Committee, headed by Celler.[48]

At the beginning of 1960, the Rules Committee had twelve members, with two southern Democrats, Smith and William M. Colmer (Democrat–Mississippi), often joining the four Republicans to effectively block progressive legislation.[49] Speaker Sam Rayburn (Democrat–Texas) and the Democratic leadership were determined to break the conservative stranglehold on the Rules Committee; he even threatened to purge Colmer from the committee. Then the House, in a bruising, bitter skirmish, voted to temporarily enlarge the committee from twelve to fifteen members for the new Eighty-Seventh Congress (1961–1962).[50] Two years later, the expansion was made permanent.

During the early 1960s, student activists and others continued the lunch counter sit-in demonstrations that began in Greensboro, North Carolina, and then spread to other forms of nonviolent protest. The reactions of many southern whites to such demonstrations, however, were anything but nonviolent. In 1960, the Supreme Court ruled that segregation within interstate travel was illegal, including segregation in bus terminals, waiting rooms, restrooms and restaurants. Student activists in the spring of 1961 tested that ruling by riding in two buses from Washington, D.C., deep into the South. They were called the Freedom Riders. While they were stopped and arrested in Virginia, the students did not meet up with violence until they disembarked at Rock Hill, South Carolina. John Lewis and another rider were severely beaten and arrested when they used a whites-only restroom. When they arrived in Anniston, Alabama, the bus driver stopped and yelled to the waiting, angry mob, "well, boys, here they are. I brought you some niggers and nigger-lovers." Local officials gave the Ku Klux Klan permission to deal with the students. One bus was firebombed, and the students were beaten by the mob. In Birmingham, police commissioner Bull Connor offered no protection. A second group of freedom riders, arriving from Nashville, were arrested by Connor; the riders had no protection and were severely beaten. Finally, the Kennedy administration announced that the Interstate Commerce Commission would ban segregation in all interstate facilities; still, the rides continued, and jails, particularly in Mississippi, filled with protesters.[51]

Moments after John F. Kennedy was sworn into office on January 20, 1961, a young black man, James Meredith, inspired by the new president, decided to enroll at the all-white University of Mississippi. Once they found out that he was black, university officials set about a strategy of "delay, diversion, and duplicity" to postpone Meredith's admission for another twenty months. There were federal and state court orders, two trials, a ruling by the U.S. Supreme Court, and finally federal marshals and 16,000 federal troops sent to maintain order. Governor Ross Barnett, defiant to the end, told a state-wide television audience, "No school will be integrated in Mississippi while I am governor." Barnett saw federal enforcement as the "greatest crisis since the War between the States. . . . We must either submit to the unlawful dictates of the federal government or stand up like men and tell them *NEVER!* We will not drink from the cup of genocide." Meredith was ultimately enrolled, but blood flowed, and lives were lost. In the rioting instigated by white protestors, two men were killed, 160 marshals and 40 soldiers were injured, and 200 individuals were arrested.[52]

The year 1963 brought several dramatic and tragic events to the nation's conscience. In May, Birmingham, Alabama, burst into conflict, with Bull Connor's police using fire hoses, electric cattle prods, and police dogs to intimidate African-American protestors who were demanding that public facilities be opened. Over 700 African-Americans, including many children, were arrested, forcing Kennedy to send in 3,000 troops to Birmingham to keep the peace. Throughout the South during the next ten weeks, in seventy-five cities, there were some 758 demonstrations, with 13,786 arrests.[53]

On a hot, sticky June 11, Alabama governor George C. Wallace stood before the entrance to Foster Auditorium, where University of Alabama students were to be officially registered for classes. At stake was the registration of two black students, Vivian Malone and James Hood. Wallace was determined to prevent their registration, and Nicholas Katzenbach, U.S. assistant attorney general, was equally determined to ensure their right to enter the public university. Wallace and Katzenbach nervously eyed each other, each reading from their prepared notes, and following a tentatively choreographed script. In the end, the Alabama National Guard was federalized, Wallace backed down, and the two black students were admitted. Wallace, with the last word, put his best spin on the episode: "Alabama is winning this fight against federal interference because we are awakening the people to the trend toward military dictatorship in this country."[54]

Buoyed by the news from Tuscaloosa, Kennedy was determined to give a nationwide speech that evening. Hastily prepared, with no rehearsal, the president informed the nation that he would soon deliver a major civil rights bill to Congress. Kennedy told the television audience that the nation was confronted by a "moral issue" that was "as old as the scriptures and is as clear as the American Constitution."[55]

It was time for Congress to act, Kennedy urged.

Making the Law: The Civil Rights Act of 1964

Kennedy's civil rights legislation was sent to Congress on June 19, 1963. The legislation was long-anticipated, and was accompanied by a 5,500-word message, in which the president urged Congress to "join with the executive and judicial branches in making it clear to all that race has no place in American life or law."[56]

Its prospects for passage, however, were not good and would require an all-out lobbying effort.[57] At the heart of the president's proposal was the controversial Title II, prohibiting racial discrimination in public accommodations: in restaurants, hotels, amusement parks, movie theaters, and retail establishments in interstate commerce. His bill also would strengthen the attorney general's authority to start school desegregation suits when requested to do so by someone unable to sue, and other provisions.

Predictably, southern lawmakers rushed to the microphone to condemn Kennedy's proposal. Strom Thurmond said it reminded him of the terrible days of Reconstruction, castigating the president's bill as "unconstitutional, unnecessary, unwise and beyond the realm of reason." James Eastland saw this as a "complete blueprint for the totalitarian state. . . . [E]very hamburger stand, every barber shop, every beauty parlor, every rooming house up to every bank and insurance company in America" would come under federal control. John C. Stennis (Democrat–Mississippi) feared that the attorney general would trample over the rights of white people: "Bobby Kennedy could ultimately have federal marshals and troops at every crossroads" and could "become the private attorney general of every member of the NAACP, CORE, and other pressure groups and agitators."[58]

The very night that Kennedy addressed the nation, Medgar Evers, a long-time local Mississippi official of the NAACP, was gunned down in his driveway as he was about to enter his home. His murderer, fertilizer salesman Byron de la Beckwith, later told a group of fellow Klansmen that "killing that nigger gave me no more inner discomfort than our wives endure when they give birth to our children. We ask them to do that for us. We should do just as much."[59] Two all-white all-male jury trials ended in mistrial in 1964 (thirty years later, in 1994, de la Beckwith was found guilty of murder, and, in 2001, died in prison).

On that same day, Martin Luther King, Jr., announced that there would be a massive march on Washington. On August 28, over 200,000, by conservative official estimates, gathered before the Lincoln Memorial, participating in the March on Washington. It was televised worldwide on the new Telsat satellite system. Kennedy had tried to dissuade civil rights leaders from coming to Washington for this mass gathering, but, as it gathered momentum, he came out in support. This was A. Philip Randolph's defining event. In 1941, Randolph, the president of the Brotherhood of Sleeping Car Porters, had planned a march on Washington, and now it was coming to fruition. John Lewis, representing SNCC, about to give a strong, controversial speech, in the end acceded to Randolph's plea to tone it down. The final speaker was Martin Luther King, Jr., who gave his iconic "I have a Dream" speech. Journalist Murray Kempton described it as "the largest religious pilgrimage of Americans that any of us is ever likely to see."[60]

Kennedy was in a difficult position. King and other black leaders publicly were chiding him for being too timid; liberal Democrats were clamoring for tough, punitive measures; and southern Democrats, already vehemently opposed to him on civil rights threatened to take out their anger on other pending administration-backed legislation. Kennedy and his backers in Congress had to cobble together a coalition of northern Democrats and moderate Republicans to come up with strong but, inevitably, compromised language.

One of the sticking points for many Republicans was the fact that Title II, the public accommodations section, was based on the commerce clause of the Constitution rather than the ostensibly more compelling Fourteenth Amendment equal protection clause. The administration reasoned that racially segregated public accommodations impeded the free flow of interstate commerce. Republicans saw this argument as specious and open-ended: did that really mean, like Eastland said, that every local barber shop and every hamburger stand would come under federal jurisdiction? Republicans also would have preferred using the Fourteenth Amendment; after all, they could point with pride that it was the Republican-controlled Civil War Congress that crafted its protections.

The decision to anchor the anti-discrimination measures in the commerce clause, in the end, may have been rooted in the politics of the Senate. By basing the authority on the commerce clause, the civil rights bill would be routed to the Senate Commerce Committee, chaired by Warren Magnuson (Democrat–Washington), a friend of the administration. But if the bill were based on the Fourteenth Amendment, it would have to begin its journey in the Senate Judiciary Committee, headed by the implacable Eastland.[61]

The Senate, no matter the committee of first jurisdiction, would be the thorniest problem, particularly with the threat of a southern filibuster. The administration decided to approach the House of Representatives first, where its chances, despite Smith and the Rules Committee, looked more promising.

On June 19, 1963, the administration's bill went to Subcommittee No. 5 of the Judiciary Committee. The subcommittee was the only one where northern Democrats dominated, and Emmanuel Celler was chair of both the subcommittee and the full Judiciary Committee. The ranking Republican was William McCulloch, a low-profile conservative representing a rural Ohio district. Deputy Attorney General Nicholas Katzenbach and his colleague Burke Marshall worked particularly with McCulloch to fashion a bi-partisan compromise bill.[62] The bill hammered out by Katzenbach and McCulloch weakened the voting rights title of the Kennedy draft. However, liberal Democrats felt blindsided by this compromise, since they hadn't been included in its deliberations. Soon, a tough, bold substitute bill appeared from the Democrats, which added a new fair employment practices section.

McCulloch saw this as nothing more than a raw power move, with Democrats trying to embarrass the Republicans. Neither House Minority Leader Charles Halleck (Indiana), minority whip Gerald R. Ford (Michigan), or McCulloch were going to stand there and take it while Democrats accused them of being weak on civil rights. The Republicans and conservative

308

Democrats threatened to have the liberal bill go directly to the floor and be cut to pieces; McCulloch vowed that he wouldn't lift a finger to help.[63]

Then came two extraordinary events. On September 15, 1963, a bomb exploded under the steps of the Sixteenth Street Baptist Church in Birmingham, Alabama, killing four African-American girls, aged eleven to fourteen. It was "Youth Day" Sunday at the church. The bombing, one of many racially motivated incidents that had occurred in Birmingham over the past two decades, attracted worldwide outrage. Martin Luther King, Jr., in his eulogy, said that the girls' death had "something to say to every minister of the gospel who has remained silent behind the safe security of stained-glass windows." It also said something to "every politician who has fed his constituents with the stale bread of hatred and the spoiled meat of racism" and to "a federal government that has compromised with the undemocratic practices of southern Dixiecrats and the blatant hypocrisy of right-wing northern Republicans." It was not just the murderers that citizens should be concerned with, but "the system, the way of life, the philosophy which produced the murderers."[64]

After Birmingham, civil rights legislation seemed all the more urgent. On November 20, the full Judiciary Committee finally reported its bill. There had been tremendous amounts of bickering, accusations, the breakup of tenuous coalitions, tensions over who could claim credit, and whom to blame. What finally emerged was a bill that was stronger than Kennedy's original bill and still acceptable to most Republicans. The compromise legislation added a measure first pushed by Republicans, a Title VII, which forbade discrimination in employment. Another key change was the strengthening of Title VI, prohibiting discrimination in federally funded programs.[65]

Then came the second shock, the assassination of John F. Kennedy in Dallas, Texas, two days later. With his death, the political landscape had now profoundly changed. The day after Kennedy was buried, President Lyndon Johnson, whose views on civil rights were suspect by many, addressed a joint session of Congress. So unlike Kennedy's mannerisms and speech, Johnson's cadence was slow, his voice laced with a Texas twang; lawmakers and dignitaries in the packed House chamber listened intently to his every word. Halfway through his speech, Johnson said:

> No memorial oration or eulogy could more eloquently honor President Kennedy's memory than the earliest possible passage of the civil rights bill for equal rights. We have talked for one hundred years or more. It is now time to write the next chapter—and to write it in the books of law.[66]

It was one of Lyndon Johnson's finest moments. Two days later, he summoned African-American civil rights leaders to the White House, one at a time, for lengthy, frank discussions. Johnson reached out to New Deal liberals, to assure them that they were in harmony with one another. While southern lawmakers were uncomfortable with his speech, they did not appear to be alarmed or shocked. This was, after all, a Texan, a southerner; in the end, they thought, one of their own. Privately, however, Johnson said to his beloved mentor, Richard Russell, "if you get in my way" on this civil rights bill, "I'm going to run you down. I want you to know that, because I care about you."[67]

The civil rights bill had not gone to the full House of Representatives, but was now bottled up in Howard Smith's Rules Committee. Then on December 9, Celler filed the inevitable discharge petition to force the bill out of Rules, hoping to get the necessary 218 signatures, so that the bill could be sent to the full House and passed before the holiday recess. But only 150 lawmakers signed on, and the discharge petition failed. But over the Christmas holiday, northern members of the House heard loud and clear from their constituents who were demanding that lawmakers support the civil rights legislation. As soon as Congress reconvened in early January 1964, many other lawmakers indicated that they were ready to sign on. Furthermore, there were rumblings in the Rules Committee itself, and by January committee members were just two votes short of having a majority ready to force the bill from Smith's hand.

On January 8, in his first State of the Union address, Lyndon Johnson implored Congress: "Let this session of Congress be known as the session which did more for civil rights than the last hundred sessions combined."[68]

The next day, Howard Smith finally relented, and began hearings on the civil rights legislation. "I know the facts of life around here," he said. He held nine days' worth of hearings, during which time twenty-eight House members from the South were witnesses against the bill, while just five members were in favor. Then, on January 30, the civil rights bill finally left the Rules Committee and was now ready for general debate by the full House.[69]

Then out of the blue, Smith introduced an amendment on the House floor, on February 8, calling for the insertion of the word "sex" into the proposed Title VII, thus prohibiting employment discrimination on the basis of gender as well as race, and national origin. Many thought he was joking or more seriously, trying to throw a monkey wrench into the provision. No, assured Smith, the insertion of the word "sex" "will help an important minority." "This bill is so imperfect," Smith said, "what harm will this little amendment do?"

> Eighty-Eighth Congress, 2nd Session (January 7– October 3, 1964)
>
> Senate: 67 Democrats; 33 Republicans
>
> House: 258 Democrats; 177 Republicans
>
> President: Lyndon B. Johnson

Every woman in the House, except for one, agreed to support Smith's amendment, no matter the motivation. Katherine St. George (Republican– New York) lectured her male colleagues: "We outlast you. We outlive you. We nag you to death. So why should we want special privileges? We want this crumb of equality." Members laughed, but not Martha W. Griffiths (Democrat–Michigan), the formidable member of the House Ways and Means Committee. In a long and impassioned plea, Griffiths made the most forceful argument, warning that if the word "sex" were not included, then "white women will be the last at the hiring gate."

Edith S. Green (Democrat–Oregon) was the only woman to oppose the amendment, arguing that, for every discriminatory action against a woman, blacks had suffered tenfold the number. She said the Smith amendment would "help destroy" this section of the bill. Emanuel Celler, no friend of the Equal Rights Amendment which he had bottled up in the Judiciary Committee for a total of twenty years, likewise pleaded that the language be dropped, saying Smith's amendment was "illogical." What were women worried about, Celler wondered: in his own house, women were not in the minority, and furthermore, he was always able to get in the two last words, "Yes, dear." Again, there were knowing guffaws from his male colleagues. Opposition also came from the Johnson administration; it did not want the Smith amendment to gum up the works.[70] But after two hours of debate, Smith's amendment passed, 168 to 133. Some observers had to be muttering about strange bedfellows as most of the old guard southern conservatives were voting to protect women and many liberal northerners were voting against the amendment.

The House heard over 120 amendments on February 10, agreed to 28 of them, mostly on technical language, and finally, after all had been dispensed with, it voted overwhelmingly to adopt the civil rights bill, 290 to 110. It was a truly bipartisan victory, with 138 Republicans joining 152 Democrats. Indeed, it was the South against everybody else: of the 110 in opposition, ninety-six came from the old Dixie.[71]

The legislation was now off to the Senate, where civil rights forces would over the course of the next four months marshal superior organization and leadership. When the House bill was walked over to the Senate, Majority Leader Mike Mansfield (Democrat–Montana) was there to intercept it at the door. If he had not, the civil rights bill automatically would have been referred to the committee of jurisdiction, the Judiciary Committee, chaired by James Eastland. Mansfield's interception was the same tactic Lyndon Johnson used in 1956, against the same committee and the same chairman. The only way around Eastland was for the Senate to act as a committee of the whole, and consider the legislation directly on the floor. Mansfield employed another tactic: he would keep the wily Richard Russell from tying up the Senate with endless parliamentary maneuvers and quorum calls. Mansfield would make sure that there was a quorum of fifty senators on the floor at all times, and only allow the Appropriations Committee to hold its regular committee session. All other Senate business would be suspended. Francis R. Valeo, Mansfield's assistant recalled, "Russell was taken aback by this. He was quite surprised. . . . Mansfield was stealing his thunder in effect."[72]

Russell warned that the embattled southern senators would resist: "We shall enter into the battle next week with the earnest hope and prayer that we may find the means and strength to bring the facts of the issue to the people of this self-governing republic before it is too late."[73] During past civil rights filibusters, the southerners formed a platoon system, where three platoons of six senators each, would take turns talking the offending legislation to death. As they had successfully done before, southern senators would talk this bill to death, water it down, or hope that the sponsors would eventually abandon it.

Johnson asked Mansfield to designate Hubert Humphrey (Democrat–Minnesota) as the floor leader; Humphrey eagerly accepted this task. Working closely with Humphrey was liberal Republican Thomas H. Kuchel of California, who was responsible for rounding up fifteen Republican senators for quorum calls.[74] Johnson wasted no time: he called Humphrey, goading him about the challenge ahead: "You have got this opportunity now, Hubert, but you liberals will never deliver. You don't know the rules of the Senate, and your liberals will be off making speeches when they ought to be present in the Senate. I know you've got a great opportunity here, but I'm afraid it's going to fall between the boards." But Humphrey swears that he knew exactly what the goading and cajoling Johnson was doing: "One thing I liked about Johnson [was that] even when he conned me I knew what was happening to me."[75]

The central strategic question was this: could the pro-civil rights Senators come up with a coalition of northern Democrats and moderate Republicans sizeable enough to invoke cloture when the inevitable southern filibuster occurred? It would take sixty-seven votes to override. The task was complicated because some senators, like the eighty-seven-year-old Carl Hayden (Democrat–Arizona), were opposed to cloture on principle, no matter what the subject. Moderate and conservative Republicans would have to be won over, despite some provisions they found objectionable in Title VII, such as the Equal Employment Opportunity Commission and provisions that cut off federal funds for noncompliance.

Everett M. Dirksen (Republican–Illinois) was key. As minority leader in the Senate, he could persuade moderate Republicans to join the Democrats, but certainly he would extract a price. But not even his aides knew where Dirksen stood on civil rights. He said he had an open mind and hadn't made any commitments or assumptions. His apparent indecision made him all the more valuable. Dirksen was a master of Senate tactics who played politics as good as any on the Hill. He was also vain, loved being the center of attention, and enjoyed the sound of his mellifluous baritone voice. Humphrey and Lyndon Johnson both worked on Dirksen, stroking his ego, giving him credit, letting him take center stage. Humphrey recalled Johnson saying to him: "You've got to play to Ev Dirksen. You've got to let him have a piece of the action. He's got to look good all the time."[76]

Thomas Kuchel would have to round up four out of every five Republican senators. Certainly northeast liberal Republicans like Kenneth Keating and

Jacob Javits of New York and Clifford Case of New Jersey would be on board, and so would some progressive Midwesterners. But six of Dirksen's colleagues, all from the prairie or mountain states, were dead set against a cloture override; the most prominent opponent was Barry Goldwater of Arizona, who was vying for the Republican Party's 1964 presidential nomination.[77] Indeed, Goldwater in early September also would vote against that year's version of Medicare-Medicaid legislation.

The Republican votes would have to come from other Midwest or mountain state Republicans, such as Len B. Jordan (Montana), Karl E. Mundt (South Dakota), Carl T. Curtis (Nebraska), or Roman Hruska (Nebraska). One key senator on the fence was conservative Bourke B. Hickenlooper of Iowa. Mansfield aide Francis Valeo recalled how Hickenlooper, and other fence-sitting Republicans, were fussed over. Hickenlooper was ushered into a meeting in Mansfield's back office in the Capitol, with Burke Marshall and Nicholas Katzenbach from the Justice Department and Mike Manatos from the White House. Mansfield told Valeo: "Go in there and talk to those lawyers . . . and tell them I'm going to bring Hickenlooper in there and they're to make any changes in the bill he wants." The senator from Iowa suggested a few minor changes, then said, "well, that's a hell of a lot better bill that it was."[78] Hickenlooper did not promise his vote, caused some heartburn later in the deliberations, but finally came through with his vote to override the veto, and brought a few of his Midwest colleagues with him.

The southern filibuster began on the procedural question: should the just-passed House bill be referred to the Eastland Judiciary Committee or go directly on the Senate calendar? Southerners filibustered for fifteen days, March 9 through March 26. Dirksen, a stickler for parliamentary procedure, sided with the southerners; surprisingly, so did Wayne L. Morse (Oregon), the fiercely independent liberal Democrat. But Humphrey reminded his colleagues of Eastland's track record: 120 out of 121 civil rights bills over the past decade had died in his committee. Thomas J. Dodd (Democrat–Connecticut) said enough was enough, that the civil rights bill had already gone through eighty-three days of testimony and 280 witnesses; it was time for the whole Senate to take up the matter.[79]

The pro-civil rights senators were impressively organized, under the leadership of Humphrey and Kuchel. Each morning, Humphrey, Kuchel, and their floor captains huddled with Justice Department officials, usually Nicholas Katzenbach, and often joined by Clarence Mitchell of the NAACP and Joseph Rauh of the Leadership Conference on Civil Rights. They published a daily bipartisan newsletter, parceling out floor responsibilities, summarizing procedures, and giving talking points on controversial issues. Further they stymied the southern strategy of insisting on repeated quorum calls, by having enough senators ready and available at all times.[80]

After three weeks of filibustering on the procedural issue, the Senate finally got down to the substance of the legislation. The longest filibuster in Senate history soon began, starting on March 30 and finally ending on June 10. For the southerners, it was a risky gamble. It was an all-or-none strategy, with no alternative southern proposal, and one that historians have viewed as fatefully flawed. Hubert Humphrey couldn't understand the southerners' tactics: "I never could quite understand why they didn't let us vote more often. If they had done so, they could have insisted that the legislative process, after all, was working because amendments were being voted on. But they didn't do that. Instead they just kept talking and talking. It seemed that they had lost their sense of direction and had little or no real plan."[81]

Russell, tired and fighting against the ravages of emphysema, knew he couldn't win over the Senate; all he could do was delay, fight for time, and hope that Johnson and the non-southerners in the Senate would give up in frustration. Russell vowed to fight "to the last ditch." Along with him were eighteen southern Democrats and one lone Republican, John G. Tower of Texas. Russell could count on the die-hards and flame-throwers, like Eastland, Thurmond, Allen J. Ellender (Louisiana), and Stennis, but some of the other southerners, like J. William Fulbright (Arkansas), Russell B. Long (Louisiana), and George A. Smathers (Florida), were not blind to the merits of the civil rights legislation, or at least understood that African-Americans soon would be a constituency to be reckoned with, if not at least courted.[82]

Still, these southerners had to participate in the filibuster and vote against civil rights reforms; it would have been political suicide to do otherwise. In a telephone conversation with President Johnson, Fulbright confessed: "Christ, I'm really over a barrel on this thing. I wish to hell I could vote with you. You know that." Johnson: "I know that, I know it." Fulbright: "I hope to hell I can get this thing out of the way, but I feel like a traitor, you know."[83]

The southerners droned on and on, day after legislative day. Despite the high stakes, the bitterness of the policy fight, there still was a measure of comity and civility among the lawmakers. Humphrey remembered Willis Robertson (Democrat–Virginia), seventy-seven years old in 1964 and filibustering against civil rights, was always good for an hour's speech, but the strain was showing. To make it a little easier on Robertson, Humphrey would interrupt and ask him a long, convoluted question. Robertson "would smile and respond," Humphrey wrote, "acknowledging without words my gesture. Afterward, we might share his Virginia sour-mash whiskey." Robertson, in turn, would help Humphrey out by coming to the Senate floor when Humphrey needed an extra body for a quorum call.[84]

One thing Russell and other southerners hoped for was that George Wallace's 1964 bid for the presidency would stir up grassroots support and demonstrate to the nation that his message resonated not just in the South but with Americans throughout the country. That support came in Wisconsin, which held its 1964 presidential primary on April 7. On that day in Milwaukee's Schroeder Hotel, a jubilant George Wallace, donning a feathered Winnebago war bonnet and joyously dancing a victory war dance, whooped, "We won without winning!" Governor John Reynolds, running as a favorite-son stand-in for Lyndon Johnson won the primary, but Wallace, with 34 percent of the vote, was the talk of politics nationwide the next day. "All Mississippi is thrilled," said a telegram from that state's governor Paul Johnson. Wallace, who entered the Wisconsin primary, his first ever in the North, had found his audience: blue-collar ethnic workers particularly in southside Milwaukee who were fed up with crime, were fearful of blacks in adjoining neighborhoods, and saw in Wallace a man who understood them. At his biggest rally at Serb Hall on Milwaukee, three thousand Polish immigrants belted out the first stanza of "Dixie" in their Old World tongue, much to Wallace's delight.[85]

Wallace went on to the Indiana primary where he won 24 percent of the vote. In Maryland, on May 20, the Alabama governor almost won the presidential primary on the strength of blue-collar Baltimore and rural white voters on the civil rights-scarred Eastern Shore. Those blue-collar workers in Baltimore had heavily backed John Kennedy in 1960, now were nearly unanimous for Wallace. But African-American voters came out in droves, and Wallace blamed them for his defeat. "If it hadn't been for the nigger bloc vote," he said, "we'd have won it all."[86]

Johnson was worried that Wallace's success in tapping into traditional Democratic northern blue-collar voters would only encourage the southerners in the Senate to continue their all-out effort to kill the civil rights legislation. While a number of northern Democratic senators dismissed the Wallace threat and its implications, Abraham Ribicoff of Connecticut did not. Wallace "has proved something. He has proved that there are many Americans in the North as well as the South who do not believe in civil rights." Ribicoff predicted that "the next twenty years will be years of strife and turmoil in the field of civil rights," with the troubles "not just in the South, but primarily in the North."[87]

While Wallace was making headlines in the northern primaries, and the filibuster continued on the floor of the Senate, minority leader Everett Dirksen began his legislative horse-trading. Hoping to get reluctant Republicans to join him, Dirksen proposed over one hundred amendments to the civil rights bill. The amendments ranged from the trivial to a "complete evisceration" of the major titles. No one knew for sure if Dirksen was serious about the amendments, whether he was trying to gain a better bargaining position, or if, ultimately, he just wanted to have his name on the bill.[88] Ultimately, Dirksen then reduced the number of amendments to ten, all of them related to the fair employment title.

The horse-trading continued, with Dirksen and the Democratic leadership walking a fine line: rounding up moderate-conservative Republicans, not irritating the increasingly impatient civil rights leaders, not upsetting the House Republicans, and not destroying the fragile balance in the Senate. On May 13, Attorney General Robert Kennedy, senators Humphrey, Dirksen, and others crafted a "clean bill," to be introduced as a substitute. Some seventy changes were made, mostly technical, and, in the end, the Humphrey–Dirksen substitute, as it was called, was even stronger than the original bill that had come over from the House.

On June 1, senators Mansfield and Dirksen finally announced their decision to file a cloture petition; it would be filed on Saturday, June 6, with the vote taking place on Monday, June 9. The floor leaders wanted to wait until after the California primary on June 2, where Barry Goldwater, who had already informed his Republican colleagues that he'd vote against a cloture petition, was running against New York governor Nelson Rockefeller. Dirksen didn't want to upset Goldwater backers in the Senate by pressing the issue. But Dirksen also wanted the civil rights issue settled by the time Republicans met in San Francisco for their presidential nominating convention in July 13.[89]

In his closing speech, Richard Russell lamented the work done by religious leaders in pressing for the civil rights legislation: "I have observed with profound sorrow the role that many religious leaders have played in urging the passage of the bill."[90] Russell, adept at the art of politics and persuasion, could not see that, for many, civil rights was a profoundly moral issue. Indeed, through their activities on Capitol Hill and grassroots measures, particularly in the Midwest, progressive church leaders and activists were deeply committed to ending racial discrimination. In a sense, it was a re-emergence of the early twentieth-century Social Gospel, and at the center was the National Council of Churches.[91] Under the leadership of the Rev. Eugene Carson Blake, the National Council, and many faith-based organizations became energetic civil rights activists.[92] Humphrey noted the important role played by the Leadership Conference on civil rights, various civil rights organizations, labor organizations, business leaders, and church organizations. "Without the clergy, we could never have passed the bill."[93]

Key Provisions of the 1964 Civil Rights Act

The act had eleven separate titles, dealing with voting rights, the extension of the Civil Rights Commission, and other provisions. The most important sections, however, were these:

- Title II, which barred discrimination on the basis of race, color, religion or national origin in any public accommodation, such as restaurants, lunch counters, movie theaters, sports arenas, and other public accommodations if they affected interstate commerce.
- Title III authorized the U.S. attorney general to pursue legal proceedings on behalf of individuals who might not have the funds or feel that bringing a suit would jeopardize their personal safety or jobs.
- Title IV called for active pursuit of desegregation in public schools and called on the attorney general to file suits to enforce the act.
- Title VI declared that any government agency receiving federal funds could lose those funds it it engaged in unlawful discrimination.
- Title VII declared it unlawful for employers, employment agencies, labor unions or training programs to discriminate on the basis of race, color, religion, sex, or national origin in hiring, discharging, and terms of conditions of employment.

On June 10, by a vote of 71 to 29, for the first time in its history, the Senate shut down debate on a civil rights filibuster. Twenty-seven Republicans joined forty-four Democrats, including the terminally ill Clair Engel from California; the back of southern resistance in the Senate had been broken. "This," said Strom Thurmond, who was about to switch over to Barry Goldwater and the Republican Party, "is a sad day for America." Liberal Republican Jacob Javits retorted, "This was one of the Senate's finest hours."[94]

The following week the Senate, by 73 to 27, passed the civil rights bill. Among those voting against the civil rights bill was Barry Goldwater, who said he was personally opposed to segregation of the races, but nevertheless labeled the bill unconstitutional. Goldwater, ignoring the political advice of his Republican colleagues who were fearful that his stand would rip apart the upcoming Republican convention, stood firm. He acknowledged getting his constitutional advice from a young Arizona lawyer, William H. Rehnquist, and a young Yale law professor, Robert Bork.[95] On July 2, the Senate's version of the bill was passed by the House by an overwhelming 289 to 126.

At last, basic guarantees of freedom and equality would now become the law of the land. At the overflowing signing ceremony, on July 2, 1964, Lyndon Johnson stated that millions of Americans had been denied essential freedoms, but no longer. "Our Constitution, the foundation of our Republic, forbids it. The principles of our freedom forbid it. Morality forbids it. And the law I sign tonight forbids it."[96]

Ceremonial signing pens, seventy-five in all, were handed out, to Dirksen and Humphrey, Celler, William McCulloch, Robert Kennedy, and a wide variety of civil rights leaders.

Just before the Republican convention in July, an informant helped the FBI locate the bodies of three civil rights workers, Andrew Goodman, Michael (Mickey) Schwerner, and James Chaney. While nearly a thousand civil rights workers, part of the Freedom Summer voting rights program, had been arrested by Mississippi lawmen that summer, Neshoba County deputy sheriff Cecil Price released the three deep in the woods into the hands of white vigilantes. Mississippi politicians dismissed reports that they had been murdered. Eastland told Lyndon Johnson that it had to be a "publicity stunt." "Who is it that would harm 'em?" Eastland asked, "There's no white organizations in that area of Mississippi. Who could possibly harm 'em?"[97]

Most Republicans in Congress supported civil rights legislation, and, without their support, the Civil Rights Act of 1964 would not have been possible. Yet their political and symbolic leader, the man running for the presidency, had voted against the civil rights legislation. Barry Goldwater, no racist himself, was widely admired and supported in the Deep South. He won the electoral votes of his home state of Arizona and five Deep South states, but was otherwise crushed in the November presidential election.

Making the Law: The Voting Rights Act of 1965

Following the *Brown* decisions, several southern states cracked down on African-American voting. In Mississippi, by the end of 1955, there were no black voters registered in fourteen counties. Louisiana officials distributed "how-to-discriminate" pamphlets to local officials, showing how to remove blacks from the voting rolls. While in Tennessee and North Carolina, black voter registration increased, in the Deep South, the numbers of registered blacks shrunk.[98]

Key Individuals in the Civil Rights Legislation

Civil rights leaders, like Martin Luther King, Jr., John Lewis, Roy Wilkins, labor, civic and church leaders, Fannie Lou Hamer, James Meredith, and thousands of courageous ordinary citizens fill the roster of those responsible for the two civil rights laws. If they did not push, agitate, and fight, sometimes at great risk to their lives, the 1960s civil rights laws would not have been possible.

In Washington, the Civil Rights Act and Voting Rights Act were two of the most contentious and bitterly fought legislative fights in American history. Three individuals were key to their success.

Lyndon B. Johnson (1908–1973) had never supported civil rights legislation during his first twenty years in Congress. But with looming national ambitions, he made an "abrupt and total reversal" and used all his power and guile to win support of the first civil rights law in the twentieth century.[99] While he maintained a low profile in the debates and proceedings for both the 1964 and 1965 laws, he was indeed the driving force behind the scenes. The historian Robert Caro has stated that "Lyndon Johnson was the greatest champion in the halls of government that black Americans, and indeed all Americans of color, had during the 20th Century. And indeed . . . with the single exception of Abraham Lincoln, he was the greatest champion with white skin that they had in the history of the republic."[100]

Hubert H. Humphrey (1911–1978) was elected to the U.S. Senate in 1948; in 1965, he became vice-president of the United States from 1965 to 1969. Humphrey ran for president in 1968 and was narrowly beaten by Richard M. Nixon. He also was an unsuccessful candidate for his party's nomination for president in 1960 and 1972. Humphrey returned to the Senate in 1971, serving until 1978. Known as the "happy warrior" for his upbeat attitude and sunny disposition, he was well admired and respected by colleagues and staff in both the House and the Senate. His strategic leadership in the Senate was central to passage of the 1964 law.

Everett M. Dirksen (1896–1969) served in the House of Representatives from 1933 through 1948, then was elected to the Senate in 1950, was chosen minority leader in 1959, and served until 1969. On most issues, Dirksen was a stout conservative, hawkish on the Vietnam war, cautious on economic and social policy. Lyndon Johnson knew that Dirksen was in a tight spot politically in supporting civil rights legislation, but, in the end, could be depended upon.

By 1964, there had been some progress in registering African-Americans in parts of the South. Tennessee had enfranchised 69 percent of its adult blacks, Florida 64 percent, and Texas 58 percent. But Mississippi was by far the worst state; it had registered just 28,500 out of 422,000 eligible black voters, a mere 6.7 percent. Historian Neil R. McMillen pointed out that there were fewer blacks eligible to vote in Mississippi for Lyndon Johnson in 1964 than for William McKinley in 1896.[101]

For many blacks in Mississippi, it wasn't a question of intimidation or pressure against them not to vote; many simply did not know that the vote was available to them. Fannie Lou Hamer remembered going to a voter registration meeting in 1962, and commenting: "until then . . . I didn't know that a Negro could register and vote. . . . I guess if I'd had any sense I'd-been a little scared, but what was the point of being scared? The only thing they could do to me was kill me and it seemed like they'd been trying to do that a little bit at a time ever since I could remember."[102]

Hamer, with a sixth-grade education, worked in the fields and as a time keeper in a plantation, had joined SNCC in 1962, to register African-Americans in Mississippi. Earlier, she had lost her job because of civil rights activities and then SNCC hired her as a field secretary. In June 1963 in Winona, Mississippi, she was thrown into jail for disorderly conduct; her offense was attempting to enter a "whites only" restaurant. In the adjoining jail cells, she heard cries and screams from other prisoners. In Hamer's words:

> The state highway patrolmen came and carried me out of the cell into another cell where there were two Negro prisoners. The patrolman gave the first Negro a long blackjack that was heavy. It was loaded with something and they had me lay down on the bunk with my face down, and I was beat. I was beat by the first Negro till he gave out. Then the patrolman ordered the other man to take the blackjack and he began to beat. . . .[103]

Hamer was ordered to sign a statement saying that she had not been mistreated and was later released. She refused medical treatment and her injuries were so severe that she became partially blind and permanently disabled.[104]

In 1964, Hamer helped organize the Mississippi Freedom Democratic Party (MFDP) as an alternative to the all-white state Democratic Party. At the Democratic National Convention that year, she testified before the credentials committee about the abuse and torture she and other African-Americans had suffered when attempting to vote. She was bitterly disappointed when the Democratic delegates failed to unseat the regular Democrats from Mississippi and gave the MFDP just two at-large seats. Nonetheless, her presence and cause made a lasting impression on the delegates and the nation.

Hamer and three others from the MFDP held a mock election against incumbent Mississippi congressmen in the November 1964 elections.[105] When the new Eighty-Ninth Congress convened on January 4, 1965, Hamer and the other women challenged the election results and tried to enter the House chamber to be sworn in. William Fitts Ryan (Democrat–New York) objected to the swearing in of the four veteran Mississippi Democrats and the freshman Republican, but then Speaker of the House Carl Albert (Democrat–Oklahoma) moved that the Mississippians be seated. On a procedural vote, Hamer and the protestors lost, but were heartened to know that 148 lawmakers had voted against the Mississippians and, by extension, against the exclusion of African-Americans from the voting booth.[106]

From the November 1964 elections, the Democrats gained thirty-five seats in the House of Representatives, giving them 295 seats to 140 for the Republicans. It was such an historic, overwhelming majority that some of them had to spill over to the Republican side of the aisle so they could all be accommodated. Yet while Democrats dominated, and while the Mississippi challenge went on, Republicans did pick up support in the South. Five new Republican congressmen were elected from Alabama, and one each from Georgia and Mississippi. It was the beginning of an historic, tectonic shift of white voters, going from a solid South of Democrats to a near solid South of Republicans in the following decades.

Martin Luther King, Jr., returning from a European trip where he received the Nobel Prize for Peace, met with Johnson in mid-December 1964. At the meeting, King pressed Johnson for a voting rights bill but Johnson was hesitant. It had been just six months since the end of the bruising fight for the 1964 Civil Rights Act, and Johnson needed southern votes for a host of other Great Society legislation. Yes, a voting rights bill was important and the time would eventually come, he told King, but it could not be in 1965.[107] What the president probably did not tell King was that he had ordered Nicholas Katzenbach to begin crafting the next civil rights bill, legislation that would provide "once and for, equal voting rights."[108]

King was exhausted, physically and psychologically. He been constantly traveling, pulled in all directions and haunted by the suspicions, then the reality, that the FBI had wiretapped and recorded his activities and were threatening to reveal damaging personal information.[109] But there was work to be done: most pressing work was voter registration, particularly in Selma, Alabama. There was a solid reason for targeting this sleepy city on Highway 80 west of Montgomery. There were 15,000 African-Americans of voting age, but just 355 were registered; white registrars were determined to stop any more blacks from voting. In addition, King knew that a protest in Selma would be just as incendiary as the protests in Birmingham the year before. Sheriff Jim Clark of Dallas County (Selma) would overreact just like Bull Connor did in Birmingham.[110] Heads might crack, but the wider world would be witness.

The Eighty-Ninth Congress began its new, boisterous session. House Republican young turks, including Donald H. Rumsfeld (Illinois), persuaded Gerald R. Ford to challenge Charles A. Halleck for the senior minority leadership position. Halleck was considered as someone who drank too much, lacked initiative, and "was deemed too old, too forbidding, too irascible"[111] to be an effective leader. Ford, just as conservative as Halleck but far more

Eighty-Ninth Congress, 1st Session
(January 4–October 23, 1965)

Senate: 68 Democrats;
32 Republicans

House: 295 Democrats;
140 Republicans

President: Lyndon B. Johnson

likeable and reliable, became the new Republican leader in the House and was less willing to sustain the southern Democratic-conservative Republican partnership.

In the Senate, the biggest change was that Hubert Humphrey, who had a central role in the 1964 civil rights fight, now was vice-president. The Democrats now held a 68–32 majority, the largest such majority since 1940, and southern Democrats seemed to have lost some of the taste for the fight. Their leader, Richard Russell, was recuperating in Georgia from a long, difficult battle with emphysema. The next senior southern senator, Allen Ellender from Louisiana, seventy-five years old, adopted the same, unimaginative and inevitably defeating defensive strategy.[112]

The 1957, 1960, and 1964 Civil Rights Acts addressed part of the problem of voter discrimination, but these laws proved to be weak and piecemeal, and enforcement through litigation was exasperatingly long and discouraging. Individual states could continue creating voting standards and restrictions, the U.S. Department of Justice would then investigate and perhaps litigate, but the Justice Department often faced federal district courts unsympathetic to the government's case.[113]

Now, by the beginning of the year, Johnson was ready to unveil his voting rights legislation. The president met several times in early 1965 with King, Randolph, Roy Wilkins, Whitney Young, Jr., and Clarence Mitchell. On January 15, Johnson, in a telephone conversation with King, said: "The greatest achievement of my administration . . . I said to a group yesterday, was the passage of the 1964 Civil Rights Act. But I think this will be bigger, because it'll do things that even the '64 act couldn't do."[114] In his State of the Union speech, Johnson pledged to send Congress a voting rights bill, and, in early February, Senate Majority Leader Mansfield, the new attorney general Katzenbach, and Senator Dirksen began the arduous process of crafting a tough, sweeping bill with severe penalties. Mansfield, rarely an angry man, gave his staff instructions to draft the simplest and harshest of bills, no more than one page long. "I want a bill," he told his staff, "that a man with a first grade-education, colored or white, can understand."[115] It took weeks of careful deliberation, but events soon overtook the legislative negotiations. In March, Selma exploded.

The Selma March

In early February, King and approximately three thousand demonstrators had been arrested in a voting drive in Selma, Alabama. Then on March 6, Governor Wallace banned a march planned from Selma to the state capital

Montgomery, calling it a danger to public safety. King was not with the marchers, but at home in Atlanta; his life had once again been threatened and he reluctantly decided to stay away. On the evening of the March 7, the civil rights leaders were to begin their fifty-four-mile march. They came down Broad Street, then reached the Edmund Pettus bridge as it crossed the Alabama River. Sheriff Jim Clark, backed by his mounted posse, ordered them to turn around and go home. The marchers refused. Clark yelled out, "Get those god-damned niggers! And get those god-damned *white* niggers."[116]

Leading the march were John Lewis and Hosea Williams. Lewis recalls what came next: "The troopers and posse men swept forward as one, like a human wave, a blur of blue shirts and billy clubs and bullwhips. We had no chance to turn and retreat. There were six hundred people behind us, bridge railings to either side and the river below." Lewis continued:

> I remember how vivid the sounds were as the troopers rushed toward us—the clunk of the troopers' heavy boots, the whoops of rebel yells from the white onlookers, the clip-clop of horses' hooves hitting the hard asphalt of the highway, the voice of a woman shouting, "Get 'em! *Get* the niggers!"[117]

More than fifty men and women had been severely injured. That evening, ABC television interrupted its Sunday night feature movie, *The Judgment at Nuremberg*, to show a fifteen-minute clip of the raw footage from Selma; 48 million viewers witnessed the brutality. It is not known if George Wallace was complicit in the clubbings and beatings, but he never issued a single word of criticism of the police or sympathy for the protestors.[118] There was a further national outcry when, on March 11, a Boston-based thirty-eight-year-old white Unitarian minister, the Rev. James Reeb, was severely beaten in Selma and died.[119]

After the bloody events in Selma, several hundred civil rights picketers, most of whom were white, camped outside the White House. Impatient with the president's failure to act quickly on the voting rights law, the protestors shouted their dismay. One sign said: "Johnson is Goldwater in disguise."

Almost on impulse, a Wallace aide suggested that the governor meet with President Johnson; this might divert attention away from Selma and give Wallace a chance to talk about the dangers posed by the civil rights agitators. Wallace agreed immediately, but later regretted his hasty decision. On Saturday, March 13, Governor Wallace met with Johnson in the Oval Office for three hours. Lyndon Johnson recalled: "I kept my eyes directly on the governor's face the entire time. I saw a nervous, aggressive man; a rough shrewd politician who had managed to touch the deepest chords of pride as well as prejudice among his people."[120] Johnson, "like some Texas python, had almost wrapped himself around the governor," pressed Wallace: governor, you can do more to desegregate the schools and increase voter registration. Wallace said he had no such power, that authority belonged to the local officials. "Don't you shit me, George Wallace!"[121] Then Johnson shoved in the rhetorical knife, "You had the power to keep the president of the United States off the [Alabama] ballot [in 1964]. Surely you have the power to tell a few poor county registrars what to do."[122] Indeed, it was not the conversation that Wallace had expected; he put on a brave face when he and the president met with reporters, then headed back to Alabama to regain his defiant composure.

On Monday, March 15, Johnson went before a joint session of Congress and gave the most memorable speech of his public life. In his slow southern drawl, he spoke in sweeping terms: "I speak tonight for the dignity of man and the destiny of democracy. I urge every member of both parties, Americans of all religions and of all colors, from every section of the country, to join me in that cause."[123] In two days, he would send a bill to Congress to eliminate illegal barriers to voting, demanding that Congress act. Millions were watching on television. During his forty-five-minute speech, the president was interrupted thirty-six times by applause and two standing ovations. The television audience could also see Senator Sam Ervin (Democrat–North Carolina) sitting with his arms folded, in "massive disapproval" and Senator Ellender "slumped gloomily" in his chair; the Virginia and Mississippi delegations, and some other southerners, boycotted the speech altogether.[124]

Voting obstacles in Virginia, South Carolina, Georgia, Alabama, Louisiana, and Mississippi would be suspended by the proposed legislation. But if those states couldn't abide having federal intervention, the course of action was simple, Johnson said: "Open your polling places to all your people. Allow men and women to register and vote whatever the color of their skin. Extend the rights of citizenship to every citizen of this land."

This was not just a southern problem nor is it a problem solely about African-Americans, Johnson said: "There is no Negro problem. There is no southern problem or northern problem. There is only an American problem." There could be no hesitation and no delay, for "the time for waiting is gone." Then, in his most memorable line, Johnson echoed the determination and goal of the civil rights movement: "It is not just Negroes, but really it is all of us, who must overcome the crippling legacy of bigotry and injustice. And . . . we. . . . shall . . . overcome." After a moment of stunned silence, the lawmakers jumped to their feet and burst into sustained, emotional applause and shouts of approval.

Former baseball great Jackie Robinson, now a columnist for the Chicago *Defender*, remarked that the president's words "lifted a weight of what seemed like a thousand pounds crushing in on the heart." Johnson biographer Robert Dallek characterized it as "Johnson's greatest speech and one of the most moving and memorable presidential addresses in the country's history."[125]

On March 17, federal district court judge Frank M. Johnson, Jr., ruled that the Selma civil rights forces had a right, guaranteed under the Constitution, to march from Selma to Montgomery, the state capital. Having watched the television news footage of "Bloody Sunday," Judge Johnson concluded that the enormity of the wrong suffered by African-Americans outweighed concerns for unobstructed highways and sidewalks. For his courageous application of the law, Frank Johnson was ostracized by the Alabama elite, had his life threatened repeatedly, and his mother's house was burned.[126]

Governor Wallace would not guarantee police protection for the demonstrators, but Lyndon Johnson would. He swiftly mobilized nearly 4,000 troops from the "Dixie" Division of the Alabama National Guard and a nearby U.S. Army base. For Johnson, having Alabama citizens defend the marchers was key: "They were not intruders forcing their way in; they were citizens of Alabama. That made all the difference in the world."[127]

The march to Montgomery, starting out with approximately 4,000 participants, lasted five days, and by the time they reached the capital, their numbers had swelled to 22,000. It was a peaceful march, but, in its aftermath, Viola Liuzzo, a Detroit civil rights volunteer, was gunned down as she helped shuttle marchers back and forth.[128]

Emmanuel Celler immediately began hearings and, on May 12, the voting rights bill was reported out of his committee and then sent to Smith's Rules Committee. Defiant to the end, Smith delayed the bill by three weeks, then, when it finally went to the full House, he delayed its passage by another five weeks of parliamentary maneuvering. On July 9, the House overwhelmingly approved its version, 333–85.

Key Provisions of the Voting Rights Act of 1965

Section 2 of the act closely followed the language of the Fifteenth Amendment, prohibiting on a nationwide basis the denial or abridgment of the right to vote based on literacy tests.

Section 5 was the most significant feature. It targeted states or their political subdivisions which had voting tests (such as literacy, good character, knowledge of the state's constitution, or others) as of November 1, 1964 and less than 50 percent of those of voting age participating in the 1964 presidential election. When those conditions existed, then the voting tests were voided and the states could not implement new changes without pre-clearance from the U.S. attorney general or the U.S. District Court in the District of Columbia. Federal examiners would be used to assist qualified voters to register and to vote, and federal observers could monitor the activities in a jurisdiction's polling place.

In the Senate, the bill was also introduced right after Johnson's speech. Sixty-six senators signed on as co-sponsors, assuring that the bill would quickly pass and would be impervious to a last-minute filibuster. The Senate version passed on May 26, by an equally overwhelming vote of 77–19.

There were some differences in the House and Senate versions, especially the inclusion of a poll-tax ban in the House, which was eventually dropped in the conference committee. Then on August 3 the House overwhelmingly adopted the voting rights legislation and the next day the Senate followed. Two southern senators, Democrats Ralph W. Yarborough of Texas and George A. Smathers of Florida, broke ranks and voted for the legislation.[129]

On August 6, 1965, Lyndon Johnson signed the Voting Rights Act into law. For this momentous occasion, he chose the ornate President's Room in the Capitol, becoming the first chief executive since Herbert Hoover to use this historic room to sign important legislation. More than one hundred lawmakers, cabinet officials, and civil rights leaders crowded into the room. In a televised ceremony, Johnson declared that "today we strike away the last major shackle of those fierce and ancient bonds" of oppression, and recalled how he and Congress quickly acted after the "outrage of Selma." He signed the law, sitting at the desk he had used to guide through the 1957 and 1960 civil rights legislation. This was also the room where Abraham Lincoln, 104 years ago to the day, had affixed his signature to legislation freeing slaves pressed into duty by the Confederacy.[130]

The ceremony then moved to the Capitol Rotunda, where Johnson said that "today is a triumph for freedom as huge as any victory that's ever been won on any battlefield." This law, he said, is righting a wrong which "no American in his heart can justify." He called the signing "a victory for the freedom of the American Negro, but it is also a victory for the freedom of the American nation." Johnson then implored to every African-American in the United States: "you must register; you must vote; you must learn so your choices advance your interests and the interests of our beloved nation. Your future and your children's future depend upon it and I don't believe you're going to let them down."[131]

There was much work to be done. Immediately the attorney general proclaimed that the Voting Rights provisions would apply to South Carolina, Georgia, Alabama, Louisiana, Mississippi, Virginia, twenty-six counties in North Carolina, and a few other jurisdictions.[132] In the six southern states which were the primary target of the law, just 1.1 million African-Americans had registered to vote, while twice that number had not registered. Right after Johnson signed the law, forty-five federal examiners, each one a volunteer and a southerner, from the Civil Service Commission offices in Dallas and Atlanta were dispatched to the affected counties armed with bundles of voter registration forms. They had been in Washington, undergoing an intensive three-day registration training seminar, even before the bill became law.[133]

The next day, Attorney General Katzenbach filed suit against the poll tax in Mississippi, federal law suits to follow challenging poll taxes in Alabama, Texas, and Virginia. The first voting suits had been filed in Mississippi in July 1961; by election time 1964, twenty-three additional suits had been filed. By the time the Voting Rights Act had been signed into law, federal lawsuits were pending in sixty of Mississippi's eighty-two counties. Martin Luther King announced, following an hour-long meeting with President Johnson, that he would now press for voting rights for African-Americans in northern cities and states.[134]

This legislative triumph, however, was soon overshadowed by the combustion of urban unrest. Just five days after President Johnson signed the historic legislation, a major race riot broke out in the Watts section of Los Angeles. This was triggered by a minor incident, an arrest of a black man on the suspicion of drunk driving. By the time the violence had ended, five days later, thousands had been arrested, thirty-four persons were killed, and property damage was more than $40 million.[135]

Aftermath

Well before the 1964 legislation was passed, the Department of Justice and the president himself were busy persuading southern business leaders to comply with the new law. On October 30, 1964, just days before the presidential election, the federal Community Relations Service published a survey of fifty-three southern and border-state cities with populations of 50,000 or more, showing "widespread compliance" with the law. In announcing the results, Lyndon Johnson thanked the many civic and labor leaders, clergy and educators, but then singled out those who deserved "special note:" the members of Congress who had opposed the civil rights bill "with all their strength and eloquence" but, now that it is enacted, are urging their constituents to comply with the "law of the land."[136]

Timeline for Civil Rights and Voting Rights
1948   Split in Democratic Party; emergence of Dixiecrat protest party; Humphrey and strong civil rights plank.
1954   *Brown* v. *Board of Education* (I); *Brown (II)* in 1955.
1957   Civil Rights Act of 1957 enacted; a weak law, but first since the 1870s.
1960   Civil Rights Act of 1960 enacted; another weak measure.
1963   Civil rights unrest in Birmingham, march on Washington, Kennedy introduces civil rights legislation.
1964   Prolonged Senate filibuster; enactment of Civil Rights Act of 1964.
1965   Beatings at Selma; enactment of Voting Rights Act of 1965.
1970s   Voting Rights Act reauthorized and extended in 1970, reinforced and extended in 1975; significant increase in black registration; opposing tactics shift to voter dilution.
1982   Extension of Voting Rights Act for twenty-five years.
2006   Another extension of Voting Rights Act for twenty-five years.

Both the 1964 Civil Rights Act and the 1965 Voting Act were immediately challenged in court, and both were upheld in unanimous opinions of the U.S. Supreme Court. Less than six months after its passage, the Supreme Court upheld Title II, the public accommodations section, of the Civil Rights Act in two companion cases. In the first, the *Heart of Atlanta Motel* v. *United States*, the Court ruled that Congress had "ample power" to protect against racial discrimination in motels and hotels serving interstate commerce. In a second case, *Katzenbach* v. *McClung*, the Court ruled that even a local establishment, Ollie's Barbecue, serving only local white folks, came under the jurisdiction of Title II because it drew a substantial portion of its food supplies from out of state.[137] Senator Eastland's fears were becoming reality.

The state of South Carolina challenged the Voting Rights Act, arguing that the Congress had exceeded its authority in trying to enforce the Fifteenth Amendment, that, by singling out certain states for special treatment, Congress had violated the principle of equality of the states, and, by not allowing judicial review of the administrative procedures, it had violated the concept of bill of attainder. The Court in *South Carolina* v. *Katzenbach* upheld the Voting Rights Act in a near-unanimous opinion, rejecting out of hand the arguments of South Carolina and the states that had joined it as friends of the court. The Court also upheld a portion of the law which had outlawed New York's state English literacy requirement, and then ruled that state poll taxes posed an "invidious discrimination" that violated the equal protection clause of the Fourteenth Amendment.[138]

But soon after Johnson's solemn declaration that "we shall overcome," the civil rights revolution began to fall apart. Urban riots were symptomatic of more profound discontentment and disillusionment of African-Americans, there was a growing backlash of blue-collar white Americans who cheered on George Wallace as he again ran for president in 1968 and 1972. Martin Luther King, SNCC, and other civil rights organizations turned against Johnson and the quagmire of the Vietnam war. King's assassination and the ensuing urban riots only heightened the disappointment, frustration, and rage, from both whites and blacks. Americans were now telling pollsters that national policy was moving too fast on civil rights reform, and the rhetoric of "law and order," "welfare cheats," and "neighborhood schools" was resonating with voters as they looked to Richard Nixon and George Wallace as alternatives to the Great Society and its excesses.[139]

Nixon focused on a "southern strategy," trying to woo disaffected white southerners away from their historic home with the Democratic Party. Nixon, he assured southerners, knew them, knew their concerns, and castigated liberals as elitists who were out of touch with the concerns of average (white) Americans. In his first State of the Union address in 1969, Nixon said, "It is time for those who make massive demands on society to make minimal demands on themselves."[140] Court-ordered school busing, the eradication of housing discrimination, advancement in employment and education, central notions of justice and fairness would take a back seat in the Nixon administration.

Despite the setbacks and the obstacles, the Civil Rights Act of 1964 has been a major accomplishment. Title II, the public accommodations section, once reinforced by the Supreme Court, became, relatively speaking, the easiest part of the Civil Rights Act to enforce. It eradicated "whites only" and "colored only" drinking fountains, restaurants, or swimming pools. In a sense, many of these were peculiarities of the old South, not problems endemic to the entire country. They were problems that were fairly straightforward, and not fraught with baggage like school desegregation, affirmative action, or employment discrimination.[141] In many ways, it just became good business for restaurants, bars, and hotels to open to a broader clientele, and certainly many national chains and franchises probably welcomed the legislation.

Civil rights and education scholar Gary Orfield argues that the law extends far beyond education and "few measures in American history have ever had so profound an effect on our schools."[142] The law has gone beyond its original purpose by developing civil rights policies to protect Hispanic children in public schools and to provide bilingual education. For Orfield, the biggest problem with enforcement of Title II protections is the continued resistance of state and local officials and the unwillingness "in the four GOP Administrations since 1964 to employ the ultimate sanctions under the law."[143]

Title VII enforcement has been most effective in cases dealing with sex discrimination. Once it became operational, the Equal Employment Opportunity Commission (EEOC) at first brushed off sex discrimination cases, but, during the first two years of enforcement, 4,000 sex discrimination complaints were filed, roughly one-quarter of the commission's case load. Ten years later, in 1975, Title VII was being characterized as "the most comprehensive and important of all federal and state laws prohibiting employment discrimination."[144]

African-American voting registration had begun in earnest before the passage of the 1965 Voting Rights Act. The Southern Christian Leadership Conference's Voter Education Project, begun in 1962 and finishing in 1964, gave funds and coordinated the activities of the NAACP, the SCLC, SNCC, CORE, and the National Urban League. The Voter Education Project was successful in many southern states, but was a failure in Mississippi.[145] Likewise, the Department of Justice had filed seventy-one suits, together with broad-based litigation against Alabama, Mississippi, and Louisiana during the eight years before passage of the Voting Rights Act.[146]

The number of African-American voters in the South increased dramatically, thanks to the Voter Education Project and, especially in areas of greatest resistance, to Voting Rights Act enforcement. With only 1.1 million African-Americans registered in 1964, the number had risen to 3.1 million in 1969, with nearly 500 African-Americans holding elective office that year in the lower South.[147]

Discrimination and voting irregularities still persisted, but the focus was now shifting from outright denial of the vote to vote dilution. By 1988, the gap between black and white registration rates had narrowed considerably.[148] The gap of 49.9 percent in Alabama in 1965 had shrunk to just 6.6 percent in 1988; in Mississippi the 63.2 percent gap closed to 6.3 percent; and in Louisiana a 48.9 percent gap in 1965 became a 2.0 gap in favor of black voters in 1988.

The more ominous problem for African-Americans and Hispanics was voter dilution. Multi-member districts, at-large elections, appointing rather than electing officials, and gerrymandering were adopted in cities throughout the South in order to dilute the strength of black neighborhoods. In 1969, a Supreme Court decision looked at such practices in Mississippi and Virginia, and ruled that any such changes were subject to the pre-clearance provisions found in section 5 of the Voting Rights Act.[149] Up until this time, the pre-clearance section was relatively unused, but now the floodgates opened. During its first five years (1965–1969), there were just 323 section 5 changes submitted to the Attorney General; during the next five years, there were 4,153 changes requested. But, in the 1980s and 1990s, the number exploded, and in 2000–2002, there were almost 50,000 such requests made.[150]

In 1970, Congress extended the Voting Rights Act for another five years. In 1975, there were extensive hearings held, and an important provision was added to assist minorities whose primary language was not English. There was a conclusive record of exclusion of voting rights to Spanish-speaking citizens, and the 1975 Voting Rights Extension required oral or written bilingual assistance for voters in jurisdictions that have significant minority voters. The pre-clearance provisions of Section 5 were extended to areas of Texas where there was considerable discrimination against citizens of Hispanic origin.

If voter dilution was now the new concern, just what constituted dilution? The Supreme Court ruled in 1980 in *City of Mobile* v. *Bolden* that any constitutional claim of minority voter dilution must include proof that there was a racially discriminatory purpose.[151] This could present a very difficult hurdle to overcome in claiming voter discrimination. The *Bolden* standard, however, was to have a short life.

In May 1981, as extension renewal deadlines approached, Congress held eighteen separate hearings in Washington, Alabama, and Texas, with a total of 122 witnesses. Don Edwards (Democrat–California), chair of the House Judiciary Subcommittee on Civil Rights, later wrote about the continued discrimination, blatant and subtle, they found: "What we learned in those eighteen days of hearings was shocking—and sad. All seven members of the subcommittee, Republicans and Democrats alike, were dismayed." The most serious abuses were suffered by Hispanics in Texas who were not protected by the Voting Rights Act until 1975.[152]

Ronald Reagan and some Republicans argued for a nationwide voting standard, but that idea was rebuffed, and the VRA extension easily passed in the House. The two Republican senators from North Carolina, Jesse Helms and John P. East, complained that there was no reward for states which had improved their voting rights enforcement since being put on the list. In the end, Robert Dole (Republican–Kansas) brokered the language which now concentrated on the results of voter dilution rather than the intent of such dilution.[153] There was a lot of infighting and back scenes maneuvering, but eventually Congress renewed section 5 of the Voting Rights Act for another twenty-five years, and decided that Section 2 should be amended to prohibit vote dilution. Even old segregationist J. Strom Thurmond and Jamie L.

Whitten (Democrat–Mississippi) voted to pass the extension of the original 1965 Act.[154]

As African-Americans gained political strength, they found that even the archest of arch-segregationists had changed their tune, if for no other reason than they needed to attract these new voters. James O. Eastland, in his last run for office, courted African-American political leaders; so too, did Strom Thurmond, who in his latter years voted for the Martin Luther King, Jr., national holiday and drew a good 20 percent of African-American voters in South Carolina. Thurmond's conversion, however, didn't impress former U.S. Civil Rights commissioner Morris Abram: "The day the blacks got the vote in South Carolina you saw Strom Thurmond referring to them no longer as 'niggers' but as 'our beloved brethren.'"[155] George Wallace, permanently crippled by an assassin's bullet and nearing the end of his life, apologized to African-Americans, meeting with leaders individually, for his views and actions of the past. As his biographer Dan Carter observed, "Black Alabamians wanted Wallace to be forgiven."[156]

Still, complaints about voting rights enforcement kept mounting. The American Civil Liberties Voting Rights Project had brought 293 cases in thirty-one states since June 1982 challenging alleged discriminatory practices and failure of states or localities to comply with the law. Nearly half (145) of those cases came in Georgia, with thirty-eight coming from South Carolina. The Department of Justice, under Section 5 of the Voting Rights Act, had issued over 1,000 objections to discriminatory voting changes since 1982.[157] In 1993, the Supreme Court ruled on another dimension of race and voting, in *Shaw* v. *Reno*,[158] where it held that the redrawn congressional districts in North Carolina amounted to racial gerrymandering. The Court required that redistricting must meet both the requirements of the Voting Rights Act and the strict scrutiny standard it established for interpreting the Fourteenth Amendment. The "bizarre" results of redistricting, which led to a black-majority congressional district 160 miles long and at times no wider than a four-lane highway, could not be justified.

At the beginning of the contentious new 104th Congress, in January 1995, the Republicans had taken over the House of Representatives for the first time since 1955. Gerald Solomon (Republican–New York), the new chairman of the Rules Committee, ordered that the portrait of former committee chairman Howard Smith be hung in the committee room. John Lewis (Democrat–Georgia), who was elected to Congress in 1987, and eight of his colleagues from the Congressional Black Caucus would have none of it. Lewis, a hero of the civil rights movement, argued that Smith was "a man who represents our dark past" and that his portrait "deeply saddened and troubled" many people. Solomon averred that he did not know of Smith's segregationist views and said that Smith had always been good to committee Republicans. The portrait came down.[159]

The Voting Rights Act, amended in 1982, would be in force until 2007, unless Congress authorized its renewal. As the deadline approached, there were rumors floating around particularly on black-oriented radio stations, newspapers, and websites that President George W. Bush and the Republican-controlled Congress had no interest in extending the legislation. There were criticisms that the Justice Department, over objections from its own civil rights lawyers, had approved Republican-backed voting programs in Texas and Georgia, to the detriment of minorities.[160]

Indeed, relations between Bush and African-Americans were tense. The president had made a point to skip the annual meeting of the NAACP for five straight years, being the only chief executive since Warren G. Harding not to have made the important gesture of attending the annual gathering. But in July 2006, on the very day that the Senate unanimously voted to extend the Voting Rights Act, Bush for the first time addressed the annual NAACP convention held in Washington. Bush, and through him the Republican Party, extended its hand to the NAACP.

Using Ronald Reagan's words, Bush called the Voting Rights Act the "crown jewel" and vowed to sign its renewal. At the same time, he acknowledged the shortcomings of the position taken by the Republican Party: "I consider it a tragedy that the party of Abraham Lincoln let go of its historic ties with the African-American community. For too long, my party wrote off the African-American vote, and many African-Americans wrote off the Republican Party." Bush continued: "I understand that many African-Americans distrust my political party." This comment provoked some of the loudest cheering during the president's speech.[161]

During the summer of 2006, in the House of Representatives, the Republican leadership had to work hard to stave off a revolt from conservative southern Republican lawmakers. The Voting Rights Act extension, named in honor of Fannie Lou Hamer, Rosa Parks, and Coretta Scott King, would maintain the Justice Department's authority to review ballot changes in the states first targeted in the original 1965 legislation.[162] The extension, like the one adopted in 1982, would be in effect for twenty-five years, until 2031.

Many of the conservative complaints centered on Section 5, the pre-clearance provisions. In the forty-year history of voting rights enforcement, just eleven Virginia counties had managed to meet federal standards and became exempt from federal jurisdiction. Lynn A. Westmoreland (Republican–Georgia) led the conservative revolt, charging that the provisions, written so long ago, did not take into account the progress made in the sixteen impacted states. "It makes no sense," Westmoreland argued, "to extend this bill as is for twenty-five years and keep Georgia in the penalty box for sixty-six years based on the results of the 1964 election." Georgia indeed had made progress: in 1965, there were just three African-American election officials; in 2006, there were more than 800. Yet, the Department of Justice had found, over the course of those forty-one years, that there were 200 incidents where Georgia state and local officials tried to dilute black voting strength.[163]

K. Michael (Mike) Conaway (Republican–Texas) argued that, by continuing to have Texas on the pre-clearance list, the extension failed to understand that the problems had been corrected. "It labels Texas as a racist state, and that's not true," implored Conway. Steve King (Republican–Iowa) led a group of eighty fellow conservatives who argued against a requirement for bilingual ballots in districts where some of the voters had limited English skills. In the end, however, the Voting Rights Act extension passed the House of Representative, 390–33, after seven hours of impassioned debate, according to one reporter, "punctuated by several shouting matches between white Republicans and black Democrats from Georgia, who accused each other of hypocrisy and distorting the facts."[164] On July 27, 2006, President Bush signed into law the twenty-five year extension.

In late 2006, the U.S. Department of Justice filed a first-of-a-kind suit under the Voting Rights Act: a suit brought in eastern Mississippi accusing blacks of suppressing the voting rights of whites. The focus was on African-American Ike Brown, the chairman of the Noxubee County Democratic Executive Committee, and, according to the *New York Times*, its "undisputed political boss." Brown was accused of "relentless voting-related racial discrimination" against whites, who are outnumbered in the rural county by more than three to one. Brown was accused of taking cues from segregationist policies of the past and applying them today to maximize black voting and power. In June 2007, a U.S. District Court judge ruled that there was ample evidence that Brown's actions violated the Voting Rights Act.[165]

The Civil Rights Act of 1964 and the Voting Rights Act of 1965 were extraordinary legislative achievements. Public accommodations quickly desegregated, barriers to voting were removed and millions of African-American registered to vote. But the promise of school integration and a healthy balance between black and white students in public education became elusive. Over the decades, federal and state policymakers, civil rights activists, and community organizations have fought bruising battles over the use of busing to achieve racial integration, affirmative action, and job creation, and dilution of voting strength.

What remain are the more intractable issues of educational and economic opportunity, social justice, and social responsibility. Further there is the new reality of the demographics of American society and the workforce. The old dynamic of African-Americans, the South, and the legacy of servitude are facing a new dynamic of immigrants, legal and otherwise, especially from Latin America, who now count as the largest minority population.[166]

11

MEDICAL CARE FOR THE ELDERLY AND POOR
The Medicare and Medicaid Act of 1965

*No longer will older Americans be denied
the healing miracle of modern medicine. No longer
will illness crush and destroy the savings that they have so
carefully put away over a lifetime so that they might enjoy
dignity in their later years.*

Lyndon B. Johnson,
at the Medicare signing ceremony (1965)

*The elderly are not primarily interested in more money,
more benefits, more handouts.*

American Medical Association (1961)

On a hot, muggy July 30, 1965, in a simple but moving ceremony in the auditorium of the Truman Presidential Library in Independence, Missouri, President Lyndon Johnson affixed his signature to the Social Security Amendments of 1965, known to all as Medicare and Medicaid. Johnson, with an entourage of forty-seven, including thirty-three members of Congress, had flown from Washington to Independence to honor his predecessor, Harry Truman. In opening the ceremonies, the eighty-one-year-old former president uncharacteristically struggled for the right words. "I am glad to have lived this long and to witness today the signing of the Medicare bill."

Lyndon Johnson, with a keen eye for staging and political symbolism, praised Truman for his advocacy of national health insurance twenty years earlier. "I'm so proud that this has come to pass in the Johnson administration," said the president. "But it was really Harry Truman of Missouri who planted the seeds of compassion and duty which have today flowered into care for the sick and serenity for the fearful."

Making Medicare and Medicaid a reality had been a long, sometimes bitter, legislative struggle reaching back to the late 1930s. Johnson acknowledged the pioneering legislative work of Robert F. Wagner, James Murray and John Dingell, Aime Forand, Wilbur Mills, Clinton Anderson, Cecil King, and the advocacy of labor leaders and representatives of the elderly. But mostly he heaped praise on Harry Truman, who, on November 15, 1945 had first urged Congress to enact national health care. The 250 dignitaries assembled in the Truman Library auditorium erupted in cheers when Johnson said, "The people of the United States love and voted for Harry Truman, not because he gave them hell—but because he gave them hope." In signing the legislation into law, Lyndon Johnson used seventy-two ceremonial pens, giving the first to Mrs. Truman and the second to President Truman. Harry Truman also became the first recipient of a Medicare card, with Lyndon Johnson's signature bearing witness. "I am a very, very happy man," the noticeably frail Truman beamed.[1]

National health care was not included in the Social Security legislation of 1935. President Roosevelt never openly endorsed it, organized labor was not strong enough to push for it, and the medical establishment was firmly against it. National health insurance gained some attention in 1938 when a national health conference was convened, and a few years later when Senators Robert F. Wagner, Sr. (Democrat–New York) and James Murray (Democrat–Montana) and Representative John D. Dingell, Sr. (Democrat–Michigan), introduced such legislation in Congress. Their measure went nowhere, but hopes for some form of national health care were revived after World War II when President Truman strongly endorsed it in late 1945. But domestic battles, particularly one of such magnitude and controversy, would be hard-fought and difficult to win, with Congress changing hands and Truman's political capital plummeting.

When Truman shocked the nation with his come-from-behind win in 1948, one organization that was most stunned was the American Medical Association. Truman and the Democratic-controlled Congress pressed for national health care, but the AMA, using the wizardry of professional political consultants, launched an effective, multi-million-dollar grassroots effort, warning citizens against government control and "socialized medicine." So effective were the AMA and its allies that Congress never even took a vote on national health insurance. For the decade of the 1950s, national health care was definitely on the back burner.

National health care advocates tried a different approach. Social security was becoming much more an integral part of the elderly's life and well-being; in the 1950s, benefits were increased and eligibility was expanded. Perhaps the best way to approach national policy was to concentrate health care on the elderly, rather than the entire population, and do it through amendments to existing Social Security legislation. Congressman Aime Forand (Democrat–Rhode Island) introduced such legislation in 1957, but it fell on deaf ears. Health care became an issue in the 1960 presidential elections, and John F. Kennedy pushed for health care, using the now-familiar term of Medicare. Each year during the Kennedy administration, Senators Cecil R. King (Democrat–California) and Clinton P. Anderson (Democrat–New Mexico) introduced medical insurance legislation, concentrating on federal assistance for hospital care. And each year the American Medical Association vigorously fought against it.

With the 1964 presidential election, the two candidates were poles apart on federal health care. President Johnson urged Medicare's passage; Arizona Senator Barry Goldwater, the Republican nominee, was four-square against it. Lyndon Johnson won an extraordinary victory in November 1964, and progressive-minded Democrats swept into Congress, giving Johnson overwhelming majorities in both chambers. The 1964 election was not a referendum on Medicare, but, nevertheless, the people, who in poll after poll had indicated that they wanted health care for the elderly, had spoken.

The one voice in Congress that mattered, more than any other in the health care fight was that of Wilbur D. Mills (Democrat–Arkansas), the chairman of the House Ways and Means Committee. Long an opponent of Medicare and the administration-backed legislation, he now saw the wisdom of medical care reform. In a brilliant stroke, he cobbled together the administration's bill (hospital coverage), with a Republican substitute (doctors' fees), and joined them with medical assistance for the poor (Medicaid). Mills characterized it as a "three-layer cake," and it soon became the law of the land.

In short order, nearly every elderly person in America was covered by Medicare and millions of poor, of whatever age, were covered by Medicaid. It was an extraordinary effort on the part of the federal and state bureaucracies to get the programs up and running and get individuals signed up for coverage. Yet, there were plenty of problems looming ahead, particularly the inability to rein in the costs of health care and medical fees. In their haste to get the programs started, President Johnson, the Department of Health, Education, and Welfare (HEW), and Congress gave doctors and hospitals wide berth in setting fees and costs, and those expenses ballooned.

Despite soaring costs and nagging questions about fraud, there was a general consensus during the first thirty years of Medicare and Medicaid that the programs were worthwhile and working. That consensus fell apart with the rise of managed care and Health Maintenance Organizations (HMOs) during the late 1980s and 1990s, the Republicans taking over Congress following the 1994 elections, and efforts to strip back benefits and privatize health care. Medicare added two other components, a short-lived program, called Medicare+Choice, permitting individuals to use the services of private health plans, and in 2003 the Medicare Prescription Drug Improvement Act.

Today, Medicare is under considerable scrutiny. There is extraordinary concern, from all sides of the political spectrum, about the rising costs of health care, prescription drugs, and the growing inter-generational gap in health coverage. There have been commissions, white papers, academic conferences, congressional investigations, and campaign promises for overhauls of the system. There are also serious consideration that the United States join the rest of the industrialized world in health care policy, by enacting universal national health care, whose benefits would be for all Americans rather than just the elderly, the disabled, and a few others.

Background

Up through the end of the nineteenth century, the federal government responded to health issues only when faced with an immediate crisis.[2] In 1793, a yellow fever epidemic prompted President George Washington to ask lawmakers to pass emergency legislation that, if needed, would temporarily move Congress out of Philadelphia. The lawmakers did not object to this cautionary move, particularly when it involved their own safety. But other federal health legislation ran into the continuing controversy between federalists who wanted some national health response and anti-federalists who insisted on state control. The federal government in 1796 imposed a quarantine against yellow fever, but later, when anti-federalists had the political upper hand, the authority to enforce a quarantine was given to the states, with the national government playing only a subordinate role. In 1813, the federal government sent agents throughout the country to provide vaccinations to prevent smallpox. Here was a unique situation: the national government, using taxpayers' money, was dealing directly with the people. This program lasted for nine years, but was promptly shifted to state authorities after a federal agent mixed up the vaccines, causing several deaths in North Carolina.[3]

In 1824, the U.S. Supreme Court ruled in *Gibbons* v. *Ogden*, a matter involving a New York state exclusive franchise for steamship navigation, that the regulation of interstate and foreign commerce was specifically assigned to Congress through Article I Section 8 of the Constitution. Advocates for the state argued that, because the state had authority over health quarantines and other matters, it should also control navigation rights on the Hudson river. Chief Justice John Marshall ruled against state interests, declaring that the Hudson was a part of interstate commerce, but he also noted that health matters, like quarantines, were not mentioned in the specific powers of Congress, and therefore became the responsibility of the states under the Tenth Amendment.[4]

As seen in the chapter on the Homestead Act, social reformer Dorothea Dix persuaded Congress to use funds from the sale of surplus federal lands to create a program for national mental health. President Franklin Pierce, however, vetoed the legislation in 1854 on the grounds that the federal government had no business getting involved in the health concerns of its citizens. Healthcare would be a matter for state or local government, and, more particularly, of private charity.[5]

In 1878, the United States faced another health crisis, a yellow fever epidemic that was spreading up the Mississippi River valley from the port of New Orleans. Altogether, some twenty to thirty thousand persons had died. In 1879, a federal bill created the National Board of Health, which was given supervisory authority over quarantine issues. The legislation was hotly debated, the sticking point being federal versus state control. Reconstruction, carpetbaggers, and federal control over local affairs were still raw subjects for many members of Congress. The law remained in effect for just four years.[6]

Then, in 1892, four ships arrived in New York harbor from Hamburg, Germany, with cholera on board. The alarm sounded, and while there was no spread of this dreaded disease in New York City, it was enough of a scare for Congress to pass legislation authorizing a federal quarantine law. That measure is still on the books.[7]

While the American focus on health issues was confined chiefly to quarantines and emergency measures, European lawmakers were creating the first measures to protect the health of individuals. In 1883, the German Reichstag adopted a compulsory sickness insurance law protecting workers in a limited number of industrial categories. Later, this law was extended to assist the elderly and workers who had suffered from industrial accidents. By 1911, at least eleven European countries had established some form of health insurance legislation.[8]

By the early years of the twentieth century, American social reformers and some politicians were looking to the European model and asking why the United States was lagging behind. Among the early American social reformers was Dr. Isaac M. Rubinow, who argued that the United States was twenty-five years behind European governments in assisting the poor, and that social insurance, especially health care, was urgently needed. The Russell Sage Foundation in 1908 sent Dr. Lee K. Frankel and Miles Dawson to Europe to study various health care systems and both the Prudential and Equitable Life insurance companies sent investigators to Europe as well. Health care surfaced in the 1912 presidential contest, when Theodore Roosevelt, running on the Progressive (Bull Moose) Party ticket, called for protections against "the hazards of sickness, irregular employment and old age through the adoption of a system of social insurance adapted to American use."[9]

The American Association of Labor Legislation (AALL), founded at the University of Wisconsin in 1906, was created both to study and to promote all aspects of worker safety, from labor union organization, advocacy of minimum wage and maximum hour legislation, workmen's compensation, unemployment, and health and safety issues. In 1912, AALL had established a committee on social insurance, the first of its kind, and by 1915 had drafted model legislation, calling for assistance to low-income workers and cash compensation, hospital and medical benefits for workers and their dependents. Progressive governor Hiram Johnson of California established the California Social Insurance Commission in 1915, and the governors of Massachusetts and Nevada also endorsed state government health insurance plans. By the following year, the AALL model legislation was introduced in a number of state legislatures.[10]

At the national level, Congress held hearings on health care legislation in 1916. The surgeon general of the United States, Dr. Rupert Blue, who at the same time was president of the American Medical Association, addressed the AMA's 1916 annual meeting, predicting that "health insurance will constitute the next great step in social legislation."[11] The Social Insurance Committee of the AMA recommended that there be compulsory government-run health insurance.

But the devil was in the details. As social insurance historian Nancy Altman described it, "The more physicians learned about the proposal, the more they opposed it, fearing it would lead to government control of medical practice."[12] State medical societies came out in opposition, so did health insurance companies, the Pharmaceutical Manufacturers' Association, and the National Association of Manufacturers, which had supported health care programs in 1916. Samuel Gompers and the American Federation of Labor opposed government-imposed programs, fearing that such programs would weaken the incentive for workers to join unions and gain those rights through collective bargaining. In 1918, California voters in a referendum rejected government health insurance and the New York state legislature voted down a health insurance proposal.

At its annual meeting in New Orleans in 1920, the House of Delegates of the AMA sharply reversed its endorsement of health care legislation made just four years earlier, issuing this policy statement:

> The American Medical Association declares its opposition to the institution of any plan embodying the system of compulsory contributory insurance against illness, or any other plan of compulsory insurance which provides for medical service to be rendered to contributors or their dependents, provided, controlled, or regulated by any state or federal government.[13]

This emphatic declaration became the rallying cry for the AMA for the next forty-five years, as it fought vigorously against the evils of "socialized medicine."

There was little interest in federal health care legislation during the 1920s. Only one such law was enacted, the Sheppard–Towner Act of 1921, which provided federal grants to states for the promotion of the "welfare and hygiene" of mothers and new-borns. This was one of the last vestiges of the Progressive era, and the law got much of its impetus from women's organizations and newly enfranchised women voters. The AMA opposed this measure, but to no avail. The Sheppard–Towner Act, however, was not renewed at the end of the decade.[14]

In 1933 and 1934, the new president Franklin Roosevelt rarely talked about national health care, but he had assured the medical profession that he would keep politics out of the discussion. He was noncommittal when the issue of national health care came up, wanting not to get involved in debate over the matter.[15] Senator Robert Wagner's original bill on social insurance had proposed the creation of a Social Insurance Board that would consider "old-age insurance . . . health insurance, and related subjects." But, because of the pressure from the AMA and Roosevelt's fear that the social security package might be scuttled, Wagner's Social Insurance Board was recast as the Social Security Board and all references to health care were deleted.[16] The Social Security Act was silent on health care. That would be another fight for another day.

The AFL under Samuel Gompers steadfastly refused to endorse health care legislation, a view not shared by all union leaders, and one that caused considerable internal tension. Now, eleven years after Gompers's death and just two months after Social Security was enacted in 1935, delegates to the AFL convention, in a major reversal of policy, unanimously endorsed health insurance legislation by the federal and state governments. Gompers's successor, William Green, openly advocated health insurance.[17]

In 1936, Roosevelt created an Interdepartmental Committee to Coordinate Health and Welfare Activities, appointing Assistant Secretary of the Treasury Josephine Roche to call a conference in July 1938 to consider proposals for government-sponsored health insurance. The National Health Conference of 1938 drew together 176 delegates from a wide variety of interests: health insurance, doctor organizations, labor groups, and those representing citizen groups in need of medical care. This conference led to the introduction of a proposal from Senator Wagner, whose 1939 legislation called for federal grants to states so that they could establish health insurance systems. The timing, however, was not very good. The 1938 elections brought a resurgence of conservative southern Democrats and Republicans to Congress; they were in no mood to approve expanded social insurance benefits. Also, the AMA and its state medical societies vigorously opposed Wagner's bill, and Roosevelt, becoming more preoccupied with impending war in Europe and the still anemic national economy, would not embrace Wagner's legislation, and it ultimately died in the House.[18]

Congress was reluctant to extend social insurance legislation, but the public was warming up to government assistance for health care. Public opinion polls taken in 1936, 1937, 1938, and 1942 asked whether government ought to help citizens pay for the medical care they needed. Three out of four people who responded in each of these polls said yes. When asked in 1944 and 1945 if it was a "good idea" to have Social Security pay for doctors' and hospital bills, the majority of respondents said "yes."[19]

While Wagner's 1939 legislation would have extended federal assistance to states for health insurance, the first real national health insurance plan was presented to Congress in 1943, again from Wagner, his Senate colleague James Murray, and Representative John Dingell, Sr. The Wagner–Murray–Dingell bill called for a federal system of hospital and medical coverage, funded by an employer/employee payroll tax through Social Security. The U.S. Surgeon General was given broad authority to set fees and limit the number of patients a doctor could attend to. But the legislation hit a brick wall: Roosevelt stayed away from it, the AMA and its allies vigorously opposed it, and Congress would not consider it. Wagner–Murray–Dingell was resubmitted in 1945, 1947, and 1949, failing every time, but certainly generating sparks of controversy every time it was introduced.[20]

The drive for national health insurance was revived when President Harry Truman sent a strong endorsement to Congress in November 1945. "Our new economic bill of rights should mean health security for all, regardless of residence, station, or race—everywhere in the United States," Truman said. The AMA and Republicans had complained that national health insurance was nothing more than such a scheme. Truman anticipated the charge: he stated that he was not recommending socialized medicine. "Socialized medicine means that all doctors work as employees of the government. The American people want no such system. No such system is here proposed."[21] Truman called for an expansion of hospitals, increased support for public health, child and maternal care, and a health insurance program that would cover everyone, even professionals, agricultural and domestic workers who were not covered by Social Security.[22]

In 1946, Senate hearings began on Truman's bill. Senator Murray chaired the Committee on Education and, as he began his opening remarks, his very irritated colleague Robert A. Taft (Republican–Ohio) blurted out: this bill is "the most socialistic measure that this Congress has ever had before it, seriously."[23] Taft had to be restrained and then escorted out of the hearings by Capitol police. Such was the mood in Congress: bitter division, finger-pointing, and vows of reprisal.

With the congressional elections of 1946, Republicans regained control of both the House and the Senate for the first time since the beginning of the New Deal. In this, the Eightieth Congress, Truman's domestic programs would face a cantankerous, reinvigorated Republican majority. Truman could no longer count on labor for support. Labor leaders were expending nearly all of their energy on a losing fight against the Taft–Hartley legislation. Furthermore, unions were now turning to contract bargaining as the solution to health care problems for their members. The United Mine Workers, under president John L. Lewis, negotiated a health, welfare, and retirement fund, supported by a royalty charge on each ton of coal extracted from the mines. The United Steelworkers pursued private solutions as well. By 1950, approximately 95 percent of the employees represented by CIO unions had managed to obtain health and welfare plans written into their collective bargaining agreements.[24]

In the presidential election year of 1948, Truman was exhausted politically, and nearly everyone with any sense of politics knew that Governor Thomas E. Dewey of New York would be the next president. Truman had angered southern Democrats by advocating strong civil rights reforms, he had irritated party liberals by equivocating on issues dear to them, his popularity with voters was scraping the bottom, and only die-hard Democrats wanted Truman to stay on the ticket. Democrats were demoralized, bitter, and sure of defeat. Republicans, particularly Dewey himself, saw the election as a slam dunk; so confident was Dewey that he shortened his campaign appearances, and talked to the press about his cabinet choices during those critical weeks before the election. The Gallup Poll stopped measuring public opinion weeks before the November election: why belabor a foregone conclusion?[25]

The AMA, like so many others, was stunned when Truman won. The Democrats had gained seventy-five seats in the House of Representatives, giving Truman a paper majority prepared to enact his national health insurance program. In his State of the Union speech before the Eighty-First Congress on January 4, 1949, Truman called for a variety of legislative actions, including a $4 billion tax increase, the repeal of Taft–Hartley, and the protection of civil rights. He did not back off from health care: "We must spare no effort to raise the general level of health in this country. In a nation as rich as ours, it is a shocking fact that tens of millions lack adequate medical care. We are short of doctors, hospitals, nurses. We must remedy these shortages. Moreover, we need—and we must have without further delay—a system of prepaid medical insurance which will enable every American to afford good medical care."[26]

This was the moment of truth for the AMA; it had to fight back with everything it could muster. First, the AMA had to replace the hidebound and reactionary Dr. Morris Fishbein, who had been the organization's chief spokesman during the 1930s and 1940s. The AMA needed the deft hand of political professionals. In 1946, it turned to the California-based public relations firm of Whitaker and Baxter for advice and counsel. Clem Whitaker and his wife Leone Baxter were veterans of high-profile gubernatorial elections and issue advocacy fights in California, and they had caught the attention of the AMA because of their role in helping the California Medical Association fight off Governor Earl Warren's state-sponsored health insurance proposal.[27]

Clem Whitaker outlined the strategy for the AMA: it had to be a simple, vigorous campaign with broad appeal, and it couldn't just look like the doctors fighting against Washington. With a staff of thirty-seven, Whitaker and Baxter set up shop in Chicago, the home of the AMA, and spent nearly $5 million in the next three-and-a-half years, particularly exploiting grassroots and direct lobbying techniques.[28]

The AMA needed both a slogan and an enemy. The label "socialized medicine" fitted perfectly: it played on the fears of some unknown socialist, even communist, menace, playing in harmony with the red-baiting of Representative Richard Nixon (Republican–California), the House Committee on Un-American Activities, and the communist and fellow-travelers charges that were later perfected by Senator Joseph McCarthy (Republican–Wisconsin). The enemy? Well it couldn't be Harry Truman who had just won an upset election. It had to be Oscar Ewing, the administrator of the Federal Security Agency, the agency that housed Social Security. Newspaper reporter Mike Gorman once asked Clem Whitaker how he planned to defeat national health care. That seemed like an impossible job, said Gorman. "Oh, that's easy," said Whitaker.

> We've been through this fight with Governor Warren's proposal for a
> state health insurance program and it's a cinch to beat it. In order to
> do so, there are only two things you have to have. First you have to
> give the program a bad name and we're going to call it "socialized

medicine" because the idea of socialism is very unpopular in the United States. . . . The second thing you have to have is a devil. You have to have a devil in the picture to paint him in all his horns and we've got that man chosen. We first thought we would center the attack on President Truman, but we've decided he is too popular; but we've got a perfect devil in this man Ewing and we're going to give him the works.[29]

The Whitaker and Baxter team gathered eight thousand endorsements from non-medical groups—from the American Legion to the General Federation of Women's Clubs, from fraternal, service, and business organizations, large and small. They all pledged their opposition to compulsory national health insurance. Whitaker and Baxter solicited favorable editorials, distributed between 40 and 50 million pieces of literature to doctors' and dentists' offices, druggists, insurance agents, and others.

There was no direct charge against Truman or his health insurance plan, but rather a broad attack against "socialized medicine." One effective broadside showed a well-known nostalgic picture of a kindly family doctor at the bedside of a sick child. The text read: "Keep Politics Out of This Picture! . . . Would you change this picture? Compulsory health insurance is political medicine. It would bring a third party—a politician—between you and your Doctor. It would bind up your family's health in red tape. It would result in heavy payroll taxes—and inferior medical care for you and your family. Don't let that happen here!"[30]

And it didn't happen. This was probably Truman's best chance of getting national health insurance enacted, but the fight was fierce and contentious, and finally national health was mired in Congress.[31] In the end Truman had given up on the prospects of national health care, there was no action in either the House or the Senate, and the AMA's "socialized medicine" campaign won out. Altogether, the AMA spent over $1.5 million in 1949 and $1.3 in 1950 for lobbying purposes; up to this point in American political history, no organization had ever spent that much money lobbying Congress.[32]

Knowing that universal national health care was a dead issue, the Truman administration started looking for something on a smaller scale. In its final days, Oscar Ewing unveiled a new plan, giving sixty days of free hospital care to all Social Security beneficiaries, that is, the elderly, widows, and orphans. The plan, introduced in late February 1952, during the lamest of lame-duck periods, went nowhere. With everyone's attention focused on the upcoming presidential election and a new administration, Ewing's proposal was barely noticed. Yet this was the seed out of which Medicare would grow.

For now, however, the fight was over. During the 1950 congressional elections, the AMA spent an unheard-of $1 million in the two-week period before the elections, and another $2 million came from tie-in advertising from groups sympathetic to the AMA.[33] Democrats lost twenty-eight seats in the

House that year and barely kept a majority in the Senate. The Republican Party platform for the 1953 presidential race condemned "federal compulsory health insurance, with its crushing cost, wasteful inefficiency, bureaucratic dead weight, and debased standards of medical care."[34] In 1952, Dwight Eisenhower, a firm opponent of "socialized medicine," was elected president and, during the same election, Republicans had recaptured majorities in both the House and the Senate.

The Eisenhower administration, through its new department of Health, Education and Welfare (HEW) and its secretary, Oveta Culp Hobby, put forth an alternative plan, which would assist the growth of private health insurance through a limited reinsurance service. This was a modest program, but it, nevertheless, raised red flags for the AMA, who, in the testimony of one of its officials, saw it as an "opening wedge" to "socialized medicine." The measure was soundly defeated in 1954, failing once more in 1956.[35]

Yet, there was growing interest at both the state and federal level in looking at the problems of health and aging. The New York legislature in 1947 became the first state lawmaking body to conduct a wide-ranging series of hearings on the problems of aging. Other states followed up with their own hearings and recommendations. The Federal Security Agency, the predecessor to the Department of Health, Education, and Welfare, convened a national conference on the problems of aging in 1950, and there were several steps by Congress to establish organizations to deal with the problems of aging. Then, in 1956, the Eisenhower administration established the Federal Council on Aging, an interdepartmental committee that advised federal agencies on issues related to the elderly.[36]

In 1956, Congress enacted a major addition to Social Security by adding benefits for the totally and permanently disabled. Organized labor, now with the merged AFL-CIO, had rallied behind the Social Security fight, and after winning that battle was determined to do more. The target now became health insurance for the elderly. Nelson H. Cruikshank, head of the AFL-CIO social security department, and his staff created legislation calling for insurance protection for surgery fees, sixty days of hospitalization and another sixty days for nursing home care, drug coverage, and other fees. The AFL-CIO presented its bill to the Ways and Means Committee, the key committee in the House of Representatives that has jurisdiction over social security legislation.[37]

The new chairman of Ways and Means, Wilbur D. Mills (Democrat–Arkansas), declined to sponsor the bill; so did two other senior members. Finally, Aime J. Forand (Democrat–Rhode Island) agreed, and, from 1957 through 1960, the Forand bill became the focus of Medicare proponents.

Why concentrate on health insurance for elderly, the most vulnerable and most expensive cohort in society? No other industrialized country that had health insurance for its citizens concentrated only on the elderly. Robert M. Ball, one of the pioneers in social insurance policy who later was commissioner of the Social Security Administration, argued that medical care for the elderly was a fall-back position. All of those who developed Medicare, Ball argued, were advocates of universal national health care, but had to face political reality. The best chance to get any coverage was to start with those who were already covered under Social Security, the elderly. "We expected Medicare to be a first step toward universal national health insurance," Ball wrote years later.[38]

The Ways and Means Committee began hearings on the Forand bill in 1958, but met with strong opposition from the Eisenhower administration. The AMA also spent a quarter million dollars lobbying to defeat the bill and, in 1960, the Ways and Means Committee rejected Forand's legislation by 17 to 8, with chairman Mills in the opposition.[39]

Two other health care approaches were considered in Congress that year. Senator Jacob Javits (Republican–New York) presented a bill which would authorize federal grants to states that helped subsidize health insurance for the elderly, with an emphasis on private insurance and voluntary participation. The second approach, which became law, was offered by Wilbur Mills and Senator Robert S. Kerr (Democrat–Oklahoma) and provided increased federal money for state programs that helped the indigent. The Kerr–Mills bill was an updated version of legislation introduced by Senator Taft to help the neediest elderly persons meet their medical expenses. Kerr–Mills required states to set up programs to assist the elderly. But Kerr–Mills was flawed and underperforming: by 1963, just thirty-two states participated and the bulk of the federal matching funds went to just five states.[40]

Aime Forand retired from Congress in 1960, but the issue of health care for the elderly did not die. Senator John F. Kennedy (Democrat–Massachusetts), after his nomination as the Democratic presidential candidate, introduced a Forand-type bill in the Senate, which was promptly defeated. Kennedy then made medical care an issue on the campaign trail. He had received only one Republican vote for his bill, and with a little campaign math and rhetoric went after his opponents: "Ninety percent of the Republicans voted against Social Security in the mid-thirties and 95 percent in 1960 voted against the medical care for the aged tied to Social Security."[41]

During his first year as president, John Kennedy urged that federal aid to education and Medicare, as it was now being called, be priority legislative items. In his first State of the Union address, Kennedy urged that medical insurance for the elderly be enacted in 1961. Then, ten days later, he sent to Congress the first ever special message devoted to health care issues. In addition to the legislation he had sponsored late in his term as senator, Kennedy urged Congress to pass legislation dealing with nursing home construction grants, hospital research and development, training programs, and the establishment of a National Institute of Child Health and Development. Each of these ideas had come from recommendations from a Kennedy transition task force headed by Wilbur J. Cohen.[42]

Cohen, one of the chief architects of federal social insurance policy and during the 1950s a professor at the University of Michigan, was appointed assistant secretary of HEW and put in charge of writing Medicare legislation. It was also Cohen's job, both in the Kennedy and then the Johnson administrations, to work closely with Wilbur Mills. As his biographer, Edward D. Berkowitz, noted, Cohen "was practically the administration's ambassador to Wilbur Mills."[43]

Administration-backed Medicare legislation was brought up in Congress by Forand's successors, Clinton P. Anderson (Democrat–New Mexico) in the Senate and Cecil R. King (Democrat–California) in the House. But the bill could not surmount the hurdle of a reluctant Ways and Means Committee, with six Democrats, including Wilbur Mills, joining ten Republicans to make a hostile majority of 16–9.[44] For the AMA and its 180,000 members, it was time to go back on high alert and, if need be, play a little rough. Cecil King was so irritated at the AMA that in March 1962, he called on the American Association of Advertising Agencies to investigate what he characterized as "lies and deception" found in AMA newspaper advertisements against the King–Anderson bill. King charged that the AMA was engaging in a "coldly calculated campaign of dishonesty" to discredit his legislation.[45]

On May 20, 1962, at a rally at Madison Square Garden in New York, some 18,000, mostly elderly citizens had paid $1 each to listen to a speech by President Kennedy; another 2,500 who did not have tickets listened outside the Garden through loudspeakers. It seemed as colorful and raucous as a campaign rally. Just the night before, the Garden had been festooned with bunting, balloons and streamers for a birthday salute to Kennedy, with Marilyn Monroe gushing her birthday wishes. This night, after the entertainment of Mitch Miller and his Sing-Along Singers, opera star Robert Merrill, and a medley from *Porgy and Bess*, the rally heard from AFL-CIO president George Meany, HEW secretary Abraham A. Ribicoff, and finally the president. Delivering his speech without notes, Kennedy said that the fight for Medicare was "not a campaign against doctors, because doctors have joined us. This is a campaign to help people meet their responsibilities." Kennedy urged the crowd at the Garden and, through closed-circuit television, the 150,000 others reportedly attending rallies in thirty-three other states, to back medical care for the aged under Social Security. Kennedy assured the receptive crowd that King–Anderson would be passed "this year or, inevitably as the tide comes in, next year."[46]

However, the AMA saw it differently. The organization rented Madison Square Garden the following night, bought time on 190 television stations throughout the country to deliver an hour-long rebuttal of the president. The AMA had wanted free network time, but was refused; Boston television stations would not show the AMA rebuttal, even when offered money. On an empty Madison Square Garden stage, facing an empty hall, Dr. Edward R. Annis, who later that year would become AMA president, characterized the King–Anderson bill as a "cruel hoax and a delusion" and told the television audience that "doctors feared that the American public is in danger of being blitzed, brainwashed, and bandwagoned."[47] Instead, Annis argued for the Kerr–Mills program, and, while he was at it, took a swipe at Britain's national health service. The *British Medical Journal* later shot back, characterizing the AMA's attack on the British system as "vulgar, cheap and nonsense," while vigorously supporting the Kennedy administration's medical plans.[48]

The AMA, however, won the debate. Kennedy's comments were off-the-cuff, sounded too much like a campaign rally, and failed to win over the skeptical television audience. The AMA, emboldened by its encounter with the president, took out full-page ads in newspapers throughout the country asking citizens to write their congressmen to stop King–Anderson. Suddenly, the mood appeared to sour on federally sponsored health care for the elderly. The AMA also formed a new entity, the American Medical Political Action Committee, arguing that "medicine must play an increasing role in day-to-day political activities." The AMA was determined to protect its friends on the Ways and Means Committee and to raise funds for like-minded candidates in the 1962 mid-term elections.[49]

The key to getting King–Anderson, or any other version of medical care for the elderly, passed into law was to convince the chairman of the House Ways and Means committee. But Wilbur Mills had been dead set against the Forand, Kennedy, and King–Anderson legislation. He preferred his own legislation, the flawed Kerr–Mills Act, which applied a means test, and helped those states that wanted to participate to assist the elderly poor. Winning over Mills was imperative, not just for medical care, but for tax reform, trade issues, and a variety of other key finance-related measures.

In the early fall of 1963, President Kennedy again paid special attention to Mills. When the president flew down to Arkansas to help dedicate a dam in Mills's congressional district, a White House aide told a reporter, "If Wilbur wanted us to go down to Heber Springs and sing 'Down by the Old Mill Stream,' we'd be glad to do it." Indeed, at the Greers Ferry Dam dedication, Kennedy flattered the Arkansas delegation by saying that "pound for pound" it wielded more influence in Washington than any other state delegation.[50] Kennedy might have been referring to long-serving senators John L. McClellan or J. William Fulbright, but mostly he was using his charm and flattery to butter up Wilbur Mills.

Making the Legislation

Kennedy made the pilgrimage to Heber Springs in early October; seven weeks later he was assassinated in Dallas. At the beginning of the second session of the Eighty-Eighth Congress, the push for Medicare now was in the hands of President Lyndon B. Johnson and his team of advisors. In February, 1964, Johnson put Wilbur Cohen, then the number three official at HEW, in full charge of the administration's Medicare efforts.[51] Presidential and congressional elections were just nine months away, and certainly health insurance would be a major topic. Republican governor Nelson Rockefeller of New York, who was a leading contender for his party's presidential nomination, had introduced a Medicare bill (Congressman John V. Lindsay of New York); so too had Senator Javits (Republican–New York). Wilbur Mills was anxious to get a Democratic proposal considered in his committee by early March, and, of course, Lyndon Johnson was keenly interested in putting a Democratic stamp on medical legislation.

Wilbur Cohen and the Social Security staff worked hard to meet Wilbur Mills's demands for background information, cost estimates, and alternative policy plans. Among the policy plans they developed would be the first draft of what later would become Medicaid, providing health insurance for welfare recipients.[52]

Throughout the Spring of 1964, Mills equivocated about Medicare: he worried about the impact of scheduled Social Security tax increases, he opposed the King–Anderson bill, and was worried about conservative Democrats on his committee who might not follow his leadership. His political worries came soon enough. Three such Democrats, John C. Watts of Kentucky, A. Sydney Herlong, Jr., of Florida, and Burr P. Harrison of Virginia, each announced intentions to vote against Medicare. This was enough for Mills to announce that he would oppose the King–Anderson medicare package and recommend instead a cash benefit increase for Social Security. Medicare could wait, Mills finally decided, until after the November election. On June 24, 1964, Mills announced that he could not support Medicare; the growing number of medical care advocates were outraged.[53]

President Johnson and his political strategist Larry O'Brien did not want to force a vote on Medicare in the Ways and Means Committee, and instead opted to add the administration's King–Anderson bill as an amendment to a proposed Social Security increase bill in the Senate. To their surprise, a modified version passed in the Senate as a rider to the Social Security bill, and leading the charge were Senators Anderson and Javits, together with Albert Gore, Sr. (Democrat–Tennessee). Barry Goldwater publicly and forthrightly opposed Medicare. He voted against it in 1960, 1962, and now in September 1964. On the Senate floor, he declared that "my fundamental objection to this proposal is that it is based on the unspoken premise that American workers . . . are incapable of deciding how to spend their money. It reveals a contempt for the intelligence and the judgment of our people. . . ."[54]

For voters, here was a clear, stark difference in policy choice: Johnson was the champion of federal medical care and Goldwater consistently opposed it. As one of Johnson's political advisors said to the president, "I don't think *you* should be kicking Goldwater, but this is a great opportunity for us to beat him to death among these older people if we play it right."[55] And beaten up Goldwater was. Johnson and his vice-presidential running mate Hubert H. Humphrey of Minnesota won decisively, with margins unequaled since Roosevelt's 1936 landslide victory over Alf Landon. Goldwater won his home state, together with the Deep South of Louisiana, Mississippi, Alabama (where

Johnson was not even on the ballot), Georgia, and South Carolina. Further, the Congress was even more firmly in the hands of Democrats. There were seventy-one new Democrats, nearly all of whom committed to Medicare's passage. As Larry O'Brien put it, "For all practical purposes, Medicare passed on Election Day. We estimated that we gained close to forty new Medicare votes in the House and at least two in the Senate. Equally important, after years of frustration with the House Ways and Means Committee, we had a seventeen-to-eight majority there."[56]

The new Eighty-Ninth Congress, which met for the first time on January 4, 1965, was overwhelmingly Democratic and ready to enact Johnson's legislation. Johnson was determined to get Medicare passed; it was one of his very few legislative defeats in 1964, and he could not let that defeat stand. In his State of the Union address delivered on the first day of Congress, Lyndon Johnson asked that Medicare be the first order of business, and, in both the House and Senate, the administration's bills were give the symbolic designation of HR-1 and S-1, respectively. On the second day of the new Congress, the Ways and Means committee membership was brought into line with the new realities of the two-to-one Democratic domination, going from fifteen Democrats to seventeen, and Republicans dropping from ten to eight. From 1961 on, every pro-Medicare Democrat who left Ways and Means had been replaced by a pro-Medicare legislator, and two anti-Medicare lawmakers were replaced by pro-Medicare ones. Johnson worked closely with Speaker of the House John W. McCormack (Democrat–Massachusetts) to revise the partisan ratio on the committee. Former Ways and Means committee staffer and political scientist John F. Manley called it the "clearest case" of packing the committee to assure Medicare's passage.[57]

On January 7, Johnson sent a special message to Congress on health care, and it looked like nothing could stop medical insurance from becoming a reality. Wilbur Mills, now at the height of his political power, counted the votes and faced a new political reality. As Lyndon Johnson wrote in his memoirs, "when the election changed the head count in Congress, [Wilbur Mills's] mind changed as well." Mills announced that he hoped to get the administration's King–Anderson bill through his committee and out to the floor of the House by mid-March. This news stunned the AMA. Doctors were furious at Mills for seemingly caving in to the administration, and he, in turn, was furious at the AMA for refusing to acknowledge political reality.[58]

> Eighty-Ninth Congress, 1st Session (January 4–October 23, 1965)
>
> Senate: 68 Democrats; 32 Republicans
>
> House: 295 Democrats; 140 Republicans
>
> President: Lyndon B. Johnson

The AMA had strongly backed Goldwater; indeed, nine of its past presidents served as health policy advisors to his campaign. But now, ignoring the inevitable, some 200 representatives of state medical societies met in Chicago and decided to press on. In a surprise move, the AMA launched a last-ditch half-million-dollar anti-Medicare campaign, and came up with their own legislative plan, called the Eldercare Program, which would provide federal and state grants, under Kerr–Mills guidelines, to subsidize private health insurance policies. Among its many communication pieces, it hired retired actor Ronald Reagan to record an appeal to the wives of AMA members, asking them to fight against Medicare and for Eldercare by writing to Congress. "If you don't do this," the actor implored, "one of these days you and I are going to spend our sunset years telling our children and our children's children what it once was like in America when men were free."[59]

But the AMA was both irritating and offending its friends. The White House, according to Larry O'Brien, was "delighted by the AMA's blind opposition to the inevitable."[60] Congressman Frank Thompson, Jr. (Democrat–New Jersey), no friend of the AMA, scoffed at the Eldercare Program, which he dubbed "Doctorcare." It was to be financed, Thompson chortled, "by a two-percent federal tax on applesauce, and the funds were to be used to provide special therapy for any physician who felt himself suffering from an urge to make house calls; if he didn't respond satisfactorily to the arguments of his colleagues over the phone, he was to be rushed to the nearest Cadillac showroom."[61]

Milton Friedman, professor of economics at the University of Chicago and policy advisor to Goldwater, might have hit the most sensitive nerve, characterizing the AMA as "perhaps the strongest trade union in the United States."[62]

Organized labor and the Democratic Party strongly backed Medicare. So too did the National Council of Senior Citizens, an organization created in 1961 as an outgrowth of the Kennedy presidential campaign's Senior Citizens for Kennedy. Aime Forand, just retired from Congress, was persuaded to lend his name as chairman of the organization. The National Council for Senior Citizens was underwritten by the AFL-CIO and the Democratic Party, and by 1963 boasted some two million members in affiliate clubs. Another organization, which would later become the dominant lobbying organization for the elderly, the National Retired Teachers Association–American Association of Retired Persons, was essentially on the sidelines, not actively promoting or trying to defeat Medicare.[63]

The American people were deeply concerned about medical care for the elderly, according to a poll taken by Louis Harris in early 1965: "So deep is the concern about medical care for the aged," Harris wrote, "that the American people would welcome any of a variety of national plans, ranging from President Johnson's medicare under Social Security to the American Medical Association's Eldercare plan with voluntary features."[64] The administration's plan was supported chiefly by citizens on the East and West coasts, Democrats, residents of urban areas, and families making less than $10,000 per year. By a two-to-one margin, respondents wanted Medicare rather than having lowered taxes, and by the same percentage, they favored Medicare over having a balanced budget.

Highlights of the Medicare-Medicaid Act of 1965

The Social Security Act Amendments of 1965 contain two key provisions, title XVIII (Medicare) and Title XIX (Medicaid). Medicare has two basic components. Part A is Hospital Insurance, which covers hospital, skilled nursing, and home health care services. It is funded by payroll taxes under Social Security and beneficiaries are those sixty-five and older who are also eligible for Social Security. Part B is Supplementary Medical Insurance, which covers the costs of physician services, outpatient care, and ambulatory services. It covers those eligible for Social Security and is funded by general revenues and by patient deductibles.

A third component is Medicaid, which provides health care insurance to persons of low income, regardless of age. It is funded jointly by the federal and state governments, with the federal government's portion coming from general revenue funds rather than payroll taxes.

The AMA-backed Eldercare Program was introduced by A. Sydney Herlong and Thomas B. Curtis (Republican–Missouri). But, to the AMA's dismay, a Republican alternative was also introduced by John W. Byrnes of Wisconsin. Byrnes's bill was patterned after the high-option plan then in use for federal employees. The Republican bill was, according to John Manley, "simple, but ingenious: an optional plan, funded by a small monthly payment from each enrollee with federal funds taken out of general revenue, included a benefits package so attractive to the elderly in terms of cost to them that practically everyone would participate."[65] But as clever as the Republican plan might be, Byrnes, an opponent of Medicare, privately conceded that his bill didn't stand a chance of passage, not against such a strong Democratic majority.[66]

In many respects, the Republican substitute answered objections from the medical lobby to the administration-backed King–Anderson bill and also went far beyond King–Anderson benefits. In theory, the Byrnes bill was a voluntary, not a compulsory, program; its benefits were generous; by being funded by general revenues and not payroll taxes, it was actuarially sound and would not hurt social security funding.[67]

Key Individuals in Medicare

Lyndon B. Johnson (1908–1973) was determined to push Medicare as his top priority in the Eighty-Ninth Congress. Medicare was a key component of the Great Society legislation, which included the Civil Rights of 1964, the Voting Rights Act of 1965, the Elementary and Secondary Education Act of 1965, the Higher Education Facilities Act of 1965, the Immigration and Nationality Services Act of 1965, and the Economic Opportunity Act of 1964.

Wilbur D. Mills (1909–1992) began service in the House of Representatives in 1939, and from 1957 through 1974 was chairman of the Ways and Means Committee. Apart from Medicare, Mills championed increases in Social Security benefits, and was also the chief tax expert in the House and responsible for the Tax Reform Act of 1969. He briefly toyed with the idea of running for president in 1972, and was involved in a tawdry scandal months before his re-election to Congress in 1974. Mills stepped down from the chairmanship of Ways and Means in 1974 and did not seek re-election in 1976.[68]

Wilbur J. Cohen (1913–1987), another product of the University of Wisconsin and a protege of Edwin Witte, at the beginning of his career had served in Washington as a technical advisor to Arthur Altmeyer and the Social Security Board and then director of the Bureau of Research and Statistics. He was professor of public welfare administration at the University of Michigan during the latter part of the Eisenhower administration, and developed health care policy alternatives for presidential candidate John F. Kennedy. He was the third-ranking official in HEW during the Kennedy Administration, and later under President Johnson was the second ranking official and most responsible for crafting the administration's medicare and other health care policies. In 1968, Cohen became secretary of HEW.[69]

On March 9, Wilbur Cohen, at the invitation of chairman Mills, appeared before the Ways and Means Committee to explain the various health care options. Cohen outlined the measures for the administration's King–Anderson bill and then outlined the Byrnes bill as well. After completing the summary of policy options, Wilbur Mills turned to his colleague, John Byrnes, and said, "You know, John, I like that part of your bill about taking care of doctor bills as well as hospital expenses."[70]

Mills had two objectives in mind, to "strike a balance between safeguarding Social Security and protecting the general operating budget."[71] The Byrnes package, which focused on doctors' bills, would be financed through the general revenue fund, not putting a strain on the payroll Social Security tax.

The third part of the Mills plan, Medicaid, would replace the 1960 Kerr–Mills legislation, making it a more uniform program and financed with a simpler method, with the federal government picking up between 50 and 80 percent of the expenses of the program. Historian Sheri I. David argues that Medicaid was "casually added as an after thought" partially to appease the AMA and its Eldercare program and to improve on the five-year-old Kerr–Mills legislation.[72]

It was a stroke of policy genius: combine the administration's bill (hospital coverage), with a Republican-backed alternative (doctors' fees), and throw in assistance to the poor (Medicaid) for good measure. It made sense politically, too: it took much of the wind out of the AMA and Republican opposition, pleased some fiscal conservatives, particularly the chairman himself, and it was, finally, legislation that Mills was confident would win passage in Congress.

That evening, March 2, Wilbur Cohen rushed into the Oval Office, as Johnson described in his memoirs, in "a state of high excitement." Cohen related to Johnson how Mills had "dropped a bombshell," putting together the administration and Republican plans so quickly and adroitly that "the

Republicans were dumbstruck" and so were the administration sponsors.[73] Mills called his bill a "three-layer cake" (hospitalization, doctors' fees, and Medicaid), and he urged Cohen to redraft the administration bill overnight to reflect the compromise. Johnson gave Cohen the approval to rework the bill, but to make sure credit came the Democrats' way: "Just tell them," Johnson said to Cohen, "to snip off that name 'Republican' and slip those little old changes into the bill."[74]

Mills's three-part Medicare package quickly sailed through the Ways and Means Committee, on a straight party-line vote of 17–8. What had made Wilbur Mills, the long-time opponent of health care legislation, change his mind? *New York Times* reporter Tom Wicker noted that, at the beginning of 1965, Mills found himself "with a majority for the bill in his committee. He found the House highly receptive and eager to pass [Medicare]. He found Mr. Johnson plugging its virtues to an already convinced public. In short, Mr. Mills faced a new situation in which it had become at least possible that his own committee might overturn him."[75]

The next day, March 26, Johnson brought Senate and House leaders to the Oval Office to make sure that everyone was on board for passing Medicare. After the meeting, they moved on to the Cabinet Room, where television cameras were ready. Johnson introduced the nine Democratic leaders, and, one by one, they each expressed their full support for Medicare. Only one hesitated, 78-year-old Harry F. Byrd, Sr. (Democrat–Virginia), the chairman of the Senate Finance Committee, and no friend of health care legislation. Byrd was reluctant to come to the White House, and thought that the meeting was about the Vietnam war, not health legislation. In the Cabinet Room, he was seated next to Johnson, and the cameras were rolling. Then came the interrogation: Johnson was sure, looking at Byrd, that his good friend from Virginia would schedule a meeting of his committee on health care, since nothing was pressing right now. Wasn't that true? All Byrd could do was gulp and meekly utter, "yes." "Good," replied Johnson, as he banged his hand on the table. After the meeting, Representative Carl Albert (Democrat–Oklahoma) observed: "that was the best example of 'The Treatment' in public that anyone ever got."[76]

On April 8, Mills introduced the 200-page bill on the floor of the full House of Representatives. He was greeted with a standing ovation. This consistent, cautious foe of health care legislation was now the new hero. That evening, the House overwhelmingly passed the Mills version of Medicare, far more than the administration had asked for, by 313 to 115, with 65 Republicans joining 248 Democrats. Leaving no stone unturned, Johnson personally phoned every doubtful member of Congress.[77]

Now it was on to the Senate. The AMA, still fighting, warned senators of the dangers of Medicare. Dr. Donovan F. Ward, president of the AMA, in May told the Senate Finance Committee that the quality of medical care would undoubtedly deteriorate if the House bill were passed, and, dusting off that old canard, admonished the senators: "this may be your last chance to weigh the consequences of taking the first step toward establishment of socialized medicine in the United States.[78]

But it was too late for the AMA. After 500 minor amendments and a spirited debate in the Senate, Medicare passed, 68–21, and soon the differences between the House and Senate versions were ironed out in conference, and by late July the legislation was ready for Johnson's signature.

Lyndon Johnson had a flair for the historic gesture. In April, he and his entourage flew down to Stonewall, Texas, where he signed the historic Elementary and Secondary Education Act, with his first public school teacher, Mrs. Katherine Deadrich Loney, at his side. Johnson then used the President's Room in the Senate wing for signing the Voting Rights Act on August 6. The Statue of Liberty was the backdrop for signing the comprehensive Immigration Reform legislation. For the Medicare signing ceremony, he chose to honor President Harry Truman, affixing his signature at the Truman presidential library, and giving the former president the first Medicare card.

As much as the AMA was the bitter foe of Medicare, Johnson knew that he needed its cooperation, grudging or otherwise. In June, the AMA House of Delegates considered nine different resolutions urging a boycott of the soon-to-be passed legislation. But Dr. James Z. Appel, the new president of AMA, warned doctors against a boycott, saying it was both unethical and a clear sign of bad citizenship. Some doctors were furious, with "Impeach Appel" telegrams pouring in to the convention. At the same meeting, the House of Delegates rejected a notion permitting African-American doctors who had been barred from local medical societies from obtaining direct membership in the AMA, and refused to endorse the Surgeon General's report that smoking was a health hazard.[79]

Johnson was worried about the AMA, but he also had their number. In a conversation with AFL-CIO president George Meany, Johnson compared the AMA to chickens:

> George, have you ever fed chickens? "No," Meany answered. Well, said Johnson, chickens are real dumb. They eat and eat and eat and never stop. Why, they start shitting at the same time they're eating, and before you know it they're knee-deep in their own shit. Well, the AMA's the same. They've been eating and eating nonstop and now they're knee-deep in their own shit and everybody knows it. They won't be able to stop anything.[80]

The day before Johnson and his entourage headed to Independence, Missouri, the president invited the leaders of the AMA to the White House. Before the doctors had a chance to say anything, Johnson launched into an extended soliloquy about his fondness for his old family doctor who took care of his ailing father and mother, and the respect that he had for the noble profession of medicine. He was certain, Johnson droned on, that doctors would cooperate with the new law, because they were interested in serving people, and he was grateful for their views, and thanked them very much for coming to the White House.[81] Here was another variation of the Johnson Treatment.

A couple of days later, the AMA announced that it would be up to individual doctors to determine whether or not they would participate. Finally, in October at the AMA annual convention, president Appel acknowledged that his organization had lost but acknowledged that "we are expected by the public, the press, and the Congress to act as reasonable and mature men and women. All of us have been concerned for years with the so-called image of the AMA and of individual physicians." Physicians, the highest paid of all professions, earning an average of $22,200 in 1964, were reluctantly accepting Medicare. In time, a full 95 percent of the doctors became participants.[82] Doctors, hospitals, and others in the medical establishment, however, may have lost the battle, but, in the details of legislation and the arcane language of rule-making, which rewarded them with few checks on cost controls, they would win the medical care war.

Aftermath

Less than a year after the legislation was enacted, Medicare began to operate on July 1, 1966. By the end of that first year, nearly all eligible elderly, almost 19 million, were enrolled in Part A, Hospital Insurance, and 93 percent, nearly 18 million, were enrolled in the Part B, the voluntary Supplemental Medical Insurance program. Robert M. Ball, the commissioner of Social Security since 1962 and a longtime veteran of federal old age programs, was put in charge. HEW hired 1,800 new employees, created twenty-one branch offices and seventy-one temporary service centers in 1965–1966.[83] It was an enormous task to get Medicare into operation, and Johnson demanded that the program go full throttle.

In doing so, however, according to Johnson domestic policy aide Joseph A. Califano, Jr., HEW caved in to the medical establishment. "We let the doctors and hospitals write reimbursement rules that would make them rich without any exposure to financial risk. In our zest to get Medicare off to a roaring start, we let them dig deep into the taxpayers' pockets."[84] Califano charged that doctors were able to persuade Congress to allow them to charge "reasonable," "customary," and "prevailing" fees but also give them the authority to control how Medicare would set such fees. But what was "reasonable" and "customary"? No one really knew what doctors were charging and there was no consensus on what should be an upper limit on payments to physicians and other medical professionals. Nonetheless, physicians' fees more than doubled in their rate of increase from 1965 to 1966.[85]

Further, hospitals were able to get interest on both current and capital debt included in the cost of reimbursement, HEW would pay for depreciation for buildings and equipment which were purchased in the first place by federal

Hill–Burton dollars, and hospitals would get accelerated depreciation. Hospitals also would get a 2 percent "plus factor," on top of actual costs, which Califano charged was "a bribe to get the hospital industry to cooperate with Medicare." During the first year of Medicare coverage, the average daily service charge in hospitals went up 21.9 percent.[86]

In more measured terms, Judith M. Feder argues that the Social Security Administration, which had jurisdiction over Medicare until 1977, was faced with two alternative approaches in implementing this new program. SSA could have used its clout to bring about hospital reforms, improve quality of care, and hold down any escalation of Medicare costs. Instead, it chose efficiency, conflict avoidance, and the check-writing function that was more familiar to the Social Security program.[87] What was important to the administration was getting the programs up and running and getting the elderly signed on.

Timeline for Medicare and Health Care Legislation

1949	National health insurance fight in Congress; AMA castigates it as "socialized medicine."
1958	First Medicare legislation introduced in House by Aime Forand.
1965	Medicare-Medicaid signed into law by Johnson, with Truman sitting at his side, July 30.
1972	Medicare expanded to include disabled people younger than 65; and people suffering from chronic kidney failure; Medicare cost control reforms.
1977	Health Care Financing Administration (HCFA) created to administer Medicare and Medicaid.
1982–83	Medicare is amended to slow rapidly rising costs by establishing fixed prices for hundreds of procedures.
1988	Catastrophic Coverage Act adds a drug benefit to Medicare. Act is repealed one year later after protests from seniors that cost is too high.
1997	Increased costs; Congress passed Balanced Budget Act to cut spending for many services, including Medicare HMOs. Move prompts widespread complaints from medical providers and results in numerous HMOs abandoning program.
2001	HCFA renamed Centers for Medicare and Medicaid Services (CMS).
2003	Medicare Modernization Act adds outpatient drug benefit for seniors, including subsidies for HMOs to boost enrollment, and mandates that Medicare conduct numerous demonstration studies on quality and payment.

There was another "problem," which mostly affected southern hospitals. In order to obtain Medicare funds, they would have to comply with the nondiscrimination provisions of Title VI of the 1964 Civil Rights Act, and would have to desegregate their facilities. The White House received plaintive phone calls. "The callers all seemed to have southern accents, and they all said they were friends of Lyndon's," wrote Merle Miller. "'They're [the hospitals] not going to change their ways overnight. You know that as well as I do. Doctors won't treat the colored, and the nurses won't treat them.' And so on."[88] But the law compelled them to comply, such was the reach of Title VI. Yet, in many communities, particularly in the rural South, historically segregated hospitals were the only health facilities available. Some certainly dragged their feet, and federal officials were faced with the perplexing question of adhering to the civil rights law or keeping a scarce health facility open to the public. Often, the answer was the latter.

Federal policymakers were faced with two nagging problems during the first several years of the new programs. The first problem was fraud. Federal prosecutors were kept busy during this period fighting against doctors and hospitals who were overbilling and filing false reimbursement claims. Yet nothing during this era compared with the fraud perpetrated in the late 1990s and into the new century by HCA, Inc., the Tennessee-based hospital management firm. In 2003, HCA, Inc. agreed to pay the United States $631 million in civil penalties and damages arising from false claims it was alleged to have made in its Medicare and other federal health care reimbursement submissions. Three years earlier, HCA subsidiaries had also pleaded guilty to criminal conduct and had been fined $840 million in penalties. In all, HCA was fined $1.7 billion, by far the largest amount in health care fraud investigations.[89]

The other, more intractable problem was rapidly escalated costs, threatening to bring down the whole system. By 1970, both policy leaders and the general public agreed that there was a crisis in American health care. Richard M. Nixon, assuming office in January 1969, declared that the country faces "a massive crisis" in health care and that, if action weren't taken soon, "we will have a breakdown in our medical system."[90] One action to restore fiscal solvency, Nixon said, was to raise the Medicare tax, which already had been increased in 1967. However, Russell B. Long (Democrat–Louisiana), the chairman of the Senate Finance Committee, countered that more taxes would not solve the problems, and he called for his committee staff to study ways to cut back on skyrocketing hospital and physician costs.

In early February 1970, the Finance Committee report was made public. It outlined soaring costs for physician services and hospitals, overbilling of services, a doubling of the cost of Medicare and a quadrupling of costs for Medicaid since the programs began four years earlier. It concluded that some doctors were taking huge sums from the federal programs, citing one New York state doctor who collected $1.4 million from Medicare and Medicaid in one year alone. The report made it clear: the Part A Hospital Insurance Trust Fund would be bankrupt by 1973 if corrective steps weren't taken. The Senate Finance Committee report also suggested some novel ideas: compare hospitals' billing practices against each other, and determine which were overcharging. Another revolutionary idea: set limits on how much doctors could charge. This struck too close to the financial heart of the AMA. As health reporter Richard Sorian described it, "once again, shrieks of 'socialized medicine' rang in the halls of Congress and on the editorial pages of many of the nation's newspapers."[91]

It took Congress a while to act, but starting in 1972 a series of Medicare reforms were put in place. Cost control measures were established for hospital rooms and physician fees, but they did little to control the steadily increasing reimbursement costs. At the same time, however, Congress expanded Medicare coverage. Some 1.7 million disabled persons under sixty-five years old were added as well as another 18,000 under sixty-five who were suffering from end-stage renal disease. Joseph Califano was particularly critical of this latter policy decision: "When Congress in 1972 legislated to provide kidney dialysis to all comers, the motivation was humane. But the costs have been staggering—not only because of the basic coverage, but also because Congress, bowing to the interests of hospitals and freestanding clinics, provided reimbursement for dialysis in these expensive settings, but not at home."[92]

Near the beginning of his presidency in March 1977, Jimmy Carter announced a major restructuring, removing the administration of Medicare and Medicaid from the Social Security Administration, and placing it in a new agency, the Health Care Financing Administration (HCFA). Medicare was no longer under the culture and mindset of Social Security, which was to efficiently serve and protect its elderly beneficiaries. HCFA was establishing a new identity and mission, that of a health-financing program with a focus on cost controls.[93]

During the 1970s, much of the interest in federal health care had shifted from reforms of Medicare and Medicaid to the creation of a national health insurance system. On the day after the Senate Finance Committee report was issued in 1970, Representative Martha W. Griffiths (Democrat–Michigan) called for scrapping Medicare and Medicaid and replacing them with a national health insurance system for all Americans through prepaid group insurance plans. Hers was one of just several proposals attempting to save money and broaden coverage.[94]

Writing early in the 1970s, former Johnson administration policy aide Larry O'Brien predicted, ". . . what Medicare was to the 1960s, national health insurance is to the 1970s. Once again, as under Eisenhower, there is a strong Republican opposition. Once again, a Kennedy [Senator Ted Kennedy] is leading the fight [in the Senate]. And once again the ultimate outcome is as inevitable as tomorrow's sunrise."[95] There were attempts in Congress in 1971 and 1974 to enact comprehensive health insurance, and, in 1974, it seemed as though it might happen. President Nixon that year predicted that "comprehensive health insurance is an idea whose time has come in America."[96] During 1974, four major plans for national health insurance were considered, including ones developed by Wilbur Mills, now in his last year of Congress, and Edward M. Kennedy (Democrat–Massachusetts). But 1974 was a year when Congress, the presidency, and the nation were consumed by Watergate and no such law was passed.

With the new Ninety-Fourth Congress, the first post-Watergate session meeting in January 1975, Democratic leaders renewed their call for universal care. But the new president, Gerald R. Ford was determined to "whip inflation now," and had promised to veto any new expensive legislation, including national health insurance.[97]

The momentum was slipping away for advocates of national health insurance. Nevertheless, President Jimmy Carter declared in 1979 that "a uniform, comprehensive national health insurance program is one of the major unfinished items on America's social agenda."[98] But no such legislation would be passed during the remaining months of the Carter administration. In the Reagan years, as political scientist Theodore R. Marmor succinctly put it, "no one of political significance advocated universal health care coverage."[99] Not until 1993 and the first year of the Clinton administration would there be a similar attempt at national health insurance policymaking.

Returning to Medicare, a Carter administration proposal attempted to control the costs of hospital care. The administration's ambitious proposal in 1979 would have applied federal government limits to the annual increase in hospital costs. Carter's proposal was backed by Paul G. Rogers (Democrat–Florida) and Henry A. Waxman (Democrat–California) in the House, but ran into the considerable opposition of Dan Rostenkowski (Democrat–Illinois). In the Senate, Edward Kennedy, who would soon challenge Carter for the Democratic nomination for the presidency, backed the legislation, but Russell Long (Democrat–Louisiana) opposed it. A compromise bill emerged, sponsored by Richard A. Gephardt (Democrat–Missouri), calling for voluntary efforts by hospitals to gradually cut back costs. This compromise, a key victory for hospital lobbyists, carried the day. For a short time, the hospitals did cut back on expenses, but, by the time Ronald Reagan had captured the White House in November 1980, voluntary cost containment was but a fleeting memory. Hospital cost increases were back with a vengeance.[100]

President Reagan promised to cut back on waste and inefficiency in government spending. Certainly one of the biggest targets might have been Medicare, with its $70 billion budget, the second largest item in the domestic budget and the fastest growing. In his first year in office, however, Reagan targeted cutbacks in traditional welfare programs, such as food stamps, AFDC, and Medicaid. In response to growing criticisms of his cuts, Reagan outlined the federal government's "social safety net," identifying those programs that would be spared from draconian reductions. The Reagan budget would not go after veterans' benefits, Head Start, summer job programs, Supplementary Security Income (SSI), or Medicare. But with mounting deficits, thanks in part to the unprecedented three-year tax cut enacted in 1981 and to the under-performing economy, Medicare became a more tempting target. Through the 1981 Omnibus Budget Reconciliation Act (OBRA) and the 1982 Tax Equity and Fiscal Responsibility Act (TEFRA) there were substantial cuts in hospital services and Medicare revenues.[101]

There was more to come. The administration, through David Stockman, the director of the Office of Management and Budget, proposed a 2 percent across-the-board cut in hospital payments, a plan grudgingly accepted by the hospital industry. The Senate Finance Committee, now under the leadership of Robert J Dole (Republican–Kansas), opted for cutting what were known as hospital ancillary charges, with gradually tighter controls. Into the debate stepped Richard S. Schweiker, the secretary of the department of Health and Human Services (HHS), who was determined to come up with a pricing policy that would be acceptable to both Congress and the hospital industry. To control hospital costs, which had been increasing by 19 percent a year since 1972, HHS policymakers called for the creation of a prospective pricing system (PPS) based on diagnosis-related groups, or DRGs.

Prospective pricing meant that costs would be set before admission to a hospital rather than after a patient was discharged. It would replace the cost-based reimbursement system, which encouraged hospitals to bill Medicare at high rates for lengthy and expensive hospital stays. The PPS program would limit reimbursement to the average price for treatment, and all hospitals would receive the same amount of reimbursement. Those inefficient hospitals, whose cost exceeded the Medicare reimbursement, would feel a financial pinch; those efficient hospitals, whose cost was less than the reimbursement, would be rewarded for their ability to keep costs down. HHS policymaking based the reimbursement on diagnosis-related groups (DRGs), a national system that identified 468 different categories of diagnosis (such as "heart failure and shock," "angina pectoris," or "respiratory infections and inflammations").

Almost reinforcing the need of and perhaps the urgency for reform, the Hospital Insurance Trust Fund issued a report soon after Schweiker's plan was made public warning that the ruinous inflation rates from the late 1970s threatened to plunge Medicare into bankruptcy. As part of the 1983 Social Security rescue package, the new Congress quickly passed the DRG-based prospective pricing legislation, just four months after Schweicker had made public his report.[102]

The DRG reimbursement system, which Theodore Marmor calls "a sophisticated form of government price controls," went into effect in October 1983.[103] The overall goal was to bring cost efficiencies to hospitals, based on a reimbursement for a fixed average cost per diagnosis. Over the next several years, Congress readjusted reimbursement rates and phased in the system, but the trend was established: better containment of hospital costs. There was a price to pay, however: hospital stays shortened, and, to some critics, were too abbreviated for good-quality recuperation, and the number of Medicare patient admissions declined.[104]

There were also attempts to cut costs on the other side of the Medicare reimbursement equation, the costs of physician care. In 1972, Congress, responding to the rapid increase in physician bills, created legislation stating that Medicare payment for physician services in any given region of the country could not rise faster than the index of earning levels for physicians. Nor could doctors charge at rates more than the 75th percentile of customary charges of area physicians; the old rate was at the 95th percentile. In 1985 and 1986, Congress passed legislation requiring physicians to meet an "inherent reasonableness" test for Medicare reimbursement. But, there was little evidence that these and earlier physician cost containment measures worked. The legislative measures did not address the heart of rising doctor bills: physicians could increase the number of procedures performed and could unbundle services, that is, divide the care into a larger number of billable units.[105]

Then came an extraordinary year in health care policymaking. On July 1, 1988, there was a ceremony in the Rose Garden at the White House, as President Reagan signed into law the Medicare Catastrophic Coverage Act (MCCA), hailed as a major $2 billion expansion of health care for the elderly. Just fifteen months later, on October 4, 1989, the House of Representatives voted to repeal this new law, and in late November the Senate agreed. Medicare Catastrophic Coverage, in the words of health care expert Marilyn Moon, was "one of the shortest-lived pieces of social legislation in the United States."[106] The legislation was primarily the work of one individual, Dr. Otis Bowen, former governor of Indiana, chairman of the 1982 Advisory Council on Social Security, and later Reagan's secretary of Health and Human Services. Building on recommendations from his 1982 findings, Bowen called for increasing Medicare coverage to include catastrophic care. Congress went further: expanded payments for nursing home care, prescription drug coverage, and more. Who would pay for this major expansion? President Reagan insisted, and lawmakers agreed, that the program be revenue-neutral, leading to an extra monthly Medicare premium and a 15 percent income-tax surtax for people over 65 who had incomes over $35,000. Roughly 5 percent of the beneficiaries would have had to pay the maximum surcharge, amounting to $800 a year, or $1,600 for a couple.

Soon, however, there was a grassroots revolt. Six thousand members resigned from the American Association of Retired Persons (AARP) because it had agreed to the legislation. The fires of protest were stoked by the National Committee to Preserve Social Security and Medicare, an organization created by a direct marketing firm, which was widely accused of generating mailing lists and membership fees and providing inaccurate information rather than benefitting seniors. Dan Rostenkowski (Democrat–Illinois), chairman of the House Ways and Means Committee, and defender of the legislation, was heckled by senior citizens, shouting "Liar, liar," "Chicken, chicken—we won't forget you at election time." Caught on television was Rostenowski trapped in his car, with old folks booing, and angrily waving signs in his face.[107]

The overwhelming percentage of seniors would not have been affected by the maximum surcharge, but it made no difference. Their protests were loud and clear: how un-American to give extra benefits and then slap a surcharge on the beneficiaries. Congress soon caved in, and the legislation passed in

July of the year before was now, in November 1989, repealed. Scare tactics by opponents, the inability to explain the sometimes confusing benefits, a heavy focus on the premium increase and the surcharge—all these led to a stunning reversal of policy.[108]

In 1991, health care became a major issue in the special election in Pennsylvania to fill the Senate vacancy caused by the death of H. John Heinz, III. Harris Wofford, the Democratic candidate who pushed comprehensive health care reform, won an upset victory over former U.S. attorney general and Pennsylvania governor Richard L. Thornburgh. Wofford's campaign was adroitly managed by James Carville. The following year, Carville was the key campaign consultant for Bill Clinton's presidential race. While the Clinton campaign's focus was on the economy, health care reform became the top policy agenda item for the new Clinton administration, with Hillary Rodham Clinton leading the drive. While the last burst of national health care policymaking came in the 1970s, the Clintons were determined that the time had come for a major transformation.

President Clinton promised to send to Congress within its first hundred days a national health care package.[109] The optimism and naivete of the new Clinton team, combined with a complicated plan crafted in secret in the White House, undisciplined policy focus, poor communication with congressional leaders, and, later, the distractions of the Whitewater scandal, forced delay in the president's presenting the plan to Congress. On September 21, 1993, President Clinton introduced his health insurance plan to a joint session of Congress, with great anticipation and approval from nearly two-thirds of the public. Hillary Clinton testified before several congressional committees, impressing lawmakers with her command of this very complicated subject. Yet, almost exactly a year later, on September 26, 1994, George J. Mitchell (Democrat–Maine), the Senate majority leader, pronounced national health care dead.

As professor Paul Starr, an advocate of the Clinton health plan, later wrote: "The collapse of health care reform in the first two years of the Clinton administration will go down as one of the greatest lost political opportunities in American history. It is a story of compromises that never happened, of deals that were never closed, of Republicans, moderate Democrats, and key interest groups that backpedaled from proposals they themselves had earlier co-sponsored or endorsed."[110]

The Clinton plan, a complex, unwieldy 1,342-page document, called for federal government enforcement of mandates for employers to provide health insurance for their employees through closely regulated health maintenance organizations (HMOs). It further called for regional insurance purchasing cooperatives and global spending caps. There were competing Democrat and Republican plans, with nearly every health care interest group endorsing some kind of proposal.[111] The Clinton program was not understood by the public. In one pointed example, when members of a focus group had the Clinton proposal described to them, 70 percent approved of it; when the name "Clinton" was attached to it, that very same proposal dropped by 30–40 percent. Big business organizations, originally interested in some sort of reform, turned against the Clinton plan. So, too, did the health care and insurance industries. Chief among the critics was the Health Insurance Association of America, which crafted an effective $15 million issue advocacy advertising program, featuring *Harry and Louise*, a well-read, concerned married couple sitting in their kitchen despairing over the supposedly unintelligible Clinton plan.[112]

Seven weeks after Senator Mitchell declared health care reform dead, the Republicans, in a stunning reversal of power, swept into the majority in the House of Representatives, gaining fifty-four seats. Thirty-four Democratic incumbents, including Speaker of the House Thomas S. Foley (Washington) and chairman of the Ways and Means Committee, Dan Rostenkowski (Illinois), were defeated; no incumbent Republicans lost. A conservative Republican era, some calling it a revolution, was about to start in Congress, with significant consequences for Medicare and other New Deal and Great Society programs.

Political scientist Jonathan Oberlander has argued that during the first three decades of Medicare there was generally a political consensus: policymaking was bipartisan and operating under the implicit notion "that federal health insurance for the elderly should take the form, in essence, of a single-payer health system."[113] Then came the 1994 elections. While Medicare was not part of the original Republican party's Contract with America, once the new Speaker of the House, Newt Gingrich (Republican–Georgia), concluded business during the symbolic first hundred days of the 1995 legislative session, he turned to Medicare reform. Fuel was added to the Republicans' fire when, in April, 1995, a report from the Medicare Trustees announced that the Medicare Trust Fund was projected to run out of money by 2001, even when using optimistic financial estimates.[114]

Skirting around the usual committee structure, Gingrich took firm control of the Medicare issue and the Republican budget. Medicare was targeted for a $270 billion, 30 percent, reduction in expenditures over a seven-year period of time. Gingrich and his colleagues were sensing a new mood in the country: a disdain toward the elderly. Old folks were no longer perceived as the weak, the frail, and the destitute, but were seen as the well-off recipients of two of the largest federal programs, Social Security and Medicare, and that they would fight tooth and nail for their largesse while younger Americans struggled with new families, higher tuition bills, and higher mortgages.[115] Some conservatives saw a receptive audience when they stoked the fires of inter-generational conflict.

The other major factor was the changing landscape for health insurance. For decades, it was the free-for-service model, found in the dominant industry provider of Blue Cross and Blue Shield. Then came managed care, through passage of the Health Maintenance Act of 1973. While they grew slowly at first, by the mid-1990s nearly 51 million individuals were enrolled in 562 various HMO plans. At the same time, there was a steep decline in traditional health plans, going from 95 percent of the employer-sponsored market in 1978 to just 14 percent by 1998. "Unmanaged" care had just one remaining stronghold: Medicare.[116]

There was extraordinary pressure to "reform" Medicare. Indeed, Republicans labeled their plan the Medicare Preservation Act, which drew support from the AMA. Democrats, predictably, saw this as a direct assault on one of their cherished social programs. President Clinton vetoed the Republican-crafted legislation, and packaged himself as the defender of Medicare and the elderly in his successful re-election bid in 1996.

Yet, there was reform during this era, culminating in the Balanced Budget Act of 1997, which targeted Medicare for significant cuts, a total of $116 billion reduction in outlays from 1998 through 2002. This law also created a Bipartisan Commission on the Future of Medicare, headed by Senator John B. Breaux (Democrat–Louisiana) and Congressman William M. (Bill) Thomas (Republican–California). The most important recommendation coming from the commission's year-long study was to make Medicare into a competitive market, a program that emphasized "premium support," a voucher plan, which would shift the responsibility of health care costs to the beneficiaries and their health coverage plans.[117] The Commission's recommendations needed a super majority, however, which it failed to achieve.

Another feature of the Balanced Budget Act was the Medicare+Choice program, which offered Medicare beneficiaries private sector health care choices. This provision received enthusiastic bipartisan support and encouragement from the managed care industry. At the time it was enacted, approximately 6 million beneficiaries, or 15 percent of the total Medicare population, were enrolled in some form of managed care plans. However, the optimism soon evaporated. In just one year after enactment, dozens of managed care programs were opting out of Medicare or reducing the number of beneficiaries they served. The reason for their dissatisfaction, according to Nancy-Ann DeParle, former head of the Health Care Financing Administration, was that managed care programs, trying to offer more attractive alternative benefits, felt they were not getting adequate reimbursement from the federal government and that they were mired in excessive regulation.[118] During the 1999–2001 contract years, some 118 Medicare+Choice plans reduced their services or withdrew from Medicare, affecting 1.65 million beneficiaries. Medicare+ Choice, created with enthusiasm, was soon destined for the scrap heap of health care policies.

Thanks to the booming U.S. economy during the mid-1990s, the 1998 federal budget was balanced for the first time since 1969, and forecast for fiscal year 2000 and beyond was for record surpluses. The reports of the Medicare Trustees were also more positive. Instead of running out of money in 2001, the Trustees' report in 1999 said there was enough in the fund to last until 2015; the following year, the report forecast sufficient funds until 2025.[119] Things were looking brighter for Medicare and its long-term financial prospects.

In his 1999 State of the Union address, President Clinton called on Congress to resurrect a major health benefit now missing in Medicare: prescription drug coverage. In 1988, as a part of the catastrophic care legislation, Congress included a prescription drug benefit, but it disappeared when the law was repealed the following year. Now it was back in full measure. Prescription drugs were now heavily marketed, increasingly used by the elderly, more expensive, and less available through managed care programs. The public, particularly the elderly, supported prescription drug coverage and it became a key issue in the 2000 presidential campaign.

On December 8, 2003, President George W. Bush signed into law the Medicare Prescription Drug, Improvement, and Modernization Act of 2003 (MMA), creating the first major benefit expansion since the program was established in 1965.[120] The law also replaced Medicare+Choice with a new program, Medicare Advantage (Part C), which expanded the number of preferred provider organizations, together with better coverage options, for elderly beneficiaries. The prescription drug component (Part D) went into effect in January 2006, with an estimated cost of $409 billion over its first ten years of operation. For many elderly it presented a bewildering array of choices and confusion in drug coverage. In addition, many elderly found themselves falling into what was called a "doughnut hole," where Medicare would not provide drug reimbursement. Medicare covers 75 percent of the first $2,250 worth of prescription drugs, then coverage drops to zero; it comes in again when patient expenses hit $5,100, where 95 percent of the cost is borne by Medicare. Between three and seven million elderly fell into the nearly $3,000 "doughnut hole" in 2006. The enormous expense of Part D, the confusion over coverage, the gap in benefits, and the failure of the legislation to require the Medicare program to negotiate the price of drugs—all these continued to be contentious issues.

By 2006, some 36.7 million individuals aged sixty-five and older, together with 7.0 million disabled persons or those with end-stage renal disease, were covered by Medicare, at a total cost of $450 billion per year. In that year, 84 percent of Medicare beneficiaries received coverage from the original Medicare programs, Part A (Hospital Insurance) and Part B (Supplementary Medical Insurance). As of January 2007, some 19 percent of beneficiaries were enrolled in Medicare Advantage, with most participating in HMOs or PPOs.[121]

What to do about Medicare? The central challenge, acknowledged by a wide range of commentators and policymakers, is controlling costs. The choices, broadly seen, are fairly simple, but politically painful and difficult to realize. Medicare costs could be shifted from the federal government to beneficiaries: instead of beneficiaries absorbing 25 percent of Part B, their premiums would increase. The federal government could restrict enrollment, such as raise the eligibility level from age sixty-five to age sixty-seven, just as Social Security does. The medical services now covered could be reduced, reconfigured, or elim-inated. Health care insurance could be turned over to the competitive private market place.[122] With such an extraordinary amount of money invested each year in the health of the elderly, and with such personal and central issues of well-being and health at stake, public policy choices will have to be weighed carefully.

In the meantime, the issue of national health care for all citizens, not just seniors, continues to draw attention in policymaking circles. Legal affairs and health care professor Timothy Stoltzfus Jost summed up an argument made by many observers of American health care:

> All other developed nations in the world, including developed countries in Western Europe, Asia, North and South America, and on the Pacific Rim, provide health care for all or most of their residents. Although private health insurance products are available for purchase on a voluntary basis in virtually every country, no other developed country relies on private insurance as does the United States to provide primary coverage for its population. All developed nations have recognized that voluntary private insurance cannot cover everyone (as it does not in the U.S.) and have developed some form of public health insurance.[123]

In the early 1940s, Representative John D. Dingell of Michigan joined Senators Robert Wagner and James Murray to advocate, unsuccessfully, a system of national health care. Dingell retired in 1955 and was replaced by his son, John D. Dingell, Jr., who in every session since has introduced some form of universal health care coverage under a single-payer model. Early in the 110th Congress (2007–2009), Dingell, now in his fifty-second year in the House, joined forces with Senator Edward Kennedy of Massachusetts to offer Medicare for All, a legislative proposal that would phase in Medicare coverage as an option for all Americans, without regard to age, over a five-year period, and would be paid for by payroll taxes. Proponents argue that this package would significantly reduce private-sector health spending, where costs now average 13 percent of payroll, and would lead to greater efficiency through a single-payer model.[124]

During the primaries in 2007 and the general election for president in 2008, health care was a central, though not dominant, policy concern. In August 2007, the American Medical Association launched a three-year, multi-million-dollar campaign to cover the one in seven Americans who are without health insurance. Its plan calls for tax credit subsidies or vouchers to help the roughly 46.6 million uninsured obtain their own insurance coverage and to foster market reforms to create affordable insurance.[125]

For all its shortcomings, Medicare has been an extraordinarily important factor in the well-being of America's elderly and disabled. For many, Medicare, together with Social Security, is the lifeline protecting them from the vicissitudes of old age. Medicare has a broad reservoir of public support, but its future is continually clouded by questions of financial viability. The Obama administration, the 111th Congress (2009–2010), and policymakers in the future will have to grapple with health care options with far-reaching consequences. Whether the answer is a cut-back on services, increase of premiums, privatization, or the larger leap to a program guaranteeing coverage for all, Medicare will sit center stage in the ongoing public policy debate about health insurance and medical coverage.

12

PROTECTING THE ENVIRONMENT

The National Environmental Policy Act of 1969

The nineteen-seventies absolutely must be the years
when America pays its debt to the past by reclaiming
the purity of its air, its waters and our living environment.
It is literally now or never.

> Richard M. Nixon, on signing NEPA into law
> (January 1, 1970)

Thank God for NEPA, because there were so many pressures
to make a selection for technology that might have been forced
upon us and that would have been wrong for the country.

> Admiral James Watkins, Secretary of Energy (1992)

The National Environmental Policy Act (NEPA) holds the
unusual honor of being the most successful environmental
law in the world and the most disappointing.

> Oliver A. Houck (2000)

Manhattan's Fifth Avenue was jammed, not with the usual taxis and delivery trucks, but with a huge, light-hearted throng of people that stretched from Forty-Third Street up sixteen blocks to Central Park. Tens of thousands packed Union Square; thousands more crowded into a block-long polyethylene "bubble" on Seventeenth Street, where they could breathe pure, filtered air. A favorite T-shirt sported a warning from the popular cartoon character Pogo: "We have met the enemy and they is us!" Throughout the country, millions of students, environmental activists, and ordinary citizens attended teach-ins, listened to speeches, and took action. Wearing gas masks, some protestors buried automobiles in mock funerals to symbolize the end of the era of fossil fuels. Some dumped buckets of rotting fish onto the marble floors of electric utility and chemical companies. Others rolled up their sleeves and cleaned up beaches, painted park benches, swept debris from drainage ditches, pulled old

367

tires, discarded car batteries, and other detritus out of rivers and streams. In Washington, while the president scoffed at the idea of celebrating Mother Nature, some of his White House staffers had their pictures taken as they rolled up their sleeves to help clean up the Potomac River. Thousands on the national Mall sang along with folk troubadours Pete Singer and Phil Ochs, "all we are saying, is give earth a chance."

This was Earth Day, April 24, 1970. The nationwide rallies, protests, and teach-ins that day were five times larger than any anti-Vietnam rally and twenty times larger than any combined civil rights marches held in recent years. Some 22 million Americans, a full one-tenth of the country's population, participated. Earth Day then was extended to Earth Week, with millions more participating in grassroots environmental activities, politicians of all stripes boasting their enthusiasm for environmental action, and companies jumping onto the environment-friendly bandwagon.[1]

Not everyone was impressed by the festivities and hoopla. *Washington Post* columnist Nicholas von Hoffman wrote that, despite good intentions, Earth Day "was turned into a muddled media carnival, a paint-up, clean-up, fix-up hoax." Our attention, he continued, "was drawn off our ecocidal destruction of man, agriculture, flora and fauna in Vietnam by such things as the full page newspaper ads by the Schlitz Brewing Company adjuring us not to drop their beer cans on the beach but in the nearest trash cans." Von Hoffman further blamed the politicians, who, he claimed, were bought off by campaign funds from major polluters, who have "slithered in to mislead the parade."[2] Another critic, Congressman Joel T. Broyhill (Republican–Virginia), saw little difference between the anti-war student protesters and the environmental crowd. At an awards dinner for the Washington, D.C., chapter of the National Police Officers Association, he labeled student protestors "screaming punks, misfits and squirts," encouraged by the media, who "just want an excuse to do something." Instead of Earth Day, Broyhill suggested to his sympathetic audience, "we need a national Shave Day and Bath Day."[3]

But other politicians were quite impressed by the numbers and the opportunities for them to demonstrate their newly found love for all things green. So many members of Congress were back home participating in rallies and parades that no business was scheduled on Capitol Hill. The executive branch was not immune from the enthusiasm of the environmental movement. Four months earlier, President Richard M. Nixon took the unusual step of signing the National Environmental Policy Act (NEPA) into law on New Year's day. While most everyone else was watching college football bowl games and enjoying a national holiday, Nixon ushered reporters into the Western White House at San Clemente, California. With his signature affixed to NEPA, the president declared that we had now entered the 1970s, the "Decade of the Environment." Never an advocate for conservation or environmental protection, Nixon was nevertheless a wily pragmatist and seized the opportunity to command center stage.

Two of the most prominent pro-environmental senators, Henry M. (Scoop) Jackson (Democrat–Washington) and Edmund S. Muskie (Democrat–Maine), not only had crafted important environmental legislation, but also were considered probable candidates for the presidency in the upcoming 1972 campaign. Nixon most certainly would be running for re-election and did not want either of these two Democrats to be too far ahead of him on this increasingly popular cause.

All of a sudden, environmentalism was in vogue. The nation's attention for the moment wasn't focused on the Vietnam war, civil rights, or the rights of women, but on preserving the land and its people. Very few members of Congress in the early 1960s considered themselves environmentalists; now, it seemed, just about every one was on board. During the latter part of 1969, NEPA sailed through Congress, by voice vote in the Senate with just token resistance in the House. There was little discussion in Congress or in the environmental press about the consequences of this new law. Just a few pages long, NEPA was written in broad language, more like constitutional prose than detailed lawmaking, leading one environmental historian to claim that it was "the most sweeping environmental law ever enacted by a United States Congress."[4]

After Earth Day came the creation of the Environmental Protection Agency, a tough, comprehensive Clean Water Act, and a burst of environmental legislation during the 1970s.[5] The production of federal environmental legislation during the 1970s was extraordinary, and at its foundation was the National Environmental Policy Act.

Background

In 1864, the American linguist, legislator, and diplomat George Perkins Marsh published *Man and Nature*,[6] a seminal book on conservation and nature. His central message was a stark warning: the earth was being modified and degraded by the relentless efforts of humans. For Marsh, the threat to nature was not simply a matter of science, but more importantly it was a matter of moral indignation: "Man has too long forgotten that the earth was given to him for usufruct alone, not for consumption, still less for profligate waste."[7] Also in the late nineteenth century, the scientist and explorer John Wesley Powell, then the director of the U.S. Geological Survey, was an important influence on the study of western ecology.

Engineer and naturalist John Muir was instrumental in the development of the nation's national park system, and emphasized preservation of natural resources. Muir's philosophy and approach differed from those of his contemporary Gifford Pinchot, who emphasized conservation of natural resources.[8] Pinchot, a professional forester, became the first head of the U.S. Forest Service during the Theodore Roosevelt administration. In 1908, Pinchot brought together the state governors, justices of the Supreme Court, and representatives from sixty-eight national societies, to focus on conservation issues and policy. Other conferences were held throughout the country, and the idea of a "conservation movement" was born.[9]

Throughout American history, Congress enacted legislation to control and protect the land. Geographer Allan K. Fitzsimmons has described four phases of early federal conservation legislation.[10] The first phase was that of exploitation, seen through the Northwest Ordinance (1787), the Homestead Act (1862), the Timber Culture Act (1877), and the Desert Land Act (1877). These laws promoted expansion and economic growth, but also permitted wastefulness and undesirable exploitation. A second phase, preservation, was largely a reaction to the first. The first national park, Yellowstone, was created in 1872, then game birds were preserved through the Lacey Act (1906) and wildlife refuges were established in 1905. The Antiquities Act (1906) protected historical sites and gave rise to the creation of national monuments; later, the Wilderness Act (1964) continued that tradition. A third phase, utilitarianism, brought multi-use management plans through the Forest Management Act (1897), the Rivers and Harbors Act (1917), the Soil Conservation Act (1935), and the Outer Continental Shelf Lands Act (1953). A fourth phase, public health, began with the Refuse Act (1899) (part of the Rivers and Harbors Act), which dealt with contamination of waterways and the dumping of wastes into navigable rivers. This pioneering law required individuals and corporations to obtain dumping permits from the Army Corps of Engineers; yet, this legislation was largely ignored by federal enforcement officials.[11] Despite these federal laws, until the 1960s environmental and conservation issues were viewed primarily as state and local problems, with little push for federal environmental protection.

The Air Pollution Act (1955) was the first federal attempt of its kind, prompted by the growing problem of smog in the fast-growing Los Angeles basin in the early 1940s and the 1948 disaster in Donora, a southwestern Pennsylvania mill town.

The Donora tragedy was especially gripping. Located on a horseshoe bend in the Monongahela River, Donora, a town of 14,000, was home to the Donora Zinc Works, a smelting operation owned by the U.S. Steel Corporation. The smoke and foul air were considered a part of life; so too was the often-present smog laden with sulfur dioxide. Town folks got used to the nuisance, considered it part of the cost of progress and a steady pay check. But in late October, 1948, in this narrow valley, the thick, noxious air was trapped in a thermal inversion, and the town was enveloped in the deadly "Donora Smog." Carbon monoxide, sulfur, and heavy metal dust became a deadly mixture breathed in by animals and humans alike. Residents soon crowded into the local hospital and rescue squads and ambulances were summoned. The elderly and those with respiratory ailments were urged to leave town, but the smog was so thick and the traffic so congested, that evacuation was impossible. During the last six days of October, twenty people died of asphyxiation, and 7,000—one half the entire population – were hospitalized or became ill. By Saturday morning, the fifth day of the smog, eleven people had died; but not until the next morning did the Donora Zinc Works finally shut down. On Sunday evening rain fell, dispersing the smog; the next day, the Zinc Works was back in operation.[12]

Seven years later, in 1955, the commonwealth of Pennsylvania passed a clean air act, the first state law to control air pollution. The Zinc Works shut down in 1957, but its passing was not mourned. The local newspaper, the Monessen *Daily Independent* editorialized: "the Zinc Works may have cost the valley more jobs than it ever supplied, and the cost to the Donora-Webster area in terms of general community welfare is probably incalculable."[13] Later in 1955 and 1970, when federal clean air legislation was being debated, the horrors of Donora were recounted.

After World War II, there was a growing appreciation of the dangers of pollution, and, with an increasingly affluent society, many Americans were rejecting the venerable notion that pollution was the price of progress.[14] They were a receptive audience for several popular books published during the 1950s and early 1960s that lamented America's wastefulness and destruction of the environment. In 1949, ecologist Aldo Leopold's *A Sand County Almanac* was an important catalyst for the growing awareness of the ecological movement and his land ethic philosophy. This book's impact has been compared to that of Henry David Thoreau's *Walden Pond*, and altogether more than 2 million copies of Leopold's book have been sold. There was renewed interest in the writings and ideas of George Perkins Marsh in the 1950s, and a growing appreciation for his pioneering work.[15] Journalist Vance Packard was the best-selling author of *The Waste Makers* (1960), which denounced planned obsolescence and the throw-away society. Scientist Paul R. Ehrlich warned of the dangers of overpopulation in his widely read *The Population Bomb* (1968). Stewart L. Udall, secretary of the interior during the Kennedy and Johnson administrations, wrote *The Quiet Crisis* (1963), a call to action for protection of the environment.[16]

The most prominent book during this era, however, was Rachel Carson's *Silent Spring*.[17] Carson, with urgency and moral suasion, documented the dangers of pesticides, in particular DDT, and the deleterious impact of bio-accumulation. Carson's findings, published in 1962, caused a sensation, prompting a furious reaction by the chemical industry, which spent well over a quarter million dollars to discredit her. The attacks got personal, accusing her of "hysteria," questioning her academic credentials, and wondering out loud how an unmarried woman could challenge the authority of the male-dominated scientific community.[18] But the *New York Times* characterized the "gentle, soft-spoken" Carson as an "unlikely candidate for the role of avenging angel."[19]

At the end of March 1963, CBS television announced that it would air "The Silent Spring of Rachel Carson" in its investigative series, *CBS Reports*. Jay McMullen, the CBS producer, had spent eight months interviewing a wide spectrum of voices, from senior government officials, like the secretary of agriculture and the surgeon general of the United States, to industry spokesmen.

With Eric Sevareid narrating the documentary, Rachel Carson came across as a "dignified, polite, concerned scientist," in contrast to the man who turned out to be her best foil, the "wild-eyed, loud-voiced" Dr. Robert White-Stevens, dressed in a white laboratory coat, who represented the chemical industry.[20] There were approximately 10 to 15 million viewers, an unusually high number for a serious television documentary, and Carson carried the day and won the argument. Historian Linda Lear, Carson's biographer, summed up the impact of the CBS documentary: "In a single evening, Jay McMullen's broadcast added the environment to the public agenda."[21]

The following day, Senator Hubert Humphrey (Democrat–Minnesota) announced that the Senate would begin a broad-scale investigation of environmental hazards, under the leadership of Abraham Ribicoff (Democrat–Connecticut). At nearly the same time, the Presidential Science Advisory Council released the findings of its study on the use of pesticides. It had been rumored that the Senate's Republican Policy Committee and the chemical industry were exerting "enormous pressure" to have the Science Advisory Council's report watered down.[22] The executive branch report was not all that environmentalists wanted, but it did call for the "elimination of the use of persistent toxic pesticides."[23]

At a May 1963 Senate hearing, Ernest Gruening (Democrat–Alaska) compared Carson's work with that of Harriett Beecher Stowe's *Uncle Tom's Cabin*, predicting that *Silent Spring* would change the course of history.[24] Writing twenty years later, Jack Lewis observed that the Environmental Protection Agency (EPA) "may be said without exaggeration to be the extended shadow of Rachel Carson."[25] However, Rachel Carson would not live to see the enormous impact generated by her book. At the time of the CBS documentary, Carson was wracked with cancer and would live just one more year.

One important political influence was Wisconsin's governor Gaylord A. Nelson, who made conservation and the environment key features of his 1960 re-election campaign. Earlier, Nelson received very positive support for his program to preserve Wisconsin wildlife areas, with funding supplied by an added 1 cent tax on cigarettes. Nelson, who later as a senator, was the driving force behind Earth Day in 1970, convinced President John F. Kennedy to go on an unprecedented eight to ten state national tour focusing on conservation issues and environmental protection. But the trip was eclipsed by the signing of the Nuclear Test Ban treaty. The test ban was news, the environment wasn't. "Most editors, most reporters didn't know a damn thing about the environment and didn't care. It wasn't an issue," Nelson recalled years later.[26]

During the Lyndon Johnson administration, particularly through the work of Secretary of the Interior Stewart L. Udall, several environmental laws were passed. Johnson pushed for the Water Quality Act of 1965, saying at the signing ceremony: "Today we begin to be masters of our environment."[27] Congress passed five other anti-pollution and conservation laws during the Great Society, including the Wilderness Act (1964), the Land and Water Conservation Fund

Act (1965), the Endangered Species Preservation Act (1965), the Solid Waste Disposal Act (1965), the National Trail System Act (1968), and the Wild and Scenic Rivers Act (1968).[28] Another law of particular interest to Johnson was the Highway Beautification Act of 1965. The law, which called for the control of outdoor advertising and junkyards along Interstate highways, was also known as Lady Bird Johnson's pet project. Overall, however, the response by both the White House and Congress to environmental issues during the 1960s was halting and piecemeal.

In the mid- and late 1960s, there were several well-publicized environmental episodes, pitting corporate interests against growing resistance from conservationists at the grassroots level.

Storm King Mountain. In 1963, the New York electric utility company, Consolidated Edison, announced that it would build a power plant on Storm King Mountain, near the Hudson River. A grassroots effort, called the Scenic Hudson Preservation Conference, led by Stephen and Beatrice Duggan, tried but failed to have the construction halted. The Federal Power Commission (FPC), which had jurisdiction over the siting and operation of power plants, determined that the plant was needed, and that questions of natural beauty and aesthetics were irrelevant issues. At the end of 1965, however, a federal court reversed the FPC, ruling in favor of Scenic Hudson, stating that the organization had standing to sue in this case. It took a full decade before Con Edison was forced to abandon its Storm King project, but an important precedent was set: a conservation group was permitted to bring suit to protect the public interest.[29]

Indiana Dunes. It was a controversy that had been brewing for nearly a half century: the clash between big steel companies and other manufacturers versus conservationists on the Indiana shoreline of Lake Michigan. By 1916, the area was a thriving industrial center for steel mills and power plants. But the Indiana shoreline was also an area of natural beauty, with its many pristine sand dunes. The largest dune was called the Indiana Slide, a 200-foot dune which had been systematically carted off in railroad boxcars by the Ball brothers of Muncie, Indiana, who manufactured glass jars, and the Pittsburgh Plate Glass Company plant based in Kokomo, Indiana. Sporadic efforts were made to save the dunes and to create a national lakeshore. Through the efforts of Senator Paul H. Douglas (Democrat–Illinois), whose Chicago constituents benefitted from the nearby Indiana recreational area, and a citizens' organization called the Save the Dunes Council, a solution was ironed out. In a compromise, the industrialists received the Burns Waterway Harbor (Port of Indiana) on Lake Michigan, and in late 1966, during the Eighty-Ninth Congress, a total of 8,330 acres of land and water were carved out for the Indiana Dunes National Lakeshore; four additional authorizations increased the park's size to 15,000 acres.[30]

Santa Barbara oil spill. At 10:45 a.m., on January 28, 1969, a Union Oil Company (Unocal) oil rig, Platform A, stationed six miles into the Pacific Ocean suffered a blowout. Over the next ten days, 200,000 gallons of crude oil spilled onto the beaches of central California, from Pismo to Oxnard, contaminating an area of over 800 square miles. Seabirds were hit particularly hard, with an estimated 3,600 birds killed. Pictures of oil-drenched birds appeared in news accounts worldwide. But Fred L. Hartley, described by the *New York Times* as "gruff, outspoken, and iron-willed," the president and chief executive of Unocal, refused to call this an environmental disaster. There were no human lives lost, reckoned Hartley. "I am amazed at the publicity for the loss of a few birds."[31] But the reaction to this ecological disaster was swift and fierce: a local grassroots organization, Get Oil Out (GOO) was formed, 100,000 people signed petitions to ban offshore oil drilling, and, more importantly, the oil spill awakened the nation to dangers of environmental catastrophe.

The Cuyahoga River. Another spectacular, but far less consequential, event occurred on June 22, 1969, when the Cuyahoga River caught fire in Cleveland, Ohio. *Time* magazine described the river: "Chocolate-brown, oily, bubbly with subsurface gases, it oozes rather than flows." This wasn't the first time that the river had caught fire; in fact, it had done so nine times before in the last 100 years. And this was certainly not the most damaging. In 1952, a fire caused $1.5 million in damage, while the 1969 fire, lasting just 30 minutes, did only about $50,000 in damage and little ecological harm. But rivers aren't supposed to catch on fire, and this unusual event created a media sensation, inspired a song by Randy Newman, "Burn On," brought attention to environmental problems, and helped speed the passage of the Clean Water Act in 1972.[32]

Environmentalism, which barely registered as a concern during the 1968 presidential election, had now reached a critical threshold in public opinion.[33] But the public was far ahead of Congress. Gaylord Nelson lamented that there were only four or five senators and an equal number of representatives who could have been considered environmentalists in the late 1960s. One of them, Senator Henry Jackson, in April 1969, told the National Audubon Society that "the public sense of priorities and those of the government are poles apart with respect to the importance of environmental matters."[34]

The public was also ahead of the older conservation groups, like the Sierra Club, the National Audubon Society, the National Wildlife Federation, the Izaak Walton League, and others. Environmental reporter Philip Shabecoff noted that these organizations were "still preoccupied by traditional land and wildlife preservation issues," and that "most—though not all—of the old guard had remained blind and deaf to the growing national anger over pollution and other environmental threats to human health." Years later, Michael McCloskey of the Sierra Club remembered that "we were taken aback by the speed or suddenness with which the new forces exploded."[35]

Suddenly, the environment—not the Vietnam war or civil rights—was the hot topic on Capitol Hill. Trying to catch up with the sentiment and anxieties of the American public, Congress exploded with more than 140 environmental bills introduced during the second half of 1968 and the first half of 1969.[36]

Making the Law

The idea of a national environmental policy act had been first introduced in 1959, when Senator James E. Murray (Democrat–Montana), offered a bill known as the Resources and Conservation Act of 1960.[37] Murray's legislation was designed to draw together the various reports and actions of the federal government in the field of conservation. He crafted legislation to create an advisory council to the president, a joint conservation committee for Congress, and an annual report on the state of conservation and natural resources. The legislation also contained a broad-ranging declaration of national conservation resources and development policy. While Murray's legislation gathered a good deal of support in the Senate, the Eisenhower administration, the timber industry, business organizations, and western lawmakers, among others, opposed it. Conservation was not a major issue in the 1960 presidential campaign; both candidates John F. Kennedy and Richard M. Nixon endorsed something of a conservation plan, but theirs fell far short of Murray's. When the senator died in 1961, so too did the legislation that he had championed.[38]

Lyndon Johnson's approach to the protection of the environment was essentially through the perspective of resource conservation. Despite some activity from White House conferences on the environment during 1965, and the Great Society environmental legislation cited above, the momentum for presidential action collapsed with the increasing difficulties of the Vietnam War.[39]

Gaylord Nelson, now a senator, proposed legislation in 1965 to create a council of environmental advisors, an idea which later was incorporated into NEPA. His legislation also would set up a system to collect data on all aspects of the environment. This was an interesting shift in emphasis from earlier legislation that would focus on specific industries or natural resources;[40] however, Nelson's bill could not muster enough support for passage.

Henry Jackson had introduced legislation in late 1967 which would create an environmental review council, call for annual environmental quality reports, and establish a program for ecological research.[41] Rather than hold hearings on his bill, Jackson decided to participate in a joint House–Senate colloquium on national emerging environmental policy. Jackson's committee staff had turned to professor Lynton K. Caldwell of Indiana University for assistance. Caldwell had written a seminal article in 1963 calling for a new federal focus on the field of environmental policy, and for years he had been the leading academic voice in this arena.[42] The counsel to the Senate Interior Committee, William Van Ness, asked Caldwell to develop a rationale and the substance of a policy for the environment for use by the committee and by Congress.[43] Caldwell's policy paper, *A National Policy for the Environment*, was the central focus of the July 1968 colloquium sponsored by the Senate's Committee on Interior and Interior Affairs and the House of Representative's Committee on Science and Astronautics, co-chaired by Senator Jackson and Congressman George P. Miller (Democrat–California).[44] Caldwell's work was also underwritten by the

Conservation Fund, which at the time was headed by Russell E. Train. About half of the Johnson administration cabinet and leading environmental scientists attended these sessions, but the public's attention was elsewhere. In this terrible year 1968, with its assassinations, riots, and never-ending Vietnam war, the public was simply not interested in the environment. Nor was the press interested; not a single newspaper reporter bothered to attend or write about the meeting.[45]

Jackson was emerging as an important voice in environmental policymaking, but another senator had made his mark years earlier. As governor of Maine from 1954 to 1958, Edmund Muskie made a name for himself as a champion of cleaning up the state's polluted rivers. Elected to the U. S. Senate in 1958, he became the chair of the Air and Water Pollution Subcommittee of the Senate Public Works Committee just four years later. Muskie had become the Senate's "Mr. Clean" and "Ecology Ed," and he was reluctant to share the mantle with other lawmakers (or presidents), particularly on such a popular, emerging issue as environmental protection. Muskie gained broad national recognition as Hubert Humphrey's vice-presidential running mate in 1968 and was a presumed presidential contender for the 1972 contest.

Jackson introduced a fairly limited bill, S. 1075, on February 18, 1969. The bill contained a preamble outlining environmental policy goals, authorized the secretary of the interior to conduct ecological research, and established a Council on Environmental Quality, which would advise the president and prepare annual reports on the environment.[46]

Similar legislation was prepared in the House of Representatives under the sponsorship of John D. Dingell, Jr. (Democrat–Michigan), the chair of House Merchant Marine and Fisheries Committee. In their original form, neither the House nor the Senate versions had the most important feature of the final legislation, the requirement of an Environmental Impact Statement (EIS).

Jackson held hearings during the Spring of 1969, and the most important contribution, the heart of the final legislation, came at the prompting of professor Caldwell, who continued to work as a consultant to Jackson's committee. Caldwell argued that a declaration of public policy for the environment wasn't enough; there also needed to be some kind of "action-forcing mechanism." Without some kind of mandatory performance requirement by the federal agencies, Caldwell later wrote, "the Act might be no more than a pious resolve which the federal bureaucracy could ignore with impunity."[47] Thus was created the requirement that all federal agencies prepare environmental impact statements for any significant action they undertook. In order to oversee and coordinate the collection of environmental data and to serve the White House and Congress in policymaking, a new agency would be created, the Council on Environmental Quality.[48]

The hearings on Jackson's bill were relatively low-profile: there was little mention in the press, little interest from lobbyists and special interests. Even the principal environmental organizations were not actively engaged. They were invited to attend the hearings, but only the Sierra Club managed to come to the Senate deliberations. According to Caldwell, the environmental groups were approached, even visited, to discuss strategy, but the groups were "disinclined to work together" and wanted to pursue their own separate agendas.[49]

The White House also didn't pay much attention to the legislation. As Jackson's biographers observed, because the legislation "was so sweeping, with so much impact on all the agencies of the federal government, no body took it seriously."[50] This was particularly evident in the reaction of Dr. Lee DuBridge, the newly appointed science advisor to the president. DuBridge, former president of California Institute of Technology, was summoned to the Jackson hearings, but, without a prepared statement, "casually, almost disdainfully" listed the reasons why the Nixon administration was against the bill or why the bill wasn't necessary. Jackson then put on his prosecutorial hat: he went through, point by point, the provisions in his bill. *Tell us, Dr. DuBridge, what is your specific objection to this provision?* DuBridge would have no objection. Then to the next provision, *what do you object to here?* Again, the science advisor had no problems with the section. In the end, DuBridge, prodded by Jackson, agreed to every provision of the bill. From that moment, the Nixon administration finally came around to supporting (and later grabbing credit for) NEPA.[51]

In the House of Representatives, Congressman John Dingell introduced his NEPA bill originally as an amendment to the Fish and Wildlife Coordination Act. Dingell's bill was less comprehensive than Jackson's and contained no "action-forcing" mechanism, but in subsequent hearings a requirement for investigative environmental findings was added by fellow Michigan Democrat, Lucien N. Nedzi. But there was a big hurdle to overcome. Once the Dingell bill had been reported out of the Merchant Marine and Fisheries Committee, on July 11, it had to go through the Rules Committee. There Wayne N. Aspinall (Democrat–Colorado), who was both a member of the Rules Committee and the chairman of the Interior and Insular Affairs Committee, raised several objections regarding jurisdiction, the vagueness and ambiguity of the bill (such as the lack of any definition of the word "environment"), and the fear that natural resource development would be hampered by the new emphasis on environmentalism. More compromises were made in the language, and finally, in early September, the House version was voted on, 372 to 15, with 43 abstentions.[52]

In the meantime, there were two major developments: a White House proposal for a cabinet-level environmental quality council and a clash between Jackson and Muskie.

President Nixon, on May 29, 1969, from his Key Biscayne, Florida, retreat issued Executive Order 11472, which established a new agency, the Environmental Quality Council (EQC). Following his election in November 1968, Nixon had established ten policy task forces, including a group on resources and the environment, headed by Russell E. Train. DuBridge sent to the White House a proposal for a cabinet-level EQC, and, in May, Nixon issued the executive order. In defending the new EQC before congressional hearings, the science advisor emphasized that the president himself would preside over the Council. With an engaged, decisive president in charge, DuBridge told the committee, environmental problems could be forcefully resolved.[53]

But Jackson, Dingell and other legislators were not buying the administration's argument. Jackson, in an interview three years later, characterized the Nixon proposal as "interdepartmental chaos," and Dingell likened the EQC to a "cockpit," where agencies would fight out their turf and jurisdiction battles. Gaylord Nelson worried that the Council would avoid controversy and not resolve any tough environmental questions. The House Appropriations Committee labeled the administration's plan a "patchwork approach," which "would be little better than nothing," and Caldwell worried that an interdepartmental body would foreclose independent review.[54]

The Jackson legislation was sent to the Senate on June 10, and, without debate and with no amendments, slipped into the "morning hour," where routine matters are usually considered; S. 1075 then passed by voice vote.[55] But two days later, Senator Muskie, along with forty co-sponsors, introduced an amendment to a water control bill, containing a provision to establish an Office of Environmental Quality in the White House. There was a serious policy difference between Jackson and Muskie: Jackson's legislation would make the federal agencies internalize environmental values through the Environmental Impact Statement requirements. But Muskie and his staff did not trust the federal agencies to police themselves. There was also a jurisdictional issue. Muskie feared that the new NEPA legislation would "debilitate" the existing goals and programs developed in Muskie's own Air and Water Pollution Subcommittee.[56] Muskie was worried that, even though federal agencies would be fully informed, in the end it was their choice on how and when to act. As Matthew J. Lindstrom and Zachary A. Smith observe, Muskie "was, as we have since learned, correct."[57] Finally, there was a personal matter: Leon Billings, an aide to Muskie, later observed that "Scoop [Jackson] wanted a piece of the action," and Muskie was "not too happy about Jackson cutting into his issue."[58]

By early October, with tempers cooled and egos put in check, Jackson and Muskie had hammered out a compromise, with Muskie gaining assurances that the environmental impact requirement would be strengthened with the insistence on "detailed statements," and that these environmental impact statements would not water down or affect the current statutory obligations of federal agencies. The House and Senate versions went to conference, and just days before their December adjournment for the holidays, the two chambers easily passed NEPA; the Senate without even a recorded vote. As historian Richard Liroff summed up, "For many legislators, undoubtedly, a vote for NEPA was symbolic—akin to a vote for motherhood and apple pie. Little did they realize, however, that in voting to enact NEPA, they were placing a potent weapon in the hands of citizen activists."[59] In one of his last speeches on the floor of the Senate before its passage, Henry Jackson said he had intended NEPA to be "the most important and far-reaching environmental and con-servation measure ever enacted by Congress."[60]

Key provisions of the National Environmental Policy Act

NEPA was extraordinary legislation, only five pages long, written in language more befitting a constitution rather than a piece of legislation; a "stunningly simple statute," in the words of law professor Bradley C. Karkkainen.[61] Lynton Caldwell later wrote about the breadth of the opening policy statement in the law: "We believed that the best way to introduce the new idea of a holistic approach to dealing with the environment was to go with a policy statement that would open people's minds to what could and should be done." The idea of NEPA was to "*establish* policy."[62]

Lawmakers and commentators have often referred to it as the "Magna Carta" of environmental legislation. Its preamble set a tone of idealism: The purposes of the National Environmental Policy Act were

- "To declare a national policy which will encourage productive and enjoyable harmony between man and his environment.
- "To promote efforts which will prevent or eliminate damage to the environment and biosphere and stimulate the health and welfare of man.
- "To enrich our understanding of the ecological system and natural resources important to the Nation."

Title I contained the Declaration of a National Environmental Policy:

The Congress, recognizing the profound impact of man's activity on the interrelations of all components of the natural environment, particularly the profound influences of population growth, high-density urbanization, indus-trial expansion, resource exploitation, and new and expanding technological advances and recognizing further the critical importance of restoring and maintaining environmental quality to the overall welfare and development of man, declares that it is the continuing policy of the federal government, in cooperation with state and local governments, and other concerned public and private organizations, to use all practicable means and measures, including financial and technical assistance, in a manner calculated to foster and promote the general welfare, to create and maintain conditions under which man and nature can exist in productive harmony, and fulfill the social, economic, and other requirements of present and future generations of Americans.[63]

Title I also required that "to the fullest extent possible" the policies, laws, and regulations of the United States be interpreted and administered according to this policy, and that "*all* agencies" of the federal government "*shall*" be required in *every* federal agency recommendation or report that proposed legislation or offered federal action which would significantly affect the quality of the environment to provide "a detailed statement"—an environmental impact statement of the proposed action, any adverse environmental effects that could not be avoided, and alternatives to the proposed action.

Before making the detailed statement, the federal agency *shall consult* with and obtain comments from other federal agencies having jurisdiction or expertise, and

---

the statement, along with comments and views, will be available to the CEQ and the public. This last point—comments from the public—was groundbreaking. Here was the opportunity for citizens and environmental organizations to have input into federal policymaking.

The Council on Environmental Quality in the Executive Office of the President was created, with the task of preparing annual reports and assisting other agencies in implementing the law, and with monitoring overall environmental progress.[64]

On January 1, 1970, at his Western White House at San Clemente, California, Richard Nixon signed NEPA into law. In his accompanying remarks, Nixon commended Senator Jackson and other lawmakers, but not Senator Muskie. Neither Nixon nor his administration had any role in the passage of NEPA, and in fact his officials had testified against the creation of the Council of Environmental Quality. Yet Nixon had the spotlight, and made it appear that NEPA was really a victory for his administration. Letters started pouring in from throughout the nation thanking Nixon for his environmental leadership.[65]

Key Individuals in Creating NEPA

Henry M. Jackson (1912–1983) served in the House of Representatives (1941–1953) and the Senate (1963–1983). He was long-time chairman of the Committee on Interior and Insular Affairs and a member of the Committee on Energy and Natural Resources. While Edmund Muskie, Gaylord Nelson, John Dingell, and a few other legislators were important in the creation of NEPA, Lynton Caldwell has written that Jackson was "the most articulate and effective advocate" of the law and "had the deepest insight into its scope and significance."[66] Jackson, a strong defender of the military, later tasted defeat from environmentalist forces when he vigorously supported the Supersonic Transport (SST), developed by home-state Boeing Corporation. Jackson was an unsuccessful candidate for the Democratic nomination for the presidency in 1972 and 1976.

Lynton Keith Caldwell (1913–2006) provided the intellectual framework for NEPA. He was a longtime political science professor at Indiana University, where he retired in 1984 as the Arthur F. Bentley Professor Emeritus. He was an author of ten books and more than 200 scholarly papers. Most important was his 1963 paper "Environment: A New Focus for Public Policy." He later summed up NEPA and its role in environmental policy in a 1998 book, *The National Environmental Policy Act: An Agenda for the Future.*

Ed Muskie, two weeks later, pooh-poohed Nixon's public commitment to the environment, calling the administration's antipollution efforts "slogan-rich and action-poor."[67] Less than a week later, Nixon upped the ante and delivered his 1970 State of the Union address, where he proposed making the 1970s an historic period where we would "transform our land into what we want it to become."[68] Three weeks later, on February 10, Nixon announced a 37-point environmental action program, something a president had never done before.

Nixon also came through with a strong commitment to the new Council on Environmental Quality. Nixon chose strong nominees for the CEQ: Russell E. Train, the former head of the Conservation Fund and now the undersecretary of the interior, would be the chairman. Joining Train were Gordon MacDonald, a geophysicist at the University of California-Santa Barbara and member of the Environmental Studies Board of the National Academy of Sciences. Robert Cahn, the third member, was a noted conservation reporter for the *Christian Science Monitor*. They constituted "a formidable trio, not one a lackey to industry," wrote historian J. Brooks Flippen.[69] Nixon had laid down the marching orders: federal agencies were to comply with the NEPA.

Before NEPA, federal agencies paid little attention to environmental issues.[70] Typically, federal agencies were focused on their mission—building roads, clearing forests, handling hazardous materials, erecting hydroelectric dams, and hundreds of other activities. They were concerned with costs, timetables, mission-oriented obstacles, not with the environmental impact of their actions, nor on the input of citizens or environmental organizations. During the hearings and testimony in 1969, the White House and federal agencies paid little attention to the proposed requirement of an environmental impact statement.[71]

Now through NEPA, the environmental impact statement was not a discretionary matter. An agency might be fulfilling its own statute, but it also had to comply with the mandates of NEPA.[72] This was a revolutionary concept. Furthermore, citizens now would have a voice, a chance to review the impact statements, make their cases, suggest alternatives, and act as watchdogs. Federal decision-making would gain a measure of transparency; indeed, another revolutionary idea.

The new law left many questions unresolved: What is the meaning of the "environment"? What does "the fullest extent possible" require? What is a "major federal action"? Do citizens have standing to sue? Environmental law was in its infancy, and there were few precedents articulated in federal courts. While there had been no discussion of judicial review in the hearings and public documents leading up to NEPA's enactment, the scope and direction of the law would largely be settled in the courts.[73]

Aftermath

In January 1970, three weeks after Nixon signed NEPA into law, Gaylord Nelson announced that he would soon introduce a constitutional amendment that recognized the right of every American to a "decent environment." In the original Senate version of NEPA, Senator Jackson had inserted an "environmental bill of rights," which declared that "each person has a fundamental and inalienable right to a healthful environment." However, this proclamation was taken out of the conference bill.[74] Nelson's constitutional amendment never went anywhere, but it was indicative of the growing interest in environmental protection.

Earth Day was held on April 22, 1970. The old guard of the environmental movement wasn't prepared for the extraordinary outpouring of interest and concern coming from millions of ordinary citizens. Nor was the White House prepared. John C. Whitaker, who had served as a Nixon White House aide for environmental issues, acknowledged that "there was little doubt that the Nixon administration took its licks on Earth Day."[75] While leading Democratic politicians, like senators (and 1972 presidential hopefuls) Muskie, Humphrey, Jackson, Birch E. Bayh of Indiana, and George S. McGovern of South Dakota spoke out on the necessity for environmental clean-up, Nixon was quiet. Two months earlier he had given his ground-breaking environmental speech to Congress, and felt it wasn't necessary to say more. There would be no White House proclamation praising Earth Day; in fact, just days before, Nixon had directed his secretary of the interior, Walter Hickel, to approve construction of the Alaska pipeline and to make public that controversial announcement on Earth Day.[76]

Yet, Nixon was about to make a major reorganization, creating a new and potentially powerful environmental agency. A presidential council on government reorganization, headed by Litton Industries chairman Roy Ash, recommended that two new agencies, the National Oceanic and Atmospheric Administration (NOAA) and the Environmental Protection Agency (EPA), be created, to provide focus and centralization for the federal government's anti-pollution activities. Nixon accepted the Ash Council's recommendations on July 2, 1970, and in December EPA was formally created. William D. Ruckelshaus, then an assistant attorney general in the Department of Justice, was selected as its first administrator.[77] At his confirmation hearing on December 1, Ruckelshaus vowed to be a strong advocate for programs that clean up the environment. Senator Muskie said to the new EPA chief, "I hope that you preempt the title that has been tossed about loosely in recent years. I hope that you become known as 'Mr. Clean'."[78] Ruckelshaus joined in the laughter, but, reporter E. W. Kenworthy surmised, "his laugh must have been a little forced: He cannot but be aware of the difficult and slippery path on which he has set foot."[79] EPA began as a large agency, with a budget of $1.28 billion and a staff of 6,673, taking over the environmental responsibilities that had been handled by sixty-three federal departments and agencies.[80]

Throughout 1970, Nixon was looking over his shoulder, not wanting Democrats to gain political advantage on the environment issue, particularly with the crucial 1970 congressional elections looming. The personal and political animosity between Muskie and Nixon played out in the intense battle over the Clean Air Act Amendments, legislation championed by Muskie. Nixon took personal interest and a strong hand in drafting the legislation. On the last day of 1970, Nixon, who was not very happy over the final version, signed the

Clean Air Act Amendments into law.[81] At the signing ceremony, Nixon claimed the "primary role" in submitting the legislation and pledged that 1971 would be the "year of action" to put the new antipollution laws into effect. Senator Muskie, "Mr. Clean," the long-time champion of environmental issues and especially this legislation, was not invited to the ceremony.[82] In his memoirs, CEQ chairman Russell Train thought the slight came across "as an act of pettiness," and probably helped highlight Muskie's role, just the opposite of what Nixon had wanted.[83]

Republicans had not done well in the 1970 congressional election, and Nixon was frustrated that environmental groups and the press were not giving him the credit he thought he deserved. Nixon saw it as a no-win situation: no matter what he did for the environment, it wasn't enough. The politics just didn't add up, either: "you can't win with the environment," Nixon said, "but they can beat you up with it."[84] The president, who ushered in the new decade of the environment with a flourish from his San Clemente office on New Year's day, would no longer be the champion or, indeed, protector of the environment. Russell Train, the president's own advisor, wrote in his memoirs that there had been no evidence that Nixon had any "real personal interest in environmental matters," and that his reaction to the issue was that of a "highly political animal." Once Muskie's presidential bid had collapsed in the snow-swept primaries of early 1972, and Nixon had won an overwhelming re-election victory against anti-war candidate George McGovern, the environment was no longer an issue for him.[85]

But the decade of the 1970s, despite Nixon's loss of enthusiasm, truly became the "decade of the environment." In 1970, NEPA was followed by Earth Day, the creation of the EPA, and, on the final day of the year, the signing into law of the Clean Air Act. Many more environmental laws were to follow during the decade of the 1970s, and were of such importance, wrote environmental reporter Philip Shabecoff, that "taken together, must be regarded as one of the great legislative achievements of the nation's history."[86] Among the laws passed were the Clean Air Act Amendments (1970), the Clean Water Act Amendments (Federal Water Pollution Control Act, 1972), the Endangered Species Act (1973), and the Toxic Substances Control Act (1976).[87]

Timeline for Environmental Legislation

1962	Publication of Rachel Carson's *Silent Spring*.
1963	Publication of Lynton K. Caldwell's, "Environment: A New Focus for Public Policy."
1964	Storm King Mountain environmental battle begins.
1969	Santa Barbara oil spill; Cuyahoga River ignites.
1969	NEPA enacted into law; signed on January 1, 1970.
1970	Earth Day; EPA created; Clean Air Act Amendments.
1970s	Decade of unprecedented federal environmental legislation.

As remarkable as this string of laws was, scientists, policymakers, activists, and lawmakers were still in the early stages of environmental policymaking during the 1970s. As political scientist Walter A. Rosenbaum reminds us, "not only the ozone hole but also global climate warming, genetically altered foods, endocrine disrupters, leaking underground storage tanks, ionizing radiation, indoor air pollution, and a multitude of other environmental issues—as well as many thousands of chemicals now common to U.S. commerce and industry—were unimagined or unknown to environmental activists."[88]

As for NEPA, its broad language left many questions to be answered, including what were the duties of federal regulators under the law and what role, if any, could citizens play in challenging agency policies? These questions were soon answered in federal court, in *Calvert Cliffs Coordinating Committee* v. *Atomic Energy Commission*.[89] The AEC (the forerunner of the Nuclear Regulatory Commission) contended that only radiation hazards had to be considered when a nuclear power company applied for an operating license or construction permits. AEC rules had prohibited outside parties, such as environmental groups, from raising non-radiological issues, such as thermal pollution from the release of water from the nuclear plants. Thus, in AEC's opinion, NEPA's requirement of environmental impact statements and public participation simply did not apply. The citizens' group argued that NEPA did apply to the deliberations of the AEC and that the Calvert Cliffs Coordinating Committee had standing to challenge the licensing of this nuclear power plant forty-five miles southeast of Washington, D.C., on the Chesapeake Bay.

Federal judge J. Skelly Wright ruled in favor of the citizens' group and chastised the Atomic Energy Commission. Wright stated that the AEC's "crabbed interpretation of the National Environmental Policy Act makes a mockery of the act" and that the AEC had failed in its duty to implement environmental safeguards.[90] He further ruled that NEPA did not permit an "escape hatch" for "foot-dragging agencies" and ordered AEC to comply with the law. "The very purpose of the National Environmental Policy Act was to tell federal agencies that environmental protection is as much a part of their responsibility as is protection and promotion of the industries they regulate," ruled Judge Wright. Following the *Calvert Cliffs* decision, the AEC ordered in early September 1971 the review of the permits and licenses of ninety-six nuclear power reactors throughout the country to now include all environmental factors.[91]

More lower federal court cases followed, with rulings generally interpreting the role of NEPA in an expansive way. Over the years, section 102 of NEPA, requiring the environmental impact statement, had been thoroughly litigated; after just eight years, there had been 1,052 NEPA-related lawsuits filed in federal courts.[92]

While the lower federal courts had been the early guardians of NEPA, the U.S. Supreme Court, through a series of decisions, had weakened the mandate of the law.[93] The first important NEPA-related case to reach the U.S. Supreme

Court was *Kleppe* v. *Sierra Club* (1976).[94] The Sierra Club had argued that the Department of the Interior could not further develop federal coal fields in a four-state great plains area without a comprehensive EIS covering the entire region. The Supreme Court, however, deferred to the judgment of the environmental agency and ruled it wasn't the place for the judiciary "to substitute its judgment for that of an agency as to environmental consequences of its actions." In another case dealing with nuclear power plants, the Supreme Court in 1978 held that the Atomic Energy Commission was in the best position to determine its own procedures.[95] The Supreme Court has generally reinforced lower court decisions, but it had not decided any NEPA cases from 1989 to 2004, and, in more recent years, only cases on marginal issues.[96]

NEPA was also intended to apply to United States activities abroad, but a number of federal agencies had tended to resist the requirements. President Jimmy Carter, in January 1979, clarified this NEPA requirement through Executive Order 12114, and reaffirmed the duty of federal agencies to consider environmental components in their projects, even if they were on foreign soil.[97]

The "Decade of the Environment" ended with the presidential elections in November 1980. With the election of former California governor Ronald W. Reagan came the opportunity for conservative forces to overturn or at least slow down the revolution in environmental lawmaking. For years in the western states, an anti-environmental movement called Operation Sagebrush had been gaining force. Now it had a friend in the White House. Law professor Joel A. Mintz characterized the changeover to the Reagan administration as a "dramatic change in the tone, structure, and operation" of EPA's enforcement program. NBC News was less nuanced, declaring this the "end of the environmental movement."[98]

Reagan's key appointments were welcome news to conservatives. The new president appointed James G. Watt to be the secretary of the interior. Watt had been the founding president of the Mountain States Legal Fund, an anti-environmental group funded in part by beer magnate Joseph Coors, which promoted the private-property-friendly concept of "wise use." The EPA would be headed by Anne M. Gorsuch (later Burford), who quickly advocated budget cuts in her agency, the elimination of its enforcement division, and other regulatory "reforms." Watt and Burford (and to a lesser degree Rita M. Lavelle, the head of the Superfund program at EPA) quickly became lightning rods for environmental critics and targets of congressional inquiry. Over a million people signed a "Dump Watt" petition that was circulated by the Sierra Club. Watt was castigated in Congress for his enthusiasm to open up nearly all public lands, ridiculed for trying to ban the musical group the Beach Boys from July 4th celebrations on the Washington Mall, and ultimately resigned in September 1983 after making a crude insensitive joke.

In March 1983, Burford was forced to resign (along with nineteen high-level EPA colleagues). She was found in contempt of Congress for refusing to turn over documents that strongly suggested partisan political advantage in the handling of Superfund monies. Lavelle was convicted of giving false testimony to congressional committees, was fined $10,000 and served four-and-one-half months of a six months' prison sentence.[99]

The Reagan administration sought to change the direction of environmental policy, not only by its senior appointments, but also by cutting budgets and exerting control over environmental regulations. Reagan tried, but failed, to cut out the Council for Environmental Quality altogether. There were severe staff cuts in CEQ and the agency barely limped along thereafter. The EPA budget and personnel were slashed: it lost one-third of its budget and one-fifth of its personnel during Reagan's first term.[100]

There was considerable backlash from the environmental community; many environmental organizations saw their membership soar as citizens became alarmed at the direction and scope of Reagan's conservation and environmental policies. Reagan tried to repair some of the damage by bringing back the respected William Ruckelshaus, then Lee Thomas, to serve as EPA administrators.

But certainly the damage had been done. As political scientist Walter A. Rosenbaum has summed up, to environmental leaders the Reagan years meant "above all, dangerous drift and indecision, almost a decade of lost opportunities and intensifying environmental ills."[101]

The summer of 1988 was miserable. As a *New York Times* editorial lamented, "People gag on ozone smog as bad as in any year on record. They can't escape the heat by visiting the seashore because the beaches are polluted. They hear warnings that even hotter years lie ahead because of the global warming caused by the predicted greenhouse effect."[102] Democratic presidential candidate Michael Dukakis promised to institute policies that would overcome the "legacy of neglect" of the Reagan years. Dukakis's opponent, George H. W. Bush, played little public role on environmental issues during his eight years as vice-president; but as head of the Reagan administration's deregulation effort he helped weaken the federal role in environmental protection. Among other things, Bush opposed automobile efficiency standards and the removal of lead from gasoline.[103]

When George H. W. Bush became president he surprised, and reassured, some environmental critics by appointing the well-respected William Reilly, president of the World Wildlife Fund, as his new administrator of EPA, and long-time environmental hand Michael Deland as the head of the Council of Environmental Quality. Bush also pushed for, and Congress enacted, the urgently needed Clean Air Act amendments, breaking a ten-year-long legislative stalemate on the issue. Yet, the Bush administration had far to go to repair the policies and practices of the Reagan administration. The EPA was still in partial shell-shock: its budget and staffing had not been restored to levels needed to meet its increasing responsibilities, and environmental issues, like many other domestic issues, were not priority items for Bush. Behind the scenes, a little-known organization, the Council on Competitiveness, chaired by

Vice-President Dan Quayle, pushed the EPA and other agencies to ease up on federal environmental regulations that would be "burdensome" to industry. Particularly troublesome for environmentalists was the administration's failure to take a leadership role in international environmental diplomacy, especially the 1992 U.N. Earth Summit in Rio de Janeiro.

While governor of Arkansas, Bill Clinton did not have much of a record as an environmental progressive, but much was expected of him and his new administration when he was elected president in 1992. The new vice-president, Al Gore, Jr., had been the Senate's leading champion of the environment and had just written a well-received book, *Earth in Balance*. The Clinton–Gore team promised a wide range of environmental protection programs, insisting that a clean environment did not have to derail economic growth.[104] Clinton appointed former Arizona governor and president of the League of Conservation Voters Bruce Babbitt as secretary of the interior, Carol Browner as administrator of the EPA, and Kathleen McGinty as head of the Council of Environmental Quality. Both Browner and McGinty had served as aides to Al Gore in the Senate. Clinton wanted to lift EPA to cabinet rank and to replace the CEQ with a more potent organization, the Office of Environmental Policy (OEP); both measures, however, were unfulfilled.

Unknown to the White House or to the Democratic leadership at the time, the window for any significant environmental legislation was closing fast. During the 103rd Congress (1993–1994), environmental policy was of relatively low priority for the administration, and only one piece of environmental legislation was passed, the California Desert Protection Act. Congress and the administration failed to get reauthorizations for the Clean Water Act, Safe Drinking Water Act, Endangered Species Act, and Superfund.[105] In the 103rd Congress, while there was little party discipline, Democrats held the majority in both the House and the Senate. Then came the election of 1994, Newt Gingrich, and the Contract with America.

In an extraordinary electoral victory, the Republican Party in 1994 claimed control of both the Senate and the House of Representatives. After forty consecutive years of being in the minority, Republicans were now in charge in the House, with Newt Gingrich (Republican–Georgia) the new Speaker. Part of the drive to get Republicans elected was the Contract with America, a policy declaration endorsed by well over 300 House Republican incumbents and candidates. One of the pledges was an old familiar conservative nostrum: get government off of our backs and "free Americans from bureaucratic red tape."[106] There was nothing in the Contract specifically mentioning the environment, but there was enormous pressure from conservative think tanks, business interests, and the drumbeat of conservative talk radio for the newly empowered conservative majority to act.

House policymakers wanted federal regulations to pass a stringent test: were the benefits of the new regulation worth the costs? Business trade associations, the National Association of Manufacturers, and two coalitions, Project Relief and the Alliance for Reasonable Regulation, all pushed for the Job Creation and Wage Enhancement Act of 1995, which would mandate cost-benefit analysis and risk assessments throughout the regulatory process.[107] Conservatives hoped that this proposal, requiring a twenty-three-step review process, would weed out unnecessary federal regulations. It easily passed in the House, but was blocked in the Senate.

Another Republican tactic was to simply cut off funding for objectionable regulatory activities. For example, in 1995 the House added seventeen riders to the EPA appropriations bill. The EPA, in effect, was told not to spend money on water-quality and drinking water standards, on economic development in wetlands areas, toxic air emissions from oil and gas refineries, and other matters. Environmental groups sprung to action, labeling this a congressional "war on the environment," and Clinton threatened a veto. This time, House Republicans had overplayed their hand and were hearing plenty from angry constituents. Finally, sixty-three Republicans, following the lead of Sherwood L. Boehlert (New York) refused to go along with its leadership's position, and the riders were removed in the House–Senate conference committee.[108]

Undeterred, Republican congressional leaders pressed for steep cuts in the budget of the EPA. Despite a Clinton budget veto, heated criticism from Secretary of the Interior Bruce Babbitt and EPA Administrator Carol Browner, and battering in public opinion polls, the Republicans did manage to cut the environmental protection budget. Yet the bruising battles of 1995 left House Majority Whip Thomas D. DeLay (Republican–Texas) frustrated: "I'll be straight with you—we have lost the debate on the environment."[109] For DeLay, this was personal. As a small business owner of a pest-control company, DeLay had repeated run-ins with environmental regulations; he had vowed to run for Congress to rid the country of the pest of burdensome regulations.

By the time of the Republican congressional takeover in 1995, NEPA had been in effect for twenty-five years. At first, in 1970–1972, federal agencies filed a flurry of environmental impact statements, 5,834 in all. By 1980, there were 966 filed, and since then there have been an average of 500–600 environmental impact statements filed each year.

Most federal actions, however, do not require environmental impact statements. There are two other important options. The most common is called the categorical exclusion (CE), usually a short statement, where it has been determined that there will be no significant impact on the human environment. Several agencies have determined in advance what will fall into categorical exclusion: for the Federal Highway Administration, landscaping, construction of bike and pedestrian lanes are excluded; the Forest Service excludes from consideration the closing of an area during a period of extreme fire danger, or adjusting special use or recreational fees. In addition, recent legislation has added specific categories to the list of categorical exclusions. For example, the Energy Policy Act of 2005 excludes projects that disturb fewer than five acres, and the Healthy Forest Restoration Act of 2003 excludes hazardous fuel reduction projects on federal land.[110]

The second category of environmental review is called the environmental assessment (EA). Roughly 50,000 environmental assessments are made each year, and those assessments will either conclude that a full environmental impact statement (EIS) is required (just over 1 percent of these assessments), or will conclude that there is a finding of no significant impact (FONSI). In the 1990s and moving into the twenty-first century, there was a trend toward preparing "mitigated FONSIs." Following the environmental assessment, the agencies would take steps to fix or reduce a problem. While controversial under some circumstances, the mitigated findings of no significant impact provided a "relief valve"; now only "very major" federal actions which could not be mitigated would be required to go through the full NEPA review with an environmental impact statement.[111]

When an agency is required to prepare an environmental impact statement, it must include several elements: (a) a brief statement of the purpose of the project and the need the agency is responding to; (b) a description of all the reasonable alternatives that would meet the project's need and purpose; (c) a description of the environment affected by the alternatives (such as endangered species, wetlands, historic sites, and so forth); and finally, (d) an analysis of the impact of each alternative. A draft EIS is developed, then, following public comment, a final version is created. After this, the lead federal agency must create a public record of decision, a necessary step before a federal project can proceed.[112]

In 2006, a total of 542 environmental impact statements were filed, coming mostly from the U.S. Forest Service (144), followed by the Federal Highway Administration (66), U.S. Army Corps of Engineers (56), and the Bureau of Land Management.[113]

As time has gone by, the EIS became a larger, more complex document, filled with data, often taking hundreds of hours, and months, even years to complete. The average length of the EIS is now over 570 pages, takes between two weeks and 18 months to prepare, and costs approximately $10,000 to $200,000.[114]

There were plenty of complaints from industry and others who had to comply with the law. For example, the executive director of the Northwest Mining Association, an organization of 1,300 members in thirty-one states and six Canadian provinces who explore and mine on western public lands, complained to the CEQ in 2006: "Something is dreadfully wrong with a process designed to provide a hard look at the impacts of major federal actions affecting the human environment, that now takes five, ten and even eighteen years to complete. What NEPA sponsor Senator Henry Jackson . . . thought would be a six to eight page document (the EIS) has, with respect to most mining projects, mushroomed to thousands and thousands of pages."[115]

Environmental impact statements suffer from another problem. Daniel A. Bronstein and his colleagues observe that many EIS documents are "heavy on data and light on analysis," that are frequently "incomprehensible and thus useless" to the concerned public.[116]

In its own evaluation of the effectiveness of NEPA, the Council of Environmental Quality found that the Act frequently "takes too long and costs too much, agencies make decisions before hearing from the public, documents are too long and technical for many people to use, and training for agency officials at times is inadequate."[117]

On environmental issues, in particular, there was a clear gap—perhaps chasm—between Republican and Democratic ideology and policymaking. The new George W. Bush administration was determined to reverse nearly all of the major environmental initiatives of the Clinton administration's EPA, Departments of Agriculture and Interior.[118] Bush withdrew U.S. participation in the Kyoto Protocol on Climate Change; Vice-President Richard Cheney developed a new energy plan behind closed doors with industry leaders, without input from environmental organizations. Former interior secretary James Watts chimed in, "everything Cheney's saying, everything the president's saying— they're saying exactly what we were saying twenty years ago, precisely. Twenty years later, it sounds like they've just dusted off the old work."[119]

The EPA, under Christine Todd Whitman, briefly withdrew the strict arsenic standards developed under the Clinton administration, undercut some of the enforcement provisions of the Clean Air Act, and even data from agency scientists became suspect. The new secretary of the interior, Gale Norton, a former Watts staffer of the Mountain States Legal Fund, reversed Clinton policies, by authorizing oil drilling near national parks and advocating opening up the Alaska Arctic National Wildlife Refuge (ANWR) to oil drilling. The Office of Management and Budget (OMB) was given greater oversight of environmental regulations, with an aggressive use of cost-benefit analysis to determine environmental risks.[120]

In 2001, the U.S. Senate was divided evenly, with fifty Republicans and fifty Democrats. Then, Senator James M. Jeffords of Vermont abruptly left the Republican Party, became an independent, and aligned with the Democrats. Jeffords was fed up with his party, including its environmental policies. As a reward for jumping parties, Democrats agreed to make him chairman of the Environment and Public Works Committee.[121] But following the November 2002 mid-term elections, Republicans regained control of the Senate, and James Inhofe (Oklahoma) replaced Jeffords as chairman of the Environment and Public Works Committee. Inhofe, one of the Senate's most conservative members, once likened the EPA to the "Gestapo," and in 2003 famously asked, "With all of the hysteria, all of the fear, all of the phony science, could it be that man-made global warming is the greatest hoax ever perpetuated on the American people? It sure sounds like it."[122]

It was time for NEPA to be reviewed and possibly re-assessed. In 2002, President George W. Bush established a NEPA task force, headed by the Council of Environmental Quality, with the mission of assisting federal agencies in updating their practices and procedures. One year later, the White House task force issued its report and recommendations, concluding that no legislative changes were needed but suggesting ways of improving its implementation.[123]

A new agency established by Congress in 1998, the U.S. Institute for Environmental Conflict Resolution, was charged with helping to implement the policy goals of NEPA. Its advisory committee in 2004 made several recommendations on how to improve the NEPA decision-making process.[124]

Then, in 2005, Congress stepped in. Richard Pombo (Republican–California), until his defeat in 2006, was chair of the powerful House Resources Committee (renamed by Democrats in 2007 the House Natural Resources Committee). Pombo had been the scourge of environmental groups, which accused him of deliberately undermining environmental legislation, particularly the Endangered Species Act, even subverting the legislative process itself.[125] Under Pombo's direction, the Resources Committee in April 2005 created a special task force to look into ways of expediting or "streamlining" the environmental impact statement process. The task force, chaired by Cathy McMorris Rodgers (Republican–Washington), began a series of eight field investigations and hearings on ways to improve the environmental impact statement process.

In October 2005, a group of 202 professors of administrative, environmental and natural resources law and policy submitted its comments to the task force.[126] The group's basic message to the McMorris Rodgers task force was that NEPA had been successful, there was no need for a new law, but that it could use stronger administrative rules and "the will to make them effective." The professors conceded that the process took time and money, but that the costs and burdens could be exaggerated: after all, only 1 percent of the 50,000 actions potentially subject to the NEPA process were required to develop an environmental impact statement. To them, full examination of the alternatives was what the NEPA process required, and that public participation is at the heart of the democratic process.

But the NEPA task force soon became the target of heated partisanship. This was to be a bipartisan task force, but, when it came time to issue the final report, it was done without Democratic input and even without notice to the Democratic members of the task force, according to a former Democratic staff member.[127]

The NEPA Task Force final report was published in early January 2006, and immediately drew heated criticism from conservationists. The Wilderness Society, for example, charged that the proposals would "significantly weaken" NEPA by making the law a voluntary obligation, by tipping alternative analysis in favor of corporate interests, and by restricting how and when the public can challenge agency decisions.[128] The Task Force made its point, but its charter expired at the end of the session, and, particularly with a new Democratically controlled 110th Congress (2007–2008), there was no further legislative effort to "streamline" NEPA.

Yet, during the 109th Congress (2005–2006), there were enacted several legislative restrictions to or exemptions from NEPA requirements. For example, the "Real I.D. Act of 2005," as part of an Emergency Supplemental Appropriations bill, permits Homeland Security to construct barriers and roads along U.S. borders without complying with NEPA. Section 390 of the Energy Policy Act of 2005 establishes a "rebuttal presumption" that new wells created out of existing wells, numerous actions causing surface disturbance of less than five acres, and new pipelines in previously approved corridors, are excluded from NEPA review. Grazing permits could be renewed on millions of acres of national forest land without NEPA review. Forest Service and Dept. of Interior regulations, adopted in 2003, categorically exclude certain timber harvesting activities from NEPA review. In addition, there have been restrictions on the substance of environmental reviews. For example, the Healthy Forests Restoration Act (2003), designed to reduce wildfires, directs the Forest Service and the Bureau of Land Management to consider only the agency's preferred alternative and a no-action alternative. Finally, there have been restrictions to public participation in the NEPA process, by narrowing and cutting back review periods.[129]

The task forces, the policy reassessments, and the legislative "streamlining" are symptomatic of the mixed reactions to NEPA. Dinah Bear, former general counsel for the Council on Environmental Quality, has written that, in professional environmental circles, NEPA elicits two typical reactions.[130] Some praise the statute, call it the "America's environmental magna carta," and defend it against all who might try to change (or "streamline") the law. Other environmentalists will argue that NEPA was important and a good law at the time of its enactment, but times have changed, so many environmental laws have been created since then to take care of specific problems, and the process of developing an environmental impact statement has become long, cumbersome, and expensive, far beyond what Henry Jackson had envisaged when he created the law.

Those who praise the law NEPA often stress its unique participatory element. Congressman Tom Udall (Democrat–New Mexico), the son of former interior secretary Stewart Udall, in 2005 called NEPA "one of the nation's most important and vibrant laws." He argued that "a central tenet of our democracy is that government should be accountable to the people, and NEPA has fundamentally served to make our democracy work better by greatly enhancing citizen participation in the process of federal agency decision making."[131]

Others, like the 202 professors who submitted a brief before the 2005 NEPA task force, argued that it is not the law suits that tell the whole story, it is the potential for legal action that matters. That potential, or perhaps threat, will ensure that "both environmental impacts (from environmental plaintiffs) and economic impacts (from industry plaintiffs) will be considered. Agency awareness of this potential is the practical enforcer of NEPA."[132]

Robert G. Dreher, of the Georgetown University Environmental Law and Policy Institute, observed in 2005 that, over its thirty-five years history, NEPA "has been extraordinarily successful in accomplishing its goals."[133] He argues that it serves as a "critical tool for democratic government decision-making, establishing an orderly, clear framework for involving the public in major decisions affecting their lives and communities."[134]

Other supporters, like Nicholas C. Yost, former general counsel for the CEQ, have noted that NEPA "may be the most imitated law in American history."[135] Over one hundred countries, including China, have adopted similar legislation. By 2003, fifteen states and the District of Columbia and Puerto Rico had state environmental policies modeled on NEPA, requiring environmental statements. Most are "carbon copies" of NEPA.[136] Some local governments, using their own versions of NEPA, have gone a step further by applying the environmental review process to land use planning and land use decisions. The state environmental policy act process is most active in California, New York, and Washington state.[137]

Defenders of the law point to its success stories. In Arizona, for example, NEPA was the vehicle that ensured public comments and public hearings after Congress created five new national monuments. In Colorado, a program to clear cut in the Grand Mesa National Forest was met with intense public opposition and the proposal was scaled back so that hundreds of thousands of acres of forested land would not be sacrificed. Old growth forests were protected in North Carolina and drinking water was protected from radioactive waste mill tailings in Utah. When the federal Department of Energy (DOE) decided in the mid-1990s to build high radioactive waste tanks at the Hanford Nuclear Plant in eastern Washington state, the NEPA analysis showed that the rationale and technical case for such tanks (and the consequent diverting of $500 million from its other cleanup activities) were flawed.[138]

Professor Oliver A. Houck, whose observation opens this chapter, has called NEPA the most successful environmental law in the world, but also the most disappointing. "The real problem with NEPA," Houck writes, "is that it attempts the impossible." In enacting NEPA, Congress was looking "for a silver bullet, the one solution for all federal actions, that would do nothing less than change the conduct of the entire government."[139]

But perhaps such change of conduct comes down to values, priorities, and political will.[140] Writing eight years before his death, Lynton Caldwell conceded that NEPA had not become the "visible centerpiece of American environmental policy."[141] He argued that this law, with so much potential, had been marginalized by the White House, misinterpreted by the judicial branch, and subject to popular indifference.

NEPA provides the framework and it articulates the values, but what is currently missing both in legislative and the executive branches is the will to make it an integral part of this nation's policy agenda.

13

THE LAWS THAT
SHAPED AMERICA

Now, there are some who question the scale of our ambitions, who suggest that our system cannot tolerate too many big plans. Their memories are short. For they have forgotten what free men and women can achieve when imagination is joined to common purpose, and necessity to courage.
President Barack Obama, Inaugural Address (2009)

Today, Washington is tied up in a Gordian knot of political gridlock. While Americans struggle to pay for health care, save for the future, care for kids and aging parents and achieve financial security, political leaders have become more polarized and less effective. Partisanship has trumped leadership. Gaining political advantage has become more important than solving the nation's problems.
William D. Novelli, president, AARP (2008)

The fifteen laws featured in this book span an extraordinary time in American history, from the last days of the Confederation Congress in 1787 to the Nixon administration and its aftermath. They were chosen because they have had a lasting impact on American society. What else might these disparate laws have in common? With just fifteen examples, it is risky to make sweeping generalizations; nevertheless, there are some interesting common features in these landmark laws.

Some Common Features

Presidential Involvement

In some of these landmark laws, the president was deeply involved. Franklin Roosevelt pushed hard for the passage of social security legislation, and considered its enactment one of his most important accomplishments. He was, as historian Arthur M. Schlesinger, Jr., noted, the "single national political leader" identified with the creation of social insurance.[1] Lyndon Johnson was heavily invested in both the Civil Rights Act and the Voting Rights Act. Much of his involvement, especially during the Civil Rights Act filibuster, was behind the scenes, while Senator leaders, particularly Hubert Humphrey, carried the burden in Congress. Johnson's swift action following the Selma, Alabama, crisis, led to the enactment of the tough enforcement provisions of the Voting Rights Act.

In some of these laws, however, there was limited presidential involvement. Franklin Pierce reluctantly endorsed the Kansas–Nebraska Act, agreed that the 1820 Missouri Compromise should be overturned, and helped resurrect festering old wounds about slavery and territory. During the heat of the 1862 congressional term, Abraham Lincoln was deeply concerned about the worsening war situation and the early losses inflicted on supposedly superior Union forces. But Lincoln played no part in the two landmark laws, the Homestead Act and the Morrill Land-Grant Act. For the first six years of his presidency, Woodrow Wilson had held firm to his belief that woman suffrage should be gained through the states, and not through a federal constitutional amendment. In early 1918, with war raging in Europe, Wilson surprised everyone by publicly endorsing national action on woman's suffrage, arguing that the amendment was "vitally essential" for the war effort.

Nor did Franklin Roosevelt play much of a role in the National Labor Relations Act. Just as Congress was about to finish its work on the bill, Roosevelt publicly endorsed it and assured the public that it was part of his "must pass" legislation. Dwight Eisenhower was eager to create an interstate highway system, outlining his plan before the National Governors Association meeting. However, he delegated to his staff most of the responsibilities to push this legislation and, unfortunately, his assistants sometimes did not have the best political judgment on this issue. On January 1, 1970, Richard Nixon, who heretofore had displayed little interest in environmental issues, suddenly took the spotlight, signing the National Environmental Policy Act, and declaring the 1970s as the "Decade of the Environment." He succeeded in stealing the political thunder from potential presidential rivals Edmund Muskie and Henry Jackson, but soon Nixon's enthusiasm for the environment waned.

Quickly Resolved and Long, Drawn-out Battles

In the late spring of 1787, the eighteen remaining delegates to the Confederation Congress quickly finished their work on the Northwest Ordinance and, on July 11, Nathan Dane slipped into the legislation the very important non-slavery provision; soon the whole bill was unanimously approved. The ratification of the Louisiana Purchase treaty took just two weeks, spurred on by a six-month deadline imposed by Napoleon himself. To get the document from Paris to New York, then to Washington, took over two months, and for Jefferson to call the Congress into emergency session and get the word out to the far reaches of the country took up further precious time. But the Senate, ratifying the treaty in late October, managed to beat the deadline with days to spare. The Marshall

Plan was expedited by the fear of economic and political collapse in war-ravaged Europe. The British could no longer support Greece and Turkey and it was evident that the United States would have to step in, and it quickly did so with the unprecedented aid package. Finally, the National Environmental Policy Act, riding the crest of national concern about environmental degradation, was quickly passed, with little opposition, and with little understanding of its long-term implications.

On the other hand, some legislation had long gestation periods. The longest of all was the fight for woman's suffrage. As Carrie Chapman Catt lamented, it took fifty-two years of political struggle, 480 campaigns at the state level, and battles in nineteen consecutive Congresses, to finally enact the Constitutional amendment. Ratification came swiftly, but not without sharp battles and setbacks. Both the Homestead Act and the Morrill Land Grant College Act had been proposed decades earlier but had been defeated or subject to presidential veto. With southern Democrats no longer tying up legislation, Republican lawmakers were able to enact these and other important pieces of legislation in the remarkable 1862 session. The fight for Medicare was also a long, drawn-out affair, preceded by the 1948 battle for national health insurance, and finally built up momentum with the election of John F. Kennedy in 1960. The overwhelming 1964 defeat of Barry Goldwater, the outspoken opponent of Medicare, by its champion, Lyndon Johnson, finally convinced the powerful chairman Wilbur Mills that the time for the legislation was ripe. Bitter fights over civil rights legislation in 1957 and 1960 finally culminated in the 1964 Civil Rights Act and the 1965 Voting Rights Act.

Driven by Public Opinion

The law that probably received the most impetus from public opinion was the National Environmental Policy Act. In 1969, there was a great surge in interest in environmental issues, fueled by the Santa Barbara off-shore oil spill and the burning of the Cuyahoga River in Cleveland. More than two hundred environment-related bills were introduced at the time, and NEPA rode a crest of public support. The Civil Rights Act and the Voting Rights Act were spurred by civil rights protests, courageous activists in voter registration drives, and northern public sentiment that demanded change. Of all the laws studied here, religious leaders and grassroots movements played an important part in making the case for civil rights reform.

By the early 1950s, there was growing public demand for the federal government to do something about the highway transportation system, and that demand led to the passage of the federal-aid highway law popularly known as the Interstate Highway Act in 1956. During the early 1960s, and especially after the 1964 presidential election, citizens were demanding the federal government do something, anything, about the rising cost of medical care for the elderly. Medicare came about because of that growing sentiment.

Big Fights in Congress

Nearly all the landmark laws produced tension and opposition in Congress, but two of these laws, in particular, touched off bitter fights. Perhaps the most contentious fight occurred during the consideration of the Kansas–Nebraska Act in 1854. Free Soil lawmakers published the vitriolic "Appeal," accusing Stephen A. Douglas of "criminal betrayal" for reviving the festering issues of slavery and territory. There were angry shouts and threats, vows of retaliation, and lingering bitterness. The legislation and its surrounding controversy tore the Democratic Party apart on sectional grounds, and destroyed the Whig Party.

In the introduction to this book, readers got a taste of the bitter fight that had surrounded the filibuster of the Civil Rights Act of 1964. Southern leaders in Congress had drawn their wagons into the circle of delay and parliamentary procedure, hoping that they could talk the bill to death, and that Congress, anxious to move on to less controversial matters, would drop the legislation for that session.

However, two laws, in particular, were passed in Congress with limited opposition. The Marshall Plan legislation (the Economic Cooperation Act of 1948), despite some bitter opposition, claimed 84 percent of the vote in the House and 90 percent of the vote in the Senate. The dangers of imminent European collapse were evident, and in a remarkable period of bipartisan foreign policymaking, and the firm warnings from Secretary of State Marshall, the legislation quickly became law. In 1969, Congress was riding a wave of public demands for environmental protection. All of a sudden, hundreds of pieces of legislation emerged, and nearly every member of Congress was claiming to be a born-again environmentalist. The National Environmental Policy Act passed overwhelmingly in the House and by voice vote in the Senate.

An Overwhelming Partisan Majority

One of the striking aspects of these landmark laws is that seven out of fifteen were created when one political party dominated in Congress and the president was of the same party. While Abraham Lincoln was not a factor in the creation of the Homestead Act or the Morrill Act, the Thirty-Seventh Congress (1861–1862) was dominated by Republicans, the Democratic opposition from the South had gone home, and Congress was able to pass a remarkable string of legislation. The Seventy-Fourth Congress (1935–1936), dominated by Democrats and with a Democrat in the White House, was able to pass the National Labor Relations Act and the Social Security Act within a matter of six weeks. Democrats had a good working majority in the Eighty-Eighth Congress (1963–1964) and increased their dominance in the Eighty-Ninth (1965–1966). But the numbers were deceiving: many of those Democrats were from the South, and virtually every southern legislator opposed the Civil Rights Act and the Voting Rights Act. Lyndon Johnson exerted pressure, Democratic congressional leaders responded with determination and that rare commodity, discipline, but in the end it took the assistance of moderate Republicans joining non-southern Democrats to craft a working majority. The overwhelming majority of Democrats elected in November 1964 assured passage of the Medicare Act.

Interest Groups and the Laws

The Nineteenth Amendment giving women the right to vote would probably have stayed off the congressional radar screen for many years had it not been for the longstanding, persistent efforts of the national and grassroots woman suffrage organizations. The GI Bill owes much to the American Legion, which basically crafted the law and advocated for Congress to give GI Joe and GI Jane their due. While many interests, from the Congress to the Eisenhower administration, wanted to create a national interstate highway system, the "Road Gang" of highway construction companies, automobile manufacturers, gas and rubber producers, and others connected with automobile transportation, were especially keen for the law.

Yet, some interest groups somehow missed the boat. The American Federation of Labor, the largest organization representing workers, sat on the sidelines while Senator Robert F. Wagner of New York and Congress crafted the National Labor Relations Act. Still in its early years as an organization, the National Retired Teachers Association–American Association of Retired People (now the AARP) also did not participate in the policy fight for Medicare. An ad-hoc organization, the National Council for Senior Citizens, funded largely by organized labor, was the main vehicle for grassroots support. Likewise, none of the old line environmental organizations seemed interested in or participated in the creation of the National Environmental Policy Act.

Other organizations fought vigorously against landmark legislation and lost. The National Association of Manufacturers (NAM) was a strenuous opponent of the National Labor Relations Act, and the American Medical Association (AMA) fought hard against the enactment of Medicare. Ironically, today the NAM website, featuring an historical timeline of the organization's activities, blandly glosses over the 1930s fight against labor unions and the New Deal. Also, the AMA, which fought so hard against Medicare, in 2007 launched a multi-million-dollar advertising campaign to fight for legislation to cover the one in seven Americans who were not covered by health insurance.

The Role of Outside Experts

In the making of three laws, outside experts, all from academic circles, were instrumental. In 1851, Jonathan B. Turner of Illinois College urged the creation of agricultural and mechanical colleges; this "Turner Plan" was widely distributed. The Illinois legislature even urged its members of Congress to push for a federal version. Six years later, in 1857, Justin Morrill introduced in Congress his version of the Turner plan.

Faculty and graduates from University of Wisconsin played a prominent role in the crafting of the Social Security Act. Economics professor John R. Commons had drafted some of the first examples of model unemployment legislation. His students and protégés included Edward Witte and Arthur Altmeyer, both key figures in the creation of Social Security. Another Wisconsin graduate, Wilbur J. Cohen, was an important participant in the crafting of Medicare and Medicaid.

Professor Lynton K. Caldwell of Indiana University first conceived of the idea of the environment as a distinct field of public policy analysis. In the Senate deliberations, Caldwell served as an advisor and pushed for an "action-forcing mechanism" to accompany a general declaration of environmental principles. That mechanism became the environmental impact state, the central component of the National Environmental Policy Act.

The Overlay of Race

To a remarkable degree, issues of race and justice weave their way through the majority of these laws. When Nathan Dane added an anti-slavery provision in the Northwest Ordinance, this law became the very first federal enactment to forbid slavery in U.S. territory. New England states were particularly concerned that, once the Louisiana territory had become settled and new slave-owning states had been carved out of the territory, the balance of economic and political power would shift against them. The Kansas–Nebraska Act was supposed to pave the way for transcontinental railroad development, but instead opened the hornet's nest of controversy concerning slavery and territories. Less than six years later, the nation was torn asunder.

The Homestead Act and the Morrill Act had been stymied in earlier legislative sessions because in part of the overtones of race and slavery. Southern politicians were suspicious of the homestead idea, although thousands of poor southern families could have benefitted from it. Even when fellow southerner Andrew Johnson championed the legislation, his voice was drowned out as that of a "Black Republican." When the second Morrill Land-Grant Act was passed in 1890, it opened the way for seventeen southern and border states to create separate black educational institutions so that they could be eligible for land-grant college funds. Mostly these black institutions provided elementary and secondary education during their early years.

Some of the most vociferous opposition to woman suffrage came from southern states. A push to give women the right to vote would upset the southern power structure. It might encourage African-American males, whose right to vote was ostensibly guaranteed by the Constitution forty years earlier, and it would put African-American females on an equal footing with whites. This was too much for several southern U.S. senators, who pushed for amendments to allow women to vote, but only white women.

The GI Bill also had its overlay of race. One of the principal authors, Representative John E. Rankin of Mississippi, the chairman of the veterans' committee in the House, fought against giving African-Americans unemployment insurance and against any possibility that educational benefits for blacks who might dare consider going to a southern whites-only college or university.

Of course, race, justice, and basic civil rights were at the forefront of the battles to enact the Civil Rights Act and the Voting Rights Act.

Change and Denouement

The Homestead Act essentially played itself out, with the final federal homestead claim handed out in Alaska over twenty years ago. The Land-Grant College act certainly was important in creating public education in America, but, with agriculture now but a small fraction of the budget, faculty, research, and students of land-grand institutions, they must reach out to new missions and challenges. The National Labor Relations Act, the most important law protecting the rights of workers and unions, continues to be the founding document, but the union movement has lost much of its former strength, and in many states constitutes less than 10 percent of the labor force. Social Security has grown from a modest program, with modest benefits and costs, to a far more comprehensive, vital, and expensive program. Like clockwork, lawmakers would raise the benefits and expand the coverage of Social Security during the 1950s and 1960s, finally indexing the benefits in the 1970s. Along with Medicare, the impact, cost, and importance of these two programs is unmatched in domestic public policy. Certainly America's greatest domestic challenges focus on how to continue to support these programs or how to move toward better solutions.

The GI Bill for World War II veterans spawned legislation for veterans serving in the Korean war and the Vietnam war, as well the most recent legislation protecting those men and women who served in the post-9/11 military. The Marshall Plan helped to stabilize western European countries both economically and politically after World War II. It is recalled, fondly, by lawmakers and other politicians who want to create a Marshall Plan for education, or health, or to combat AIDS, or many other causes.

The Interstate Highway system is now complete, but now comes the difficult and very expensive challenge of maintaining and rebuilding the transportation infrastructure. The deadly collapse of the bridge across an Interstate connector in Minneapolis reminds us of the looming crisis of aging infrastructure not only in the Interstate system but particularly in surface transportation throughout the country.

With NEPA, the promise and impact of the environmental impact statement has been blunted by court rulings and by congressional action that has carved out exceptions and qualifications to the law's requirements.

Other Laws in Recent Years

During every two-year session of Congress, roughly 10,000 bills are introduced; perhaps 500, or 4 percent, will become law.[2] The last piece of landmark legislation examined here is the National Environmental Policy Act, enacted forty years ago. Are there no laws since then, from the turbulent days of Richard Nixon's presidency to the waning days of George W. Bush's administration, that deserve mention? Indeed, there were more than a dozen laws that I considered, but ultimately decided not to include, and there are two which deserve our attention and will most likely be judged by historians and policymakers as landmark laws.

If there were room for more legislation, I would have included the following. The *Immigration and Nationality Act* (1965), another law enacted during the Great Society era, abolished the old system of national origins quotas and imposed separate ceilings on non-Western hemisphere and Western hemisphere immigrants. This law, also known as the Hart–Cellar Act of 1965, became an important vehicle in shifting immigration away from its European focus to worldwide inclusion. From its enactment until 1995, over 18 million legal immigrants, triple the number from the previous thirty years, had immigrated to the United States.[3] The Immigration and Nationality Act, though amended several times, remains the foundation of current immigration policies.

Through the *Elementary and Secondary Education Act (ESEA)* (1965) the federal government overturned its long-standing policy of noninvolvement in the funding public school education. "No law I have signed or will sign means more to the future of America," Lyndon Johnson intoned at the signing ceremony on April 11, 1965. There had been bitter policy fights throughout American history on the role of federal involvement in schools, particularly because of the factors of federal aid to parochial or non-parochial schools, race and segregation, apportionment formulas, and the fears of federal intrusion into public education.[4] ESEA has provided billions of dollars in federal assistance to states to help support their primary and secondary schools. The latest version of ESEA came in 2002 when President George W. Bush signed into law what became popularly known as the *No Child Left Behind Act*. This important, but controversial, law provided over $11 billion in federal financial assistance to target public schools that were educating low-income children and another $10 billion for teacher recruitment and training and other programs.

Another important measure was *Title IX of the Education Amendments* (1972), which prohibited gender discrimination in federally funded education programs. While it did not specifically target these areas, since its passage the law has helped revolutionize women's sports and athletic participation at all levels, and has led to many gains for women and girls in others fields of endeavor. Since 2002, following the death of one of its co-authors, the law has been called the *Patsy Mink Equal Opportunity in Education Act*.[5]

During the Ninety-Seventh Congress (1981–1983), the first years of the Reagan administration, the most important piece of legislation was the *Economic Recovery Tax Act* (1981), which called for massive individual and business tax cuts. It was a centerpiece of the Reagan attempt to cut taxes, trim the size of the federal government, and institute the questionable theory of supply side economics. The legislation was also known as the Kemp–Roth Tax Cut, named after its principal authors Representative Jack F. Kemp (Republican–New York) and Senator William V. Roth, Jr. (Republican–Delaware). Many Republicans saw the tax cuts as a way to "starve the beast," that is, take tax money away from the federal bureaucracy so that the government would not be able to fund unnecessary and extravagant programs.[6] But, government spending was not limited, or impeded, by the tax-cutting legislation. Pet projects, essential services, and uncontrollable obligations kept the spending spigot wide open. One of the unintended, but inevitable, outcomes was a significant increase in the annual federal deficit during the Reagan years.

During George H. W. Bush's term as president (1989–1993), the 101st Congress (1989–1991) enacted the *Americans with Disabilities Act* (1990), which prohibited discrimination against the disabled in employment, public services, and accommodations. Also enacted in 1990 were the *Clean Air Act Amendments*, which imposed tougher regulations for the control of smog and toxic emissions. Congress had been deadlocked for a decade before coming up with this important compromise legislation.

During the first term of Bill Clinton's presidency (1993–1997), Congress enacted the *Family and Medical Leave Act* (1993), requiring businesses to provide up to twelve weeks of unpaid leave for a worker for the birth or adoption of a child. Congress also enacted the *Health Insurance Portability and Accountability Act* (1996), which provided "portability" for the health insurance of workers who moved from job to job, lost their jobs, or were self-employed. A major change in welfare policy came through the *Personal Responsibility and Work Opportunity Reconciliation Act* (1996), which ended the federal guarantee of cash welfare payments to low-income mothers and their children. While much of the 105th Congress (1997–1999) was consumed with the efforts to impeach President Clinton, law makers did enact the *Transportation Equity Act for the Twenty-first Century (TEA-21)* (1998), which authorized nearly $218 billion for surface transportation over a six-year period.

Several laws stood out during the presidency of George W. Bush (2001–2009). In response to the Enron collapse and other corporate misdeeds, the 107th Congress (2001–2003) passed the *Sarbanes–Oxley Act (Corporate Fraud Accountability Act)* (2002), which developed or enhanced laws dealing with the governance of publicly held corporations and accounting firms. The law was named after its two chief sponsors, Senator Paul S. Sarbanes (Democrat–Maryland) and Representative Michael G. Oxley (Republican–Ohio). Then Congress created the *Department of Homeland Security* in 2002, transferring to this agency many of the law enforcement programs from twenty-two existing federal agencies. As mentioned above, the No Child Left Behind law was also enacted during this session of congress.

During the 108th Congress (2003–2004), Congress enacted the *Medicare Prescription Drug Improvement and Modernization Act* of 2003, producing the largest and most expensive overhaul of Medicare in its history. Congress also enacted the latest in a series of transportation funding measures, with the *Safe, Accountable, Flexible Transportation Equity Act: A Legacy for Users (SAFETEA-LU)* (2005), which added over $285 billion into surface transportation infrastructure improvements.

Other laws from recent times as well as throughout American history are highlighted in the Appendix.

The Next Two Landmark Laws

Yet, two recent laws stand out. Both were passed in the rush of the moment, both were motivated by fear of the unknown, and in the end both greatly enhanced the powers of the executive branch. In enacting both laws, the usual deliberative, procedural steps in the legislative process were tossed aside, and it is safe to say that most members of Congress comprehended only the vaguest outlines of what they were voting on. We will be studying their lasting impact on American society for decades to come. The first law, passed in the aftermath of the 9/11 terrorist attacks, was the USA PATRIOT Act,[7] enacted with overwhelming support in October 2001. The second law, passed under the threat of an unpredictable global financial meltdown, was the Emergency Economic Stabilization Act, enacted in early October 2008.

The Patriot Act

The Patriot Act was described at the time of its enactment as "perhaps the longest, broadest, most sweeping piece of legislation in American history."[8] This 342-page measure was signed into law on October 26, 2001, six weeks after the September 11 terrorist attacks and three days after it was introduced in Congress. Both the Congress and the president were under enormous pressure to do something, and the end result was controversial legislation that greatly enhanced the authority and powers of the executive branch of government.

On the morning after the terrorist attacks, Assistant Attorney General Viet Dinh brought together Justice Department lawyers and policy experts to review federal law on surveillance and security. As *Washington Post* reporter Robert O'Harrow, Jr., observed, over a period of the next six weeks, "behind a veneer of national solidarity and bipartisanship, Washington leaders engaged in pitched, closed-door arguments over how much new power the government should have in the name of national security. They were grappling not only with the specter of more terrorist attacks but also with the chilling memories of Cold War red-baiting, J. Edgar Hoover's smear campaigns, and Watergate-era wiretaps."[9]

In early years, Congress had put restraints on executive power involvement in domestic surveillance. In 1978, President Jimmy Carter signed into law the Foreign Intelligence Surveillance Act (FISA), which defined broad surveillance authority for the federal government, but also set clear limits on its power. Title III of the Omnibus Crime Control and Safe Streets Act of 1968 regulated electronic eavesdropping, and the so-called "pen register, trap and trace" rules were enacted in the Electronic Communications Privacy Act of 2000.

Now, those provisions were about to be undone by the rush to create anti-terrorist legislation. Long-time civil liberties advocates like Morton Halperin of the Council on Foreign Relations and James X. Dempsey of the Center for Democracy and Technology worried that Congress would grant dramatic new powers to the administration, and civil liberties protections be damned.[10] Halperin, Dempsey and Marc Rotenberg from the Electronic Privacy Information Center, prepared a manifesto, "In Defense of Freedom at a Time of Crisis," which was signed by representatives from more than 150 disparate groups, from civil libertarians to gun owners, warning of the overreach of the Patriot Act.[11] In the Senate, at the center of the debate was Patrick J. Leahy (Democrat–Vermont), chairman of the Senate Judiciary Committee and a long-time proponent of civil liberties, who also urged caution, warning his colleagues and the administration not to rush headlong into creating an unwise law.

Critics recalled the abuses of the FBI counterintelligence, in a program called COINTELPRO, which tried to undermine political activists and tried systematically to undermine the credibility of Dr. Martin Luther King, Jr., and others. The Church Committee, named after its chairman Senator Frank F. Church (Democrat–Idaho), in the mid-1970s uncovered an extraordinary range of domestic spying carried out against religious organizations, politicians, women's rights advocates, and anti-war groups.[12]

Political scientist Barbara Sinclair, writing about the legislative process in 2000, argued that "unorthodox" procedures in the Congress have become increasingly used.[13] Certainly that was the case with both the Patriot Act and the Emergency Economic Stabilization Act, where formal legislative procedures were swept aside.

An agreed-upon congressional version of the Patriot Act was brushed aside, the White House and Attorney General John Ashcroft insisted that an administration-sponsored bill be substituted, that it not be amended, and that it be passed within a week.

The Patriot Act was rushed through: there was no federal agency review apart from the Attorney General's own staff, no public hearings, no committee mark up, very little floor debate, no conference report.[14] The final version of the legislation did not reach lawmakers' desks until minutes before the vote. No Member of Congress had a chance to fully read, comprehend, or even question the content of this enormously important legislation.

There were ten titles in the Patriot Act, nearly all of what President Bush and Attorney General Ashcroft and his team wanted. (1) The federal government was given broader authority, for both law enforcement and anti-terrorist purposes, to intercept terrorists' communications. (2) Likewise, the federal government gained increased authority under anti-money-laundering laws and regulations to deny terrorist access to funds. (3) The law tightened international borders, making it more difficult for foreign terrorists to enter the United States, and making it easier for the federal government to expel terrorists. (4) New federal crimes were promulgated, such as outlawing terrorist attacks on mass transit. Finally, (5) there were a number of changes to existing anti-terrorism laws.[15]

There were some provisions inserted by Senator Leahy and Congressman Richard K. Armey (Republican–Texas) to safeguard the monitoring of e-mail messages and grand jury disclosures. Armey also insisted upon having sunset provisions, so that the entire legislation would have to come up for reauthorization in four years.

The Patriot Act easily passed in the Senate, 98–1, with only Senator Russell Feingold (Democrat–Wisconsin) forcefully dissenting. The House of Representatives gave its resounding approval, 357–66, with most of the dissenters coming from Democratic members.

In the effort to make the United States more secure from terrorist activities, the Patriot Act has had a far-reaching impact on American society, particularly air travel, immigration, high education, libraries, banking, and scientific research.[16]

In March 2006, the Patriot Act was reauthorized, but this time it was subject to intense debate, the threat of a filibuster, accusations that Democrats had been barred from conference meetings, two temporary extensions, and finally a somewhat closer vote in both the House and the Senate. The reauthorization package made fourteen of the original sections permanent, sunset two provisions, and made a few modifications.

However unsightly might have been the process of making the Patriot Act, Congress had overwhelming support from the public. The public was strongly in favor of the Patriot Act when it was enacted, and five years later, in January 2006, a CNN/USA Today/Gallup Poll should that only 7 percent of Americans thought that the Act should be eliminated. There was also solid evidence that most Americans did not know what provisions the Act contained.[17]

In March 2007, Congress sent a stinging, bipartisan message to both the White House and the Justice Department that one little-observed provision of the Patriot Improvement and Reauthorization Act of 2005 would be eliminated. Senator Dianne Feinstein (Democrat–California) charged that this section was added during conference without the knowledge of any senator, whether Republican or Democrat. The Act had authorized the attorney general to replace U.S. attorneys without the usual Senate confirmation. In the wake of the firing of eight U.S. attorneys, Congress was in no mood to extend more power to the executive branch.[18]

The Patriot Act substantially increased the powers of federal law enforcement; whether it has been instrumental in halting terrorist activity and preventing another 9/11, however, is yet to be determined.

The Emergency Economic Stabilization Act of 2008

Certainly there had been warnings: the subprime mortgage collapse had been evident well over a year earlier. In March 2008, the federal government offered $29 billion in credit following the collapse of investment firm Bear Stearns; in May, the government returned to taxpayers a $168 billion economic stimulus package; on September 6, Fannie Mae and Freddie Mac, the two giant U.S. mortgage companies, were taken over by the federal government, with promises to infuse hundreds of billions of dollars.

Then on Friday, September 12, 2008 at 6 p.m., just after the financial markets had closed in New York for the week, thirty of Wall Street's top executives were summoned to the headquarters of the New York Federal Reserve bank. Meeting them there were Treasury Secretary Henry M. Paulson, Jr. and Ben S. Bernanke, chairman of the Federal Reserve System. The financiers were told bluntly: Lehman Brothers was on the brink of bankruptcy and Merrill Lynch might be next. Paulson and Bernanke emphasized that there would be no government bailout, and that these two venerable icons of Wall Street were on their own. The thirty leaders were also told, "come back in the morning and be prepared to do something."

On a Saturday of high stakes poker, the government made good on its promise and refused to bail out Lehman Brothers, but Bank of America came to the rescue and bought out Merrill Lynch. On Sunday, the government called for an extraordinary four-hour trading session, described by one trader as "utter chaos," to help Lehman Brothers unwind its trades. Then AIG, one of the largest American insurance firms, requested a bridge loan of $40 billion from the federal government, just to stay afloat. By Monday, Lehman Brothers declared bankruptcy. Then the government on September 16 took over an 80 percent share of AIG with a $85 billion (later $143 billion) Federal Reserve loan.

Then came the biggest request for bailout funds, up to $700 billion in financial aid. Over the period of many months, a small team of Treasury Department experts had worked in secret on a bailout plan; now it was about to be unveiled.[19] On the evening of Thursday, September 18, Bernanke and Paulson gave the sobering news to congressional leaders assembled in the office of Speaker Nancy Pelosi (Democrat–California). For ten minutes, Bernanke laid out the scenario of American, perhaps even worldwide, financial doom unless Congress acted forcefully and quickly. The prospects were so sobering and dire, that Bernanke swore the lawmakers to secrecy on some of the potential implications.[20]

Presidential politicking soon got involved, as Senator John McCain (Republican–Arizona) abruptly suspended his campaign and talked about cancelling the next night's first presidential debate with Senator Barack Obama (Democrat–Illinois), and flew to Washington, vowing to take control of the crisis. But McCain's efforts fell flat. President Bush called on both McCain and Obama to meet with him, and the presidential candidates sat stone-faced and quiet in the Cabinet Room as the administration outlined its plan.

That night, Wednesday, September 24, President Bush delivered his first prime-time televised speech in over a year. "Our entire economy is in danger," the president warned, noting that "America could slip into a financial panic." Bush was addressing the nation, trying to put in simple and plain terms what was at stake if Congress did not act to approve the $700 billion bailout plan. "Ultimately, our country could experience a long and painful recession," he warned. "Fellow citizens, we must not let this happen."

But the public reaction against what was now being labeled the "Wall Street Bailout," was fierce, swift, and angry. Radio talk shows, bloggers, and especially telephone callers to congressional offices were brimming with resentment, anger and distrust, fearing that a bailout would only help out the greedy, smart-money Wall Streeters or the unwitting or unscrupulous people who tried to buy homes they could not afford. The House e-mail system became so overloaded with angry messages that it collapsed.

Finally, on Sunday evening, hours before the Asian markets opened on Monday morning, the bill was drafted. To the surprise of many in Washington and in the financial markets, the House of Representatives turned down the legislation, with many conservative Republicans joined by a few liberal Democrats to bring about its defeat, 228–205. Jeb Hensarling (Republican–Texas), a leader of the rock-ribbed conservative element in his party, blasted the legislation as being on "the slippery slope to socialism." As the "no" votes accumulated, and defeat looked probable, the stock market panicked. "The market's down more than 600 points—700, 800? What's it going to take?" screamed Republican whip Joseph Crowley of New York. In fact, it was a 777 point loss on the Dow Jones Industrial Average of the New York Stock Exchange, the biggest one-day loss since the Great Depression. That one-day loss alone was valued at more than the total combined cost to this date of the Iraq and Afghanistan wars.[21] Republican leaders, like Crowley, hoped to corral reluctant colleagues and persuade them to change their votes, but many of them made a quick exit from the House Chamber, heading to their offices or to the airport.[22]

Immediately after the House vote, the U.S. Chamber of Commerce, normally an ally of the many conservative Republicans who voted against the bill, blasted out a threatening e-mail to reluctant lawmakers: "Make no mistake: When the aftermath of congressional inaction becomes clear, Americans will not tolerate those who stood by and let the calamity happen."[23]

The legislation was a tough sell. Coming without warning, the bill was offered by an administration (and particularly a president) with historic low approval ratings, asking Congress to approve the largest ever lay out of funds for any activity, flying directly in the face of free-market, hands-off conservative ideology, seen by an angry public as nothing more than corporate welfare for the rich and greedy, with no assurance that the legislation would remedy the problems of the credit crunch, and dire warnings from the White House, the Treasury, and business leaders that legislation had to be enacted as soon as possible, or America's standing in the world would collapse. Many in Congress felt that they had a gun at their head; at the same time, angry constituents were lighting fires of protest at their feet. No lawmaker wanted to be faced with this impossible set of policy options so late in the lame duck president's term and so close to their own re-election.

After the House rejected the first version of the bill, the Senate then over-whelmingly approved it, but in doing so added "sweeteners" to make it more palatable to wavering colleagues. On Friday, October 3, one week after the administration said it absolutely had to have passage, the House responded by voting, 263–171, for the $700 billion package, along with another $149 billion in tax breaks and special favors. In the end, to help draw in reluctant colleagues, Congress added other "extenders" that had nothing to do with the issue of a bailout: tax breaks for NASCAR racetrack builders ($109 million), no increase in the alternative minimum tax ($62 billion), incentives to promote alternative energy ($17 billion); assistance to rum producers in Puerto Rico and the Virgin Islands ($192 million), and others. It became, truly, the Mother of All Bailouts. What started out as a three-page proposal from Secretary Paulson's office two weeks earlier became a 340-page piece of legislation hurriedly signed into law by President Bush. By the end of the day, however, the stock market had plunged once more.

Will the $700 billion (or is it $850 billion?) bailout legislation stabilize the markets, unfreeze the credit, and restore confidence in American and inter-national financial markets? Or is this just the tip of the iceberg, with global financial repercussions still yet unknown? Finance ministers met in Washington in early October, and planned coordinated efforts to shore up the credit markets. In September, Secretary Paulson had opposed the idea of the federal government taking an equity stake in the banking industry. But in an historic, unprecedented move, the Bush administration reversed that decision in mid-October by partially nationalizing nine major American banks, investing $250 billion in them. The immediate impact was the largest percentage gain in the Dow Jones industrial average, 11 percent in one day, reversing some of the mammoth losses that occurred the week before.

Whatever the outcome, the partial nationalization of the banking industry and this extraordinary legislation, rushed through Congress, generating such opposition and anger, represent a true watershed event in American history. Ronald Reagan's cheerful and optimistic belief in the "miracle of the marketplace," relying on the forces and impulses of private capitalism, where winners are rewarded and losers just have to try harder, had met the cold, hard reality of the financial collapse. Here was a new reality, and only federal government intervention could mitigate the damage. Congressman Barney Frank (Democrat–Massachusetts), chairman of the House Financial Services Committee and a key player in the legislation, summed up the dilemma: "The private sector got us into this mess. The government has to get us out of it."[24]

Will the bailout and partial nationalization of the banks work? The best minds in the world of finance and economics simply do not know.

What Is Yet to Come

Each year, Congress and the White House face the challenges of crafting public policy and making laws. In recent years, however, Congress has been bogged down in bitter partisanship and has accomplished little. Harry Truman once blasted the Eightieth Congress (1947–1948), calling it the "Do-Nothing Congress." But, as congressional scholar Norman J. Ornstein recently asked, "What would Harry Truman say about the One Hundred Ninth Congress? Harry Truman would apologize to the Eightieth Congress."[25] That session of Congress, 2005–2006, met for the fewest number of days in over forty years and accomplished very little. When Democrats took over Congress during the 110th Congress (2007–2008), much more was expected by their leaders and supporters. But with the partisan margins so thin, particularly in the Senate, the result was little improvement over the poor performance of the previous Congress.

As expressed by William Novelli, the president of AARP, at the beginning of this chapter, Congress, no matter which party is in the majority, seems to be stuck in gridlock. With gridlock comes stalemate, and the failure to enact much-needed legislation.

On its website, AARP proclaims that Americans should "Demand a world where our elected officials stop bickering and work together." "Take action alongside millions of Americans who are tired of Washington gridlock standing in the way of affordable, quality health care and long-term financial security." This plea is linked to a website called DividedWeFail.org, sponsored by an unlikely alliance of the AARP, Business Roundtable, Service Employees International Union (SEIU), and the National Federation of Independent Business (NFIB), whose mascot is a purple (not red or blue) donkey-like elephant (or elephant-like donkey). DividedWeFail's goal: break the gridlock.

Legislative gridlock is nothing new. Congressional scholars like David Mayhew and Sarah A. Binder have studied the causes and implications of gridlock over the course of many decades.[26] More recently scholars Thomas E. Mann and Norman J. Ornstein have depicted Congress as the "broken branch" of government.[27] They write that "over the past two decades, we have grown more and more dismayed at the course of Congress." At first, it was the arrogance of the Democrats who had been in legislative power for thirty-five years and the shrillness of Republican frustrations at being in the minority. But, Mann and Ornstein write, Republicans, once in power in 1995, were no better. In the new century, neither party could hold a solid majority, partisanship became even more shrill, accountability and ethical behavior were given short shift, and the climate on Capitol Hill became "unsettling and destructive."[28]

Congress was simply not a pleasant place to work: across-the-aisle friendship, cooperation, and comity have long since evaporated. I spent three years in a senior staff position for a member of Congress in the late 1980s, and thought at the time that Congress was a difficult, unfriendly place. But compared to the toxic atmosphere of the 1990s and carrying over into the 2000s, the 1980s must seem like a relatively calm chapter in legislative history.

But as with many of the battles told in this book, comity, trust, and co-operation —as welcome as they are—are not necessary ingredients in the creation of great legislation. Just as important are political leadership, imagination, stamina, and persistence.

The last few paragraphs of this book were written following the inauguration of Barack Obama as the forty-fourth president of the United States and strong Democratic gains in Congress. The 111th Congress (2009–2010) has 262 Democrats, 178 Republicans, and 1 vacancy, while the Senate has 56 Democrats, 41 Republicans, 2 Independents who caucus with the Democrats, and 1 still contested seat. These are not the overwhelming margins found in the Eighty-Ninth Congress (1965–1966), the Seventy-Fourth (1935–1936), or the Thirty-Seventh (1861–1862). But certainly enough of a partisan leverage for Democrats to gain victories, if they can stay together and not fall apart on ideological grounds. This is the first time since 1994 that a Democratic president will work with a Democratic majority in both Houses of Congress. President Obama has promised to work with Republicans and craft bipartisan solutions, but the tough reality of lawmaking will undoubtedly test the lofty notion of bipartisanship.

Their work will be cut out for them: an economy in crisis, enormous deficit spending, federal government commitments to at least $7.8 trillion in loans, investments, and guarantees, and a legacy of legislative and executive neglect.

What will be the next laws that shape America? Hundreds of billions, even a trillion dollars will be borrowed simply to kick-start the faltering U.S. economy. What funds will be left for other much-needed programs? Certainly two pieces of landmark legislation, Social Security and Medicare, beg the attention of Congress and the White House to make them solvent over the long haul or to make adjustments in their fundamental policy goals. The crisis in non-Medicare health systems, likewise, cries out for a solution. Do Congress, the White House, and the complex of stakeholders have the imagination, drive, and fortitude to craft a national health care package that so eluded lawmakers in 1948 and in 1993?

From the days of Richard Nixon to the present, presidents and lawmakers have decried America's dependence on foreign sources of oil, but the percentage of such oil has grown steadily over the past forty years. For decades, America has prospered because of its reliance on readily available and relatively cheap sources of energy. But that era is over, and what we face are hard, expensive, and difficult choices (and some interesting opportunities) that may involve fundamental changes in lifestyle and expectations. Again, do members of Congress and the White House have what it takes to meet those challenges?

I conclude this book with a glimpse at one of our most intriguing and difficult policy challenges, the reality of global warming. In late June 1988, James E. Hansen, a NASA scientist, testified before the Senate Energy and Natural Resources Committee, and forcefully warned the legislators about the immediate threat of global warming. It was a sweltering day in Washington, the air conditioning was not working properly in the Dirksen Senate Office Building, and lawmakers, staff, and witnesses were in their shirt sleeves, sweating. Despite the discomfort, this was an historic day: a respected senior scientist, sounding the alarm to a threat that few in Congress understood. Before Hansen's testimony, "global climate change was not on the political agenda. It was something that a few environmentalists and a few politicians . . . were talking about," observed Jonathan Lash, president of the environmental organization World Resources Institute.[29] In August of 1988, while running for the presidency, Vice-President George H. W. Bush called for an early international conference to discuss greenhouse gases and the depletion of the ozone layer.

Nineteen years later, in 2007, former vice-president Al Gore, Jr., shared the Nobel Prize for Peace with the United Nations Intergovernmental Panel on Climate Change. Gore had dedicated much of the time since his presidential defeat in 2000 to the issue of global warming, putting together a PowerPoint presentation, showing it to more than 2,000 audiences, and having it become the basis for an Academy Award-winning documentary, *Inconvenient Truth*.[30]

Yet, from the time of Hansen's testimony to Gore's award-winning documentary, Congress had not passed any major law mandating cuts in greenhouse emissions. In fact, during that interval, the total emissions of carbon dioxide in the United States had climbed by 18 percent.[31] The best possibility for climate change legislation was a cap-and-trade bill crafted by Senators Joseph I. Lieberman (Independent–Connecticut) and John W. Warner (Republican–Virginia). But the legislation was pulled from the Senate floor in June 2008 after its sponsors realized that it could not overcome a probable filibuster.

This pleased James M. Inhofe (Republican–Oklahoma), the senator who once called global warming "the greatest hoax ever perpetuated on the American people." Inhofe saw the failure of the Lieberman–Warner bill as proof that Americans aren't listening to Hansen and his crowd. "Hansen, Gore, and the media have been trumpeting man-made climate doom since the 1980s. But Americans are not buying it."[32] Yet, most Americans were understanding the challenges associated with global warming and were becoming increasingly worried.[33]

The Bush White House had a different agenda. Earlier in 2007, a House committee heard from government scientists who complained of White House pressure to emphasize the uncertainty of global climate change. Then the director of the Centers for Disease Control and Prevention (CDC), Dr. Julie Gerberding, testified before the Senate Environment and Public Works

Committee in October 2007 on the health effects of global warming. Her earlier draft, containing specific examples of potential health risks, was "eviscerated," according to one CDC scientist, by the Office of Management and Budget (and perhaps the CEQ). Whole sections were removed to give what the White House said was a "balanced view" of the subject of global warming.[34]

Global climate change presents one of the biggest challenges to policymakers. The variables are so great, the costs for remediation are unknown but probably staggering, the rewards uncertain, and the risks yet to be fully identified. International cooperation is essential, requiring at times the subordination of national goals and aspirations, even strains on a nation's concept of sovereignty.

Like climate change, the challenges presented in these areas of public policy are extraordinary and daunting. They require skilled, imaginative policymakers and political leaders who can use their negotiating skills and political muscle. That's a tall order, but certainly not an insuperable one.

It would give me no greater pleasure than to write a second edition of this book, telling the story of how Congress and the president successfully crafted legislation on national health care, or energy transformation, or global warming, adding another landmark to the laws that shaped America.

APPENDIX

Other Major Legislation

Many other laws were considered for this book and they merit our attention as important pieces of law and public policy. What follows is a roll call of such legislation, along with several treaties and constitutional amendments, presented chronologically from the First to the 107th Congress. In a number of instances, these laws appear in the chapters of this book either as antecedents to or as follow-up legislation to the fifteen laws that shaped America.[1]

Beginning of the Republic to 1829

From the presidency of George Washington (1789–1797) to that of John Quincy Adams (1825–1829), Congress met for twenty two-year sessions. Most of the important pieces of legislation occurred during the formative years of 1789–1791. During that First Congress (1789–1791), the essentials of federal government were established. Separate laws created the Departments of State, War, Treasury, and the Office of the Postmaster General. In addition, the *Judiciary Act of 1789* organized the federal judicial system, established the Supreme Court with five members, created circuit and district courts, and established the office of the Attorney General. The *Bill of Rights*, the first Ten Amendments to the U.S. Constitution, was proposed in September 1789, then ratified by the states in December 1791. The first *Copyright Law* (1790) gave fourteen years of copyright protection to plays, maps and books. A new *Permanent Seat of Government* (1790) was created, a ten-mile square district straddling the banks of the Potomac River; in 1800, Washington, D.C., would be the new seat of federal power. Another important enactment was the *Funding and Assumption Act* (1790) which provided for the payment of the nation's foreign and domestic debt, and permitted the federal government to assume the indebtedness of the states. Finally, the *First Bank of the United States* (1791) was incorporated as a national bank, with $10 million in capital stock.

By contrast, the Second Congress (1791–1793) enacted only one piece of major legislation, the *Fugitive Slave Act* (1793), which authorized slave owners or their agents to seize and return fugitive slaves; state officials were required to enforce this law. During the Third and Fourth Congresses (1793–1797)

413

lawmakers focused on western lands, relations with Native American tribes, and foreign affairs. Congress passed the *Land Act* (1796), which provided for the surveying of the Northwest Territory, set the price of two dollars per acre for land sold in plots of 640 acres each, and established land offices in Cincinnati and Pittsburgh. Congress also enacted the *Indian Intercourse Act* (1796), which established the boundary lines between the United States and various Indian tribes, and also prohibited the purchase of Indian lands except by treaty or convention. Two important treaties were ratified during this time, the controversial *Jay's Treaty* (1795) between England and the United States and *Pinckney's Treaty* (1796) between Spain and the United States which recognized U.S. land claims to the Mississippi River, established commercial relations between the two countries, and most importantly guaranteed free navigation on the Mississippi for American settlers and traders.

During the Fifth and Sixth Congresses (1797–1801) when John Adams was president, only one set of laws stands out, the notorious four *Alien and Sedition Acts* (1798). The first, called the Naturalization Act, stated that no alien could become a U.S. citizens unless he had declared his intention five years in advance. The second, the Alien Act, called for the deportation of certain undesirable aliens and required a license for others for a two-year period. The third, the Alien Enemies Act, empowered the president to arrest, imprison, or banish persons who were subject to an alien power. Finally, the Sedition Act called for the arrest and imprisonment of any person, citizen, or alien, who attempted to impede the lawful process of government, foment insurrection, write, publish, or utter any false or malicious statement about the president, vice-president, Congress or the government of the United States. These laws were set to expire at the end of Adams's term, March 3, 1801, and, wisely, they did.

During the eight-year administration of Thomas Jefferson (1801–1809), there were just two major legislative actions. In the Eighth Congress (1803–1805), in a special session, the Senate ratified the *Louisiana Purchase Treaty*, the subject of Chapter 1. In 1807 Congress approved the *Slave Trade Prohibition Act*, which prohibited the importation of slaves into any part of the United States after January 1, 1808. While its provisions were often ignored, this measure put into law the provision in the U.S. Constitution which forbade interference with the slave trade for the first twenty years of the Republic, that is, until 1808, but banned the importation thereafter.

Just one key legislative act stands out during the presidency of James Madison (1809–1817). The War Hawks in Congress—John C. Calhoun of South Carolina, Henry Clay of Kentucky, and Felix Grundy of Tennessee, among others—demanded war be declared against Great Britain. In June 1812, a bitterly divided Congress voted at President Madison's request for a *Declaration of War on Britain and Ireland*.

During the eight years of James Monroe's presidency (1817–1825), one treaty and one piece of legislation stand out, both dealing with American expansionism. During the Fifteenth Congress (1817–1819), the *Adams–Onis (Transcontinental) Treaty* (1821) was ratified, with the United States acquiring Florida from Spain and defining the western boundary of the Louisiana Territory. Through this treaty, the United States renounced its earlier claims to Texas. In March 1820, Congress enacted the *Missouri Compromise*, authorizing the inhabitants of Missouri to form a constitution and state government, and stipulating that slavery would be "forever prohibited" in the remainder of the Louisiana Territory north of 36°30′ degrees latitude, with the exception of the new state of Missouri. The Missouri Compromise was held unconstitutional in part in the *Dred Scott* v. *Sanford* decision of the Supreme Court in 1857, and by the *Kansas–Nebraska Act of 1854*, the subject of Chapter 2.

During John Quincy Adams's presidency (1825–1829), one legislative action stands out: the so-called *Tariff of Abominations* (1828). The Twentieth Congress (1827–1829) passed this legislation which exacted exceedingly high tariffs of 41 percent on most imported raw material, but had somewhat lower duties on woolen goods for New England manufacturers.

From Andrew Jackson through the Civil War (1829–1865)

Except for the administrations of Andrew Jackson, James K. Polk, and Abraham Lincoln, this period was marked by relatively weak presidents, and growing sectional tensions within Congress and the country, culminating in the Civil War.

The controversial *Indian Removal Act* (1830) was enacted during the Twenty-First Congress (1829–1831). Just after taking office, Andrew Jackson pushed for this legislation, not only giving the president the power to negotiate treaties with Indians living east of the Mississippi River but also authorizing resettlement of all eastern Indians to lands in the West. By 1837 the Jackson administration had removed, through force or voluntarily, some 46,000 Native Americans from east of the Mississippi. The Twenty-Second Congress (1831–1833) enacted the *Tariff Act of 1832*, drawing protest and outrage from the South. South Carolina threatened to leave the Union, and official protests were lodged by the legislatures of Georgia, Mississippi, and Virginia. The threats of nullification were tempered by two laws enacted the next year, the *Compromise Tariff of 1833*, which somewhat modified the Tariff Act and the *Force Bill* (1833), which authorized the president to use army and navy to execute revenue laws and collect duties.

Probably the most important presidential veto in American history came in 1832 when Jackson refused to renew the charter of the Bank of the United States. There were sharp protests, particularly from Henry Clay of Kentucky and Daniel Webster of Massachusetts, but Congress failed to override Jackson's veto.

From the Twenty-Third Congress (1833–1835) during Jackson's second administration through the Twenty-Eighth Congress (1843–1845) in the last years of the John Tyler administration, there were no important pieces of legislation. During the Twenty-Ninth Congress (1845–1847), with James K. Polk as president, Congress passed the *Declaration of War with Mexico* (1846) and the *Tariff Act* (1846), which lowered tariff rates. Following the war, the Thirtieth Congress (1847–1849) enacted the *Treaty of Guadalupe–Hidalgo* (1848). The treaty ended the Mexican–American war, with Mexico ceding all claims to Texas north of the Rio Grande River, California, and New Mexico, and the United States paying $15 million to Mexico along with accepting $3.2 million in outstanding claims by American citizens against the Mexican government.

The next important pieces of legislation were collectively known as the *Compromise of 1850*. The Thirty-First Congress (1849–1851) saw sectional rivalries heat up after the cession of Texas to the United States. The Compromise consisted of a series of laws passed in September 1850: California was admitted into the Union as a free state; territorial governments and boundaries were established for Utah and New Mexico, with the provision that their status as free or slave states would be determined by the territories themselves through their constitutions; the slave trade would be abolished in the District of Columbia by 1851; the 1793 Fugitive Slave Act was amended by removing the cases from states and appointing federal commissioners to conduct hearings and issue arrest warrants, and prohibiting slaves from having the right to trial by jury or to testify on their own behalf; finally, the Texas–New Mexico boundary was established, and Texas was paid $10 million in compensation for its loss of New Mexico lands. In 1854, the Thirty-Third Congress (1853–1855) passed the highly controversial *Kansas–Nebraska Act*, which repealed the Missouri Compromise of 1820.

Following Abraham Lincoln's election in 1860, southern states began their movement towards secession. Before the breakup of the Union, Congress passed the *National Telegraph Act* (1860) for the construction of a telegraph line between San Francisco and the western border of Missouri. At the end of the tumultuous Thirty-Sixth Congress (1859–1861), South Carolina, then Mississippi, Florida, Alabama, Georgia, Louisiana, and Texas left the Union (and the Congress); the other southern states would soon join them. Without their southern colleagues, northern legislators quickly passed bills creating the free territories of Colorado, Nevada, and Dakota, all in the last few weeks of the Congress.

The first session of the Thirty-Seventh Congress (1861–1863) convened on July 4, 1861. By then the Civil War was in full force and President Lincoln asked for, and Congress obliged him with, unprecedented authority to fight the insurrection. The *National Loan Act* (1861) authorized the Treasury to borrow $250 million over the next twelve months to prosecute the war; the *Revenue Act* (1861) inaugurated a $20 million tax on real estate, customs and excise taxes, and a 3 percent income tax on annual individual income of over $800. Then

Congress passed the *First Confiscation Act* (1861), which freed slaves who were employed as soldiers or laborers by the rebellious states.

The second session, in 1862, proved to be a period of enormous long-term legislative consequences. It produced two of the major pieces of legislation found in Chapter 3, the *Homestead Act* and the *Morrill Land-Grant College Act*. In addition, $150 million in paper currency, "greenbacks," was authorized through the *Legal Tender Act* (1862); portions of the law, however, were found unconstitutional in 1870 in *Hepburn* v. *Griswold*. Congress authorized the Union Pacific Railroad and the Central Pacific Railroad to build a rail and telegraph line between Omaha and San Francisco in the *Pacific Railroad Act* (1862). The Department of Agriculture, the Internal Revenue Bureau within the Department of the Treasury, and a National Banking System (1863) were created. A *Second Confiscation Act* (1862) authorized the federal government to free slaves in areas captured by Northern troops.

In 1863, West Virginia was admitted into the Union, and the free territories of Arizona and Idaho were created. The first nationwide draft was created in the *Conscription Act* (1863), but eligible men could provide a substitute or pay a $300 fee and be excused from service. This year also saw the creation of the National Academy of Science. The *Freedmen's Bureau Act* (1865) was established to provide clothing, food, and shelter to the poor, refugees, and freedmen from the rebellious states. The Thirteenth Amendment (1865) to the Constitution abolished slavery and involuntary servitude, except for punishment of a crime.

Reconstruction through the End of the Century (1865–1900)

Congress was faced with the pressures of reconciliation, punishment, and return of the southern states to the Union. The first major piece of legislation in the Thirty-Ninth Congress (1865–1867) was the *Fourteenth Amendment* (1866) to the Constitution, which declared for the first time that all persons born or naturalized in the United States were citizens, and added the equal protection and due process class to guard against state abuses. Then Congress enacted the *First Reconstruction Act* (1867), which divided the former Confederacy, with the exception of Tennessee which was about to be readmitted into the Union, into five military districts. The ten rebellious states would be readmitted into the Union only after calling constitutional conventions, establishing state governments with black male suffrage, and ratifying the Fourteenth Amendment. In a clash of politics between President Andrew Johnson and the Radical Republicans in Congress, Johnson was nearly convicted of an impeachable offense for violating the *Tenure of Office Act* (1867), which required prior congressional approval for a president to remove a cabinet officer.

During the Fortieth Congress (1867–1869), federal lawmakers enacted three more Reconstruction laws and, through the *Omnibus Act* (1869), six rebellious states were readmitted into the Union after having framed a republican government and ratified the Fourteenth Amendment. The *Fifteenth Amendment* (1870), which prohibited discrimination against black male voters, was ratified. The most important piece of legislation not dealing with the aftermath of the Civil War and Reconstruction was the *Alaska Purchase Treaty* (1867).

During the first administration of Ulysses S. Grant (1869–1873), Congress through a series of laws readmitted four former rebellious states, established the Department of Justice, and, through the *Judiciary Act of 1869*, enlarged the Supreme Court to its current size of eight associate and one chief justice. To combat vigilante activities of the Ku Klux Klan and to protect African-American voters, Congress enacted the *First Force Act* (the *Ku Klux Klan Act*) (1870), which was ruled unconstitutional in parts, and the *Second Force Act* (the *Second Ku Klux Klan Act*) (1871).

A *Third Force Act* (the *Third Ku Klux Klan Act*) (1871) was enacted in the Forty-Second Congress (1871–1873) in an attempt to stop further intimidation by whites in the South, and an *Amnesty Act* (1872) was enacted, removing the political and civil disabilities from all but 500–600 ex-Confederate leaders. In recognition of the growing importance of the West, Congress designated the first protected national park in the *Yellowstone National Park Act* (1872). The *Civil Rights Act* (1875) was enacted in the Forty-Third Congress (1873–1875) to guarantee to blacks all rights in public accommodations and public conveyances; much of the law later was ruled unconstitutional in the *Civil Rights Cases* (1883). In the last days of the Grant Administration, the Republican-controlled Senate and Democratic-controlled House created an *Electoral Commission* (1877) to determine which set of electoral returns to accept from the hotly contested presidential contest between Republican Rutherford B. Hayes and Democrat Samuel J. Tilden.

There was a dearth of significant legislation from the Forty-Fifth (1877–1879) to the Fifty-Sixth (1899–1901) Congresses, during the administrations of Hayes (1877–1881), James A. Garfield (1881), Chester A. Arthur (1881–1885), Grover Cleveland (1885–1889 and 1893–1897), Benjamin Harrison (1889–1893), and William McKinley (1897–1901). Several states were admitted into the Union, Hawaii was annexed, and through a series of laws, immigration was tightened, particularly with the exclusion of Chinese. There were, however, three significant acts. The *Pendleton Act* (1883) created the modern civil service system, the Civil Service Commission, and protected federal workers from political or electoral obligation. Four years later, the *Interstate Commerce Act* (1887) was enacted, creating the Interstate Commerce Commission (ICC), outlawing discriminatory and unreasonable rates and authorizing the ICC to investigate and prohibit railroad rate abuses. A third major law was the *Sherman Antitrust Act* (1890), giving the federal government power to prosecute any corporation that attempted to restrain interstate trade and attempted to monopolize commerce.

APPENDIX

The Progressive Era up to the New Deal
(1901–1932)

One of the first pieces of business of the Fifty-Seventh Congress (1901 1903) and the first year of Theodore Roosevelt's presidential term was to open up the Panama Canal, through the *Hay–Pauncefote Treaty*, giving the United States the right to build and operate the canal; the *Spooner (Isthmus Canal) Act* (1902) authorizing the funds to purchase and operate the canal; and, in 1904, the *Hay–Bunau–Varilla Treaty*, which granted the United States full and permanent sovereignty over the Panama Canal ten-mile wide zone. The United States had acquired the Philippine Islands through the peace treaty ending the Spanish–American war (1898), and through the *Philippine Government Act* (1902) gave U.S. protection to the citizens of the Philippines. Also enacted in 1902 was the *National Reclamation Act*, to build canals and dams in the West. During the Fifty-Ninth Congress (1905–1907), Congress enacted on the same day the *Meat Inspection Act* and the *Pure Food and Drug Act* (1906), which regulated the labeling and branding of foods and drugs, and made it a crime to manufacture or sell adulterated or mislabeled foods or drugs.

While the United States had a national income tax during the Civil War, its provisions expired in 1872; another attempt at an income tax in 1894 was ruled unconstitutional. During the first year of William Howard Taft's presidency, progressive lawmakers were able to push through the legislation for the *Sixteenth Amendment* to the Constitution authorizing the federal income tax; four years later, in 1913, the ratification process was completed. Through the *Mann–Elkins Act* (1910), the telegraph, telephone, cable, and radio companies were brought under the jurisdiction of the Interstate Commerce Commission, as well as the railroads. Through the *Seventeenth Amendment* to the Constitution, approved in 1912 and ratified in 1913, U.S. senators would now be directly elected by popular vote rather than by state legislators.

A number of pieces of important legislation were passed during the first administration of Woodrow Wilson (1913–1917). During the Sixty-Third Congress (1913–1915), lawmakers enacted the *Federal Reserve Act* (1913), creating the Federal Reserve Board and the national banking system. The *Federal Trade Commission Act* (1914) created the Federal Trade Commission, giving it power to prevent unfair business practices and investigate suspect activities of corporations and businesses. In the Sixty-Fourth Congress (1915–1917), the federal government first gave funds to states to establish rural postal roads and developed a system of highway classification in the *Federal-Aid Road Act* (1916) and established the *National Park Service* (1916). Congress also enacted the *Keating–Owen Child Labor Act* (1916), which prohibited child labor in interstate commerce, and set minimum ages and maximum hours that children could work; two years later, it was ruled unconstitutional in *Hammer* v. *Dagenhart* (1918).

The Sixty-Fifth Congress (1917–1919) focused on World War I. On April 6, 1917, Congress declared that a *State of War with Germany* existed. It enacted a *Selective Service Act* (1917), requiring all men from twenty-one to thirty (and later forty–five) to register for military service. It created fines and prison terms for those found guilty of sabotage, spying, or refusing military service in the *Espionage Act* (1917), which was later reinforced by the *Sabotage Act* (1918). The Sixty-Sixth Congress (1919–1921) passed the *Nineteenth Amendment* (1919) to the Constitution, extending the right to vote to women. The states ratified the amendment in 1920. The fascinating, tortuous fight for women's suffrage is the subject of Chapter 4. A landmark measure not enacted was an American endorsement of the League of Nations, Wilson's most significant defeat.

During Warren Harding's administration (1921–1923), Congress clamped down on immigration through the *Immigration Quota Act* (1921), limiting the number of persons of any particular nationality to 3 percent of that nationality's population in the 1910 census. When Calvin Coolidge was president, the Sixty-Eighth Congress (1923–1925) enacted the *Rogers Foreign Service Act* (1924), which reorganized and combined the U.S. diplomatic and consular services into a unified Foreign Service of the United States and professionalized the diplomatic corps. A *Child Labor Amendment* (1924) to the Constitution was proposed, seeking uniformity in child labor standards throughout the nation, but it was not ratified by the required number of states. Following the disastrous floods on the Mississippi River in 1927, Congress enacted the *Flood Control Act* (1928) to authorize a ten-year flood control program in the Mississippi Valley.

During Herbert C. Hoover's administration, the Seventy-First Congress (1929–1931) adopted the *Smoot–Hawley Tariff Act* (1930), which dramatically raised import duties on imported agricultural products; this had the unintended consequence of drying up international trade and exacerbating the growing worldwide economic depression. During the Seventy-Second Congress (1931–1933), lawmakers enacted the *Reconstruction Finance Corporation* (1932) to provide $2 billion in loans to banks, mortgage, and insurance companies and railroads. The *First Glass–Steagall Act* (1932) permitted the Federal Reserve banks to use government bonds and securities in addition to commercial paper as collateral, significantly increasing the amount of available credit. The *Norris–LaGuardia Anti-Injunction Act* (1932) restricted the use of court injunctions to prevent strikes and labor boycotts and prohibited "yellow-dog" contracts, which forced workers to pledge not to join a union as a condition of their employment. Two constitutional amendments were approved. The *Twentieth*, the so-called "Lame Duck" amendment, moved the presidential term up from March 4 to January 20 and began the legislative term on January 3; the *Twenty-First Amendment* repealed the Eighteenth Amendment and ended Prohibition. Both new amendments became effective in 1933, the first year of the Franklin D. Roosevelt administration.

New Deal to New Frontier (1933–1963)

Congress and the Roosevelt Administration produced an extraordinary amount of significant legislation, particularly during the first four years. In 1932, Roosevelt defeated Hoover, Democrats swept into the majority in both the House and the Senate, and the Depression worsened. What followed was the most productive and concentrated period of law and policymaking in United States history. During their first 100 days in office, Roosevelt and the Seventy-Third Congress approved fourteen significant pieces of legislation. Among them was the *Emergency Banking Relief Act* (1933), to stave off the banking crisis and authorize the Reconstruction Finance Corporation to provide temporary funds to solvent banks. The *Civilian Conservation Corps* (1933) was created to provide jobs for a quarter million young men. The *Agricultural Adjustment Act* (1933) helped farmers, who were some of the hardest hit during the Depression, to stave off bankruptcies and foreclosures by controlling agricultural production, paying farmers to limit production of seven basic commodities, and providing refinancing of mortgages. This legislation was found unconstitutional by the Supreme Court and eventually was replaced by a second Agricultural Adjustment Act in 1938. The *Tennessee Valley Authority Act* (1933) created a public corporation to build hydroelectric dams, provide electricity, and develop flood control programs and other public works projects for the Tennessee River Valley. The Bank Act of 1933 (*Second Glass–Steagall Act*) created the Federal Deposit Insurance Corporation, separated banking into deposit and investment affiliates, permitted branch banking, and gave the Federal Reserve Board further powers to prevent bank speculation. During the next year, the *Securities Exchange Act* (1934) created the Securities and Exchange Commission to regulate the operation of the stock markets. Also in 1934, Congress enacted the *Taylor Grazing Act*, prohibiting the sale of 80 million acres of public domain grasslands in the West.

During the Seventy-Fourth Congress (1935–1937), several major pieces of legislation were enacted. The *National Labor Relations Act (Wagner Act)* and the *Social Security Act*, the subjects of Chapters 6 and 7, were passed within six weeks of each other in the summer of 1935. Also enacted during this period was the *Banking Act* (1935), which reorganized the Federal Reserve Board, giving it authority to control monetary reserves, discount operations, interest rates, and the purchase of government securities. The *Public Utility Holding Company Act* (1935) gave the Federal Power Commission and the Federal Trade Commission the authority to regulate the interstate transmission of electricity and gas, restricting monopolistic utility practices. The *Rural Electrification Act* (1936) permitted the Rural Electrification Administration to make loans to electric cooperatives, opening up much of rural America to electricity for the first time. Finally, the *Walsh–Healey Government Contracts Act* (1935) assured a prevailing minimum wage and maximum working hours based on a forty-hour week and eight-hour day, and prevented child and convict labor for all persons employed by contractors working for the federal government.

During the Seventy-Fifth Congress (1937–1939) in Roosevelt's second administration, the *Civil Aeronautics Act* (1938) was enacted to meet the growing regulatory and safety demands of the airline industry. Also, the *Federal Fair Labor Standards Act* (1938) established a federal minimum wage (twenty-five cents an hour), a maximum work week of forty-four hours during the first year of employment, forty-two after the second, and forty hours thereafter for all firms engaged in interstate commerce. This law exempted farmers, domestic workers, and professionals. Further, child labor was prohibited; workers had to be eighteen or over for hazardous work, sixteen and over for regular work. In the next session of Congress, federal employees were banned from participating in political campaigns and election activity through the *Hatch Act* (1939).

With the war in Europe becoming a grim reality, Congress enacted four important prewar pieces of legislation, First, the *Neutrality Act* (1939) repealed an earlier arms embargo clause and permitted belligerents, mainly Britain, to purchase armaments from the United States. Then Congress passed the *Alien Registration Act (Smith Act)* (1940), requiring the registration and fingerprinting of all foreign nationals and making it unlawful to advocate the overthrow of the government. The first peacetime national draft was enacted through the *Selective Training and Service Act* (1940), requiring the registration of all men between twenty-one and thirty-five years of age. The Seventy-Seventh Congress (1941–1943) enacted the fourth major prewar law, the *Lend-Lease Act* (1941), authorizing the United States to sell, lend, or lease any defense equipment to any country whose defense was vital to the defense of the United States. This broadly worded act, together with a $7 billion appropriation, was vital in propping up Britain and other allies. In separate enactments, Congress on December 8 and 11, 1941, declared war with Japan, Germany, and Italy. Through the first and second *War Powers Acts* (1941, 1942), the president was given extraordinary latitude to conduct the war, and, through the *Emergency Price Control Act* (1942), the Office of Price Administration was created and given power to stabilize and control prices and rents. During the Seventy-Eighth Congress (1943–1945), a pay-as-you-go federal income tax withholding system was created through the *Current Tax Payment Act* (1943); also enacted was *Servicemen's Readjustment Act (GI Bill)* (1944), the subject of Chapter 7.

During the Seventy-Ninth Congress (1945–1947), World War II came to an end, Franklin Roosevelt died, and Harry S. Truman succeeded him. Two important provisions dealing with international relations were enacted: the *U.S. Participation in the United Nations Act* (1945), providing for U.S. membership in the United Nations, and the *Bretton Woods Agreements Act* (1945), authorizing the United States to join the International Monetary Fund and the International Bank for Reconstruction and Development. All parts of America's atomic energy program were transferred to a five-member Atomic Energy Commission through the *Atomic Energy Act* (1946). In addition, Congress enacted the *Fulbright Scholars Program* (1946) for the international exchange of college and university students, and the *Hill–Burton Hospital Survey and Construction Act* (1946), authorizing federal grants to states for hospital construction.

During the Eightieth Congress (1947–1948), Democrats lost control of both the House and Senate for the first time since 1933, the first year of Roosevelt's administration. It was a time of intense partisan bickering on domestic issues, but a rather unusual period of bipartisan cooperation in foreign policy. The *Twenty-Second Amendment* (1947, ratified 1951) limited presidents to two four-year terms or ten years altogether. The *Taft–Hartley Labor–Management Relations Act* (1947) was enacted, over the veto of Truman, curtailing a number of union practices, including closed shop agreements and secondary strikes. Aid to Greece and Turkey was provided in 1947, through the *Greek–Turkey Aid Act*, following the announcement that Britain could no longer sustain its power and assistance in that area of the Mediterranean. The next year, Congress enacted one of the major laws in this book, the *Marshall Plan (Economic Cooperation Act)* (1948), the subject of Chapter 8. Finally, the *National Security Act* (1947) replaced the War and Navy Departments with what eventually would become the Department of Defense; it created the Joint Chiefs of Staff, the National Security Council, and the Central Intelligence Agency.

During the Eighty-First Congress (1949–1951), with Truman re-elected president and the Congress returning to Democratic hands, the *North Atlantic Treaty* (1949) was concluded, creating the North Atlantic Treaty Organization, which pledged to promote the stability and mutual defense of the twenty signatory countries. With the growing concern about loyalty and espionage in the United States, Congress enacted the *McCarran Internal Security Act* (1950), over Truman's veto, requiring Communist organizations to register with the Department of Justice and provide membership information. In the following Congress, the *McCarran–Walter Immigration and Nationality Act* (1952) revised and codified the immigration laws, preserving the national origin quota system created in the 1920s; this also was enacted over Truman's veto. In 1952, the *Korean GI Bill of Rights (Veterans Readjustment Assistance Act)* was enacted, to assist returning veterans of the Korean war.

At the end of Dwight D. Eisenhower's first term as president, the Eighty-Fourth Congress (1955–1957) enacted the *Interstate Highway Act (Federal-Aid Highway Act)* (1956), the subject of Chapter 9, together with the companion financing legislation, the *Highway Revenue Act* (1956). The *Social Security Act* was amended to provide a disability benefit for workers between fifty and sixty-four with long-term disabilities. In 1958 the Eighty-Fifth Congress (1957–1958), in response to the Sputnik threat from the Soviet Union, enacted the *National Defense Education Act*, establishing a $1 billion national program to improve the teaching of mathematics, science, and foreign languages. Following six years of investigation into corrupt and mismanaged labor practices, the Eighty-Sixth Congress (1959–1961) passed the *Landrum–Griffin Labor-Management Reporting and Disclosure Act* (1959), requiring all unions to hold national elections, adopt constitutions and bylaws, and prepare annual reports. Through the

Twenty-Third Amendment (1960, ratified in 1961), citizens of the District of Columbia were permitted to vote in presidential elections and were assigned three delegates in the Electoral College.

During John F. Kennedy's administration (1961–1963), the Eighty-Seventh Congress (1961–1963) enacted the *Organization for Economic Cooperation and Development Convention* (1961), creating the Organization for Economic Cooperation and Development (OECD), a consultative body consisting of the United States, Canada, and eighteen European countries, to encourage economic growth and trade. The *Area Redevelopment Act* (1961) developed a fund to finance industrial redevelopment loans and rural redevelopment loans, vocational training, and retraining for workers in rural America. Congress enacted the *Peace Corps Act* (1961), putting into legislation what Kennedy had earlier established by executive order. The *Arms Control and Disarmament Act* (1961) established an independent U.S. Arms Control and Disarmament Agency to conduct research, negotiations, and inspections for nuclear disarmament. The *Twenty-Fourth Amendment* (1962, ratified 1964) outlawed poll taxes or other such taxes as conditions to vote.

Great Society (1964) to the Present

Three laws from the Great Society years of the Lyndon Johnson Administration are featured in this book: the *Civil Rights Act* (1964) together with the *Voting Rights Act* (1965) in Chapter 10, and *Medicare and Medicaid Act* (1965) in Chapter 11. When Johnson retired from office in 1969, his former cabinet members presented him with a plaque listing the 207 landmark laws enacted during his five-plus years in office.[2] Certainly 207 laws may have been enacted, but the cabinet was overstating their importance by designating them all as "landmark." Nevertheless, the Eighty-Eighth (1963–1965) and Eighty-Ninth (1965–1967) Congresses, in particular, produced an extraordinary amount of important legislation. Not since the New Deal, and not afterwards, has such a stream of important legislation come from Washington.

In August 1963, while Kennedy was still president, Congress passed the *Nuclear Test Ban Treaty*, between the United States, the Soviet Union, and later over one hundred other signatories, prohibiting the participants from conducting nuclear weapons tests in outer space, under water, or in areas outside of the control of the signatory country. Three weeks after Kennedy's assassination, Congress enacted the *Vocational Education Act* (1963), broadening the reach of federal training and authorizing permanent federal assistance to states for such education.

With Johnson now president, several major pieces of legislation were enacted. The one with the biggest impact and drama was the *Civil Rights Act* (1964), but Congress also enacted the *Urban Mass Transportation Act* (1964), the first major federal initiative toward developing a comprehensive and coordinated plan for urban mass transit. The *Economic Opportunity Act* (1964) established the Office of Economic Opportunity and several programs for disadvantaged and poor people. The *Food Stamp Act* (1964) created a federal program, administered by the states, to assist poor families and individuals with their nutrition needs. Congress also enacted the *Wilderness Act* (1964) which designated 9.1 million acres of national forest lands as wilderness and prohibited the use of airplanes, permanent roads, commercial buildings, and mining in those areas.

One of the most controversial actions of Congress, in retrospect, was the *Gulf of Tonkin Resolution* (1964), giving the president near-blanket authority to repel armed attack against U.S. forces in Vietnam. Following Johnson's landslide victory in November 1964 against Barry Goldwater, and with huge, sympathetic majorities in both the House and the Senate in the new Eighty-Ninth Congress (1965–1967), major pieces of legislation came tumbling out. Not only the *Voting Rights Act* (1965) and the *Medicare and Medicaid Act* (1965), but also the *Immigration and Nationality Act* (1965), which abolished the old system of national origins quotas and imposed separate ceilings on non-Western hemisphere and Western hemisphere immigrants. The federal government became more involved in education through the *Elementary and Secondary Education Act* (1965), which provided over $1 billion in federal grants to states for their primary and secondary schools. The *Higher Education Act* (1965) created a National Teacher Corps and provided $840 million in aid to poor and middle-class college students and graduate programs for public school teachers. Military veterans were given assistance through the *Veterans Readjustment Benefits Act* (1966). The National Endowment for the Arts and the National Endowment for the Humanities were created and given funding through the *National Foundation on the Arts and Humanities Act* (1965). New federal cabinet-level departments were created through the *Department of Housing and Urban Development Act* (1965) and the *Department of Transportation Act* (1966). Congress passed major legislation to assist the elderly through a federal grant program in the *Older Americans Act* (1965) and to assist schools in poor areas with the *Child Nutrition Act* (1966). Transportation issues were addressed through the *Motor Vehicle Air Pollution Control Act* (1965); the *National Traffic and Motor Vehicle Safety Act* (1966), which set safety standards for all new automobiles; and the *Highway Safety Act* (1966), which required the states to develop their own programs of high-way safety.

Following this burst of major legislation, the final two years of Lyndon Johnson's presidency were consumed by the growing bitterness and disaffection toward the war in Vietnam. A major domestic issue was civil unrest and crime. In response, Congress enacted the *Omnibus Crime Control and Safe Streets Act* (1968), which created the Law Enforcement Assistance Administration, gave federal grants to state and local governments, and broadened the authority of police to use wiretaps. The Corporation for Public Broadcasting was established through the *Public Broadcasting Act* (1967), and the *Civil Rights Act* (1968) was enacted to protect against discrimination in housing.

During the Nixon administration, in the Ninety-First and Ninety-Second Congresses (1969–1973), a number of significant pieces of legislation were enacted, including the *National Environmental Policy Act* (1969), the subject of Chapter 12. Several other environmental laws were enacted, including the *Clean Air Act* (1970), which set specific deadlines for auto emissions and required states to establish air quality programs, and the *Water Quality Improvement Act* (1970), which gave the federal government authority over oil spills and made oil companies liable for cleanup, the *Federal Water Pollution Control Act Amendments* (1972), and the *Coastal Zone Management Act* (1972). The *Voting Rights Act Amendments* (1970) extended the 1965 Voting Rights Act and lowered the voting age to eighteen for all federal, state, and local elections; however, the Supreme Court ruled that Congress did not have the authority to lower the voting age for state and local elections, which was then covered through the *Twenty-Sixth Amendment* (1971) to the Constitution. The *Equal Rights Amendment* was approved in Congress in 1972, but died in 1982, falling three states short of the required thirty-eight needed for ratification. Another important breakthrough was *Title IX of the Education Amendments* (1972), which prohibited gender discrimination in federally funded education and in the years since its passage has revolutionized women's sports and athletic participation at all levels. Amtrak, the national passenger rail service, was created through the *Rail Passenger Service Act* (1970), and federal mass transit funds were provided through the *Urban Mass Transit Assistance Act* (1970). The food stamp program was given nationwide standards through the *Food Stamp Act* (1970).

The Watergate affair and the charges of impeachment against President Richard Nixon dominate our memory of the Ninety-Third Congress (1973–1975). Nevertheless, some major pieces of legislation were also enacted. The *War Powers Resolution* (1973) required the president to consult with Congress before committing U.S. armed forces into hostilities and required a termination after sixty days unless Congress declared war. The *Trans-Alaska Pipeline Authorization Act* (1973) called for the construction of the oil pipeline from Prudhoe Bay to the port of Valdez. Two additional environmental laws were enacted, the *Endangered Species Act* (1973) and the *Safe Drinking Water Act* (1974). The *Congressional Budget and Impoundment Control Act* (1974) created the Congressional Budget Office, revised the federal budget calendar, and created new budget committees in Congress. Minimum federal funding standards for private pensions were established through the *Employee Retirement Income Security Act (ERISA)* (1974). Further, the *Federal Election Campaign Act Amendments* (1974) established campaign spending and contribution limits; some of these provisions were negated by the Supreme Court in *Buckley* v. *Valeo* (1976).

During the administration of Gerald R. Ford (1974–1977), New York City received emergency federal funds through the *New York City Seasonal Financing Act* (1975), and the Consolidated Rail Corporation (ConRail) acquired the bankrupt Penn Central Railroad and other lines through the *Railroad Revitalization and Regulatory Reform Act* (1976). The Ninety-Fourth Congress

(1975–1977) also enacted two environmental laws, the first to regulate toxic wastes, the *Toxic Substances Control Act* (1976), and the second to create a federal solid waste program, the *Resource Conservation and Recovery Act* (1976).

In President Jimmy Carter's term of office (1977–1981), two cabinet-level departments were created, the *Department of Energy* (1977) and the *Department of Education* (1979). The Ninety-Fifth Congress (1977–1979) enacted the *Panama Canal Treaty* (1978), returning the canal to Panama, and the *Airline Deregulation Act* (1978), which deregulated the commercial passenger air traffic and phased out the Civil Aeronautics Board. Several environmental measures became law, the most important of which were the *Surface Mining Control and Reclamation Act* (1977), which set environmental standards for all surface coal mining, and the *Comprehensive Environmental Response, Compensation, and Liability Act ("Superfund")* (1980), setting up a $1.6 billion fund to clean up the worst of the nation's toxic waste sites. The Ninety-Sixth Congress (1979–1981) also loaned the Chrysler Corporation funds to stave off bankruptcy in the *Chrysler Corporation Loan Guarantee Act* (1979).

From the mid-1950s until 1980, Congress had been controlled by the Democratic Party in both the House and the Senate. During Ronald Reagan's first administration (1981–1985), the Senate now was controlled by Republicans, while Democrats were in the majority in the House. During the Ninety-Seventh Congress (1981–1983), the most important piece of legislation was the *Economic Recovery Tax Act* (1981), which called for massive individual and business tax cuts. The *Nuclear Waste Policy Act* (1982) called for the president to recommend two sites for the permanent storage of nuclear wastes. During the Ninety-Ninth Congress (1985–1987), the Defense Department was reorganized through the *Goldwater–Nichols Act (Department of Defense Reorganization Act)* (1986) and a major set of changes in the federal tax law was created through the *Tax Reform Act* (1986). The *Water Quality Act* (1987), providing a ten-year re-authorization for construction of sewage treatment facilities, was enacted over President Reagan's veto.

During George H. W. Bush's term as president (1989–1993), the 101st Congress (1989–1991) enacted the *Americans with Disabilities Act* (1990), which prohibited discrimination against the disabled in employment, public services, and accommodations. The *Clean Air Act Amendments* (1990) imposed tougher regulations for the control of smog and toxic emissions. The 102nd Congress (1991–1993) enacted the *Intermodal Surface Transportation Efficiency Act (ISTEA)* (1991), providing nearly $120 billion for highway improvements and $31 billion for mass transit programs over a six-year period. Congress also enacted the *Strategic Arms Reduction Treaty (START)* (1991) with Russia and three other former Soviet states to reduce nuclear weapons.

During the first term of Bill Clinton's presidency (1993–1997), Congress enacted the *Family and Medical Leave Act* (1993), requiring businesses to provide up to twelve weeks of unpaid leave for a worker for the birth or adoption of a child. The 103rd Congress (1993–1995) also enacted the *Brady Handgun Violence*

Prevention Act (1993), requiring a waiting period for the purchase of a handgun. The *Violent Crime Control and Law Enforcement Act* (1994) authorized $30 billion over six years to fight against violent crime. During Clinton's second term, the 104th Congress (1995–1997) enacted the *Telecommunications Act* (1996) allowing the seven regional Bell Telephone companies to enter into the long-distance telephone market. The *Health Insurance Portability and Accountability Act* (1996) provided a "portability" of health insurance for workers who moved from job to job, lost their jobs, or were self-employed. A major change in welfare policy came through the *Personal Responsibility and Work Opportunity Reconciliation Act* (1996), which ended the federal guarantee of cash welfare payments to low income mothers and their children. While much of the 105th Congress (1997–1999) was consumed with the impeachment of President Clinton, lawmakers did enact the *Transportation Equity Act for the Twenty-first Century (TEA-21)* (1998), which authorized nearly $218 billion for surface transportation over a six-year period.

Several laws stood out in the Presidency of George W. Bush, which began in 2001. The *USA Patriot Act* (2001), in response to the September 11th terrorist attacks, broadly expanded the power of federal law enforcement agencies to gather and share information and to increase penalties for terrorist activities. The *No Child Left Behind Act* (2001) required states to develop and implement annual reading and math assessment programs and to create teacher quality programs. The *Bipartisan Campaign Reform Act (BCRA)* (2002) banned corporate, union, and individual soft money in federal campaigns, and doubled the amount of money that individuals could contribute to federal candidates. In response to the Enron collapse and other corporate misdeeds, the 107th Congress (2001–2003) passed the *Sarbanes–Oxley Act (Corporate Fraud Accountability Act)* (2002). Then Congress created the *Department of Homeland Security* in 2002, transferring to this agency many of the law enforcement programs from twenty-two existing federal agencies.

During the 108th Congress (2003–2004), Congress enacted the *Do-Not-Call Implementation Act* of 2003 establishing the Federal Trade Commission's Do Not Call Registry to ward against unsolicited commercial telemarketing calls. Also enacted was the *Partial-Birth Abortion Act* of 2003 prohibiting late-term abortions. The *Medicare Prescription Drug Improvement and Modernization Act* of 2003 produced the largest and most expensive overhaul of Medicare in its history. During the 109th Congress (2005–2006), Congress enacted the *Energy Policy Act* of 2005 providing loan guarantees and incentives for energy development. *Safe, Accountable, Flexible Transportation Equity Act: A Legacy for Users (SAFETEA-LU)* (2005) added over $285 billion into surface transportation infrastructure improvements. During the 110th Congress (2007–2008), the *Post-9/11 Veterans Educational Assistance Act* (the new GI Bill) of 2008 expanded the educational benefits to military service personnel serving since September 11, 2001. Finally, in its last days before the presidential election, Congress enacted the highly controversial and very expensive *Emergency Economic Stabilization Act of 2008.*

NOTES

PREFACE

Epigraph quote from Hughes speech at an American Law Institute dinner, Washington, D.C., February 23, 1924, in "Too Many Laws Here and 'Law Factories,' Declares Hughes," *The New York Times*, February 24, 1924, 1.

1. Seventeen Southern Democratic Senators were joined by a lone Republican, John Tower of Texas. *1964 Congressional Quarterly Almanac*, 357.
2. *1964 CQ Almanac*, 367. Byrd's filibuster was not the longest in the history of civil rights deliberations. The record belonged to Senator J. Strom Thurmond (Democrat–South Carolina) when he spoke against final clearance of the 1957 civil rights bill with a filibuster of twenty-four hours and eighteen minutes. Thurmond switched party allegiance, becoming a Republican in 1964 and backed Barry Goldwater for president.
3. *1964 CQ Almanac*, 368. He said he might vote for final passage, but, in the end, Goldwater voted against this historic legislation.
4. Robert C. Albright, "Senator Engle Dies of Brain Tumor," *The Washington Post*, July 31, 1964, B5; Marjorie Hunter, "Packed Senate Galleries Tense; 10-Minute Vote Makes History," *The New York Times*, June 11, 1964, 21.
5. Stephen W. Stathis, *Landmark Legislation 1774–2002: Major U.S. Acts and Treaties* (Washington, D.C.: CQ Press, 2003), v.
6. National Archives and Records Administration (NARA) in association with National History Day and USA Freedom Corps, "Our Documents," available at http://www.ourdocuments.gov.; Indiana University Center on Congress, "Notable Members of Congress and the Laws They Sponsored," available at the Indiana University website, at http://congress.indiana.edu/learn_about/notable_members/notable_main.htm. David R. Mayhew, *Divided We Govern: Party Control, Lawmaking, and Investigations, 1946–1990* (New Haven: Yale University Press, 1991); Paul C. Light, *Government's Greatest Achievements: From Civil Rights to Homeland Defense* (Washington, D.C.: Brookings Institution, 2002); Louis Jacobson, "Ten Bills That Really Mattered," *Roll Call*, May 3, 2005. Stathis, *Landmark Legislation 1774–2002*; Stathis includes legislation passed during the Continental Congress and the U.S. Congress Assembled, 1774–1788. Brian K. Landsberg, ed. in chief, *Major Acts of Congress*, 3 vols. (New York: Macmillan Reference, 2004).

1 WESTWARD EXPANSION: THE NORTHWEST
ORDINANCE OF 1787 AND THE LOUISIANA PURCHASE
RATIFICATION OF 1803

Epigraph quotes from Francis S. Philbrick, *The Rise of the West: 1754–1830* (New York: Harper & Row, 1965), 130, and Bernard DeVoto, "Celebrating 150 Years of the Louisiana Purchase," *Collier's* (March 21, 1953): 44–47, quoted in Jon Kukla, *A Wilderness So Immense: The Louisiana Purchase and the Destiny of America* (New York: Alfred A. Knopf, 2003), frontispiece.

1. Louise Phelps Kellogg, "France and the Mississippi Valley: A Resume," *The Mississippi Valley Historical Review* 18 (1) (June, 1931): 4.
2. Ibid.
3. Ibid., 6. The great early work on La Salle and western discovery is Francis Parkman, *La Salle and the Discovery of the Great West* (Williamston, Mass.: Corner House Publishers, 1968, 1897 ed.) and Francis Parkman, *France and England in North America*, 2 vols. (New York: Library of America, 1983, 1877 ed.).
4. Marion E. Cross, trans., *Father Louis Hennepin's Description of Louisiana: Newly Discovered to the Southwest of New France by Order of the King* (Minneapolis: University of Minnesota Press, 1938), 4. Neither Joliet, Marquette, de La Salle, nor Hennepin, however, was the first European to reach the Mississippi River. Over a century earlier, in May 1539, explorer Hernando de Soto anchored in a bay called Espiritu Santo (Tampa Bay, Florida), with one thousand well-armed soldiers. He set off on a three-year march through present-day Florida, Georgia, Alabama, Mississippi, crossing the Mississippi River in the northern portion of the state, and ending in Arkansas. It was a bloody march, with de Soto's forces encountering and killing thousands of Native Americans along the way. De Soto, stricken with a fever, died in 1542 on the banks of the Mississippi, while the battered remnants of his party floated down the river, eventually reaching the Spanish settlement of Punuca in Mexico. On de Soto's bloody exploration, see David Ewing Duncan, *Hernando de Soto: A Savage Quest in the Americas* (New York: Crown Publishers, 1995). Gavin Menzes, *1421: The Year China Discovered America* (New York: William Morrow, 2002), asserts that the Chinese may have been to the Mississippi more than one hundred years before de Soto.
5. Parkman, *France and England in North America*, vol. 2, 534, and Jay Gitlin, "Children of Empire or Concitoyens? Louisiana's French Inhabitants," in *The Louisiana Purchase: Emergence of an American Nation*, ed. Peter J. Kastor (Washington, D.C.: CQ Press, 2002), 25.
6. Fred Anderson, *Crucible of War: The Seven Years' War and the Fate of Empire in British North America, 1754–1766* (New York: Vintage Books, 2000), 5–7.
7. Peter J. Kastor, "Introduction" in *The Louisiana Purchase*, ed. Kastor, 2, and Gitlin, "Children of Empire or Concitoyens?" 25. Under the 1763 treaty, the trading of land and influence was worldwide: France ceded Senegal to Britain; Cuba and the Philippines were given back to Spain; in East India, France was permitted to return to its posts, but not in Bengal, which now came under British influence.
8. Bernard Bailyn, *Voyagers to the West: A Passage in the Peopling of America on the Eve of the Revolution* (New York: Alfred A. Knopf, 1986), 26.
9. Jack N. Rakove, "Ambiguous Achievement: The Northwest Ordinance," in *Northwest Ordinance: Essays on Its Formulation, Provisions and Legacy*, ed. Frederick D. Williams (East Lansing: Michigan State University, 1989), 5.
10. Philbrick, *The Rise of the West*, 104.
11. Robert F. Berkhofer, Jr., "Jefferson, the Ordinance of 1784, and the Origins of the American Territorial System," *The William and Mary Quarterly* 29 (2) (April, 1972): 233.

12. Rakove, "Ambiguous Achievement," 10–11.

13. Philbrick, *The Rise of the West*, 115.

14. Don E. Fehrenbacher, *The Dred Scott Case: Its Significance in American Law and Politics* (New York: Oxford University Press, 1978), 75; also Merrill Jensen, "The Cession of the Old Northwest," *The Mississippi Valley Historical Review* 23 (1) (June 1936): 27.

15. Jensen, "The Cession of the Old Northwest," 28.

16. The Mohawks, Oneidas, Cayugas, Senecas, Onondagas, and Tuscaroras comprised the Iroquois Confederacy.

17. Jensen, "The Cession of the Old Northwest," 41–48.

18. Fehrenbacher, *The Dred Scott Case*, 76 and Peter S. Onuf, *Statehood and Union: A History of the Northwest Ordinance* (Bloomington: Indiana University Press, 1987), 25.

19. Peter S. Onuf, *Jefferson's Empire: The Language of American Nationhood* (Charlottesville: University Press of Virginia, 2000), 143–44.

20. Fehrenbacher, *The Dred Scott Case*, 77.

21. Garry Wills, *"Negro President": Jefferson and the Slave Power* (Boston: Houghton Mifflin Company, 2003), 22.

22. Ibid., 23.

23. Richard P. McCormick, "The 'Ordinance' of 1784?" *The William and Mary Quarterly* 50 (1) Law and Society in Early America (January, 1993): 120.

24. Onuf, *Statehood and Union*, 31.

25. Dennis Denenberg, "The Missing Link: New England's Influence on Early National Educational Policies," *The New England Quarterly* 52 (2) (June, 1979): 221.

26. David Carleton, *Landmark Congressional Laws on Education* (Westport, Conn.: Greenwood Press, 2002), 15–16.

27. Fehrenbacher, *The Dred Scott Case*, 79. On the background and constitutionality of the Northwest Ordinance, see Denis F. Duffey, "The Northwest Ordinance as a Constitutional Document," *Columbia Law Review* 95 (4) (May, 1955): 929–68.

28. Onuf, *Statehood and Union*, 58.

29. Fehrenbacher, *The Dred Scott Case*, 81.

30. Staughton Lynd, "The Compromise of 1787," *Political Science Quarterly* 81 (2) (June, 1966): 237.

31. Paul Finkelman, "Slavery and the Northwest Ordinance: A Study in Ambiguity," *Journal of the Early Republic* 6 (4) (Winter, 1986): 359.

32. Dane, Nathan. "Letter, July 16, 1787." Original manuscript in the Wisconsin Historical Society Archives (SC 1423). Online facsimile available at the Wisconsin Historical Society website at http://www.wisconsinhistory.org/turningpoints/search.asp?id=22.

33. David P. Currie, *The Constitution in Congress: The Federalist Period, 1789–1801* (Chicago: The University of Chicago Press, 1997), 103.

34. William Wirt Blume, "Legislation on the American Frontier: Adoption of Laws by Governor and Judges: Northwest Territory 1788–1798; Indiana Territory 1800–1804; Michigan Territory 1805–1823," *Michigan Law Review* 60 (3) (January, 1962): 317–72.

35. Onuf, *Statehood and Union*, 55.

36. Currie, *The Constitution in Congress*, 104.

37. Ibid., 105.

38. Patrick J. Furlong, "Putting the Ordinance to Work in the Northwest," in *The Northwest Ordinance 1787: A Bicentennial Handbook*, ed. Robert M. Tayloyr, Jr. (Indianapolis: Indiana Historical Society, 1987), 80–81.

39. Ibid., 81–82.

40. Ibid., 87.

41. Ibid., 83.

42. Reprinted in Taylor, ed., *The Northwest Ordinance 1787*, following 30; emphasis in the original.
43. Bernard W. Sheehan, "The Indian Problem in the Northwest: From Conquest to Philanthropy," in *Launching the Extended Republic: The Federalist Era*, eds. Ronald Hoffman and Peter J. Albert (Charlottesville: University Press of Virginia, 1996), 191–92.
44. Onuf, *Statehood and Union*, 140.
45. Marc Mahan, "The Life of Nathan Dane," The Nathan Dane Archival Collaborative. Available at the Primary Research website at http://primary research.org/PRTHB/Dane/biography.htm.
46. Anthropologist G. Michael Pratt of Heidelberg College identified the site in 1995. Library of Congress Bicentennial website, "Fallen Timbers Battlefield," http://www.loc.gov/gov/bicentennial/propage/OH/oh-9_h_kaptur5.html.
47. Milo M. Quaife, *Checagou: From Indian Wigwam to Modern City, 1673–1835* (Chicago: University of Chicago Press, 1933).
48. "Treaty of Greenville," Ohio Historical Society website, available at http://www. ohiohistorycentral.org/ohc/history/h_indian/document/tgreenev.shtml.
49. Paul Finkelman, "Evading the Ordinance: The Persistence of Bondage in Indiana and Illinois," *Journal of the Early Republic* 9 (Spring, 1989): 21; Wills, "*Negro President*", 23–4.
50. Finkelman, "Evading the Ordinance," 38.
51. John Chester Miller, *The Wolf by the Ears* (New York: The Free Press, 1977), 143.
52. Finkelman, "Evading the Ordinance," 40. Indiana Constitution, 1816, Art. VIII, sec. 1.
53. Finkelman, "Evading the Ordinance," 38–49.
54. Duffey, "The Northwest Ordinance as a Constitutional Document," 930.
55. Jurgen Herbst, "The Development of Public Universities in the Old Northwest," in *Northwest Ordinance*, ed. Williams, 97.
56. Carleton, *Landmark Congressional Laws on Education*, 22–23, and Edward Danforth Eddy, Jr., *Colleges for Our Land and Time: The Land-Grant Idea in American Education* (New York: Harper and Brothers, 1957), 21–22.
57. R. Douglas Hurt, "Historians and the Northwest Ordinance," *The Western Historical Quarterly* 20 (3) (August 1989): 261–62.
58. Ibid., 280.
59. Kastor, *The Louisiana Purchase*, 2.
60. James E. Lewis, Jr., *The Louisiana Purchase: Jefferson's Noble Bargain?* (Charlottesville: The Thomas Jefferson Foundation, 2003), 21.
61. Alexander DeConde, *This Affair of Louisiana* (New York: Charles Scribner's Sons, 1976), 45–47.
62. Kukla, *A Wilderness So Immense*, 75; and more fully on Gardoqui's diplomatic efforts, see chs. 3–5.
63. Harry Ammon, *James Monroe: The Quest for National Identity* (Charlottesville: University Press of Virginia, 1990), 53–59, at 56.
64. DeConde, *This Affair of Louisiana*, 50.
65. Kukla, *A Wilderness So Immense*, 205, and DeConde, *This Affair Louisiana*, 49.
66. James R. Sofka, "Thomas Jefferson and the Problem of World Politics," in *The Louisiana Purchase*, ed. Kastor, 52.
67. Philbrick, *The Rise of the West*, 202; also Ron Chernow, *Alexander Hamilton* (New York: Penguin Press, 2004), 485–503.
68. DeConde, *This Affair of Louisiana*, 34–35.
69. Arthur Preston Whitaker, "France and the American Deposit at New Orleans," *The Hispanic American Historical Review* 11 (4) (November, 1931): 486–87, and Peter J. Kastor, *The Nation's Crucible: The Louisiana Purchase and the Creation of America* (New

Haven: Yale University Press, 2004), 37. Throughout this narrative, there are three members of the South Carolina Pinckney family involved. Thomas Pinckney (1750–1828) was U.S. Minister to Britain (1792–1796) and sent as envoy extraordinary to Spain (1794–1795) to negotiate the Treaty of San Lorenzo (Pinckney's Treaty). His brother, Charles Cotesworth Pinckney (1746–1825), was sent to France in 1796 as U.S. Minister, but was rebuffed; the following year, he, Elbridge Gerry, and John Marshall were sent to France, and were involved in what became known as the XYZ Affair. Charles Pinckney (1757–1824), cousin of Thomas and Charles C., was U.S. Minister to Spain, 1801–1804. See Frances Leigh Williams, *A Founding Family: The Pinckneys of South Carolina* (New York: Harcourt Brace Jovanovich, 1978).

70. Thomas M. Ray, "'Not One Cent for Tribute': The Public Addresses and American Popular Reaction to the XYZ Affair, 1798–1799," *Journal of the Early Republic* 3 (4) (Winter, 1983): 389–412.

71. Alexander DeConde, *The Quasi-War: The Politics and Diplomacy of the Undeclared Naval War with France, 1797–1801* (New York: Scribners, 1966) and William Stinchcombe, *The XYZ Affair* (Westport, Conn.: Greenwood Press, 1980). The loan and bribe were carried out by Mme de Villette, a friend of Talleyrand; the three individuals (XYZ in the diplomatic dispatches) who tried to negotiate this transaction were Jean Conrad Hottinguer and Lucien Hauteval, Swiss citizens, and a Mr. Bellamy, an American banker in Hamburg.

72. DeConde, *This Affair of Louisiana*, 89–92.

73. Ibid., 93–95.

74. Irving Brant, *James Madison: Secretary of State 1800–1809* (Indianapolis: Bobbs-Merrill, 1953), 65.

75. Wills, *"Negro President,"* 35, and Wendell G. Schaeffer, "The Delayed Cession of Spanish Santo Domingo to France, 1795–1801," *The Hispanic American Historical Review* 29 (1) (February, 1949): 46–68.

76. Wills, *"Negro President."*

77. Ralph Ketcham, *James Madison: A Biography* (New York: Macmillan, 1971), 417.

78. Ibid.

79. DeConde, *This Affair of Louisiana*, 107; George Dangerfield, *Chancellor Robert R. Livingston of New York 1746–1813* (New York: Harcourt, Brace and Company, 1960), 311–17.

80. Sofka, "Thomas Jefferson and the Problem of World Politics," 58.

81. Dumas Malone, *Jefferson and His Time*, vol. 4, *Jefferson the President: First Term, 1801–1805* (Boston: Little, Brown and Company, 1970), 260, 264–65; E. Wilson Lyon, "Introduction" to Francois Barbe-Marbois, *The History of Louisiana: Particularly of the Cession of that Colony to the United States of America* (Baton Rouge: Louisiana State University Press, 1977, 1830 ed.), xliv; and Dangerfield, *Chancellor Robert R. Livingston*, 353.

82. "The Louisiana Purchase Legislative Timeline, 1802–1807," U.S. Library of Congress, American Memory Series. Presidential messages and legislative documents available at the American Memory website of the Library of Congress, at http://memory/loc.gov/ammem/amlaw/louisiana.html.

83. Brown, *The Constitutional History of the Louisiana Purchase*, 4, and Dangerfield, *Chancellor Robert R. Livingston of New York*, 314.

84. E. Wilson Lyon, "Introduction" in Barbe-Marbois, *The History of Louisiana*, lxvi.

85. Ibid., lxii–lxiii.

86. Dangerfield, *Chancellor Robert R. Livingston of New York*, 371.

87. Ibid., 360–61; Ammon, *James Monroe*, 209; and Henry Adams, *History of the United States of America During the First Administration of Thomas Jefferson, 1801–1805* (New York: Library of America, 1986, [1889–91]), 320.

88. Ammon, *James Monroe*, 207–15; Dangerfield, *Chancellor Robert R. Livingston of New York*, 358–71; Adams, *History of the United States*, 319–35.
89. *National Intelligencer*, July 4, 1803, reprinted in *The Louisiana Purchase*, ed. Kastor, 202; see also Betty Houchin Winfield, "Public Perception and Public Events: The Louisiana Purchase and the American Partisan Press," in *The Louisiana Purchase*, ed. Kastor, 38–50.
90. Malone, *Jefferson the President: First Term, 1801–1805*, 297, and Adams, *History of the United States*, 358.
91. Malone, *Jefferson the President: First Term, 1801–1805*, 303.
92. Lewis, Jr., *The American Union and the Problem of Neighborhood*, 30.
93. Adams, *History of the United States*, 355.
94. Brown, *The Constitutional History of the Louisiana Purchase*, 20–29.
95. Currie, *The Constitution in Congress: The Jeffersonians*, 98.
96. Dangerfield, *Chancellor Robert R. Livingston of New York*, 373.
97. Malone, *Jefferson the President: First Term, 1801–1805*, 302.
98. Dangerfield, *Chancellor Robert R. Livingston of New York*, 373.
99. Adams, *History of the United States*, 352, and quote from Gates, in Kastor, *The Louisiana Purchase*, frontispiece.
100. Malone, *Jefferson the President: First Term, 1801–1805*, 303.
101. Brown, *The Constitutional History of the Louisiana Purchase*, 33. Finally, in 1828, Chief Justice John Marshall laid to rest the question of constitutional authority to acquire territory in *American Insurance Co.* v. *Canter*, 1 Peters 511 (1828), when he declared: "The Constitution confers absolutely on the Government of the Union the powers of making war, and of making treaties; consequently, that Government possesses the power of acquiring territory, either by conquest or by treaty."
102. Currie, *The Constitution in Congress: The Jeffersonians*, 99 n. 90, emphasis in the original.
103. Reginald Horsman, "The Dimensions of an 'Empire for Liberty': Expansion and Republicanism, 1755–1825," *Journal of the Early Republic* 9 (1) (Spring, 1989): 7.
104. Ketcham, *James Madison*, 421.
105. Horsman, "The Dimensions of an 'Empire for Liberty,'" 9.
106. Brown, *The Constitutional History of the Louisiana Purchase*, 34.
107. William Lee Miller, *Arguing About Slavery: The Great Battle in the United States Congress* (New York: Alfred A. Knopf, 1996), 168–69.
108. DeConde, *This Affair of Louisiana*, 186.
109. Charles de Secondat, baron de Montesquieu, *The Spirit of the Laws* (Geneva, 1748), trans. Thomas Nugent; ed. Franz Neumann (New York: 1949); book 8, section 16, cited in Kukla, *A Wilderness So Immense*, 65.
110. Horsman, "The Dimensions of an 'Empire for Liberty,'" 7.
111. DeConde, *This Affair of Louisiana*, 191.
112. Ibid., 187.
113. Currie, *The Constitution in Congress: The Jeffersonians*, 98.
114. John Upton Terrell, *Zebulon Pike: The Life and Times of an Adventurer* (New York: Weybright and Talley, 1968).
115. Albert F. Simpson, "The Political Significance of Slave Representation, 1787–1821," *The Journal of Southern History* 7 (3) (August, 1941): 324.
116. Miller, *The Wolf by the Ears*, 130.
117. David M. Potter, *The Impending Crisis, 1848–1861*. Completed and edited by Don E. Fehrenbacher (New York: Harper and Row, 1976), 53; U.S. Census Bureau figures cited in *The Louisiana Purchase*, ed. Kastor, 273. Actual numbers for Louisiana in 1860 were 357,456 whites; 331,726 slaves; and 18,647 free people of color.
118. Miller, *The Wolf by the Ears*, 144.

119. Ibid., 143, and Robert E. Bonner, "Empire of Liberty, Empire of Slavery," in *The Louisiana Purchase*, ed. Kastor, 132.
120. Miller, *The Wolf by the Ears*, 145.
121. Kastor, "Introduction," in *The Louisiana Purchase*, ed. Kastor, 7.
122. Elizabeth Gaspar Brown, "Legal Systems in Conflict: Orleans Territory 1804–1812," *The American Journal of Legal History* 1 (1) (January, 1957): 35, 53. Brown noted that to date, "no fully satisfactory explanation for this fact [preference for the Code Napoleon] has been offered." At 53.
123. Kastor, *The Nation's Crucible*, 164.
124. Ibid., 165.
125. Louisiana State Museum website, "The Cabildo," available at http://lsm.crt.state.la.us/cabildo/cab6.htm.
126. John M. Murrin, "The Jeffersonian Triumph and American Exceptionalism," *Journal of the Early Republic* 20 (1) (Spring, 2001): 1–4.

2 SLAVERY AND THE TERRITORIES: THE KANSAS–NEBRASKA ACT OF 1854

Epigraph quotes from Douglas in Robert W. Johannsen, *Stephen A. Douglas* (Urbana: University of Illinois Press, 1973, 1997 ed.), 434; James M. McPherson, *Battle Cry of Freedom: The Civil War Era* (New York: Oxford University Press, 1988), 121; and Robert V. Remini, *The House: The History of the House of Representatives* (New York: HarperCollins Publishers and Smithsonian Books, 2006), 150.

1. Robert V. Remini, *Martin Van Buren and the Making of the Democratic Party* (New York: Columbia University Press, 1959).
2. Jean H. Baker, *Affairs of Party: The Political Culture of Northern Democrats in the Mid-Nineteenth Century* (Ithaca: Cornell University Press, 1983), 19.
3. Lynn L. Marshall, "The Strange Stillbirth of the Whig Party," *The American Historical Review* 72 (2) (January, 1967): 445, and Michael F. Holt, *The Rise and Fall of the American Whig Party* (New York: Oxford University Press, 1999).
4. Holt, *American Whig Party*, 209.
5. Tyler Anbinder, *Nativism and Slavery: The Northern Know Nothings and the Politics of the 1850s* (New York: Oxford University Press, 1992), ch. 10.
6. David M. Potter, *The Impending Crisis, 1848–1861*. Completed and edited by Don E. Fehrenbacher (New York: Harper and Row, 1976), 29.
7. Don E. Fehrenbacher, *Sectional Crisis and Southern Constitutionalism* (Baton Rouge: Louisiana State University Press, 1980, 1995 ed.), 10; Howard A. Ohline, "Republicans and Slavery: Origins of the Three-Fifths Clause in the United States Constitution," *The William and Mary Quarterly* 3rd Ser. 28 (4) (October, 1971): 563–84.
8. Fehrenbacher, *Sectional Crisis*, 11–12.
9. Donald R. Hickey, "New England's Defense Problems and the Genesis of the Hartford Convention," *The New England Quarterly* 50 (4) (December, 1977): 587–604; Albert F. Simpson, "The Political Significance of Slave Representation, 1787–1821," *The Journal of Southern History* 7 (3) (August, 1941): 315.
10. Simpson, "Political Significance of Slave Representation," 315.
11. Leonard L. Richards, *The Slave Power: The Free North and Southern Domination, 1780–1860* (Baton Rouge: Louisiana State University Press, 2000), 54–55.
12. Richards, *The Slave Power*, 56–57; Simpson, "The Political Significance of Slave Representation," 323 n. 34; also Garry Wills, *"Negro President": Jefferson and the Slave Power* (Boston: Houghton Mifflin Company, 2003); Paul Finkelman, *Slavery and the Founders*, 2nd ed. (Armonk, N.Y.: M. E. Sharpe, 2001), 203.
13. William H. Freehling, *The Road to Disunion*, vol. 1 *Secessionists at Bay, 1776–1854* (New York: Oxford University Press, 1990), 146–47.

14. Slavery had officially ended in Massachusetts, New Hampshire, Connecticut, Rhode Island, Pennsylvania, and Vermont before 1789; New York enacted gradual emancipation in 1799 and in 1817; New Jersey enacted gradual emancipation in 1804. Many northerners sold their slaves to southerners, and slavery lingered in many of the northern states for years. See, for example, David Menschel, "Abolition Without Deliverance: The Law of Connecticut Slavery 1784–1848," *Yale Law Journal* 111 (2001): 183–222, and Joanne Pope Melish, *Disowning Slavery: Gradual Emancipation and Race in New England, 1780–1860* (Ithaca, N.Y.: Cornell University Press, 1998). On Maryland and the waning influence of the slave economy, see Freehling, *The Road to Disunion*, 32–33. Delaware had a small slave population and, by 1860, 90 percent of its blacks were free. See Harold Hancock, "Civil War Comes to Delaware," *Civil War History* 2 (1956): 29–56. A useful collection of materials is found in the Slavery in the North website, http://www.slavenorth.com/index.html.

15. Freehling, *The Road to Disunion*, 142.

16. Potter, *The Impending Crisis*, 54–55; Jefferson quote from Paul L. Ford, ed., *The Works of Thomas Jefferson*, 12 vols. (New York: Putnam's, 1904–1905), vol. XII, 158.

17. Freehling, *The Road to Disunion*, 144.

18. Glover Moore, *The Missouri Controversy, 1819–1821* (Lexington: University of Kentucky Press, 1953), 50–55, 57–58.

19. On the history of Slave Power, the Slave Power thesis and its critics, see Richards, *The Slave Power*.

20. Freehling, *The Road to Disunion*, 147–48; Michael F. Holt, *The Political Crisis of the 1850s* (New York: John Wiley, 1978), 229.

21. Eric Foner, *Free Soil, Free Labor, Free Men* (New York: Oxford University Press, 1970, 1995), 87–88.

22. Quoted in ibid., 150.

23. Avery O. Craven, *Civil War in the Making, 1815–1860* (Baton Rouge: Louisiana State University, 1958), 40–41.

24. Freehling, *The Road to Disunion*, 152–53; Richards, *The Slave Power*, and Fehrenbacher, *The South and Three Sectional Crises*, 23.

25. Moore, *The Missouri Controversy*, 348.

26. Robert V. Remini, *John Quincy Adams* (New York: Times Books, 2002). In "Martin Van Buren and the Tariff of Abominations," *The American Historical Review* 63 (4) (July, 1958): 903–17, Remini noted that, contrary to generally accepted accounts, Van Buren did not introduce the Tariff of Abominations with the purpose of defeating it.

27. Freehling, *The Road to Disunion*, 255.

28. Alfred H. Kelley and Winfred A. Harbison, *The American Constitution: Its Origins and Development*, 4th ed. (New York: W. W. Norton, 1970), 304–16.

29. Harlow W. Sheidley, "The Webster–Hayne Debate: Recasting New England's Sectionalism," *The New England Quarterly* 67 (1) (March, 1994): 5–29. Webster in 1830 belonged to the anti-Jackson forces; he began his congressional career during the Thirteenth Congress (1813–1814) as a Federalist from New Hampshire; later he was an Adams senator from Massachusetts, then in the Twenty-Fifth Congress (1837–1838) became a Whig. *Biographical Dictionary of the United States Congress, 1774–Present*; online version available at http://bioguide.congress.gov.

30. Kelley and Harbison, *The American Constitution*, 306–11.

31. Ibid.

32. Freehling, *The Road to Disunion*, 308; this section relies heavily on Freehling's extensive analysis of the gag rule crises, chs. 17–19.

33. Clement Eaton, "Censorship of the Southern Mails," *The American Historical Review* 48 (2) (January, 1943): 269.

34. Herbert Aptheker, *Nat Turner's Slave Rebellion* (New York: Humanities Press, 1966), and Stephen B. Oates, *The Fires of Jubilee: Nat Turner's Fierce Rebellion* (New York. Harper and Row, 1975).

35. Freehling, *The Road to Disunion*, 309.

36. Eaton, "Censorship of the Southern Mails," 271–72.

37. David C. Frederick, "John Quincy Adams, Slavery, and the Disappearance of the Right of Petition," *Law and History Review* 19 (1) (Spring, 1991): 120–21; Eaton, "Censorship of the Southern Mails," 273.

38. Freehling, *The Road to Disunion*, 310–11.

39. Ibid., 328.

40. Frederick, "John Quincy Adams," 132. Pinckney was the son of Charles Pinckney (1757–1824), representative, senator, and governor of South Carolina, and U.S. minister to Spain during the time of the Louisiana Purchase.

41. Remini, *The House*, 129.

42. Adams quoted in Freehling, *The Road to Disunion*, 344; Frederick, "John Quincy Adams," 134–38.

43. Frederick, "John Quincy Adams," 138.

44. Ibid.,139.

45. Paul Boyer, et al., *The Enduring Vision* 2 vols., 4th ed. (Boston: Houghton Mifflin, 2000), 436–37.

46. Robert William Fogel, *Without Consent or Contract: The Rise and Fall of American Slavery* (New York: W. W. Norton, 1989), 65; Stephen John Hartnett, *Democratic Dissent and the Cultural Fictions of Antebellum America* (Urbana: University of Illinois Press, 2002), ch. 3.

47. William J. Cooper, Jr., *The South and the Politics of Slavery, 1826–1856* (Baton Rouge: Louisiana State University Press, 1978), 176.

48. Michael A. Morrison, *Slavery and the American West: The Eclipse of Manifest Destiny and the Coming of the Civil War* (Chapel Hill: University of North Carolina Press, 1997), 13–38.

49. Eric Foner, "The Wilmot Proviso Revisited," *The Journal of American History* 56 (2) (September, 1969): 267, and Boyer, *The Enduring Vision*, 436.

50. Foner, "The Wilmot Proviso Revisited," 268.

51. Ibid.

52. Freehling, *The Road to Disunion*, 418–21; Hartnett, *Democratic Dissent*, ch. 3; Cooper, *The South and the Politics of Slavery*, 186–88.

53. Foner, "The Wilmot Proviso Revisited," 274. Oregon expansionists wanted the boundary line at 54°40' north latitude, the southern border of Russia's Alaskan territory; the Polk administration settled for the 49° north latitude, the current Canadian–American border.

54. Quoted in Holt, *The Political Crisis of the 1850s*, 51; emphasis in the original.

55. Foner, "The Wilmot Proviso Revisited," 276.

56. Joseph G. Rayback, *Free Soil: The Election of 1848* (Lexington: University Press of Kentucky, 1970), 42.

57. Ibid., 24.

58. Quoted in Avery Craven, *The Coming of the Civil War* (Chicago: University of Chicago Press, 1942, 1963), 226. Stephens was the vice-president of the Confederacy and later served five months in federal prison. He was subsequently elected senator when Georgia was readmitted into the Union. Thomas E. Schott, *Alexander H. Stephens of Georgia: A Biography* (Baton Rouge: Louisiana State University Press, 1988).

59. Rayback, Free Soil, 26–27; Holman Hamilton, *Prologue to Conflict: The Crisis and Compromise of 1850* (Lexington: University of Kentucky Press, 1964), 8.

60. Rayback, *Free Soil*, 28.
61. Ibid., 45, and Foner, "The Wilmot Proviso Revisited," 278.
62. Brian G. Walton, "The Elections for the Thirtieth Congress and the Presidential Candidacy of Zachary Taylor," *The Journal of Southern History* 35 (2) (May, 1969): 202.
63. Potter, *The Impending Crisis*, 141–42; John Niven, *Salmon P. Chase: A Biography* (New York: Oxford University Press, 1995).
64. Morrison, *Slavery and the American West*, 96–97.
65. Ibid., 101–103.
66. Ibid.
67. Ibid., 103–104.
68. Hamilton, *Prologue to Conflict*, 15–19.
69. Ibid., 34.
70. K. Jack Bauer, *Zachary Taylor: Soldier, Planter, Statesman of the Old Southwest* (Baton Rouge: Louisiana State University Press, 1985), 297.
71. Johannsen, *Stephen A. Douglas*, 262; Hamilton, *Prologue to Conflict*, 44–45.
72. Glyndon G. Van Deusen, *The Life of Henry Clay* (Boston: Little, Brown, 1937), 399.
73. Clay quote from Freehling, *The Road to Disunion*, 495; Hamilton, *Prologue to Conflict*, 54–59. On Clay, Calhoun, and Webster, the "Great Triumvirate," see the fascinating "impersonations" (in the author's words) of them in Stephen B. Oates, *The Approaching Fury: Voices of the Storm, 1820–1861* (New York: HarperCollins, 1997).
74. Van Deusen, *The Life of Henry Clay*, 400–401; Clay quote cited from *Congressional Globe*, 31st Congress, 1st sess., App. 115–27.
75. Craig R. Smith, *Daniel Webster and the Oratory of Civil Religion* (Columbia, Mo.: University of Missouri Press, 2005), 224.
76. McPherson, *Battle Cry of Freedom*, 70.
77. Calhoun quoted in Smith, *Daniel Webster*, 225.
78. *Dartmouth College* v. *Woodward*, 4 Wheaton 518 (1819).
79. Smith, *Daniel Webster*, 234–35.
80. Hamilton, *Prologue to Conflict*, 84–86; Johannsen, *Stephen A. Douglas*, 277–78.
81. McPherson, *Battle Cry of Freedom*, 74.
82. Bauer, *Zachary Taylor*, 314–16.
83. Smith, *Daniel Webster*, 238–51.
84. Douglas quoted in Johannsen, *Stephen A. Douglas*, 296–97.
85. Holt, *The Political Crisis of the 1850s*, 90.
86. Hamilton, *Prologue to Conflict*, 189.
87. McPherson, *Battle Cry of Freedom*, 78.
88. Potter, *The Impending Crisis*, 138–41; Samuel Shapiro, "The Rendition of Anthony Burns," *The Journal of Negro History* 44 (1) (January, 1959): 34–51; *Prigg* v. *Pennsylvania*, 16 Peters 539 (1842).
89. Granville D. Davis, "Arkansas and the Blood of Kansas," *The Journal of Southern History* 16 (4) (November, 1950): 431.
90. Kelly and Harbison, *The American Constitution*, 377.
91. Eugene H. Rosenboom, *A History of Presidential Elections: From George Washington to Richard M. Nixon* (New York: Macmillan, 1970), 145–47.
92. Allan Nevins, *Ordeal of the Union*, vol. 2, *A House Dividing, 1852–1857* (New York: Charles Scribner's Sons, 1947), 38.
93. Ibid., 78–79.
94. Holt, *The Political Crisis of the 1850s*, 141.
95. Nevins, *Ordeal of the Union*, vol. 2, 78–79.
96. Potter, *The Impending Crisis*, 146–47; Roy Gittinger, "The Separation of Nebraska and Kansas from the Indian Territory," *The Mississippi Valley Historical Review* 3 (4) (March, 1917): 442–61.

97. Nevins, *Ordeal of the Union*, vol. 2, 92.
98. Potter, *The Impending Crisis*, 154–55.
99. Robert R. Russel, "The Issues in the Congressional Struggle Over the Kansas–Nebraska Bill, 1854," *The Journal of Southern History* 29 (2) (May, 1963): 192.
100. Johannsen, Stephen A. Douglas, ch. 14.
101. Nicole Etcheson, *Bleeding Kansas: Contested Liberty in the Civil War Era* (Lawrence: University Press of Kansas, 2004), 15; Russel, "Kansas–Nebraska Bill, 1854," 187–210.
102. Nevins, *Ordeal of the Union*, vol. 2, 94; Johannsen, *Stephen A. Douglas*, 406.
103. McPherson, *Battle Cry of Freedom*, 123.
104. Johannsen, *Stephen A. Douglas*, 408–409.
105. Ibid., 409.
106. Potter, *The Impending Crisis*, 160.
107. Ibid., 160–61.
108. Johannsen, *Stephen A. Douglas*, 414–15.
109. Roseboom, *A History of Presidential Elections*, 151.
110. Johannsen, *Stephen A. Douglas*, 418–21.
111. Ibid., 418–19.
112. Potter, *The Impending Crisis*, 163.
113. Johannsen, *Stephen A. Douglas*, 419.
114. Nevins, *Ordeal of the Union*, vol. 2, 114.
115. Douglas quoted in Johannsen, *Stephen A. Douglas*, 421.
116. Douglas quoted in ibid.
117. Douglas quoted in ibid.
118. *United States Statutes at Large*, 10 (Boston: Little Brown, 1855), 277, reproduced in the Avalon Project, Yale University, http://www.yale.edu/lawweb/avalon/kanneb.htm.
119. Johannsen, *Stephen A. Douglas*, 424.
120. Holt, *The Political Crisis of the 1850s*, 148.
121. Ibid., 149.
122. Seward quoted in Nevins, *Ordeal of the Union*, vol. 2, 118; Sumner speech, February 21, 1854, from American Memory section of Library of Congress website, http://memory.loc.gov/cgi-bin/query/r?ammen/rbaapc:@field(DOCID)+@lit(rbaapc28500div0).
123. Russel, "Kansas–Nebraska Bill, 1854," 207–10. The vote on final passage in the Senate was 35–13 in favor (May 25); in the House, it was 113–100 (May 22).
124. Douglas quoted in Johannsen, *Stephen A. Douglas*, 434.
125. William E. Gienapp, *The Origins of the Republican Party, 1852–1856* (New York: Oxford University Press, 1987), 81.
126. Nevins, *Ordeal of the Union*, vol. 2, 121.
127. Holt, *The Political Crisis of the 1850s*, 150.
128. Quoted in Gienapp, *The Origins of the Republican Party*, 87.
129. Holt, *American Whig Party*, 839.
130. Anbinder, *Nativism and Slavery*, 20–21.
131. Ibid., 43–44.
132. William E. Gienapp, "Nativism and the Creation of a Republican Majority in the North before the Civil War," *The Journal of American History* 72 (3) (December 1985): 532.
133. McPherson, *Battle Cry of Freedom*, 140.
134. Ibid., 543.
135. Joel H. Silbey, "After 'The First Northern Victory': The Republican Party Comes to Congress, 1855–1856," *Journal of Interdisciplinary History* 20 (1) (Summer, 1989): 1.

136. Fred Harvey Harrington, "'The First Northern Victory,'" *The Journal of Southern History* 5 (2) (May, 1939): 186. Banks began his congressional career in 1853 as a Democrat, then switched to the American party, then the Republican (until 1858); following service in the Union army, he returned to Congress as a Union Republican, then a Republican, an Independent, then back to the Republican party. Banks was also an unsuccessful candidate for Congress in 1872 on the Liberal and Democratic tickets. U.S. Congress, *Biographical Directory of the United States Congress, 1774–Present*, online version, available at http://bioguide.congress. gov/biosearch/biosearch1.asp.

137. Etcheson, *Bleeding Kansas*, 2.

138. Quoted in McPherson, *Battle Cry of Freedom*, 147.

139. McPherson, *Battle Cry of Freedom*, 146–47.

140. Harrington, "'The First Northern Victory,'" 205.

141. Manisha Sinha, "The Caning of Charles Sumner: Slavery, Race, and Ideology in the Age of the Civil War," *Journal of the Early Republic* 23 (2) (Summer, 2003): 233. Much has been written about caning and its impact; for standard references, see ibid., n. 2. David Donald, *Charles Sumner and the Coming of the Civil War* (New York: Alfred A. Knopf, 1960), 282–347; Michael D. Pierson, "'All Southern Society Is Assailed by the Foulest Charges': Charles Sumner's 'The Crimes Against Kansas,' and the Escalation of Republican Anti-Slavery Rhetoric," *The New England Quarterly* 68 (4) (December, 1995): 531–57.

142. Quoted in Donald, *Charles Sumner and the Coming of the Civil War*, 285.

143. Sinha, "The Caning of Charles Sumner," 245.

144. "The Sumner Outrage!" *The New York Daily Times*, May 31, 1856, 1.

145. Sinha, "The Caning of Charles Sumner," 247.

146. Ibid., 256.

147. Etcheson, *Bleeding Kansas*, 106–13.

148. Paul Finkelman, *Dred Scott v. Sandford: A Brief History with Documents* (Boston: Bedford Books, 1997), 45. The most comprehensive analysis is Don E. Fehrenbacher, *The Dred Scott Case: Its Significance in American Law and Politics* (New York: Oxford University Press, 1978).

149. Quote in Finkelman, *Dred Scott v. Sandford*, 49.

150. Kenneth M. Stampp, *America in 1857: A Nation on the Brink* (New York: Oxford University Press, 1990), 108–109; Finkelman, *Dred Scott v. Sandford*, 50.

151. Potter, *Impending Crisis*, 297.

152. MacPherson, *Battle Cry of Freedom*, 162–63.

153. Stampp, *America in 1857*, 282.

154. Quoted in Johannsen, *Stephen A. Douglas*, 591.

155. Reinhard H. Luthin, "Abraham Lincoln Becomes a Republican," *Political Science Quarterly* 59 (3) (September, 1944): 420–38.

156. "House Divided" speech from Roy P. Basler, ed., *The Collected Works of Abraham Lincoln*. 9 vols. (New Brunswick, N.J.: Rutgers University Press, 1953–1955), II, 461–69; Don E. Fehrenbacher, "The Origins and Purpose of Lincoln's 'House-Divided' Speech," *The Mississippi Valley Historical Review* 46 (4) (March, 1960): 615–43. Harry V. Jaffa, *Crisis of the House Divided: An Interpretation of the Lincoln–Douglas Debates* (Seattle: University of Washington Press, 1959).

157. McPherson, *Battle Cry of Freedom*, 212–13.

158. Ibid., 219.

159. Rosenboom, *History of Presidential Elections*, 182–84.

3 THE PROMISE OF LAND: THE HOMESTEAD ACT OF 1862 AND THE MORRILL LAND-GRANT COLLEGE ACT OF 1862

Epigraph quotes from George W. Julian, "The Spoliation of the Public Lands," *The North American Review* 141 (345) (August, 1885): 175, and Morrill quoted in James Grey, *Open Wide the Door: The Story of the University of Minnesota* (New York: G. P. Putnam, 1958), 201. Earlier, Julian had commented that the Homestead Act "has probably done more to make the American name honored and beloved among civilized nations than any single act of legislation since the formation of the government." George Julian, "Our Land Policy," *Atlantic Monthly* XLIII (1879): 328.

1. Paul W. Gates, "Public Land Issues in the United States," *The Western Historical Quarterly* 2 (4) (October, 1971): 372.
2. Douglas W. Allen, "Homesteading and Property Rights; Or, 'How the West Was Really Won,'" *Journal of Law and Economics* 34 (1) (April, 1991): 6.
3. Paul W. Gates, *The Economic History of the United States*, vol. III, *The Farmer's Age: Agriculture 1815–1860* (New York: Holt, Rinehart and Winston, 1960), 51.
4. Benjamin H. Hibbard, *A History of the Public Land Policies* (Madison: University of Wisconsin Press, 1965), 69.
5. Allen, "Homesteading and Property Rights," 7–8, and John Mayfield, *The New Nation, 1800–1845*, rev. ed. (New York: Hill and Wang, 1982, 1961), 53.
6. George Dangerfield, *The Awakening of American Nationalism 1815–1828* (New York: Harper Torchbooks, 1965), 75.
7. Hibbard, *A History of the Public Land Policies*, 93–100.
8. Allen, "Homesteading and Property Rights," 8.
9. Paul W. Gates, *The Wisconsin Pine Lands of Cornell University: A Study in Land Policy and Absentee Ownership* (Ithaca: Cornell University Press, 1943), 1.
10. David P. Currie, "The Constitution in Congress: The Public Lands, 1829–1861," *The University of Chicago Law Review* 70 (3) (Summer, 2003): 787–90.
11. Malcolm J. Rohrbough, *The Land Office Business: The Settlement and Administration of American Public Lands, 1789–1837* (New York: Oxford University Press, 1968), 295.
12. Currie, "The Constitution in Congress: The Public Lands, 1829–1861," 783–85.
13. Robert D. Ilisevich, *Galusha A. Grow: The Peoples' Candidate* (Pittsburgh: University of Pittsburgh Press, 1988), 58, and St. George L. Sioussat, "Andrew Johnson and the Early Phases of the Homestead Bill," *The Mississippi Valley Historical Review* 5 (3) (December, 1918): 256–57. This section relies heavily on Ilisevich's analysis.
14. Ilisevich, *Galusha A. Grow*, 58–59.
15. George M. Stephenson, *The Political History of the Public Lands from 1840 to 1862* (New York: Russell and Russell, 1967, 1917), 115.
16. Robert W. Johannsen, *Stephen A. Douglas* (Urbana: University of Illinois Press, 1997), 318.
17. Quote from Daniel Walker Howe, *What Hath God Wrought: The Transformation of America, 1815–1848* (New York: Oxford University Press, 2007), 147; Ilisevich, *Galusha A. Grow*, 64.
18. Ilisevich, *Galusha A. Grow*, 68.
19. Ibid., 75.
20. Currie, "The Constitution in Congress: The Public Lands, 1829–1861," 803–804; Gates, *The Wisconsin Pine Lands of Cornell University*, 12–13; Thomas J. Brown, *Dorothea Dix: New England Reformers* (Cambridge: Harvard University Press, 1998).
21. Gates, *The Wisconsin Pine Lands of Cornell University*, 12–13.
22. Hans L. Trefousse, *Andrew Johnson: A Biography* (New York: W. W. Norton, 1989), 110–11.

23. Quoted in Stephenson, *The Political History of the Public Lands*, 159–60.

24. Ibid., 161; Trefousse, *Andrew Johnson*, 112.

25. Stephenson, *The Political History of the Public Lands*, 195–97; Trefousse, *Andrew Johnson*, 120–21.

26. Philip Shriver Klein, *President James Buchanan: A Biography* (University Park, Pa.: Pennsylvania State University Press, 1962), 345–46.

27. Ilisevich, *Galusha A. Grow*, 189–90.

28. Paul W. Gates, *Fifty Million Acres* (Ithaca: Cornell University Press, 1953), 89.

29. Jeter Allen Isely, *Horace Greeley and the Republican Party, 1853–1861* (Princeton: Princeton University Press, 1947), 291.

30. Ilisevich, *Galusha A. Grow*, 190; Trefousse, *Andrew Johnson*, 121–22.

31. Republican Platform of 1860 in *History of American Presidential Elections, 1789–1968*, ed. Arthur M. Schlesinger, Jr., vol. 2, *1848–1896* (New York: Chelsea House, 1971), 1126.

32. Harold M. Hyman, *American Singularity: The 1787 Northwest Ordinance, the 1862 Homestead and Morrill Acts, and the 1944 G.I. Bill* (Athens, Ga.: University of Georgia Press, 1986), 24; George N. Rainsford, *Congress and Higher Education in the Nineteenth Century* (Knoxville: University of Tennessee Press, 1972), 7; Robert H. Land, "Henrico and Its College," *William and Mary Quarterly* 2nd Ser. 18 (1938): 470.

33. The colleges are listed here by founding name, date, religious affiliation, and current name and date: Harvard College (1636, Congregational; Harvard University, 1780); College of William and Mary (1693, Episcopal); Collegiate School (1701, Congregational; Yale College, 1745; Yale University, 1887); College of New Jersey (1747, Presbyterian; Princeton University, 1896); King's College (1754, Episcopal; Columbia College, 1787; Columbia University, 1912); College, Academy and Charitable School (1755, Episcopal; University of Pennsylvania, 1791); College of Rhode Island (1765, Baptist; Brown University, 1804); Queen's College (1766, Dutch Reform; Rutgers College, 1825; Rutgers University, 1924); Dartmouth College (1769, Congregational). Donald G. Tewksbury, *The Founding of American Colleges and Universities Before the Civil War* (New York: Arno Press, 1969; 1932), Table IV, 32–54.

34. Hyman, *American Singularity*, 25.

35. Jurgen Herbst, "The Development of Public Universities in the Old Northwest," in *Northwest Ordinance: Essays on Its Formulation, Provisions and Legacy*, ed. Frederick D. Williams (East Lansing: Michigan State University Press, 1988), 98.

36. Rainsford, *Congress and Higher Education*, 16–17; John S. Brubacher and Willis Rudy, *Higher Education in Transition: A History of American Colleges and Universities, 1636–1968*, revised and enlarged ed. (New York: Harper and Row, 1968), 224–27.

37. Rainsford, *Congress and Higher Education*, 19–20.

38. *U.S. Statutes at Large*, vol. 6, 255; Rainsford, *Congress and Higher Education*, 21–22; quote from Budd Whitebook, *The George Washington University: In and Of the District of Columbia* (Washington, D.C.: George Washington University, 2003), 7.

39. Gates, *The Wisconsin Pine Lands of Cornell University*, 4; Rainsford, *Congress and Higher Education*, 22.

40. Rainsford, *Congress and Higher Education*, 24, citing David Madsen, *The National University—Enduring Dream of the U.S.* (Detroit: Wayne State University Press, 1966), 167–69; Gates, *The Wisconsin Pine Lands of Cornell University*, 3.

41. Betty Hollow, *Ohio University, 1804–2004: The Spirit of a Singular Place* (Athens: Ohio University Press, 2003).

42. Edward Danforth Eddy, Jr., *Colleges for Our Land and Time: The Land-Grant Idea in American Education* (Westport, Conn.: Greenwood Press, 1957), 187. The states were Louisiana (admitted in1812), Indiana (1816), Mississippi (1817), Illinois (1818),

Alabama (1819), Missouri (1821), Arkansas (1836), Michigan (1837), Iowa (1846), California (1850), Oregon (1858), and Kansas (1861).

43. *Dartmouth College* v. *Woodward*, 4 Wheaton 518 (1819).

44. Webster quote from Richard Hofstadter and Wilson Smith, eds., *American Higher Education. A Documentary History*, vol. 1 (Chicago: University of Chicago Press, 1961), 212.

45. Paul Westmeyer, *A History of American Higher Education* (Springfield, Ill.: Charles C. Thomas, 1985), 18.

46. Tewksbury, *The Founding of American Colleges*, 170. The two state universities in Ohio were Ohio University (1804) and Miami University (1809).

47. Ibid.

48. Colin B. Burke, *American Collegiate Populations: A Test of the Traditional View* (New York: New York University Press, 1982), 17, 54–55, cited in Roger L. Williams, *The Origins of Federal Support for Higher Education: George W. Atherton and the Land-Grant College Movement* (University Park, Pa.: Pennsylvania State University Press, 1991), 16. Earlier studies by Tewksbury, *The Founding of American Colleges*, 28, and Westmeyer, *A History of American Higher Education*, 24, had much higher estimates of antebellum college mortality rates.

49. Carl L. Becker, *Cornell University: Founders and the Founding* (Ithaca: Cornell University Press, 1967, 1943), 26–27; Mary Turner Carriel, *The Life of Jonathan Baldwin Turner* (Urbana: University of Illinois Press, 1961, 1911).

50. Gates, *The Wisconsin Pine Lands of Cornell University*, 4, and Allan Nevins, *Ordeal of Union*, vol. 2, *A House Dividing* (New York: Charles Scribner's Sons, 1947), 191.

51. John H. Florer, "Major Issues in the Congressional Debate of the Morrill Act of 1862," *History of Education Quarterly* 8 (4) (Winter, 1968): 459.

52. "Congressional Apportionment," U.S. House of Representatives, Clerk of the House website, available at http://clerk.house.gov/histHigh/Congressional_ History/congApp.html.

53. Morrill's recollection from his 1874 private papers, quoted in William Belmont Parker, *The Life and Public Services of Justin Smith Morrill* (Boston: Houghton Mifflin Co., 1924), 266.

54. Florer, "Major Issues in the Congressional Debate of the Morrill Act of 1862," 460, and Coy F. Cross II, *Justin Smith Morrill: Father of the Land-Grant Colleges* (East Lansing: Michigan State University Press, 1999), 80.

55. Cross, *Justin Smith Morrill*, 80–81.

56. Ibid., 81.

57. Rice and Mason quoted in Eddy, *Colleges for Our Land and Time*, 31; Clay quoted in Gates, *The Wisconsin Pine Lands of Cornell University*, 5.

58. Gates, *The Wisconsin Pine Lands of Cornell University*, 8.

59. Earle D. Ross, "The Agricultural Backgrounds and Attitudes of American Presidents," *Social Forces* 13 (1) (October, 1934–May, 1935), 41. Calvert was vice-president of the U.S. Agricultural Society, and founded in 1856 the first agricultural research college in America, later the Maryland Agricultural College at College Park. He served one term in the U.S. Congress (1861–1863) as a Unionist from his home state of Maryland. Biographical Directory of the U.S. Congress, "Charles Benedict Calvert," online version, http://bioguide. congress.gov.

60. Morrill, writing in 1874, quoted in Parker, *Justin Smith Morrill*, 268.

61. James T. DuBois and Gertrude Mathews, *Galusha A. Grow: Father of the Homestead Law* (Boston: Houghton Mifflin, 1917), 246.

62. Ernest B. Furguson, *Freedom Rising: Washington in the Civil War* (New York: Alfred A. Knopf, 2004), 116.

63. Ilisevich, *Galusha A. Grow*, 201–12; James A. Rawley, *The Politics of Union: Northern Politics During the Civil War* (Hinsdale, Ill.: Dryden Press, 1974), 34.
64. Rawley, *The Politics of Union*, 36–38.
65. Furguson, *Freedom Rising*, 118–24; James M. McPherson, *Battle Cry of Freedom: The Civil War Era* (New York: Oxford University Press, 1988), 334–49; and DuBois and Mathews, *Galusha A. Grow*, 249. The budget for the Thirty-Sixth Congress (1859–1861) had been $66 million. Total Union wartime expenses amounted to $3.3 billion, of which approximately 21 percent was paid through taxes. Thirty percent of the United States wartime expenditures in World War I was paid for by taxes; and 42 percent came from taxes in World War II. Rawley, *The Politics of Union*, 49–50.
66. Leonard P. Curry, *Blueprint for Modern America: Nonmilitary Legislation of the First Civil War Congress* (Nashville: Vanderbilt University Press, 1968), 102–103.
67. Ibid., 103–106.
68. Ibid., 105–106; Ilisevich, *Galusha A. Grow*, 210. Curry noted that it "would seem to be impossible to determine the actual vote" on the Homestead bill in the House, with three varying tallies, from 105, 106, and 114 votes for, and 16 or 18 votes against; at 106, n. 9.
69. Ilisevich, *Galusha A. Grow*, 210–11; Curry, *Blueprint for Modern America*, 108.
70. Jay Richter, "The Origin and Development of the Land-Grant College in the United States," *The Journal of Negro Education* 31 (3), The Negro Public College (Summer, 1962): 233.
71. Curry, *Blueprint for Modern America*, 109–10.
72. Wilkinson quoted in Gates, *The Wisconsin Pine Lands of Cornell University*, 8–9.
73. Russell I. Thackrey, *The Future of the State University* (Urbana: University of Illinois Press, 1971), 8.
74. Becker, *Cornell University*, 34–35; Frederick Rudolph, *The American College and University: A History* (New York: Alfred A. Knopf, 1962), 250–51; Scott Key, "Economics or Education: The Establishment of American Land-Grant Universities," *The Journal of Higher Education* 67 (2) (March–April, 1996): 215–16.
75. Morrill, writing in 1874, quoted in Parker, *Justin Smith Morrill*, 270.
76. Lincoln quoted in James G. Randall, *Lincoln the President*, vol. 3, *Midstream* (New York: Dodd, Mead, 1952), 143; Eldon L. Johnson, "Misconceptions About the Early Land-Grant Colleges," *Journal of Higher Education* 52 (4) (July–August, 1981): 335.
77. "News from Washington," *The New York Times*, May 22, 1862, 5.
78. Marion Clawson, *Uncle Sam's Acres* (Westport, Conn.: Greenwood Press, 1951), 93.
79. National Park Service, Homestead National Monument of America website, http://www.nps.gov/home/homestead_act.html and http://www.nps.gov/home/scrapbook.html. The Freeman farm is now the site of the Homestead National Monument of America.
80. Addison Erwin Sheldon, *Histories and Stories of Nebraska* (1913), cited in Legends of America website, http://legendsofamerica.com.
81. Folke Dovring, "European Reactions to the Homestead Act," *The Journal of Economic History* 22 (4) (December, 1962): 469.
82. Paul Wallace Gates, "Federal Land Policy in the South, 1866–1888," *Journal of Southern History* 6 (3) (August, 1940): 304.
83. Gates, "Federal Land Policy in the South, 1866–1888," passim.
84. Clawson, *Uncle Sam's Acres*, 93.
85. Allen, "Homesteading and Property Rights," 9; Paul W. Gates, "The Homestead Law in an Incongruous Land System," *The American Historical Review* 41 (1936): 662.
86. Allen, "Homesteading and Property Rights," 7–8.
87. Donald Worster, *An Unsettled Country: Changing Landscapes of the American West* (Albuquerque: University of New Mexico Press, 1994), 9–14. The principal

biography of Powell is Wallace E. Stegner, *Beyond the Hundredth Meridian: John Wesley Powell and the Second Opening of the West* (Boston: Houghton Mifflin, 1962, 1954).

88. Worster, *An Unsettled Country*, 13.
89. Ibid., 15–16.
90 Ibid., 17.
91. Frederick Jackson Turner, *The Frontier in American History* (New York: H. Holt and Company, 1920), "The Significance of the Frontier in American History," 1–18; quote on 1.
92. An extraordinary number of works have been written about the Turner thesis, in its defense and in criticism. See William Cronon, "Revisiting the Vanishing Frontier: The Legacy of Frederick Jackson Turner," *The Western Historical Quarterly* 18 (2) (April, 1987): 157–76, and Allan G. Bogue, "Frederick Jackson Turner Reconsidered," *The History Teacher* 27 (2) (February, 1994): 195–221.
93. Shelly C. Dudley, "The First Five: A Brief Overview of the First Reclamation Projects," in Waterhistory.org, a website of the International Waterway History Association, http://www.waterhistory.org/histories/reclamation.
94. Donald E. Worster, *Rivers of Empire: Water, Aridity, and the Growth of the American West* (New York: Pantheon Books, 1985), 130–31.
95. Gates, "Public Land Issues in the United States," 371.
96. National Park Service, "Found: America's Last Homesteader!," http://nps.gov/home/homesteader.html.
97. Robert E. Pierre, "Homesteading Reborn for a New Generation," *The Washington Post*, April 5, 2004, A1.
98. Eddy, *Colleges for Our Land and Time*, 47–48.
99. Vernon Carstensen, "A Century of Land-Grant Colleges," *The Journal of Higher Education* 33 (1) (January, 1962): 33.
100. Williams, *The Origins of Federal Support for Higher Education*, 46–49.
101. Allan Nevins, *The State Universities and Democracy* (Urbana: University of Illinois Press, 1962), 29; Allan Nevins, *The Origin of the Land-Grant Colleges and State Universities: A Brief Account of the Morrill Act of 1862* (Washington, D.C.: Civil War Centennial Commission, 1962), 4.
102. Nevins, *The State Universities and Democracy*, 29–30, and Gates, *The Wisconsin Pine Lands of Cornell University*, 41.
103. Nevins, *The State Universities and Democracy*, 30.
104. Ibid., 31–32. Caleb Cushing (1800–1879) had a lengthy record of public service, including election to Congress, Attorney General under Franklin Pierce, service in the diplomatic corps, and an unsuccessful nomination as Chief Justice of the United States under U. S. Grant.
105. Becker, *Cornell University*, 84–85. Cornell's wealth came from stock in Western Union.
106. Williams, *The Origins of Federal Support for Higher Education*, 47, and Earle D. Ross, "The Great Triumvirate of Land-Grant Educators: Gilman, White, and Walker," *The Journal of Higher Education* 32 (9) (December, 1961): 480–88.
107. Brubacher and Rudy, *Higher Education in Transition*, 231.
108. Johnson, "Misconceptions About the Early Land-Grant Colleges," 336.
109. Ibid., and Eddy, *Colleges for Our Land and Time*, 67–68.
110. Williams, *The Origins of Federal Support for Higher Education*, 3.
111. John Aubrey Douglas, "Creating a Fourth Branch of State Government: The University of California and the Constitutional Convention of 1879," *History of Education Quarterly* 32 (1) (Spring, 1992): 31–72.
112. Ibid., 40–48.
113. Williams, *The Origins of Federal Support for Higher Education*, 120–21.
114. Ibid., 153–55.

115. Earle D. Ross, *Democracy's College: The Land-Grant Movement in the Formative State* (New York: Arno Press, 1969; Iowa State University, 1942), 178–79.

116. Fred Humphries, "Land-Grant Institutions: Their Struggle for Survival and Equality," in *A Century of Service: Land-Grant Colleges and Universities, 1890–1990* (New Brunswick, N.J.: Transaction Publishers, 1992), 4. Just three black institutions received 1862 Morrill funds: Alcorn State University in Mississippi (established in 1871); Hampton Institute in Virginia (1872); and Claflin University in South Carolina (1872). In 1897, Kentucky State College eventually received funds under the original Morrill Act. D. O. W. Holmes, "Seventy Years of the Negro College: 1860 to 1930," *Phylon (1940–1956)* 10 (4) (Fourth Quarter, 1949): 311.

117. The following are the 1890 Morrill colleges, with the date they were established, the year each state accepted the terms of the 1890 Morrill Act, and the institution's current name.

   State Agricultural and Mechanical Institute, Normal, Alabama, 1875–1891 (Alabama A&M University); Agricultural, Mechanical and Normal College, Pine Bluff, Arkansas, 1872–1891 (University of Arkansas at Pine Bluff); State College for Colored Students, Dover, Delaware, 1891–1891 (Delaware State University); Florida Agricultural and Mechanical College for Negroes, Tallahassee, Florida, 1887–1891 (Florida A&M University); Georgia State Industrial College, Industrial College, Georgia, 1890–1890 (Georgia State Industrial College); Kentucky State Industrial College, Frankfort, Kentucky, 1887–1893 (Kentucky State University); Southern University and Agricultural and Mechanical College, Scotlandville, Louisiana, 1880–1893 (Southern University and Agricultural and Mechanical College); Princess Anne Academy, Princess Anne, Maryland, 1887–1892 (University of Maryland-Eastern Shore); Alcorn Agricultural and Mechanical College, Alcorn, Mississippi, 1871–1890 (Alcorn State University); Lincoln University, Jefferson City, Missouri, 1866–1891 (Lincoln University); The Negro Agricultural and Normal University, Greensboro, North Carolina, 1894–1891 (North Carolina Agricultural and Technical University); Colored Agricultural and Normal University, Langston, Oklahoma, 1897–1899 (Langston University); State Colored Normal, Industrial, Agricultural and Mechanical College of South Carolina, Orangeburg, South Carolina, 1896–1896 (South Carolina State University); Tennessee Agricultural and Industrial State Teachers College, Nashville, Tennessee, 1913–1891 (Tennessee State University); Prairie View State Normal and Industrial College, Prairie View, Texas, 1879–1891; Virginia State College for Negroes, Ettrick, Virginia, 1883–1891 (Virginia State University); West Virginia State College, Institute, West Virginia, 1891–1892 (West Virginia State College). Holmes, "Seventy Years of the Negro College," 311–12.

118. Humphries, "Land-Grant Institutions," 4–5.

119. Holmes, "Seventy Years of the Negro College," 308.

120. Humphries, "Land-Grant Institutions," 5.

121. Ibid.

122. Hyman, *American Singularity*, 72–73.

123. Ibid., 73. More recently established University of Houston and Texas Southern University also received a portion of the oil income. Predominantly black Texas Southern was the university created in response to the Supreme Court decision of *Sweatt* v. *Painter*, which in 1947 required the state of Texas to admit a black student to a state-supported law school. Rather than admitting Heman Marion Sweatt to an all-white university law school, the Texas legislature chose to duplicate those facilities by establishing in 1947 the Texas Southern University for Negroes. Texas Southern University, now one of the most ethnically diverse universities in Texas, is not a land-grant institution.

124. Westmeyer, *A History of American Higher Education*, 65.
125. Ibid., 149, and University of Alaska-Fairbanks website, http://www.uaf.edu/uaf/about/history.html.
126. Martin C. Jischke, "Adapting Justin Morrill's Vision to a New Century: The Imperative of Change for Land-Grant Universities," address given at the National Association of State Universities and Land-Grant Colleges Annual Meeting, San Diego, California, November 14, 2004. Available at the Cooperative State Research, Education, and Extension Service, U.S. Department of Agriculture website, http://www.crees.usda.gov/newsroom/speeches/04morrill.html. "The World's 200 Top University Rankings," *The (London) Times Higher Education Review*, November 5, 2004, lists eleven land-grant institutions among the world's top 100 universities.
127. Neil E. Harl, "Relevance of the Land Grant Mission in the Twenty-First Century," paper presented at Kansas State University, Manhattan, Kansas, November 18, 2003, available at the Iowa State University website, http://www.econ.iastate.edu/faculty/harl/RelevanceoftheLandGrandMission.pdf; Mark G. Yudof, "Is the Public Research University Dead?" *Chronicle of Higher Education*, January, 2002, B-24.
128. Harl, "Relevance of the Land Grant Mission in the Twenty-First Century," 9.
129. Jischke, "Adapting Justin Morrill's Vision to a New Century."
130. Ibid.

4 WOMEN'S RIGHT TO VOTE:
THE NINETEENTH AMENDMENT TO THE U.S.
CONSTITUTION (1919)

Epigraph quote from Declaration of Sentiments and Resolutions in George Klosko and Margaret G. Klosko, *The Struggle for Women's Rights: Theoretical and Historical Sources* (Upper Saddle River, N.J.: Prentice Hall, 1999), 100; suffragist banner, U.S. National Archives and Records Administration website, exhibit on the Constitution, available at http://www.archives.gov/exhibit_hall/charters_of_freedom/constitution/19th_amendment.htm.

1. "Wilson Takes Office To-Day as 28th President," *The New York Times*, March 4, 1913, 1. This section relies on contemporary newspaper accounts from *The New York Times* and *The Washington Post*, March 3–5, 1913.
2. Doris Stevens, *Jailed for Freedom: American Women With the Vote* (Troutdale, Oregon: NewSage Press, 1995, 1920), 35.
3. Linda J. Lumsden, *Inez: The Life and Times of Inez Milholland* (Bloomington: Indiana University Press, 2004), 81–91.
4. John T. Woolley and Gerhard Peters, *The American Presidency Project* [online]. Santa Barbara, Calif.: University of California (hosted), Gerhard Peters (database). Available from World Wide Web: http://www.presidency.ucsb.edu/ws/?pid=25831.
5. Carrie Chapman Catt and Nettie Rogers Shuler, *Woman Suffrage and Politics: The Inner Story of the Suffrage Movement* (New York: Charles Scribner's Sons, 1926), 472.
6. Judith Apter Klinghoffer and Lois Elkins, "'The Petticoat Electors': Women's Suffrage in New Jersey, 1776–1807," *Journal of the Early Republic* 12 (Summer, 1992): 150.
7. Robert J. Dinkin, *Before Equal Suffrage: Women in Partisan Politics from Colonial Times to 1920* (Westport, Conn.: Greenwood Press, 1995), 19–20, and Klinghoffer and Elkins, "'The Petticoat Electors'," passim.
8. Dinkin, *Before Equal Suffrage*, 101–12.

9. Anne M. Boylan, "Women and Politics in the Era before Seneca Falls," *Journal of the Early Republic* 10 (3) (Autumn, 1990): 363–64; Louise M. Young, "Women's Place in American Politics: The Historical Perspective," *Journal of Politics* 38 (3) 200 Years of the Republic in Retrospect: A Special Bicentennial Issue (August, 1976): 307.

10. While many thousands of women participated in abolitionist activity, several women stood out, making an important impact on both the anti-slavery movement and later the cause of women's rights. Frances Wright (1795–1852) wrote forcefully about the abolition of slavery, opposition to organized religion, reform of divorce and marriage laws, birth control, and universal public education. She became an important force in the working-class political movement in New York, won a seat in the New York legislature, running on the "Fanny Wright" party. A second important writer, intellectual, and member of the New England transcendentalist movement was Margaret Fuller (1810–1850) who wrote *Woman in the Nineteenth Century* (1845), a feminist classic which helped frame the Seneca Falls conference, and conducted her famous seminars that helped radicalize many prominent Boston women.

    Two other important figures were the Grimke sisters, Angelina (1805–1879) and Sarah (1792–1873), daughters of a wealthy South Carolina slaveholding family, who became powerful anti-slavery speakers and forceful writers. Their agitation brought the wrath of New England clergy, and a pastoral letter from the Council of Congregational Ministers, was read in all Congregational churches in July 1837, warning that the sisters threatened "permanent injury to the female character." Sarah Grimke's *Letters on the Equality of the Sexes*, published in 1837, drew the analogy between the condition of women and slavery and was a foretaste of the developing women's rights movement. Other women, particularly followers of abolitionist William Lloyd Garrison, lectured and traveled widely: Abigail Kelley Foster (1810–1887), Lucy Stone (1818–1893), along with African-American activists Frances Ellen Watkins Harper (1825–1911), Maria Stewart (1803–1879), Sarah Parker Remond (1826–1894), and Sojourner Truth (ca. 1797–1883). Young, "Women's Place in American Politics," 313–15; Elizabeth Frost-Knappman and Kathryn Cullen-DuPont, *Women's Suffrage in America*, updated ed. (New York: Facts on File, 2005), 436, 452. Mari Jo Buhle and Paul Buhle, eds., *The Concise History of Woman Suffrage: Selections from the Classic Work of Stanton, Anthony, Gage, and Harper* (Urbana: University of Illinois Press, 1978), 69–70; Alison M. Parker, "The Case for Reform Antecedents for the Woman's Rights Movement," in *Votes for Women: The Struggle for Suffrage Revisited*, ed. Jean H. Baker (New York: Oxford University Press, 2002), 29–30. Judith E. Harper, *Susan B. Anthony: A Biographical Companion* (Santa Barbara, Calif.: ABC-CLIO, 1998), 5; Suzanne M. Marilley, *Woman Suffrage and the Origins of Liberal Feminism in the United States, 1820–1920* (Cambridge: Harvard University Press, 1996), ch. 1.

11. Eleanor Flexner and Ellen Fitzpatrick, *Century of Struggle: The Woman's Rights Movement in the United States*, enlarged ed. (Cambridge: Belknap Press of Harvard University Press, 1996, 1959), 39–40; Young, "Women's Place in American Politics," 316.

12. Young, "Women's Place in American Politics," 317.

13. Frost-Knappman and Cullen-DuPont, *Women's Suffrage in America*, 49.

14. Elizabeth Cady Stanton, Susan B. Anthony, and Matilda J. Gage, eds., *History of Woman Suffrage*, vol. I (New York: Arno and The New York Times, 1969, 1881), 35; Paula Baker, "The Domestication of Politics: Women and American Political Society," 1780–1920, *American Historical Review* 89 (3) (June, 1984): 634.

15. Miriam Gurko, *The Ladies of Seneca Falls: The Birth of the Woman's Rights Movement* (New York: Schocken Books, 1974), 2; Elisabeth Griffith, *In Her Own Right: The Life of Elizabeth Cady Stanton* (New York: Oxford University Press, 1984), 47–61.

16. Frost-Knappman and Cullen-DuPont, *Women's Suffrage in America*, 73.
17. Elizabeth Cady Stanton, *Eighty Years and More: Reminisces 1815–1897* (Boston: Northeastern University Press, 1993, 1898), 148.
18. Ibid. Philip S. Foner noted that only one man played a prominent role in the Seneca Falls proceedings, and that was Frederick Douglass. Philip S. Foner, ed., *Frederick Douglass on Women's Rights* (Westport, Conn.: Greenwood Press, 1976), 3.
19. Quoted in Andrea Moore Kerr, *Lucy Stone: Speaking Out for Equality* (New Brunswick: Rutgers University Press, 1992), 60.
20. Ibid., 1, 61. Stone (1818–1893) graduated from Oberlin College (the only coeducational college in the country at the time); in 1855 she married Henry Browne Blackwell, but retained her maiden name (another first). She presided over the Woman's Rights Convention in New York, and in 1866 organized the American Equal Rights Association. Antoinette Brown was also an early graduate of Oberlin, the first woman ordained as a minister.
21. Kerr, *Lucy Stone*, 60–61.
22. Harper, *Susan B. Anthony*, 20–34. Susan B. Anthony (1820–1906).
23. Frost-Knappman and Cullen-DuPont, *Women's Suffrage in America*, 447–48; Griffith, *In Her Own Right*. Elizabeth Cady Stanton (1815–1902).
24. Harper, *Susan B. Anthony*, 36.
25. Young, "Women's Place in American Politics," 321.
26. Section 2 of the Fourteenth Amendment reads, in part: "But when the right to vote at any election . . . is denied to any of the male inhabitants of such State . . . the basis of representation therein shall be reduced in the proportion which the number of male citizens shall bear to the whole number of male citizens twenty-one years of age in such State." Young, "Women's Place in American Politics," 321.
27. Harper, *Susan B. Anthony*, 93.
28. Tilton later became involved in what could only be described as one of the scandals of the century. The complicated, convoluted scandal involved charges of extramarital relations between Tilton's wife, Elizabeth Richards Tilton, and Henry Ward Beecher, the renowned liberal Congregational minister and best friend of Theodore Tilton. It had all the hallmarks of the juiciest soap opera: illicit love, betrayal, blackmail, subterfuge, and free love. Victorian Claflin Woodhull, tipped off by Elizabeth Cady Stanton, published a complete expose of the long-simmering rumors of the affair. There was a nearly seven-month long trial, a hung jury, and the story dominated the press from 1872 through 1875. Beecher had been president of the American Woman Suffrage Association (AWSA) and Theodore Tilton was president of the National Woman Suffrage Association (NWSA). The Beecher–Tilton affair also fixed in the popular mind and the press the picture of the suffrage movement as immoral and tainted. Both organizations suffered, and lost membership, and their message and purpose were crippled for years. Kerr, *Lucy Stone*, 164–65, 176; Altina L. Waller, *Reverend Beecher and Mrs. Tilton: Sex and Class in Victorian America* (Amherst: University of Massachusetts Press, 1982).
29. Kerr, *Lucy Stone*, 120. The old three-fifths clause of the Constitution, which permitted southern states to count their slaves as three-fifths of a person for the purposes of representation, was now moot. Recently liberated blacks, now citizens, would swell the representation of the South by another fifteen seats in Congress, next time there was a census and the states were readmitted into the Union.
30. Harper, *Susan B. Anthony*, 50–51.
31. Garth E. Pauley, "W. E. B. Du Bois on Woman Suffrage: A Critical Analysis of His Crisis Writings," *Journal of Black Studies* 30 (3) (January, 2000): 388.
32. Cited in Buhle and Buhle, *The Concise History of Woman Suffrage*, 254.

33. Ibid., 258.
34. "Equal Rights: Anniversary of the American Equal Rights Association," *The New York Times*, May 13, 1869, 1.
35. Cited in Buhle and Buhle, *The Concise History of Woman Suffrage*, 259; Pauley, "W. E. B. Du Bois on Woman Suffrage," 387–90.
36. Alexander Keyssar, *The Right to Vote: The Contested History of Democracy in the United States* (New York: Basic Books, 2000), 185.
37. Among the states ratifying were those under Reconstruction governments: North Carolina, Louisiana, South Carolina, Arkansas, Florida, Alabama, Missouri, Mississippi, and Texas.
38. Harper, *Susan B. Anthony*, 36.
39. 88 U.S. 162 (1875); opinion by Chief Justice Morrison Waite.
40. Jennifer K. Brown, "The Nineteenth Amendment and Women's Equality," *Yale Law Journal* 102 (8), Symposium: Economic Competitiveness and the Law (June, 1993): 2177–82.
41. Keyssar, *The Right to Vote*, 183.
42. David Morgan, *Suffragists and Democrats: The Politics of Woman Suffrage in America* (East Lansing: Michigan State University Press, 1972), 18; Dinkin, *Before Equal Suffrage*, 101–103.
43. Flexner and Fitzpatrick, *Century of Struggle*, 171–77; Suzanne M. Marilley, "Frances Willard and the Feminism of Fear," *Feminist Studies* 19 (1) (Spring, 1993): 123–46.
44. Jane Jerome Camhi, *Women Against Women: American Anti-Suffragism, 1880–1920* (New York: Carlson Publishing, 1994), 27 n. 12; Griffith, *In Her Own Right*, 126.
45. "Shall the Sisters Vote?" *The Washington Post*, January 27, 1887, 2.
46. "Woman Suffrage in the Senate," *The New York Times*, January 26, 1887, 4.
47. Beverly Beeton, "Woman Suffrage in Territorial Utah," in *Battle for the Ballot: Essays on Woman Suffrage in Utah, 1870–1896*, ed. Carol Cornwall Madsen (Logan: Utah State University Press, 1997), 116–17, originally published in *Utah Historical Quarterly* 46 (Spring, 1978): 100–20.
48. Beeton, "Woman Suffrage in Territorial Utah," 130–31. Belva Lockwood (1830–1917) was the first woman lawyer to practice before the U.S. Supreme Court; later, she was the sponsor of Samuel R. Lowery, the first African-American from the South to be admitted to practice before the U.S. Supreme Court. Frost-Knappman and Cullen-DuPont, *Women's Suffrage in America*, 441–42.
49. Allison Sneider, "Woman Suffrage in Congress: American Expansion and the Politics of Federalism, 1870–1890," in Baker, *Votes for Women*, 78.
50. Catt and Shuler, *Woman Suffrage and Politics*, 495–96.
51. Griffith, *In Her Own Right*, 203–4; Vivian Gornick, *The Solitude of Self: Thinking About Elizabeth Cady Stanton* (New York: Farrar, Straus and Giroux, 2005).
52. Harper, *Susan B. Anthony*, 252–54; Griffith, *In Her Own Right*, 210–15.
53. Ida Husted Harper, *The Life and Work of Susan B. Anthony*, vol. 3 (New York: Arno and *The New York Times*, 1969, 1908), 1376.
54. Ibid., ch. 70.
55. Quoted in Robert Booth Fowler and Spencer Jones, "Carrie Chapman Catt and the Last Years of the Struggle for Woman Suffrage: 'The Winning Plan,'" in Baker, *Votes for Women*, 133.
56. Fowler and Jones, "Carrie Chapman Catt," 133–34.
57. Catt and Shuler, *Woman Suffrage and Politics*, 268.
58. Fowler and Jones, "Carrie Chapman Catt," 135.
59. Wyoming (1869 as territory; 1890 as state); Colorado (1893); Utah (territory, 1879; rescinded 1887; 1896 as state); Idaho (1896); Washington (territory, 1883; 1910 as state); California (1911); Arizona (1912); Oregon (1912); Kansas (1912); Nevada (1914); Montana (1914). Only four other states granted full suffrage before the

Nineteenth Amendment was ratified: New York (1917), South Dakota (1918), Oklahoma (1918), and Michigan (1918). Counting those states giving less than full suffrage, there were 30 states granting women voting rights prior to the passage of the Nineteenth Amendment.

60. Holly J. McCammon and Karen E. Campbell, "Winning the Vote in the West: The Political Successes of the Women Suffrage Movements, 1866–1919," *Gender and Society* 15 (1) (February, 2001): 55–82; also, Holly J. McCammon, Karen E. Campbell, Ellen M. Granberg, and Christine Mowery, "How Movements Win: Gendered Opportunity Structures and U.S. Women's Suffrage Movements, 1866 to 1919," *American Sociological Review* 66 (February, 2001): 49–70.

61. Cahmi, *Women Against Women*, 124. Madeleine Dahlgren was the widow of Admiral John A. Dahlgren, and Eleanor Sherman was the wife of General William T. Sherman.

62. Thomas Jablonsky, "Female Opposition: The Anti-Suffrage Campaign," in Baker, *Votes for Women*, 119–21.

63. Sally Hunter Graham, *Woman Suffrage and the New Democracy* (New Haven: Yale University Press, 1996), 34–35.

64. Jablonsky, "Female Opposition," 121. Josephine Dodge (1855–1928) was a prominent advocate of the day nursery movement for working-class mothers, came from and married into prominent, wealthy families. The NAOWS was formed in her Park Avenue apartment in New York; she edited *The Woman's Protest*, and remained president of the organization until it moved its headquarters to Washington, D.C., in 1917. Minnie Bronson served in a variety of jobs with the federal government, investigation working conditions for women and children, and served as general secretary of NAOWS. Camhi, *Women Against Women*, biographical appendix, 238–41.

65. Camhi, *Women Against Women*, 2.

66. Jablonsky, "Female Opposition," 121–23.

67. Richard Barry, "Why Women Oppose Woman Suffrage," *Pearson's Magazine* (March, 1910): 329, cited in Camhi, *Women Against Women*, 57.

68. Aileen S. Kraditor, *The Ideas of the Woman Suffrage Movement, 1890–1920* (New York: Columbia University Press, 1965), 14–42; Thomas J. Jablonsky, *The Home, Heaven, and Mother Party: Female Anti-Suffragists in the United States, 1868–1920* (New York: Carlson Publications, 1994), and Camhi, *Women Against Women*, chs. 1, 2.

69. Kraditor, *The Ideas of the Woman Suffrage Movement*, ch. 2, passim.

70. Kristy Maddux, "When Patriots Protest: The Anti-Suffrage Discursive Transformation of 1917," *Rhetoric & Public Affairs* 7 (3) (2004): 283–310.

71. Ibid., 296–305.

72. Jablonsky, *The Home, Heaven, and Mother Party*, 65.

73. Morgan, *Suffragists and Democrats*, ch. 11; Catt and Shuler, *Woman Suffrage and Politics*, ch. 5. On support and opposition to woman suffrage in state referendums, see Eileen L. McDonagh and H. Douglas Price, "Woman Suffrage in the Progressive Era: Patterns of Opposition and Support in Referenda Voting, 1910–1918," *American Political Science Review* 79 (2) June, 1985): 415–35.

74. Jablonsky, *The Home, Heaven, and Mother Party*, ch. 5.

75. Kenneth R. Johnson, "White Racial Attitudes as a Factor in the Arguments Against the Nineteenth Amendment," *Phylon* 31 (1) (First Quarter, 1970): 32.

76. Ibid., 33. Underneath the senator's nose, black citizens of Florida, particularly women, were mobilizing for the vote in the months before passage of the Nineteenth Amendment. Blacks, however, were crushed by the Ku Klux Klan and other white supremacists in what has been considered the bloodiest election day in modern American history, the election of 1920. Paul Ortiz, *Emancipation Betrayed: The Hidden History of Black Organizing and White Violence in Florida from Reconstruction to the Bloody Election of 1920* (Berkeley: University of California Press, 2005).

77. Johnson, "White Racial Attitudes," 35.
78. Paul E. Fuller, *Laura Clay and the Woman's Rights Movement* (Lexington: University Press of Kentucky, 1975), ch. 9; Kenneth R. Johnson, "Kate Gordon and the Woman-Suffrage Movement in the South," *Journal of Southern History* 38 (3) (1972): 365–92.
79. Frost-Knappman and Cullen-DuPont, *Women's Suffrage in America*, 292.
80. Ellen Carol DuBois, *Harriot Stanton Blatch and the Winning of Woman Suffrage* (New Haven: Yale University Press, 1977), 3.
81. Inez Haynes Irwin, *Angels and Amazons* (Garden City, N.Y.: Doubleday, Doran & Co., 1934), 319, retold in Jacqueline Van Voris, *Carrie Chapman Catt: A Public Life* (New York: The Feminist Press, 1996, 1987), 128.
82. Frost-Knappman and Cullen-DuPont, *Women's Suffrage in America*, 294–95; David Von Drehle, *Triangle: The Fire that Changed America* (New York: Atlantic Monthly Press, 2003).
83. Michael McGerr, "Political Style and Women's Power, 1830–1930," *The Journal of American History* 77 (3) (December, 1990): 876–77.
84. Cahmi, *Women Against Women*, 122; Sharon Hartman Strom, "Leadership and Tactics in the American Woman Suffrage Movement: A New Perspective from Massachusetts," *The Journal of American History* 62 (2) (September, 1975): 296–315.
85. Robert Booth Fowler, *Carrie Catt: Feminist Politician* (Boston: Northeastern University Press, 1986), 143–45.
86. Ibid., 145.
87. DuBois, *Harriot Stanton Blatch*, 3, 274–75.
88. Fowler, *Carrie Catt*, 146–47
89. Catt and Shuler, *Woman Suffrage and Politics*, 316–17; Graham, *Woman Suffrage and the New Democracy*, ch. 5.
90. Gayle Veronica Fischer, "The Seventy-Fifth Anniversary of Woman Suffrage in the United States: A Bibliographic Essay," *Journal of Women's History* 7 (3) (Fall, 1995): 184.
91. McGerr, "Political Style and Women's Power," 874.
92. Quoted in Christine A. Lunardini and Thomas J. Knock, "Woodrow Wilson and Woman Suffrage: A New Look," *Political Science Quarterly* 95 (Winter, 1980–1981): 657.
93. Stevens, *Jailed for Freedom*, 37–38.
94. Arthur S. Link et al., eds., *The Papers of Woodrow Wilson, December 2, 1913–May 5, 1914*, vol. 29 (Princeton: Princeton University Press, 1979), 21–22; Kendrick A. Clements and Eric A. Cheezum, *Woodrow Wilson* (Washington, D.C.: CQ Press, 2003), 119.
95. Lunardini and Knock, "Woodrow Wilson and Woman Suffrage," 661.
96. Clements and Cheezum, *Woodrow Wilson*, 94, 98.
97. Catt and Shuler, *Woman Suffrage and Politics*, 259–60.
98. The dispatch from German Foreign Secretary Zimmermann to the German Minister in Mexico City stated that, in the event Germany and the United States went to war, the Minister should propose to Mexico that it enter the war against the United States and receive in return "the lost territory in Texas, New Mexico, and Arizona." Further, President Carranza of Mexico should ask Japan to join the coalition. Arthur S. Link, *Woodrow Wilson and the Progressive Era, 1910–1917* (New York: Harper Torchbooks, 1963, 1954), 271.
99. Catt and Shuler, *Woman Suffrage and Politics*, 318; Graham, *Woman Suffrage and the New Democracy*, 111.
100. Graham, *Woman Suffrage and the New Democracy*, 113.
101. "Wilson Backs Amendment for Woman Suffrage," *The New York Times*, January 10, 1918, 1; "See Suffrage Victory," *The Washington Post*, January 9, 1918, 2.

102. Catt and Shuler, *Woman Suffrage and Politics*, 321.
103. "House for Suffrage, 274–136," *The New York Times*, January 11, 1918, 1; Catt and Shuler, *Woman Suffrage and Politics*, 322. New York had thirty-nine representatives, but there were four vacancies at the time of the vote.
104. "Suffragists Add Four to Senate List," *The Washington Post*, January 13, 1918, 4.
105. Ray Stannard Baker, *Woodrow Wilson: Life and Letters* (New York: Doubleday, 1913–1946), vol. VIII, 412. Letter from Wilson to Senator Christie Benet, September 18, 1918.
106. For short biographical sketches of eighty-eight major figures in the suffragist struggle, see Frost-Knappman and Cullen-DuPont, *Women's Suffrage in America*, 426–52.
107. Benet's career in the Senate lasted only from July 6 through November 5, 1918. *Biographical Directory of the United States Congress, 1774–Present*, online version.
108. Lunardini and Knock, "Woodrow Wilson and Woman Suffrage," 668.
109. Senate deliberations and Wilson speech from newspaper articles from the *The New York Times*, September 20–October 3, 1918.
110. Clements and Cheezum, *Woodrow Wilson*, 120–21.
111. "Suffragist Burn Wilson in Effigy; Many Locked Up," *The New York Times*, February 10, 1919, 1.
112. Flexner and Fitzpatrick, *Century of Struggle*, 309.
113. Ibid., 307.
114. Morgan, *Suffragists and Democrats*, 129.
115. "President Wilson's Message to Congress," *The New York Times*, May 21, 1919, 4.
116. Anne F. Scott and Andrew M. Scott, *One Half the People: The Fight for Woman Suffrage* (Philadelphia: J. B. Lippincott, 1975), 163.
117. Eileen L. McDonagh, "Issues and Constituencies in the Progressive Era: House Roll Call Voting on the Nineteenth Amendment, 1913–1919," *The Journal of Politics* 51 (1) (February, 1989): 128–29.
118. P. Orman Ray, "The World-Wide Woman Suffrage Movement," *Journal of Comparative Legislation and International Law*, 3rd Ser. 1 (3) (1919): 220–38.
119. Graham, *Woman Suffrage and the New Democracy*, 128–29.
120. Frost-Knappman and Cullen-DuPont, *Women's Suffrage in America*, 455. Illinois won the race to be the first to ratify, but a clerk's error caused the Illinois legislature to redo its work; that permitted Wisconsin to claim bragging rights as the first state to ratify. Flexner and Fitzpatrick, *Century of Struggle*, 309.
121. Morgan, *Suffragists and Democrats*, 146.
122. A. Elizabeth Taylor, "Tennessee: The Thirty-Sixth State," in Marjorie Spruill Wheeler, ed., *The Woman Suffrage Movement in Tennessee, the South, and the Nation* (Knoxville: University of Tennessee Press, 1995), 60; Catt and Shuler, *Woman Suffrage and Politics*, 398–413.
123. Van Voris, *Carrie Chapman Catt*, 160.
124. Jablonsky, "Female Opposition," 125.
125. Flexner and Fitzpatrick, *Century of Struggle*, 314, and *The New York Times* accounts, August, 1920.
126. Quoted from Catt and Shuler, *Woman Suffrage and Politics*, 451.
127. "Colby Proclaims Woman Suffrage," *The New York Times*, August 27, 1920, 1.
128. Morgan, *Suffragists and Democrats*, 153.
129. Frost-Knappman and Cullen-DuPont, *Women's Suffrage in America*, 353–55; Fowler, *Carrie Catt*, 155–58.
130. Sara Alpern and Dale Baum, "Female Ballots: The Impact of the Nineteenth Amendment," *Journal of Interdisciplinary History* 16 (1) (Summer, 1985): 43–67.
131. Baker, "The Domestication of Politics," 643–44.
132. Graham, *Woman Suffrage and the New Democracy*, 107–108.

133. Paul Kleppner, "Were Women to Blame? Female Suffrage and Voter Turnout," *Journal of Interdisciplinary History* 12 (4) (Spring, 1982): 621–43; Alpern and Baum, "Female Ballots."

134. Dinkin, *Before Equal Suffrage*, 136.

135. M. Margaret Conway, Gertrude A. Steuernagel, and David W. Ahern, *Women and Political Participation: Cultural Change in the Political Arena* (Washington, D.C.: CQ Press, 1997), 80; Kay Lehman Schlozman, Nancy Burns, and Sidney Verba, "Gender and Pathways to Participation: The Role of Resources," *Journal of Politics* 56 (November, 1994): 963–90.

136. Conway et al., *Women and Political Participation*, 91.

137. Felton, the widow of William Harrell Felton (Democrat–Georgia), served just one day before her husband's successor was chosen. With her ceremonial one-day service, Rebecca Felton became (a) the first woman in the Senate, (b) the oldest senator (eighty-seven) to be selected; and (c) the senator with the shortest service. Other widows and special appointments with short service were Rose McConnell Long (Democrat–Louisiana), the wife of Huey P. Long (Democrat–Louisiana), who served for nearly twelve months (January 1936–January 1937); Dixie Bibb Graves (Democrat–Alabama), the wife of Governor Bibb Graves, who served out the 5-month term (August 1937–January 1938) of Hugo L. Black (Democrat–Georgia) when he became a member of the U.S. Supreme Court; Gladys Pyle (Republican–South Dakota), who served out the remaining four months (November 1938–January 1939) of Peter Norbeck (Republican–South Dakota); Vera Cahalan Bushfield (Republican–South Dakota), served three months (October–December 1938), upon the death of her husband, Harlan J. Bushfield (Republican–South Dakota); Eva Kelley Bowring (Republican–Nebraska) served from April through November, 1954, upon the death of Dwight Palmer Griswold (Republican–Nebraska), then Hazel Hempel Abel (Republican–Nebraska) served from November through December 1954, to fill the remainder of Griswold's term; Elaine S. Edwards (Democrat–Louisiana) served from August through November 1972, upon the death of Allen J. Ellender (Democrat–Louisiana); Muriel Humphrey (Democrat–Minnesota) served from January through November 1978, upon the death of her husband, Hubert H. Humphrey, Jr. (Democrat–Minnesota); Maryon Allen (Democrat–Alabama), served from June through November 1978, upon the death of her husband, James Browning Allen (Democrat–Alabama); Joceyln Burdick (Democrat–North Dakota), served from September to December 1992, upon the death of her husband Quentin N. Burdick (Democrat–North Dakota). Sheila Frahm (Republican–Kansas) served from June to November 1996, and was an unsuccessful candidate for the remainder of the term of Robert Dole, who resigned to run for the presidency. Jean Carnahan (Democrat–Missouri) was appointed in January 2001 to fill the vacancy caused by the death of her husband, Governor Mel Carnahan, who was elected to office posthumously in November 2000; she served until November 25, 2002. Two widows of senators were elected on their own right: Hattie Wyatt Caraway (Democrat–Arkansas, 1931–1945) and Margaret Chase Smith (Republican–Maine, 1949–1973). U.S. Senate website, "Women in the Senate," available at http://www.senate.gov/artandhistory/history/common/briefing/women_senators.html.

138. Barbara Mikulski (Democrat–Maryland, sworn in 1987); Dianne Feinstein (Democrat–California, 1993); Barbara Boxer (Democrat–California, 1993); Patty Murray (Democrat–Washington, 1993); Kay Bailey Hutchison (Republican–Texas, 1993); Olympia J. Snowe (Republican–Maine, 1995); Mary Landrieu (Democrat–Louisiana, 1997); Susan Collins (Republican–Maine, 1997); Blanche Lincoln (Democrat–Arkansas, 1999); Deborah Stabenow (Democrat–Michigan, 2001); Maria E. Cantwell (Democrat–Washington, 2001); Lisa Murkowski

(Republican–Alaska, 2002); Claire McCaskill (Democrat–Missouri, 2007); Amy Klobuchar (Democrat–Minnesota, 2007); Jeanne Shaheen (Democrat–New Hampshire, 2009); Kay Hagen (Democrat–North Carolina, 2009); and Kirsten E. Gillibrand (Democrat–New York). U.S. Senate website, "Women in the Senate."

139. "Women in Elective Office 2006," Center for American Women and Politics, Eagleton Institute of Politics, Rutgers, The State University of New Jersey website, available at http://www.cawp-rutgers.edu/Facts/Officeholders/cawpfs.html.

5 PROTECTING THE WORKING FAMILY: THE NATIONAL LABOR RELATIONS ACT OF 1935

Epigraph quote of Green from Irving Bernstein, *The Turbulent Years: A History of the American Worker, 1933–1941* (Boston: Houghton Mifflin Company, 1970), 349; "Wagner, Robert Ferdinand," *West's Encyclopedia of American Law*, eds. Jeffrey Lehman and Shirelle Phelps, vol. 10, 2nd ed. (Detroit: Gale, 2005), 262; Karl E. Klare, "Judicial Deradicalization of the Wagner Act and the Origins of Modern Legal Consciousness," *Minnesota Law Review* 62 (1978): 265. Ronald A. Wykstra and Eleanour V. Stevens, *Labor Law and Public Policy* (New York: Oyssey Press, 1970), 37.

1. *Commonwealth* v. *John Hunt et al.*, 4 Metcalf 111 (1842). Philip S. Foner, *History of the Labor Movement in the United States*, vol. 1: *From Colonial Times to the Founding of the American Federation of Labor* (New York: International Publishers, 1947), 162–65; Wykstra and Stevens, *Labor Law and Public Policy*, 38–46.

2. Foner, *History of the Labor Movement in the United States*, vol. I: 218.

3. Foster Rhea Dulles and Melvyn Dubofsky, *Labor in America: A History*, 4th ed. (Arlington Heights, Ill.: Harlan Davidson, 1984, 1949), 70–89.

4. Ibid., 82.

5. Ibid., 88.

6. Ibid.

7. Howard Kimeldorf and Judith Stepan-Norris, "Historical Studies of Labor Movements in the United States," *American Review of Sociology* 18 (1992): 504; Dulles and Dubofsky, *Labor in America*, 100-102.

8. Dulles and Dubofsky, *Labor in America*, 105–106.

9. Wykstra and Stevens, *Labor Law and Public Policy*, 47; Melvyn Dubofsky, *The State and Labor in Modern America* (Chapel Hill: University of North Carolina Press, 1994), 8–12.

10. Leon Fink, *Workingmen's Democracy: The Knights of Labor and American Politics* (Urbana: University of Illinois Press, 1983); Kimeldorf and Stepan-Norris, "Historical Studies of Labor Movements in the United States," 504; Dulles and Dubofsky, *Labor in America*, 117–18, ch. 8.

11. Dulles and Dubofsky, *Labor in America*, 142–56. The Federation of Organized Trades and Labor Unions, an alliance formed by a meeting of union officials and the Knights of Labor in 1881, was the transitional body preceding the 1886 formation of the AFL.

12. Dulles and Dubofsky, *Labor in America*, 155; Philip S. Foner, *History of the Labor Movement in the United States*, vol. 2: *From the Founding of the American Federation of Labor to the Emergence of American Imperialism* (New York: International Publishers, 1955), 171. The strongest unions under the AFL umbrella were the United Brotherhood of Carpenters and Joiners (57,000 members), Cigar Makers' Union (27,000); Iron and Steel Workers' Union (24,000), Iron Molders' Union (23,000), and the Typographical Union (28,000).

13. Foner, *History of the Labor Movement in the United States*, vol. 2, 206.

14. Dulles and Dubofsky, *Labor in America*, 157–59; Foner, *History of the Labor Movement in the United States*, vol. 2, 206–18.

15. H. Paul Jeffers, *An Honest President: The Life and Presidencies of Grover Cleveland* (New York: William Morrow, 2000), 290–309; Dulles and Dubofsky, *Labor in America*, 162–70; Foner, *History of the Labor Movement in the United States*, vol. 2, 261–78.

16. Dulles and Dubofsky, *Labor in America*, 202.

17. Philip S. Foner, *History of the Labor Movement in the United States*, vol. 3: *The Policies and Practices of the American Federation of Labor, 1900–1909* (New York: International Publishers, 1964), 367–92; Dulles and Dubofsky, *Labor in America*, 200–14.

18. E. Edward Herman and Alfred Kuhn, *Collective Bargaining and Labor Relations* (Englewood Cliffs, N.J.: Prentice-Hall, 1981), 13.

19. Kimeldorf and Stepan-Norris, "Historical Studies of Labor Movements in the United States," 506.

20. *Adair* v. *United States*, 208 U.S. 161 (1908) and *Coppage* v. *Kansas*, 236 U.S. 1 (1915); *Hitchman Coal and Coke Company* v. *Mitchell*, 245 U.S. 229 (1917). Alfred H. Kelly and Winfred A. Harbison, *The American Constitution: Its Origin and Development*, 4th ed. (New York: W. W. Norton, 1970, 1948), 532–33; Joel I. Seidman, "The Yellow Dog Contract," *Quarterly Journal of Economics* 46 (2) (February, 1932): 348–61. The term "yellow dog," a term that has been around since the 1830s, referred to a cowardly common cur or mongrel dog, a symbol of utter worthlessness. Robert Hendrickson, ed., *Facts on File Encyclopedia of Word and Phrase Origins*, 3rd ed. (New York: Checkmark Books, 2004). The Hitchman contract read: "I am employed by and work for the Hitchman Coal & Coke Co. with the express understanding that I am not a member of the United Mine Workers of America and will not become so while an employee . . . and that the Hitchman . . . is run nonunion and agrees with me that it will run nonunion while I am in its employ. . . ." Irving Bernstein, *The Lean Years: A History of the American Worker, 1920–1933* (Boston: Houghton Mifflin, 1966), 197.

21. Bernstein, *The Lean Years*, 200.

22. *In re Debs*, 158 U.S. 564 (1895); Harry A. Millis and Emily Clark Brown, *From the Wagner Act to Taft–Hartley: A Study of National Labor Policy and Labor Relations* (Chicago: University of Chicago Press, 1950), 8.

23. Felix Frankfurter and Nathan Greene, *The Labor Injunction* (New York: MacMillan, 1930), 1; Dulles and Dubofsky, *Labor in America*, 172.

24. Bernstein, *The Lean Years*, 200, 407. Parker was nominated by President Hoover to the U.S. Supreme Court in 1930. He became the first nominee in thirty-six years to be rejected by the Senate, in no small part because of his action in the Red Jacket injunction. The official name of the lead plaintiff was the Red Jacket Consolidated Coal and Coke Company.

25. *Loewe* v. *Lawlor*, 208 U.S. 274 (1908); Wykstra and Stevens, *Labor Law and Public Policy*, 55–63.

26. *Gompers* v. *Buck Stove & Range Company*, 221 U.S. 418 (1911).

27. *Duplex Printing Press Company* v. *Deering*, 254 U.S. 443 (1921); Herman and Kuhn, *Collective Bargaining and Labor Relations*, 38–39.

28. R. W. Fleming, "The Significance of the Wagner Act," in Milton Derber and Edwin Young, eds., *Labor and the New Deal* (Madison: University of Wisconsin Press, 1967), 124; Edward Berman, *Labor and the Sherman Act* (New York: Harper, 1930); Herman and Kuhn, *Collective Bargaining and Labor Relations*, 37.

29. Herman and Kuhn, *Collective Bargaining and Labor Relations*, 40.

30. David Brody, *Labor in Crisis: The Steel Strike of 1919* (Philadelphia: Lippincott, 1965); and David M. Kennedy, *Over Here: The First World War and American Society* (New York: Oxford University Press, 1980), 270–79.

31. Millis and Brown, *From the Wagner Act to Taft–Hartley*, 16.

32. Ibid., 15–18.
33. Willliam E. Leuchtenberg, *The Perils of Prosperity, 1914–1932*, 2nd ed. (Chicago: University of Chicago Press, 1993, 1958), 99.
34. *Adkins* v. *Children's Hospital*, 261 U.S. 525 (1923); Bernstein, *The Lean Years*, 227–32.
35. Ibid., 215–20; Herman and Kuhn, *Collective Bargaining and Labor Relations*, 41.
36. Howard Zinn, *La Guardia in Congress* (Westport, Conn.: Greenwood Press, 1972, 1959), 227. Compare with Irving Bernstein, who wrote that La Guardia "had no prior connection with anti-injunction legislation," but introduced the Norris bill in the House and "thereby won the right to place his name on the measure." Bernstein, *The Lean Years*, 413.
37. Frankfurter and Greene, *The Labor Injunction*. Frankfurter and Greene dedicated their work to "Mr. Justice Brandeis: For whom law is not a system of artificial reason, but the application of ethical ideals, with freedom at the core." Other academics and legal scholars included Donald Richberg of Chicago, professor Herman Oliphant of Johns Hopkins University, Edwin E. Witte of the University of Wisconsin, and Francis B. Sayre of Harvard University. Zinn, *La Guardia in Congress*, 227.
38. Zinn, *La Guardia in Congress*, 227; Richard Lowitt, *George W. Norris: The Persistence of a Progressive, 1913–1933* (Urbana: University of Illinois Press, 1971), 518–27; Bernstein, *The Lean Years*, 411–13; Ralph K. Winter, Jr., "Labor Injunction and Judge-Made Labor Law: The Contemporary Role of Norris-La Guardia," *Yale Law Journal* 70 (1) (November, 1960), 70–102.
39. Republican La Guardia, certainly aware of the political albatross named Herbert Hoover, toyed with the idea of switching to the Democratic party. But his nemesis, Tammany boss Jimmy Hines, had the last word, and refused to appoint La Guardia as the Democratic candidate in 1932. In the end, Franklin Roosevelt won New York's Twentieth Congressional District by 20,000 votes, and La Guardia lost to Tammany-backed James Lanzetta by 1,200 votes. That was La Guardia's first congressional defeat; he demanded a recount, but Congress upheld the Lanzetta victory. Thomas Kessner, *Fiorello H. La Guardia and the Making of Modern New York* (New York: McGraw-Hill, 1989), 193–95.
40. Lowitt, *George W. Norris*, vol. 1, 525–26.
41. David M. Kennedy, *Freedom from Fear: The American People in Depression and War, 1929–1945* (New York: Oxford University Press, 1999), 292; Richard C. Wilcock, "Industrial Management's Policies Toward Unionism," in *Labor and the New Deal*, eds. Derber and Young, 288–90; Edward Berkowitz and Kim McQuaid, "Businessman and Bureaucrat: The Evolution of the American Social Welfare System, 1900–1940," *Journal of Economic History* 38 (1), The Tasks of Economic History (March 1978): 120–42.
42. Arthur M. Schlesinger, Jr., *The Age of Roosevelt: The Coming of the New Deal* (Boston: Houghton Mifflin, 1958), 90.
43. Bernstein, *The Lean Years*, 96.
44. Irving Bernstein, *The Turbulent Years*, 1–2.
45. Patrick Maney, "The Forgotten New Deal Congress," in *The American Congress: The Building of Democracy*, ed. Julian E. Zelize (Boston: Houghton Mifflin, 2004), 446.
46. Melvyn Dubofsky and Warren Van Tine, *John L. Lewis: A Biography* (New York: Quadrangle/New York Times Book Co., 1977), 181–82.
47. Gerald T. Dunne, *Hugo Black and the Judicial Revolution* (New York: Simon and Schuster, 1977), 145.
48. Ibid., 147–48; Marian C. McKenna, *Franklin Roosevelt and the Great Constitutional War: The Court-Packing Crisis of 1937* (New York: Fordham University Press, 2002), 74–75.
49. Schlesinger, *The Coming of the New Deal*, 94.

50. Frank Freidel, *Franklin D. Roosevelt: Launching the New Deal* (Boston: Little, Brown, 1973), 422–24; Leon H. Keyserling, oral history interview, Harry S. Truman Library, May 3, 1971, Washington, D.C., available at the Truman Presidential Library website, at http://trumanlibrary.org/oralhist/keyserl.htm. The Wagner group included his legislative aide, Simon Rifkind, economist Harold G. Moulton of the Brookings Institution and labor manager Meyer Jacobstein; its plan called for permitting trade associations to draw up codes, grant labor wages and hours protection, and right of labor to collectively bargain. The Department of Commerce group was headed by Assistant Secretary John Dickinson, and associated with Frances Perkins and Rexford G. Tugwell, Jerome Frank, and Frank's aide, Leon Keyserling. Tugwell wrote the draft, including enforcement provisions, of levying a processing tax like that found in the recently enacted agriculture legislation. The Moley group included General Hugh Johnson and Donald R. Richberg, who, as legal counsel to railroad unions, had helped draft the Railway Labor Act of 1926. The original draft came from a plan for recovery by Gerard Swope, the president of General Electric. Irving Bernstein, *The New Deal Collective Bargaining Policy* (Berkeley and Los Angeles: University of California Press, 1950), 29–33.
51. The legislation was formulated by Dickinson, Johnson, Wagner, Tugwell, Richberg, Perkins, Charles Wyzanski the labor department's solicitor, and Lewis W. Douglas, the budget director. Freidel, *Franklin D. Roosevelt*, 422–24.
52. J. Joseph Huthmacher, *Senator Robert F. Wagner and the Rise of Urban Liberalism* (New York: Atheneum, 1968), 147; Keyserling Oral History, 5; William E. Leuchtenburg, *Franklin D. Roosevelt and the New Deal, 1932–1940* (New York: Harper and Row, 1963), 107.
53. McKenna, *Franklin Roosevelt and the Great Constitutional War*, 77–78. Section II of the NIRA authorized $3.3 billion to be spent by a new Public Works Administration (PWA) and the Reconstruction Finance Corporation (RFC) to build highways, dams, and federal buildings.
54. Bernard Bellush, *The Failure of the NRA* (New York: Norton, 1975), 1.
55. Huthmacher, *Senator Robert F. Wagner*, 155.
56. For an insider, rambling account, see Hugh S. Johnson, *The Blue Eagle from Egg to Earth* (New York: Doubleday, Doran, 1935).
57. Peter F. Kihss, "Blue Eagle's Defeat Blasted Great Vision," *The Washington Post*, June 3, 1935, B3.
58. Leuchtenburg, *Franklin D. Roosevelt and the New Deal*, 66.
59. Huthmacher, *Senator Robert F. Wagner*, 160. On creation of the NLB, see Edward Berkowitz and Kim McQuaid, *Creating the Welfare State: The Political Economy of Twentieth-Century Reform*, 2nd ed. (New York: Praeger, 1988), 96–101.
60. Ibid., 161; Millis and Brown, *From the Wagner Act to Taft–Hartley*, 23; James A. Gross, *The Making of the National Labor Relations Board*, vol. I: *1933–1937* (Albany: State University of New York Press, 1974), 37–39.
61. Millis and Brown, *From the Wagner Act to Taft–Hartley*, 23–24.
62. Bernstein, *The New Deal Collective Bargaining Policy*, 59.
63. Dubofsky, *The State and Labor in Modern America*, 121.
64. Frances Perkins, *The Roosevelt I Knew* (New York: Viking Press, 1946), 304.
65. Huthmacher, *Senator Robert F. Wagner*, 164–65; Millis and Brown, *From the Wagner Act to Taft–Hartley*, 24; Bernstein, *The New Deal Collective Bargaining Policy*, 57–75.
66. Millis and Brown, *From the Wagner Act to Taft–Hartley*, 25–26.
67. Rhonda F. Levine, *Class Struggle and the New Deal: Industrial Labor, Industrial Capital, and the State* (Lawrence: University Press of Kansas, 1988), 114.
68. Bernstein, *The Lean Years*, 217.
69. Ibid., 217–317; Levine, *Class Struggle and the New Deal*, 115–31.

70. Bellush, *The Failure of the NRA*, 136.

71. Anthony J. Badger, *The New Deal: The Depression Years, 1933–1940* (Chicago: Ivan R. Dee, 2002, 1989), 89–91.

72. Jordan A. Schwarz, *The New Dealers: Power Politics in the Age of Roosevelt* (New York. Alfred A. Knopf, 1993), chapter 4: "Hugh Johnson: Raising Prices," 96–105; Bellush, *The Failure of the NRA*, 136–57.

73. "President Back Today in Unequaled Power as GOP Rout Grows," *The Washington Post*, November 8, 1934, 1.

74. Bernstein, *The Lean Years*, 323.

75. Theodore C. Alford, "New Faces in the Senate: Harry Truman of Missouri," *The Washington Post*, November 12, 1934, 9. Alford, the Washington correspondent for the *Kansas City Star*, said of Truman: "He is not considered brilliant, either as an orator or as a scholar, but has great personal charm and is a tireless worker. He has never had time to develop hobbies."

76. "First Lady Decides to Serve Wine at White House Parties," *The Washington Post*, November 9, 1934, 1. At the press conference announcing this momentous event, Mrs. Roosevelt announced that she would not be indulging, and that just two glasses would be available, not the old practice of having a different wine after each course.

77. McKenna, *Franklin Roosevelt and the Great Constitutional War*, 89.

78. Ibid.

79. Kenneth S. Davis, *FDR: The New Deal Years* (New York: Random House, 1986), 525; for a full discussion of the 1934 legislation, see Bernstein, *The New Deal Collective Bargaining Policy*, 57–75.

80. Bernstein, *The New Deal Collective Bargaining Policy*, 87–88; Gross, *The Making of the National Labor Relations Board*, 130–48.

81. Davis, *FDR: The New Deal Years*, 525; for a full discussion of the 1934 legislation, see Bernstein, *The New Deal Collective Bargaining Policy*, 57–75.

82. Davis, *FDR: The New Deal Years*, 525; Leuchtenburg, *Franklin D. Roosevelt and the New Deal*, 150.

83. Louis Stark, "Wagner Predicts New Labor Risings," *The New York Times*, March 12, 1935, 12; "Wagner Retorts to Labor Bill Foes," *The New York Times*, April 29, 1935, 4.

84. Mark Barenberg, "The Political Economy of the Wagner Act: Power, Symbol, and Workplace Cooperation," *Harvard Law Review* 106 (7) (May, 1993): 1386.

85. "Company Unions Hit Wagner Bill," *The New York Times*, March 27, 1935, 2.

86. Louis Stark, "Labor Mobilizes Congress Lobbies," *The New York Times*, April 30, 1935, 6.

87. Bernstein, *The New Deal Collective Bargaining Policy*, 118.

88. Perkins, *The Roosevelt I Knew*, 239.

89. "High Court Laughs in Schechter Case," *The New York Times*, May 4, 1935, 2.

90. *Schechter* v. *United States*, 295 U.S. 495 (1935).

91. McKenna, *Franklin Roosevelt and the Great Constitutional War*, 102–104; Alpheus T. Mason, *Brandeis: A Free Man's Life* (New York: Viking, 1946), 620. On the same day, the Court, in unanimous opinions, invalidated the Frazier–Lemke Act on mortgage moratoria (*Louisville Bank* v. *Radford*, 295 U.S. 555) and curtailed the president's power to remove members of independent regulatory commissions (*Humphrey's Executor* v. *United States*, 295 U.S. 602). William E. Leuchtenberg, *The Supreme Court Reborn: The Constitutional Revolution in the Age of Roosevelt* (New York: Oxford University Press, 1995), 89.

92. McKenna, *Franklin Roosevelt and the Great Constitutional War*, 113–14; Leuchtenberg, *The Supreme Court Reborn*, 90; Davis, *FDR: The New Deal Years*, 514–21.

93. Bellush, *The Failure of the NRA*, 172.

94. Huthmacher, *Senator Robert F. Wagner*, 201; Robert S. McElvaine, *The Great Depression: America, 1929–1941* (New York: Times Books, 1984), 259–63; Otis L. Graham, Jr., "Historians and the New Deals: 1944–1960," *The Social Studies* 54 (April 1963): 133–40; Schlesinger, *Politics of Upheaval*, 392–408.

95. Jerold S. Auerbach, *Labor and Liberty: The La Follette Committee and the New Deal* (Indianapolis: Bobbs-Merrill, 1966), 53.

96. Dexter Perkins, *The New Age of Franklin Roosevelt, 1932–1945* (Chicago: University of Chicago Press, 1964), 39; Cortner, *The Jones & Laughlin Case*, 61–62.

97. Cortner, *The Jones & Laughlin Case*, 65.

98. "NAM Historical Highlights," National Association of Manufacturers website, available at http://www.nam.org. NAM blandly described its activities of seventy years ago: "In 1934, concern over many of President Franklin Roosevelt's New Deal proposals and key labor issues prompted the NAM to launch a public relations campaign 'for the dissemination of sound American doctrines to the public.'"

99. "58 Lawyers Hold Labor Act Invalid," *The New York Times*, September 19, 1935, 1.

100. "Labor Act Ruling Attacked by Ickes," *The New York Times*, September 20, 1935, 13.

101. Auerbach, *Labor and Liberty*, 56–59.

102. Patrick J. Maney, *"Young Bob" La Follette: A Biography of Robert M. La Follette, Jr., 1895–1953* (Columbia: University of Missouri Press, 1978), 171–72; Bernstein, *The Turbulent Years*, 450–51. La Follette, who succeeded his father, began service in the Senate as a Republican in 1925; in 1934 he was re-elected to the Senate on the Progressive party ticket, then ran, but lost, as a Republican in 1946. Gross, *The Making of the National Labor Relations Board*, 212–23. On La Follette's Republican primary loss to Joseph McCarthy and La Follette's later suicide, see Patrick J. Maney, "Joe McCarthy's First Victim," *Virginia Quarterly Review* (Summer, 2001).

103. Maney, *"Young Bob" La Follette*, 211.

104. Auerbach, *Labor and Liberty*, and Maney, *"Young Bob" La Follette*, chs. 10 and 12.

105. Maney, *"Young Bob" La Follette*, 170.

106. Ibid., 176.

107. Ibid., 185.

108. *United States* v. *Butler*, 297 U.S. 1 (1936), overturned the Agricultural Adjustment Act; *Carter* v. *Carter Coal Company*, 298 U.S. 238 (1936), struck down the Guffey Bituminous Coal Act; and *Morehead* v. *New York ex rel. Tipaldo*, 298 U.S. 587 (1936), overturned the New York minimum wage law.

109. Leuchtenberg, *The Supreme Court Reborn*, 215.

110. Cortner, *The Jones & Laughlin Case*, 105–106.

111. Kennedy, *Freedom from Fear*, 330.

112. Kelly and Harbison, *The American Constitution*, 759–62.

113. Leuchtenberg, *The Supreme Court Reborn*, 133–34.

114. McKenna, *Franklin Roosevelt and the Great Constitutional War*, 285.

115. Ibid., 280–337; Leuchtenburg, *The Supreme Court Reborn*, 132–62; Kelly and Harbison, *The American Constitution*, 761–64.

116. *West Coast Hotel* v. *Parrish*, 300 U.S. 379 (1937), at 391. This decision overruled *Adkins* v. *Children's Hospital*, 261 U.S. 525 (1923).

117. Kelly and Harbison, *The American Constitution*, 763–64; McKenna, *Franklin Roosevelt and the Great Constitutional War*, 419. On the "switch in time" issue, see the major arguments in Leuchtenberg, *The Supreme Court Reborn*, 310 n. 17.

118. Cortner, *The Jones & Laughlin Cases*, 79. *NLRB* v. *Jones & Laughlin Steel Corp.*, 301 U.S. 1 (1937); *NLRB* v. *Fruehauf Trailer Co.*, 301 U.S. 49 (1937); *NLRB* v. *Friedman-Harry Marks Clothing Co.*, 301 U.S. 58 (1937); *Associated Press Co.* v. *NLRB*, 301 U.S. 103 (1937); and *Washington, Virginia and Maryland Coach Co.* v. *NLRB*, 301 U.S. 142 (1937).

119. Cortner, *The Jones & Laughlin Cases*, 122.
120. Gross, *The Making of the National Labor Relations Board*, 189.
121. 301 U.S. at 37.
122. Ibid.
123. Arthur Krock, "Five Cases Decided," and Louis Stark, "Labor Will Drive for a New Power," *The New York Times*, April 13, 1937, 1.
124. Gross, *The Making of the National Labor Relations Board*, 237–38.
125. "The Court Surveys Anew the Sweep of Industry," *The New York Times*, April 18, 1937, 61.
126. Bernstein, *The Turbulent Years*, 663.
127. Dubofsky and Van Tine, *John L. Lewis*, 205.
128. Lichtenstein, *Labor's War at Home*, 10.
129. Bernstein, *The Turbulent Years*, 453–54; Kenneth Warren, *Big Steel: The First Century of the United States Steel Corporation, 1901–2001* (Pittsburgh: University of Pittsburgh Press, 2001). By 2005, U.S. Steel had shrunk to 42,000 employees.
130. Bernstein, *The Turbulent Years*, 519–54, quote at 525.
131. Nelson Lichtenstein, *The Most Dangerous Man in Detroit: Walter Reuther and the Fate of American Labor* (New York: Basic Books, 1995), 84–87; Stephen H. Norwood, *Strikebreaking and Intimidation: Mercenaries and Maculinity in Twentieth-Century America* (Chapel Hill: University of North Carolina Press, 2002), ch. 5: "Harry Bennett, the Cult of Muscularity, and Anti-Labor Terror, 1920–1945."
132. Walter Galenson, *The CIO Challenge to the AFL: A History of the American Labor Movement, 1935–1941* (Cambridge: Harvard University Press, 1960), ch. 2; Kennedy, *Freedom from Fear*, 317–19.
133. Quote from Bernstein, *The Turbulent Years*, 695; Galenson, *The CIO Challenge to the AFL*, 43; Kennedy, *Freedom from Fear*, 316.
134. Dulles and Dubofsky, *Labor in America*, 271.
135. *NLRB* v. *MacKay Radio and Telegraph*, 304 U.S. 333 (1939), on replacement workers; *NLRB* v. *Fansteel Metallurgical Corp.*, 306 U.S. 240 (1939), on sit-down strikes. R. Alton Lee, *Eisenhower and Landrum–Griffin: A Study in Labor-Management Politics* (Lexington: University Press of Kentucky, 1990), 2–3.
136. James T. Patterson, *Congressional Conservatism and the New Deal: The Growth of the Conservative Coalition in Congress, 1933–1939* (Westport, Conn.: Greenwood Press, 1981, 1967), 316–17; James T. Patterson, *Mr. Republican: A Biography of Robert A. Taft* (Boston: Houghton Mifflin Company, 1972), 353.
137. Milton Derber, *The American Idea of Industrial Democracy, 1865–1965* (Urbana: University of Illinois Press, 1970), 368–69.
138. James T. Patterson, *Grand Expectations: The United States, 1945–1974* (New York: Oxford University Press, 1996), 43.
139. Robert J. Donovan, *Conflict and Crisis: The Presidency of Harry S. Truman, 1945–1948* (New York: W. W. Norton, 1977), 209–18.
140. Michael K. Honey, "Operation Dixie, the Red Scare, and the Defeat of Southern Labor Organizing," in Robert W. Cherny, William Issel, and Kieran Walsh Taylor, eds., *American Labor and the Cold War: Grassroots Politics and Postwar Political Culture* (New Brunswick: Rutgers University Press, 2004), 216.
141. Dulles and Dubofsky, *Labor in America*, 344.
142. R. Alton Lee, *Truman and Taft–Hartley: A Question of Mandate* (Lexington: University of Kentucky Press, 1966), 15; Patterson, *Mr. Republican*, 353.
143. Robert W. Cherny, William Issel, and Kieran Walsh Taylor, "Introduction," in *American Labor and the Cold War*, ed. Cherny et al., 2–3; Robert A. Taft, "The Taft-Hartley Act: A Favorable View," *Annals of the American Academy of Political and Social Science* 274 (March 1951): 195–99. The Taft–Hartley Act was officially the Labor–Management Relations Act of 1947.

144. Lee, *Truman and Taft–Hartley*, 1.
145. Donovan, *Conflict and Crisis*, 301; Lee, *Truman and Taft–Hartley*, 80–81.
146. Huthmacher, *Senator Robert F. Wagner*, 337.
147. Alonzo L. Hamby, *Beyond the New Deal: Harry S. Truman and American Liberalism* (New York: Columbia University Press, 1973), 185.
148. Huthmacher, *Senator Robert F. Wagner*, 338.
149. Quoted in Dulles and Dubofsky, *Labor in America*, 361.
150. Adam K. McAdams, *Power and Politics in Labor Legislation* (New York: Columbia University Press, 1964), 1.
151. Walter Galenson, *The American Labor Movement, 1955–1995* (Westport, Conn.: Greenwood Press, 1996), 7–9.
152. Lee, *Eisenhower and Landrum–Griffin*, viii.
153. McAdams, *Power and Politics in Labor Legislation*, 1.
154. U.S. Census Bureau, *Statistical Abstract of the United States: 2006*, table 648: Union Members by Selected Characteristic: 2004.
155. North Carolina (2.7 percent); South Carolina (3.0 percent); Arkansas and Mississippi (both 4.8 percent). U.S. Census Bureau, *Statistical Abstract of the United States: 2006*, table 649: Labor Union Membership by State: 1983 and 2004.
156. Hoyt M. Wheeler, *The Future of the American Labor Movement* (Cambridge: Cambridge University Press, 2002), 3–4; Kate Bronfenbrenner and Tom Juravich, "It Takes More Than House Calls: Organizing to Win with a Comprehensive Union-Building Strategy," in Kate Bronfenbrenner, Sheldon Friedmin, Richard W. Hurd, Rudolph A. Oswald, and Ronald L. Seeber, eds., *Organizing to Win* (Ithaca, N.Y.: ILR Press, 1997), 19–36; and Michael Goldfield, *The Decline of Organized Labor in the United States* (Chicago: University of Chicago Press, 1987), ch. 6. For an analysis of the scholarly work on the NLRA during its fifty years with suggestions for future research, see John Thomas Delaney, David Lewin, and Donna Sockell, "The NLRA at Fifty: A Research Appraisal and Agenda," *Industrial and Labor Relations Review* 39 (1) (October 1985): 46–75.

6 THE GRAND CONTRACT: THE SOCIAL SECURITY ACT OF 1935

Epigraph quotes from Roosevelt in "Social Security: Will It Replace the Hazards of the Machine Age?" *The Washington Post*, August 18, 1935, B3; William E. Leuchtenburg, *Franklin D. Roosevelt and the New Deal: 1932–1940* (New York: Harper and Row, 1963), 132, and Gaylord Nelson, "Foreward," to Robert M. Ball, *Social Security Today and Tomorrow* (New York: Columbia University Press, 1978), vii.

1. Carlos A. Schwantes, *Coxey's Army: An American Odyssey* (Lincoln: University of Nebraska Press, 1985).
2. Larry DeWitt, "Historical Background and Development of Social Security," from the Social Security Administration website, http://ssa.gov/history/briefhistory 3.html. The last Civil War pension, going to a surviving widow, was paid out in 1999. On Civil War pensions, see Theda Skocpol, *Protecting Soldiers and Mothers: The Political Origins of Social Policy in the United States* (Cambridge: Belknap Press of Harvard University, 1992), and Dixon Wecter, *When Johnny Comes Marching Home* (Cambridge: Houghton Mifflin Company, 1944).
3. Edwin Amenta and Bruce G. Carruthers, "The Formative Years of U.S. Social Spending Policies: Theories of the Welfare State and the American States During the Great Depression," *American Sociological Review* 53 (October, 1988): 661; Joseph P. Harris, "The Social Security Program of the United States," *American Political Science Review* 30 (3) (June, 1936): 460–62; Roy Lubove, *The Struggle for Social Security, 1900–1935* (Cambridge: Harvard University Press, 1948), 27–28.

4. Edward Berkowitz and Kim McQuaid, *Creating the Welfare State: The Political Economy of Twentieth-Century Reform*, rev. 2nd ed. (New York: Praeger, 1988), 46; Lubove, *The Struggle for Social Security*, 61.

5. Paul A. Rauschenbush, "The Wisconsin Idea: Unemployment Reserves," *Annuals of the American Academy of Political and Social Science* 170, Social Insurance (November, 1933): 65–75; on John R. Commons, Nancy J. Altman, *The Battle for Social Security: From FDR's Vision to Bush's Gamble* (Hoboken, N.J.: John Wiley and Sons, 2005), 12–20; and Arthur M. Schlesinger, Jr., *The Age of Roosevelt: The Coming of the New Deal* (Boston: Houghton Mifflin Company, 1958), 301–303.

6. Schlesinger, *The Coming of the New Deal*, 301.

7. J. Joseph Huthmacher, *Senator Robert F. Wagner and the Rise of Urban Liberalism* (New York: Atheneum, 1968), 174.

8. Schlesinger, *The Coming of the New Deal*, 301.

9. *Report to the President of the Committee on Economic Security* (1935), 68, table 13, cited in Harris, "The Social Security Program of the United States," 470; Robert K. Burns, "Economic Aspects of Aging and Retirement," *American Journal of Sociology* 59 (4) (January, 1954): 384.

10. Fraternal Order of Eagles website, www.foe.com. When Social Security eventually passed, one of the ceremonial signing pens went to the Fraternal Order of Eagles, from Roosevelt, himself a member of that organization. Senator Wagner and Representative Lewis were also members of the Fraternal Order of Eagles.

11. DeWitt, "Historical Background and Development of Social Security."

12. Edwin E. Witte, "Old Age Security in the Social Security Act," *Journal of Political Economy* 45 (1) (February, 1937): 7.

13. Edwin Amenta, *When Movements Matter: The Townsend Plan and the Rise of Social Security* (Princeton: Princeton University Press, 2006); Edwin Amenta, Bruce G. Carruthers, and Yvonne Zylan, "A Hero for the Aged? The Townsend Movement, the Political Mediation Model, and U.S. Old-Age Policy, 1934–1950," *American Journal of Sociology* 98 (2) (September, 1992): 315; Robert S. McElvaine, *The Great Depression: America, 1929–1941* (New York: Times Books, 1984), 241–43; Edward D. Berkowitz, *America's Welfare State: From Roosevelt to Reagan* (Baltimore: Johns Hopkins University Press, 1991), 18–21; Michael E. Parrish, *Anxious Decades: America in Prosperity and Depression* (New York: Norton, 1992), 329. The $200 a month in 1933 would be $2,709 a month in 2005.

14. McElvaine, *The Great Depression*, 242; Leuchtenburg, *Franklin D. Roosevelt and the New Deal*, 106.

15. McElvaine, *The Great Depression*, 242.

16. Altman, *The Battle for Social Security*, 26–27; Greg Mitchell, *Campaign of the Century: Upton Sinclair's E.P.I.C. Race for Governor of California and the Birth of Media Politics* (New York: Atlantic Monthly Press, 1991). One year before the gubernatorial election, Sinclair optimistically wrote a book, *I, Governor of California and How I Ended Poverty, A True Story of the Future*. After his defeat, the prolific Sinclair wrote *I, Candidate for Governor and How I Got Licked*. For a copy of his EPIC plan, see the Social Security Administration website, http://www.ssa.gov/history/epic.html.

17. T. Harry Williams, *Huey Long* (New York: Alfred A. Knopf, 1970), ch. 24; Leuchtenburg, *Franklin D. Roosevelt and the New Deal*, 98–100; Glen Jeansonne, *Gerald L. K. Smith: Minister of Hate* (New Haven: Yale University Press, 1988), 46–63. For Long's February 23, 1934, "Every Man a King" address, see the U.S. Senate website, http://www.senate.gov/artandhistory/history/common/generic/Speeches_Long_EveryManKing.htm.

18. McElvaine, *The Great Depression*, 238; Alan Brinkley, *Voices of Protest: Huey Long, Father Coughlin and the Great Depression* (New York: Vintage, 1983), ch. 4. In the Spring of

2006 the largest talk show audience belonged to Rush Limbaugh (13.5 million-plus per week), Sean Hannity (12.5 million-plus), Michael Savage (8.25 million-plus), and Dr. Laura Schlessinger (8 million plus). By the early 2000s, total U.S. population had topped 300 million; it was 122 million in the early 1930s. Survey from *Talkers* magazine, online at its website, http://www.talkers.com.

19. Anthony J. Badger, *The New Deal: The Depression Years, 1933–1940* (Chicago: Ivan R. Dee, 2002, 1989), 290.

20. Brinkley, *Voices of Protest*, 193.

21. Frances Perkins, *The Roosevelt I Knew* (New York: Viking Press, 1946), 278.

22. Altman, *The Battle for Social Security*, 27–28.

23. Franklin D. Roosevelt, Address to Congress, June 8, 1934, available at the Social Security Administration website, http://ssa.gov/history/fdrstmts.html.

24. Altman, *The Battle for Social Security*, 26–27.

25. Paul H. Douglas, *Social Security in the United States: An Analysis and Appraisal of the Federal Social Security Act* (New York: Whittlesey House, 1936), 84–85; Harris, "The Social Security Program of the United States," 470.

26. Perkins, *The Roosevelt I Knew*, 282–83.

27. Berkowitz and McQuaid, *Creating the Welfare State*, 115; Harris, "The Social Security Program of the United States," 462.

28. Witte wrote extensively on the creation and impact of the social security legislation. The most important writing is Edwin E. Witte, *The Development of the Social Security Act* (Madison: University of Wisconsin Press, 1962).

29. Harris, "The Social Security Program of the United States," 463.

30. Franklin D. Roosevelt, Address to Advisory Council of the Committee on Economic Security on the Problems of Economic and Social Security, November 14, 1934, available at the Social Security Administration website, http://ssa.gov/history/fdrstmts.html.

31. Perkins, *The Roosevelt I Knew*, 286; speech by Frances Perkins recounting this story before SSA employees, October 23, 1962, available at the "A Tea Party That Changed History," at the Social Security Administration website, http://www.ssa.gov/history/tea.htm.

32. Edwin E. Witte, "Social Security: A Wild Dream or a Practical Plan?" (1938) in Robert J. Lampman, ed., *Social Security Perspectives: Essays by Edwin E. Witte* (Madison: University of Wisconsin Press, 1972), 3, and Edwin E. Witte, "Postwar Social Security," ch. xv in Seymour E. Harris, ed., *Postwar Economic Problems* (New York: McGraw-Hill, 1943), 263–77, reprinted in *Social Security Perspectives*, ed. Lampman, 15–29, at 15.

33. Douglas, *Social Security in the United States*, 86. Douglas later became U.S. Senator from Illinois, serving from 1949 to 1967.

34. Theda Skocpol and Edwin Amenta, "Did Capitalists Shape Social Security?" *American Sociological Review* 50 (4) (August, 1985): 572; Douglas, *Social Security in the United States*, 95–96; Epstein quote from "Hits Payroll Tax for Age Pensions," *The New York Times*, February 8, 1935, 4; Arthur J. Altmeyer, *The Formative Years of Social Security* (Madison: University of Wisconsin Press, 1966), 33.

35. Long quoted in Robert C. Albright, "Leaders Ask For Caution on 'Security,'" *The Washington Post*, January 20, 1935, 1.

36. Merrill C. Murray, "Social Insurance Perspectives: Background Philosophy and Early Program Developments," *Journal of Insurance* 30 (2) (June, 1963): 190–91; and Douglas, *Social Security in the United States*, 97–99.

37. Schlesinger, *The Coming of the New Deal*, 308–309. On the payroll tax, see Mark H. Leff, "Taxing the 'Forgotten Man': The Politics of Social Security Finance in the New Deal," *Journal of American History* 70 (2) (September 1983): 359–81.

38. "See Vast Loan Use for Security Fund," *The New York Times*, February 9, 1935, 2; Schlesinger, *The Coming of the New Deal*, 310.
39. Berkowitz and McQuaid, *Creating the Welfare State*, 126.
40. Witte, "Old Age Security in the Social Security Act," 11.
41. Ibid., 12.
42. Quoted in McElvaine, *The Great Depression*, 257.
43. Robert C. Lieberman, "Race, Institutions, and the Administration of Social Policy," *Social Science History* 19 (Winter, 1995): 511–42; Gareth Davies and Martha Derthick, "Race and Social Welfare Policy: The Social Security Act of 1935," *Political Science Quarterly* 112 (2) (1997), quote from 220; Jill S. Quadagno, *The Color of Money: How Racism Undermined the War on Poverty* (New York: Oxford University Press, 1994); Linda Gordon, *Pitied but Not Entitled: Single Mothers and the History of Welfare, 1890–1935* (Ithaca: Cornell University Press, 1994).
44. Davies and Derthick, "Race and Social Welfare Policy," 224–26, Witte quoted on 225.
45. Elliot A. Rosen, *Roosevelt, the Great Depression, and the Economics of Recovery* (Charlottesville: University of Virginia Press, 2005), 168–69.
46. "Business Men Hear Wagner Back Bill," *The New York Times*, March 8, 1935, 5.
47. Witte, *The Development of the Social Security Act*, 95; "Townsend Queried on Pension Plan," *The New York Times*, February 17, 1935, 18.
48. Perkins, *The Roosevelt I Knew*, 278–79.
49. "House Routs Radical Bills for Security," *The Washington Post*, April 19, 1935, 1; Witte, *The Development of the Social Security Act*, 98–99.
50. Ibid.
51. Schlesinger, *The Coming of the New Deal*, 311.
52. Larry DeWitt, "Never a Finished Thing: A Brief Biography of Arthur Joseph Altmeyer: The Man FDR Called 'Mr. Social Security,'" available at the Social Security Administration website, http://www.ssa.gov/history/bioaja.html.
53. Schlesinger, *The Coming of the New Deal*, 311.
54. Perkins, *The Roosevelt I Knew*, 301.
55. He is author of *The Formative Years of Social Security*.
56. Wilbur J. Cohen, "Edwin E. Witte (1887–1960): Father of Social Security," *Industrial and Labor Relations Review* 14 (1) (October, 1960): 7–9.
57. Altmeyer, *The Formative Years of Social Security*, 42.
58. Franklin Waltman, Jr., "Roosevelt Signs Security Bill to Benefit 30 Million Citizens," *The Washington Post*, August 15, 1935, 1.
59. Frances Perkins, "Social Security: The Foundation," *The New York Times*, August 18, 1935, SM1.
60. Schlesinger, *The Coming of the New Deal*, 313; McElvaine, *The Great Depression*, 257.
61. Altmeyer, *The Formative Years of Social Security*, 43.
62. Perkins, *The Roosevelt I Knew*, 299–300.
63. Eric R. Kingson and Edward D. Berkowitz, *Social Security and Medicare: A Policy Primer* (Westport, Conn.: Auburn House, 1993), 27.
64. Gerald D. Nash, Noel H. Pugach, and Richard F. Tomasson, eds., *Social Security: The First Half Century* (Albuquerque: University of New Mexico Press, 1988), 14.
65. Sylvester J. Scheiber and John B. Shoven, *The Real Deal: The History and Future of Social Security* (New Haven: Yale University Press, 1999), 53–54.
66. Leuchtenburg, *Franklin D. Roosevelt and the New Deal*, 195. Ronald Reagan in 1984 accomplished an equally impressive feat, capturing every state except Minnesota and the District of Columbia, in defeating Walter Mondale, 525 to 13.
67. Marian C. McKenna, *Franklin Roosevelt and the Great Constitutional War: The Court Packing Crisis of 1937* (New York: Fordham University Press, 2002), 432–34; Larry DeWitt, "The Supreme Court Rulings on the Social Security Act," Social Security

Administration, 1999, available at the Social Security Administration website at http://www.ssa.gov/history/court.html.

68. McKenna, *Franklin Roosevelt and the Great Constitutional War*, 433. *Steward Machine Company* v. *Davis*, 301 U.S. 548 (1937); *Helvering et al. v. Davis*, 301 U.S. 619 (1937). A third decision was *Carmichael* v. *Southern Coal & Coke and Gulf States Paper*, 301 U.S. 495 (1937).

69. William Haber and Wilbur J. Cohen, eds., *Readings in Social Security* (New York: Prentice-Hall, 1948), 145; Altmeyer, *The Formative Years of Social Security*, 83.

70. Bruce J. Dierenfield, *Keeper of the Rules: Congressman Howard W. Smith of Virginia* (Charlottesville: University Press of Virginia, 1987), 57.

71. Altmeyer, *The Formative Years of Social Security*, 86–87; "The Candler Building: Home of Social Security 1936–1960," Social Security Administration website, http://www.ssa.gov/history/ssa/CandlerFactSheet.htm.

72. James E. Pate, "Administering Social Security," *Social Forces* 17 (3) (March, 1939): 333.

73. Schlesinger, *The Coming of the New Deal*, 315. The first chairman of the Social Security Board was John G. Winant, later the U.S. Ambassador to Great Britain. Altmeyer took over as chairman in 1937.

74. DeWitt, "Never a Finished Thing," 14.

75. Berkowitz and McQuaid, *Creating the Welfare State*, 131.

76. Included in the Social Security Advisory Group were Gerard Swope of General Election, Marion B. Folsom of Eastman, Kodak, and E. R. Stettinius of U.S. Steel. Labor leaders included Sidney Hillman of the Amalgamated Clothing Workers and Philip Murray of the CIO. Paul Douglas of the University of Chicago and Edwin E. Witte also were members. Edward D. Berkowitz, "The First Advisory Council and the 1939 Amendments," in Berkowitz, ed., *Social Security After Fifty* (Westport, Conn.: Greenwood Press, 1987), 55–78.

77. On the work of the 1939 Advisory Council, and subsequent councils, see Brown, *An American Philosophy of Social Security*, ch. 3. Letter from Franklin D. Roosevelt to Arthur J. Altmeyer, April 28, 1938, available at the Social Security Administration website, http://www.ssa.gov/history/fdrstmts.html, 20.

78. "Legislative History: 1939 Amendments," Social Security Administration website, http://www.ssa.gov/history/1939amends.html.

79. Franklin D. Roosevelt, "Presidential Statement on Signing Some Amendments to the Social Security Act, August 11, 1939," available at the Social Security Administration website, http://ssa.gov/history/fdrstmts.html.

80. Robert J. Rosenthal, "Organized Labor's Social Security Program: 1948," *Social Forces* 26 (3) (March, 1948): 337; Martha Derthick, *Policymaking for Social Security* (Washington: Brookings Institution, 1979), ch. 5.

81. DeWitt, "Historical Background and Development of Social Security," 29.

82. Ibid., 27.

83. Ibid.

84. Edward D. Berkowitz, *Mr. Social Security: The Life of Wilbur J. Cohen* (Lawrence: University Press of Kansas, 1995), 70; Wilbur J. Cohen, "Aspects of Legislative History of the Social Security Act Amendments of 1950," *Industrial and Labor Relations Review* 4 (2) (January 1951): 187–99.

85. Berkowitz, *Mr. Social Security*, 72–76.

86. Social Security Administration, *Brief History of Social Security*, 29. On programs for the handicapped, see Edward D. Berkowitz, *Disabled Policy: America's Programs for the Handicapped* (Cambridge: Cambridge University Press, 1987).

87. Social Security Administration, *Brief History of Social Security*, 30.

88. Derthick, *Policymaking for Social Security*, 381–84.

89. Ball, *Social Security Today and Tomorrow*, 13–14 n. 14.

90. Ibid., 14.
91. See Edward D. Berkowitz, *Robert Ball and the Politics of Social Security* (Madison: University of Wisconsin Press, 2003).
92. "Summary of Social Security Amendments of 1983," available at the Social Security Administration website, http://www.ssa.gov/history/1983amend.html; and Geoffrey Kollman, *Social Security: Summary of Major Changes in the Old-Age Benefits Program*, (Washington, D.C.: Congressional Research Service, U.S. Congress, 2000).
93. Social Security Administration, *Brief History of Social Security*, 33; *Budget of the United States Government, Fiscal Year 2008, Social Security Administration*, available at http://www.gpoaccess.gov/usbudget/fy08/pdf/budget/ssa.pdf.
94. Jeffrey H. Birnbaum, "Private-Account Concept Grew From Obscure Roots," *The Washington Post*, February 22, 2005, A1.
95. Peter J. Ferrara, *Social Security: The Inherent Contradiction* (San Francisco: Cato Institute, 1980). Ferrara also wrote *Social Security: Averting the Crisis* (Washington, D.C.: Cato Institute, 1982) and *Social Security Reform: The Family [Security] Plan* (Washington, D.C.: Heritage Foundation, 1982).
96. Stuart Butler and Peter Germanis, "Achieving a 'Leninist' Strategy," *Cato Journal* 3 (2) (Fall, 1983): 548, available at the Cato Institute website, at http://www.cato.org/pubs/journal/cj3n2/cj3n2-11.pdf.
97. Birnbaum, "Private-Account Concept Grew From Obscure Roots," A1.
98. Roger Lowenstein, "A Question of Numbers," *The New York Times Magazine*, January 16, 2005, 40; Stephen Moore, *Bullish on Bush: How George Bush's Ownership Society Will Make America Stronger* (New York: Madison Books, 2004).
99. Robert Pear, "Social Security Enlisted to Push Its Own Revision," *The New York Times*, January 16, 2005, 1; Daniel Gross, "Social Security Bashing: An Historical Perspective," *The New York Times*, January 16, 2005, 6; Jennifer Jerit and Jason Barabas, "Bankrupt Rhetoric: How Misleading Information Affects Knowledge about Social Security," *Public Opinion Quarterly* 70 (3) (Fall 2006): 278–303; Joshua Green, "The Rove Presidency," *The Atlantic*, September 2007, 52–72.
100. "Social Security Around the World," *The Washington Post*, April 11, 2005. Glenn Frankel, "For Many, It's Back to the State" (on Britain), and Monte Reel, "A Safety Net with Some Holes" (on Chile). Academic studies of privatization include Martin Feldstein, ed., *Privatizing Social Security* (Chicago: University of Chicago Press, 1998); with chapters on Chile, Sebastian Edwards, "The Chilean Pension Reform: A Pioneering Program," 33–62; and Britain, Alan Budd and Nigel Campbell, "The Roles of the Public and Private Sectors in the U.K. Pension System," 99–134; Jonathan Gruber and David A. Wise, eds., *Social Security and Retirement around the World* (Chicago: University of Chicago Press, 1999).
101. Among the many calls for reform is Peter A. Diamond and Peter R. Orszag, *Saving Social Security: A Balanced Approach* (Washington, D.C.: Brookings Institution, 2004). A summary of recent legislative action on Social Security reform is Dawn Nuschler, *Social Security Reform* (Washington, D.C.: Congressional Research Service, Library of Congress, 2006).
102. *FY 2008 Budget, Social Security Administration*.
103. Heather Boushey, *Social Security: The Most Important Anti-Poverty Program for Children* (Washington, D.C.: Center for Economic and Policy Research, 2005).
104. Benjamin I. Page, "Is Social Security Reform Ready for the American Public?" in *Social Security and Medicare*, eds. Sheila Burke, Eric Kingson, and Uwe Reinhardt (Washington, D.C.: National Academy of Social Insurance, 2000), 188.
105. Quote from 1976, available at the Hubert H. Humphrey Institute, University of Minnesota website, http://www.hhh.umn.edu/humphrey-forum/quot.htm.

7 THE PROMISE TO AMERICA'S VETERANS:
THE GI BILL OF 1944

Epigraph quote from Clark Kerr, "Expanding Access and Changing Missions: The Federal Role in U.S. Higher Education," *The Educational Record* 75 (4) (Fall, 1994): 27; quote from Peter F. Drucker, *Post-Capitalist Society* (New York: Harper-Business, 1993), 3. The term "GI" has long been associated with American servicemen. "GI" originally meant "galvanized iron," a term used by U.S. Army clerks to designate items such as a trash can (GI can); then it was used to describe "government-issued" items, such as clothing or equipment; later it became a colloquial expression for members of the armed services, especially enlisted soldiers. *Webster's New World Dictionary of the American Language*, Second College Edition (New York: Prentice Hall Press, 1986).

1. William H. Glasson, *Federal Military Pensions in the United States* (New York: Oxford University Press, 1918), 12–17. In 1624, twelve years before the Plymouth Colony's action, the General Assembly of Virginia passed a series of laws, one of which contained a pension provision. However, that law did not receive the necessary ratification from the parent company in England; thus the Plymouth Colony's action is credited as the first pension in the colonies, at 14.

2. Richard H. Kohn, "The Social History of the American Soldier: A Review and Prospectus for Research," *The American Historical Review* 86 (3) (June, 1981): 558, and Ron Chernow, *Alexander Hamilton* (New York: Penguin Press, 2004), 176–77.

3. Glasson, *Federal Military Pensions in the United States*, 19.

4. *United States Statutes at Large*, 2d Cong., 1st Sess., 273.

5. Glasson, *Federal Military Pensions in the United States*, 96.

6. Michael J. Bennett, *When Dreams Came True: The GI Bill and the Making of Modern America* (Washington, D.C.: Brassey's, 1996), 37.

7. Glasson, *Federal Military Pensions in the United States*, 96.

8. James W. Oberly, "Gray-Haired Lobbyists: War of 1812 Veterans and the Politics of Bounty Land Grants," *Journal of the Early Republic* 5 (1) (Spring, 1985): 35. See also, James W. Oberly, *Sixty Million Acres: American Veterans and the Public Lands before the Civil War* (Kent, Ohio: Kent State University Press, 1990).

9. Oberly, "Gray-Haired Lobbyists," 36–47.

10. Ibid., 58.

11. Wallace E. Davies, "The Mexican War Veterans as an Organized Group," *The Mississippi Valley Historical Review* 35 (2) (September, 1948): 221.

12. William H. Glasson, "The National Pension System as Applied to the Civil War and the War with Spain," *Annals of the American Academy of Political and Social Science* 19 (March, 1902): 222.

13. Donald L. McMurry, "The Political Significance of the Pension Question, 1885–1897," *The Mississippi Valley Historical Review* 9 (1) (June, 1922): 23–26. The Confederate veteran received virtually nothing. As Dixon Wecter put it, "His contract was null and void. His government, the party of the first part, existed no longer. Not until years later did small state pensions begin." Dixon Wecter, *When Johnny Comes Marching Home* (Cambridge: Houghton Mifflin Company, 1944), 119–20.

14. McMurry, "The Political Significance of the Pension Question, 1885–1897," 23.

15. Kenneth E. Cox, "The Greatest Legislation," *The American Legion Magazine*, June 2004, excerpted on the U. S. Congress, House Committee on Veterans' Affairs website, http://veterans.house.gov/benefits/gi60y/greatleg.html, and Glasson, "The National Pension System as Applied to the Civil War and the War with Spain," 205.

16. McMurry, "The Political Significance of the Pension Question, 1885–1897," 28 n. 22.

17. Larry M. Logue, "Union Veterans and Their Government: The Effects of Public Policies on Private Lives," *Journal of Interdisciplinary History* 22 (3) (Winter, 1992): 426; H. Paul Jeffries, *An Honest President: The Life and Presidencies of Grover Cleveland* (New York: William Morrow, 2000), 163–69, and McMurry, "The Political Significance of the Pension Question, 1885–1897," 29–30.

18. Glasson, "The National Pension System as Applied to the Civil War and the War with Spain," 50.

19. McMurry, "The Political Significance of the Pension Question, 1885–1897," 35–36.

20. Theda Skocpol, *Protecting Soldiers and Mothers: The Political Origins of Social Policy in the United States* (Cambridge: Belknap Press of Harvard University, 1992), 102, and Kohn, "The Social History of the American Soldier," 559.

21. Roy V. Peel, "The 'Separateness' of the Veteran," *Annals of the American Academy of Political and Social Science* (238) (March, 1945): 171.

22. J. M. Stephen Peeps, "A B.A. for the G. I. . . . Why?" *History of Education Quarterly* 24 (4) (Winter, 1984): 515, and Theodore R. Mosch, *The GI Bill: A Breakthrough in Educational and Social Policy in the United States* (Hicksville, N.Y.: Exposition Press, 1975), 15–16.

23. Mosch, *The GI Bill*, 14.

24. Ibid., 23.

25. Ibid., 16.

26. Bennett, *When Dreams Came True*, 47–48.

27. The Veterans of Foreign Wars (VFW), based in Kansas City, Missouri, was created in 1914 through the merger of two organizations, the American Veterans of Foreign Service and the National Society of the Army of the Philippines; those organizations were created to aid veterans of the Spanish–American War (1898) and Philippines Insurrection (1899–1902). "VFW at a Glance," Veterans of Foreign Wars official website, http://www.vfw.org.

28. Bennett, *When Dreams Came True*, 57–58.

29. "House Agrees to Vote Today on Bonus Bill," *The Washington Post*, June 14, 1931, 1.

30. Talcott W. Powell, *Tattered Banners* (New York: Harcourt, Brace and Company, 1933), 6.

31. John W. Killigrew, "The Army and the Bonus Incident," *Military Affairs* 26 (2) (Summer, 1962): 59.

32. Ibid., 59–60.

33. Ibid., 61.

34. John R. M. Wilson, "The Quaker and the Sword: Herbert Hoover's Relations with the Military," *Military Affairs* 38 (2) (April, 1974): 41; see Paul Dickson and Thomas B. Allen, *The Bonus Army: An American Epic* (New York: Walker and Company, 2005).

35. David M. Kennedy, *Freedom from Fear: The American People in Depression and War, 1929–1945* (New York: Oxford University Press, 1999),139; Kenneth S. Davis, *FDR: The New Deal Years, 1933–1937* (New York: Random House, 1986, 1979), 57–59; and Frank Freidel, *Franklin D. Roosevelt: Launching the New Deal* (Boston: Little, Brown, 1973), 244–48.

36. Quoted in Harold M. Hyman, *American Singularity: The 1787 Northwest Ordinance, the 1862 Homestead and Morrill Acts, and the 1944 GI Bill* (Athens, Ga.: The University of Georgia Press, 1986), 64.

37. John Bound and Sarah Turner, "Going to War and Going to College: Did World War II and the GI Bill Increase Educational Attainment for Returning Veterans?" *Journal of Labor Economics* 20 (4) (2002): 788.

38. An earlier presidential committee, the Post-war Manpower Conference (PMC), had studied a variety of veterans and demobilization issues, and had issued its

report in July 1943. Roosevelt had regarded the work of the PMC as preliminary and exploratory. Keith W. Olson, *The GI Bill, the Veterans, and the Colleges* (Lexington: University Press of Kentucky, 1974), 9.

39. Robert C. Albright, "President's Veteran Plan Applauded," *The Washington Post*, July 30, 1943, 1.

40. Mosch, *The GI Bill*, 38.

41. John H. Crider, "President Urges Congress to Back Post-War Education of Veterans," *The New York Times*, October 28, 1943, 1.

42. Roosevelt cited in Peel, "The 'Separateness' of the Veteran," 169.

43. Olson, *The GI Bill, the Veterans, and the Colleges*, 13.

44. Bennett, *When Dreams Came True*, 135.

45. Davis R. B. Ross, *Preparing for Ulysses: Politics and Veterans During World War II* (New York: Columbia University Press, 1969), 99 and 99, n. 42. Ross noted that Omar Ketchum of the Veterans of Foreign Wars (VFW) earlier used the phrase "GI Bill of Rights" on January 12, 1944 during House hearings.

46. Ibid., 94–95.

47. Ibid., 102.

48. Ibid.

49. "Spanish Vets Press for Rise in Pensions," *The Washington Post*, January 10, 1944, 3.

50. Ross, *Preparing for Ulysses*, 104.

51. "Disable Group Fears Long Delay on Claims Under Centralized Service for Veterans," *The New York Times*, May 9, 1944, 34.

52. "Urges Amending 'GI Bill,'" *The Washington Post*, May 15, 1944, 19.

53. Ross, *Preparing for Ulysses*, 90–91.

54. Ibid., 106.

55. "Atherton Assails Rankin for Delay," *The New York Times*, April 22, 1944, 14.

56. Ross, *Preparing for Ulysses*, 108.

57. "House Group Backs 'GI Rights Bill,'" *The New York Times*, May 4, 1944, 17.

58. "Atherton Assails Rankin for Delay," *The New York Times*, April 22, 1944, 14.

59. "Legion Seeks Nation's Aid for GI Bill," *The Washington Post*, March 13, 1944, 4.

60. Mosch, *The GI Bill*, 41.

61. Peel, "The 'Separateness' of the Veteran," 169.

62. Bennett, *When Dreams Came True*, 77–78.

63. Ibid., 79–80.

64. "House Divided on Veterans' Bill," *The New York Times*, May 12, 1944, 10.

65. Kathleen McLaughlin, "House by 387 to 0 Approves GI Bill," *The Washington Post*, May 19, 1944, 20.

66. Ross, *Preparing for Ulysses*, 117, and Bennett, *When Dreams Come True*, 181–92.

67. "Roosevelt Signs "GI Bill of Rights,'" *The New York Times*, June 23, 1944, 1.

68. Mosch, *The GI Bill*, 40.

69. Walter Goodman, *The Committee: The Extraordinary Career of the House Committee on Un-American Activities* (Baltimore, Md.: Penguin Books, 1969), 12.

70. Olson, "The GI Bill and Higher Education," 598.

71. Atherton biographical sketch, Online Archive of California, available at http://www.oac.cdlib.org/finaid/ark:/13030/tf709nb53x/bioghist/39460293.

72. Hyman, *American Singularity*, 65.

73. R. Alton Lee, "The Army 'Mutiny' of 1946," *The Journal of American History* 53 (3) (December, 1966): 556.

74. United States President's Commission on Veteran's Pensions, *The Historical Development of Veterans' Benefits in the United States*, 84t Cong., 2nd sess., House Committee Print No. 244, Staff Report No. 1, May 9, 1956, 54, quoted in Mosch, *The GI Bill*, 1.

75. Mosch, *The GI Bill*, 1.

76. Lee, "The Army 'Mutiny' of 1946," 557.
77. Ibid., 559.
78. Ibid., 561–63.
79. Wecter, *When Johnny Comes Marching Home*, 112, and Lee, "The Army 'Mutiny' of 1946," 557.
80. Bound and Turner, "Going to War and Going to College," 787–90.
81. Elizabeth A. Edmondson, "Without Comment or Controversy: The GI Bill and Catholic Colleges," *Church History* 71 (4) (December, 2002): 826.
82. Joseph Shiffman, "The Education of Negro Soldiers in World War II," *The Journal of Negro Education* 18 (1) (Winter, 1949): 23.
83. Mosch, *The GI Bill*, 23.
84. Ibid., 24.
85. Edwin Kiester, Jr., "The GI Bill May Be the Best Deal Ever Made by Uncle Sam," *Smithsonian* 25 (8) (November, 1994): 131, and Edmondson, "Without Comment or Controversy," 832.
86. Quoted in Olson, "The GI Bill and Higher Education," 604.
87. Ibid. and Olson, *The GI Bill, the Veterans, and the Colleges*, 25.
88. Kiester, "The GI Bill May Be the Best Deal Ever Made by Uncle Sam," 131, also, Marc Leepson, "The Big One," *GW Magazine* (Fall, 1995): 13.
89. Edmondson, "Without Comment or Controversy," 822.
90. Olson, "The GI Bill and Higher Education," 596.
91. Chester E. Finn, Jr., *Scholars, Dollars, and Bureaucrats* (Washington, D.C.: Brookings Institution, 1978), 62.
92. Olson, "The GI Bill and Higher Education," 600.
93. Benjamin Fine, "GI Called Credit to U.S. Education," *The New York Times*, July 23, 1951, 10.
94. Olson, "The GI Bill and Higher Education," 604.
95. Edmondson, "Without Comment or Controversy," 836.
96. Benjamin Fine, "14 Billions Spent in 7 Years to Educate 8 Million GI's," *The New York Times*, July 22, 1951, 1.
97. Ira Katznelson, *When Affirmative Action Was White: An Untold History of Racial Inequality in Twentieth-Century America* (New York: Norton, 2005), 68.
98. Benjamin Fine, "Millions in Waste Charged in Schooling for Veterans," *The New York Times*, February 6, 1950, 1.
99. Olson, *The GI Bill, the Veterans, and the Colleges*, 104.
100. Mosch, *The GI Bill*, 90–91.
101. Marcus Stanley, "College Education and the Midcentury GI Bills," *Quarterly Journal of Economics* 118 (2) (May, 2003): 671–78, and Bound and Turner, "Going to War and Going to College," 792.
102. Mosch, *The GI Bill*, 52–55, and Olson, *The GI Bill, the Veterans, and the Colleges*, 104–105.
103. Public Law 550, 82nd Congress, 1952.
104. Mosch, *The GI Bill*, 51.
105. "History of GI Bill," GI Bill website, http://www.gibill.va.gov/education/GI_Bill.htm.
106. Ibid.
107. Michael B. Tannen, "Is the Army College Fund Meeting Its Objectives?" *Industrial and Labor Relations Review* 41 (1) (October, 1987) 50–51.
108. Ibid., 52.
109. Ibid.
110. G. V. (Sonny) Montgomery with Michael B. Ballard and Craig S. Piper, *Sonny Montgomery: The Veteran's Champion* (Jackson: University Press of Mississippi, 2003), 71.

111. "History of GI Bill," GI Bill website, http://www.gibill.va.gov/education/GI_Bill.htm.
112. William Celis III, "50 Years Later, the Value of the GI Bill is Questioned," *The New York Times*, June 22, 1994, B7, and Greg Winter, "From Combat to Campus on the GI Bill," *The New York Times*, January 16, 2005, Education Life 4A, 8.
113. Remarks of Congressman Smith, May 11, 2004, from House Committee on Veterans' Affairs website, http://veterans.house.gov/benefits/gi60th/intro.html.
114. Remarks of Congressman Brown, May 11, 2004, from House Committee on Veterans' Affairs website, http://veterans.house.gov/benefits/gi60th/intro.html.
115. Remarks of Secretary Principi, June 18, 2004, from House Committee on Veterans' Affairs website, http://veterans.house.gov/benefits/gi60th/intro.html.
116. Kerr, "Expanding Access and Changing Missions."
117. Olson, "The GI and Higher Education," 608, and Celis, "50 Years Later, the Value of the GI Bill is Questioned," B7.
118. Kerr, "Expanding Access and Changing Missions."
119. David Carleton, *Landmark Congressional Laws on Education* (Westport, Conn.: Greenwood Press, 2002).

8 THE RECOVERY OF WESTERN EUROPE: THE MARSHALL PLAN OF 1948

Epigraph quotes from Harry S. Truman, *Memoirs: Years of Trial and Hope*, vol. 2 (New York: Doubleday and Company, 1956), 110, and Helmut Schmidt, "Miles to Go: From American Plan to European Union," *Foreign Affairs* (May/June, 1997): 213.

1. Robert J. Donovan, *The Second Victory: The Marshall Plan and the Postwar Revival of Europe* (New York: Madison Books, 1987), 11.
2. Schmidt, "Miles to Go," 213.
3. Daniel Barbezat, "The Marshall Plan and the Origin of the OEEC," in *Explorations in OEEC History*, ed. Richard T. Griffiths (Paris: Organization for Economic Cooperation and Development, 1997), 34, and Cabell Phillips, *The Truman Presidency: The History of a Triumphant Succession* (New York: Macmillan Company, 1966), 176.
4. Barry Eichengreen and Marc Uzan, "The Marshall Plan: Economic Effects and Implications for Eastern Europe and the Former USSR," *Economic Policy* 7 (14) Eastern Europe (April, 1992): 16–17.
5. Walt W. Rostow, "Lessons of the Plan: Looking Forward to the Next Century," *Foreign Affairs* 76 (3) The Marshall Plan and Its Legacy (May/June, 1997): 207, and Robert E. Wood, "From the Marshall Plan to the Third World," in *Origins of the Cold War: An International History*, eds. Melvyn P. Leffler and David S. Painter (London: Routledge, 2002), 203–204.
6. Truman, *Memoirs: Year of Decisions*, vol. 1 (New York: Doubleday and Company, 1956), 227–28.
7. James Lachlan MacLeod, "The Most Unsordid Act in History?" *History News Network* website, http://hnn.us/articles/1712.html. See also Charles Burton Marshall, "The Lend-Lease Operation," *Annals of the American Academy of Political and Social Science* 225, Nutrition and Food Supply: The War and After (January, 1943) 183–89, and Warren F. Kimball, *The Most Unsordid Act: Lend-Lease, 1939–1941* (Baltimore: Johns Hopkins University Press, 1969).
8. Truman, *Memoirs: Year of Decisions*, 228.
9. Henry Pelling, *Britain and the Marshall Plan* (New York: St. Martin's Press, 1988), 3–4.
10. Robert J. Donovan, *Conflict and Crisis: The Presidency of Harry S. Truman, 1945–1948* (New York: W. W. Norton, 1977), 185–86, and Pelling, *Britain and the Marshall Plan*, 4, 5.

11. Roy Jenkins, "Special Relationships: The Postwar Bequest," *Foreign Affairs* 76 (3) The Marshall Plan and Its Legacy (May/June, 1997): 201–202. Jenkins was Home Secretary and Chancellor of the Exchequer, in two Labour governments, from 1965 to 1976; served as President of the European Community.

12. Pelling, *Britain and the Marshall Plan*, 5.

13. William Hillman, *Mr. President: The First Publication from the Personal Diaries, Private Letters, Papers and Revealing Interviews of Harry S. Truman* (New York: Farrar, Straus and Young, 1952), 23.

14. Donovan, *Conflict and Crisis*, 279.

15. George F. Kennan, *Memoirs: 1925–1950* (Boston: Little, Brown, 1967), 292–93.

16. The Long Telegram is excerpted in Kennan, *Memoirs*, appendix C: Excerpts from Telegraphic Message from Moscow of February 22, 1946, 547–59.

17. Wilson D. Miscamble, *George F. Kennan and the Making of American Foreign Policy, 1947–1950* (Princeton: Princeton University Press, 1992), 27.

18. Robert A. Pollard, "The National Security State Reconsidered: Truman and Economic Containment, 1945–1950," in *The Truman Presidency*, ed. Michael J. Lacey (Cambridge: Cambridge University Press, 1989), 212.

19. Miscamble, *George F. Kennan*, 27, and John Lewis Gaddis, *The United States and the Origins of the Cold War, 1941–1947* (New York: Columbia University Press, 1972), chs. 9, 10.

20. Susan M. Hartmann, *Truman and the 80th Congress* (Columbia, Mo.: University of Missouri Press, 1971), 4.

21. Ibid., 6.

22. Joseph C. Goulden, *The Best Years, 1945–1950* (New York: Atheneum, 1976), 257.

23. Joseph Bledsoe Bonds, *Bipartisan Strategy: Selling the Marshall Plan* (Westport, Conn.: Praeger, 2002), 1, and Hartmann, *Truman and the 80th Congress*, 12.

24. Donovan, *Conflict and Crisis*, 260.

25. David McCullough, *Truman* (New York: Simon and Schuster, 1992), 479.

26. Ibid., 478.

27. Alonzo L. Hamby, *Man of the People: A Life of Harry S. Truman* (New York: Oxford University Press, 1995), 388.

28. Ibid.

29. Dean Acheson, *Present at the Creation: My Years in the State Department* (New York: W. W. Norton, 1969), 140–41.

30. Charles E. Bohlen, *Witness to History: 1929–1969* (New York: W. W. Norton, 1973), 259.

31. Miscamble, *George F. Kennan*, 5.

32. Ibid., 13–14.

33. Truman, *Memoirs: Years of Trial and Hope*, 99.

34. Joseph M. Jones, *The Fifteen Weeks (February 6–June 4, 1947)* (New York: Viking Press, 1955), 7.

35. Ibid., 9.

36. Walter Millis, ed., and E. S. Duffield, *The Forrestal Diaries* (New York: Viking Press, 1951), 245.

37. Jones, *The Fifteen Weeks*, 8.

38. Donovan, *Conflict and Crisis*, 278.

39. Acheson, *Present at the Creation*, 219. "They were all there, the majority and minority potentates," in Acheson's words: from the Senate: H. Styles Bridges (Republican– New Hampshire, chairman of the Joint Committee on Foreign Economic Cooperation); Arthur H. Vandenberg (Republican–Michigan, chairman of the Committee on Foreign Relations), Alben W. Barkley (Democrat–Kentucky, Minority Leader), Tom Connally (Democrat–Texas, ranking member, Committee on Foreign Relations); from the House, Joseph W. Martin, Jr.

(Republican–Massachusetts, Speaker of the House), Charles A. Eaton (Republican–New Jersey, chairman of Committee on Foreign Affairs), Sol Bloom (Democrat–New York, ranking member of the Committee on Foreign Affairs), and Sam Rayburn (Democrat–Texas, Minority Leader). Congressman John Taber (Republican–New York, chairman Appropriations Committee) could not make the meeting. Inexplicably, Senator Robert A. Taft was not invited; Vandenberg quickly drew this omission to the President's attention.

40. Hamby, *Man of the People*, 391.
41. Acheson, *Present at the Creation*, 219. As one historian observed, Acheson "enunciated a primitive version of the domino theory." Scott Jackson, "Prologue to the Marshall Plan: The Origins of the American Commitment for a European Recovery Program," *The Journal of American History* 65 (4) (March, 1979): 1049; also James A. Robinson, *Congress and Foreign Policy-Making: A Study in Legislative Influence and Initiative* (Westport, Conn.: Greenwood Press, 1980; reprint from Dorsey Press, 1962), 40.
42. Acheson, *Present at the Creation*, 219.
43. "Greek Crisis Cited Against Military Cuts," *The New York Times*, March 3, 1947. Cannon's remark might also have applied to the suggestion of Senator Richard B. Russell, Jr. (Democrat–Georgia), made the same day that England, Ireland, Wales, and Scotland should become American states.
44. Walter Lippmann, "The Greek Commitment," *The Washington Post*, March 4, 1947, 9.
45. President Truman's Remarks to Congress, March 12, 1947, in *The Washington Post*, March 13, 1947, 1.
46. C. P. Trussell, "Congress Is Solemn: Prepares to Consider Bills After Hearing the President Gravely," *The New York Times*, March 13, 1947, 1.
47. Diane B. Kunz, "The Marshall Plan Reconsidered: A Complex of Motives," *Foreign Affairs* 76 (3) The Marshall Plan and Its Legacy (May/June, 1997): 163.
48. Robert C. Albright, "Both Foreign Affairs Groups Meeting Today on Proposal," *The Washington Post*, March 13, 1947, 1, and Johnson Warns of 'Invasion,'" *The New York Times*, March 12, 1947, 4.
49. David M. Crawford, "United States Foreign Assistance Legislation, 1947–1948," *Yale Law Review* 58 (6) (May, 1949): 872–73.
50. Hamby, *Man of the People*, 391.
51. Melvin P. Leffler, "The American Conception of National Security and the Beginnings of the Cold War, 1945–48," *The American Historical Review* 89 (2) (April, 1984): 368.
52. Bohlen, *Witness to History*, 261.
53. W. Averell Harriman oral history, conducted by Richard D. McKinzie and Theodore A. Wilson, Washington, D.C., 1971, for the Truman Presidential Library, 7; available at http://www.trumanlibrary.org/oralhist/harriman.htm.
54. Eichengreen and Uzan, "The Marshall Plan," 21.
55. Bohlen, *Witness to History*, 262.
56. Ibid., 263.
57. Ibid.
58. George C. Marshall, interview conducted by Harry B. Price and Roy E. Foulke, October 30, 1952; Harry B. Price Papers, Truman Presidential Library.
59. Melvyn P. Leffler, *A Preponderance of Power: National Security, the Truman Administration, and the Cold War* (Stanford: Stanford University Press, 1992), 157, 189.
60. Walter Lippmann, "Cassandra Speaking," *The Washington Post*, April 5, 1947, 5.
61. Ronald Steel, *Walter Lippman and the American Century* (Boston: Little, Brown, 1980), 440–42; on State Department paternity claims, see Charles P. Kindleberger, *Marshall Plan Days* (Boston: Allen & Unwin, 1987), 25–32.

62. Walter Isaacson and Evan Thomas, *The Wise Men: Six Friends and the World They Made* (New York: Simon and Schuster, 1986), 405–406.
63. Jackson, "Prologue to the Marshall Plan," 1046.
64. Michael J. Hogan, *The Marshall Plan: America, Britain, and the Reconstruction of Western Europe, 1947 1952* (Cambridge: Cambridge University Press, 1987), 40–44, and Jones, *The Fifteen Weeks*, 231 ff.
65. Hogan, *The Marshall Plan*, 40. Hogan identifies Joseph Jones, Ben T. Moore, Harold Van B. Cleveland as "leading apostles" for European economic integration; they were joined by Paul R. Porter, Charles H. Bonesteel, and Charles P. Kindleberger.
66. "Policy with Respect to American Aid to Western Europe," enclosed with Kennan to Acheson, May 23, 1947, U.S. Department of State, *Foreign Relations of the United States*, vol. III (Washington, D.C.: U.S. Government Printing Office, 1967–1988), 223–30, cited in Miscamble, *George F. Kennan*, 50–51.
67. Miscamble, *George F. Kennan*, 51.
68. Isaacson and Thomas, *The Wise Men*, 408 and James Chace, *Acheson: The Secretary of State Who Created the American World* (New York: Simon and Schuster, 1998), 170–73. Bilbo, charitably described in his later years as a racist demagogue, was found guilty by a Senate committee of accepting bribes from contractors during World War II, and was denied his Senate seat at the beginning of the Eightieth Congress. He died in August 1947.
69. Chace, *Acheson*, 171, and Joseph M. Jones to Walter Lippmann, May 7, 1947, in Marshall Plan collection, Truman Library, available from http://www.truman library.org/whistlestop/study_collections/marshall/large/folder2.
70. Crawford, "United States Foreign Assistance Legislation, 1947–1948," 873; citing Sen. Doc. No. 111, 80th Cong., 1st Session 2 (1947). The Acheson speech, "The Requirements of Reconstruction," is reprinted in Robert Dallek, ed., *The Dynamics of World Power: A Documentary History of United States Foreign Policy, 1945–1973*, vol. 1, Western Europe (New York: Chelsea House Publishers, 1973), 47.
71. Will Clayton letter to Herbert Elliston, January 26, 1953, in *Selected Papers of Will Clayton*, ed. Frederick J. Dobney (Baltimore: Johns Hopkins Press, 1971), 208–10.
72. "The European Crisis," in *Selected Papers of Will Clayton*, 201–204, emphasis in the original; Gregory Fossedal and Bill Mikhail, "A Modest Magician: Will Clayton and the Rebuilding of Europe," *Foreign Affairs* 76 (3) The Marshall Plan and Its Legacy (May/June 1997), 195; and Gregory A. Fossedal, *Our Finest Hour: Will Clayton, the Marshall Plan, and the Triumph of Democracy* (Stanford, Calif.: Hoover Institution Press, 1993).
73. Miscamble, *George F. Kennan*, 52.
74. Chace, *Acheson*, 177, and Forrest C. Pogue, *George C. Marshall: Statesman*, vol. 4 (New York: Viking, 1987), 207.
75. Phillips, *The Truman Presidency*, 184–85.
76. Marshall interview, Price Papers, 1.
77. Marshall to Conant, in Meredith Hindley, "How the Marshall Plan Came About," from National Endowment for the Humanities website, http://www.neh.gov/humanities/1998–11/Marshall.html. Bert McCormick was Colonel Robert R. McCormick, long-time owner of the *Chicago Tribune*, staunch conservative and vocal isolationist. See Richard Norton Smith, *The Colonel: The Life and Legend of Robert R. McCormick, 1880–1955* (Boston: Houghton Mifflin, 1997).
78. Robert H. Ferrell, "George C. Marshall," in *The American Secretaries of State and Their Diplomacy*, ed. Robert H. Ferrell (New York: Cooper Square Publishers, Inc., 1966), 111.
79. Arthur Hartman, "The Challenge of the Marshall Plan," in *Present at the Creation: The Fortieth Anniversary of the Marshall Plan*, ed. Armand Clesse and Archie C. Epps (New York: Harper & Row, 1990), 10.

80. George C. Marshall, "Address at Harvard Commencement, June 5, 1947," in *Present at the Creation*, ed. Clesse and Epps, xv–xix.
81. Hogan, *The Marshall Plan*, 44.
82. Charles L. Mee, Jr., *The Marshall Plan: The Launching of the Pax Americana* (New York: Simon and Schuster, 1984), 168. John Gimbel observes: "Current mythology on the Marshall Plan notwithstanding, records now available show conclusively that there was no plan when . . . Marshall spoke at Harvard . . ." *The Origins of the Marshall Plan* (Stanford: Stanford University Press, 1976), 6.
83. Leonard Miall oral history interview, conducted by Philip C. Brooks, June 16, 1974, for the Truman Presidential Library. Available at http://www.truman library.org/oralhist/miall.htm. Alan Bullock, *Ernest Bevin: Foreign Secretary 1945–1951* (New York: W. W. Norton, 1983), 404. However, several news accounts appeared in the next day's *The New York Times* and *The Washington Post*, along with the full text in both newspapers.
84. Bullock, *Ernest Bevin*, 404.
85. Ibid., 405.
86. Pelling, *Britain and the Marshall Plan*, 11.
87. Bohlen, *Witness to History*, 265, and Leffler, *A Preponderance of Power*, 184.
88. Madeleine K. Albright, Commencement Address at Harvard University, June 5, 1997, available at the U.S. Agency for International Development website, http://www.usaid.gov/multimedia/video/marshall/albright.html. On Czechoslovakia and the Soviet takeover, see Josef Korbel, *The Communist Subversion of Czechoslovakia, 1938–1948: The Failure of Coexistence* (Princeton: Princeton University Press, 1959). Korbel was in the unique position of being the father of one secretary of state, Albright, and the professor of another, Condoleezza Rice.
89. Mee, *The Marshall Plan*, 150–51.
90. Barbezat, "The Marshall Plan and the Origin of the OEEC," 34. Charles P. Kindleberger, who was executive secretary for the State Department's working committee on the Marshall Plan, wrote that the CEEC request was closer to $30 billion: $19.9 billion from the United States and $8.3 billion for net imports from the rest of the American continent. Charles P. Kindleberger, "In the Halls of the Capitol," *Foreign Affairs* (May/June, 1997), 186; Phillips, *The Truman Presidency*, 186–87; William C. Mallalieu, "The Origins of the Marshall Plan: A Study in Policy Formation and National Leadership," *Political Science Quarterly* 73 (4) (December, 1958): 481–504.
91. Phillips, *The Truman Presidency*, 187.
92. Ibid. and Harry B. Price, *The Marshall Plan and Its Meaning* (Ithaca: Cornell University Press, 1955), 50–55.
93. Donovan, *Conflict and Crisis*, 261.
94. Vandenberg, *The Private Papers of Senator Vandenberg*, 1, and Donovan, *Conflict and Crisis*, 258.
95. C. David Tompkins, *Senator Arthur H. Vandenberg: The Evolution of a Modern Republican, 1884–1945* (Lansing: Michigan State University Press, 1970), 235–58.
96. Donovan, *Conflict and Crisis*, 258.
97. Pogue, *George C. Marshall: Statesman*, 234–35.
98. Ibid., 236.
99. I. F. Stone, *The Truman Era* (New York: Random House, 1972), 71.
100. Harold L. Hitchens, "Influences on the Congressional Decision to Pass the Marshall Plan," *The Western Political Quarterly* 21 (1) (March, 1968): 51–52; Lester Markel et al., *Public Opinion and Foreign Policy* (New York: Harper, 1949), 9.
101. Hitchens, "Influences on the Congressional Decision to Pass the Marshall Plan," 59–60. Data from survey by Rep. Max Schwabe (Republican–Missouri).
102. Bonds, *Bipartisan Strategy*, ch. 9.

103. Hitchens, "Influences on the Congressional Decision to Pass the Marshall Plan," 53–54.
104. Herbert Agar, *The Price of Power: America Since 1945* (Chicago: University of Chicago Press, 1957), 78–79.
105. Edward T. Folliard, "U.S. Is Striving to Prevent Third World War, He Tells Lawmakers," *The Washington Post*, December 20, 1947, 1; Phillips, *The Truman Presidency*, 191; and Felix Belair, Jr., "Truman Requests 17 Billion for ERP," *The New York Times*, December 20, 1947, 1.
106. Jackson, "Prologue to the Marshall Plan," 1044.
107. Donovan, *Conflict and Crisis*, 287.
108. Willard Thorp, "The Origins of the Marshall Plan," in *Present at the Creation*, ed. Clesse and Epps, 22.
109. Bonds, *Bipartisan Strategy*, 117–18.
110. James Reston, "Marshall Always Patient, But Adamant on His Plan," *The New York Times*, January 9, 1948, 3.
111. Felix Belair, Jr., "President Rejects Hoover's Program for Checks on ERP," *The New York Times*, January 23, 1948, 1; Hartmann, *Truman and the 80th Congress*, 160–61.
112. Harriman oral history, 12.
113. Mee, *Marshall Plan*, 239–40.
114. Hitchens, "Influences on the Congressional Decision to Pass the Marshall Plan," 61.
115. Steel, *Walter Lippman and the American Century*, 450.
116. Vandenberg, *The Private Papers of Senator Vandenberg*, 389.
117. Ferdinand Kuhn, Jr., "Vandenberg Calls on Senate for Swift Approval of ERP to Help Head Off Third War," *The Washington Post*, March 2, 1948, 1.
118. James T. Patterson, *Mr. Republican: A Biography of Robert A. Taft* (Boston: Houghton Mifflin, 1972), 388.
119. Hartmann, *Truman and the 80th Congress*, 162–63.
120. Bonds, *Bipartisan Strategy*, 189; Robinson, *Congress and Foreign Policy-Making*, 42; Hoffman quoted in Price, *The Marshall Plan and Its Meaning*, 55.
121. Harold Hinton, "Aid Bill Is Signed by Truman as Reply to Foes of Liberty," *The New York Times*, April 4, 1948, 1.
122. Robert A. Dahl, *Congress and Foreign Policy* (New York: Harcourt, Brace, 1950), 228–30.
123. Bonds, *Bispartisan Strategy*, 190–91.
124. Robert A. Dahl, *Congress and Foreign Policy* (New York: Harcourt, Brace, 1950), 228–30.
125. Barbezat, "The Marshall Plan and the Origin of the OEEC," 35.
126. When he arrived in Washington, Hoffman stunned Vandenberg by saying he did not want the job and told Truman the same thing. Truman told him, "I'm expecting you to say yes." Hoffman said he'd think about it. The next afternoon, Hoffman held a press conference to discuss a recent trip to Asia he made on behalf of the government. In middle of the session, there was a bulletin from White House announcing Hoffman had accepted position as head of ECA. At that point, of course, he could not decline. United States Department of State, "The Marshall Plan: Origins and Implementation" (Washington, D.C.: Government Printing Office, 1987), 8, and Cabell Phillips, "The Man Who Will Spend $17,000,000,000," *The New York Times*, July 25, 1948, Magazine, 6.
127. Department of State, "The Marshall Plan," 9.
128. Hadley Arkes, *Bureaucracy, the Marshall Plan, and the National Interest* (Princeton: Princeton University Press, 1972), 156 ff., and Paul G. Hoffman, *Peace Can Be Won* (Garden City, N.Y.: Doubleday and Company, 1951), 90–91.

129. Department of State, "The Marshall Plan," 12–13.
130. Kindleberger, "In the Halls of the Capitol," 190.
131. Phillips, *The Truman Presidency*, 193, and Mee, *The Marshall Plan*, 246.
132. Hogan, *The Marshall Plan*, 135.
133. David S. Painter, "Oil and the Marshall Plan," *The Business History Review* 58 (3) (Autumn, 1984): 362, and Kunz, "The Marshall Plan Reconsidered," 168.
134. Daniel Schorr, "Marshall Plan Memories," *The New Leader*, June 30, 1997, 4–5.
135. Irwin M. Wall, *The United States and the Making of Postwar France, 1945–1954* (Cambridge: Cambridge University Press, 1991), 159; Hogan, *The Marshall Plan*, 157–59.
136. Donovan, *The Second Victory*, 62–63.
137. Herbert C. Mayer, *German Recovery and The Marshall Plan, 1948–1952* (New York: Edition Atlantic Forum, 1969), 15.
138. Mayer, *German Recovery and The Marshall Plan, 1948–1952*, 32. In 1948, Greece reached just 77 percent of its 1938 levels, while Italy had reached 81 percent. The 1948 average for all participating countries was 99 percent, and if Western Germany were excluded, the average was 114 percent of the 1938 levels.
139. Charles S. Maier, "Introduction" in *The Marshall Plan and Germany: West German Development within the Framework of the European Recovery Program*, ed. Charles S. Maier with Gunter Bischof (New York: Berg, 1991), 5.
140. Mayer, *German Recovery and The Marshall Plan*, 25. The program was called Government Aid and Relief to Occupied Areas (GARIOA).
141. Werner Abelshauser, "American Aid and West German Economic Recovery: A Macroeconomic Perspective," in *The Marshall Plan and Germany*, ed. Maier, 405, and Helge Berger and Albrecht Ritschl, "Germany and the Political Economy of the Marshall Plan, 1947–1952: A Re-Revisionist View," in *Europe's Post-War Recovery*, ed. Barry Eichengreen (Cambridge: Cambridge University Press, 1995), 199.
142. Quoted in Abelshauser, "American Aid and West German Economic Recovery," 406–407, emphasis in the original. Erhard allowed, however, that "during the first year, they [Marshall Plan monies] did save the people of West Berlin from starving."
143. Jean Edward Smith, *Lucius D. Clay: An American Life* (New York: Henry Holt, 1990), 484–86.
144. Thomas Schwartz, "European Integration and the 'Special Relationship': Implementing the Marshall Plan in the Federal Republic," in *The Marshall Plan and Germany*, ed. Maier, 172.
145. Abelshauser, "American Aid and West German Economic Recovery," 409.
146. Konrad Adenauer, *Memoirs 1945–53*, trans. by Beate Ruhm von Oppen (London: Weidenfeld and Nicolson, 1966), 101.
147. Wall, *The United States and the Making of Postwar France*, 2.
148. Axel Krause, "Maurice Schumann: Senator and Former Foreign Minister of France," *Europe*, April 1997, 365.
149. Chiarella Esposito, *America's Feeble Weapon: Funding the Marshall Plan in France and Italy, 1948–1950* (Westport, Conn.: Greenwood Press, 1994), and Jeffrey G. Giague, Review of Chiarello Esposito, *America's Feeble Weapon: Funding the Marshall Plan in France and Italy, 1948–1950*, H-France, H-Net Review, April, 1997, available from http://www.h-net.msu.edu/reviews/showrev.cgi?path=26394870 875024.
150. Hogan, *The Marshall Plan*, 380.
151. Kennedy quoted in USAID website, http://www.usaid.gov/about_usaid/usaid hist.html.
152. Truman, *Memoirs: Years of Trial and Hope*, 119.
153. Arkes, *Bureaucracy, the Marshall Plan, and the National Interest*, 3.

154. Charles S. Maier, "American Visions and British Interests: Hogan's Marshall Plan," *Reviews in American History* 18 (1) (March, 1990): 103.
155. Alan S. Milward, *The Reconstruction of Western Europe, 1945–1961* (Berkeley: University of California Press, 1984), and Milward, "Was the Marshall Plan Necessary?" *Diplomatic History* (1989): 231–53; Charles S. Maier, "The Two Postwar Eras and the Conditions for Stability in Twentieth-Century Western Europe," *The American Historical Review* 86 (April, 1981).
156. Milward, *The Reconstruction of Western Europe*, 5, 465–66.
157. Ibid., 465–66; 469–70.
158. Barry Eichengreen and Marc Uzan, "The Marshall Plan: Economic Effects and Implications for Eastern Europe and the Former USSR," *Economic Policy* 7 (14) Eastern Europe (April, 1992): 15.
159. Hogan, *The Marshall Plan*, 445.
160. Ibid., 427–29.
161. Bevin's speech excerpted in part in "America's Great Heart," *The Washington Post*, March 25, 1948, 15.
162. Adenauer oral history, 4.
163. Bernard Gwertzman, "Bonn to Give $47-Million in Honor of Marshall Plan," *The New York Times*, June 6, 1972, 1.

9 RIBBONS OF HIGHWAY: THE INTERSTATE HIGHWAY ACT OF 1956

Epigraph quote from "President-Elect Dwight D. Eisenhower on Good Roads," available from the U.S. Department of Transportation, Federal Highway Administration (FHWA) website, www.fhwa.dot.gov/infrastructure/history.htm, and Tom Lewis, *Divided Highways: Building the Interstate Highways, Transforming American Life* (New York: Viking Penguin, 1997), xiv.

1. The Interstate Highway System is also found on the island of Oahu, Hawaii; but there are no Interstate roads in Alaska. Not all state capitals, however, are connected with the Interstate system. Dover, Delaware; Jefferson City, Missouri; Carson City, Nevada; Pierre, South Dakota; and Juneau, Alaska, are the five capital cities not connected. Dan McNichol, *The Roads that Built America: The Incredible Story of the U.S. Interstate System* (New York: Barnes and Noble Books, 2003), 151.
2. Available from http://www.eisenhower.utexas.edu/highway. Other wonders included the Hoover Dam and the Golden Gate Bridge.
3. McNichol, *The Roads that Built America*, 206, and Dan McNichol, "Big Dig Nearing Light of Costly Tunnel's End," *The New York Times*, July 25, 2004, 15–16.
4. A third federal program for highways is the federal domain roads program, which channels federal funds for highways and roads that run through national forests and parks, military bases, and Native American reservations.
5. The official name of the legislation was the Highway Act of 1956, Public Law 84–627. The system was designated the National System of Interstate and Defense Highways; in 1990, it was renamed the Dwight D. Eisenhower System of Interstate and Defense Highways.
6. "Target: $27 Billion, The 1955 Estimate." Available from the FHWA website, www.fhwa.dot.gov/infrastructure/history.htm.
7. Charles L. Dearing, *American Highway Policy* (Washington, D.C.: The Brookings Institution, 1941), 31–32.
8. David P. Currie, "The Constitution in Congress: The Public Lands, 1829–1861," *The University of Chicago Law Review* 70 (3) (Summer, 2003): 784; Dearing, *American Highway Policy*, 32–37. The old National Road closely follows the present-day U.S. 40.

9. Lewis, *Divided Highways*, 6.
10. McNichol, *The Roads that Built America*, 36.
11. James J. Flink, "Three Stages of American Automobile Consciousness," *American Quarterly* 24 (4) (October, 1972): 453.
12. Wayne E. Fuller, "Good Roads and Rural Free Delivery of Mail," *The Mississippi Valley Historical Review* 42 (1) (June, 1955): 76.
13. Frederic L. Paxson, "The Highway Movement, 1916–1935," *The American Historical Review* 51 (2) (January, 1946): 240.
14. Fuller, "Good Roads and Rural Free Delivery of Mail," 67–83. The rural mail carrier had an incentive to push for better roads: poor roads meant that the letter carrier had to work all the harder to deliver mail and it might also have meant that he would have to forfeit part of his pay because of undelivered mail.
15. McNichol, *The Roads that Built America*, 37–38. In Germany, Karl Benz already had been producing automobiles for the commercial market in 1890, and, by 1895, automobiles were a common sight on the streets of Paris; considerable worldwide attention was paid to the first long-distance auto race, a 727-mile course from Paris to Bordeaux and back in June 1895. Flink, "Three Stages of American Automobile Consciousness," 453.
16. Flink, "Three Stages of American Automobile Consciousness," 454.
17. Earle letter reprinted in Tom Kuennen, *Paving the Way to Prosperity* (Washington, D.C.: American Road and Transportation Builders Association, 2002), 6–7. In 1902, the organization was known as the American Road Makers; in 1910, it became the American Road Builders Association (ARBA), then American Road and Transportation Builders Association (ARTBA) in 1977.
18. Paxson, "The Highway Movement, 1916–1935," 238–39. In 1973, AASHO became the American Association of State Highway and Transportation Officials (AASHTO), and represents state transportation interests in all of the forms of travel: air, highway, public transportation, rail and water.
19. Carl Graham Fisher, an Indiana businessman, founded the Prest-O-Lite Company, which made automobile headlights. In 1912, he purchased Miami Beach, Florida, then in 1915 created the Dixie Highway. By 1917, he was worth $50 million, but, following the devastating Miami hurricane of 1927 and the stock market crash in 1929, Fisher was bankrupt by 1930. Jerry M. Fisher, *Pacesetter: The Untold Story of Carl G. Fisher* (Fort Bragg, Calif.: Lost Coast Press, 1998), and John B. Rae, *The Road and the Car in American Life* (Cambridge: MIT Press, 1971), 36.
20. Lewis, *Divided Highways*, 51, and Paxson, "The Highway Movement," 241–42.
21. Richard F. Weingroff, "Federal Aid Road Act of 1916: Building the Foundation," available from the FHWA website, www.fhwa.dot.gov/infrastructure/history. htm. The president of the American Automobile Association was John A. Wilson, brother of Woodrow Wilson. Fuller, "Good Roads and Rural Free Delivery of Mail," 81 n. 51.
22. Quoted in Fuller, "Good Roads and Rural Free Delivery of Mail," 79.
23. John Chynoweth Burnham, "The Gasoline Tax and the Automobile Revolution," *The Mississippi Valley Historical Review* 48 (3) (December, 1961): 435–36.
24. Dearing, *American Highway Policy*, 103.
25. Burnham, "The Gasoline Tax and the Automobile Revolution," 446.
26. Ibid., 456–57.
27. Dwight D. Eisenhower, *At Ease: Stories I Tell to Friends* (Garden City, N.Y.: Doubleday & Company, Inc., 1967), chapter 11, "Through Darkest America with Truck and Tank." Richard F. Weingroff, "The Man Who Changed America, Part 1," *Public Roads* (March/April, 2003), available from the FHWA website, www.fhwa.dot.gov/infrastructure/history.htm, and Paxson, "The Highway Movement, 1916–1935," 243–44.

28. Dwight D. Eisenhower, *Mandate for Change, 1953–1956* (Garden City, N.Y.: Doubleday & Company, Inc., 1963), 548.

29. Flink, "Three Stages of Automobile Consciousness," and Bruce E. Seely, *Building the American Highway System: Engineers as Policy Makers* (Philadelphia: Temple University Press, 1987), 72.

30. Richard F. Weingroff, "From 1916 to 1939: The Federal-State Partnership at Work," available from the FHWA website, www.fhwa.dot.gov/infrastructure/history.htm, and Seely, *Building the American Highway System*, 73.

31. Weingroff, "From 1916 to 1939: The Federal-State Partnership at Work."

32. Lewis, *Divided Highways*, 49.

33. Lee Mertz, "Origins of the Interstate," available from the FHWA website, www.fhwa.dot.gov/infrastructure/history.htm. Richard Weingroff, historian of the FHWA, writes that it, indeed, is not legend, but fact: the map that Roosevelt drew is in the National Archives. See Richard F. Weingroff, "Essential to the National Interest," *Public Roads* 69 (5) (March/April 2006), available online at http://www.tfhrc.gov/pubrds/06mar/07.htm. Weingroff correspondence with the author, August 27, 2007.

34. "Super Roads Are Studied in Work Plan," *The Washington Post*, February 20, 1935.

35. Mertz, "Origins of the Interstate," and Seely, *Building the American Highway System*, 169–77.

36. Owen D. Gutfreund, *Twentieth-Century Sprawl: Highways and the Reshaping of the American Landscape* (New York: Oxford University Press, 2004), 39, and Seely, *Building the American Highway System*, 170–71.

37. Lewis, *Divided Highways*, 48.

38. Gutfreund, *Twentieth-Century Sprawl*, 37–38.

39. Seely, *Building the American Highway System*, 175–76.

40. "Futurama at Fair Is Viewed in Test," *The New York Times*, April 16, 1939, 3; "Fair Visitors 'Fly' Over U.S. of 1960," *The New York Times*, April 19, 1939, 17; "Futurama Is Voted the Most Popular," *The New York Times*, May 17, 1939, 19; and Paul Mason Fotsch, "The Building of a Superhighway Future at the New York World's Fair," *Cultural Critique* 48 (Spring, 2001): 66, 68. In addition, several documentary films were shown at the world's fair and drew large crowds. The most popular, by far, was *The City*, written by urban critic and intellectual Lewis Mumford with music by Aaron Copland. The documentary was, in the opinion of urban studies professor Owen D. Gutfreund, a "superbly effective manifesto for anti-urban city planning, centered around an outright rejection of existing urbanization patterns in favor of new-construction suburban subdivisions in the garden-city tradition, beyond the limits of existing metropolitan areas, linked to other settlements by newly built highways." Gutfreund, *Twentieth-Century Sprawl*, 41–42.

41. Mark H. Rose, *Interstate: Express Highway Politics, 1941–1956* (Lawrence: The Regents Press of Kansas, 1979), 2.

42. James A. Dunn, Jr., *Miles to Go: European and American Transportation Policies* (Cambridge: MIT Press, 1981), 120–21.

43. McNichol, *The Roads that Built America*, 102.

44. Richard O. Davies, *The Age of Asphalt: The Automobile, the Freeway, and the Condition of Metropolitan America* (Philadelphia: J. B. Lippincott Company, 1975), 3–4.

45. American Road Builders' Association, "Presentation of the Bartlett Award to William Randolph Hearst, Jr.," January 1956, reprinted in Mertz, "Origins of the Interstate."

46. "President-Elect Dwight D. Eisenhower on Good Roads," available from the FHWA website, www.fhwa.dot.gov/infrastructure/history.htm.

47. Quote from Address of President, delivered by Vice-President Richard Nixon to the Governors Conference, Lake George, New York, July 12, 1954, available from the FHWA website, www.fhwa.dot.gov/infrastructure/history.htm.
48. Ibid.
49. Weingroff, "The Man Who Changed America, Part 1."
50. Seely, *Building the American Highway System*, 214.
51. Weingroff, "The Man Who Changed America, Part 1."
52. Lewis, *Divided Highways*, 98–102. Eisenhower, later in his memoirs, singled out Weeks for praise: "great highway system will stand in part as a monument to the man in my Cabinet who headed the department responsible for it . . . Secretary of Commerce Sinclair Weeks." Eisenhower, *Mandate for Change*, 549.
53. Lewis, *Divided Highways*, 102.
54. Richard F. Weingroff, "General Lucius D. Clay: The President's Man," available from the FHWA website, www.fhwa.dot.gov/infrastructure/history.htm.
55. Davies, *The Age of Asphalt*, 18.
56. "Summary of Clay Committee Hearings, October 7 and 8, 1954," John S. Bragdon Files, Eisenhower Library, Abilene, Kansas, reprinted in Davies, *The Age of Asphalt*, 56–59; 60.
57. Lewis, *Divided Highways*, 112. See James A. Dunn, Jr., *Driving Forces: The Automobile, Its Enemies and the Politics of Mobility* (Washington, D.C.: Brookings Institution, 1998), 36, for a delineation of the highway coalition into taxing groups and spending groups.
58. Eisenhower, *Mandate for Change*, 548.
59. Dwight D. Eisenhower, *Public Papers of the Presidents of the United States: Dwight D. Eisenhower, 1953–1961*, 8 vols (Washington, D.C.: GPO); vol. 19 (1955), 275–80.
60. Attachment to memorandum from Emmett Welch to Floyd D. Peterson, office of General John S. Bragdon. Available from the FHWA website, www.fhwa.dot.gov/infrastructure/history.htm.
61. Richard F. Weingroff, "Senator Harry Flood Byrd of Virginia: The Pay-As-You-Go Man," available from the FHWA website, www.fhwa.dot.gov/infrastructure/history.htm.
62. Weingroff, "General Lucius D. Clay;" Kyle Longley, *Senator Albert Gore, Sr.: Tennessee Maverick* (Baton Rouge: Louisiana State University Press, 2004), 124–26.
63. "General Lucius D. Clay's Testimony," available from the FHWA website, www.fhwa.dot.gov/infrastructure/history.htm.
64. Eisenhower, *At Ease*, 502.
65. Congressional Quarterly, *Congress and the Nation, 1945–1964* (Washington, D.C.: Congressional Quarterly Service, 1965), 531.
66. Mark H. Rose, *Interstate: Express Highway Politics, 1939–1989*, rev. ed. (Knoxville: University of Tennessee Press, 1990), 92.
67. Burnham, "The Gasoline Tax and the Automobile Revolution," 457. The petroleum business "never fully understood that the success and growth of the gasoline tax—as a toll that paid for improved highways—indicated that Americans in general agreed to finance the automobile revolution."
68. Dunn, *Miles to Go*, 121.
69. Robert Thruelson, "Coast to Coast Without Stopping," *Saturday Evening Post* October 20, 1956, 23, quoted in Davies, *The Age of Asphalt*, 22.
70. Congressional Quarterly, *Congress and the Nation, 1945–1964*, 531.
71. Robert Griffith, "Dwight D. Eisenhower and the Corporate Commonwealth," *The American Historical Review* 87 (1) (February, 1982): 106 and Rose, *Interstate*, 92.
72. Eisenhower, *At Ease*, 166
73. Quoted in Leonard Downie, Jr., "The Contractors: Their Politics and Influence," *The Washington Post Magazine*, September 30, 1973, 23.

74. Gore, Boggs, Eisenhower, and Frank Turner (but not George Fallon) were honored in June 1996 as "The Visionaries" at the fortieth anniversary of the Interstate Highway System. At the ceremony, Vice President Al Gore, Jr., commented that he vividly remembered as an eight-year-old boy watching his father debate policy matters concerning the building of the Interstate highway system. The younger Gore's phrase "Information Superhighway," first used in the 1970s, was inspired by his father's work. "Visionaries of the Interstate Honored at Gala Celebration," available from the FHWA website, http://www.fhwa.dot.gov/infrastructure/rw961.htm.

75. Richard F. Weingroff, "Federal-Aid Highway Act of 1956: Creating the Interstate System," available from the FHWA website, www.fhwa.dot.gov/infrastructure/history.htm.

76. *America' Highways, 1776–1976: A History of the Federal-Aid Programs.* (Washington, D.C.: Federal Highway Administration, U.S. Department of Transportation, 1976), 185–87, and Bruce E. Seely, "Francis C. Turner: Father of the U.S. Interstate Highway System," *TR News* 213 (March–April, 2001), 5–14, available from Transportation Research Board, National Research Council website, http://trb.org//publications/trnews/trnews213.pdf.

77. Davies, *The Age of Asphalt*, 4.

78. Helen Leavitt, *Superhighway—Superhoax* (Garden City, N.Y.: Doubleday & Company, Inc., 1970), 187–88.

79. Congressional Quarterly, *Congress and the Nation, 1945–1964*, 531–32.

80. Leavitt, *Superhighway—Superhoax*, 188–89, and Congressional Quarterly, *Congress and the Nation, 1945–1964*, 533–35. Historian Bruce E. Seely noted that, in the end, "congressional hearings revealed only that the Bureau [of Public Roads] was, as always, cautious with taxpayer money." Seely, "Francis C. Turner," 8.

81. Robert A. Caro, *The Powerbroker: Robert Moses and the Fall of New York* (New York: Alfred A. Knopf, 1974), 838–39.

82. Ibid., 840–41.

83. Memorandum for the Record. Meeting in the President's Office: Interim Report on the Interstate Highway Program, April 6, 1960. Dwight D. Eisenhower Presidential Library. Available from http://www.eisenhower.archives.gov/dl/InterstateHighways/meetingofApril61960ReInterstateHighwayProgram040860Pg1.pdf.

84. Editorial, November 20, 1966, quoted in Leavitt, *Superhighway—Superhoax*, 69.

85. Alan Altshuler and David Luberoff, *Mega-Projects: The Changing Politics of Urban Public Investment* (Washington, D.C.: The Brookings Institution and Lincoln Institute of Land Policy, 2003), 83.

86. Davies, *The Age of Asphalt*, 33.

87. Lewis, *Divided Highways*: see chapter eight for a detailed, fascinating account of the New Orleans Interstate fight and the battles in other urban areas.

88. *Citizens to Preserve Overton Park, Inc., et al. v. Volpe, Secretary of Transportation, et al.*, 401 U.S. 402 (1971); and McNichol, *The Roads that Built America*, 159–61.

89. Robert C. Albrook, "50 mph Traffic Loop Would 'Feed' Central D.C.," *The Washington Post*, December 4, 1955, E1, and Leavitt, *Superhighway—Superhoax*, 91–109, for an account of the Washington, D.C., Interstate battles.

90. A. Q. Mowbray, *Road to Ruin* (Philadelphia: J. B. Lippincott, 1969), 224; Natcher quote from Robert L. Asher, "Halt to Subway Money Is Threatened if D.C. Freeway Foes Continue Attack," *The Washington Post*, August 9, 1966, A1.

91. Drew Pearson and Jack Anderson, "Highway Lobby Rolls Roughshod," *The Washington Post*, July 15, 1968, B11. Voting for the bill were the Members of Congress in the immediate suburban district of Maryland (Republicans Gilbert Gude and Democrat Hervey Machen) and Virginia (Republicans Joel Broyhill and

William Scott); also helping out was chairman of the overall committee, Representative George Fallon of Baltimore.

92. George M. Smerk, *Urban Mass Transportation: A Dozen Years of Federal Policy* (Bloomington, Ind.: Indiana University Press, 1974), 19.

93. Edward Weiner, *Urban Transportation Planning in the United States: An Historical Overview*, 5th ed. (Washington, D.C.: Department of Transportation, 1997), ch. 4, available from the U.S. Department of Transportation website, http://tmip.fhwa. dot.gov/clearinghouse/docs/utp. The planning process became known as the 3C process, relating to the Act's requirement that it be "continuing, comprehensive, and cooperative."

94. Quoted in Glenn Yago, *The Decline of Transit: Urban Transportation in German and U.S. Cities, 1900–1970* (New York: Cambridge University Press, 1984), 198.

95. Dunn, *Miles to Go*, 122. The court ruling was *State Highway Commission of Missouri* v. *Volpe*.

96. Ibid., 125.

97. Quoted in Richard F. Weingroff, "Creating a Landmark: The Intermodal Surface Transportation Efficiency Act of 1991," available from the FHWA website, www.fhwa.dot.gov/infrastructure/history.htm.

98. Altshuler and Luberoff, *Mega-Projects*, 115, and U.S. Congress, Congressional Research Service, *Air Quality and Transportation Enhancement Provisions in the Intermodal Surface Transportation Efficiency Act of 1991*. 97th Congress. Report No. 97–902 (updated June 10, 1998), written by David M. Bearden. The $6 billion went for the Congestion Mitigation and Air Quality (CMAQ) program. ISTEA was crafted under the congressional leadership of Democratic Senators Daniel Patrick Moynihan (New York), Harry Reid (Nevada), and Lloyd Bentsen (Texas), and Democratic Representatives Robert Roe (New Jersey), Norman Mineta (California), and Republicans E. G. (Bud) Shuster (Pennsylvania), and John Paul Hammerschmidt (Arkansas).

99. McNichol, *The Roads that Built America*, 240–45. The elevated Interstate highway should not be confused with the more famous Green Monster, the left field wall at Boston's Fenway Park.

100. Ibid., 245.

101. The 2005 highway act is officially the Safe, Accountable, Flexible, and Efficient Transportation Equity Act (SAFE-TEA) of 2005. Alaska, while ranking forty-seventh in population, received the third highest amount of earmarked money. "Fresh Pork, Coming to a District Near You," *The New York Times*, August 7, 2005, WK3.

102. John R. Meyer and Jose Gomez-Ibanez, *Autos Transit and Cities* (Cambridge: Harvard University Press, 1981), 7.

103. Texas Transportation Institute, *2004 Urban Mobility Study* (September 2004), http://mobility.tamu.edu/ums. Quote from press release accompanying the report, http://tti.tamu.edu/media/releases/2004/mobility.stm.

104. Anthony Downs, *Stuck in Traffic: Coping with Peak-Hour Traffic Congestion* (Washington, D.C.: The Brookings Institution Press, and Cambridge: The Lincoln Institute of Land Policy, 1992), 11.

105. Table summarizing these policy options, their effectiveness, costs, difficulty of implementation, and political acceptability in Downs, *Stuck in Traffic*, 152–53. See also Anthony Downs, *Still Stuck in Traffic: Coping with Peak-Hour Traffic Congestion* (Washington, D.C.: Brookings Institution Press, 2004).

106. Downs, *Stuck in Traffic*, 164.

107. Quoted in Mitchell Gordon, *Sick Cities: Psychology and Pathology of American Urban Life* (Baltimore: Penguin Books, 1965), 13.

108. Dolores Hayden, *Building Suburbia: Green Fields and Urban Growth, 1820–2000* (New York: Pantheon Books, 2003), 168–70.

109. Joel Garreau, *Edge City: Life on the New Frontier* (New York: Doubleday, 1991).
110. Ibid., 7, and ch. 11, "The List: Edge Cities, Coast to Coast."
111. Robert E. Lang, *Edgeless Cities: Exploring the Elusive Metropolis* (Washington, D.C.: Brookings Institution Press, 2003), 1.
112. A good summary of automobile and highway critics is found in Dunn, *Driving Forces*; Lewis Mumford, *The Highway and the City* (New York: Harcourt, Brace, 1963); Jane Jacobs, *The Death and Life of Great American Cities* (New York: Random House, 1961); Mowbray, *Road to Ruin*; Leavitt, *Superhighway—Superhoax*; Hayden, *Building Suburbia*; Emma Rothschild, *Paradise Lost: The Decline of the Auto-Industrial Age* (New York: Random House, 1973); James J. Flink, *The Car Culture* (Cambridge: MIT Press, 1975) and *The Automobile Age* (Cambridge: MIT Press, 1988); Kay, *Asphalt Nation*, 345; and Deborah Gordon, *Steering a New Course: Transportation, Energy, and the Environment* (Washington, D.C.: Island Press, 1991).
113. Wendell Cox and Jean Love, "Forty Years of the U.S. Interstate Highway System: An Analysis. The Best Investment a Nation Ever Made." American Highway Users Alliance, June, 1996. The American Highway Users Alliance was chartered by General Motors chairman Alfred P. Sloan in 1932 as the National Highway Users Conference, central force in the "Road Gang" mentioned in connection with the 1944 legislation. It has approximately 100 corporate/association members and 500 individual members.
114. Cox and Love, "Forty Years of the U.S. Interstate Highway System," passim.
115. An excellent analysis of the inherent advantages of highway policy promotion is found in Dunn, *Driving Forces*, 25–27.
116. Data from the Texas Transportation Institute cited in Lisa Caruso, "Mapping a New Route," *National Journal*, October 18, 2008, 32.

10 JUSTICE, EQUALITY, AND DEMOCRACY'S PROMISE:
THE CIVIL RIGHTS ACT OF 1964 AND THE VOTING
RIGHTS ACT OF 1965

Epigraph quotes from Robert D. Loevy, ed., *The Civil Rights Act of 1964: The Passage of the Law That Ended Racial Segregation* (Albany: State University of New York Press, 1997), 40.

1. Robert Mann, *The Walls of Jericho: Lyndon Johnson, Hubert Humphrey, Richard Russell, and the Struggle for Civil Rights* (New York: Harcourt Brace, 1996), 18; Robert A. Caro, *Master of the Senate: The Years of Lyndon Johnson* (New York: Knopf, 2002), 440–43.
2. Mann, *The Walls of Jericho*, 19. Mann credits Milton Stewart, leader of the New York contingent from the Americans for Democratic Action (ADA), with contributing substantially to the speech.
3. Ibid., 20–21.
4. David McCullough, *Truman* (New York: Simon and Schuster, 1992), 640.
5. Ibid., 640–43.
6. John N. Popham, "Southerners Name Thurmond to Lead Anti-Truman Fight," *The New York Times*, July 18, 1948, 1.
7. "Thurmond Warns of Rights Strife," *The New York Times*, August 1, 1948, 44; "Thurmond Hits Truman, Dewey, Wallace as Leading U.S. to 'Rocks of Totalitarianism,'" *The New York Times*, August 12, 1948, 44; "Thurmond Attacks Civil Rights Points," *The New York Times*, October 3, 1948, 40; "States Rights Democrats Frown at Name 'Dixiecrats' Devised to Fit Paper's Headline," *The New York Times*, September 5, 1948, 5.
8. Hubert H. Humphrey, Oral History, Interview I, August 17, 1971, Lyndon B. Johnson Library, conducted by Joe Frantz, 6.

9. On the history of Jim Crow laws, see C. Vann Woodward, *The Strange Career of Jim Crow*, 3rd rev. ed. (New York: Oxford University Press, 1974, 1955). Woodward notes that the origin of the term "Jim Crow" is "lost in obscurity." A song and dance called "Jim Crow" was performed in 1832 and the term became an adjective in 1838. At 7 n. 5.

10. Aldon D. Morris, *The Origin of the Civil Rights Movement: Black Communities Organizing for Change* (New York: The Free Press, 1986), 1–2.

11. Harvard Sitkoff, *The Struggle for Black Equality: 1954–1992*, rev. ed. (New York: Hill and Wang, 1993, 1981), 4–5.

12. On civil rights in the New Deal era, see Harvard Sitkoff, *A New Deal for Blacks: The Emergence of Civil Rights as a National Issue*, vol. 1: *The Depression Decade* (New York: Oxford University Press, 1978).

13. On the NAACP strategy, see Thurgood Marshall, "An Evaluation of Recent Efforts to Achieve Racial Integration in Education Through Resort to the Courts," *Journal of Negro Education* 21 (3), The Courts and Racial Integration in Education (Summer, 1952): 316–27; Sitkoff, *The Struggle for Black Equality*, 18–21. On *Brown v. Board of Education*, see James T. Patterson, *Brown* v. *Board of Education: A Civil Rights Milestone and its Troubled Legacy* (New York: Oxford University Press, 2001), and Richard Kluger, *Simple Justice: The History of Brown v. Board of Education and Black America's Struggle for Equality* (New York: Knopf, 2004, 1975).

14. McCullough, *Truman*, 588–89, quote from 589; Robert J. Donovan, *Conflict and Crisis: The Presidency of Harry S Truman, 1945–1948* (New York: W. W. Norton, 1977), 333–35.

15. Russell L. Riley, *The Presidency and the Politics of Racial Inequality: Nation-Keeping from 1931 to 1965* (New York: Columbia University Press, 1999), 160–61; William C. Berman, *The Politics of Civil Rights in the Truman Administration* (Columbus: Ohio State University Press, 1970). The Report of the President's Committee on Civil Rights, *To Secure These Rights* (1947), Truman Presidential Library, available at http://www.trumanlibrary.org/civilrights/srights1.htm.

16. Donovan, *Conflict and Crisis*, 336.

17. Harry S. Truman, Special Message to the Congress on Civil Rights, February 2, 1948, John T. Woolley and Gerhard Peters, *The American Presidency Project* [online]. Santa Barbara, Calif.: University of California (hosted). Gerhard Peters (database). Available at http://presidency.ucsb.edu/?pid=13006.

18. George Gallup, "Southern Voters 9–1 Against 'Rights' Bills," *The Washington Post*, April 4, 1948, B1; "Byrd Says 'Rights' Mean Dictatorship," *The New York Times*, February 20, 1948, 3.

19. Alfred H. Kelly and Winfred A. Harbison, *The American Constitution: Its Origins and Development*, 4th ed. (New York: W. W. Norton, 1970), 921–22.

20. *Sipuel v. Board of Regents*, 332 U.S. 631 (1948) (law school education in Oklahoma); *Sweatt v. Painter*, 339 U.S. 629 (1950) (law school education in Texas); *McLaurin v. Oklahoma State Regents*, 339 U.S. 637 (1950) (graduate school education).

21. 347 U.S. 483 (1954). On the decision, see Patterson, *Brown v. Board of Education*, 65–69.

22. Alpheus T. Mason, *The Supreme Court from Taft to Warren* (Baton Rouge: Louisiana State University Press, 1958), 189–90.

23. *Bolling v. Sharpe*, 347 U.S. 497 (1954).

24. Kelly and Harbison, *The American Constitution*, 927; Patterson, *Brown v. Board of Education*, 84.

25. Kelly and Harbison, *The American Constitution*, 927–28.

26. Caro, *Master of the Senate*, 785–86; Kelly and Harbison, *The American Constitution*, 752. Neither Lyndon Johnson nor his senate colleagues from Tennessee, Albert A. Gore, Sr., or C. Estes Kefauver, signed the Southern Manifesto. All three

harbored burning national ambitions, and Kefauver became the Democratic vice-presidential candidate in 1956.

27. Kluger, *Simple Justice*, 753.
28. Patterson, *Brown v. Board of Education*, 109–13; Benjamin Fine, "Arkansas Troops Bar Negro Pupils; Governor Defiant," *The New York Times*, September 5, 1957, 1. Stikoff, *The Struggle for Black Equality*, 31. "Text of Address by the President of the United States, Delivered from His Office at the White House, Tuesday, September 24, 1957," available from the Eisenhower Presidential Library, www.eisenhower.archives.gov/dl/LittleRock/PressRelease924571.pdf.
29. Eisenhower quoted in Burk, *The Eisenhower Administration and Black Civil Rights*, 238; Wilkins quoted in Sitkoff, *The Struggle for Black Equality*, 36. For a more sympathetic view of Eisenhower and civil rights, see David A. Nichols, *A Matter of Justice: Eisenhower and the Beginning of the Civil Rights Revolution* (New York: Simon and Schuster, 2007).
30. Yasuhiro Katagiri, *The Mississippi State Sovereignty Commission: Civil Rights and States' Rights* (Jackson: University Press of Mississippi, 2001).
31. William S. White, "The Southern Democrat Now Takes Over," *The New York Times*, January 9, 1955, Sunday Magazine, 9. Also, William S. White, *The Citadel: The Story of the U.S. Senate* (New York: Harper, 1957).
32. Robert V. Remini, *The House: The History of the House of Representatives* (Washington, D. C.: Library of Congress and Smithsonian Books, 2006), 376.
33. On Russell's career and role in civil rights legislation: Gilbert C. Fite, *Richard B. Russell, Senator from Georgia* (Chapel Hill: University of North Carolina Press, 1991); Mann, *The Walls of Jericho*; Caro, *Master of the Senate*; Spencer Rich, "Mitchell Looks Back on Three Decades of Civil Rights Activism," *The Washington Post*, August 22, 1978, A3.
34. Delivered May 27, 1954; excerpted in a pamphlet written by Judge Tom P. Brady, "Black Monday: Segregation or Amalgamation . . . America Has Its Choice," in Carson et al., *The Eyes on the Prize Civil Rights Reader*, 92. Brady wrote that Eastland's speech was the "tersest, the clearest and the most accurate analysis of the segregation problem yet propounded. This speech should go into the homes of every white and Negro in the South. It will do much to extinguish the widely scattered, smoldering fires of racial hate the decision [*Brown*] has rekindled." At 93.
35. Bruce J. Dierenfield, *Keeper of the Rules: Congressman Howard W. Smith of Virginia* (Charlottesville: University of Virginia Press, 1987); Smith quote from 198; Charles O. Jones, "Joseph G. Cannon and Howard W. Smith: An Essay on the Limits of Leadership in the House of Representatives," *Journal of Politics* 30 (3) (August 1968): 617–46; Remini, *The House*, 402.
36. Caro, *Master of the Senate*, for the story of Johnson's rise to power in the Senate and the creation of the 1957 Civil Rights Act.
37. Mack C. Shelley II, *The Permanent Majority: The Conservative Coalition in the United States Congress* (University, Ala.: University of Alabama Press, 1983), 66, cited in Nicole L. Gueron, "An Idea Whose Time Has Come: A Comparative Procedural History of the Civil Rights Acts of 1960, 1964, and 1991," *Yale Law Journal* 104 (5) (March 1995), 1224.
38. Richard W. Bolling, *House Out of Order* (New York: E. P. Dutton, 1965), 174.
39. In 1975, the Senate reduced the number of votes required from two-thirds (67 of the 100 senators) to three-fifths (60 of the 100 Senators).
40. Thurmond switched his party allegiance from Democrat to Republican in 1964.
41. On Brownell's relations with Eisenhower, see Herbert Brownell and John P. Burke, *Advising Ike: Memoirs of Attorney General Herbert Brownell* (Lawrence: University Press of Kansas, 1993).
42. On the 1957 Civil Rights Act, Robert Fredrick Burk, *The Eisenhower Administration and Black Civil Rights* (Knoxville: University of Tennessee Press, 1984), 204–28;

Caro, *Master of the Senate*, part IV; Riley, *The Presidency and the Politics of Racial Inequality*, 184–89.

43. Morris, *The Origins of the Civil Rights Movement*.
44. Gueron, "An Idea Whose Time Has Come," 1213–14.
45. Ibid.; on the Civil Rights Act of 1960, see Daniel M. Berman, *A Bill Becomes a Law: Congress Enacts Civil Rights Legislation* (New York: Macmillan, 1966).
46. "Eisenhower Signs Civil Rights Bill," *The New York Times*, May 7, 1960, 12; Marshall quoted by Berman, *A Bill Becomes a Law*, 135.
47. David J. Garrow, *Bearing the Cross: Martin Luther King, Jr., and the Southern Christian Leadership Conference* (New York: William Morrow, 1986), 138–39.
48. Robert Dallek, *An Unfinished Life: John F. Kennedy, 1917–1963* (Boston: Little, Brown, 2003), 380–81.
49. Jones, "Joseph G. Cannon and Howard W. Smith," 635.
50. Dallek, *An Unfinished Life*, 329.
51. The vote in the House was 217–212 in favor of expanding the Rules Committee.
52. *Boynton v. Virginia*, 364 U.S. 454 (1960); David Halberstam, *The Children* (New York: Fawcett Books, 1998) John Lewis with John D'Orso, *Walking with the Wind: A Memoir of the Movement* (San Diego: Harcourt Brace, 1999); Jim Peck, *Freedom Ride* (New York: Simon and Schuster, 1998), and James Farmer, *Lay Bare the Heart* (New York: Plume Books, 1985).
53. Nadine Cohodas, "James Meredith and the Integration of Ole Miss," *Journal of Blacks in Higher Education* 16 (Summer 1997): 112–22; author quote from 113, Barnett quote from 120; Nadine Cohodas, *The Band Played Dixie* (New York: Free Press, 1997).
54. "Civil Rights, 1963," The Dirksen Congressional Center website, http://congresslink.org/civilrights/1963.htm.
55. Dan Carter, *The Politics of Rage: George Wallace, the Origins of the New Conservatism, and the Transformation of American Politics* (New York: Simon and Schuster, 1995), 141–52, quote at 151.
56. John F. Kennedy, "Radio and Television Report to the American People on Civil Rights," June 11, 1963, from the John F. Kennedy Presidential Library website, http://www.jfklibrary.org.
57. Tom Wicker, "Kennedy Asks Broad Rights Bill as 'Reasonable' Course in Crisis; Calls for Restraint by Negroes," *The New York Times*, June 20, 1963, 1.
58. Dallek, *An Unfinished Life*, 640–41.
59. Lawmakers quoted in "Rights Plan Hit by Southern Bloc," *The New York Times*, June 20, 1963, 18.
60. Carter, *The Politics of Rage*, 153–54.
61. Lewis, *Walking the Wind*, 214–27; A. Philip Randolph, "Why Should We March," *Survey Graphic*, November 1942, 488–89, excerpted in Alan F. Westin, ed., *Freedom Now! The Civil Rights Struggle in America* (New York: Basic Books, 1964), 75–78. Murray Kempton, "The March on Washington," *The New Republic*, September 14, 1963, 19–20.
62. David B. Filvaroff and Raymond E. Wolfinger, "The Origin and Enactment of the Civil Rights Act of 1964," in *Legacies of the 1964 Civil Rights Act*, ed. Bernard Grofman (Charlottesville: University Press of Virginia, 2000), 9–32.
63. Filvaroff and Wolfinger, "The Origin and Enactment of the Civil Rights Act of 1964," 18–19. Hugh Davis Graham, *The Civil Rights Era: Origins and Development of National Policy, 1960–1972* (New York: Oxford University Press, 1990), 80–81.
64. King eulogy from James M. Washington, ed., *A Testament of Hope: The Essential Writings and Speeches of Martin Luther King, Jr.* (San Francisco: Harper and Row, 1986), 221, excerpted in Renee C. Romano, "Narratives of Redemption: The Birmingham Church Bombing Trials and the Construction of Civil Rights

Memory," in *The Civil Rights Movement in American Memory*, ed. Renee C. Romano and Leigh Raiford (Athens, Ga: University of Georgia Press, 2006), 97. On the Birmingham bombings, Diane McWhorter, *Carry Me Home: Birmingham, Alabama, the Climatic Battle of the Civil Rights Movement* (New York: Simon and Schuster, 2001).

65. Filvaroff and Wolfinger, "The Origin and Enactment of the Civil Rights Act of 1964," 20–21.

66. Lyndon B. Johnson, Address before a Joint Session of Congress, November 27, 1963, John T. Woolley and Gerhard Peters, *The American Presidency Project* (online). Santa Barbara, Calif.: University of California (hosted). Gerhard Peters (database). Available at http://presidency.ucsb.edu/?pid+25988.

67. Mann, *The Walls of Jericho*, 384–85; Taylor Branch, *Pillar of Fire: America in the King Years, 1963–65* (New York: Simon and Schuster, 1998), 187.

68. Lyndon B. Johnson, State of the Union Address, January 8, 1965, available from Woolley and Peters, *The American Presidency Project*, available from http://www.presidency.ucsb.edu/ws/?pid=26787.

69. Joseph L. Rauh, Jr., "The Role of the Leadership Conference on Civil Rights in the Civil Rights Struggle of 1963–1964," in *The Civil Rights Act of 1964*, ed. Loevy, 62–63.

70. Marie Smith, "Should Sex Amendment Be in Rights Bill?" *The Washington Post*, February 11, 1964, 35; E. W. Kenworthy, "Jobs Issue Blocks Attempt in House to Vote on Rights," *The New York Times*, February 9, 1964, 1. Carl M. Brauer, "Women Activists, Southern Conservatives, and the Prohibition of Sex Discrimination in Title VII of the 1964 Civil Rights Act," *Journal of Southern History* 49 (1) (February, 1983): 37–56; Cynthia Deitch, "Gender, Race, and Class Politics and the Inclusion of Women in Title VII of the 1964 Civil Rights Act," *Gender and Society* 7 (2) (June, 1993): 183–203.

71. Graham, *The Civil Rights Era*, 142–43.

72. Francis R. Valeo, Oral History Interviews, Senate Historical Office, Washington, D.C. Interview 8. "Civil Rights Act of 1964," September 18, 1085, 313, conducted by Donald A. Ritchie.

73. Quoted in John G. Stewart, "The Civil Rights Act of 1964: Strategy," in *The Civil Rights Act of 1964*, ed. Loevy, 198.

74. Clifford M. Lytle, "The History of the Civil Rights Bill of 1964," *Journal of Negro History* 51 (4) (October, 1966): 294.

75. Humphrey oral history, III, June 21, 1977; interviewed by Michael L. Gillette, 6, Lyndon B. Johnson library.

76. Ibid.

77. Edward L. Schapsmeier and Frederick H. Schapsmeier, *Dirksen of Illinois: Senatorial Statesman* (Urbana: University of Illinois Press, 1985), 156–57. The Republicans dead set against overriding a filibuster were John Tower (Texas), Edwin L. Meecham (New Mexico), Milward L. Simpson (Wyoming), Wallace Bennett (Utah), and Milton Young (North Dakota).

78. Valeo oral history, 322–23.

79. Graham, *The Civil Rights Era*, 144–45.

80. Mann, *The Walls of Jericho*, 396–98.

81. Hubert H. Humphrey, *The Education of a Public Man: My Life and Politics* (Minneapolis: University of Minnesota Press, 1991), 208

82. Mann, *The Walls of Jericho*, 400–1.

83. Jonathan Rosenberg and Zachary Karabell, *Kennedy, Johnson, and the Quest for Justice: The Civil Rights Tapes* (New York: W. W. Norton, 2003), 298; a slightly different version is in Michael R. Beschloss, ed., *Taking Charge: The Johnson White House Tapes, 1963–1964* (New York: Simon & Schuster, 1997), 334. Telephone conversation between Johnson and Fulbright, April 29, 1964.

84. Humphrey, *The Education of a Public Man*, 365, n. 5.
85. Richard C. Haney, "Wallace in Wisconsin: The Presidential Primary of 1964," *Wisconsin Magazine of History* (Summer, 1978): 259–78; Carter, *The Politics of Rage*, 202–209, Wallace quoted on 205.
86. Carter, *The Politics of Rage*, 213–15, quote at 215.
87. E. W. Kenworthy, "Senators Doubt Wallace Impact on Rights Action," *The New York Times*, May 21, 1964, 1.
88. Filvaroff and Wolfinger, "The Origin and Enactment of the Civil Rights Act of 1964," 25–26.
89. John G. Stewart, "Tactics II," in *The Civil Rights Act of 1964*, ed. Loevy, 287–90.
90. Quoted in Humphrey, *The Education of a Public Man*, 46.
91. James T. Findlay, "Religion and Politics in the Sixties: The Churches and the Civil Rights Act of 1964," *Journal of American History* 77 (1) (June, 1990): 66–92.
92. Findlay, "Religion and Politics in the Sixties," 76.
93. Humphrey, *The Education of a Public Man*, 209.
94. Robert E. Baker, "Senate Stops Filibuster, 71 to 29," *The Washington Post*, July 11, 1964, A1.
95. Nick Kotz, *Judgment Days: Lyndon Baines Johnson, Martin Luther King Jr., and the Laws that Changed America* (Boston: Houghton Mifflin, 2005), 152; Branch, *Pillar of Fire*, 356–57.
96. Lyndon B. Johnson, "Radio and Television Remarks Upon Signing the Civil Rights Bill," available at http://www.presidency.ucsb.edu/ws/?pid=26361.
97. Beschloss, ed., *Taking Charge*, 432–33; Carter, *The Politics of Rage*, 222–23.
98. Burk, *The Eisenhower Administration and Black Civil Rights*, 206.
99. Caro, *Master of the Senate*, xv, xxiii.
100. Robert Caro, "Lyndon Johnson: Power and Personality," Fourteenth Annual Theodore H. White Lecture on Press and Politics (Cambridge: Harvard University, Kennedy School of Government, 2003), at 28.
101. Neil R. McMillen, "Black Enfranchisement in Mississippi: Federal Enforcement and Black Protest in the 1960s," *Journal of Southern History* 43 (3) (August, 1977): 352.
102. Fanny Lou Hamer, "To Praise Our Bridges," in *The Eyes on the Prize*, ed. Carson, 177.
103. Ibid., 178.
104. Charles Rabb, "Mississippi Negroes Give Grim View of Intimidation in Voter Registration," *The Washington Post*, June 9, 1964.
105. The Mississippi Freedom Democratic Party candidates were Aaron Henry, Annie Devine, Virginia Gray, and Hamer. "Johnson Big Victor in 'Freedom' Voting," *The New York Times*, November 3, 1964, 28.
106. Quote from Joseph A. Loftus, "Five Mississippians Seated by House," *The New York Times*, January 5, 1965, 17; Robert E. Baker, "Mississippi's Delegates Win Seats in House," *The Washington Post*, January 5, 1965, A9. The five Mississippi lawmakers were veteran Democrats William M. Colmer, Jamie L. Whitten, Thomas G. Abernethy, and John Bell Williams; the Republican newcomer was Prentiss Walker.
107. Garrow, *Bearing the Cross*, 368.
108. Johnson, *The Vantage Point*, 161.
109. James T. Patterson, *Grand Expectations: The United States, 1945–1974* (New York: Oxford University Press, 1996), 579.
110. Garrow, *Bearing the Cross*, 368–75.
111. Remini, *The House*, 403.
112. Mann, *The Walls of Jericho*, 464–65.
113. "The Voting Rights Act of 1965," 467–68.
114. Telephone conversation between Johnson and King, January 15, 1965, in Beschloss, ed., *Reach for Glory*, 159.

115. McNeil, *Dirksen*, 253.
116. Carter, *The Politics of Rage*, 248–9. On Selma, Garrow, *Bearing the Cross*, 357–430; Taylor Branch, *At Canaan's Edge: America in the King Years, 1965–68* (New York: Simon and Schuster, 2006), 68–170; Charles E. Fager, *Selma 1965* (New York: Scribner's, 1974).
117. Lewis, *Walking in the Wind*, 200.
118. Carter, *The Politics of Rage*, 248–9.
119. There was no similar national outcry when African-American Jimmy Lee Jackson was killed earlier by an Alabama state trooper.
120. Johnson, *The Vantage Point*, 162.
121. Miller, *Lyndon*, 431, and Carter, *Politics of Rage*, 252–53 ("Texas python" description).
122. Branch, *At Canaan's Edge*, 98.
123. Lyndon B. Johnson, "Special Message to Congress: The American Promise," March 15, 1965. Wooley and Peters, *The American Presidency Project*, available at http://www.presidency.ucsb.edu/ws/?pid=26805.
124. Tom Wicker, "Johnson Urges Congress at Joint Session to Pass Law Insuring Negro Vote," *The New York Times*, March 16, 1965, 1.
125. Jackie Robinson, "Three Cheers for LBJ," *The Chicago Defender*, April 3, 1965, 8; Dallek, *Flawed Giant*, 218.
126. On Frank Johnson, see Jack Bass, *Taming the Storm: The Life and Times of Judge Frank M. Johnson, Jr. and the South's Fight Over Civil Rights* (New York: Doubleday, 1993).
127. Johnson, *The Vantage Point*, 163.
128. Branch, *Pillar of Fire*, 571–610.
129. John Tower (Republican–Texas) was absent from the vote, but announced that he was against passage. The other Republican voting against the legislation was Strom Thurmond of South Carolina. "Senate Roll-Call Vote on Voting Rights Bill," *The New York Times*, August 4, 1965, 13; *Congress and the Nation*, vol. 2, 1965–1968 (Washington, D.C.: Congressional Quarterly Service, 1969), 356–64.
130. Lawson, *Black Ballots*, 321.
131. "Text of Johnson's Statement on Voting Rights Law," *The New York Times*, August 7, 1965, 8; Robert E. Baker, "LBJ Signs Vote Rights Bill Today," *The Washington Post*, August 6, 1965, A1.
132. The law also applied to one county in Arizona and Alaska. In November, 1965, coverage was extended to two more Arizona counties, one county in Hawaii, and one in Idaho. Kelly and Harbison, *The American Constitution*, 965.
133. John Herbers, "U.S. Voting Aides Depart for South," *The New York Times*, August 7, 1965, 1.
134. Neil R. McMillen, "Black Enfranchisement in Mississippi: Federal Enforcement and Black Protest in the 1960s," *Journal of Southern History* 43 (3) (August, 1977): 356; Jesse W. Lewis, Jr., "King Sees Shift to North in Negro Rights Drive," *The Washington Post*, August 6, 1965, A4.
135. Gerald Horne, *Fire This Time: The Watts Uprising and the 1960s* (Charlottesille: University Press of Virginia, 1995).
136. "Provisions of the Civil Rights Act of 1964," *1964 CQ Almanac*, 378.
137. *Heart of Atlanta Motel* v. *United States*, 379 U.S. 241 (1964); *Katzenbach* v. *McClung*, 379 U.S. 294 (1964). In a third case, *Hamm* v. *City of Rock Hill*, 379 U.S. 306 (1964), the Court ruled that, with the passage of Title II, Congress in effect abated pending and future state criminal prosecutions of sit-in cases. A new federal law, the Court reasoned, now protected what was formerly illegal under state and local law. Four Justices dissented in *Hamm*, saying that Congress would have had to specifically make such an abatement.
138. *South Carolina* v. *Katzenbach*, 383 U.S. 301 (1966); on English literacy requirement, *Katzenbach* v. *Morgan*, 384 U.S. 641 (1966); on poll taxes, *Harper* v. *Virginia Board*

of Elections, 383 U.S. 667 (1966). The Twenty-Fourth Amendment to the Constitution, ratified in 1964, forbade the poll tax in federal elections.

139. Garth E. Pauley, *The Modern Presidency and Civil Rights: Rhetoric on Race from Roosevelt to Nixon* (College Station: Texas A&M University Press, 2001), 200–201.

140. Woodward, *Strange Career of Jim Crow*, 211.

141. See Randall Kennedy, "The Struggle for Racial Equality in Public Accommodations," in *Legacies of the 1964 Civil Rights Act*, ed. in Grofman, 156–66.

142. Gary Orfield, "The Civil Rights Act and American Education," in *Legacies of the 1964 Civil Rights Act*, ed. in Grofman, 89–128, at 127.

143. Ibid.

144. Brauer, "Women Activists, Southern Conservatives," 37. On Title VII, see Paul Burnstein, "The Impact of EEO Law: A Social Movement Perspective," in *Legacies of the 1964 Civil Rights Act*, ed. in Grofman, 129–55.

145. Paul E. Jaubert and Ben M. Crouch, "Mississippi Blacks and the Voting Rights Act of 1965," *Journal of Negro Education* 46 (2) (Spring, 1977): 160; Pat Watters and Reese Cleghorn, *Climbing Jacob's Ladder: The Arrival of Negroes in Southern Politics* (New York: Harcourt, Brace & World, 1967).

146. Richard J. Timpone, "Mass Mobilization or Government Intervention? The Growth of Black Registration in the South," *The Journal of Politics* 57 (2) (May, 1995): 427. On the aftermath of the Voting Rights Act, see Bernard Grofman, Lisa Handley, and Richard G. Niemi, *Minority Representation and the Quest for Voting Equality* (Cambridge: Cambridge University Press, 1992); Harrell R. Rodgers, Jr., and Charles S. Bullock III, *Law and Social Change: Civil Rights Laws and Their Consequences* (New York: McGraw-Hill, 1972); Harold W. Stanley, *Voter Mobilization and the Politics of Race: The South and Universal Suffrage, 1952–1984* (New York: Praeger, 1987).

147. Kelly and Harbison, *The American Constitution*, 967–8.

148. Grofman, Handley, and Niemi, *Minority Representation and the Quest for Voting Equality*, 23–24.

149. *Allen* v. *State Board of Elections*, 393 U.S. 544 (1969); Keyssar, *The Right to Vote*, 289–315.

150. Victor Andres Rodriguez, "Section 5 of the Voting Rights Act of 1965 After *Boerne*: The Beginning of the End of Preclearance?" *California Law Review* 91 (2003): 782.

151. 446 U.S. 55 (1980).

152. Don Edwards, "Voting Rights Act of 1965," in Lorn S. Foster, ed., *The Voting Rights Act: Consequences and Implications* (New York: Praeger, 1985), 7; John Herbert Roper, The Voting Rights Extension Act of 1982," *Phylon* 45 (3) (Third Quarter, 1984): 188.

153. On this era, see Raymond Wolters, *Right Turn: William Bradford Reynolds, the Reagan Administration, and Black Civil Rights* (New Brunswick, N.J.: Transaction, 1996), ch. 8.

154. Roper, "The Voting Rights Extension Act of 1982," 188.

155. Gerald S. and Deborah H. Strober, *"Let Us Begin Anew:" An Oral History of the Kennedy Presidency* (New York: HarperCollins, 1993), 277, cited in Riley, *The Presidency and the Politics of Racial Inequality*, 265.

156. Carter, *Politics of Rage*, 461.

157. American Civil Liberties Union, "The Case for Extending and Amending the Voting Rights Act" (2006), available from the ACLU website, http://www.aclu.org/votingrights/gen/24393res20060306.html.

158. 509 U.S. 630 (1993).

159. David Rosenbaum, "Offending Portrait Succumbs to Black Lawmakers' Protest," *The New York Times*, January 25, 1995, A19.

160. Dan Eggen, "Staff Opinions Banned in Voting Rights Cases," *The Washington Post*, December 10, 2005, A3.

161. Michael M. Grynbaum, "Bush Moves to 'Heal Old Wounds,'" *Boston Gobe*, July 21, 2006, A2.

162. The official name of the legislation is the "Fannie Lou Hamer, Rosa Parks, and Coretta Scott King Voting Rights Act Reauthorization and Amendments Act of 2006," Public Law 109–246.
163. Bob Kemper, "Voting Rights Focus on Georgia," *Atlanta Journal-Constitution*, July 10, 2006, 1A; Bob Kemper and Carlos Campos, "Voter Law a Divisive Issue for Georgians," *Atlanta Journal-Constitution*, July 21, 2006; Leadership Conference on Civil Rights website, http://www.RenewTheVote.org.
164. Bob Kemper, "Voting Act OK'd in Tense House," *Atlanta Journal-Constitution*, July 14, 2006, 1A.
165. Adam Nossiter, "U.S. Says Blacks in Mississippi Suppress White Vote," *The New York Times*, October 11, 2006, 18; "Whites Faced Election Bias in Mississippi, Judge Rules," *The Washington Post*, June 30, 2007, A30.
166. See Hugh Davis Graham, *Collision Course: The Strange Convergence of Affirmative Action and Immigration Policy in America* (New York: Oxford University Press, 2002).

11 MEDICAL CARE FOR THE ELDERLY AND POOR: THE MEDICARE AND MEDICAID ACT OF 1965

Epigraph quote from Johnson, transcript of remarks, in *The New York Times*, July 31, 1965, 9; the American Medical Association, testimony at hearing on *Health Services for the Aged under the Social Security Insurance System*, U.S. House of Representatives, Committee on Ways and Means, August 2, 1961, 1327–32, reprinted in Eugene Feingold, *Medicare: Policy and Politics: A Case Study and Policy Analysis* (San Francisco: Chandler Publishing Co., 1966), 28.

1. Edward T. Folliard, "Medicare Bill Signed by Johnson," *The Washington Post*, July 31, 1965, A1; John D. Morris, "President Signs Medicare Bill; Praises Truman," *The New York Times*, July 31, 1965, 1. Larry DeWitt, "The Medicare Program as a Capstone to the Great Society—Recent Revelations in the LBJ White House Tapes," unpublished essay, May 2003. Available at http://www.larrydewitt.net/Essays/MedicareDaddy.htm. DeWitt is an historian with the Social Security Administration.
2. Carleton B. Chapman and John M. Talmadge, "Historical and Political Background of Federal Health Care Legislation," *Law and Contemporary Problems* 35 (2), Health Care: Part 1 (Spring, 1970), 334.
3. Ibid., 334–36.
4. 22 U.S. 1 (1824); Chapman and Talmadge, "Historical and Political Background of Federal Health Care Legislation," 336.
5. Monte M. Poen, *Harry S. Truman Versus the Medical Lobby* (Columbia: University of Missouri Press, 1979), 9.
6. Chapman and Talmadge, "Historical and Political Background of Federal Health Care Legislation," 338.
7. Ibid., 339–40.
8. Forrest A. Walker, "Compulsory Health Insurance: 'The Next Great Step in Social Legislation,'" *Journal of American History* 56 (2) (September, 1969): 290; Arthur P. Miles, *An Introduction to Public Welfare* (Boston: D.C. Heath, 1949), 152–71.
9. Walker, "Compulsory Health Insurance," 291. Rubinow first called for reform in "Labor Insurance," *Journal of Political Economy* 12 (June, 1904), and his work included *Social Insurance: With Special Reference to American Conditions* (New York: Henry Holt, 1913) and *Quest for Security* (1934). Theodore M. Brown and Elizabeth Fee, "Isaac Max Rubinow: Advocate for Social Insurance," *American Journal of Public Health* 92 (8) (2002): 1224–25. On early efforts for government-sponsored health care, see Poen, *Harry S. Truman Versus the Medical Lobby*, 1–14.

10. Peter A. Corning, *The Evolution of Medicare . . . From Idea to Law*, Social Security Administration, 1969, ch. 1. Available at http://www.ssa.gov/history/corning. html. On AALL's efforts to pass health insurance in New York state, see Beatrix Hoffman, *The Wages of Sickness: The Politics of Health Insurance in Progressive America* (Chapel Hill: University of North Carolina Press, 2000).

11. Quoted in Walker, "Compulsory Health Insurance," 290.

12. Nancy J. Altman, *The Battle for Social Security: From FDR's Vision to Bush's Gamble* (Hoboken, N.J.: John Wiley, 2005), 18.

13. Cited in Odin W. Anderson, "Compulsory Medical Care Insurance, 1910–1950," *Annals of the American Academy of Political and Social Science* 273, Medical Care for Americans (January, 1951): 108.

14. Chapman and Talmadge, "Historical and Political Background of Federal Health Care Legislation," 341; J. Stanley Lemons, "The Sheppard–Towner Act: Progressivism in the 1920s," *Journal of American History* 55 (4) (March, 1969): 776–86. The law was named for its chief sponsors, Senator Morris Sheppard (Democrat– Texas) and Representative Horace Mann Towner (Republican–Iowa).

15. Jaap Kooijman, "Soon or Later On: Franklin D. Roosevelt and National Health Insurance, 1933–1945," *Presidential Studies Quarterly* 29 (2) (June, 1999): 337, 345.

16. Chapman and Talmadge, "Historical and Political Background of Federal Health Care Legislation," 342; Paul Starr, *The Social Transformation of American Medicine* (New York: Basic Books, 1982), 266–70.

17. Alan Derickson, "Health Security for All? Social Unionism and Universal Health Insurance," *Journal of American History* 80 (4) (March: 1994) 1337–39.

18. David R. Hyde, Payson Wolff, Ann Gross, Elliott Lee Hoffman, "The American Medical Association: Power, Purpose, and Politics in Organized Medicine," *Yale Law Journal* 63 (1953–1954), 1008, 1010; Starr, *The Social Transformation of American Medicine*, 275–58. On the earlier years of the AMA, see Oliver Garceau, *The Political Life of the American Medical Association* (Cambridge: Harvard University Press, 1941). Further, see Nancy Tomes, "Merchants of Health: Medicine and Consumer Culture in the United States, 1900–1940," *Journal of American History* 88 (2) (September, 2001): 519–47.

19. Starr, *The Social Transformation of American Medicine*, 278. In 1944, 58 percent said it was a "good idea," and 68 percent said the same in 1945.

20. Derickson, "Health Security for All?," 1340; Hyde et al., "The American Medical Association," 1009; Chapman and Talmadge, "Historical and Political Background of Federal Health Care Legislation," 343; Starr, *The Social Transformation of American Medicine*, 280–89; Poen, *Harry S. Truman Versus the Medical Lobby*, 29–65.

21. Edward T. Folliard, "Truman Plan for Health Insurance Starts Row," *The Washington Post*, November 20, 1945, 1; Felix Belair, Jr., "Truman Asks Law to Force Insuring of Nation's Health," *The New York Times*, November 20, 1945, 1.

22. Starr, *The Social Transformation of American Medicine*, 281.

23. Derickson, "Health Security for All?," 1342.

24. Ibid., 1246, 1351.

25. Zachary Karabell, *The Last Campaign: How Harry Truman Won the 1948 Election* (New York: Alfred A. Knopf, 2000); Richard Norton Smith, *Thomas E. Dewey and His Times* (New York: Simon and Schuster, 1982).

26. Harry S. Truman, Annual Message to the Congress on the State of the Union, January 5, 1949 in John Woolley and Gerhard Peters, *The American Presidency Project* (online), Santa Barbara, Calif.: University of California (hosted), Gerhard Peters (database). Available from http://www.presidency.ucsb.edu/?pid=13293.

27. Hyde et al., "The American Medical Association," 1011. On the Warren health care plan, see Daniel J. B. Mitchell, "Impeding Earl Warren: California's Health

Insurance Plan that Wasn't and What Might Have Been," *Journal of Health Politics, Policy and Law* 27 (6) (December, 2002): 947–76.

28. Feingold, *Medicare*, 98. On the Whitaker and Baxter-led campaign, see Stanley Kelley, Jr., *Professional Public Relations and Political Power* (Baltimore: Johns Hopkins University Press, 1966, 1957), 67–106; Poen, *Harry S. Truman Versus the Medical Lobby*, 144–45.

29. Gorman recounted this conversation to Oscar Ewing. Oral History Interview with Oscar R. Ewing, Truman Presidential Library. Conducted May 1, 1969, at Chapel Hill, N.C., by J. R. Fuchs. Available from http://www.trumanlibrary.org/oralhist/ewing3.htm.

30. Poem, *Harry S. Truman Versus The Medical Lobby*, 100; Kelley, *Professional Public Relations and Political Power*, 81.

31. Theodore R. Marmor, *The Politics of Medicare*, 2nd ed. (Hawthorne, N.Y.: Aldine de Gruyter, 2000), 8; "Social Security Medicare Program Enacted," *1965 CQ Almanac* (Washington, D.C.: Congressional Quarterly, Inc., 1966), 246.

32. "Social Security Medicare Program Enacted," 247.

33. Feingold, *Medicare*, 98–100.

34. James L. Sundquist, *Politics and Policy: The Eisenhower, Kennedy, and Johnson Years* (Washington, D.C.: The Brookings Institution, 1968), 291.

35. Ibid., 291–92; quote from testimony of David B. Allman, chairman, AMA legislative committee. Colin Gordon, *Dead on Arrival: The Politics of Health Care in Twentieth-Century America* (Princeton: Princeton University Press, 2003), 23–25.

36. Sundquist, *Politics and Policy*, 295–96.

37. Ibid., 296.

38. Robert M. Ball, "What Medicare's Architects Had in Mind," *Health Affairs* 14 (4) (Winter, 1995): 62. Among those whom Ball singles out as leaders in developing Medicare were Nelson Cruikshank of AFL-CIO Social Security Department; Lisabeth Schorr, director of AFL-CIO health insurance; Wilbur Cohen, who later became secretary of HEW; Alvin David, assistant director of the Bureau of Old-Age, Survivors and Disability Insurance at the Social Security Administration; Bill Fullerton and Irv Wolkstein who worked under David; Ida Mirriam, who headed the Bureau of Research and Statistics at SSA. Ball was commissioner of SSA from 1962 to 1973; Hess was in charge of Disability Insurance program, later in charge of Medicare, then the acting commissioner of SSA after Ball.

39. E. Richard Brown, "Medicare and Medicaid: The Process, Value, and Limits of Health Care Reforms," *Journal of Public Health Policy* 4 (3) (September, 1983): 341; Rowland Evans and Robert Novak, *Lyndon B. Johnson: The Exercise of Power* (New York: New American Library, 1966), 223–24. On the struggles over the Forand bill, Sundquist, *Politics and Policy*, 296–302, and Sheri I. David, *With Dignity: The Search for Medicare and Medicaid* (Westport, Conn.: Greenwood Press, 1985), 3–15.

40. Gordon, *Dead on Arrival*, 26–7; on Kerr-Mills, see David, *With Dignity*, 33–47.

41. Sundquist, *Politics and Policy*, 307.

42. David, *With Dignity*, 49–66, at 53.

43. Edward D. Berkowitz, *Mr. Social Security: The Life of Wilbur J. Cohen* (Lawrence: University Press of Kansas, 1995), 161.

44. Tom Wicker, "Medicare's Progress," *The New York Times*, March 25, 1965, 49.

45. Richard Harris, *A Sacred Trust* (New York: New American Library, 1966), 123; (quote) "AMA Inquiry Sought," *The New York Times*, March 19, 1962, 38.

46. Clayton Knowles, "Kennedy Exhorts Public to Support Medical Care Bill," *The New York Times*, May 21, 1962, 1; Harris, *A Sacred Trust*, 141–45.

47. Harris, *A Sacred Trust*, 143.

48. Peter Kihss, "AMA Rebuttal to Kennedy Sees Aged Care 'Hoax,'" *The New York Times*, May 22, 1962, 1; "British Call Views of AMA 'Nonsense,'" *The New York Times*, July 14, 1962, 7.

49. Donald Jackson, "Doctors Get Call to Act in Politics," *The New York Times*, June 25, 1962, 10; Sundquist, *Politics and Policy*, 311.

50. Tom Wicker, "President Visits Arkansas Today," *The New York Times*, October 3, 1963, 18; John F. Kennedy, "Remarks in Heber Springs, Arkansas, at the Dedication of Greers Ferry Dam," October 3, 1963. John Woolley and Gerhard Peters, *The American Presidency Project* (online). Santa Barabara, Calif.: University of California (hosted), Gerhard Peters (database). Available from http://www.presidency.ucsb.edu/ws/?pid=9455.

51. Berkowitz, *Mr. Social Security*, 215. Anthony J. Celebrezze was secretary of HEW; the principal deputy was Ivan Nestigen.

52. Berkowitz, *Mr. Social Security*, 214–15.

53. Ibid., 213–14; Julian E. Zelizer, *Taxing America: Wilbur D. Mills, Congress, and the State, 1945–1975* (Cambridge: Cambridge University Press, 1998), 227; Sundquist, *Politics and Policy*, 311–17.

54. "Goldwater, Johnson on Medicare," *The Washington Post*, September 3, 1964, A15.

55. Quote from Gordon, *Dead on Arrival*, 27, emphasis in the original; "Goldwater, Johnson on Medicare," *The Washington Post*, September 3, 1964, A15; Howard A. Rusk, "Candidates on Health: I," *The New York Times*, October 18, 1964, 77.

56. Lawrence F. O'Brien, *No Final Victories: A Life in Politics From John F. Kennedy to Watergate* (New York: Ballantine Books, 1976), 188–89; Lyndon B. Johnson, *Vantage Point: Perspectives of the Presidency 1963–1969* (New York: Holt, Rinehart and Winston, 1971), 213.

57. John F. Manley, *The Politics of Finance: The House Committee on Ways and Means* (Boston: Little, Brown, 1970), 27; also John F. Manley, "Wilbur D. Mills: A Study in Congressional Influence," *American Political Science Review* 63 (2) (June, 1969): 441–64.

58. Harris, *A Sacred Trust*, 179.

59. Richard Sorian, *The Bitter Pill: Tough Choices in America's Health Policy* (New York: McGraw-Hill, 1988), 92–93.

60. O'Brien, *No Final Victories*, 189; Sundquist, *Politics and Policy*, 317–21.

61. Harris, *A Sacred Trust*, 180–1.

62. Austin C. Wehrwein, "AMA Is Continuing Fight Against Medical-Care Bill," *The New York Times*, October 18, 1964, 76.

63. Henry J. Pratt, "Old Age Associations in National Politics," *Annals of the American Academy of Political and Social Science* 415, Political Consequences of Aging (September 1974), 109–12; Sundquist, *Politics and Policy*, 310–411, 314.

64. Louis Harris, "Public Feels Deeply About Need to Get Health Plan Started," *The Washington Post*, March 8, 1965, A2.

65. Manley, *The Politics of Finance*, 119.

66. Harris, *A Sacred Trust*, 179–81.

67. Ibid., 119–20. Manley credits William Quealy, the minority counsel for the Ways and Means Committee, for his role in creating the Byrnes bill.

68. On Mills and the Ways and Means Committee, see Manley, *The Politics of Finance*, and Zelizer, *Taxing America*.

69. Cohen's biographer is Edward D. Berkowitz, *Mr. Social Security*.

70. Merle Miller, *Lyndon: An Oral Biography* (New York: G. P. Putnam's Sons, 1980), 410; Berkowitz, *Mr. Social Security*, 227–32. In his recollection twenty-two years later, Mills said "I whispered in his [Byrnes's] ear, 'John, I wish you'd offer a motion to include it.' 'I'd be glad to.'" Transcript, Wilbur Mills Oral History Interview II, March 25, 1987, by Michael L. Gillette, Internet Copy, Lyndon B. Johnson Library, 1.

71. Eric Patashnik and Julian Zelizer, "Paying for Medicare: Benefits, Budgets, and Wilbur Mills's Policy Legacy," *Journal of Health Politics, Policy and Law* 26 (1) (February, 2001): 20.

72. David, *With Dignity*, 148–49.
73. Johnson, *Vantage Point*, 215.
74. Eric F. Goldman, *The Tragedy of Lyndon Johnson* (New York: Knopf, 1969), 290, cited in Allen J. Matusow, *The Unraveling of America: A History of Liberalism in the 1960s* (New York: Harper and Row, 1984), 227.
75. Tom Wicker, "What Changed Mills's Mind?" *The New York Times*, April 11, 1965, E9.
76. "Byrd Promises LBJ Action on Medicare," *The Washington Post*, March 27, 1965, A2. The Democratic leaders invited to the White House were, from the House, Wilbur Mills, Cecil King, John McCormack, Hale Boggs (Louisiana), Carl Albert, and from the Senate, Clinton Anderson, George A. Smathers (Florida), Mike Mansfield (Montana), and Harry Byrd.
77. Miller, *Lyndon*, 411. Johnson characterized Mills: "so long the villain of the act [Medicare], was now a hero to the old folks." Johnson, *Vantage Point*, 215.
78. "AMA Head Sees Decline in Care," *The New York Times*, May 12, 1965, 21.
79. Austin C. Wehrwein, "AMA Chiefs Ask Delay on Boycott," *The New York Times*, June 24, 1965, 46. The AMA had received a five-year $10-million grant from the tobacco industry to study the health effects of smoking.
80. Robert Dallek, *Flawed Giant: Lyndon Johnson and His Times, 1961–1973* (New York: Oxford University Press, 1998), 209–10.
81. Miller, *Lyndon*, 412.
82. Morton Mintz, "AMA Counselor Chills Medicare Boycott Idea," *The Washington Post*, October 3, 1965, A14; Wehrwein, "AMA Is Continuing Fight Against Medical-Care Bill," 76; and Johnson, *Vantage Point*, 218.
83. David, *With Dignity*, 143–44.
84. Joseph A. Califano, Jr., *America's Health Care Revolution: Who Lives? Who Dies? Who Pays?* (New York: Random House, 1986), 142–43. Califano later served as secretary of the Department of Health, Education and Welfare in the Carter Administration (1977–1979).
85. Marmor, *The Politics of Medicare*, 89.
86. Califano, *America's Health Care Revolution*, 144; Marmor, *The Politics of Medicare*, 89. Matusow, *The Unraveling of America*, 232. The 2 percent hospital bonus was eliminated in 1969.
87. Judith M. Feder, *Medicare: The Politics of Federal Hospital Insurance* (Lexington, Mass.: D. C. Heath, 1977).
88. Miller, *Lyndon*, 412.
89. "Largest Health Care Fraud Case in U.S. History Settled. HCA Investigation Nets Record Total of $1.7 Billion," U.S. Department of Justice press release, June 26, 2003. Available from the Department of Justice website, http://www.usdoj.gov/opa/pr/2003/June/03_civ_386.htm.
90. Quoted in Starr, *The Social Transformation of American Medicine*, 381.
91. Richard D. Lyons, "Medicare Study in Senate Seeks Urgent Reforms," *The New York Times*, February 9, 1970; Sorian, *Bitter Pill*, 95–97, quote on 97.
92. Califano, *America's Health Care Revolution*, 146; Sorian, *The Bitter Pill*, 97–99; Judith Bentkover, Philip Caper, Mark Schlesinger, and Joel Suldan, "Medicare's Payment of Hospitals," in David Blumenthal, Mark Schlesinger, and Pamela Brown Drumheller, eds., *Renewing the Promise: Medicare and Its Reform* (New York: Oxford University Press, 1988), 90–114; Marilyn Moon, *Medicare Now and in the Future*, 2nd ed. (Washington, D.C.: Urban Institute Press, 1996), 33–35.
93. Jonathan Oberlander, *The Political Life of Medicare* (Chicago: University of Chicago Press, 2003), 125–26; Robert A. Derzon, "The Genesis of HCFA," *CMS Reflections*, July 26, 2005, available at http://content.healthaffairs.org.
94. Eve Edstrom, "Health Insurance for All Proposed," *The Washington Post*, February 10, 1970, A2.

95. O'Brien, *No Final Victories*, 190–91.
96. Quoted in Rick Mayes, *Universal Coverage: The Elusive Quest for National Health Insurance* (Lanham, Md.: Lexington Books, 2001), 1.
97. Ibid., 97; Karen Davis, *National Health Insurance* (Washington, D.C.: The Brookings Institution, 1975), 166–71.
98. Mayes, *Universal Coverage*, 1.
99. Marmor, *The Politics of Medicare*, 115.
100. Sorian, *Bitter Pill*, 99–102.
101. Ibid., 102–109; Benkover et al., "Medicare's Payment to Hospitals," 94.
102. Benkover et al., *Medicare's Payment to Hospitals*, 94–6; Sorian, *Bitter Pill*, 110–21; Moon, *Medicare Now and in the Future*, 55–9.
103. Marmor, *The Politics of Medicare*, 109.
104. Moon, *Medicare Now and in the Future*, 55–60.
105. David Blumenthal and William Hsiao, "Payment of Physicians Under Medicare," in *Renewing the Promise*, ed. Blumenthal, Schlesinger, and Drumheller, 120–21.
106. Moon, *Medicare Now and in the Future*, 115.
107. Martin Tolchin, "Retreat in Congress: The Catastrophic-Care Debacle," *The New York Times*, October 9, 1989, 1; Bill Peterson, "Rostenkowski Heckled by Senior Citizens," *The Washington Post*, August 18, 1989, A4.
108. Moon, *Medicare Now and in the Future*, 135–7.
109. On the political dynamics of the Clinton health care proposal, see Haynes Johnson and David Broder, *The System: American Politics at the Breaking Point* (Boston: Little, Brown, 1997). Also, Jacob S. Hacker, *The Road to Nowhere: The Genesis of President Clinton's Plan for Health Security* (Princeton: Princeton University Press, 1997); Theda Skocpol, *Boomerang: Health Care Reform and the Turn Against Government* (New York: W. W. Norton, 1996); and Nicholas Lham, *A Lost Cause: Bill Clinton's Campaign for National Health Insurance* (Westport, Conn.: Praeger, 1996). On the role of Hillary Rodham Clinton, see Carl Bernstein, *A Woman in Charge: The Life of Hillary Rodham Clinton* (New York: Alfred A. Knopf, 2007). On the loss of business support, see Peter Swenson and Scott Greer, "Foul Weather Friends: Big Business and Health Care Reform in the 1990s in Historical Perspective," *Journal of Health Politics, Policy and Law* 27 (4) (August, 2002): 605–38.
110. Paul Starr, "What Happened to Health Care Reform?" *The American Prospect* 20 (Winter, 1995): 20–31; see Paul Starr, *The Logic of Health Care Reform: Why and How the President's Plan Will Work*, rev. and expanded ed. (New York: Penguin Books, 1994, 1992).
111. Starr, "What Happened to Health Care Reform?" 21.
112. Ben Goddard of Goddard-Claussen/First Tuesday, a California-based political consulting firm, was the creator of the Harry and Louise ads. Robin Toner, "Harry and Louise and a Guy Named Ben," *The New York Times*, September 30, 1994, A22. Also, Darrell West, Diane Heath, and Chris Goodwin, "Harry and Louise Go to Washington: Political Advertising and Health Care Reform," *Journal of Health Politics, Policy and Law* 21 (1996): 35–36.
113. Oberlander, *The Political Life of Medicare*, 157.
114. "Summary of Findings," 1995 Report of the Medicare Trustees, available from the Social Security Administration website, www.ssa.gov/history/reports/trust/trustreports.html. Robert Pear, "More Dire Warnings About Social Security," *The New York Times*, April 4, 1995, D24.
115. Ibid., 166–67.
116. National Institutes of Health, National Center for Health Statistics, *Health, United States, 2004*, table 134: Health Maintenance Organizations (HMOs) and Enrollment. Oberlander, *The Political Life of Medicare*, 169–71. By 2003, 71.8 million individuals were enrolled in HMOs.

117. Library of Congress, Congressional Research Service, *Medicare: Changes to Balanced Budget Act of 1997*, written by Jennifer O'Sullivan, Carolyn Merck, Madeleine Smith, Sibyl Tilson (November 19, 1999), 1; Oberlander, *The Political Life of Medicare*, 184–89; Marmor, *The Politics of Medicare*, 117–49.

118. Nancy-Ann DeParle, "As Good As It Gets: The Future of Medicare+Choice," *Journal of Health Politics, Policy and Law* 27 (3) (June 2002), 497. HCFA has since been renamed as the Centers for Medicare and Medicaid Services (CMS).

119. Oberlander, *The Political Life of Medicare*, 190.

120. Library of Congress, Congressional Research Service, *Overview of the Medicare Prescription Drug, Improvement, and Modernization Act of 2003*, written by Jennifer O'Sullivan, Hinda Chaikind, Sibyl Tilson, Jennifer Boulanger, and Paulette Morgan (December 6, 2004); Marilyn Moon, "How Beneficiaries Far Under the New Medicare Drug Bill," *The Commonwealth Fund*, June 2004.

121. Library of Congress, Congressional Research Service, *Medicare: A Primer*, written by Jennifer O'Sullivan (October 30, 2006), 11; testimony of Peter R. Orszag, Director of the Congressional Budget Office, before the Subcommittee on Health, House Committee on Ways and Means, March 21, 2007.

122. Library of Congress, Congressional Research Service, *Social Security and Medicare: The Economic Implications of Current Policy*, written by Marc Labonte (December 6, 2006); Moon, *Medicare Now and in the Future*; Shea McClanahan, Kenneth Apfel, and Paisa Fatehi, "Health Insurance for Older Americans: Assessing Medicare's Past, Present, and Future," in Kenneth Apfel and Betty Sue Flowers, eds., *Big Choices: The Future of Health Insurance for Older Americans* (Austin: University of Texas, 2004), 125–26.

123. Timothy Stoltzfus Jost, "Why Can't We Do What They Do? National Health Reform Abroad," *Journal of Law, Medicine and Ethics* 32 (3) (Fall, 2004): 433.

124. Office of Senator Edward M. Kennedy, press release, "Kennedy and Dingell Fight for Medicare for All," April 25, 2007, available from the Kennedy Senate website, http://kennedy.senate.gov/newsroom. For background on Medicare for All, see Eva DuGoff, "Medicare for All: Issues of Policy and Politics," *The Current* (The Public Policy Journal of the Cornell Institute for Public Affairs), 10 (2) (Spring, 2007): 85–102; Olga Pierce, "The 'Medicare for All' Strategy," *United Press International*, April 26, 2007.

125. "AMA Launches Multi-Million Dollar Campaign to Cover the Uninsured," available at www.medicalnewstoday.com. American Medical Association, *Expanding Health Insurance: The AMA Proposal for Reform* (2007), available at http://ama-assn.0rg/ama1/pub/upload/mm/363/ehi1012.pdf.

12 PROTECTING THE ENVIRONMENT: THE NATIONAL ENVIRONMENTAL POLICY ACT OF 1969

Epigraph quotes from Nixon, in "Nixon Promises an Urgent Fight to End Pollution," *The New York Times*, January 2, 1970, 1; Testimony of Admiral James Watkins before the House Armed Services Committee (1992), cited in the Council on Environmental Quality, *The National Environmental Policy Act: A Study of its Effectiveness After 25 Years*, at 13, available from the Council on Environmental Quality website, http://ceq.eh.doe.gov/nepa/nepa25fn.pdf. Oliver A. Houck, "'Is That All?' A Review of *The National Environmental Policy Act, An Agenda for the Future*, By Lynton Caldwell," *Duke Environmental Law & Policy Forum* 11 (Fall, 2000): 173. Although it was signed into law on January 1, 1970, the official name of the law is the National Environmental Policy Act of 1969.

1. Adam Rome, "'Give Earth a Chance': The Environmental Movement and the Sixties," *The Journal of American History* 90 (2) (September 2003): 525; *American*

Heritage, October 1993; Gaylord Nelson, "Earth Day 25 Years Later," *EPA Journal*, Winter, 1995, 9–10; Denis Hayes, "Earth Day!," *Mother Earth News*, April/May, 2005, 24; Joseph Lelyveld, "Millions Join Earth Day Observances Across the Nation," *The New York Times*, April 23, 1970, 1; J. Brooks Flippen, *Nixon and the Environment* (Albuquerque: University of New Mexico Press, 2000), 15.

2. Nicholas von Hoffman, "Earth Day: 'A Net Loss,'" *The Washington Post*, April 27, 1970, C1.

3. Carl Bernstein, "Protestors Rouse Fury of Broyhill," *The Washington Post*, May 15, 1970, B11.

4. Richard A. Liroff, *A National Policy for the Environment* (Bloomington: Indiana University Press, 1976), 3.

5. Norman J. Vig and Michael E. Kraft, *Environmental Policy in the 1990s* (Washington, D.C.: CQ Press, 1990), appendix 1: "Major Federal Laws on the Environment, 1969–1989."

6. George Perkins Marsh, *Man and Nature*, ed. David Lowenthal (Cambridge: Belknap Press of Harvard University Press, 1965, 1864).

7. Marsh quoted in Grant McConnell, "Prologue: Environment and the Quality of Political Life," in *Congress and the Environment*, ed. Richard A. Cooley and Geoffrey Wandesforde-Smith (Seattle: University of Washington Press, 1970), 5.

8. John M. Meyer, "Gifford Pinchot, John Muir, and the Boundaries of Politics in American Thought," *Polity* XXX (2) (Winter, 1997): 267–84. Michael Cohen, *The Pathless Way: John Muir and American Wilderness* (Madison: University of Wisconsin Press, 1984); Gifford Pinchot, *Breaking New Ground* (New York: Harcourt, Brace and Company, 1947); M. Nelson McGreary, *Gifford Pinchot: Forester—Politician* (Princeton: Princeton University Press, 1960); and Roderick Nash, *Wilderness and the American Mind*, rev. ed. (New Haven: Yale University Press, 1973).

9. McConnell, "Prologue: Environment and the Quality of Political Life," 4.

10. Allan K. Fitzsimmons, "Environmental Quality as a Theme in Federal Legislation," *Geographic Review* 70 (3) (July, 1980): 314–27.

11. J. Clarence Davies III and Barbara S. Davies, *The Politics of Pollution*, 2nd ed. (Indianapolis: Bobbs-Merrill, 1975); Michael E. Kraft and Norman J. Vig, "Environmental Policy from the Seventies to the Nineties: Continuity and Change," in *Environmental Policy in the 1990s*, ed. Vig and Kraft, 11.

12. David Templeton, "Cleaner Air Is Legacy Left by Donora's Killer 1948 Smog," *Pittsburgh Post-Gazette*, October 29, 1998; Jeff Gammage, "20 Died, The Government Took Heed. In 1948, a Killer Fog Spurred Air Cleanup," *Philadelphia Inquirer*, October 28, 1998. The Donora smog reminded some of the 1930 smog and the deaths of more than sixty people in the Meuse Valley and the industrial factories in Liege, Belgium. Four years after Donora, London experienced a deadly fog, causing 3,000 deaths in the first few days of December, 1952. Michelle L. Bell and Devra Lee Davis, "Reassessment of the Lethal London Fog of 1952: Novel Indicators of Acute and Chronic Consequences of Acute Exposure to Air Pollution," *Environmental Health Perspectives* 109 (3) (June, 2001): 389–94.

13. Templeton, "Cleaner Air Is Legacy Left by Donora's Killer 1948 Smog," and Monessen newspaper editorial cited in David Hess, "Historic Marker Commemorates Donora Smog Tragedy," Pennsylvania Department of Environmental Protection website, available at http://www.depweb.state.pa.us/heritage/cwp/view.asp?A=3&Q=533403.

14. Adam Rome, "'Give Earth a Chance,'" 526.

15. Aldo Leopold, *A Sand County Almanac, and Sketches Here and There* (New York: Oxford University Press, 1949); Aldo Leopold Foundation website, www.aldoleopold.org. Daniel W. Gade, "The Growing Recognition of George Perkins Marsh," *Geographic Review* 73 (3) (July, 1983): 341–44; David Lowenthal, *George Perkins Marsh:*

Prophet of Conservation (Seattle: University of Washington Press, 2000). For an understanding of the ecology crisis and Christian doctrine, see Lynn White, Jr., "The Historic Roots of Our Ecologic Crisis," *Science* 155 (3767) (March 10, 1967): 1203–207.

16. Vance O. Packard, *The Waste Makers* (New York: D. McKay, 1960); Paul R. Erhlich, *The Population Bomb* (New York: Ballantine Books, 1968); Stewart L. Udall, *The Quiet Crisis* (New York: Holt, Rhinehart and Winston, 1963.

17. Rachel Carson, *Silent Spring* (Greenwich, Conn.: Fawcett, 1962). The conservative magazine *Human Events* invited like-minded scholars in 2005 to compile a list of the ten "most harmful" books from the nineteenth and twentieth centuries. Leading the list were Karl Marx, *The Communist Manifesto*, Adolph Hitler, *Mein Kampf*, Mao Zedong, *Quotations from Chairman Mao*, then Alfred Kinsey, *The Kinsey Report*. Not reaching the top fifteen, but still receiving votes as the worst books were Carson, *Silent Spring*, Ehrlich, *The Population Bomb*, Charles Reich, *The Greening of America*, Club of Rome, *The Limits of Growth*. Human Events website, available at http//:humanevents.com/article.php?id=7591.

18. Linda Lear, *Rachel Carson: Witness for Nature* (New York: Henry Holt, 1997), 428–30.

19. "Critic of Pesticides: Rachel Louise Carson," *The New York Times*, June 5, 1963, 59.

20. Lear, *Rachel Carson*, 446–56, quote at 449.

21. Ibid., 450.

22. Ibid., 447.

23. David Michaels, "Environmental Health Science and the Legacy of Popular Literature," *Environmental Health Perspectives* 111 (1) (January, 2003): A14–15.

24. Lear, *Rachel Carson*, 454.

25. Jack Lewis, "The Birth of EPA," originally in the *EPA Journal*, November, 1985; from the EPA website, http://www.epa.gov/history/topics/epa/5c.htm. After Senator Benjamin L. Cardin (Democrat–Maryland) announced in 2007 that he intended to submit a resolution honoring Rachel Carson on the one hundredth anniversary of her birth, his colleague Tom Coburn (Republican–Oklahoma) threatened to use Senate rules and block the legislation. Coburn charged that Carson was using "junk science," and on his Senate website argued that one to two million people die every year because of malaria. "This book," Coburn noted, "was the catalyst in the deadly worldwide stigmatization against insecticides, especially DDT." David A. Fahrenthold, "Bill to Honor Rachel Carson on Hold," *The Washington Post*, May 23, 2007, B1. On the benefits of DDT, see Janet Raloff, "The Case for DDT: What Do You Do When a Dreaded Environmental Pollutant Saves Lives?" *Science News* 58 (1) (July, 2000): 12–14.

26. Oral History Interview, Gaylord Nelson, conducted by Don Nicoll, Washington, D.C., December 5, 2000; The Edmund S. Muskie Archives and Special Collections Library, Bates College.

27. Lyndon B. Johnson, *The Vantage Point: Perspectives of the Presidency 1963–1969* (New York: Holt, Rinehart and Winston, 1971), 337.

28. Richard J. Lazarus, *The Making of Environmental Law* (Chicago: University of Chicago Press, 2004), 52.

29. National Resources Defense Council, "E-Law: What Started it All?" Available from the Natural Resources Defense Council website, http://nrdc.org/legislation/helaw.asp.

30. James J. Kyle, "Indiana Dunes National Lakeshore: The Battle for the Dunes," in *Congress and the Environment*, ed. Cooley and Wandesford-Smith, 16–31; "Indiana Dunes National Lakeshore History," U.S. Department of the Interior, National Park Service website, http://www.nps.gov/indu/historyculture/index.htm.

31. Wolfgang Saxon, "Fred L. Hartley, 73, Built Unocal Into Multibillion Dollar Company," *The New York Times*, October 21, 1990. Robert O. Easton, *Black Tide:*

The Santa Barbara Oil Spill and Its Consequences (New York: Delacorte Press, 1972); Mark H. Lytle, *America's Uncivil Wars: The Sixties Era, From Elvis to the Fall of Richard Nixon* (New York: Oxford University Press, 2006).

32. "The Cities: The Price of Optimism," *Time* (August 1, 1969), available at http://www.time.com/time/magazine/article/0,9171,901182,00.html; "Cuyahoga River Fire," Ohio Historical Society website, available at http://www.ohio historycentral.org/entry.php?rec=1642; Jonathan H. Adler, "Smoking Out the Cuyahoga Fire Fable," *National Review Online*, n.d., available at http://www. nationalreview.com.

33. Fitzsimmons, "Environmental Quality as a Theme," 319.

34. Quoted in Richard A. Cooley and Geoffrey Wandesford-Smith, "Conclusions: Congress and the Environment of the Future," in *Congress and the Environment*, ed. Cooley and Wandesford-Smith, 229.

35. Philip Shabecoff, *A Fierce Green Fire: The American Environmental Movement* (New York: Hill and Wang, 1993), 118.

36. Victor B. Scheffer, *The Shaping of Environmentalism in America* (Seattle: University of Washington Press, 1991), 143.

37. For background and a detailed study of the enactment of NEPA, see Terence T. Finn, *Conflict and Compromise: Congress Makes a Law. The Passage of the National Environmental Policy Act*. Unpublished dissertation, Department of Government, Georgetown University, 1972, 8.

38. Ibid., 8–49.

39. Matthew J. Lindstrom and Zachary A. Smith, *The National Environmental Policy Act: Judicial Misconstruction, Legislative Indifference and Executive Neglect* (College Station: Texas A&M Press, 2001), 29.

40. Ibid. Nelson's bill was the Ecological Research and Surveys Bill of 1965 (S. 2282). Lindstrom and Smith point out that this is the first time the term "ecology" appeared in a federal legislative proposal.

41. Finn, *Conflict and Compromise*, 376.

42. Lynton K. Caldwell, "Environment: A New Focus for Public Policy," *Public Administration Review* 23 (September, 1963): 132–39. Other academic writings during the early 1970s included Cooley and Wandesford-Smith, eds., *Congress and the Environment* (1970); Harold Sprout and Margaret Sprout, *Towards a Politics of the Planet Earth* (New York: Von Nostrand Reinhold, 1971); Richard A. Faulk, *This Endangered Planet: Prospects and Proposals for Human Survival* (New York: Random House, 1971); Davies and Davies, *The Politics of Pollution*. See Robert V. Bartlett and James N. Gladden, "Lynton K. Caldwell and Environmental Policy: What Have We Learned," in Lynton K. Caldwell, *Environment as a Focus for Public Policy*, ed. Robert V. Bartlett and James N. Gladden (College Station: Texas A&M University Press, 1995), 27–41.

43. The Caldwell paper was entitled "A National Policy for the Environment," reprinted in Caldwell, *Environment as a Focus for Public Policy*, ed. Bartlett and Gladden, 139–66. On the developments in 1968, see Finn, *Conflict and Compromise*, 240–59.

44. Congressman George Paul Miller, who served in the House from 1945 to 1972, should not be confused with Congressman George Miller, also a Democrat from California, who began his service in 1975. They are not related.

45. Russell E. Train, *Politics, Pollution and Pandas: An Environmental Memoir* (Washington, D.C.: Island Press, 2003), 52; William W. Prochnau and Richard W. Larsen, *A Certain Democrat: Senator Henry M. Jackson, A Political Biography* (Englewood Cliffs, N.J.: Prentice-Hall, 1972), 69.

46. Liroff, *A National Policy for the Environment*, 17–18; Lindstrom and Smith, *The National Environmental Policy Act*, 34–35.

47. Lynton Keith Caldwell, *The National Environmental Policy Act: An Agenda for the Future* (Bloomington: Indiana University Press, 1998), 44.

48. Lindstrom and Smith, *The National Environmental Policy Act*, 36.

49. Lynton K. Caldwell, "An Interview with Lynton Caldwell on the National Environmental Policy Act (NEPA)," *Environmental Practice* 5 (4) (December, 2003): 282.

50. Prochnau and Larsen, *A Certain Democrat*, 273. DuBridge had also been science advisor for President Harry Truman.

51. Ibid., 274; also, Finn, *Conflict and Compromise*, 378–88.

52. Lindstrom and Smith, *The National Environmental Policy Act*, 40–43.

53. Finn, *Conflict and Compromise*, 378–88.

54. Ibid., 388, 391–93.

55. Lindstrom and Smith, *The National Environmental Policy Act*, 40.

56. Liroff, *A National Policy for the Environment*, 18–20; Lindstrom and Smith, *The National Environmental Policy Act*, 44–47. Also, Paul Charles Milazzo, *Unlikely Environmentalists: Congress and Clean Water, 1945–1972* (Lawrence: University Press of Kansas, 2006), 112–14.

57. Lindstrom and Smith, *The National Environmental Policy Act*, 46.

58. Flippen, *Nixon and the Environment*, 113; on the career of Muskie, see David Nevin, *Muskie of Maine* (New York: Random House, 1972).

59. Liroff, *A National Policy for the Environment*, 5.

60. *Congressional Record*, vol. 115, 40416.

61. Bradley C. Karkkainen, "Toward a Smarter NEPA: Monitoring and Managing Government's Environmental Performance," *Columbia Law Review* 102 (4) (May, 2002): 909.

62. Caldwell, "An Interview with Lynton Caldwell on the National Environmental Policy Act (NEPA)," 282–83. Emphasis in the original.

63. 42 U.S.C. sec. 4331(a) (1982).

64. On the first five years of the CEQ and its annual reports, see Edwin S. Mills and Frederick M. Peterson, "*Environmental Quality*: The First Five Years," *The American Economic Review* 65 (3) (June, 1975): 259–68. All italics are in the original.

65. Flippen, *Nixon and the Environment*, 51.

66. Caldwell, *The National Environmental Policy Act*, xx.

67. E. W. Kenworthy, "Muskie Calls President's Antipollution Drive 'Slogan-Rich and Action-Poor,'" *The New York Times*, January 16, 1970, 19.

68. Richard M. Nixon, Annual Message to Congress on the State of the Union, January 22, 1970. John T. Woolley and Gerhard Peters, *The American Presidency Project* (online). Santa Barbara, California: University of California (hosted), Gerhard Peters (database). Available from http://www.presidency.ucsb.edu/ws/?pid=2921.

69. Flippen, *Nixon and the Environment*, 52. On the career of Russell E. Train, see J. Brooks Flippen, *Conservative Conservationist: Russell E. Train and the Emergence of American Environmentalism* (Baton Rouge: Louisiana State University Press, 2006).

70. Serge Taylor, *Making Bureaucracies Think: The Environmental Impact Statement Strategy of Administrative Reform* (Stanford: Stanford University Press, 1984), 251.

71. Flippen, *Nixon and the Environment*, 48.

72. Daniel R. Mandelker, *NEPA Law and Litigation*, 2nd ed. (Thomson/West, 2007), 1:1.

73. Liroff, *A National Policy for the Environment*, 31.

74. E. W. Kenworthy, "Senator Nelson to Ask for Antipollution Measure," *The New York Times*, January 20, 1970, 29.

75. John C. Whitaker, *Striking a Balance: Environmental and Natural Resources Policy in the Nixon-Ford Years* (Washington, D.C.: American Enterprise Institute for Public Policy Research, 1976), 7.

76. Ibid., 6–7.
77. Joel A. Mintz, *Enforcement at the EPA: High Stakes and Hard Choices* (Austin: University of Texas Press, 1995), 20.
78. Elsie Carper, "Nominee Vows Pollution Fight," *Washington Post*, December 2, 1970, A27.
79. E. W. Kenworthy, "Nixon Has a New Aspirant for Title 'Mr. Clean,'" *The New York Times*, December 6, 1970, 24.
80. Scheffer, *The Shaping of Environmentalism in America*, 143–44.
81. Lazarus, *The Making of Environmental Law*, 76.
82. Don Oberdorfer, "Muskie Not Invited to Air Law Signing," *The Washington Post*, January 1, 1971, A2.
83. Train, *Politics, Pollution and Pandas*, 86.
84. Lazarus, *The Making of Environmental Law*, 77; Flippen, *Nixon and the Environment*, 134.
85. Train, *Politics, Pollution and Pandas*, 79.
86. Shabecoff, *A Fierce Green Fire*, 129.
87. Among the other federal laws passed during the 1970s are the Resources Recovery Act (1970); Federal Environmental Pesticides Control Act (1972); Marine Protection Act (1972); Coastal Zone Management Act (1972); Safe Drinking Water Act (1974); Federal Land Policy and Management Act (1976); National Forest Management Act (1976); Surface Mining Control and Reclamation Act (1977); and Public Utility Regulatory Policies Act (1978).
88. Walter A. Rosenbaum, *Environmental Politics and Policy*, 5th ed. (Washington, D.C.: CQ Press, 2002), 6.
89. 449 F. 2d 1109 (D.C. Circuit, 1971).
90. 449 F. 2d 1109 at 1117. On decision, see Bart Barnes, "A-Plant Safeguards Held Faulty by Court," *The Washington Post*, July 24, 1971, A1.
91. Richard D. Lyons, "AEC Will Review Reactor Permits," *The New York Times*, September 4, 1971, 1.
92. Taylor, *Making Bureaucracies Think*, 72. Council of Environmental Quality, *Annual Report* (1979), cited in Taylor, *Making Bureaucracies Think*, 72 n.
93. Lindstrom and Smith, *The National Environmental Policy Act*, 123.
94. 427 U.S. 390 (1976).
95. *Vermont Nuclear Power Corp.* v. *Natural Resources Defense Council, Inc.*, 435 U.S. 519 (1978).
96. Mandelker, *NEPA Law and Litigation*, 1:12.
97. Caldwell, "The World Environment," 323.
98. Mintz, *Enforcement at the EPA*, 40; Gil Troy, *Morning in America: How Ronald Reagan Invented the 1980s* (Princeton: Princeton University Press, 2005), 141.
99. Mintz, *Enforcement at the EPA*, 40–59; Norman J. Vig, "Presidential Leadership and the Environment: From Reagan to Clinton," in *Environmental Policy in the 1990s*, ed. Vig and Kraft, 98–101.
100. Vig, "Presidential Leadership and the Environment," 99.
101. Walter A. Rosenbaum, *Environmental Politics and Policy*, 6th ed. (Washington, D.C.: CQ Press, 2005), 8.
102. "Electoral Dynamite: The Environment," *The New York Times*, September 1, 1988, A24.
103. "Mr. Bush on the Environment," *The New York Times*, September 2, 1988, A20; "Electoral Dynamite: The Environment."
104. Vig, "Presidential Leadership and the Environment," 106; Rosenbaum, *Environmental Politics and Policy*, 6th ed., 70.
105. Vig, "Presidential Leadership and the Environment," 108–109.
106. On the Republican 1995 legislative revolution, see James G. Gimpel, *Fulfilling the Contract: The First Hundred Days* (Boston: Allyn and Bacon, 1996), and specifically

on environmental policy, Michael E. Kraft, "Environmental Policy in Congress: Revolution, Reform, or Gridlock?" in *Environmental Policy in the 1990s*, ed. Vig and Kraft, 119–39.

107. Kraft, "Environmental Policy in Congress," 129–31.

108. Ibid., 132–33.

109. Ibid., 137.

110. Kristina Alexander, *Overview of National Environmental Policy Act (NEPA) Requirements* (Washington, D.C.: Congressional Research Service, Library of Congress, January 11, 2008), Report RS20621; 3–5. See also National Resources Defense Council, "NEPA: Core Environmental Safeguard Under Growing Attack," January, 2006, available from NRDC website, http://www.wilderness.org/OurIssues/NEPA/index.cfm.

111. Submission by Professors of Administrative, Environmental and Natural Resources Law and Policy to the United States House of Representatives Task Force on the National Environmental Policy Act, October 10, 2005, 6, available at http://republicans.resourcescommittee.house.gov/archives/ii00/nepatask force/archives/debbiesease_attachA.pdf. See, also, Karkkainen, "Toward a Smarter NEPA." Robert L. Glicksman, David L. Markell, Daniel R. Mandelker, A. Dan Tarlock, and Frederick R. Anderson, *Environmental Protection: Law and Policy*, 4th ed. (New York: Aspen Publishers, 2003), 260.

112. Linda Luther, *The National Environmental Policy Act: Streamlining NEPA*. Report RL33267 (Washington, D.C.: Library of Congress, Congressional Research Service, Januay 9, 2007), 6–7. See also Linda Luther, *The National Environmental Policy Act: Background and Implementation* Report RL33152 (Washington, D.C.: Library of Congress, Congressional Research Service, November 16, 2005).

113. Data from NEPAnet, "Calendar Year 2006 Filed EISs," available at www.nepa. gov/nepa/Calendar_Year_2006_Filed_EISs.pdf, and "Environmental Impact Statements Filed 1970 through 2006," available at www.nepa.gov/nepa/EIS_by_Year_1970_2006.pdf.

114. Submission by Professors, citing CEQ reports, 5–6.

115. Letter from Northwest Mining Association, Laura Skaer, executive director, on NEPA Modernization (CE), to the Council on Environmental Quality, November 24, 2006, available at www.ceq.hss.doe.gov/ntf/ceqcomments/Northwest_Mining_Assoc_Comments_on_CEs.pdf.

116. Daniel A. Bronstein et al., "The National Environmental Policy Act at 35," *Environmental Practice* (7) (1) (2005): 3.

117. Council on Environmental Quality, *The National Environmental Policy Act: A Study of its Effectiveness After Twenty-five Years*.

118. Lazarus, *Making of Environmental Law*, 239. For a polemic against the Bush administration's environmental policies, see Robert F. Kennedy, Jr., "Crimes Against Nature," *Rolling Stone*, December 11, 2003.

119. "Watt Applauds Bush Energy Strategy," *Denver Post*, May 16, 2001.

120. Lazarus, *Making of Environmental Law*, 240–42.

121. James M. Jeffords, with Yvonne Daley and Howard Coffin, *An Independent Man: Adventures of a Public Servant* (New York: Simon and Schuster, 2001).

122. James M. Inhofe, "The Science of Climate Change," floor statement, U.S. Senate, July 28, 2003, available from Senator Inhofe's website, http://.inhofe.senate.gov/pressreleases/climate.htm.

123. The NEPA Task Force Report to the Council on Environmental Quality, "Modernizing NEPA Implementation" (September 24, 2003), available from the NEPA website, http://www.nepa.gov/ntf/report/finalreport.pdf.

124. The U.S. Institute for Environmental Conflict Resolution (ECR) was part of the Morris K. Udall Foundation, an independent federal agency of the executive

branch, based in Tucson, Arizona. The ECR website is http://www.ecr.gov; the report is found at http://www.ecr/gov/pdf/BR.pdf. See Bronstein et al., "The National Environmental Policy Act at 35," 3–5.

125. Erica Rosenberg, "Life Under the Republicans: The Subversion of Democracy in the House Resources Committee," *Hastings West-Northwest Journal of Environmental Law and Policy* 13 (Summer, 2007): 233–246.

126. Submission by Professors and Letter accompanying Submission by Professors, from Oliver Houck, professor, Tulane University Law School.

127. Rosenberg, "Life Under the Republicans," 245.

128. "Proposed Pombo Changes to National Environmental Policy Act Receive Close Scrutiny," The Wilderness Society news release, January 19, 2006, available from The Wilderness Society website, http://www.wilderness.org/NewsRoom/Release/20060119.cfm.

129. Robert G. Dreher, *NEPA Under Siege: The Political Assault on the National Environmental Policy Act* (Washington, D.C.: Georgetown Environmental Law & Policy Institute, Georgetown University Law Center, 2005), 8–10. Available at www.law.george town.edu/gelpi/research_archive/nepa/NEPAUnderSiegeFinal.pdf.

130. Dinah Bear, "Some Modest Suggestions for Improving Implementation of the National Environmental Policy Act," *Natural Resources Journal* 43 (2003): 932.

131. Tom Udall, "What Doesn't Need Fixing in NEPA," *The Environmental Forum* (May/June, 2005): 40, available from the NEPA website, http://www.nepa.gov/ntf/articles/Forum_NEPA_Task_Force_M-J_2005.pdf. Udall was ranking Democratic member on the 2005–2006 Task Force on Improving the National Environmental Policy Act.

132. Submission by Professors, 7.

133. Dreher, *NEPA Under Siege*, 4.

134. Ibid., 7.

135. Nicholas C. Yost, "Don't Undermine But Streamline Implementation," *The Environmental Forum* (May/June, 2005), 41.

136. Glicksman et al., *Environmental Protection*, 253.

137. Ibid.

138. Wilderness Society, "Measure Twice, Cut Once. NEPA: Preventing Mistakes and Making Good Projects Better Since 1970," (October, 2005), available from the Wilderness Society website, http://www.wilderness.org/Library/Documents/upload/NEPA-SuccessStories-20051021.pdf. See also Submission by Professors, Appendix: The Role of NEPA Alternatives, 20–26; and Dreher, *NEPA Under Siege*, 4–7.

139. Houck, "Is That All?" 177.

140. Lindstrom and Smith, *The National Environmental Policy Act*, 140.

141. Caldwell, *The National Environmental Policy Act*, 146.

13: THE LAWS THAT SHAPED AMERICA

Epigraph quotes from President Barack Obama, *Inaugural Address*, January 20, 2009, reprinted in *Newsweek*, Commemorative Inaugural Edition, n.d., 26–29, at 28; Novelli, "Cutting Political Gridlock," *AARP Bulletin*, January 2008, available at http://www.aarp.org/issues/dividedwefail/about_us/cutting_political_grid lock.htm.

1. Arthur M. Schlesinger, Jr., *The Age of Roosevelt: The Coming of the New Deal* (Boston: Houghton Mifflin Company, 1958), 311.

2. Glenn S. Krutz, "Issues and Institutions: Winnowing in the U.S. Congress," *American Journal of Political Science* 49 (2) (April, 2005): 1.

3. Center for Immigration Studies, "Three Decades of Mass Immigration: The

Legacy of the 1965 Immigration Act," September 1995, available from the CIS website, http://www.cis.org/articles/1995/back395.html. The law was named after its two principal sponsors, Senator Philip Hart (Democrat–Michigan) and Representative Emanuel Celler (Democrat–New York). See Charles Hirschman, "Immigration and the American Century," *Demography* 42 (4) (November, 2005): 595–620.

4. Samuel Halperin, "ESEA Ten Years Later," *Educational Researcher* 4 (8) (September, 1975): 5–9.

5. National Coalition of Women and Girls in Education, *Title IX at 35: Beyond the Headlines* (2008), available from the NCWGE website, http://www.ncwge.org/PDF/TitleIXat35.pdf.

6. William A. Niskanen, "Limiting Government: The Failure to 'Starve the Beast,'" *Cato Journal*, Fall, 2006. On the concept of "starve the beast," see Bruce Bartlett, "'Starve the Beast': The Origins and Development of a Budgetary Metaphor," *The Independent Review*, 12 (1) (Summer, 2007): 5–26, available from http://www.independent.org/pdf/tir/tir_12_01_01_bartlett.pdf.

7. The USA PATRIOT Act is an acronym for the official title: Uniting and Strengthening America by Providing Appropriate Tools Required to Intercept and Obstruct Terrorism Act. This clumsy title is but the latest attempt at legislative cleverness or obfuscation. Throughout this chapter, the law will be referred to as the Patriot Act.

8. Herbert N. Foerstal, *The Patriot Act: A Documentary and Reference Guide* (Westport, Conn.: Greenwood Press, 2008), xvii.

9. Robert O'Harrow, Jr., "Six Weeks in Autumn," *The Washington Post Magazine*, October 27, 2002, 06.

10. Ibid.

11. Foerstel, *The Patriot Act*, 30–31.

12. The fourteen reports of the Church Committee are available at the website of the Assassination Archives and Research Center, http://www.aarclibrary.org/publib/contents/church/contents_church_reports.htm.

13. Barbara Sinclair, *Unorthodox Lawmaking: New Legislative Processes in the United States Congress*, 2nd ed. (Washington, D.C.: CQ Press, 2000).

14. Kam C. Wong, *The Impact of USA Patriot Act on American Society: An Evidence Based Assessment* (New York: Nova Science Publishers, 2007), 47–48.

15. Summarized in Howard Ball, *The USA Patriot Act* (Santa Barbara, Calif.: ABC-CLIO, 2004).

16. Wong, *The Impact of USA Patriot Act on American Society*, 6.

17. Ibid., 351.

18. Foerstel, *The Patriot Act*, 203–207. Feinstein comments, March 19, 2007, upon introduction of S. 214, 110th Congress.

19. Eamon Javers and Lisa Lerer, "The $700 Billion Man," *Politico*, October 7, 2008, 15.

20. Lori Montgomery and Paul Kane, "Bush Enacts Historic Financial Rescue: House Passes Plan by Wide Margin, but Stocks Keep Falling," *The Washington Post*, October 4, 2008, A1, 9.

21. Estimates from the Congressional Budget Office cited in David Rothkopf, "9/11 Was Big. This Is Bigger," *The Washington Post*, October 5, 2008, B1.

22. Montgomery and Kane, "Bush Enacts Historic Financial Rescue," A9.

23. Jeanne Cummings, "Chamber on Offense Against Bailout Defectors," *Politico*, September 30, 2008, 10.

24. Eamon Javers, "What if the Bailout Passes but Doesn't Work," *Politico*, September 23, 2008, 16.

25. Quoted in Scott Shepard, "109th May Be the Real 'Do Nothing' Congress," The

[Raleigh-Durham, N.C.] *News and Observer*, available on its website, News Observer.com, http://www.newsobserver.com/politics/story/519951.html. See also, Thomas E. Mann and Norman J. Ornstein, *The Broken Branch: How Congress Is Failing America and How to Get It Back on Track* (New York: Oxford University Press, 2006).

26. David R. Mayhew, *Divided We Govern: Party Control, Lawmaking, and Investigations, 1946–1990* (New Haven: Yale University Press, 1991); Sarah A. Binder, "The Dynamics of Legislative Gridlock, 1947–96," *American Political Science Review* 93 (3) (September, 1999): 513–33; Sarah A. Binder, *Stalemate: Causes and Consequences of Legislative Gridlock* (Washington, D.C.: Brookings Institution, 2003).

27. Mann and Ornstein, *The Broken Branch.*

28. Ibid., ix–xii.

29. David A. Fahrenthold, "Turning Up the Heat on Climate Issue," *The Washington Post*, June 23, 2008, A3.

30. *An Inconvenient Truth* (2006), Paramount Classics and Participant Productions, directed by Davis Guggenheim; produced by Laurie David, Lawrence Bender, and Scott Z. Burns.

31. Fahrenthold, "Turning Up the Heat on Climate Issue."

32. Ibid.

33. For an analysis of two decades of public opinion studies on this subject, see Matthew C. Nisbet and Teresa Myers, "Twenty Years of Public Opinion About Global Warming," *Public Opinion Quarterly* 71 (3) (2007): 444–70.

34. Climate Science Watch, "White House 'Eviscerated' Centers for Disease Control on Climate Change Health Impacts," October 23, 2007, available from the Climate Science Watch website, http://www.climatesciencewatch.org/index. php/csw/details/cdc_testimony_censorship. For earlier White House efforts to control information about science, see Tarek Maassarani, *Redacting the Science of Climate Change: An Investigative and Synthesis Report* (Washington, D.C.: Government Accountability Project, 2007), available from the GAP website, http://www. whistleblower.org/doc/2007/Final%203.28%20Redacting%20Climate%20 Science%20Report.pdf.

APPENDIX: OTHER MAJOR LEGISLATION

1. Much of the material in this section is distilled from Stephen W. Stathis, *Landmark Legislation 1774–2002: Major U.S. Acts and Treaties* (Washington, D.C.: CQ Press, 2003) and Brian K. Landsberg, editor-in-chief, *Major Acts of Congress*, 3 vols. (New York: Macmillan Reference, 2004).

2. The plaque is reproduced on the frontispiece of Lyndon B. Johnson, *The Vantage Point: Perspectives of the Presidency 1963–1969* (New York: Holt, Rinehart, and Winston, 1971).

INDEX